Program of the

Twelfth Annual Conference of the Cognitive Science Society

25-28 July 1990
Cambridge, Massachusetts

 LAWRENCE ERLBAUM ASSOCIATES, PUBLISHERS
1990   Hillsdale, New Jersey   Hove and London

Distributed by

Lawrence Erlbaum Associates, Inc.
365 Broadway
Hillsdale, New Jersey 07642

ISBN 0-8058-0938-4

ISSN 1047-1316

The Twelfth Annual Conference of the Cognitive Science Society

July 25-28, 1990

Cambridge, Massachusetts

Conference Chair: Massimo Piattelli-Palmarini (MIT)

Scientific Advisors: Beth Adelson (Tufts), Stephen M. Kosslyn (Harvard), Steven Pinker (MIT), Kenneth Wexler (MIT)

Reviewers

Richard Alterman
William Bechtel
Thomas Bever
Lawrence Birnbaum
Paul Bloom
Michael Brent
Yves Chauvin
Michelene Chi
Garrison Cottrell
Stephen Crain
Bonnie Dorr
Kevin Dunbar
Michael Dyer
Jeffrey Elman
Nancy Etcoff
Brian Falkenhainer
Douglas Fisher
Margot Flowers
Kenneth Forbus
David Forster
Deborah Frisch
Dedre Gentner
Mark Gluck
Robert Goldstone

Arthur Graesser
Ken Haase
Kristian Hammond
Gilbert Harman
Keith Holyoak
Michael Jordan
John Kim
Eric Lormand
Maryellen MacDonald
Charles Martin
Robert Mathews
Douglas Medin
Scott Meredith
Janet Metcalfe
Nancy Nersessian
Allen Newell
Padraig O'Seaghdha
Christopher Owens
Caroline Palmer
Michael Pazzani
Steven Pinker
Peter Pirolli
Alan Prince
Lauren Resnick
Whitman Richards

Eric Ristad
Jay Rueckl
Dirk Ruiz
Mark Seidenberg
Colleen Seifert
Lokendra Shastri
Jeff Shrager
Thomas Shultz
Paul Smolensky
James Spohrer
Robert Stalnaker
Josh Stern
Katia Sycara
Carol Tenny
Paul Thagard
Elise Turner
Roy Turner
Kurt VanLehn
Stella Vosniadou
David Waltz
Kenneth Wexler
Tony Wilkie
Jeremy Wolfe
Roy Zito-Wolf

Proceedings of the
Twelfth Annual Conference of the Cognitive Science Society
Cambridge, Massachusetts - July 25/28, 1990

PAPER PRESENTATIONS

Group I: Reasoning

Group II: Language

Group III: Vision

Group IV: Learning and Memory

Group V: Cognition in Context

POSTER PRESENTATIONS

Invited Symposia

Submitted Symposia

Author Listing

Beth Adelson
Department of Computer Science
Tufts University
Medford, MA 02155

Phil Agre
Department of Computer Science
University of Chicago
1100 E. 58th Street
Chicago, IL 60637

David W. Aha
Department of Computer Science
University of California at Irvine
Irvine, CA 92717

Subutai Ahmad
International Computer Science Institute
1947 Center Street
Berkeley, CA 94704

Woo-Kyoung Ahn
Department of Psychology
University of Michigan
Ann Arbor, MI 48104

Venkat Ajjanagadde
4260 Chestnut Street, Apt. B8
Philadelphia, PA 19104

Richard Alterman
Computer Science Department
Brandeis University
Waltham, MA 02254

John R. Anderson
Department of Psychology
Carnegie Mellon University
Pittsburgh, PA 15213-3890

Michael A. Arbib
Center for Neural Engineering
University of Southern California
Los Angeles, CA 90089-2520

Yigal Arens
Information Sciences Institute
4676 Admiralty Way, Suite 1001
Marina Del Rey, CA 90292

Judith Avrahami
The Goldie Rotman Center for Cognitive
Science in Education
School of Education
The Hebrew University of Jerusalem
Jerusalem 91905
ISRAEL

Bernard Baars
The Wright Institute
2728 Durand Avenue
Berkeley, CA 94704

Norman I. Badler
Department of Computer and Information
Science
University of Pennsylvania
Philadelphia, PA 19104-6389

William Ball
Department of Psychology
Carnegie Mellon University
Pittsburgh, PA 15213

Raju S. Bapi
Department of Mathematics
University of Texas
Arlington, TX 76019-9408

John A. Bateman
Information Sciences Institute
4676 Admiralty Way
Marina del Rey, CA 90292-6695

Elizabeth A. Bates
Department of Cognitive Science, D-015
University of California at San Diego
La Jolla, CA 92093

Malcolm I. Bauer
Cognitive Science Laboratory
Princeton University
221 Nassau Street
Princeton, NJ 08542

Irving Biederman
Department of Psychology
University of Minnesota
Minneapolis, MN 55455

Lawrence Birnbaum
Department of Electrical Engineering and
Computer Science
Northwestern University
Evanston, IL 60201

C. Franklin Boyle
CDEC
Carnegie Mellon University
Pittsburgh, PA 15213

Nick Braisby
Centre for Cognitive Science
University of Edinburgh
2 Buccleuch Place
Edinburgh EH8 9LW
SCOTLAND

Matthew Brand
Institute for the Learning Sciences
Suite 300
1890 Maple Avenue
Evanston, IL 60201

Michael R. Brent
Artificial Intelligence Laboratory
Massachusetts Institute of Technology
545 Technology Square
Cambridge, MA 02139

Brent C.J. Britton
Media Lab, E15-412
Massachusetts Institute of Technology
77 Massachusetts Avenue
Cambridge, MA 02139

Gail A. Bruder
Department of Psychology
State University of New York at Buffalo
Buffalo, NY 14260

Bruce D. Burns
Department of Psychology
University of California, Los Angeles
Los Angeles, CA 90024

Claire Cardie
Department of Computer and Information
Science
University of Massachusetts
Amherst, MA 01003

Roger Chaffin
Trenton State College
Trenton, NJ 08625

David J. Chalmers
Center for Research on Concepts and
Cognition
Indiana University
510 North Fess Street
Bloomington, IN 47408

B. Chandrasekaran
Laboratory for Artificial Intelligence
Research, Department of Computer and
Information Science
The Ohio State University
Columbus, OH 43210

Yam San Chee
Department of Information Systems and
Computer Science
National University of Singapore
Lower Kent Ridge Road
Singapore 0511
REPUBLIC OF SINGAPORE

Axel Cleeremans
Department of Psychology
Carnegie Mellon University
Pittsburgh, PA 15213

Catherine A. Clement
Psychology Department
Eastern Kentucky University
Richmond, KY 40475-3108

Jonathan D. Cohen
Western Psychiatric Institute and Clinic
University of Pittsburgh
Pittsburgh, PA 15260

Gregg Collins
Northwestern University
Institute for the Learning Sciences
Suite 300
1890 Maple Avenue
Evanston, IL 60201

Albert T. Corbett
Department of Psychology
Carnegie Mellon University
Pittsburgh, PA 15213-3890

Rosalind A. Crawley
Department of Psychology
University of Durham
Durham DH1 3LE
ENGLAND

Steven Cushing
Department of Computer Science B-4
Boston University
755 Commonwealth Avenue
Boston, MA 02215

Judy DeLoache
Department of Psychology
University of Illinois
603 East Daniel Street
Champaign, IL 61820

Lisa Dent
School of Computer Science
Carnegie Mellon University
Pittsburgh, PA 15213

Eric A. Domeshek
Institute for the Learning Sciences
Northwestern University
Evanston, IL 60201

Barry B. Druhan
Department of Psychology
236 Audubon Hall
Louisiana State University
Baton Rouge, LA 70803

Kevin Dunbar
Department of Psychology
McGill University
1205 Dr. Penfield Avenue
Montréal, PQ H3A 1B1
CANADA

Dewey I. Dykstra, Jr.
Department of Physics
Boise State University
Boise, ID 83727

Gillette Elvgren III
School of Computer Science
Carnegie Mellon University
Pittsburgh, PA 15213

Jill Fain Lehman
School of Computer Science
Carnegie Mellon University
Pittsburgh, PA 15213

Brian Falkenhainer
Xerox Palo Alto Research Center
3333 Coyote Hill Road
Palo Alto, CA 94304

Anne L. Fay
Department of Psychology
Carnegie Mellon University
Pittsburgh, PA 15213-3890

Michael Fehling
Intelligent Systems Laboratory
321 Terman Center
Stanford University
Stanford, CA 94305-4025

Jerome A. Feldman
International Computer Science Institute
1947 Center Street, Suite 600
Berkeley, CA 94704

Christiane Fellbaum
Cognitive Science Laboratory
Princeton University
221 Nassau Street
Princeton, NJ 08542

Charles Fisher
The San Francisco Psychoanalytic Institute
2420 Sutter Street
San Francisco, CA 94115

Kenneth D. Forbus
Qualitative Reasoning Group
Beckman Institute
University of Illinois
405 North Mathews Avenue
Urbana, IL 61801

Dean Foster
Center for Decision Research
Graduate School of Business
University of Chicago
1101 East 58th Street
Chicago, IL 60637

Bradley Franks
Centre for Cognitive Science
University of Edinburgh
2 Buccleuch Place
Edinburgh EH8 9LW
SCOTLAND

George W. Furnas
Bell Communications Research
435 South Street, MRE 2M-397
Morristown, NJ 07960

Dedre Gentner
Psychology Department
University of Illinois at Urbana
6032 E. Daniel Street
Champaign, IL 61820

Edward Gibson
Department of Philosophy
Carnegie Mellon University
Pittsburgh, PA 15213-3890

Vittorio Girotto
Istituto di Psicologia
Centro Nazionale delle Ricerche
Viale K. Marx 15
I-00137 Roma
ITALY

Rainer Goebel
Fachbereich Psychologie
Universität Marburg
Gutenbergstrasse 18
D-3550 Marburg
WEST GERMANY

Robert L. Goldstone
Department of Psychology
University of Michigan
Ann Arbor, MI 48109

Renison J. Gonsalves
Department of Educational Services
Brooklyn College
Bedford Avenue and Avenue H
Brooklyn, NY 11210

Kenneth C. Gray
Department of Psychology
University of Michigan
Ann Arbor, MI 48104

James G. Greeno
School of Education
SU/Education Bldg. 1353096
Stanford University
Stanford, CA 94305

Mary Hare
Center for Research in Language, C-008
University of California at San Diego
La Jolla, CA 92093

Catherine L. Harris
Department of Cognitive Science, D-015
University of California at San Diego
La Jolla, CA 92093

Barbara Hemforth
Fakultät für Psychologie
Ruhr-Universität Bochum
Postfach 102148
D-4630 Bochum 1
WEST GERMANY

James Hendler
Computer Science Department
University of Maryland
College Park, MD 20742

Thomas R. Hinrichs
School of Information and Computer Science
Georgia Institute of Technology
Atlanta, GA 30332

Douglas R. Hofstadter
Center for Research on Concepts and
Cognition
Indiana University
510 North Fess Street
Bloomington, IN 47405

Susan Hollbach Weber
International Computer Science Institute
1947 Center Street, Suite 600
Berkeley, CA 94704

Keith J. Holyoak
Department of Psychology
Pranz Hall
University of California
Los Angeles, CA 90026

Eduard Hovy
Information Sciences Institute
4676 Admiralty Way, Suite 1001
Marina Del Rey, CA 90292

John E. Hummel
Department of Psychology
University of Minnesota
Minneapolis, MN 55455

Lawrence Hunter
National Library of Medicine
Bldg. 38A, MS-54
Bethesda, MD 20894

Douglas Jackson
School of Education
SU/Education Bldg. 1353096
Stanford University
Stanford, CA 94305

Rick L. Jenison
Department of Psychology
University of Wisconsin
Madison, WI 53706

Peggy L. Jennings
Department of Psychology
Oregon Hall
University of Oregon
Eugene, OR 97403

Hollyn M. Johnson
Department of Psychology
University of Michigan
Ann Arbor, MI 48104

Eric K. Jones
Institute for the Learning Sciences
Northwestern University
1890 Maple Avenue
Evanston, IL 60201

Gregory V. Jones
Department of Psychology
University of Warwick
Coventry CV4 7AL
ENGLAND

Jacqueline A. Jones
Department of Computer Science
Brooklyn College
Brooklyn, NY 11210

Jugal K. Kalita
Department of Computer and Information
Science
University of Pennsylvania
Philadelphia, PA 19104-6389

Nancy G. Kanwisher
Department of Psychology
University of California at Berkeley
Berkeley, CA 94720

Yaakov Kareev
The Goldie Rotman Center for Cognitive
Science in Education
School of Education
The Hebrew University of Jerusalem
Jerusalem 91905
ISRAEL

Steven W. Keele
Department of Psychology
Oregon Hall
University of Oregon
Eugene, OR 97403

Angela Kennedy Hickman
School of Computer Science
Carnegie Mellon University
Pittsburgh, PA 15213

Hyun-Kyung Kim
Qualitative Reasoning Group
Beckman Institute
University of Illinois
405 North Mathews Avenue
Urbana, IL 61801

David Klahr
Department of Psychology
Carnegie Mellon University
Pittsburgh, PA 15213-3890

David Kleinman
Department of Psychology
University of Durham
Durham DH1 3LE
ENGLAND

Boicho Nikolov Kokinov
Institute of Mathematics
Bulgarian Academy of Sciences
Bl. 8, Acad. G. Bonchev Street
Sofia 1113
BULGARIA

John F. Kolen
Laboratory for AI Research, Department of
Computer and Information Science
The Ohio State University
Columbus, OH 43210

Janet L. Kolodner
School of Information and Computer Science
Georgia Institute of Technology
Atlanta, GA 30332-0280

Margaret Korpi
School of Education
SU/Education Bldg. 1353096
Stanford University
Stanford, CA 94305

Chris A. Kortge
Department of Psychology
Stanford University
Stanford, CA 94305

Bernadette Kowalski
Department of Computer Science
Carnegie Mellon University
Pittsburgh, PA 15213

Bruce Krulwich
Northwestern University
Institute for the Learning Sciences
Suite 300
1890 Maple Avenue
Evanston, IL 60201

John Laird
Artificial Intelligence Laboratory
University of Michigan
Ann Arbor, MI 48105

Jill H. Larkin
Department of Psychology
Carnegie Mellon University
Pittsburgh, PA 15213

George Lakoff
International Computer Science Institute
1947 Center Street
Berkeley, CA 94704

David B. Leake
Center for Research on Concepts and
Cognition
Indiana University
510 North Fess Avenue
Bloomington, IN 47408

Paolo Legrenzi
Dipartimento di Psicologia
Via dell'Università 7
I-34127 Trieste
ITALY

Wendy Lehnert
Department of Computer and Information
Science
University of Massachusetts
Amherst, MA 01003

Géraldine Legendre
Department of Linguistics
University of Colorado
Boulder, CO 80309-0430

Daniel Levine
Department of Mathematics
University of Texas
Arlington, TX 76019-9408

Steven L. Lytinen
Artificial Intelligence Laboratory
University of Michigan
Ann Arbor, MI 48109

Siobhan B.G. MacAndrew
Department of Psychology
University of Warwick
Coventry CV4 7AL
ENGLAND

Arthur B. Markman
Department of Psychology
Beckman Institute
University of Illinois
405 North Mathews Avenue
Urbana, IL 61801

Joel D. Martin
School of Information and Computer Science
Georgia Institute of Technology
Atlanta, GA 30332

Thomas Mastaglio
Department of Computer Science
University of Colorado
Campus Box 430
Boulder, CO 80309-0430

Robert C. Mathews
Department of Psychology
236 Audubon Hall
Louisiana State University
Baton Rouge, LA 70803

Robert McCartney
Department of Computer Science and
Engineering, U-155
University of Connecticut
Storrs, CT 06269-3155

James L. McClelland
Department of Psychology
Carnegie Mellon University
Pittsburgh, PA 15213

Vera Michalchik
School of Education
SU/Education Bldg. 1353096
Stanford University
Stanford, CA 94305

Risto Miikkulainen
Artificial Intelligence Laboratory
Computer Science Department
University of California
Los Angeles, CA 90024

Benjamin O. Miller
Department of Computer Science
Brooklyn College
Brooklyn, NY 11210

Donald H. Mitchell
Amoco Production Company
Tulsa Research Center, P.O. Box 3385
Tulsa, OK 74102

Melanie Mitchell
Center for Research on Concepts and
Cognition
Indiana University
510 North Fess Street
Bloomington, IN 47405

Yoshiro Miyata
Department of Computer Science
University of Colorado
Boulder, CO 80309-0430

Ira A. Monarch
Department of Philosophy
Carnegie Mellon University
Pittsburgh, PA 15213

Stephen T. Morgan
Department of Psychology
University of Wisconsin
Madison, WI 53706

Michael C. Mozer
Department of Computer Science
University of Colorado
Boulder, CO 80309-0430

Kenneth S. Murray
Department of Computer Science
University of Texas at Austin
Austin, TX 78712

N. H. Narayanan
Laboratory for Artificial Intelligence
Research, Department of Computer and
Information Science
Ohio State University
Columbus, OH 43210

Nancy J. Nersessian
Princeton University
Program in History of Science
Princeton, NJ 08544

Sheldon Nicholl
Department of Computer Science
University of Illinois
405 North Mathews Avenue
Urbana, IL 61801

Dan Oblinger
Qualitative Reasoning Group
Beckman Institute
University of Illinois
405 North Mathews Avenue
Urbana, IL 61801

Gregg C. Oden
Department of Psychology
University of Wisconsin
Madison, WI 53706

Stellan Ohlsson
Learning Research and Development Center
University of Pittsburgh
LRDC Building, 3939 O'Hara Street
Pittsburgh, PA 15260

Stephen Omohundro
International Computer Science Institute
1947 Center Street
Berkeley, CA 94704

Christopher Owens
Computer Science Department
University of Chicago
1100 East 58th Street
Chicago, IL 60637

Vimla Patel
Cognitive Studies in Medicine
McGill University
3655 Drummond Street, Rm. 529
Montréal, PQ H3G 1Y6
CANADA

Michael J. Pazzani
Department of Information and Computer
Science
University of California
Irvine, CA 92717

Theresa Louise Penberthy
School of Information and Computer Science
Georgia Institute of Technology
Atlanta, GA 30332-0280

Sandra L. Peters
Department of Computer Science
230 Computing Center
State University of New York at Buffalo
Amherst, NY 14260

Jordan B. Pollack
Laboratory for Artificial Intelligence
Research, Department of Computer and
Information Science
Ohio State University
2036 Neil Avenue
Columbus, OH 43210

Ian Pratt
Department of Computer Science
University of Manchester
Manchester M13 9PL
ENGLAND

Yulin Qin
Department of Psychology
Carnegie Mellon University
Pittsburgh, PA 15213

Alex Quilici
Artificial Intelligence Laboratory
Computer Science Department
3531 Boelter Hall
University of California at Los Angeles
Los Angeles, CA 90024

Clark N. Quinn
Learning Research and Development Center
University of Pittsburgh
LRDC Building, 3939 O'Hara Street
Pittsburgh, PA 15260

Ashwin Ram
School of Information and Computer Science
Georgia Institute of Technology
Atlanta, GA 30332-0280

William J. Rapaport
State University of New York
Department of Computer Science
226 Bell Hall
Buffalo, NY 14260

Mary Jo Rattermann
Department of Psychology
University of Illinois
603 East Daniel Street
Champaign, IL 61820

Michael Redmond
School of Information and Computer Science
Georgia Institute of Technology
Atlanta, GA 30332-0280

Brent Reeves
Department of Computer Science
University of Colorado
Campus Box 430
Boulder, CO 80309-0430

Brian J. Reiser
Cognitive Science Laboratory
Princeton University
221 Nassau Street
Princeton, NJ 08542

Ellen Riloff
Department of Computer and Information
Science
University of Massachusetts
Amherst, MA 01003

Scott P. Robertson
Department of Psychology
Rutgers University
Busch Campus
New Brunswick, NJ 08903

Lewis G. Roussel
Department of Psychology
236 Audubon Hall
Louisiana State University
Baton Rouge, LA 70803

Peter A. Sandon
Department of Mathematics and Computer
Science, Computer Science Program
Bradley Hall
Dartmouth College
Hanover, NH 03755

Don L. Scarborough
Department of Psychology
Brooklyn College
Brooklyn, NY 11210

Jeffrey C. Schlimmer
School of Computer Science
Carnegie Mellon University
Pittsburgh, PA 15213

Walter Schneider
Learning Research and Development Center
University of Pittsburgh
LRDC Building, 3939 O'Hara Street
Pittsburgh, PA 15260

Lael J. Schooler
Department of Psychology
Carnegie Mellon University
Pittsburgh, PA 15213

Christian D. Schunn
Department of Psychology
McGill University
1205 Dr. Penfield Avenue
Montréal, PQ H3A 1B1
CANADA

Erwin M. Segal
Center for Cognitive Science
Department of Psychology
State University of New York
Buffalo, NY 14260

Colleen M. Seifert
Department of Psychology
University of Michigan
Ann Arbor, MI 48104

David Servan-Schreiber
School of Computer Science
Carnegie Mellon University
Pittsburgh, PA 15213

Emile Servan-Schreiber
Department of Psychology
Carnegie Mellon University
Pittsburgh, PA 15213-3890

Judith M. Shedden
Learning Research and Development Center
University of Pittsburgh
LRDC Building, 3939 O'Hara Street
Pittsburgh, PA 15260

Jeff Shrager
Xerox Palo Alto Research Center
3333 Coyote Hill Road
Palo Alto, CA 94304

Thomas R. Shultz
Department of Psychology
Stewart Biological Sciences Building
McGill University
1205 Dr. Penfield Avenue
Montréal, PQ H3A 1B1
CANADA

Glenn Silverstein
Department of Information and Computer
Science
University of California
Irvine, CA 92717

Herbert A. Simon
Department of Psychology
Carnegie Mellon University
Pittsburgh, PA 15213

Malathi Sivaramakrishnan
Cognitive Studies in Medicine
McGill University
3655 Drummond Street, Rm. 529
Montréal, PQ H3G 1Y6
CANADA

David B. Skalak
Department of Computer and Information
Science
University of Massachusetts
Amherst, MA 01003

Stephen Slade
Computer Science Department
Yale University
P.O. Box 2158, Yale Station
New Haven, CT 06520-2158

Steven L. Small
Department of Neurology
322 Scaiffe Hall
University of Pittsburgh
Pittsburgh, PA 15260

Paul Smolensky
Department of Computer Science
Institute of Cognitive Science
University of Colorado
Boulder, CO 80309-0430

James C. Spohrer
Advanced Technology Group
Apple Computer, MS: 76-3A
20450 Stevens Creek Boulevard
Cupertino, CA 95014

Rosemary J. Stevenson
Department of Psychology
University of Durham
Durham DH1 3LE
ENGLAND

Suzanne Stevenson
Department of Computer Science
University of Maryland
College Park, MD 20742

Andreas Stolcke
Department of Electrical Engineering and
Computer Science
University of California
Berkeley, CA 94720

Gerhard Strube
Fakultät für Psychologie
Ruhr-Universität Bochum
Postfach 102148
D-4630 Bochum 1
WEST GERMANY

Katia P. Sycara
The Robotics Institute
Carnegie Mellon University
Pittsburgh, PA 15213

James W. Tanaka
Department of Psychology
Carnegie Mellon University
Pittsburgh, PA 15213

John Theios
Department of Psychology
University of Wisconsin
Madison, WI 53706

David S. Touretzky
School of Computer Science
Carnegie Mellon University
Pittsburgh, PA 15213

Kurt VanLehn
Department of Psychology
Carnegie Mellon University
Pittsburgh, PA 15213

Michael R. Waldmann
Institut für Psychologie
Universität Frankfurt
Georg-Voigt Strasse 8
D-6000 Frankfurt-am-Main 11
WEST GERMANY

DeLiang Wang
Center for Neural Engineering
University of Southern California
Los Angeles, CA 90089-2520

Leo Wanner
Project Komet
GMD-IPSI
Dolivostr. 15
D-6100 Darmstadt
WEST GERMANY

Nigel Ward
Computer Science Division
571 Evans Hall
University of California at Berkeley
Berkeley, CA 94720

Kim Weber
Department of Psychology
Rutgers University
Busch Campus
New Brunswick, NJ 08903

Deirdre W. Wheeler
Department of Linguistics
University of Pittsburgh
Pittsburgh, PA 15260

Janyce M. Wiebe
Department of Computer Science
University of Toronto
Toronto, Ontario M55 1A4
CANADA

Mark Wiesmeyer
Artificial Intelligence Laboratory
University of Michigan
Ann Arbor, MI 48105

David C. Wilkins
Department of Computer Science
University of Illinois
405 North Mathews Avenue
Urbana, IL 61801

Garry Wilson
Department of Psychology
University of Durham
Durham DH1 3LE
ENGLAND

Heike Wrobel
Fakultät für Psychologie
Ruhr-Universität Bochum
Postfach 102148
D-4630 Bochum 1
WEST GERMANY

Horng Jyh P. Wu
Artificial Intelligence Laboratory
University of Michigan
Ann Arbor, MI 48105

Berrin A. Yanikoglu
Department of Mathematics and Computer
Science, Computer Science Program
Bradley Hall
Dartmouth College
Hanover, NH 03755

Ilan Yaniv
Center for Decision Research
Graduate School of Business
University of Chicago
1101 East 58th Street
Chicago, IL 60637

Colleen M. Zeitz
Learning Research and Development Center
University of Pittsburgh
3939 O'Hara Street
Pittsburgh, PA 15260

Roland Zito-Wolf
Computer Science Department
Brandeis University
Waltham, MA 02254

Ingrid Zukerman
Department of Computer Science
Monash University
Clayton VIC 3168
AUSTRALIA

EFFECT OF STRUCTURE OF ANALOGY AND DEPTH OF ENCODING ON LEARNING COMPUTER PROGRAMMING

Yam San CHEE
Department of Information Systems and Computer Science
National University of Singapore

Abstract

This research addresses the need for effective ways of teaching computer programming. It focuses on two aspects of instruction. First, the research investigates the use of analogy in teaching programming. It extends existing research by investigating what constitutes a *good* analogy. Second, the research investigates the effect of depth of encoding on programming performance.

The factors *analogy* and *encoding* were manipulated in a 3 x 2 factorial design. Analogy was operationalized by varying the clarity and systematicity/abstractness of the analogies used. Encoding was operationalized by varying the frequency with which deep encoding and elaboration of learned material were invoked by the presentation of questions on the learned material. The dependent variables were score obtained on program comprehension and program composition tasks and the time taken to perform the tasks. Research subjects were 15- to 17-year-olds without prior exposure to computer programming. Differences in mathematics ability and age were controlled.

The results provide empirical support for a predictive theory of the relative goodness of competing analogies. They provide only marginal support for depth of encoding (as operationalized) in learning computer programming effectively. *Post hoc* data analysis suggests that good analogies assist the learning of semantics but not syntax. Furthermore, the effect of encoding was only apparent in learning syntax but not semantics.

Introduction

The traditional approach to teaching computer programming by emphasizing programming language statements (Mayer, 1979; Spohrer & Soloway, 1986) has proved unsatisfactory. Such an approach fails to assist in the acquisition of a useful mental model of the notional machine underlying the programming language (Bayman & Mayer, 1983) and to facilitate the transition from programming knowledge to programming behavior (Anderson, Farrell & Sauers, 1984).

Explanatory Analogy

Analogies are a useful tool for learning and instruction (see, for example, Norman, 1980; Rumelhart & Norman, 1981). The validity of this claim has been demonstrated in the domain of learning computer programming (Mayer, 1975, 1976). Analogies can provide the required mental model of the notional machine. They can also facilitate the transition from programming knowledge to behavior as novices attempt to execute their mental model. Simons (1984) posits that analogies assist learning by making abstract information imaginable and concrete, by providing an existing schema as the basis for the formation of a new schema, and by making relevant anchoring ideas available so that new information can be actively integrated with prior knowledge.

Gentner (1982) postulates the characteristics of analogy that contribute to explanatory power. Her postulation is based on a well-defined theory of structure-mapping (Gentner, 1983) that distinguishes between *attributes* and *relations* on one hand and between *first-order relations* and *higher-order relations* on the other.

An explanatory analogy may be viewed in terms of three properties of internal structure: clarity, richness, and systematicity/abstractness (Gentner, 1982). *Clarity* refers to how base nodes are mapped onto target nodes. A violation occurs if one base node maps to two or more distinct target nodes *or* if two or more distinct base nodes map to the same target node. *Richness* refers to predicate density: that is, for a given set of nodes, the average number of predicates per node that can be plausibly mapped from base to target. *Systematicity/abstractness* refers to the degree to which the imported predicates belong to a mutually constraining conceptual system. Higher-order relations that link lower-order relations are the essence of systematicity. Highly systematic mappings are generally also abstract because they contain a greater proportion of higher-order relations.

The Theory of the Structure of Explanatory Analogies is derived, in part, from distinctions drawn by Gentner (1982) between good and bad explanatory analogies. It states that important, regularly occurring structural differences exist between good explanatory analogies and weak explanatory analogies. In particular, (1) good explanatory analogies possess clarity; weak explanatory analogies do not; (2) good explanatory analogies are higher in systematicity and abstractness than weak explanatory analogies; and (3) good explanatory analogies are lower or equal in richness to weak explanatory analogies.

The theory is used as the basis for distinguishing between the explanatory power of alternative analogies in this research. For achievement in both program comprehension and program composition, learning with an analogy that possesses the structural properties of good explanatory analogy is expected to result in a better learning outcome than learning with an analogy that possesses the structural properties of weak explanatory analogy.

Depth of Encoding

Learning outcomes depend not only on the quality of instruction but also on the efficacy of cognitive processing *during* the learning phase. Good learning outcomes are associated with depth of encoding (Craik & Lockhart, 1972). Greater depth implies a greater degree of semantic or cognitive analysis on the part of the student, resulting in superior understanding, recall, and retention of material learned. The initial encoding of learned material can pass through further elaboration whereby more associations are formed between newly acquired knowledge and prior knowledge. The establishment of these associations leads to better integration of new knowledge with old knowledge and improved understanding of learned material.

Depth of encoding also results in better recall because of a more persistent memory trace (Craik & Lockhart, 1972), with deeper levels of encoding associated with more elaborate, stronger, and more lasting traces. In addition, retention is a function of depth of encoding, as well as other factors such as the amount of attention devoted to a stimulus and the time available for processing the stimulus.

Based on the foregoing, the quality of students' learning when acquiring knowledge related to a new and unfamiliar domain should be significantly affected by the depth of encoding they achieve during learning. Deeper encoding should be facilitated by presenting instructional material in relatively short segments followed by questions on the material just learned. The presentation of questions forces students to try to actively understand the instructional material so that they can answer the questions correctly. Consequently, deep encoding and elaboration receive active support. The presentation of questions in short segments also eases the burden of learning because a lighter cognitive load is placed upon memory.

Where students complete their study of the entire instruction set *before* attempting questions on the materials learned, depth of encoding is less well supported. The absence of questions that evoke deeper processing of instructional material during learning results in more superficial processing and, consequently, in poorer understanding, poorer retention, and poorer recall ability. Furthermore, when students are required to answer questions only at the end of the instruction set, the cognitive load on memory is very great because students have to draw their answers from across the *entire* instruction set.

Thus, deep encoding is expected to result in better understanding, retention, and recall of learned material, and hence in superior programming task performance compared to shallow encoding that occurs when the entire instruction set is studied before questions on the instruction set are attempted.

Hypotheses Tested

The research hypotheses are based on four theoretical constructs: (1) explanatory power of analogy, (2) depth of encoding, (3) quality of program comprehension, and (4) quality of program composition.

Hypothesis 1	The quality of program comprehension when learning with a good analogy is better than the quality of program comprehension when learning with a weak analogy or without an analogy.
Hypothesis 2	The quality of program comprehension when learning with a weak analogy is better than or equal to the quality of program comprehension when learning without an analogy.
Hypothesis 3	The quality of program comprehension when learning with deep encoding is better than the quality of program comprehension when learning with shallow encoding.
Hypothesis 4	The differences in quality of program comprehension when learning with a good analogy, a weak analogy, and without an analogy will be greater when learning with shallow encoding than when learning with deep encoding; that is, there will be an interaction effect between the explanatory power of analogy and the depth of encoding.
Hypothesis 5	The quality of program composition when learning with a good analogy is better than the quality of program composition when learning with a weak analogy or without an analogy.
Hypothesis 6	The quality of program composition when learning with a weak analogy is better than or equal to the quality of program composition when learning without an analogy.

In general, the above hypotheses follow from the preceding discussion. In Hypothesis 4, an analogy is postulated to possess an *integrating* function in addition to the functions of concretizing, structurizing, and active assimilation. Hypotheses 5 and 6 are similar to Hypotheses 1 and 2 and are based on the expectation that mastery of syntax and semantics is an essential component of program coding ability.

Method

Design   The factors *analogy* and *encoding* were manipulated in a 3 x 2 factorial design. Analogy comprised three levels: (1) good analogy, (2) weak analogy, and (3) no analogy (a control condition). Encoding comprised two levels: (1) deep, and (2) shallow. The experiment was conducted in two phases: a program comprehension phase followed by a program composition phase. Two dependent variables were used in each phase. The dependent variables in the program comprehension phase were (a) program comprehension score, and (b) time taken to answer comprehension questions. The dependent variables in the program composition phase were (a) program composition score, and (b) time taken to answer composition questions. Both the program comprehension and program composition scores are performance metrics obtained by applying a predetermined scoring template to subjects' responses. The experimental design incorporated two covariates: mathematics ability and age.

Subjects Subjects were school students between the ages of 15 and 17 years. They were unexposed to computer programming. Ninety valid subjects' responses were obtained; 60 were boys and 30 were girls. They were assigned randomly to treatment conditions.

Materials

Treatment Materials. The treatment materials comprised three sets of instruction on programming in BASIC: (1) the good analogy set, (2) the weak analogy set, and (3) the no analogy set. In the good analogy set, the instructional materials were woven around an analogy that dealt with a master processor and his three assistants – the assigner, the reader, and the printer – working together in a room to perform the operations of a notional computer. Data were input either through an input slot or via data cards that came through an input window on an input wall. Data were output via an output window on an output wall. Window boxes in the room stored the values of variables whose names were written on the boxes. In the weak analogy set, the underlying analogy was similar but less elaborate. There was only one window through which both input and output were handled. In addition, the names of the three assistants were generalized to "assistant," "messenger," and "helper" in order to facilitate the one-to many and many-to-one object mappings in the weak analogy. Finally, the no analogy set presented the instructional material without reference to any analogy.

The instructional materials covered the program statements LET, PRINT, END, REM, INPUT, DATA, READ, GO TO, and IF/THEN. Looping constructs were taught using the IF/THEN and GO TO statements.

The exact length of the instructional materials was controlled. To compensate for the additional text required to present the analogy material, filler text (which presented a brief history of computers) was added to the weak analogy and no analogy materials so that the word count for each set of instructional materials was identical.

The good and weak analogy treatment materials instantiated the Theory of the Structure of Explanatory Analogies. The instructional materials contained the base of the analogy (good or weak) woven into the instruction on BASIC.

A sample of the good and weak analogies, depicted in propositional network form, is shown at the end of this paper. Networks 1 and 9 depict those portions of the base of the good analogy and weak analogy respectively that deal with the organization of the computer. The corresponding targets of the good and weak analogies are depicted in Networks 5 and 13.

Object mappings between base and target may be inferred directly by the positions the object nodes occupy in two-dimensional space. In the weak analogy networks, however, this method does not apply if an object participates in a one-to-many or many-to-one mapping. In such instances, the object mapping is specifically shown using a striped arrow.

Relation mappings from base to target are inferred via the identical positions that the relations occupy in the two-dimensional space of the propositional networks. Exceptions to this rule again occur in the weak analogy networks, and they occur when object nodes do not map one-to-one from base to target. Unlike object nodes, however, relations that map across always do so with the same name. First-order relations are depicted by normal arrows; higher-order relations are depicted by heavy arrows. Higher-order relations constrain lower-order relations in accordance with structure-mapping theory.

The operationalization of the Theory of the Structure of Explanatory Analogies can be summarized as follows. First, the good analogy possesses clarity because all object mappings from base to target are one-to-one; the weak analogy does not possess clarity because it contains two one-to-three and three one-to-two mappings. Second, the richness (predicate density) of the good analogy is 2.00, and the richness of the weak analogy is 1.85. From a practical viewpoint, richness may be regarded as equal; the closeness of the richness measures is not surprising given that *both* the good and weak analogies aim to explain the operations of the notional computer. Third, the good analogy possesses higher systematicity/abstractness than the weak analogy because 1 third-order relation, 9 second-order relations, and 78 first-order relations were mapped to the target in the good analogy compared with no third-order relations, 6 second-order relations, and 57 first-order relations being mapped across in the weak analogy.

Test Materials. The test materials comprised two sets of questions. The first set was designed to test program comprehension. It was divided into eight parts: (1) Elements of the BASIC language; (2) The replacement statement LET; (3) The PRINT statement; (4) Review: LET, PRINT, and END; (5) The INPUT statement; (6) The DATA and READ statements; (7) The unconditional transfer statement GO TO; and (8) The decision statement IF/THEN.

The second set of questions was designed to test program composition. The set comprised seven questions in increasing order of difficulty and covered the full range of BASIC statements presented.

Procedure The study was conducted in two sessions. Session 1 (the program comprehension phase) commenced at 10:00 a.m. On average, the session lasted 2 1/2 hours. Session 2 (the program composition phase) commenced after a lunch break of about one hour. The session lasted 1 1/2 hours on average.

3

The encoding factor (deep versus shallow) was operationalized by administering the instructional materials and test questions differently in Session 1. In the deep encoding condition, subjects alternated between reading instructional material on BASIC and answering questions on the material just read. In the shallow encoding condition, subjects read the entire set of instructional materials. They then answered each set of questions in the same order as subjects in the deep encoding condition.

After subjects had been instructed on how the experiment would be conducted, the experiment proper commenced. Subjects were told to begin reading the instructional materials placed before them. As they completed the reading, each raised their hand to indicate to the researcher that they had done so.

If subjects were in the deep encoding condition, they were given the first set of printed questions to answer. The researcher asked them to start work and started the stopwatch. On completion of the set of questions, subjects stopped the stopwatch and raised their hand. The researcher then recorded the time taken on the question sheet. The question sheet was then put away. The next set of instructional materials was then given to the subject. Subjects continued by alternating between reading instructional material and answering questions until the last set of questions was answered.

If subjects were in the shallow encoding condition, they first read the entire set of instructional materials. They then answered each set of questions in the same order and following the same procedure as subjects in the deep encoding condition.

Upon completing Session 1, subjects were released for lunch. When they returned for Session 2, they were instructed on the conduct of the experiment in the program composition phase. They were then given 10 minutes to review the instructional materials they had read in Session 1. The researcher then started each subject on the program composition task and, at the same time, started the stopwatch.

When subjects completed the program composition questions, they stopped the stopwatch and raised their hand. The researcher recorded the time taken on the question sheet. Subjects who completed the experimental task were each paid $20.

Scoring   Subjects' responses to the program comprehension and program composition questions were scored according to a template designed by the researcher. The scoring scheme was devised to reward the demonstration of correct knowledge of BASIC and to maximally discriminate between the levels of achievement attained by subjects. An independent check of scoring reliability was performed.

Results and Discussion
Program Comprehension
Figure 1 shows the means for program comprehension score. The program comprehension data were analyzed using ANCOVA and MANCOVA. Hypotheses

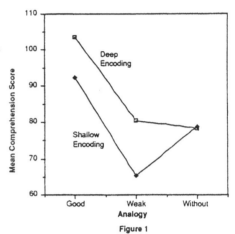

Figure 1

1 and 2 were evaluated using planned comparisons. Hypothesis 1 was confirmed when quality of program comprehension was evaluated in terms of program comprehension score ($p = .001$). It was also confirmed when quality of program comprehension was evaluated in terms of program comprehension score and time ($p = .003$).

Similarly, Hypothesis 2 was confirmed when quality of program comprehension was evaluated in terms of program comprehension score ($p = .499$). The proposition was also supported from a multivariate viewpoint ($p = .395$).

Consistent support for Hypotheses 1 and 2 when evaluated in terms of program comprehension score as well as program comprehension score and time confirms that the quality of program comprehension when learning with a good analogy is significantly better than that associated with learning with a weak analogy or without an analogy, and the quality of program comprehension when learning with a weak analogy and when learning without an analogy are not significantly different. Given the mix of clarity, richness, and systematicity/abstractness operationalized in the experiment, the theory's prediction that these characteristics effectively define good analogy is supported.

Hypothesis 3 was marginally supported when evaluated in terms of program comprehension score ($p = .055$). Despite the lack of statistical significance, the overall (weighted average) program comprehension scores were in the predicted direction (Deep Encoding, $M = 86.5$; Shallow Encoding, $M = 77.4$). The marginal significance of the univariate result may be due the task complexity and constrained experimental learning time that did not allow the expected benefit of deep encoding on the creation and restructuring of knowledge to materialize fully. A deep, semantic appreciation of the notional computer's operations requires that the knowledge acquired be assimilated and restructured over the course of learning. However, restructuring is associated with knowledge understanding but requires time to take effect (Norman, 1978).

Hypothesis 4, the posited interaction between the analogy and encoding factors, was not supported when the quality of program comprehension was evaluated in terms of program comprehension score and also in terms of program comprehension score and time. Thus, the expectation that the analogy would help subjects in the shallow encoding condition more than subjects in the deep encoding condition was not confirmed. Instead, the data suggest that the analogy and encoding factors are independent.

Program Composition

Figure 2 shows the means for program composition score. The program composition data were analyzed using covariance analysis. However, a test of the homogeneity of regression assumption revealed that the assumption was violated for the dependent variable program composition time.

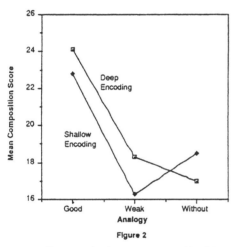

Figure 2

Consequently, the program composition data were analyzed using a covariance model proposed by Searle (1979). *Covariate-adjusted observations* were obtained by rearrangement of the model equation, and the model was estimated using MANOVA.

Using planned comparisons, Hypothesis 5 was supported when evaluated in terms of covariate-adjusted program composition score ($p = .014$). It was also supported when evaluated in terms of covariate-adjusted program composition score and time ($p = .044$). Hypothesis 6 was supported when evaluated in terms of covariate-adjusted program composition score ($p = .998$) and also when evaluated in terms of covariate-adjusted program composition score and time ($p = .613$). The non-significant result indicates equality between the weak analogy and no analogy treatment conditions.

The consistent program composition results show that the Theory of the Structure of Explanatory Analogies is also supported with respect to program composition. Note that the analogy factor accounted for 6.6% of the explained variance of program composition score but accounted for 12.0% of the explained variance of program comprehension score. A *transfer of learning* from program comprehension to program composition is thus evident. The smaller effect of type of analogy on program composition is consistent with the expectation that the explanatory power of analogy facilitates performance in program composition via achievement in program comprehension.

Post Hoc Analysis

While scoring subjects' responses to the program comprehension questions, it was noticed that the variability of scores on questions that focused on the syntactic rules of BASIC statements was consistently smaller than it was on questions that focused on the conceptual understanding associated with the operations of the notional computer. This phenomenon suggested that it might be fruitful to investigate the data further by distinguishing between scores on syntax-oriented questions and scores on semantics-oriented questions. Accordingly, the program comprehension data were subclassified into syntax scores and semantics scores and analyzed further via a *post hoc* analysis.

The data for the *post hoc* analysis were analyzed using ANCOVA and MANCOVA. The dependent variables were syntax score and semantics score. The experimental design was identical to that used in the main analysis.

Model estimation revealed that for syntax score, the analogy factor was significant ($p = .015$); the encoding factor was also significant ($p = .012$). For semantics score, however, only the analogy factor was significant ($p = .003$). From a multivariate viewpoint, both the analogy factor and the encoding factor were significant ($p = .001$ and $p = .043$ respectively).

Planned comparisons were performed to evaluate Hypotheses 1 and 2 for syntax, semantics, and both syntax and semantics. For syntax, the good analogy versus weak analogy and no analogy comparison was marginally significant ($p = .056$), while the weak analogy versus no analogy comparison was significant ($p = .027$).

For semantics, the good analogy group was significantly better than the weak analogy and no analogy groups ($p = .001$), and the weak analogy and no analogy groups were not significantly different ($p = .841$). That is, the comparisons were consistent with the results obtained for the composite program comprehension score.

Some interesting insights are obtained from the above analysis. The significance of the analogy factor on both syntax score and semantics score and the significance of the encoding factor only on syntax score suggest that the analogy treatment affects performance on both syntax and semantics, while the encoding treatment affects performance on syntax only.

Furthermore, it becomes clear that the marginal significance of the encoding factor on the composite program comprehension score ($p = .055$) was attributable to the effect of deep encoding on syntax ($p = .012$), not on semantics ($p = .117$). This result suggests that students learn the technical (rule-like) nature of syntactic knowledge effectively when such knowledge is tested shortly after it is presented. In effect, the quick application of newly-acquired syntactic knowledge assists students in assimilating the rules associated with syntax and helps to drill them in the application of such rules.

By contrast, the lack of significance of the encoding factor on semantics suggests that, contrary to the intended outcome of the encoding treatment, a deep semantic understanding of program statements was not achieved probably because of the limited exposure that students were given to programming. The hypothetical time division associated with complex learning proposed by Norman (1978) suggests that the bulk of knowledge restructuring (and hence deep semantic understanding) occurs during the central phase of learning, after sufficient time has been spent on the accretion of knowledge. Given the restricted learning time in the experiment (approximately four hours), the relatively small amount of time spent on restructuring appears to be due to the use of analogy rather than the use of deep encoding.

Examination of the weighted average means for syntax shows that the good analogy and no analogy groups were more alike than different, while the weak analogy group was unlike both (Good Analogy, $M = 25.5$; Weak Analogy, $M = 20.6$; No Analogy, $M = 24.1$). This result suggests that the weak analogy harmed the acquisition of syntactic knowledge, and the good analogy did not assist the acquisition of such knowledge. However, for semantics, the good analogy group was distinct from the weak analogy and no analogy groups (Good Analogy, $M = 72.6$; Weak Analogy, $M = 52.0$; No Analogy, $M = 54.6$). Thus, the good analogy assisted the acquisition of semantic knowledge but not syntactic knowledge.

Research Conclusions

The Theory of the Structure of Explanatory Analogies was empirically tested. The research supported the theory's prediction that clarity and systematicity/abstractness are structural characteristics of analogy that effectively capture the strength of its explanatory power. *Post hoc* analysis further revealed that good analogy assists the acquisition of semantic programming knowledge but not syntactic programming knowledge.

From the viewpoint of experimental methodology, the *explicit* operationalization and measurement of systematicity and abstractness has shown that these structural characteristics of analogy can be derived objectively and in a manner that possesses empirical validity. Thus, the usefulness of the syntactic perspective on knowledge representation based on the concepts of systematicity and abstractness has been demonstrated.

References

Anderson, J. R., Farrell, R. & Sauers, R. (1984). Learning to Program in LISP. *Cognitive Science*, 8, 87-129.

Bayman, P. & Mayer, R. E. (1983). A diagnosis of beginning programmers' misconceptions of BASIC programming statements. *Communica-*

tions of the ACM, 26, 677-679.

Craik, F. I. M. & Lockhart, R. S. (1972). Levels of processing: A framework for memory research. *Journal of Verbal Learning and Verbal Behavior*, 11, 671–684.

Gentner, D. (1982). Are scientific analogies metaphors? In D. S. Miall (Ed.), *Metaphor: Problems and Perspectives*, pp. 106-132. Brighton, Sussex: The Harvester Press.

Gentner, D. (1983). Structure-mapping: A theoretical framework for analogy. *Cognitive Science*, 7, 155-170.

Mayer, R. E. (1975). Different problem-solving competencies established in learning computer programming with and without meaningful models. *Journal of Educational Psychology*, 67, 725-734.

Mayer, R. E. (1976). Some conditions of meaningful learning for computer programming: Advance organizers and subject control of frame order. *Journal of Educational Psychology*, 68, 143-150.

Mayer, R. E. (1979). A psychology of learning BASIC. *Communications of the ACM*, 22, 589-593.

Norman, D. A. (1978). Notes toward a theory of complex learning. In A. M. Lesgold, J. W. Pellegrino, S. Fokkema & R. Glaser (Eds.), *Cognitive Psychology and Instruction*, pp. 39-48. NY: Plenum.

Norman, D. A. (1980). Teaching, learning, and the representation of knowledge. In R. E. Snow, P. A. Frederico & W. E. Montague (Eds.), *Aptitude, Learning, and Instruction*, Volume 2, pp. 237-244. Hillsdale, NJ: Lawrence Erlbaum Associates.

Rumelhart, D. E. & Norman, D. A. (1981). Analogical processes in learning. In J. R. Anderson (Ed.), *Cognitive Skills and their Acquisition*, pp. 335-359. Hillsdale, NJ: Lawrence Erlbaum Associates.

Searle, S. R. (1979). Alternative covariance models for the 2-way crossed classification. *Communications in Statistics – Theory and Methods*, A8, 799-818.

Simons, P. R. J. (1984). Instructing with analogies. *Journal of Educational Psychology*, 76, 513-527.

Spohrer, J. C. & Soloway, E. (1986). Novice mistakes: Are the folk wisdoms correct? *Communications of the ACM*, 29, 624-632.

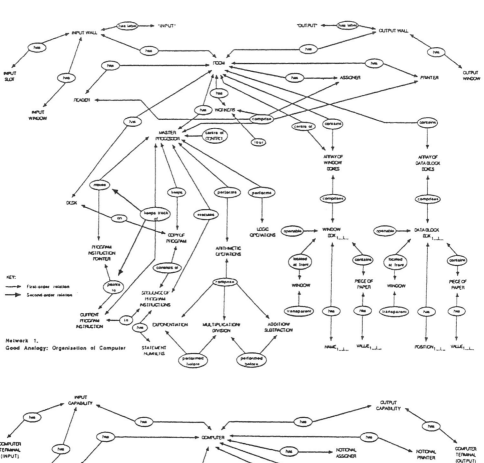

Network 1.
Good Analogy: Organisation of Computer

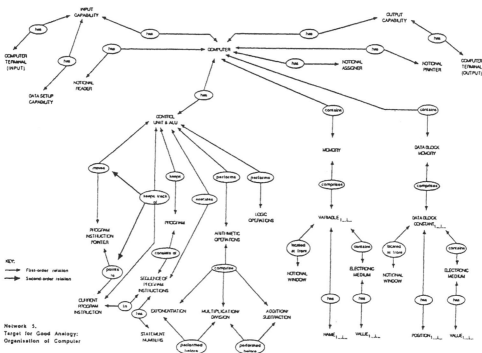

Network 5.
Target for Good Analogy:
Organisation of Computer

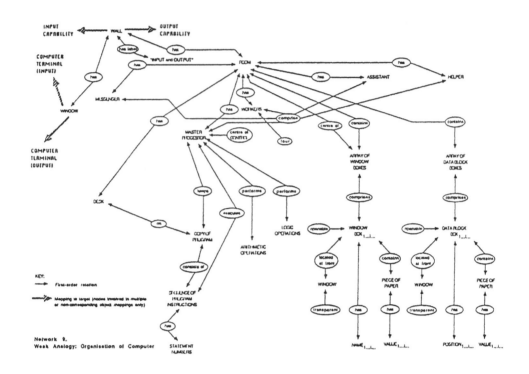

Network 9.
Weak Analogy: Organisation of Computer

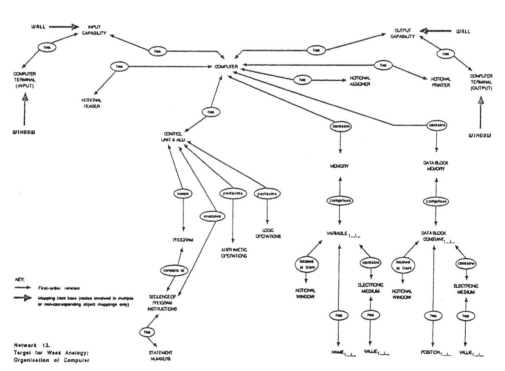

Network 13.
Target for Weak Analogy:
Organisation of Computer

8

Evaluating and Debugging Analogically Acquired Models

Beth Adelson
Dept. of Computer Science
Tufts University
Medford, MA 02155 [1]

Abstract

We describe elements of a cognitive theory of analogical reasoning. The theory was developed using protocol data and has been implemented as a computer model. In order to constrain the theory, it has been developed within a problem-soving context, reflecting the purpose of analogical reasoning. This has allowed us to develop: A purpose-constrained mapping process which makes learning and debugging more tractable; An evaluation process that actively searches for bugs; And a debugging process that maintains functional aspects of base models, while adding target-appropriate causal explanations. The active, knowledge-based elements of our theory are characteristic of mechanisms needed to model complex problem-solving.

1. Introduction: Motivation and Goals

The research described here is part of an attempt to develop a cognitive theory of analogical reasoning. Because the purpose of analogical reasoning is to learn and solve problems, we have developed our theory within a problem-solving context. This approach provides powerful insights into the phenomenon and constraints on the theory.

Recent research suggests a class of theories which rests on the processes of retrieval, mapping, evaluation, debugging and generalization (Carbonell, 1983 & 1986; Falkenhainer, Forbus & Gentner, 1986; Holyoke & Thagard 1985 & in press; Burstein & Adelson 1987; Kolodner, 1985; Kedar-Cabelli, 1984). Our work extends existing cognitive theories of analogical reasoning by specifying the processes of mapping, evaluation and debugging as active; constrained by the problem-solving context; and dependent on knowledge about function, structure and mechanism [2]. In our theory, the mapping process can be focussed so that partial domain models, sufficient for the immediate problem-solving purpose, can be mapped. This incremental learning strategy renders both mapping and debugging more tractable (Adelson & Burstein, 1987). A detailed description of our theory of mapping can be found in Adelson (1989), here we focus on evaluation and debugging:

1. Active Evaluation: An intelligent problem-solver needs to be able to identify the bugs inherent in an analogically acquired domain model. Our system searches for bugs in newly mapped domain models. It does so by comparing the nature of the actions and objects in the newly mapped model to the nature of the actions and objects appropriate in the domain being mapped into. This allows the system to identify the aspects of the model that are inappropriate and therefore unlikely to hold in the domain being mapped into. Our system also has knowledge about the way in which analogical correspondences are meant to be understood across domains. These aspects of our system reflect powerful elements of human reasoning.

2. Active Debugging: Once the buggy portion of a model has been identified it must be replaced by a representation that is accurate in the new domain. Our system constructs and runs simulations in both source and target domains in order to identify mechanisms with *analogous functionality*. This allows the system to correct mapped models, maintaining the functionality provided by the analogical example while building a representation of a mechanism appropriate to the target domain. Here too our system's behavior characterizes the constrained way in which analogical examples are understood and used.

2. Protocol Data Illustrating the Issues

[1] Thanks to Michael Brent and Mike Futeran. Also thanks to Dedre Gentner, Brian Falkenhainer and Ken Forbus for their loan of SME.
This work was funded by Carnegie-Mellon's NSF funded EDRC and by a grant from NSF's Engineering Directorate.

[2] The spirit of Carbonell's (1986) work on derivational analogy; Holyoke & Thagard's (in press) work on multiple constraint satisfaction; Kedar-Cabelli's (1984) work on purpose-guided reasoning, Burstein's (1983) work on causal reasoning and Falkenhainer, Forbus & Gentner's (1986) work on structure mapping is consonant with our view of analogical reasoning as an active, knowledge intensive process.

In developing our theory we have repeatedly drawn on the protocol data described below. These data yield insights into processes that need to be described in implementing a cognitive problem-solver.

The Protocol:

In collecting our data we video-taped a tutor teaching a student about stacks. The tutor's goal was to have the student be able to write Pascal procedures for pushing and popping items on to and off of stacks. At the beginning of the protocol session the student had just completed an introductory programming course in which he had learned about some basic programming constructs and about elementary data structures such as arrays and simple linked lists. (He had not learned about using a linked list as a stack.) The tutor had the intention of building upon the student's existing knowledge of Pascal through the use of analogy.

The relevant events of the protocol can be summarized as follows:

Learning about the behavior of a stack:

The tutor told the student that stacks are so named because their behavior is analogous to the behavior of the device that holds plates in a cafeteria. The student then proceeded to think of ways in which he might have previously encountered the use of stacks in programming; he suggested that stacks might be useful in implementing subroutine calls. He then stated that, in general, when a task had an unmet precondition it would be useful to delay execution of the task by pushing it onto a stack.

Learning about the mechanism underlying the behavior:

The tutor told the student that the mechanism of the computer science stack is in some sense analogous to the mechanism of the cafeteria stack. In order to achieve 'last in first out' (LIFO) behavior items are pushed *and* popped at the top of the cafeteria stack. The student drew a diagram of a cafeteria stack and noted that *push* causes the stack's spring to compress and *pop* causes it to expand.

Implementing push and pop in the target domain:

The student then wrote the code for *push* and *pop*. After writing *push*, however, the student asked if the capacity limitation which results when the spring is fully compressed is relevant in the new domain. The tutor told the student that the *physical* elements of the analogy (springs, movement of plates, etc.) do not apply. The student then asked if the concept of capacity limitation applies even if the spring doesn't. The tutor responded that although capacity limitation is an important concept, the student should disregard it for now.

3. Issues for Specifying a Theory of Analogical Problem-Solving

As diagrammed in Figure 1, the class of model to which our system belongs, contains a mapper, an evaluation and debugging mechanism, and a problem-solving component. The mapper takes as input a base domain model and a list of the correspondences between elements in the base model and already known target elements. The mapper produces tentative target domain models which are then debugged and evaluated. The debugged models are then used to in problem-solving. Additonally, in our system, the output of the debugger can be used to guide subsequent mappings.

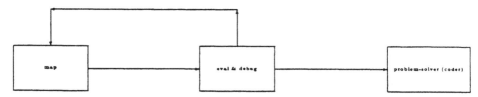

Figure 1: Components of the Analogical Reasoner

3.1. Purpose-Constrained Mapping

Purpose provides an essential constraint in problem-solving, but current implementations of cognitive theories do not make sufficient use of this constraint[3]. The argument for why purpose is necessary in constraining

---

[3]Thagard and Holyoke (in press), and Kedar-Cabelli, (1986) also stress the theoretical importance of purpose.

human problem-solving runs as follows. Understanding a complex domain requires understanding a number of distinct aspects of the domain and the relationships among those aspects (Burstein, 1986; Collins &Gentner, 1983; Adelson, 1984). Given the constraints of the cognitive system, it is not possible to learn all of these various aspects at one time. Rather, to make learning of a complex domain more tractable, students and instructors typically focus on individual, purpose-related aspects of the domain and, one at a time, map partial models from more familiar analog domains (Burstein & Adelson, 1987 & in press)[4]. In our computational description, the learning process starts with this selection and mapping of purpose-constrained aspects of the target domain. Our mapping mechanism focuses on partial models of the base domain whose type reflects the problem solver's purpose, and maps these models *separately*, type by type, over to the target domain[5].

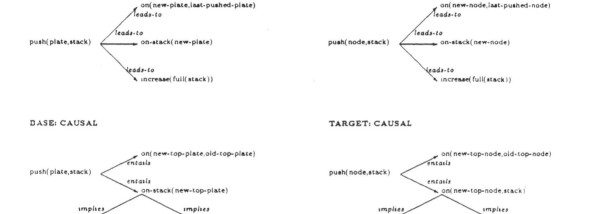

Figure 2: Behavioral and Causal Models (top and bottom) in the Base and Target Domains (left and right)

The following illustrates a mapping produced by our system:
In this example our overall goal is to have the system model the problem-solving in our protocol. That is, we want the system to learn about computer science stacks and stack operations by analogy to cafeteria stacks and to produce the code for the operations *push* and *pop*. To accomplish this, the system begins by following the tutor's suggestion to focus initially on the behavioral model for *push*[6]. It selects that model from a base domain containing behavioral and causal models of both *push* and *pop*. The selected model is then mapped into the target domain. The behavioral and causal models for *push* in the base domain can be seen in the left half of Figure 2 (top and bottom respectively).

In the upper right of the figure we see the behavioral model of the target domain produced by our mapping mechanism. What is important to note here[7] is that the nature of the models allows them to be used in the problem-solving that is the system's ultimate goal. That is, the models in the figure describe the chains of events

---

[4] Our protocol data illustrates this process. The student acquired a sophisticated understanding of the behavior of a stack before learning about the mechanism supporting the behavior.

[5] See Burstein & Adelson (in press) for an explanation of the difference between models of varying types.

[6] The tutor also supplies a list of base and target domain correspondences stating for example, that *push* in the base corresponds to *push* in the target and plates correspond to nodes.

[7] Space limitations force us to omit several points about the models. The assertions in the model can be formalized to allow, for example, the deduction that the pushed node becomes the new top node. Additionally, the predicates do have an underlying

11

that occur when domain operations are performed (Schank & Riesbeck, 1981; Schank & Abelson, 1977). As a result, they can be run on the system's *simulation machine* (Adelson, 1989; Forbus, 1985; de Kleer & Brown, 1985). This allows them not only to be examined by a debugger (Sections 3.2.1 and 3.2.2) but also to be used to generate Pascal code after debugging.

The following section describes how our system debugs the newly mapped model of *push* so that problem-solving can be carried out successfully.

3.2. Debugging a Newly Mapped Model

3.2.1 Actively Seeking out Bugs

In our theory, debugging is characterized by an *active* search for bugs. The base domain model is known, by definition, to provide an imperfect model of the target domain. The base model may contain inappropriate elements that require deletion or transformation; or it may require additional knowledge specific to the target domain.

Our current example illustrates the case in which a newly mapped model contains a concept that is inappropriate in the target domain. Looking at the behavioral model in the target domain (Figure 2, upper right) we see that it pushing a node onto a stack which is implemented as a list of nodes, leads to the stack being more full. However, the system contains prior knowledge about the target domain which asserts that lists of nodes are used when a data structure without a pre-specified capacity limitation is desired[8]. Since linked lists have no specified capacity limitation there is an inconsistency between the newly mapped model and prior knowledge of the target domain. The system must have the ability to notice and resolve this inconsistency.

Identifying and Fixing Bugs in a Runnable Model:

Here we describe how the system's evaluation and debugging mechanism resolves the 'fullness' bug in the course of evaluating the behavioral model of *push*. The system's *evaluator* traverses a newly mapped model in an attempt to determine whether each element it encounters is appropriate in light of the domain the model has been mapped into. In order to allow the evaluator to carry out the evaluation the system has been given several kinds of knowledge:

K1. Any element that occurs in a model has a definition, a *template* consisting of a set of features (Burstein, 1983; Waltz, 1982; Winston, 1977 & 1982). Elements in the model are either objects (e.g. *stack*) or predicates which describe attributes of, or actions on the object (e.g. *fullness* or *push* respectively). For objects, one feature in the template specifies the class it belongs to. For predicates the class of both the predicate and its arguments are listed. For example, the predicate *full* is defined as a measurement of the capacity of some argument which must be a limited-capacity container.

K2. The system knows not only which objects and predicates are appropriate to each domain, but also which *classes* of objects and predicates. For example, the system knows that integer variables in particular, and data structures in general, are appropriate in the computer domain.

K3. The system has general knowledge about how analogical correspondences are meant to be taken. For example, the system contains knowledge that physical contiguity in the base can be appropriately thought of as corresponding to virtual contiguity in the target.

The system uses the knowledge described above in applying rules which allow it to evaluate each element in the newly mapped model. The rules are:

R1 Infer that an element currently in the target domain is appropriate in the new model.

R2. If the element is not currently in the target domain but it is of a *class* currently in the target domain, infer that a modified version of the element is appropriate in the new model and use existing domain information

---

semantics. For example, the value of full results from dividing the current number of plates by the maximum number of plates. Along these lines, the models in the figure have substantially less detail than the actual models used by the system.

[8] For this example we have supplied the system with the same knowledge of the target domain that our novice programmer had. We have given it models for performing typical operations on variables, arrays and linked lists. It also has world knowledge about boxes and containers.

about the class to modify the element[9].

R3. If the element belongs to a class that has a corresponding class in the target (point K3), infer that a modified version of the element belongs and use existing domain information about the coresponding class to modify the model.

R4. A predicate can only be applied to an argument of an appropriate type. That is fullness cannot be predicated of a container without capacity limitations (point K1).

We see each of the above rules (and the knowledge they embody) being applied as we follow the evaluator tracing through the model for *push*. Starting at the root of the tree, the evaluator encounters the element *push*. Because the tutor had specified that *push* in the base corresponded to an asserted, but as yet undefined, version of *push* in the target the system infers that *push* is appropriate to the model and turns to the predicates that follow from it.

The template for the predicate *on* states that it is a "physical contiguity relation". The system knows that physical contiguity in the base corresponds to virtual contiguity in the target (Rule R3). It therefore makes this change to the predicate's template and then infers that the predicate holds. This is an example of the system's ability to interpret analogical correspondences in an appropriate, non-literal manner.

The evaluator comes to the next predicate that *push* leads to. Although *on-stack* does not yet exist in the target, its definition states that it is a "membership relation". The system finds that other predicates in the target are membership relations (e.g. *in-set*) and therefore hypothesizes that the predicate holds (Rule R2).

The evaluator turns to the predicate *full*, it finds that *full* is potentially appropriate in that it already exists in the target as knowledge that arrays can be full (Rule R1). However, the evaluator finds that fullness can only be predicated of containers having capacity limitations (Rule R4). It knows that the stack is being implemented as a list of nodes and that lists do not have capacity limitations. The system suggests that the concept fullness should be removed from the model. It then removes fullness. At this point, if the system is told that the problem arose because no capacity limited containers were being used in this example it will also remove all other predicates whose definitions involve capacity limitations.

But more mileage can be gotten out of this evaluation. The system has just mapped and debugged the behavioral model. It can now to go back and map the causal model using information gained in debugging the behavioral one. When this mapping begins the system will take note of any elements that have been deleted from the behavioral model (in this example, *full*); pieces of the causal model that only support an element already deleted from the behavioral will not be mapped. As a result of our strategy of incrementally mapping partial models and using earlier mappings to guide subsequent ones, the debugging of potentially complex causal models can be made considerably simpler.

3.2.2 Transforming a Mapped Model: Reasoning About Simulations

In the example just described we considered the case where an element needs to be deleted. Our system also handles the case in which a model needs to be corrected by being *transformed* through finding additional correspondences between elements of the base and target domains.

The case in which a model needs this type of transformation is illustrated by the example in which the goal is to implement a stack using an array rather than a linked list. The representation of the base domain is the same as it was for our earlier example. Prior knowledge of the target domain still consists of information about variables and arrays but not about linked lists. The system again has runnable models for typical operations such as initialization and search.

The behavioral model of push is again mapped into the target domain. This time no changes are made in the behavioral model; the fullness of the stack is found to be consistent with the system's knowledge of the capacity limitation of an array. After mapping the behavioral model, the system maps the causal model of the stack into the target domain and then begins to evaluate and debug it. During this process the system questions the tutor on the appropriateness of the spring in the causal model (see Figure 2, bottom right). The tutor tells the system that the domain-appropriate *functional analog* of the spring needs to be found. In finding the functional analog

---

[9]Space constraints preclude a description of some of the methods that have been developed to modify 'almost right' elements.

of the spring the system will draw on several types of *relational knowledge* which comprise the system's causal ontology[10]:

RK1. The system contains functional to structural mappings; knowledge relating state changes and the mechanisms causing them (Adelson, 1984; de Kleer & Brown, 1985; Forbus, 1985; Kuipers, 1985). For example, it knows that 'changes in fullness are supported by changes in the mechanism comprised of the spring, the set of plates, etc'[11].

RK2. The system has knowledge relating actions and the state changes they produce. It knows, therefore that 'pushing leads to changes in fullness'.

RK3. The system also has knowledge relating actions and the mechanisms involved. It knows that 'pushing involves a change in the spring'.

In order to find the piece of target domain mechanism with the same function as the spring, the system will find what sort of state change in the base is associated with a particular change in the spring. It will then turn to the target look at the parallel state change and determine what piece of mechanism is effected in the way that the spring was. To do this the system first needs to focus on the base and find what state changes the spring is involved in. It examines its knowledge of functional to structural mappings (RK1) and finds that the spring is involved in changes in fullness. Now, in order to find out the nature of the relationship between changes in fullness and changes in the spring, the system looks for a simulation in which both fullness (RK2) and the spring (RK3) will change. It finds that simulating *push* will produce the needed information. The simulation is run, providing the system with values for the fullness of the stack and the compression of the spring before and after the simulation is run. The system then compares the direction of change in both fullness and spring compression and finds that there is a positive relationship between the two [12].

The system now needs to find what piece of mechanism in the *target* domain changes for the same reason and in the same way as the spring (i.e. increases with fullness). The system begins by looking for an operation in which fullness increases. It will then run this operation and look for pieces of mechanism that register increases in fullness.

Target domain knowledge about the relation between actions and state changes (RK2) asserts that initializing an array causes fullness to increase; the system simulates the process and finds that in the target, it is the array-index that increases with fullness. As a result of this process, in which corresponding simulations are sought, run and evaluated for the purpose of finding functionally analogous mechanisms the system correctly hypothesizes that the array index is the analog of the spring[13].

Space limitations prevent further description of our system, but the debugging process does not end here. Now that the models mapped from the base domain have had changes made to them, they must be checked to see that they are still sufficient. This is done through a series of simulations designed to test that the models still exhibit aspects of LIFO behavior that the system knows are important. For example, pushing and then popping a set of elements must result in reversing their ordering. Additionally, the system must eventually produce both box and arrow and pascal versions of push and pop (Adelson et al, 1988).

4. Summary & Conclusions

we have presented a discussion of three of our system's mechanisms: one for mapping, one for evaluating mapped models and one for debugging inconsistencies. We have implemented a purpose-constrained mapper that reflects the way students limit their focus of attention. The strategy results in incremental learning which makes both mapping and debugging more tractable. We have also implemented an evaluation mechanism that identifies inconsistencies as elements of newly mapped models are checked to see if they are the sort of elements that are known to exist in the target domain. In doing so the evaluation mechanism uses knowledge about the nature

---

[10] These relations are learned in that the system notices and stores these types of relations whenever it acquires a new model.

[11] The system's knowledge does not contain any explicit statement concerning *how* changes in fullness are related to changes in the spring. This is what needs to be determined.

[12] Currently the system can recognize positive and negative correlations, as well as the lack of relationship between two state variables. It is possible to expand this part of the system to include the recognition of more complex, but regular relationships.

[13] When more than one piece of mechanism is found, the system has the ability to use functional information decide on the better analog.

of the base and target domains and they way in which relations apply across analogous domains. Finally, we have presented a debugging mechanism that maintains functional aspects of base models while adding target-appropriate causal explanations. The development of the mechanisms has been possible because we have worked within a problem-solving context, reflecting the purpose of analogical reasoning.

5 References

Adelson, Beth. Cognitive modeling: Uncovering how designers design. *The Journal of Engineering Design.*. Vol 1,1. 1989

Adelson, Beth. When novices surpass experts: How the difficulty of a task may increase with expertise. *Journal of Experimental Psychology: Learning, Memory and Cognition*, July 1984.

Adelson, B., Gentner, D., Thagard, P., Holyoak, K., Burstein, M., and Hammond, K. The Role of Analogy in a Theory of Problem-Solving *Proceedings of the Eleventh Annual Meeting of the Cognitive Science Society*, 1988.

Burstein, Mark H. Causal Analogical Reasoning. *Machine Learning: Volume I*. Michalski, R.S., Carbonell, J.G. and Mitchell, T.M. (Ed.). Los Altos, CA: Morgan Kaufman Publishers, Inc., 1983.

Burstein, Mark H. Concept Formation by Incremental Analogical Reasoning and Debugging. *Machine Learning: Volume II* Michalski, R.S., Carbonell, J.G. and Mitchell, T.M. (Ed.) Morgan Kaufmann Publishers, Inc., Los Altos, CA 1986.

Burstein, M. and Adelson, B. Mapping and Integrating Partial Mental Models. *Proceedings of the Tenth Annual Meeting of the Cognitive Science Society*, 1987.

Burstein, M. and Adelson, B. Analogical Reasoning for Learning. in *Applications of Artificial Intelligence to Educational Testing.* R. Freedle (Ed.) In press. Erlbaum: Hillsdale, NJ.

Carbonell, Jaime G. Transformational Analogy: Problem Solving and Expertise Acquisition. *Machine Learning: Volume I*. Michalski, R.S., Carbonell, J.G. and Mitchell, T.M. (Ed.), Los Altos, CA: Morgan Kaufman Publishers, Inc., 1983.

Carbonell, Jaime G. Derivational Analogy: A Theory of Reconstructive Problem Solving and Expertise Acquisition. *Machine Learning: Volume II*. Michalski, R.S., Carbonell, J.G. and Mitchell, T.M. (Ed.), Los Altos, CA: Morgan Kaufman Publishers, Inc., 1986

de Kleer, J. and Brown, J. S. A Qualitative Physics based on Confluences In *Qualitative Reasoning about Physical Systems* D Bobrow editor, MIT Press 1985.

Falkenhainer, B., Forbus, K. and Gentner, D. The Structure-Mapping Engine. In *Proceedings of AAAI-86*. Los Altos, CA: Morgan Kaufman, 1986.

Forbus, Ken. Qualitative Process Theory In *Qualitative Reasoning about Physical Systems* D. Bobrow editor, MIT Press 1985

Gentner, Dedre. Structure-Mapping: A theoretical framework for analogy. *Cognitive Science*, 1983, 7(2), 155-70.

Holyoke, K. and Thagard, P. Analogical Mapping by Constraint Satisfaction. Cognitive Psychology. In Press.

Kolodner, J. In *Proceedings of the Seventh Annual Conference of the Cognitive Science Society*. Boulder, CO: Cognitive Science Society, 1985.

Kuipers, B. Commonsense Reasoning About Causality. In *Qualitative Reasoning about Physical Systems* D. Bobrow editor. MIT Press 1985.

Kedar-Cabelli, S. Analogy with Purpose in Legal Reasoning from Precedents. Technical Report 17. Laboratory for Computer Science Rutgers. 1984.

Schank, R., and Abelson, B. Scripts, Plans, Goals and Understanding. Hillsdale, NJ: Erlbaum, 1977.

Schank, R. and Riesbeck, C. Inside Computer Understanding. Erlbaum: Hillsdale, NJ. 1981.

Waltz, D. Event shape diagrams. In Proceedings of the National Conference on AI. 1982.

Winston, P. Learing new principles from precedents and exercises. *AI.* 1982.

Analogical Process Performance

Clark N. Quinn
Learning Research and Development Center[1]
University of Pittsburgh

Abstract

Analogy is one of the primary mechanisms of cognition, particularly in problem-solving and learning. However, people do not use analogies very effectively. I postulate seven separate processes for analogy that could be responsible for weak analogical reasoning and test those processes independently. The results suggest that performance on analysis of the problem and performance on confirmation of the appropriateness of the analogy both might be suspect in analogical deficits.

Various analyses of the component processes of analogy in problem-solving have been performed. Clement (1981, 1986) has investigated how subjects approached new problems by forming analogies to old ones and has derived process specifications from empirical observation. Sternberg (1977a, 1977b) has specified the steps in analogy for problems where the base domain is known. Holland, Holyoak, Nisbett, and Thagard (1986) have developed a model of induction that includes an account of analogical processes. Gentner (1989) has also outlined a theory of processes in analogy. In contrast to the psychological approaches, Hall (1989) has developed a synthesis with which to analyze the various artificial intelligence models of analogy. These specifications are summarized in Table 1.

Clement	Gentner	HHNT	Hall	Sternberg	Quinn
		Represent		Encode	Analysis
Generate	Access	Select	Recognize		Access
	Map	Map	Elaborate	Map	Map
Confirm	Soundness		Evaluate	Justify	Confirm
					Transfer
Predict				Apply	Solve
Transfer	Store	Transfer	Consolidate		Transfer

Table 1.

Comparison of these analyses of analogy indicates that none of the above specifications includes all the steps that can be involved in the use of analogies. Under Quinn in Table 1 is the analysis proposed for consideration here. This analysis includes an exhaustive list of the processes involved in analogical problem solving. These steps are:

1. *analyze* the target problem to be understood;

2. *access* a familiar base domain;

3. *map* relations between the base and the target;

4. *confirm* the analogy;

5. *transfer* the problem statement of the target to the base domain representation;

6. *solve* the problem for the base domain;

7. *transfer* the solution to the target problem.

---

[1] Based on research performed while the author was at the University of California, San Diego

The first four steps may need to be repeated until a base analogy is successfully accessed and confirmed as being an appropriate model for the target. Some parts of the elaboration of the representations resulting from later processes may actually be accomplished by preceding processes, for instance the transfer of the problem from the target to the base domain may be accomplished as a result of the access and mapping processes. This still requires specification of all the processes, however, as no process can be assumed to be completely subsumed.

This model for analogy leads to predictions about performance. Prior research (Gick & Holyoak, 1980, 1983) has suggested, in a coarse analysis, that accessing an adequate analogy is less likely than successful exploitation of a provided analogy. Which of the cognitive processes of analogy are entailed in obtaining a relevant analogy and which in the subsequent use? Further, which of the processes involved in accessing an analogy might contribute to deficits in performance?

A fine-grained view of access should include the processes of analysis of the problem, access of a base domain, a mapping between the two domains, and confirmation of the analogy. Use of a given analogy, however, should incorporate the processes of mapping between the domains, transfer of the problem to the familiar base domain, solution of the problem in the base domain, and transfer to the target of the solution. Gick & Holyoak found that, given a hint to use a previous problem, subjects are quite adept at using the suggested analogy to generate an acceptable solution. This suggests that the processes involved in use of an analogy, mapping, transfer, and solution, should be adequate.

On the other hand, Gick and Holyoak found that subjects were unlikely to recall a recently presented analogical solution. Which processes might be inadequate in the access of an analogy? When presented with analogies, subjects correctly rate good analogies as better than poor ones (Gentner & Landers, 1985; Ratterman & Gentner, 1987). This would indicate that the subjects can confirm analogies adequately. Mapping has already been identified as a process that should be well practiced and effective. The problem then is to decide whether it is the analysis process or the access process that introduces the performance deficits. The analysis process yields a representation of the target problem that is then used as a basis for the selection of the base domain. The access process is determined by the representation of the target problem. Gentner (1982) has effectively argued that the access is "ballistic" in the sense that the base domain accessed is wholly determined by the representation and once the access process is launched it proceeds without possible intervention to produce a base domain representation. Given a surface representation of the target domain, the access process should return a base domain that matches on surface features. Similarly, if the analysis process results in a deep representation of the problem, the base accessed should return a useful deep analogy. This suggests that analysis is the culpable process. The expectation is that performance on analysis is inadequate. Other processes should have adequate performance.

Experiment: Component Process Performance

This experiment tested the processes independently to determine which processes were culpable in inefficient analogical performance. The processes tested were analysis, access, mapping, confirmation, transfer, and solution.

Method

The processes were tested by having the subject perform the appropriate subsequent process on a problem with the previous processes performed. For example, a subject might be instructed to perform the mapping between one domain, elaborated by the analysis process, and a new domain from the access process.

Each of the six processes was tested in six domains. Testing each process in order or in random order on the same or different domains could lead to contamination effects. For this reason the process factor had to be conducted between subjects. Each subject could perform the process in each of the six domains. This led to a two factor design with one between-subjects factor (task) and one within-subjects factor (domain).

Background knowledge could strongly influence performance on any of the analogical processes. Ideally, subjects would be presented with suitable artificial material so that all subjects share equal knowledge of the base domain and the target. A more practical answer may be to have a variety of analogies over a spectrum of domains, and to allow the subjects to self-evaluate their knowledge of the domain. However, a pilot study (Quinn, 1989) assessed and revealed no effect of self-rated domain knowledge on performance.

Materials. The materials consisted of a workbook containing the six problems. Since there were six different tasks that were administered between subjects, there were six different types of books. Each book consisted of six randomly-ordered problems, each problem in a different domain, all testing the performance of a single process.

I obtained or created six analogies, each with a paired target and base domain. These analogies are drawn from the literature, from my own experience, or were created for the experiment. They cover a broad range of likely experience, from some that require very specific knowledge to some that are likely to be familiar to most every subject.

Within each analogy, I created questions that addressed the specific processes required for analogy. For analysis, subjects were given the target problem and asked *not* to solve the problem, but, rather, merely to analyze the problem, performing all the steps necessary to solve the problem. If the subjects *thought* they had an answer, they were asked to perform the steps that justified their answer. In the access task, the subjects read a target problem and were asked to think of a similar problem. They were instructed that the specifics of the situation might be very similar or widely different. For the mapping task, subjects were given both a target and base domain, with the target domain elaborated, and asked to elaborate the base domain and to establish the correspondences between the two domains. Subjects were instructed to confirm an analogy between two given domains by rating the quality of the match and, more important, justifying their decision. In the transfer task, subjects were given both target and base domains and a particular situation in one domain. They were then asked to find the equivalent situation in the other domain. Transfer was examined as a single process since the cognitive processes operating on the two representations should be perform equivalently in either direction. The transfer process task was balanced between the two directions: transfer of the problem to the base domain and transfer of the solution back to the target domain. The final process tested was solution of a problem. Subjects were given a problem in the base domain and asked to find the solution.

Subjects. The subjects were 86 students in a cognitive psychology course. Participation in the experiment was voluntary. The topic of analogy was part of the course content, but was not presented before the administration of the experiment. These students were predominantly upper-division college students. While their generally high level of college experience *could* conceivably create a pattern of excellent performance on analogical processes, no explicit training is typically encountered in the curriculum and, in fact, their performance on some processes was less than perfect. Subjects with incomplete workbooks were eliminated from analysis. This eliminated 16 of the 86 subjects, leaving a total of 70 subjects for analysis: 11 in analysis, 8 access, 13 mapping, 13 confirmation, 12 transfer, and 13 solution.

Scoring. The data collected from this experiment consisted of six written answers for each subject. Each question was from a different domain. The subjects' answers differ in qualitative ways from the ideal answer. They can range from the subject having performed the wrong task or not having performed any task at all to an essentially perfect performance. Important distinctions between these two extremes are having performed the task but incompletely or poorly or having performed the task adequately but not exceptionally. These four distinctions were assigned a numerical score from one to four: a one (1) represented either no performance or performance of the wrong task, a two (2) was assigned for performing the correct task but not so as to allow the acceptable performance of subsequent processes, a three (3) was assessed for adequate performance of the task allowing subsequent processes to perform correctly, and a four (4) indicated performance of the task including extra performance that indicated an exceptional comprehension of the task.

This conceptual scoring system had to be interpreted differently for each task. While the criteria to determine whether the subject had performed either not at all or the wrong task were clear, the other performance levels had to have requirements specific for each task. For analysis, to receive an adequate evaluation, subjects had to either re-represent the problem, specify the causal structure, or list the possible solutions. Adequate performance on access required the subjects to access a base domain that had a causal structure that matched the target domain. For acceptable mapping performance, subjects had to determine the corresponding elements in the base domain for all the elements that were elaborated from the target domain. Adequate confirmation was based on using the deep structure of the two domains to evaluate and justify the confirmation decision. Performing transfer to an acceptable level consisted of interpreting the equivalent perturbation in one domain given a modification to the other domain. Finally, a workable solution was required to determine the ability of the solution process. In all domains, performance less than this level resulted in a rating of a two (or a one if a different procedure was performed) while a four was assigned for elaboration on a task beyond the acceptable level.

Results

Coding. Two independent raters scored the data. One rater scored all the responses while a second rater performed a validity check. Several revisions of the rating process led to a procedure producing reliability greater than ninety percent.

Analysis. One of the original six domains was found inadequate because of an incomplete specification of the confirmation task and was eliminated. This left five domains for the six processes.

Process	n	Mean	SD
Analysis	55	2.2364	0.6657
Access	40	2.8500	0.8638
Map	65	3.0462	0.6233
Confirm	65	2.6923	0.7484
Transfer	60	3.4333	0.6475
Solve	65	3.4615	0.6393

Table 2.

A two factor mixed analysis of variance was performed, with six levels of the between subjects factor (process) and five levels of the within subjects factor (domain). There was a significant effect of process $F(5,65)=15.108$, $p<.001$ but no effect of domain $F(4,260)=.81$, $p=.519$.

Performance on analysis was the worst, followed by confirmation and then access. Mapping was adequate and both transfer and solution were performed quite well (see Figure 1).

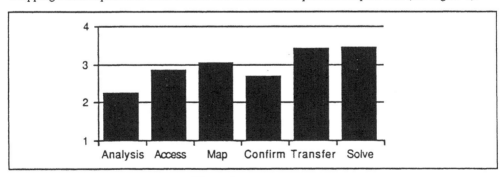

Figure 1.

19

The interaction between process and domain was significant F(20,260)=3.779, p<.001. This makes the main effect of process harder to interpret. However, as can be seen from Figure 3, there are a few isolated sources that constitute the majority of the interaction. Two of these sources are the good performance on analysis t(53)=-2.317, p=.012 and the weak performance on access t(38)=2.894, p=.0031 for the fifth pair of domains. Overall, patterns indicated by the means are maintained. The interaction can be seen in Figure 2.

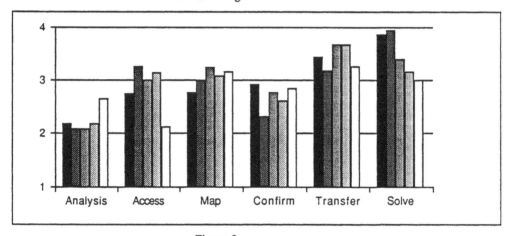

Figure 2.

Discussion

My original hypothesis was that performance on analysis should be inadequate, while performance on other processes should be adequate. These predictions were partially born out by the results of the experiment. Performance on analysis was less than adequate. Unexpectedly, the performances on access and confirmation were also less than adequate. This might be a result of one unusually low domain score for access, but it also might reflect a natural difficulty with access. Perhaps the specification of the analysis in the problems was not enough to ensure adequate access.

Performance on mapping was, on average, of a level sufficient to allow the subsequent processes to apply while performance on transfer and solution were above this level. Performance on solution was surprising, considering that problem-solving behavior has typically been considered weak. The answer may lie in the familiar domains that serve as the base problem for solution.

The result on confirmation is more surprising and harder to explain. Certainly, the task for confirmation here is different than in prior studies. In this study, subjects must explain their confirmation rating, and it is the explanation, not the rating, that receives evaluation. In the previous studies by Gentner (Gentner & Landers, 1985; Ratterman & Gentner, 1987), the subjects were evaluated on their judgement of the quality of the match. Justification may be a more complex and difficult task. Whether or not subjects actually understand the quality of the analogy, they may not be able to express that judgement well.

Another unanswered question about confirmation is whether subjects would use low-rated analogies. The experiments only determined how good the subjects thought the analogies were. One possibility is that subjects may ignore information on the quality of a match in their use of analogies, accepting inadequate base domains whether or not they have the ability to judge them. The cognitive overhead in evaluating the quality of a match, despite any ability to perform the evaluation, prevents this step from being accomplished. Another possibility is that the subjects simply use too low a threshold to confirm analogies. The subjects may have some evaluation of the analogies, and can recognize the relative quality of analogies, but accept the weak analogies.

Again, it might be that the processing load of returning to the analysis and access steps requires too much effort.

Despite the unanswered questions, the performance indications for the identified processes support both the existence of these processes as components of analogy and the utility of the process approach as a framework within which to view analogy. The use of the process approach succeeded in partially succeeded in predicting weak processes of analogy and serves as a guide within which to conduct more discussion about analogical performance deficits.

References

Clement, J. (1981). Analogy generation in scientific problem solving. *Proceedings of the Third Annual Meeting of the Cognitive Science Society*. Berkeley, CA.

Clement, J. (1986). Methods for evaluating the validity of hypothesized analogies. *Proceedings of the Eighth Annual Meeting of the Cognitive Science Society*.

Gentner, D. (1982). *Structure-mapping: a theoretical framework for analogy*. ONR report 5192.

Gentner, D. (1989). Mechanisms of analogical learning. In S. Vosniadou & A. Ortony (Eds.) *Similarity and analogy in reasoning and learning*. London: Cambridge University Press.

Gentner, D., & Landers, R. (1985). Analogical reminding: a good match is hard to find. *Proceedings of the International Conference on Systems, Man and Cybernetics*. Tucson, AZ.

Gick, M. L., & Holyoak, K. J. (1980). Analogical problem solving. *Cognitive Psychology*. 12, 306-355.

Gick, M. L., & Holyoak, K. J. (1983). Schema induction and analogical transfer. *Cognitive Psychology*. 15, 1-38.

Hall, R. P. (1989). Computational approaches to analogical reasoning: a comparative analysis. *Artificial Intelligence*. 39, 39-120.

Holland, J. H., Holyoak, K. J., Nisbett, R. E., & Thagard, P. R. (1986). *Induction: processes of inference, learning and memory*. Cambridge, MA: The MIT Press.

Holyoak, K. J, and Thagard, P. (1989) Analogical mapping by constraint satisfaction. *Cognitive Science*, 13, 3.

Quinn, C. N. (1989). *Analogical process performance and training*. Unpublished doctoral dissertation.

Ratterman, M. J., & Gentner, D. (1987). Analogy and similarity: determinants of accessibility and inferential soundness. *Proceedings of the Ninth Annual Conference of the Cognitive Science Society*.

Sternberg, R. J. (1977a). *Intelligence, information processing, and analogical reasoning*. Hillsdale, NJ: Lawrence Erlbaum Associates, Inc.

Sternberg, R. J. (1977b). Component processes in analogical reasoning. *Psychological Review*. 84, 4, 353-378.

The Effects of Familiar Labels on Young Children's Performance in an Analogical Mapping Task[*]

Mary Jo Rattermann   Dedre Gentner   Judy DeLoache
University of Illinois University of Illinois University of Illinois
Dept. of Psychology   Dept. of Psychology   Dept. of Psychology

Abstract

This research investigates the role of language in children's ability to perform an analogical mapping task. We first describe the results of a simple mapping task in which preschool children performed poorly. In the current study, we taught the children to apply relational labels to the stimuli and their performance improved markedly. It appears that relational language can call attention to domain relations and hence improve children's performance in an analogical mapping task.

A computer simulation of this mapping task was performed using domain representations that differed in their degree of elaboration of the relational structure. The results of the simulation paralleled the experimental results: that is, given deeply elaborated representations, SME's preferred interpretation produced the correct mapping response, while when given shallow representations its preferred interpretation produced an object similarity response. Taken together, the empirical and computational findings suggest that development of analogy and similarity may be explainable in large measure by changes in domain representation, as opposed to maturational changes in processing. They further suggest that relational language may be an important influence on this development.

Introduction

One of the developing child's major achievements is the acquisition of language. This acquisition process pervades almost every aspect of the young child's daily life. Our question in this research concerns the possible effects of language on one aspect of the child's developing abilities: the use of object similarity and relational similarity. Children and adults perform very differently in tasks which require the use of object similarity and/or relational similarity. For example, when given a metaphor such as "A cloud is like a sponge" young children (five years old) produced similarity comparisons based on common object-attributes (e.g., "they both are round and fluffy") while adults produced similarity comparisons based on common relational structures ("they both store water and then later give it back to you") (Gentner, 1988).

This and related developmental differences have led many researchers to suggest that young children use an inherently different mode of processing than adults. Piaget (Piaget, Montangero & Billeter, 1977) proposed that children lack the basic cognitive competence to perform an analogical mapping between objects. This ability is dependent upon cognitive

[*] This work was supported by Center for the Study of Reading contract NIE 400-81-0030. The authors would like to thank Art Markman, Rebecca Campbell, and Jennifer Glenn for their help in the preparation of this paper, and Phyllis Koenig for the wonderful penguins.

structures and processes which do not emerge until they reach the formal operations period of development (approximately 14 years of age). Others propose that children are not "fundamentally different kinds of thinkers" than adults but rather that it is deficiencies in children's knowledge that limits their performance (Brown, 1989; Carey, 1984). The domain-knowledge account would emphasize that metaphor and analogy tasks like the ones described above require knowledge that young children may not possess or may not reliably represent: for instance, knowledge of the causal relations within the two domains.

In this research we sought to (1) trace possible changes in children's ability to perform relational mappings; (2) to investigate whether any such changes could be explained in terms of changes in domain representations and (3) in particular, whether use of relational labels would play a causal role. We wanted to study the child's ability to extract relational similarity from a situation in which other solutions are in principle possible. Therefore, we designed a task in which object similarity was pitted against relational similarity. We then observed whether the child would carry out the relational mapping between the two structures. To further investigate the effects of object similarity, we manipulated the degree of similarity in the object matches by varying the perceptual richness and distinctiveness of the stimulus (Tversky, 1977). With this task we established that preschool age children have difficulty focussing on relational similarity when there is a competing object similarity. We then asked whether language can help children extract relational similarity under these conditions. We first review the basic task and then discuss the language manipulation we used to try to improve children's performance.

The Basic Task

We presented three- and four-year-old children and adults with a simple mapping game in which both object similarity and relational similarity were manipulated (Rattermann, Gentner & DeLoache, 1989). The child and the experimenter each had a set of three objects (clay pots or blue plastic boxes)'which increased in size along a continuum from left to right. (See Figure 1.).

Figure 1a.
SIMPLE

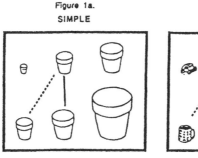

Figure 1b.
RICH

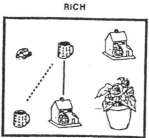

Figure 1. Stimulus sets used in mapping task.

The objects in Row 1 are the experimenter's set and the objects in Row 2 are the child's set.

The experimenter and the child played a game in which the experimenter hid a sticker under the child's set and the child tried to find it. The child was told that if he watched the experimenter as she placed a sticker under one of the objects in her set, he could use the hiding place of her sticker as a clue to the location of his own sticker. We introduced a tension between object similarity and relational similarity by staggering the size of the objects within the triads, creating both a possible object match and a possible relational match (a cross-mapping of the stimuli (Gentner & Toupin, 1986)). That is, if the experimenter's set contained objects of size 1, 2, and 3 the child's set contained objects of size 2, 3, and 4. The task was designed so that the relational response was always correct: the correct response was always based on relative size (e.g., largest object to largest object) and relative position.[1] The child was shown the correct answer and if correct was allowed to keep the sticker. In Figure 1a, the solid line represents the correct relational response, which the child will make if he is able to align the two structures relationally, while the dotted line represents the object-based response which the child will make if he responds on the basis of object similarity rather than relational similarity.

We found an age shift in the performance of this task. The three- and four-year-old children performed quite poorly (an average of 47% relational responses across both ages), while the adults performed extremely well (an average of 87% relational responses). We also found the effect of stimulus richness predicted by Tversky's contrast model; the children performed significantly better with the simple stimulus objects (an average of 54% relational responses for the three-year-olds and 62% for the four-year-olds) than with the rich stimulus objects (an average of 32% relational responses for the three-year-olds and 38% for the four-year-olds), suggesting that the presence of rich, distinctive object matches creates a salient alternative to the relational response (at least for young children). In contrast, when simple objects are used, the resulting object similarity matches are less compelling and therefore less likely to make a competitive alternative to the relational response.[2]

Can Language Promote a Relational Focus?

A growing body of research has investigated the hypothesis that young children use words to focus attention on certain kinds of information. (Gelman & Markman, 1987; Waxman & Gelman, 1986). Gelman and Markman (1987) investigated the role of common word labels on three- and four-year-old children's willingness to extrapolate characteristics between objects. They presented children with a picture of a standard object, e.g., a bluebird, and taught the children a characteristic of this object (e.g. "feeds its baby mashed up food."). The children were then shown a set of several objects, some which shared perceptual similarity

_____

1. The relations of relative size and relative position were perfectly correlated. That is, the middle-sized object was also the object in the middle position.

2. Adults performed roughly equal with the rich and the simple stimuli, suggesting that they can focus on relational commonalities relatively independent of object similarity.

with the standard and some which shared category membership (and therefore a common label) with the standard. When no labels were used the children, as expected, extended the characteristic to objects on the basis of shared perceptual similarity with the standard (e.g. a blue butterfly). When these new objects shared a category label with the standard (e.g. a blackbird) the children extended the characteristic based on the common label and, to a lesser extent, the shared perceptual similarity.

Given this evidence suggesting that labels can direct children's attention to taxonomic <u>object</u> concepts, the question we posed was whether relational labels can direct children's attention to relations. In particular, could the use of relational labels in the perceptual-mapping task influence children to respond relationally. To label the key relative-size relation we chose to use simple, familiar labels: "Daddy", "Mommy," and "Baby". "Daddy", "Mommy," and "Baby" are very salient relations to young children; in fact, children in the previous study occasionally used these labels spontaneously.[3] If the use of relational labels leads children to perform the mapping task correctly, this will support the position that developmental improvement can be accounted for by changes in representation (e.g. through accretion of knowledge) rather than by maturational change in underlying intellectual competence; and, more specifically, it will support the idea that acquisition of language is a contributor to this progression.

Method and Procedure

 Training. A graded training procedure was used to introduce the "Daddy," "Mommy," "Baby" labels to the children. We used a family of stuffed teddy bears and a family of stuffed penguins in the training task. In the first phase the experimenter's set contained a large and a small penguin, while the child's set contained a large and a small bear. This meant that there was no object identity match yet, and the child was only confronted with two animals in each set. The experimenter explained the task to the child by saying "These bears and these penguins are each a family. In the your bear family, this (pointing to the larger bear) is the Daddy and this (pointing to the smaller bear) is the Mommy. In my penguin family this is the Daddy (pointing to the larger penguin) and this is the Mommy (pointing to the smaller penguin)."

The child was asked to repeat the labels. After the child could label all the stimuli in both sets the experimenter asked "If I put my sticker under my Daddy (Mommy) penguin, your sticker is under your Daddy (Mommy). Look, my sticker is under my Daddy; where do you thing your sticker is?" The child was then allowed to search for the sticker. Phase 2 was identical to Phase 1 except for the addition of a small bear and a small penguin resulting in two families consisting of three animals to which the labels "Daddy," "Mommy," and "Baby" were applied.

---

3. An alternative would have been to use "Big," "Medium," and "Little," however, young children are often quite slow to acquire relational terms such as "big" and "little," "high" and "low," etc. and they are often applied attributionally before they are applied relationally (Donaldson & Wales, 1970; Smith, Rattermann and Sera, 1988).

In Phases 3 and 4 we introduced competing object identity choices. That is, we tried to created the same tension that the children would face later in the mapping task. To do this, we gave both the experimenter and the child families of penguins. The sizes of the penguins were designed to create a cross-mapping between the stimuli in the experimenter's set and the child's set (e.g., the experimenter's family might contain sizes 1,2, and 3 and the child's family might contain sizes 2, 3, and 4). In phase 3 only two penguins were used in each family, while in phase 4 there were three penguins in each set. (See Figure 2.) Throughout the training task the child labeled both the experimenter's objects and the child's objects after every other trial.

Figure 2. Stimulus set used in Phase 4 of training.

Mapping Task. After the training, each child was tested using the perceptual-mapping task using the stimuli described above (See Figure 1). Both the rich and the sparse stimuli were used, with half the children being tested with the sparse stimuli then the rich and the other half tested in the opposite order. Each child performed 28 trials; 14 sparse trials and 14 rich trials. The family labels were used in the same manner as in the training task.

Results
As can be seen in Figure 3, the children's performance in the labeled conditions was significantly higher than their performance when labels were not used with both the sparse stimuli ($\underline{t}$ (34) = 4.792, $\underline{p}$<.001) and the rich stimuli ($\underline{t}$(34)=5.423, $\underline{p}$<.001). The use of relational labels helped the three-year-olds truly respond relationally even in the face of a very tempting object choice.
There was also a small effect of object richness in that the few mistakes the children made in this study were made in the rich object condition. A 2 (Order of stimulus type) x 2 (Random

26

order) x 2 (Object complexity) analysis of variance confirmed a
significant effect of Object complexity $\underline{F}$ (1,20) = 4.44 $\underline{p}$ < .047.

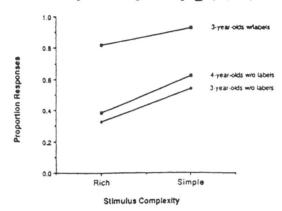

Figure 3. Results of labeling and non-labeling tasks.

<u>Simulation</u>
     The use of relational labels helped the young children in
our task to respond relationally. In fact, the familiar
relational labels allowed the three-year-olds in this experiment
to surpass the performance of the four-year-olds in the original
mapping task suggesting a role of language in the perception of
similarity.
     More generally, this improvement in children's performance
with relational labels strengthens the case for the domain-
knowledge account of the development of similarity. That is, it
suggests that children's model of processing is the same as that
of adults. To further test this hypothesis, we carried out a
computer simulation of the performance of children and adults in
this task (Gentner, Markman, Rattermann & Kotovsky, 1990;
Rattermann & Gentner, 1990). We gave propositional
representations of the stimuli used in these experiments to the
Structure-mapping Engine (SME) (Falkenhainer, Forbus & Gentner,
1986; 1989). (See Figure 4.) Based on the hypothesis that the
accretion of domain knowledge is driving changes in similarity
use, we formed two different knowledge representation of the
stimulus sets.

     We begin by making several working assumptions. We assume
that children can vary in the degree of higher-order relations[4]
present in their representation of the stimuli. We further
assume that one role of language is to make the relational
structure salient and increase the probability that the higher-
order relations will be represented. Finally, we assume that
children, in the absence of relational labels, possess shallow
representations of the stimuli consisting of object attributes
and first-order relations (The portion of Figure 4 in the dashed
box.). When labels are provided they aid the children in forming

<hr>

4. First-order relations are relations between objects, object-attributes or functions. Higher-order
   relations are relations between relations.

27

a systematic representation containing object attributes and an
elaborated higher-order relational structure. Specifically, we
assume that the higher-order relation of <u>steady change in size</u> is
more likely to be represented when relational labels are used.
In order to mimic the simple and the rich stimulus sets, we
varied the number of object attributes; the rich objects
possessed five attributes and the simple objects possessed three
attributes. Given the systematic representations of the stimulus
sets, SME's preferred mapping[5] was based on relational
similarity for both the rich and the simple stimulus sets. Given
shallow representations, however, SME's preferred mapping was
based on relational similarity with the simple stimulus sets but
based on object similarity with the rich stimulus sets. These
results mimic our findings with the developmental task.

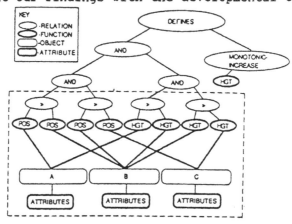

Figure 4: Knowledge representation used in simulation of developmental results.

Conclusions

In conclusion, this research suggests that the use of
familiar relational labels can improve children's ability to
perform analogical mappings. There is support, both empirical
and computational, for the conjecture that children and adults
may use the same type of similarity processes and that it is
changes in domain representations rather than changes in
cognitive competence that cause the observed developmental
improvement and (2) the acquisition and use of language –
specifically relational language – is an important contributor to
this development.

References

Brown, A. L. (1989). Analogical learning and transfer: What
      develops? In S. Vosniadou & A. Ortony (Eds.), <u>Similarity and
      analogical reasoning</u> (pp. 369–412). London: Cambridge
      University Press.
Carey, S. (1984). Are children fundamentally different kinds of
      thinkers and learners than adults? In S. Chipman, J. W.

---

5. SME performs local matches and by taking advantage of connectivity produces structurally consistent
interpretations of analogies. It then performs structural evaluations of each interpretation. We based
our results on SME's preferred evaluations.

Segal, & R. Glaser (Eds.), <u>Thinking and learning skills:</u>
<u>Current research and open question</u> (Vol. 2, pp. 485-517).
Hillsdale, NJ: Erlbaum.

Crisafi, M. A., & Brown, A. L. (1986). Analogical transfer in
very young children: Combining two separately learned
solutions to reach a goal. <u>Child Development</u>, <u>57</u>, 953-968.

Donaldson, M., & Wales, R. (1970). On the acquistion of some
relational terms. In J. R. Hayes (Ed.), <u>Cognition and the</u>
<u>development of language</u> (pp. 269-278). New York: Wiley.

Falkenhainer, B., Forbus, K. D. & Gentner, D. (1986). <u>The</u>
<u>structure-mapping engine</u> (Tech. Rep. No. UIUCDC-R86-1275).
Urbana, IL: University of Illinois, Department of Computer
Science. Also appears in <u>Proceedings of the Fifth National</u>
<u>Conference on Artificial Intelligence</u> (pp.272-277),
Philadelphia, PA: Morgan Kaufmann.

Falkenhainer, B., Forbus, K., & Gentner, D. (1989/90). The
structure-mapping engine: Algorithm and examples. <u>Artificial</u>
<u>Intelligence</u>, <u>41</u>, 1-63.

Gelman, S. A., & Markman, E. M. (1987). Young children's
inductions from natural kinds: The role of categories and
appearances. <u>Child Development</u>, <u>58</u>,1532-1541.

Gentner, D. (1988). Metaphor as structure mapping: The
relational shift. <u>Child Development</u>, <u>59</u>, 47-59.

Gentner, D., Markman, A., Rattermann, M.J., & Kotovsky, L. (1990)
Similarity is like analogy. Paper presented at the Midwest
Artificial Intelligence and Cognitive Science Conference,
Carbondale, Illinois.

Gentner D., & Toupin, C. (1986). Systematicity and surface
similarity in the development of analogy. <u>Cognitive Science</u>,
<u>10</u>, 277-300.

Piaget, J., Montangero, J., & Billeter, J. (1977). Les correlats.
In J. Piaget (Ed.), <u>L'Abstraction reflechissante</u>. Paris:
Presses Universitaires de France.

Rattermann, M.J., & Gentner, D. (1990). The development of
similarity use: It's what you know, not how you know it.
Paper presented at the Midwest Artificial Intelligence and
Cognitive Science Conference, Carbondale, Illinois.

Rattermann, M. J., Gentner, D., & DeLoache, J. (1989). Effects of
competing surface similarity on children's performance in an
analogical task. Poster presented at the biennial Meeting of
the Society for Reasearch in Child Development, Kansas City,
Missouri.

Smith, L. B., Rattermann, M. J., & Sera, M. (1988). "Higher" and
"lower": Comparative and categorical interpretations by
children. <u>Cognitive Development</u>, <u>3</u>, 341-358.

Tversky, A. (1977). Features of similarity. <u>Psychological Review</u>,
<u>84</u>, 327-352.

Waxman, S. & Gelman, R. (1986). Preschoolers use of
superordinate relations in classification and language.
<u>Cognitive Development</u>, <u>1</u>, 139-156.

Representational Issues in Analogical Transfer

Colleen M. Seifert   Kenneth C. Gray

Department of Psychology
University of Michigan

Abstract

Lack of transfer may result in part from a critical, though often ignored factor: the form of the initial representation of information during the process of analogical transfer. Using a Gick and Holyoak (1980, 1983) replication, in which subjects read a story in the guise of a memory experiment, subjects were later required to solve a problem which could be solved using an analogous strategy suggested by the story. Transfer performance was measured by the presence or absence of this target solution in subjects' protocols. The text of the original General story (from Gick & Holyoak) was modified slightly in one condition, where one role in the story was replaced by another type of actor. The changes were minor, as shown by the fact that the story modification did not affect similarity ratings between the story and problem. However the changes did appear to affect subjects' initial representation of the story and, as a result, improve subsequent transfer to the problem. The results indicate that forming an initial representation of the story that is congruent with important features of the problem is critical for analogical transfer. Subjects' abstraction of a general problem solving schema is an inadequate explanation of these results.

Introduction

Contrary to naturally occurring examples of analogical reminding, many psychological experiments have demonstrated that people have a difficult time remembering and utilizing prior examples that are only abstractly related to the current situation (Holyoak & Nisbett, 1988). Despite all the attention lack of analogical transfer has received, key factors remain to be addressed about the transfer problem. In this paper, we argue that the case against analogical reminding is limited by a failure to adequately take into account subjects' initial memory representation of presented material.

Analogical transfer is important to study because of its obvious significance in learning and problem solving (Ross, 1987). In addition, however, we believe that investigating analogy is an appropriate method to gain insight about the representation of information in memory. Retrieval has often been assumed to be an automatic process that is dependent solely on matching an input to the contents of memory (Holyoak & Nisbett, 1988). Our basic contention is that such a "simple memory" model of episode retrieval will not account for the examples of reminding that do occur in the world. This "simple memory" model, which underlies many investigators' approaches to analogical transfer, involves the use of an overall similarity metric to identify the episode in memory with the most feature overlap (after Tversky, 1977). However, it appears that content feature matching alone is not sufficient to account for the richness of analogy observed in natural settings. Instead, we argue for a more complex model of memory-based analogy, where the determining factor in retrieval is the quality of the original encoding. For example, a great deal of inference is required to fully understand a story containing abstract relations as well as content features. Analogical transfer will not occur if the understander fails to perform elaborative inferences describing the relations between features in the example. Building an initial representation that contains both the abstract and content features is critical for any later analogical use based upon them. Thus, the ability to use analogies depends on efforts towards elaborative encoding of initial episodes. That encoding may be the key to analogy is supported by Gick and Holyoak (1983), where multiple exemplars in encoding produced better transfer rates, and by Seifert, McKoon, Abelson, and Ratcliff (1986), where abstract remindings occurred when subjects were given plenty of time to encode and summarize the initial stories.

How might representation play a role in lack of transfer? Consider Gick and Holyoak (1980, 1983), which concluded that people are unable to apply a general strategy learned in one situation to another. In one of their experiments, subjects read a story under the guise of a memory experiment. The story, titled "The General", describes a general's exploits in overthrowing a dictator (see Table

31

1). Following the story, subjects were given a problem to solve, Duncker's (1945) ray problem (also included in Table 1).

Table 1

The General

A small country was ruled from a strong fortress by a dictator. The fortress was situated in the middle of the country, surrounded by farms and villages. Many roads led to the fortress through the countryside. A rebel general vowed to capture the fortress. The general knew that an attack by his entire army would capture the fortress. He gathered his army at the head of one of the roads, ready to launch a full-scale direct attack. However, the general then learned that the dictator had planted mines on each of the roads. The mines were set so that small bodies of men could pass over them safely, since the dictator needed to move his troops and workers to and from the fortress. However, any large force would detonate the mines. Not only would this blow up the road, but it would also destroy many neighboring villages. It therefore seemed impossible to capture the fortress. However, the general devised a simple plan. He divided his army into small groups and dispatched each group to the head of a different road. When all was ready he gave the signal and each group marched down a different road. Each group arrived together at the fortress at the same time. In this way, the general captured the fortress and overthrew the dictator.

The Ray Problem

Suppose you are a doctor faced with a patient who has a malignant tumor in his stomach. It is impossible to operate on the patient, but unless the tumor is destroyed the patient will die. There is a kind of ray that can be used to destroy the tumor. If the rays reach the tumor all at once at a sufficiently high intensity, the tumor will be destroyed.   Unfortunately, at this intensity the healthy tissue that the rays pass through on the way to the tumor will also be destroyed. At lower intensities the rays are harmless to healthy tissue, but they will not affect the tumor either. What type of procedure might be used to destroy the tumor with the rays, and at the same time avoid destroying the healthy tissue?

General Story and Ray/Tumor Problem from Gick and Holyoak (1980, 1983).

The plan used by the general to capture the fortress may be adapted into an analogous solution to the ray problem. The doctor can direct several low intensity rays from different sources to converge on the tumor. Gick and Holyoak's results were that only thirty percent of subjects applied the strategy from The General story to the ray problem. Even when told to use the same solution, only some of the subjects (75%) were able to apply it correctly. According to Gick and Holyoak (1983), analogical transfer depends on subjects' ability to abstract a "convergence schema" from the story and problem. The schema, as proposed by Gick and Holyoak, describes problem types for which the convergence solution is an appropriate plan. It contains commonalities between separate episodes only in terms of problem solving actions and states.

In our view, the convergence schema cannot be the sole determinant of transfer. In order to be reminded of the prior story, one must have encoded that story with a similar set of dominating features. Subjects' original encoding may not have included the particular inferences necessary to generate the connection between the stories. Of course, it may be possible upon reflection to identify an analogous relationship; however, the critical question in spontaneous analogy is not whether you can generate such a link given the two cases, but whether each case individually sets up a memory representation such that they are likely to be similarly encoded into memory.

From this perspective, it becomes clear that an important factor is how each episode is structured for presentation, so that the dominant features one expects to be encoded a priori are in fact the ones encoded by subjects. In the present experiment, we attempted to manipulate the representation formed for the story to affect the rate of transfer to the problem.

The present experiment is, in part, a replication of Gick and Holyoak's (1980, 1983) transfer experiments. Subjects are presented with a story which introduces a solution to a problem. Later, they are given an analog problem in a different domain to solve. One condition included the story and problem as in Gick and Holyoak (1980), as shown in Table 1. In a second condition minor modifications were made to the story in an effort to alter subjects' initial representations of the story to facilitate transfer to the problem. Specifically, the problem suggests the need to destroy an "enemy within" the body-- the tumor. However, this role is more difficult to observe in The General story. In the original story, the presence of the dictator was the status quo. As far as the reader can tell, the dictator had always controlled the fortress. A representation of this point may be quite different from that for the tumor in the analogous portion of the ray problem. A tumor is an object that has appeared (possibly suddenly) in the body. It would not be represented as the status quo. Rather, the appearance of a tumor is more like a sudden invasion of some foreign agent. The new version of The General story, shown in Table 2, retells the story, simply replacing the dictator from the original version with "terrorists".

Table 2

The General- Terrorist version

A small country was ruled from a strong fortress by a dictator. The fortress was situated in the middle of the country, surrounded by farms and villages. Many roads led to the fortress through the countryside. **A small group of terrorists had taken over and barricaded themselves in the fortress. An army** general vowed to capture the fortress. The general knew that an attack by his entire army would capture the fortress. He gathered his army at the head of one of the roads, ready to launch a full-scale direct attack. However, the general then learned that the **terrorists** had planted mines on each of the roads. The mines were set so that small bodies of men could pass over them safely, since the **terrorists** needed to move troops and workers to and from the fortress. However, any large force would detonate the mines. Not only would this blow up the road, but it would also destroy many neighboring villages. It therefore seemed impossible to capture the fortress. However, the general devised a simple plan. He divided his army into small groups and dispatched each group to the head of a different road. When all was ready he gave the signal and each group marched down a different road. Each group arrived together at the fortress at the same time. In this way, the general captured the fortress and overthrew the **terrorists**.

Revised General Story - terrorist version. Items in boldface were changed in this version from the original in Table 1.

By replacing the dictator with terrorists in the new version, we have highlighted this perspective, call it the "enemy within" perspective in The General story. When a memory representation for the terrorist version is set up, it should now reflect the "enemy within" perspective. The terrorist version thus highlights an additional commonality with the ray problem. Note that this new commonality is not part of the convergence schema.

Method

Subjects. Subjects were 36 University of Michigan undergraduates who participated for credit in a psychology course.

Materials. Duncker's (1945) ray problem and The General analog from Gick and Holyoak (1980, 1983) were used, along with The General- terrorist version. All materials are displayed in Tables 1 and 2.

Procedure. 21 subjects read the original version of The General and 15 subjects read the terrorist version for 3 minutes. They were then asked to write their recall of the story. After protocols were written, subjects attempted to solve the radiation problem. Following this, subjects were given a hint to "propose a solution suggested by the story." Finally, subjects were asked if they had seen the story or problem before in any context (and if so, discarded from the analysis).

Results

Table 1 shows the proportion of subjects who proposed the convergence solution to the ray problem after reading the original and the terrorist versions of The General. The left columns indicates the proportion who transferred the solution strategy spontaneously, without any hint to use the story. The second column gives the total proportion of subjects who transferred successfully after being told to use the story (this column includes the subjects from the first column). The last column gives the proportion of subjects who did not propose the convergence solution.

Table 1

	Before Hint	After Hint	No Transfer
Original Version	.19	.62	.38
Terrorist Version	.40	.60	.40

A chi-square test for association revealed that the proportion of subjects who transferred before the hint was significantly greater in the terrorist story condition ($\chi^2(2) = 3.94$, $p < .025$).

Discussion

The modifications in the General story, though minor in amount of textual change, were successful in increasing the rate of transfer. The point made by this manipulation is more subtle than saying that more similar stories result in better transfer; rated similarity when given both analogues is the same in the original and the changed versions. An independent group of 19 subjects given either the original version and the ray problem, or the terrorist version and the ray problem were asked to rate the similarity of problem to story on a scale from 0 - 10, where 0 was labelled "not at all similar" and 10 was labelled "extremely similar." No explicit instructions regarding similarity judgments were given. The mean ratings given were 7.9 for the original version and 7.6 for the terrorist version. This difference is not significant ($t(17) = 0.21$, $p > .8$).

Therefore, the changes in the terrorist version did not result in a "more similar" judgment when story and problem are compared. Instead, the representation formed when reading the changed story resulted in better analogical access and transfer when tested on the ray problem. The critical point to be made here is that the features likely to be used at encoding will dominate any use of the episode in analogical processing. Therefore, care must be taken to determine the nature of the representation built for each single presentation of each example, rather than the perceived similarity during comparison.

The ability to be reminded based on abstract features requires encoding both episodes with similar features. Because the analogues used in experiments require a fairly sophisticated representational system to characterize the target similarities, care must be taken to ensure that the representation subjects take away from their presentation must be ones that are candidates for transfer. Because of the dependence on materials, and in particular the use of a small set of classic examples for replications and extensions, conclusions are dependent on ensuring that the materials satisfy the above constraints. When they do, they provide a methodology for examining the features people encode about the world that do lead to transfer to new problem domains.

Acknowledgements

This research was sponsored by a contract between The University of Chicago and The University of Michigan under ONR contract No. N00014-88-K-0295. The authors wish to thank Kristian Hammond and Susan Chipman.

References

Duncker, K. (1945). On problem solving. *Psychological Monographs*, 58(270).

Gick, M., & Holyoak, K. (1980). Analogical problem solving. *Cognitive Psychology*, 12, 306-355.

Gick, M., & Holyoak, K. (1983). Schema induction and analogical transfer. *Cognitive Psychology*, 15.

Holyoak, K. & Nisbett, R. (1988). Induction. In E. Smith and R. Sternberg (Eds.) *The Psychology of Human Thought* (pp.50-91). Cambridge: Cambridge University Press.

Ross, B. H. (1987). This is like that: The use of earlier problems and the separation of similarity effects. *Journal of Experimental Psychology: Learning, Memory and Cognition*, 13(4), 629-639.

Seifert, C. M., McKoon, G., Abelson, R. P., & Ratcliff, R. (1986). Memory connections between thematically similar episodes. *Journal of Experimental Psychology: Human Learning and Memory*, 12 (2), 220-231.

Tversky, A. (1977). Features of similarity. *Psychological Review*, 84, 327-352.

Analogical Mapping During Similarity Judgments[*]

Arthur B. Markman
University of Illinois
Department of Psychology
Beckman Institute

Dedre Gentner
University of Illinois
Department of Psychology
Beckman Institute

Abstract

We propose that carrying out a similarity comparison of two objects or scenes requires that their components be aligned in a manner akin to analogical mapping. We present an experiment which supports this claim and then examine a computer simulation of these results which is consistent with the idea that a process of mapping and alignment occurs during similarity judgments.

Introduction

A process for calculating the similarity of two things has been assumed by nearly every model of categorization (Medin and Shaffer, 1978, Smith and Medin, 1981) and problem solving (Ross, 1984, Gick and Holyoak, 1985). A better comprehension of the processes which govern similarity would result in a deeper understanding of the mechanisms which control many other cognitive processes.

The pioneering work of Tversky (1977) established that the similarity between two items is a function of the elements which the two items have in common (common features) and the elements possessed by one item but not by the other (distinctive features). In addition to outlining the importance of common and distinctive features, Tversky and his colleagues have set out a number of ways in which the salience of common and distinctive features can be determined (Tversky, 1977, Gati and Tversky, 1984).

Although the importance of common and distinctive features cannot be overstated, Tversky's work has not addressed the problem of how the representations of the objects are compared in order to determine which elements are common and which elements are distinctive. However, some recent work has begun to address this issue (Markman, Medin and Gentner, under revision, Goldstone, Gentner and Medin, 1989). This work suggests that object representations are aligned through a process akin to the mapping processes which have been proposed for analogical reasoning (Gentner, 1983, 1989, Holyoak and Thagard, 1989 and Hall, 1989).

In this paper we first outline how analogical mapping may be applicable to similarity. We then present an experiment designed to test whether mapping is a part of similarity judgments. Finally, we will examine the results of a computer simulation of this experiment.

Similarity and Structure Mapping

We will discuss the applicability of mapping to similarity with respect to Gentner's structure-mapping theory (SMT) (Gentner, 1983, 1989) specifically, but the general points are compatible with many current theories of analogical mapping (cf. Hall, 1989 for a review). According to SMT, the comparison of two scenes requires that their relational structures be

[*] This work was supported by Office of Naval Research contract N00014-89-J1272, National Science Foundation grant BNS 87-20301, and a University of Illinois Cognitive Science/Artificial Intelligence Fellowship. The authors would like to thank Ken Forbus, Douglas Medin, Janice Skorstad, Laura Kotovsky and Mary Jo Rattermann for their helpful comments on previous drafts of this manuscript. Thanks to Robert Parish for holding down the middle. A special thanks to Julie Hays for running subjects.

aligned. Thus, objects which play a common role in both scenes are likely to be placed in correspondence, while identical objects which play different roles in their respective scenes are unlikely to be placed in correspondence. In addition, Gentner's systematicity and structural consistency principles reflect subjects' tendency to preserve relational structure (e.g. causal relations, goals, or other higher order relations) even when the objects themselves are dissimilar.

Recent research has shown that similarity judgments are sensitive to the relational structure of the stimuli (Markman, Medin and Gentner, submitted, Goldstone, Medin and Gentner, 1989, Rattermann and Gentner, 1987). For example, Rattermann and Gentner found that subjects considered pairs of stories that had similar relational structure and different characters to be more similar than pairs that had similar characters and a different relational structure. However, sensitivity to relations yields only indirect evidence that an analogical mapping process takes place during similarity judgments. The following experiment will address this question more directly.

Experiment 1

This experiment was designed to test the claim that an analogical mapping process takes place during similarity judgments. Subjects were shown a base scene and a target scene (see Figure 1). One of the objects in the base scene was highlighted and the subject was asked which objects 'goes with' that object in the target scene. We call this task one-shot mapping (1map).

In each pair of scenes one object was *cross-mapped*. Gentner and Toupin (1986) define a cross-mapping as a comparison in which there are perceptually similar objects in two scenes, but the perceptually similar objects play different roles in the relational structure of each scene. For example, in Figure 1, the two women are highly similar perceptually. However, in the top scene the woman is receiving food while in the bottom scene she is giving food away. Thus, the perceptually similar objects play different roles in their respective scenes.

Using this tension between perceptual similarity and relational similarity, we examined subjects preferences in three conditions. The first group of subjects (1map), was shown the pair of scenes. The experimenter pointed to the cross-mapped and asked the subject to point to the object in the target which 'went with' the cross-mapped object. The second group of subjects (3map) was asked to give the objects that 'went with' three of the significant objects in the target scene including the cross-mapped object. Finally, the third group of subjects (sim->1map) was asked to rate the similarity of the two scenes first, and then they were asked to point to the object that 'went with' the cross-mapped object.

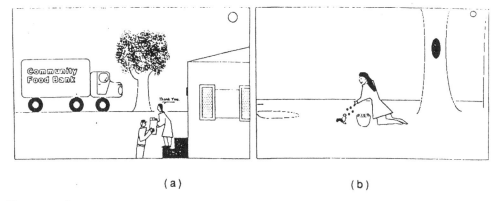

(a)   (b)

Figure 1. Sample stimulus in Experiment 1a.

We predicted that the subjects in the 1map condition would tend to select the nearly identical object in the other scene. Since these subjects need only map a single object, they have no reason to consider the relational structure of the two scenes and thus will be guided by object similarity.

Furthermore, we predicted that subjects in the 3map condition who were asked to map three of the objects which play a role in the relational structure would tend to map objects based on the relational structure of the scenes. These subjects must consider how to make three consistent mappings. If the two cross-mapped objects are placed in correspondence, there is no justification for placing any of the other objects in correspondence. As a result, these subjects should be more likely to preserve the relational structure of the scenes, which would provide support for all three object mappings.

The key prediction, however, centers on the the sim->1map condition, where subjects first performed a similarity judgment and then perform a single mapping. We predicted that these subjects would also be likely to map objects based on the relational structure of the scenes. If, as we believe, similarity judgments require that the relational structures of the scenes be aligned, then subjects' mappings following a similarity judgment should reflect this relational structure.

Method

Stimuli. The set of stimulus pictures portrayed causal higher order relations (*causal HOR*). These pictures presented scenes with a goal structure or causal structure. For example, in the pictures shown in Figure 1 someone is giving food to someone else. Each of these pictures had a cross-mapping as well.

Procedure. Subjects were run one at a time. They were seated at a table with an experimenter seated behind them. Subjects participated in only one experimental condition. The experimenter had no knowledge of the hypothesis being tested.

Subjects in the one-shot mapping (1map) condition were shown each of the base/target pairs in turn. The experimenter pointed to the cross-mapped object and asked the subject to point to the object in the other picture that went with that object. The subject's response was recorded and the next pair of pictures was presented. After completing the mapping task, subjects rated the similarity of each pair on a scale from 1 to 9.

Subjects in the three mappings (3map) condition were also shown each of the base/target pairs. However, in this case, the experimenter pointed (one at a time) to each of the three objects which made up the central relational structure of the scene. Subjects were asked to point to the objects which went with each of those objects. The cross-mapped object was always tested first. After completing the mapping task, these subjects were also asked to rate the similarity of all of the pairs of pictures.

Subjects in the similarity first then one-shot mapping task (sim->1map) first rated the similarity of a pair of pictures and then were shown the cross-mapped object and asked which object in the other picture went with it.

Finally, a control condition was run. It could be argued that any effects found in the sim->1map condition arise because subjects have greater exposure to the pictures in this condition before performing the one-shot mapping. In order to control for this possibility, one final group of subjects was shown the set of pictures one at a time and told to study them carefully for a later memory experiment. The subject saw each picture for five seconds, roughly the amount of time subjects see the pictures while making similarity comparisons. After examining the entire set of pictures, subjects in the control condition performed the 1-shot mapping task.

Design. There were 4 (3 mapping conditions and control) between subjects conditions in this design. Order of stimulus presentation was counterbalanced.

Subjects. Subjects were 24 undergraduates from the University of Illinois who received course credit for their participation in a single 15 minute session. Subjects were randomly assigned to one of six experimental conditions.

Results. Subjects' responses were recorded as being either object-based mappings, relation-based mappings or spurious mappings. Object-based mappings were those choices which placed the cross-mapped objects in correspondence. Relation-based mappings were those choices which preserved the relational structure of the scenes. Any other choice was considered a spurious mapping. The number of spurious mappings was less than 1% of the total number of responses and will not be considered further here. The proportion of relational responses on the cross-mapped object for each subject is shown in Figure 2.

As predicted, subjects who performed a similarity judgment prior to mapping made more relational responses than subjects who did not perform a similarity judgment prior to mapping. A one-way analysis of variance on the three experimental conditions indicates that, as predicted, there is a significant effect of mapping condition ($F_{(2.21)}=3.76$, $p<.05$). A planned comparison indicates that significantly more relational responses were given in the sim->1map condition than in the 1map condition ($F_{(1,21)}=7.51$, $p<.01$ one-tailed). More relational responses were given in the 3map condition than in the 1map condition, but this difference was only marginally significant ($F_{(1,21)}=2.233$, $.05<p<.1$, one tailed). Finally, there was significantly more responding in the sim->1map condition than in the control condition ($t_{(14)}=2.326$, $p<.05$ one tailed).

Proportion of relational responses by condition in experiment 1.

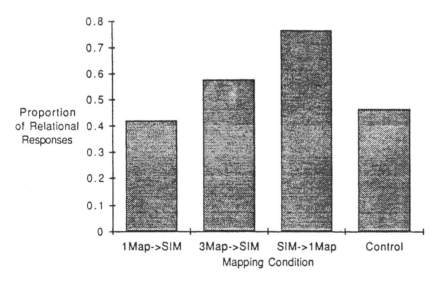

Figure 2. Graph of proportion of relational responses made by subjects in each of the mapping conditions in Experiment 1.

A correlation was done between the mean similarity judgments for each stimulus pair in each condition and the total number of relational responses given to that stimulus pair. This correlation was performed to ensure that subjects in the sim->1map condition did not simply find the stimulus pairs more similar than subjects in other conditions and thus gave more relational responses to stimuli in this condition. As expected, the correlation between similarity and number of relational responses across all mapping conditions is not significant (r(22)=.35, p>.05). Separate correlations between mean similarity and number of relational responses were also determined for each mapping condition. The correlation in the sim->1map condition were significant. (r(6)=.64 p<.05 one tailed). The correlations were not significant for any of the other conditions.

Discussion

As predicted, subjects in the sim->1map condition made more relational responses than subjects in either the 1map or control conditions. This means that, given a task that ostensibly requires object alignment, subjects prefer to preserve the relations between objects. These results support the claim that an alignment process similar to analogical mapping takes place during similarity judgments.

Furthermore, the correlation between number of relational responses given to an item and the mean similarity rating is only significant in the sim->1map condition. Since prior research indicates that similarity judgments are highly sensitive to relational structure (Markman, Medin and Gentner, under revision, Goldstone, Medin and Gentner, 1989), we interpret this correlation to indicate that, when subjects were aware of the common relational structure, they placed objects in correspondence based on their role within the relational structure. Furthermore, the non significant correlation in the 1map case indicates that, although subjects may have chosen their mapping based on the similarity between the objects, their global similarity judgments were still based on the relational similarity of the scenes.

A simulation using the Structure Mapping Engine (SME)

A computer simulation of the mapping process for the causal HOR stimulus was performed using the structure mapping engine (SME) program which was designed to implement the structure mapping theory of analogical mapping (Falkenhainer, Forbus and Gentner, 1986, 1989). The stimulus pictured in Figure 1 was encoded into a propositional representation used by SME. The representation of the scene in Figure 1a is depicted graphically in Figure 3.[1] In order to capture the cross-mapping the cross-mapped objects were given identical descriptions including a number of shared attributes, but the objects played different roles in their respective relational structures.

SME generates all possible interpretations of the match between two scenes. SME begins by proposing local matches between identical predicates in the base and target. These local matches are then connected into larger mappings provided that these matches fit into a consistent relational structure. Next, these larger matches are combined together into maximal sets with the proviso that they are structurally consistent. These maximal sets, called GMAPs, are then evaluated for their systematicity (see Falkenhainer, et. al. 1989 and Forbus and Gentner, 1989 for a discussion of the evaluation procedure). For these simulations, SME was configured using literal similarity rules which allow the system to map both attributes and relations. This configuration allows both object similarity and relational similarity to play a role in the generation of GMAPS.

For the causal HOR stimulus pair, the relational interpretation was clearly preferred. The GMAP with the highest evaluation score placed the woman receiving food and the squirrel receiving food in correspondence, as well as the man giving food and the woman giving food. The

---

[1]The representation of the causal HOR in Figure 4a is slightly simplified. All of the objects shown in the scene were included in the representation and various relations were placed between these stimuli. In order to conserve space, only two of those objects were included in the figure.

mapping preferred by SME is the same mapping preferred by subjects in the sim->1map condition where 7/8 (88%) of the subjects chose the relational interpretation.

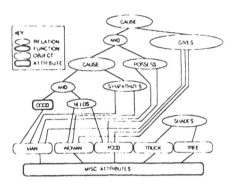

Figure 3. Propositional representation of scene in Figure 1a. This representation was used in the SME simulation of Experiment 1.

SME was also able to generate the object match interpretation of the scenes. This GMAP was given a lower evaluation score than the relational interpretation, but was given a higher evaluation score than any of the other interpretations. The simulation results are consistent with subjects' data here as well. Recall that subjects rarely (less than 1% of all trials) gave a response other than an object match or a relational match. Like human subjects, SME did not generate any highly-rated GMAPS corresponding to a spurious match.

Conclusion

The results of the experiment performed here support the claim that, in order to compute similarity, subjects must perform a relational mapping to achieve a structural alignment between the two scenes. This pattern of results is consistent with an SME simulation of the data. Thus, structure-mapping theory predicts that subjects will place objects in correspondence based on their position within the representational structure. The consistency of the predictions of structure-mapping theory with the data obtained from this similarity study demonstrate the degree to which the processes of analogical mapping and similarity judgments are alike.

References

Falkenhainer, B, Forbus, K. D., and Gentner, D. (1989). The Structure Mapping Engine: Algorithm and Examples. _Artificial Intelligence_. 41(1), 1-63.

Forbus, K. D. and Gentner, D. (1989). Structural Evaluation of Analogies: What Counts? in the proceedings of the 11th Annual Conference of the Cognitive Science Society. Ann Arbor, MI.

Gati, I. and Tversky, A. (1984). Weighting Common and Distinctive Features in Perceptual and Conceptual Judgments. _Cognitive Psychology_. 16, 341-370.

Gentner, D. (1983). Structure Mapping: A theoretical framework for analogy. <u>Cognitive Science</u>. 7, 155-170.

Gentner, D. and Toupin, C. (1986). Systematicity and Surface Similarity in the Development of Analogy. <u>Cognitive Science</u>. 10, 277-300.

Gick, M. L. and Holyoak, K. J. (1983). Schema Induction and Analogical Transfer. <u>Cognitive Psychology</u>. 15, 1-38.

Goldstone, R. L., Medin, D. L., and Gentner, D. (1989). Relations Relating Relations. in the proceedings of the11th Annual Conference of the Cognitive Science Society. Ann Arbor, MI.

Hall, R. P. (1989). Computational Approaches to Analogical Reasoning: A comparative analysis. <u>Artificial Intelligence</u>. 39, 39-120.

Holyoak, K. J. and Thagard, P. (1989). Analogical Mapping by Constraint Satisfaction. <u>Cognitive Science</u>. 13, 295-355.

Markman, A. B., Medin, D. L., and Gentner, D. (in revision). An analysis of the Perceptual-Verbal Distinction in Similarity Judgments.

Ross, B. (1984). Remindings and their Effects in Learning a Cognitive Skill. <u>Cognitive Psychology</u>. 16, 371-416.

Smith, E. and Medin, D. L. (1981). <u>Concepts and Categories</u>. Cambridge, MA: Harvard University Press.

Tversky, A. (1977). Features of Similarity. <u>Psychological Review</u>. 84(4), 327-352.

Goal Similarity in Analogical Problem Solving

Bruce D. Burns

University of California, Los Angeles

Abstract

The role of goal similarity in analogical problem solving was investigated using highly simplified chess positions. Goal similarity was manipulated by instructing subjects to make an attacking or defensive move. Subjects received training positions, followed by a set of testings positions, each solvable by mapping to a training position. A normal chess position was also given. Testing positions maximally similar to training positions (including similarity of goals) were responded to most quickly, though this effect was not found for all positions. It was also found that when subjects had to avoid a fatal threat in a normal chess position, they were more likely to successfully defend against that move if they were told that they were losing than if told they were winning. The results indicate that goal similarity influences analogical problem solving.

Introduction

Seeing a new problem as analogous to an old problem can help develop a solution (Brown, Kane, & Echols, 1986; Carbonell, 1983; Gick & Holyoak, 1980, 1983). To do this requires retrieval of a source analogue and construction of a mapping between the source and the target analogue. How these analogical processes can be achieved remains uncertain. The goals of a cognitive system have often been proposed as important factors in analogy mapping, because the purpose of analogy mapping in problem solving is to accomplish the goals of the problem solving. This has led many artificial intelligence theorists to argue for the importance of goal accomplishment to retrieval of analogies (e.g., Carbonell, 1983, 1986; Hammond, 1989; Schank, 1982; Winston, 1980, 1982), as well as more psychologically orientated theorists (e.g., Holyoak and Thagard, 1989; Gentner, 1989) to argue that goal similarity has a role in analogical mapping.

This research was supported by Contract MDA 903-89-K-0179 from the Army Research Institute. I wish to thank Ramin Gabizadeh for data collection and Keith Holyoak for extensive comments. Correspondence should be sent to Bruce Burns, Department of Psychology, UCLA, Los Angeles, CA 90024, USA; or e-mail burns@cognet.ucla.edu

For the concept of goal similarity to be meaningful it needs to be distinguished from the more general influences of semantic similarity and structural consistency. The degree of semantic similarity relates to the similarity of the elements of a source and target analogy. Structural consistency refers to the degree to which the elements play similar roles in the analogues, which can be equated with a simple criterion for mapping: If two propositions are mapped, then their constituent predicates and arguments should also be mapped. There is a reasonable amount of psychological evidence that semantic similarity (e.g., Holyoak & Koh, 1987; Ross, 1987) and structural consistency (e.g., Gentner & Toupin, 1986; Holyoak & Koh, 1987; Ross, 1987, 1989) influence analogical mapping, although there is disagreement on exactly how these factors affect mapping. How, or whether, goal similarity is distinct from these factors is disputed. One reason for this dispute is that, despite the popularity of goal similarity in theories of analogical mapping and problem solving, there is very little psychological evidence that it plays a role. One suggestive study was that of Brown et al. (1986). They found that children who were directed to focus on the goal structure of a problem were better able to transfer solutions to analogous problems than were children not so directed. Despite this, both groups were able to recall the goals when later tested, suggesting that their poor performance was not due to a simple memory failure. However, it is possible that the directions acted as a hint, thus aiding retrieval.

The present study aimed to find evidence that goal similarity plays a role in analogical problem solving, and to develop a task suitable for the further study of the its effects. If goal similarity has been a slippery concept, this is partly due to the lack of a operational definition that might be provided by a task that can demonstrate its effects.

The Task

The problem solving task used in this study is novel and therefore it is necessary to explain its nature and rationale in some detail. The task involved highly simplified chess positions. Chess was chosen largely because it is possible to clearly define goals in terms of attacking and defensive

45

moves. Different players given exactly the same position can have different goals (e.g., attack or defence) without requiring an overt change of the semantic or structural components of the problem.

The use of naive subjects dictated the use of a simple task. The positions consisted of two chess pieces on the board and one piece presented off the board, but waiting to be put on the board. For the attacking goal the task involved the subjects placing the piece that was off the board onto the board so as to guarantee that this piece would be able to capture an opposition piece on its next move. This next move occurs after one of those opposing pieces had had an opportunity to move. The task when the goal was defensive was the opposite of the attacking task: the subject must avoid the capture of a piece. The subject legally moved one of the white pieces already on the board in anticipation that the black piece off the board was about to be placed onto the board in an attempt to complete an attacking manoeuver similar to the one the subject used in the attacking task.

To help subjects achieve these goals they were trained on examples of two simple chess tactics known as *pins* and *forks*. These tactics are known by any experienced chess player, but they will not be familiar to novices. A fork manoeuver involves the attacking piece being placed so as to simultaneously attack two opposition pieces. Because the defending side's move consists of moving only one piece, only one piece will be able to escape the attack leaving the other to be captured. For a pin manoeuver the attacking piece is placed such that only one piece is directly attacked, but if this piece moves away then the one behind it can be captured. Hence a capture is still guaranteed. Examples of these training positions are presented in Figure 1 (an attacking bishop pin), Figure 2 (an example of a successful solution of the attacking bishop pin position), and Figure 3 (a successful solution to the defensive version of the bishop pin position).

After training on one of four attacking examples and on one of four defending examples, the subjects were given 40 testing trials consisting of similar simplified chess positions. Each testing position was a transformations of one of the eight training positions. Each transformation involved the same manoeuver (e.g., attacking bishop pin) but had the pieces changed (a change in semantic similarity), the relationship of the pieces to each other changed (structure inconsistency), or the goal changed (from attack to defence, or vice-versa). Because a subject received only two of the eight training positions (each involving a different manoeuver), transfer of

a manoeuver was required when the subject was given one of the other training positions as a testing position. Therefore each testing position was classified by the type of transfer that would be required to get from the manoeuver used in one of the training position that the subject had been given, to the manoeuver in the training position of which the testing position was a transformation. The four transfer conditions were *similar, attack/defence, fork/pin,* and *bishop/rook.*

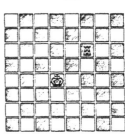

Figure 1. An attacking bishop pin position, as presented to a subject.

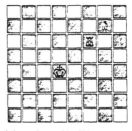

Figure 2. A solution to the attacking bishop pin position presented above.

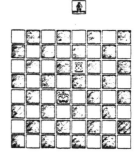

Figure 3. A solution to the defensive version of the bishop pin position presented above.

The similar condition involved the positions

that used the same manoeuver (e.g., attacking rook fork) as that used in one of the subject's training positions and hence they differed the least from the training position. Of course, a subject's training position given as a testing trial would fall into this condition, though it could no longer be considered an analogue because it would actually be identical to the training position. The attack/defence condition involved a testing position that kept the rook/bishop and pin/fork characteristics of the manoeuver constant, but swapped attack for defence or vice-versa. This condition is considered to involve a change of goal. The fork/pin condition kept the attack/defence and bishop/rook characteristics of the required manoeuver the same, but swapped fork for pin, or vice-versa. This is considered to represent a structural change of the manoeuver. The bishop/rook condition involves positions that maintain the attack/defence and fork/pin characteristics but swap between rooks and bishops as the attacking piece. This is considered to primarily be a semantic change of the manoeuver, but because rooks and bishops move differently some structural change is unavoidable.

Due to the transformation of the training position, some form of transfer would be required to map even to a testing position that was a transformations of one the testing positions that the subject had been given. To control this it will be possible to directly compare positions that were constructed using the same type of transformation, but represent different transfer conditions.

Note that over subjects, each testing position appeared in each transfer condition, so that which condition a testing position was part of depended solely on what the subject's training positions were. Response time was used as the measure of performance because most of these positions are simple enough to be eventually solved by exhaustive search.

To investigate the effect of goal similarity, the comparison of the similar and the attack/defence conditions is most critical. If goal similarity is important for mapping or retrieval, then subjects should perform better on the positions in the similar condition than they do in the attack/defence condition. If subjects find the attack/defence positions harder then this will provide evidence that changing the goal makes problem solving harder and hence support the claim that goal similarity affects the analogical mapping and/or retrieval. It could be argued that differences in difficulty could be due simply to the attacking and defending tasks being different; there might be no transfer because training for one goal does not help with the other.

However, there is in fact an intimate link between these two tasks. To solve a defending position requires knowledge of the attacking move. Subjects could not be sure that their solution to a defending position is correct unless they know what the threatened attack is, hence training on the attacking manoeuver should help the subject solve the defensive version of the manoeuver. Successful training on the defensive manoeuver involves becoming aware of the attacking form of that manoeuver.

Better performance should also be found in the similar condition as compared to the fork/pin and bishop/rook conditions, as previous work on problem solving tasks provide ample evidence that structure and semantics affect analogical mapping. The finding of such differences is important, however, because it would lend support to the assumption that solving the task involves mapping to the training positions.

A further attempt to investigate the effects of goals involved attempting to manipulate goals at the time of solving a problem. In a final position, subjects were given a full chess position and instructed to try to make the best move they could as though it were a normal chess position. This position involved a fatal move which was either available to the subject or that the subject had to identify so that they could defend against it. To manipulate goals, subjects were told either that they were winning or losing. This information is in fact irrelevant to selection of a correct move, but may have altered their immediate goal in the position. Subjects who were told they are winning would be more likely to make aggressive moves than those told they were losing. If goals are important then it would be predicted that telling a subject that they are winning should help them find the correct attacking move in the appropriate position, while telling subjects that they are losing should assist them in finding the correct defensive move when it is required.

Method

Subjects

A total of 81 subjects participated in the experiment. All subjects were from an introductory psychology subject pool at the University of California, Los Angeles. Seven subjects were eliminated because they failed to complete the task in the available time and two were eliminated because they never understood the requirements of the task. This left a sample of 72 subjects (53 male, 19 female).

Materials and Apparatus

All positions and instructions were presented by an Apollo series 4000 workstation with a 19 in. color monitor. Subjects made their responses using a mouse with three buttons. Response times were measured to an accuracy of one second.

Training positions

There were three factors each with two levels (fork or pin; bishop or rook; attack or defence) that were crossed, yielding eight training positions. However, only four different training conditions were used as each player was given two training positions that were the exact opposite of each other. For example, if one of the training positions was a bishop, pin, attack, then the other position would be a rook, fork, defence. In this way the subject was exposed to all possible elements. In particular, they became familiar with both the attacking and the defending task. It was especially important that the subject got a chance to clarify the nature of the defending task, since it is a more complex task than the attacking task.

Several constraints were applied to the construction of the eight training positions. The first constraint was that every attacking position must not only have a valid attacking solution, but must also have a defensive solution, because the same position was given as a defensive task. In effect, this means that there were only four different basic positions. The defensive versions of the training positions simply involved changing the goals and the colors of the pieces. Second, an attacking position should allow a pin solution, or a fork solution. Third, because of the restriction that an attacking piece cannot be placed onto a square where it could be immediately captured, it is not possible to create a fork position where one of the defending pieces is the same as the attacking piece. Hence one defending piece was always the opposite (in terms of rook and bishop) of the attacking piece and the other was a king. The use of a king made it easier to fulfill some of the other constraints. A fourth constraint was that it had to be taken into account that the training positions would be used as the basis for the construction of testing positions. The training positions therefore needed to be transformable in the appropriate ways.

Testing positions

Each testing position was based on one of the four basic training positions, but transformed in various ways. A total of 10 transformations were applied to each of the four basic training positions, yielding a total of 40 testing positions. Five of these transformations (*identical, rotation, change-piece, change-structure,* and *queen*) appeared for every training position. An identical transformation was the training position itself, which never appeared until at least the 22nd trial, by which time the subject had been exposed to all other possible manoeuvers. The rotation transformation was the training position rotated. The change-piece transformation was the same as the training position except that the defending piece that wasn't a king was replaced by a knight. The change-structure transformation replaced a defending piece and changed the relative position of the defenders (but an attacking maneuver of a similar type was still possible). The queen transformation used a queen as the attacking piece but allowed a similar attacking manoeuver to that used in the transformed training position. For fork training positions, five other types of more complicated transformations were used, but for pins (which are less flexible) these five were repeated so that each pin transformation was presented as both an attacking and a defending position.

As was the case for the training positions, there are many ways to construct the testing positions, but each must have both an attacking and a defending solution. The testing positions included 20 defending positions and 20 attacking. In order for all of the positions to be presented in both attacking and defending forms, two testing sets were formed. These two sets were identical, including the order of positions, except that every position that appeared as attacking in one set appeared as a defending position in the other set.

The order in which positions appeared was determined once. Order was determined by random selection, but simpler transformations had to appear before a more complex transformation of the same training position. Attacking and defending positions alternated, with odd numbered trials being attacking in one testing set and even numbered trials being attacking in the other. An equal number of pin and fork moves had to be attacking and defending.

Because the two training positions the subject received were maximally dissimilar, it was clear which transfer condition a testing position belongs to for each training condition. There was always one training position that was only one factor (attack/defence, fork/pin, or rook/bishop) different from the manoeuver used in the testing position, while the other was different by two factors (except for the similar condition where one training position has all three factors the same). Hence one training position was always clearly more similar to a given testing position than was the other training position.

It was this more similar training position that determined to which transfer condition a testing position belonged.

The final position was constructed so as to be a plausible chess position but with no worthwhile captures possible for either side. However, a fatal knight move was available to one side that would fork the other side's king and queen. Such a move is extremely dangerous because it guarantees the capture of the queen, which is the most powerful piece on the board. There was also a distractor move available, involving an attack on the other queen that is pointless at best, but is actually a losing move.

In the attacking version the subject had the opportunity to make the fatal move. In the defending version the identical position was used but with the colors reversed so that now white (the subject) must try to avoid this dangerous move, a task that could be easily accomplished if the subject realizes that it must be done. The attacking version of the position is presented in figure 4 with white about to move.

Figure 4. Final position (attacking version) with white about to move.

Procedure

Subjects were shown how the computer represented chess pieces and how to use the mouse to move pieces. They were told to follow the instructions that appeared on the screen, but that they could ask the experimenter questions if they were unclear with regard to any of the instructions.

The instructions first made clear that subjects would not see normal chess positions; in particular, kings were not special as they are in normal chess. Subjects were then given practice at detecting captures and were familiarized with using the mouse to move the pieces. Next, the subjects were presented with their attacking training position.

They were to place the white piece on the board so as to guarantee the capture of a black piece no matter what move black subsequently made. It was emphasized that they could not place their piece on a square where it could immediately be captured. It was also made clear that it did not matter what happened to the white piece once it had captured a black piece, and therefore it was irrelevant if the piece they were to capture was protected by the other black piece.

The computer indicated if the subject's response was correct or incorrect. If an incorrect move was made, the computer displayed a correct response. This display lasted 10 s and showed the problem position with the white (attacking) piece placed on a correct square. To complete this stage subjects had to solve the position three times in a row. There were three different versions of the training position, each only differing from the others by a simple translation across the board.

The second set of practice trials presented subjects with their defending training position. Subjects were instructed that they were now to legally move one of the white pieces on the board so as to avoid the capture of a white piece. They were instructed that black was going to try to attack them in a similar way to that which the subject had used during the attacking training, but that they had a chance to pre-empt the placing of the attacking piece. If they made the right move at this stage then it would not matter where black placed their piece: black would not be able to force the capture of a white piece.

The link between attack and defence was made very explicit in the subjects instructions. They were advised to first think of where black was going to place their piece, and to then think how they could render that move harmless. It was also made clear that they had to be careful because even if they avoided one threat they might leave themselves open to another. Subjects were given similar feedback and the same completion criterion as they had for attacking training.

Subjects were then given the 40 testing trials from the randomly assigned testing set. No feedback was given at this stage, but subjects should have been able to recognize when they had made a correct move. After completing all testing trials subjects were told that they would be presented with a normal chess position and that they were to make the best move they could find. They were instructed that the relative value of pieces should be taken into account just as in normal chess (a factor that had been irrelevant up to this point). To guide them, a table giving the relative value of each piece was displayed. Whether the subject saw the attacking or the defending position was crossed with assignment to the winning or the losing condition. Subjects in the winning condition were instructed, "In your position, white is WINNING and is on the ATTACK". Subjects in the losing condition were instructed, "In your position, white is LOSING and is on the DEFENSIVE".

Results

The defending positions in which a queen was the attacking piece were inherently very difficult, as reflected in very low solution rates and very long response times. For this reason these moves were eliminated from the analysis of response time data, as were the attacking versions of these positions.

The other positions had a very high solution rate, particularily the attacking positions with 98% correct solutions. Defending positions were obviously harder but still had an 82% solution rate. As error rates were low, response times were analyzed. Analyses of response time data did not distinguish between correct and incorrect solutions. In an essentially self-terminating task such as this, response times will be greater for incorrect solutions than for correct ones. If response times for incorrect moves were eliminated, information about difficulty would be lost (as long as subjects were motivated).

Table 1
Means and standard deviations (in parenthesis) of response times for each transfer condition and for attacking and defending positions in seconds, collapsed across all transformation positions.

	similar	attack/ defence	fork/ pin	rook/ bishop	Total
Attacking	15.6 (10.5)	17.1 (10.0)	21.2 (23.5)	16.6 (13.9)	17.6
Defending	29.8 (30.5)	36.4 (36.8)	31.1 (29.3)	37.4 (39.0)	33.7
Overall	22.7 (23.9)	26.8 (28.6)	26.2 (27.0)	27.0 (31.0)	25.7

The mean response times for the attacking and defending positions in each of the four transfer conditions are presented in Table 1, collapsed over all transformations. A 2x4 between-subjects analysis of variance revealed a significant main effect of whether the position was attacking or defending, $F(1,2440) = 225$, $p<.01$, $(MS_e = 703)$. This simply confirms the expectation that the defending positions are more difficult than the attacking positions. The

predicted main effect of transfer condition was obtained, $F(3,2440) = 3.48$, $p<.05$, as was a significant interaction between the two variables, $F(3,2440) = 5.45$, $p<.01$.

The nature of the interaction was examined by looking at the attacking and defending positions separately (see Table 1 for means). For attacking positions there was a significant effect of transfer condition ($F[3,1220] = 7.88$, $p<.01$, $MS_e = 238$). However, planned comparisons revealed only that the fork/pin condition was significantly slower than the similar condition ($F[1,1220] = 20.34$, $p<.01$). There were no significant differences between the similar condition and the attack/defence condition ($F[1,1220] = 1.39$, $p<.25$) or the bishop/rook condition ($F[1,1220] = .67$, $n.s.$).

For defending positions there was also an effect of transfer condition ($F[3,1220] = 3.77$, $p<.025$, $MS_e = 1167$). The planned comparisons revealed that the similar condition was significantly faster than the bishop/rook condition ($F[1,1220] = 7.55$, $p<.01$), and the attack/defence ($F[1,1220] = 5.78$, $p<.01$), but not significantly faster than the pin/fork condition ($F[1,1220] = .21$, $n.s.$).

In order to investigate the differences for particular transformation positions, pin positions were examined. Because every subject received every pin position (which was not the case for forks) a more powerful repeated measures analysis could be used. The mean response times for each pin transformation position for each transfer condition are presented in Table 2.

Table 2
Mean response times (s) for pin positions for each transformation position in each transfer condition.

	Transformation			
	identical	rotation	change-piece	change-structure
similar	15.3	19.3	26.4	27.4
defence/attack	19.7	28.3	30.2	29.5
pin/fork	22.4	30.0	31.4	28.2
bishop/rook	21.2	29.2	28.1	23.3

For the identical transformation a multivariate analysis of variance revealed a significant effect of transfer, $F(3,69)=5.88$, $p<.01$. Planned univariate contrasts revealed significant differences between the similar condition and each of the other three transfer conditions: for similar with defence/attack, $F(1,71)=4.54$, $MS_e=160$, $p<.05$; with pin/fork, $F(1,71)=8.19$, $MS_e=226$, $p<.01$; and with bishop/rook, $F(1,71)=8.23$, $MS_e=155$, $p<.01$. Similar results were obtained for the rotation transformation in which a significant effect of transfer condition was obtained, $F(3,69)=5.49$, $p<.01$.

Planned univariate contrasts showed significant differences between the similar condition and each of the other three transfer conditions: for similar with defence/attack, $F(1,71)=4.65$, $MS_e=627$, $p<.05$; with pin/fork, $F(1,71)=6.51$, $MS_e=636$, $p<.05$; and with bishop/rook, $F(1,71)=7.84$, $MS_e=452$, $p<.01$. However there were no effects of transfer condition for the change-piece ($F[3,69]=.26$, $n.s.$) or the change-structure ($F[3,69]=.77$, $n.s.$) transformations.

Responses on the final position were analyzed by classifying all moves as correct or incorrect. A correct move in the attacking condition (when the subject had a chance to make the fatal move) was only recorded if they made the knight forking move. A correct move in the defending position (when the subject is threatened by the fatal move) is any move that renders the knight move harmless.

Table 3
Number of correct and incorrect solutions given to the final position in the attacking condition as a function of subject being given winning or losing manipulation.

	attacking position		defending position	
	winning	losing	winning	losing
Correct	5	9	0	4
Incorrect	6	8	16	9

The frequencies for correct and incorrect moves, for both attacking and defending positions, as a function of whether the subject was told that they were winning or losing, are presented in Table 3. There were no significant differences for attacking positions, $X^2(1) = .15$, $n.s.$, however the defending position yield a significant difference ($X^2[1] = 9.16$, $p<.005$) indicating that subjects were more likely to solve the problem, by recognizing the need for defence, when they were told that they were losing, rather than winning.

Discussion

These results provide support for the claim that goal similarity plays a role in analogical problem solving. In doing so they indicate that this task may be a useful one for further investigating the role of goal similarity in analogical processes. The overall findings, and those from the similar and rotation transformation positions, indicated that response times were faster if goals were kept consistent between the training and testing positions. This result is strengthened by the fact that the similar position appeared after many other attacking and defending positions had been seen and solved by the subjects. The fact that the conditions that we would expect to be hard to map, the fork/pin and bishop/rook conditions, were also generally slower then the similar condition supports the contention that mapping is being used to help solve positions.

The lack of a transfer position effect for the change-piece transformation positions is interesting. It appears to indicate that changing a piece is more than a simple semantic change. It may constitute a structural change, due to the fact that different pieces move differently. Hence changing a piece may change how the pieces relate to each other, even without changing their positions.

It is still not conclusively established, however that ease of analogical retrieval or mapping caused the faster responses in the similar conditions. Further research should try to establish directly how well subjects retrieve or map to these positions. Including a recognition task would be one way to do this. Another way to make the task more sensitive to mapping effects is to present ambiguous positions with multiple valid solutions and observe if subjects favor solutions that map most closely to their training positions

The finding that the goals at the time of test can influence solutions provides a powerful demonstration of the effects of influencing the subjects goals. This is particularly so since no other changes are made and the information that is provided is not directly relevant to determining the optimal move. However it is possible that this result could be explained in terms of demand characteristics. In future research this problem could be addressed by using less explicit instructions. It should also be noted that in this experiment the final position was not designed as an analogical task, as there is nothing provided as an explicit source analogue. Future studies could turn this into an analogical task by attempting to provide an explicit source. How well subjects could find such embedded analogues is unclear, but this ability could be examined by using a recognition task in which subjects would have to recognize an embedded analogy present in a full position (again goal similarity, structural, and semantic factors could be again manipulated).

This study did not examine skilled chess play; however the results have implications for chess skill, if they prove to be extendable to skilled chess players. If chess skill is based on analogical processes, then it would provide an explanation for the characteristic of chess masters that deGroot (1965) found that most distinguished them from less skilled players: that they simply selected better moves to examine in the first place. Because neither he nor the players were able to explain this,

51

deGroot ascribed it to intuition, but its almost perceptual quality seems to fit quite well into an analogical framework.

In conclusion, this study provided support for the claim that goal similarity plays a role in problem solving, in that responses were made more quickly if consistent goals were given. This advantage may well be due to the improvement in the ease of analogical mapping that consistent goals provided, although further research is required to establish this with more confidence. The fact that this task is sensitive to such effects may mean it can be used to test different models of analogical mapping and problem solving. Such models often differ crucially in the ways they handle goals.

References

Brown, A. L., Kane, M. J., & Echols, C. H. (1986). Young children's mental models determine analogical transfer across problems with a common goal structure. *Cognitive Development, 1*, 103-121.

Carbonell, J. (1983) Learning by analogy: Formulating and generalizing plans from past experience. In R. Michalski, J. Carbonell, & T. Mitchell, (Eds.), *Machine learning: An artificial intelligence approach*. Los Altos: Tioga, 137-161.

Carbonell, J. (1986) Derivational analogy: A theory of reconstructive problem solving and expertise acquisition. In R. Michalski, J. Carbonell, & T. Mitchell (Eds.), *Machine learning: An artificial intelligence approach*, vol 2. Los Altos: Morgan Kaufman, 371-392.

deGroot, A. D. (1965). *Thought and choice in chess*. The Hague: Mouton.

Gentner, D. (1989). The mechanisms of analogical learning. In S. Vosniadou & A. Ortony (Eds.), *Analogy, similarity, and thought*. Cambridge, Mass.: Cambridge University Press.

Gentner, D., & Toupin, C. (1986). Systematicity and surface similarity in the development of analogy. *Cognitive Science, 10*, 277-300.

Gick, M. L., & Holyoak, K. J. (1980). Analogical problem solving. *Cognitive Psychology, 12*, 306-355.

Gick, M. L., & Holyoak, K. J. (1983). Schema induction and analogical transfer. *Cognitive Psychology, 15*, 1-38.

Hammond, K. (1989). *Case-based planning*. Boston: Academic Press.

Holyoak, K. J., & Koh, K. (1987). Surface and structural similarity in analogical transfer. *Memory & Cognition, 15*, 332-340.

Holyoak, K. J., & Thagard, P. (1989). Analogical mapping by constraint satisfaction. *Cognitive Science*, 13, 295-355.

Schank, R. C. (1982). *Dynamic memory*. Cambridge: Cambridge University Press.

Ross, B. (1987). This is like that: The use of earlier problems and the separation of similarity effects. *Journal of Experimental Psychology: Learning, Memory, and Cognition, 13*, 629-639.

Ross, B. (1989). A further analysis of the access and use of earlier problems: Distinguishing different superficial similarity effects. *Journal of Experimental Psychology: Learning, Memory, and Cognition, 15*, 456-468.

Winston, P. H. (1980). Learning and reasoning by analogy. *Communications of the ACM, 23*, 689-703.

Winston, P. H. (1982). Learning new principles from precedents and exercises. *Artificial Intelligence, 19*, 321-350.

Internal Analogy: A Model of Transfer within Problems

Angela Kennedy Hickman
School of Computer Science
Carnegie Mellon University
Pittsburgh, PA 15213
ach@ml.ri.cmu.edu

Jill H. Larkin
Department of Psychology
Carnegie Mellon University
Pittsburgh, PA 15213
larkin@tulip.psy.cmu.edu

Abstract

Understanding problem solving and methods for learning is a main goal of cognitive science. Analogical reasoning simplifies problem solving by transferring previously learned knowledge from a source problem to the current target problem in order to reduce search. To provide a more detailed analysis of the mechanisms of transfer, we describe a process called *internal analogy* that transfers experience from a completed subgoal in the same problem to solve the current target subgoal. We explain what constitutes an appropriate source problem and what knowledge to transfer from that source, in addition to examining the associated memory organization. Unlike case-based reasoning methods, this process does not require large amounts of accumulated experience before it is effective; it provides useful search control at the outset of problem solving. Data from a study of subjects solving DC-circuit problems designed to facilitate transfer supports the psychological validity of the mechanism.

1. Introduction

Analogical reasoning is an effective method of recycling past experience to guide problem solving. To begin the analysis of this process, we formulate the following five steps. First, the problem solver must determine a set of candidate sources. The utility of the procedure relies on the identification of the relevant knowledge. Second, one solution must be retrieved to function as the actual source. Third, the source solution must be reinstantiated and modified to solve the target problem. Fourth, the new solution should be stored so that the problem solver can reason from it to solve future problems. Fifth, the problem solver should receive some knowledge of results concerning the effort required to perform the analogy and the successfulness of the procedure. This information can be used to provide feedback to the retrieval steps of the process.

Although analogy has been explored previously [1, 2, 7, 8, 16, 17], most of the work has focused on the mapping procedure outlined in step three above. [11], [12] and [19] have addressed memory organization (related to steps one, two, and four above) in detail, but their ideas have not been integrated with an analogical mechanism. ICARUS [14] and EUREKA [10] have incorporated the whole process to some extent. However, neither system embeds its solution within a general implementation of a problem solver (for example, EUREKA is not capable of backtracking). As a result, they cannot solve problems which are as difficult as those reported in this study.

This paper addresses the first four steps of the process with a transfer mechanism called *internal* analogy, which works on similar subgoals of a single problem. This is in contrast to *within-domain* and *cross-domain* analogy which transfer knowledge across separate problems from the same domain and different domains, respectively. Work in progress using derivational analogy [4] in PRODIGY [3, 22] is beginning to address most of the steps above, but for cross-problem, within-domain analogy.

Our internal analogy mechanism is tightly integrated into a general problem solver for the physical sciences, RFERMI, and is effective in reducing search [9]. Unlike case-based reasoning methods, the process does not require large amounts of accumulated experience before it is effective; it provides useful search control at the outset of problem solving. In addition, psychological predictions drawn from the computational model of internal analogy were supported by data from a study of subjects solving DC-circuit and fluid statics problems that were designed to facilitate transfer.

The next section presents the implementation of the internal analogy algorithm in RFERMI, as well as an example trace of the non-learning system. Section 3 contains the psychological predictions derived from the computational model and the analysis of the data we collected. We conclude with a discussion evaluating internal analogy.

2. Computational Model

The internal analogy process described in the preceding section is implemented in a problem solver for the physical sciences named RFERMI. This system is a rule-based version of the FERMI system [15] and is based in part on studies of effective representations and methods for solving physics problems [5, 18]. Its task domains range from linear algebra and DC-circuits to fluid statics and classical mechanics. RFERMI maintains a principled decomposition of knowledge in order to retain the power of its domain specific knowledge while utilizing the cross-domain applicability of its more general knowledge.

RFERMI's declarative knowledge of scientific principles is organized in a *quantity hierarchy* which is stored as frames. The frame system used to implement the hierarchy is a component of FRulekit [20], a forward chaining production system. Through the use of inheritance, this hierarchy efficiently stores knowledge about quantities such as resistances, pressure drops, potential drops, and two dimensional areas.

RFERMI's procedural knowledge, as organized in its *actions hierarchy*, is of two types. First, domain specific knowledge is stored in *puller* frames that are interpreted into FRulekit rules. These pullers encode equational knowledge, such as Ohm's law, and procedures, such as those for finding the pressure drop between two points in a static liquid or the electro-magnetic force of a battery. Second, RFERMI's more general and widely applicable knowledge, such as its iterative decomposition procedure, constitute its *methods*. Methods are associated with generalized quantities so that a quantity inherits access to a method from superordinate quantities. For example, potential drop inherits access to the path invariance method from scalar field difference, which is a generalized quantity. Therefore, the method for equating potential drops along two alternate paths can be used to solve for a potential drop.

Although the system is implemented in a forward chaining production system, it maintains a backward chaining control structure via the goal monitor. The space it searches while solving for an unknown quantity is structured in a traditional AND-OR manner. When there are multiple means for pursuing a goal (i.e., pullers and methods) an OR node is generated, and when a method spawns a conjunctive set of unmet subgoals (i.e., unknown quantities) an AND node is generated. RFERMI organizes its search in a manner combining depth-first and breadth-first expansion. At OR nodes, it contains heuristic preferences for using the specific puller knowledge over the more general methods.

As an example, we present RFERMI's problem solving without learning on the problem in Figure 2-1(see Figure 2-2). The system first solves for I_2 by applying a puller. Lines 7-14 show that it solves for R_1 by generating subgoals for V_{ab} and I_1. V_{ab} is solved using a puller, which results in R_1's solution. In line 16, RFERMI chooses a different puller to solve I_3 than it used to solve I_1. (It could reduce the required search by solving I_3 in a similar manner since the goals are analogical and the system solved I_1 with relatively little effort.) In both cases, both pullers were applicable, and the system chose randomly. However, this line of reasoning ends in goal circularity (see line 20) since V_{cd} has already been posted. In lines 21-23, it tries another instantiation of the same puller, which also results in goal circularity. Finally, in lines 24-29, it obtains the value of V_{cd} by using the puller that solved I_1. The end of the trace shows how R_4 is solved.

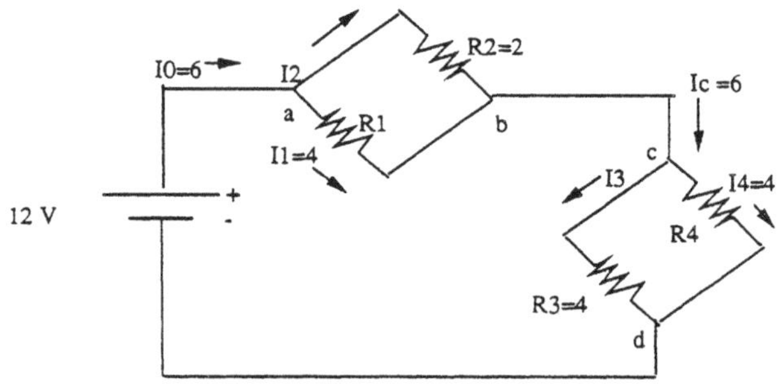

Figure 2-1: Problem 5.

The implementation of internal analogy in RFERMI relies on the trace facility of the problem solver. While solving a problem, the system stores the expanded goal tree along with the status of each goal (succeeded, failed, or pending). For goals that succeed, the instantiated productions that achieved the goal are also stored. As shown by the internal analogy algorithm in Figure 2-3, when the system begins to solve a new target subproblem, it checks if it has previously solved a goal of the same quantity type. (For example, I_1 is of the same quantity type as I_3 in Figure 2-1 since they are both currents.) If so, the most recently solved

54

1. Post Goals:	I_2, R_1, I_3, R_4	
2. Choose Goal:	I_2	
3. Apply Puller:	$I_2 = I_0 - I_1$	current flowing into a = current flowing out of a
4. Lookup:	$I_0 = 6$	
5. Lookup:	$I_1 = 4$	
6. Compute:	$I_2 = 2$	
7. Choose Goal:	R_1	
8. Apply Puller:	$R_1 = V_{ab} / I_1$	Ohm's law (V=IR)
9. Apply Puller:	$V_{ab} = I_2 R_2$	Ohm's law (V = IR)
10. Lookup:	$I_2 = 2$	
11. Lookup:	$R_2 = 2$	
12: Compute:	$V_{ab} = 4$	
13. Lookup:	$I_1 = 4$	
14. Compute:	$R_1 = 1$	
15. Choose Goal:	I_3— internal analogy would apply	
16. Apply Puller:	$I_3 = V_{cd} / R_3$	Ohm's law (V = IR)
17. Apply Puller:	$V_{cd} = I_4 R_4$	Ohm's law (V = IR)
18. Lookup:	$I_4 = 4$	
19. Apply Puller:	$R_4 = V_{cd} / I_4$	Ohm's law (V = IR)
20. Fail Circular Goal:	V_{cd}	
21. Apply Puller:	$V_{cd} = I_3 R_3$	Ohm's law (V = IR)
22. Apply Puller:	$I_3 = V_{cd} / R_3$	Ohm's law (V = IR)
23. Fail Circular Goal:	V_{cd}	
24. Apply Puller:	$I_3 = I_c - I_4$	current flowing into c = current flowing out of c
25. Lookup:	$I_c = 6$	
26. Lookup:	$I_4 = 4$	
27. Compute:	$I_3 = 2$	
28. Lookup:	$R_3 = 4$	
29. Compute:	$V_{cd} = 8$	
30. Lookup:	$R_3 = 4$	
31. Compute:	$I_3 = 2$	
32. Choose Goal:	R_4— internal analogy would apply	
33. Apply Puller:	$R_4 = V_{cd} / I_4$	Ohm's law (V = IR)
34. Lookup:	$V_{cd} = 8$	
35. Lookup:	$I_4 = 4$	
36. Compute:	$R_4 = 2$	

Figure 2-2: RFERMI's behavior on Problem 5 with no learning.

instance is chosen as the *candidate* source. If the candidate source succeeded and no more information was known about it than is known about the current problem, then it is chosen as the *actual* source. Otherwise, it is rejected because the system had additional knowledge during the previous problem solving which may have been crucial to its success. Without that knowledge, it may be unable to recycle the old solution to solve the current target problem. The failure case is decided in just the opposite manner. If the candidate source failed and contained no less information than the current problem, it is chosen. Otherwise, it is rejected. This check ensures that RFERMI does not choose a source that failed because there was less information available to the problem solver and prematurely fail the current target as a result. The mapping proceeds based on the success or failure of the source. If the source failed, then the processing of the current goal is suspended and another goal is explored. If all other problem solving fails, this goal may be later reopened. If, on the other hand, the source succeeded, its solution is appropriately reinstantiated for the current subgoal, and the solution is replayed. Since this newly solved subgoal is contained in the current problem, it is available to the algorithm as a future candidate source.

```
1. IF there are untested previously explored subgoals of the same type as target
2.          THEN candidate := most recently explored same-type subgoal
3.          ELSE fail internal-analogy
4. IF candidate succeeded
5.          THEN IF information-content(candidate) <= information-content(target)
6.                      THEN source := candidate & reinstantiate the source solution
                        to solve the target
7.                      ELSE tested(source) := TRUE & internal-analogy(target)
8.          ELSE IF information-content(candidate) >= information-content(target)
9.                      THEN source := candidate & suspend(target)
10.                     ELSE tested(source) := TRUE & internal-analogy(target)
```

Figure 2-3: The internal analogy algorithm.

Steps 5 and 8 of the algorithm in Figure 2-3 compare the amount of information known about a candidate goal at the time it was solved with the amount of information known about the current target goal. This comparison is carried out in RFERMI by calculating the set of variables in the left hand sides of the rules that solved the candidate source goal and that had known values. We call this the *information content* of the candidate source. The information content of the current target goal is computed by calculating the set of these same variables that have known values in the current working memory. For example, suppose the candidate source goal is to find the potential drop between points a and b in a circuit, and the resistance and the current between those two points were known. Now suppose the current target goal is to find the potential drop between points c and d in the same circuit, and the equation that solved the candidate source goal was potential-drop = current * resistance. If the resistance between c and d is known but the current is not, then the information content of the candidate source goal is said to be greater than that of the target goal (because the current was known in the candidate source goal).

Step 6 of Figure 2-3 reinstantiates and replays the solution of the source problem in order to solve the target problem. RFERMI carries out this step by instantiating the productions that solved the source goal in the current working memory and applying them. We call this *operator-driven mapping*, and it answers the important question that Structure Mapping [7] inadvertently poses: how does one identify the salient structure to map? We operationally define the salient structure to be the relevant variables that are tested in the left-hand sides of the operators that solved the source goal.

As a last comment, we mention that it is especially important to only suspend the processing in Step 9 of Figure 2-3. The system cannot terminally fail the goal because one of RFERMI's other general methods may still solve the problem, although more expensively.

The internal analogy mechanism described above has proven to be an effective learning mechanism in RFERMI. Detailed theoretical and empirical analyses of the search reduction it provides are described in [9].

3. Protocol Data

If, as hypothesized, the internal analogy mechanism embedded in RFERMI has any psychologically validity, then the computational model described in the previous section predicts that subjects will exhibit the following behaviors during problem solving:

- Knowledge will be transferred from either previously successful or previously failed goals.

- The source will be of the same quantity type as the target and have a compatible information content.

- Problem solving using analogy will require less effort (search) than would otherwise be necessary.

- Transfer from previously failed problem solving will enable the subject to know that a particular procedure as instantiated at the current point will fail. Thus, he should choose a different procedure.

• Transfer from previously successful problem solving will allow the subject to know precisely which procedures to choose to calculate the quantity and all its subquantities. For problems in the physical sciences, this means that the subject should know which equations to reuse to solve the unknown. However, these equations must be reinstantiated to reflect the new problem solving context.

• Since RFERMI randomly selects among its applicable pullers for solving any given subgoal, we predict that subjects will show individual differences in their problem solving behavior. The system also has two different control strategies: one strictly depth first and the other more breadth first. It's problem solving differs according to the current control strategy. As a result, we predict further individual differences will arise from the subjects' varied control strategies.

To test the predictions, we studied subjects solving problems from two of RFERMI's task domains, DC-circuits and fluid statics. These problems were designed to facilitate three kinds of transfer: internal analogy, within-domain analogy, and cross-domain analogy. The four subjects had all earned an A or a B in a year-long college physics course, but they had not solved any problems in these domains for several years. We chose subjects with this level of proficiency because we believed that they would be the most likely to exhibit the desired transfer. Subjects with a high level of expertise tend to use compiled knowledge rather than analogical reasoning; subjects with very little expertise tend to use brute force search. The subjects were given a remedial, which was in a two-column format, covering the knowledge necessary for the experiment. The left column contained the circuit information, and the right column contained the fluid statics information. Analogical concepts were presented directly across the page from each other. In order to verify the remediation, the subjects were asked to explain sparse written solutions to three example problems. These example problems were also designed to serve as analogical sources for the five problems that the subjects were asked to solve next.

We observed all three types of transfer. However, the more local types of transfer happened more frequently; only one instance of cross-domain transfer occurred. Due to space limitations, we discuss the subjects' behavior only on Problem 5, which was shown in Figure 2-1 and designed to facilitate internal analogy. Below we demonstrate that RFERMI with the internal analogy mechanism models the subjects' behavior well. The mechanism also reduces the search previously required to solve I_3 and R_4 by about 50% (compare lines 15-36 of Figure 2-2 with lines 16-30 of Figure 3-1).

We begin by comparing the behavior produced by RFERMI with internal analogy to that of Subject 1 on the example problem (see Figure 3-1). Problem solving for both proceeds similarly, except for the following differences which are unimportant with respect to the analogical mechanism. Between lines 2 and 3 of the figure, Subject 1 does some erroneous problem solving and decides to start over. As can be seen in lines 3 and 18 of the protocol, the system always posts an equation with the desired unknown on the left hand side, while the subject posts the version of the current invariance equation that corresponds to the associated prose in the remedial. In lines 8 and 10 of the protocol, Subject 1 posts incorrect equations; this will have interesting side effects later in the problem solving. The problem solver represents potential drops as a drop between two points, regardless of the path. The subject, however, clearly distinguishes potential drops with the same endpoints over different paths; this leads to his extra step in line 9. Occasionally, Subject 1 will take an arithmetical "shortcut" by not restating the implied left-hand side of the equation or by reducing fractions to their lowest terms (lines 11-12, 26-27 and 29).

Ignoring these small differences, RFERMI models the subject extremely well. Both solve equations for I_2 and R_1 in a straightforward manner. At line 17, the system's analogical mechanism is invoked because it is has solved a goal of the same quantity type with a compatible information content, I_2 (I_0 and I_1 are known while I_2 is unknown at line 3, and I_c and I_4 are known while I_3 is unknown at line 18). It retrieves the productions that solved I_2 and reinstantiates them. This saves the system search time in two ways. First, it does not have to compute which productions to apply— the analogy mechanism specifies them. Second, there are other applicable pullers at this point that would require more problem solving effort if they were used, as shown in lines 15-31 of Figure 2-2. Subject 1 also recognizes that I_3 is an analogical goal to I_2 at line 17: he states, "this (pointing to I_3) is just like that (pointing to I_2)". Then, he quickly reinstantiates the equation that he used in line 3 and solves for I_3. Similar recycling of past experience occurs for both the problem solver and the subject in lines 22-30 while solving for R_4. When Subject 1 says, "back to here," in these lines, he is pointing to the equation $R_1 = I_1/V_{r1}$ which he wrote in line 8. The subject analogizes from the incorrect equations in lines 8 and 10 and reuses them in lines 24 and 25, which causes him to derive an incorrect answer for R_4. Had he used the correct equations earlier, he would have solved this problem

	FERMI	Subject 1
1. Post Goals:	I_2, R_1, I_3, R_4	I_2, R_1, I_3, R_4
2. Choose Goal:	I_2	I_2
3. Apply Puller:	$I_2 = I_0 - I_1$	$I_0 = I_1 + I_2$
4. Lookup:	$I_0 = 6$	$I_0 = 6$
5. Lookup:	$I_1 = 4$	$I_1 = 4$
6. Compute:	$I_2 = 2$	$I_2 = 2$
7. Choose Goal:	R_1	R_1
8. Apply Puller:	$R_1 = V_{ab} / I_1$	$R_1 = I_1 / V_{r1}$
9. Apply Method:		$V_{r1} = V_{r2}^1$
10. Apply Puller:	$V_{ab} = I_2 R_2$	$V_{r2} = I_2 / R_2$
11. Lookup:	$I_2 = 2$	$= 2/$
12. Lookup:	$R_2 = 2$	2
13. Compute:	$V_{ab} = 4$	$V_{r1} = 1$
14. Lookup:	$I_1 = 4$	$I_1 = 4$
15. Compute:	$R_1 = 1$	$R_1 = 4$
16. Choose Goal:	I_3	I_3
17. Analogize:	*Fires analogy to I_2*	*"This is just like that."*
18. Apply Puller:	$I_3 = I_c - I_4$	$I_c = I_3 + I_4$
19. Lookup:	$I_0 = 6$	$I_c = 6$
20. Lookup:	$I_4 = 4$	$I_4 = 4$
21. Compute:	$I_3 = 2$	$I_3 = 2$
22. Choose Goal:	R_4	R_4
23. Analogize:	*Fires analogy to R_1*	*"Back to here."*
24. Apply Puller:	$R_4 = V_{cd} / I_4$	$R_r = I_4 / V_{r4}$
25. Apply Puller:	$V_{cd} = I_3 R_3$	$V_{r3} = I_3/R_3$
26. Lookup:	$I_3 = 2$	$= 1/$
27. Lookup:	$R_3 = 4$	2
28. Compute:	$V_{cd} = 8$	$V_{r4} = 1/2$:Apply Method
29. Lookup:	$I_4 = 4$	$4/.5 = 8$:Compute
30. Compute:	$R_4 = 2$	$R_4 = 8$

Figure 3-1: The behavior of RFERMI with learning
and Subject 1 on Problem 5.

correctly.

All four subjects performed internal analogy on Problem 5, but each exhibited a different control structure. Subject 1 backward chained much like RFERMI, while Subject 4 demonstrated more expertise in the domain and forward chained. This behavior is consistent with the results reported in [21] that show that experts tend to forward chain in search spaces that they expect to be small. Subject 2 began by backward chaining and switched to forward chaining as he gathered more experience in the domain. Subject 3 struggled to complete the problem and explored the subgoals in a nonstandard order. We now examine each of the other subject's problem solving more closely.

In contrast to Subject 1, Subject 4 solves the problem by forward chaining. This subject maps the

---

[1]The potential drop between any two points is the same regardless of the path chosen between the points.

analogical subgoals explicitly by their quantity type and information content. At the outset of the problem solving, he says, "So, I have two resistors where the current is given and the resistance is left unknown (R_1 and R_4) and two resistors where the resistance is given and the current is left unknown (R_2 and R_3)". He proceeds to solve for I_2 and R_1. At this point he says, "similar situation here," and solves for I_3, reusing the the equation that solved I_2 reinstantiated for the current goal. In a similar fashion, he uses the equations that solved R_1 to solve R_4. This subject, like Subject 2 and Subject 1 on other problems, tends not to verbalize the uninstantiated equation during the replay of the analogy but verbalizes the instantiated form instead.

Subject 3, who begins backward chaining and switches to forward chaining, states early in his problem solving that $I_1=I_4=4$ and $I_0=I_c$. When he solves I_2, he immediately states the same answer for I_3, without additional computation. It appears that his analogical reasoning is more advanced than RFERMI's. In addition to reposting and reinstantiating equations, this subject is able to recognize when the relevant variables have exactly the same value, and the answer can be recycled directly. With this straightforward extension added to the system, it could gain an even greater reduction in search. The point at which Subject 3 switches to forward chaining is also significant: he finishes solving for V_{ab}, and he recycles the equation he used in a newly instantiated form for V_{cd}. The switch from backward chaining to forward chaining seems to be triggered, at least in part, by an analogical goal.

Subject 2 is considerably less skilled at solving these types of problems than the other subjects. He struggles to solve any of the subgoals using the same knowledge encoded in RFERMI's pullers, methods, and algebra module. When he does finally solve I_2 and R_1, however, he immediately restates the current invariance relation and quickly solves I_3 and R_4. There is nothing in his analogical transfer that we did not observe in the previous three protocols.

4. Discussion and Conclusions

Although the subjects showed individual differences in their control strategies, the basic components of the analogical reasoning were those that the computational mechanism predicted. The subjects transferred knowledge from successful problem solving in order to reduce the effort required to solve the target subgoal. They simply reposted the previously successful equations and reinstantiated them in the current context. In every instance, the sources and targets were of the same quantity type and had compatible information contents.

The system models Subject 1 well in its current state. With a forward chaining control strategy, it could easily model Subject 4 as well. To model Subject 2, one additional capability must be added to the system: it should recognize those occasions when the equations need not be reinstantiated but the value may be directly recycled. Even though the computational model focused our attention toward particular problem solving behavior in the protocols, the protocols continue to suggest useful extensions to the system.

Relaxing the notion of compatible information content will provide internal analogy with a more flexible matching mechanism than either SOAR's chunking [13] or macro-operators [6] possesses. This will allow our learning method to provide search control when the others cannot. Extending the implementation to effect within-domain and cross-domain transfer will also increase its utility.

In conclusion, our study of internal analogy has described a new process for transferring knowledge within a single problem. It has also provided a more complete analysis of the processes needed for analogical transfer than has previously been presented. We specify what constitutes an appropriate source and what knowledge to transfer to the target. In addition, the mechanism is tightly integrated into a general problem solver and does not require an alternate reasoning engine or large case libraries. The psychological validity of the mechanism has also been supported through the psychological data presented.

Acknowledgements This research was supported in part by DARPA contract number F33615-87-C-1499 Amendment 20, and AIP-ONR contract number N00014-86-K-0678-N123. Angela Kennedy Hickman was also partially supported during this research by a Zonta International Amelia Earhart fellowship. We would like to thank Peter Shell for his invaluable contribution to the implementation. Jaime Carbonell, Jill Fain Lehman and David Plaut increased the clarity and the content of the paper through their comments. Sandra Esch and David Plaut assisted in setting up the lab for the experiments.

References

1. Adelson, Beth, "Analogical Reasoning: Problem-Driven Mapping and Debugging," Tech. report, Department of Computer Science, Tufts University, 1989.

2. Anderson, J. R., "A Theory of the Origins of Human Knowledge," *Artificial Intelligence*, Vol. 40, 1989, pp. 313-351.

3. Carbonell, J. G. and Veloso, M. M., "Integrating Derivational Analogy into a General Problem Solving Architecture," *Proceedings of the First Workshop on Case-Based Reasoning*, Morgan Kaufmann, May 1988.

4. Carbonell, J. G., "Derivational Analogy: A Theory of Reconstructive Problem Solving and Expertise Acquisition," in *Machine Learning, An Artificial Intelligence Approach, Volume II*, Michalski, R. S., Carbonell, J. G. and Mitchell, T. M., eds., Morgan Kaufmann, 1986, pp. 371-392.

5. Chi, M. T. H., Feltovich, P. J. and Glaser, R., "Categorization and representation of physics problems by experts and novices," *Cognitive Science*, Vol. 5, 1981, pp. 121-152.

6. Fikes, R. E. and Nilsson, N. J., "STRIPS: A New Approach to the Application of Theorem Proving to Problem Solving," *Artificial Intelligence*, Vol. 2, 1971, pp. 189-208.

7. Gentner, D., "Structure mapping: A theoretical framework for analogy," *Cognitive Science*, Vol. 7, 1983, pp. 155-170.

8. Gick, M. L. and Holyoak, K. J., "Analogical Problem Solving," *Cognitive Psychology*, Vol. 12, 1980, pp. 306-355.

9. Hickman, A. Kennedy, Shell P. and Carbonell, J. G., "Internal Analogy: Reducing Search during Problem Solving," *Proceedings of AAAI-90*, 1990, (submitted).

10. Jones, R., *A Model of Retrieval in Problem Solving*, PhD dissertation, Department of Information and Computer Science, University of California, Irvine, 1989.

11. Kolodner, J. L., "Maintaining Organization in a Dynamic Long-Term Memory," *Cognitive Science*, Vol. 7, 1983, pp. 243-280.

12. Kolodner, J. L., "Reconstructive Memory: A Computer Model," *Cognitive Science*, Vol. 7, 1983, pp. 281-328.

13. Laird, J. E., Rosenbloom, P. S. and Newell, A., "Chunking in SOAR: The Anatomy of a General Learning Mechanism," *Machine Learning*, Vol. 1, No. 1, 1986, pp. 11-46.

14. Langley, P., Thompson, K., Iba, W. F., Gennari, J. and Allen, J. A., "An Integrated Cognitive Architecture for Autonomous Agents," Tech. report 89-28, Department of Information and Computer Science, University of California, Irvine, 1989.

15. Larkin, J. H., Reif, F., Carbonell, J. G. and Gugliotta, A., "FERMI: A Flexible Expert Reasoner with Multi-Domain Inferencing," *Cognitive Science*, Vol. 12, 1988, pp. 101-138.

16. Lewis, C., "Why and How to Learn Why: Analysis-based Generalization of Procedures," *Cognitive Science*, Vol. 12, 1988, pp. 211-256.

17. Pirolli, P., "A Model of Purpose-driven Analogy and Skill Acquisition in Programming," *The 9th Annual Conference of The Cognitive Science Society*, Lawrence Earlbaum Associates, 1987, pp. 609-621.

18. Reif, F. and Heller, J. I., "Knowledge structure and problem solving in physics," *Educational Psychologist*, Vol. 17, 1982, pp. 102-127.

19. Schank, R. C., "Language and Memory," *Cognitive Science*, Vol. 4, 1980, pp. 243-284.

20. Shell, P. and Carbonell, J. G., "The FRuleKit Reference Manual", CMU Computer Science Department internal paper.

21. Simon, D. P. and Simon, H. A., *Individual Differences in Solving Physics Problems*, Lawrence Earlbaum Associates, Hillsdale, New Jersey, 1978, ch. 13.

22. Veloso, M. M. and Carbonell, J. G., "Learning Analogies by Analogy - The Closed Loop of Memory Organization and Problem Solving," *Proceedings of the Second Workshop on Case-Based Reasoning*, Morgan Kaufmann, May 1989.

Making SME greedy and pragmatic

Kenneth D. Forbus   Dan Oblinger
Qualitative Reasoning Group

Beckman Institute, University of Illinois
Phone: (217) 333-0193; Internet: forbus@p.cs.uiuc.edu

Abstract: The Structure-Mapping Engine (SME) has successfully modeled several aspects of human analogical processing. However, it has two significant drawbacks: (1) SME constructs all structurally consistent interpretations of an analogy. While useful for theoretical explorations, this aspect of the algorithm is both psychologically implausible and computationally inefficient. (2) SME contains no mechanism for focusing on interpretations relevant to an analogizer's goals. This paper describes modifications to SME which overcome these flaws. We describe a *greedy merge algorithm* which efficiently computes an approximate "best" interpretation, and can generate alternate interpretations when necessary. We describe *pragmatic marking*, a technique which focuses the mapping to produce relevant, yet novel, inferences. We illustrate these techniques via example and evaluate their performance using empirical data and theoretical analysis.

1 Introduction

The importance of analogy in human reasoning makes it a natural focus for cognitive simulation. The Structure-Mapping Engine (SME)[6,7], has been used to successfully model several aspects of human analogical processing. As a simulation of Gentner's Structure-Mapping theory [9,10], SME has been used to model human soundness judgements [13], to study the representational and processing choices in analogical processing [8], and as part of a model of sequence learning [14]. SME has also been used in an AI system which learns qualitative physics by analogy [3].

We believe several features of SME are accurate reflections of human analogical processing, including the emergence of global interpretations from local matches, the use of structural evaluation criteria as a default means of judging a comparison, the ability to generate novel candidate inferences, and the ability to construct and compare multiple interpretations of a comparison. However, the current SME algorithm has several drawbacks. First, SME constructs all structurally consistent interpretations of an analogy. This is often useful for theoretical explorations, since it allows one to know for certain the best possible interpretation of a given comparison. But it is extremely implausible psychologically. There are in the worst case a factorial number of potential solutions, making exhaustive enumeration impossible under any reasonable assumptions about human processing constraints. Even for theoretical explorations, as we tackle more realistic representations (c.f., [8]) this aspect of SME has become a stumbling block. To use SME as a central component in larger-scale simulations and AI systems, a more practical algorithm is needed. Here we describe a *greedy algorithm* which efficiently provides good approximations to the "best" interpretation. Although any greedy algorithm must sometimes fail to deliver optimal solutions, we demonstrate that in fact on this task it performs superbly.

The second drawback is that SME does not focus the mapping process according to the goals of the system. Such influences can be incorporated into analogical processing in several ways. Standard structure-mapping postulates that goals help determine both what gets matched and how the match is evaluated, but excludes them from the mapping stage itself [11]. Holyoak and Thagard's ACME model [12] blends structural, semantic, and pragmatic considerations into weights in a connectionist network, using a relaxation scheme to derive a single solution as an approximate best mapping. In addition to biasing preference for correspondences according to relevance, they allow *queries* to be inserted in the target description. If the query is supported by the match it is construed as the candidate inference of the analogy. A different approach is used by Falkenhainer's *contextual structure mapping* [3,5], which provides an elegant account of how to relax both the identicality and 1:1 constraints of structure-mapping when doing so provides more useful conjectures for the analogizer.

This paper describes a new technique, *pragmatic marking*, which is consistent with both standard and contextual structure mapping. The idea is to filter what subsets of local matches are

Figure 1: An example of SME input descriptions

We use this simple example for illustration only, realistic representations are typically much larger. The italicized numbers are not part of the representation, but have been introduced to provide a convenient means for refering to subexpressions later on.

Base domain:

```
1 (IMPLIES  2 (AND  3(SENSITIVE-TO  4 LITMUS32  5 ALCOHOL-VAPOR)  6 (INSIDE  7 COOLANT  8 SUMP)
                10 (HELD-CLOSE LITMUS32 SUMP))
          11 (DETECTABLE  12 (GIVES-OFF COOLANT ALCOHOL-VAPOR)))
13 (IMPLIES  14 (LIQUID COOLANT)  15 (POSSIBLE (GIVES-OFF COOLANT ALCOHOL-VAPOR)))
16 (IMPLIES  17 (DECREASED  19 (PRESSURE SUMP))
          20 (INCREASED  21 (FLOW-RATE  22 (FLOW  23 STILL SUMP COOLANT  24 PIPE))))
26 (IMPLIES  27 (INCREASED (PRESSURE SUMP))
          28 (DECREASED (FLOW-RATE (FLOW STILL SUMP COOLANT PIPE))))
29 (IMPLIES  30 (DECREASED  31 (AREA PIPE)) (DECREASED (FLOW-RATE (FLOW STILL SUMP COOLANT PIPE))))
32 (IMPLIES  33 (INCREASED (AREA PIPE)) (INCREASED (FLOW-RATE (FLOW STILL SUMP COOLANT PIPE))))
33 (CAUSE  34 (GREATER  35 (PRESSURE STILL) (PRESSURE SUMP)) (FLOW STILL SUMP COOLANT PIPE))
36 (FLAT-TOP COOLANT)
```

Target domain:

```
1 (INCREASED  2 (FLOW-RATE  3 (FLOW  4 EFFLUENT  5 HEAT-SINK  6 HEAT  7 HX)))
8 (DETECTABLE  9 (GIVES-OFF EFFLUENT  10 RADIATION))
11 (CAUSE  12 (CONTAINS EFFLUENT  13 STRONGTIUM) (GIVES-OFF EFFLUENT RADIATION))
14 (LIQUID EFFLUENT)
15 (FLAT-TOP EFFLUENT)
16 (GREATER  17 (TEMPERATURE EFFLUENT)  18 (TEMPERATURE HEAT-SINK))
```

considered by whether or not they can support candidate inferences relevant to the analogizer's stated goal. Unlike ACME's query mechanism, this technique does not require the actual form of the candidate inference to be specified in advance. Thus our technique is better able to support the use of analogy in modeling problem-solving and discovery.

Section 2 reviews the SME algorithm using an example. Section 3 describes the *GreedyMerge* algorithm for efficiently combining local matches into consistent global interpretations. We analyze its theoretical properties and we demonstrate empirically that it tends to be optimal, in that the first interpretation it provides is usually the same as the best interpretation found by the exhaustive SME merge algorithm. Section 4 describes pragmatic marking, analyzes its complexity, and illustrates it by example. Finally, we discuss our plans for future work.

2 How SME works

Here we sketch the standard SME algorithm to provide the backdrop for our improvements (see [7] for details). SME takes as input two propositional descriptions, a *base* and a *target*. It produces as output a set of global interpretations (gmaps) of the comparision. Each gmap contains a set of *correspondences* linking items in the base and target (including both entities and statements about them), a *structural evaluation score* which provides an indication of match quality, and a set of *candidate inferences*. The candidate inferences are statements in the base which can be hypothesized to hold in the target as a result of the gmap's correspondences. Each candidate inference is a surmise, and hence must be evaluated by other means to ensure its validity.

Figure 1 shows a simple example we use through the paper for clarity. Consider a case-based design system, which already had designed a still and was now working on a recycling plant. The base domain shows part of what it might retain about the still, and the target shows part of the description of the new design. This analogy can help solve two problems: how one might detect radiation in the effluent and how one might increase the rate of waste heat removal.

SME begins the mapping process by computing *match hypotheses* (MH's), each representing

Figure 2: Hypothesized local matches for the comparison

Each match hypothesis has the form $< Base, Target >$, where *Base* and *Target* are expression numbers from Figure 1. The roots of the graph are circled, and the pmap defined by each root is indicated by dotted lines. The thick lines indicate nogoods. Only structurally consistent MH's are shown for clarity.

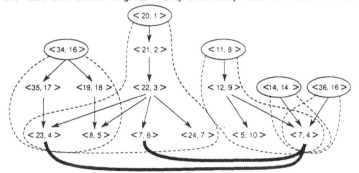

a potential correspondence between an item of the base and an item of the target[1]. Figure 2 depicts the match hypotheses for our example. These local matches must be carefully filtered and combined to build structurally consistent interpretations. First, MH's involving items whose arguments cannot be placed in correspondence are eliminated from further consideration. In our example, the hypothesized match between these two statements

```
B:  (CAUSE (GREATER (PRESSURE STILL) (PRESSURE SUMP)) (FLOW STILL SUMP COOLANT PIPE))
T:  (CAUSE (CONTAINS EFFLUENT STRONGTIUM) (GIVES-OFF EFFLUENT RADIATION))
```

fails because neither of the corresponding arguments can match, while

```
B:  (DETECTABLE (GIVES-OFF COOLANT ALCOHOL-VAPOR))
T:  (DETECTABLE (GIVES-OFF EFFLUENT RADIATION))
```

is locally consistent, given the hypothesized pairings between COOLANT and EFFLUENT and between ALCOHOL-VAPOR and RADIATION. (These pairings can be considered as the *arguments* of the match hypothesis.) Next, SME installs local consistency constraints (*nogoods*) between pairs of MH's to mark potential violations of the 1:1 constraint. That is, the MH which maps COOLANT to EFFLUENT cannot ever be part of the same interpretation as the MH which maps COOLANT to HEAT. These local inconsistencies are propagated up the argument structure of the match hypotheses, to rule out MH's whose argument matches do not suggest consistent correspondences. Those MH's which remain become the grist for gmap construction.

Constructing maximal sets of MH's is the goal of gmap construction. A gmap is maximal if adding another MH causes structural inconsistancy. It is useful to view the set of match hypotheses as a partial order, with the MH's concerning object correspondences forming the bottom elements and inclusion relationships determined by the argument structure. Call an MH a *root* if it is consistent and is not an argument of some other match hypothesis. The roots of this graph are the initial gmap candidates, or pmaps, for "partial mappings" (Again, see Figure 2).

So far, the computational complexity is low. If n is the number of items in the base and target, then finding match hypotheses and local inconsistent combinations are both $O(n^2)$, and the various propagation steps are $O(log(n))$. Exhaustively combining pmaps into gmaps is the expensive part. It begins cheaply, by taking the union of the constraints for each pmap's correspondences to

---

[1]The rules which guide MH construction are programmable. To simulate structure-mapping, attributes and relational items must have identical functors. Different rule sets can be used to implement context-sensitive methods for relaxing identicality [5] and even simulate certain aspects of ACME[4].

compute what it is inconsistent with ($O(n^2)$). The standard SME algorithm builds every possible complete gmap by making successive merges, subject to these consistency constraints, until no larger combinations can be built. If p is the number of pmaps, there are at worst $p!$ gmaps. This, of course, is expensive. Typical examples perform much better than this, due to the strong filtering effects of structural consistency. As [7] reports, on many complex examples SME takes only a few seconds of CPU time. However, we have found examples that can produce thousands of gmaps, and take days of CPU time to compute.

Finally, the structural evaluation and candidate inferences for each gmap are computed. These operations are of low complexity [7]. The structural evaluation score computation is irrelevant for this paper, see [7,8] for details. The only important feature is that the structural score of a gmap is the sum of its MH's scores, so it can easily be computed for pmaps and combined during merging.

Candidate inferences are computed by finding structure in the base which is consistent with a gmap's correspondences, but is not in fact included in them. Thinking now of the base domain as a graph, we are seeking structures which are roots (e.g., they are not themselves arguments of another item) and which have some, but not all, of their subitems mapped by the correspondences. Such items comprise potential new knowledge about the target, and are carried over by making the substitutions defined by the correspondences. Skolem functions are provided for base objects not mentioned in the correspondences. One candidate inference from a gmap resulting from our example comparison is:

(CAUSE (GREATER (TEMPERATURE EFFLUENT) (TEMPERATURE HEAT-SINK)) (FLOW EFFLUENT HEAT-SINK HEAT HX))

because the base structures *34* and *22* can map onto the target structures *16* and *3* respectively, while *33* in the base has no correspondence in the target (see Figures 1 and 2).

We believe the ability to generate structurally justifiable conjectures about the target is a central feature of analogy, responsible for its important role in creative problem solving and discovery (c.f. [2]). The rest of this paper shows how to achieve uniformly low complexity in gmap construction (at the cost of not always providing the optimum answer) and how to tune SME to produce novel candidate inferences relevant to the analogizer's goals.

3 Greed

The *greedy method* is a standard technique for combining a set of constrained, local solutions into a good global solution. The idea is that (a) finding a global solution can be modeled as deciding which local solutions to include and (b) some indication of "quality" exists for ordering local solutions[1]. Roughly, it works like this: Pick the best local solution. This rules out other choices, namely those which are inconsistent with the one picked. Throw away those which are inconsistent with your first choice. Now augment your solution with the best of the remaining local solutions. Again, this may rule out further choices, so one continues filtering and selecting until no more choices remain. The result is a single solution which is often, but not always, optimal.

The simplest version of *GreedyMerge* casts gmap construction as a sequence of decisions about which pmaps should be combined. The ordering is provided by the pmap's structural evaluation score. Starting with the largest, each pmap is merged into the solution under construction, unless doing so would violate structural consistency. If a pmap is inconsistent with the solution, it is skipped. By starting with the largest we improve our chances of getting the best solution.

The attraction of greedy methods is low complexity. Their drawbacks are (1) the solution may not be optimal and (2) obtaining useful alternative interpretations can be difficult. Whether or not the first problem is significant for natural representations is an empirical question addressed below. The second problem is very important. We view the ability to generate multiple interpretations of an analogy as critical. Even with a firm goal in mind, there can still be several ways to interpret an analogy (c.f. the Contras example in [12]).

There are several ways that multiple interpretations could be generated. One algorithm we explored generated an approximation of the top n gmaps based on their structural evaluation. This is often not a good strategy. Consider a very large base and a medium-sized target, so that many small, semi-independent pmaps are formed as well as several large ones. The gmaps for such comparisons can often be divided into several families of basically different interpretations, with each family member varying only in which small pmaps are included. In such cases the top n gmaps

Figure 3: Greedy Merge Algorithm
We assume that the standard SME algorithm has been executed up to the stage of constructing pmaps.

1. Place pmaps in descending order based on their structural evaluation score.
2. PMAPS ← the set of pmaps; USED ← { }
3. Repeat for desired number of interpretations
   3.1. MAPPING ← {PMAP$_i$} ∋ PMAP$_i$ ∉ USED
        and ∀$j < i$ PMAP$_j$ ∈ USED
   3.2. For each PMAP∈ PMAPS
        3.2.1. If PMAP is consistent with MAPPING Then
              3.2.1.1. MAPPING ← MAPPING ∪ PMAP
              3.2.1.2. USED ← USED ∪ {PMAP}
   3.3 Output MAPPING

Figure 4: Empirical Results of *GreedyMerge*

	Types Of Analogies		
	Object	Physical Systems	Stories
Number of matches	8	20	28
Min/Max number of gmaps	1/3	3/81	3/160
Min/Max GreedyMerge time (Sec.)	0/0.6	0.03/1.3	0.5/7
Min/Max FullMerge time (Sec.)	0/2.6	0.6/235	0.6/3335
Percentage of cases Greedy is optimal	100%	85%	96%
Lowest ratio Greedy Score / Best Score	100%	67%	91%

are likely to be trivial variations on the top theme, and since these will largely share the same set of candidate inferences, this is often undesirable. What we usually want is an alternate interpretation which is radically different. This suggests generating subsequent gmaps by starting with pmaps which are as large as possible but inconsistent with previously generated interpretations.

The algorithm we currently use (see Figure 3) starts by greedily generating the best gmap, and ensures that its gmaps are representative by always starting an alternate interpretation from a seed pmap which has never been used in any other interpretation. By adding the unused pmap first we ensure that we get a significantly different interpretation – it must be different since it contains a (hopefully large) structure which is inconsistent with all previously generated gmaps. Since the candidate inferences are based on the MHs these are also likely to be different. Note *GreedyMerge* reduces to the original greedy algorithm when generating only one interpretation. Each successive gmap starts with the largest unused pmap. All interpretations generated are maximal since *GreedyMerge* always attempts to add all pmaps to the interpretation during construction.

GreedyMerge is $O(nlog(n))$ in the number of pmaps, and $O(n)$ in the number of interpretations generated. The number of pmaps is $O(n^2)$ in the size of the base and target, in worst case. In practice the number of pmaps tends to be much smaller, since only plausible MH's are generated, and these tend to cluster into reasonably large pmaps.

GreedyMerge has been tested on over fifty different analogies, ranging from comparisons between physical phenomon, short stories, and object descriptions, drawn from the library of SME examples. Figure 4 summarizes the results. The stories show the most dramatic speedup – one story could not be included because the exhaustive algorithm failed to terminate after several days of computation, yet *GreedyMerge* found a reasonable interpretation in under a minute. And in most cases the first gmap generated by *GreedyMerge* was identical to the best gmap found by the exhaustive merge algorithm.

Why does *GreedyMerge* do so well? Typically, these large examples have a few large pmaps, only some of which are mutually inconsistent, and a much larger set of small pmaps. Thus the first few decisions are the really critical ones, and they are relatively easy to make. When will *GreedyMerge* fail? There are two kinds of cases where it should do poorly. The first is when there are many large pmaps with a high degree of mutual inconsistency, since many more decisions have to be correct, and hence the chance of error grows. This was the problem in the few cases (4 out of 56) where a non-optimal solution was generated. The second is when an initial, large pmap is inconsistent with every member of a large set of small but mutually compatible pmaps which in fact outweigh the initial one. We do not know how likely such situations are in natural representations. Fortunately, the ability to generate radically different interpretations provides a way to recover from such problems.

4 Pragmatism

The power of analogy comes from its ability to shed new light on the target by importing knowledge from the base. Retaining this ability using $GreedyMerge$ requires modifying SME further. The reason is that the structurally best match may not always provide the most relevant inferences [3,5]. Returning to our example, the structurally best interpretation places the two flows in correspondence. But what if our goal is to propose how to detect strongtium in the recycler's effluent? As we find below, an interpretation which maps COOLANT to EFFLUENT is better for this purpose, even though a smaller structure is mapped. When using the original SME merge algorithm, one simply searches the interpretations to find a relevant inference. Since $GreedyMerge$ is not exaustive, we must take care to ensure that relevant interpretations are actually generated.

Unfortunately, the techniques used by ACME provide no leverage here. Their techniques seem most useful for modeling instructional analogies, where a teacher may explicitly provide correspondences or point out which facts are most important. Here there is no correspondence involving the base fact that we wish to bring over, so it cannot be given extra weight or identified a priori as interesting. Introducing a query fact in the target does not help – if we knew the form of the query fact, we wouldn't need analogy to solve the problem. To get the novel inferences required for analogical problem solving requires a more generative solution.

Our *pragmatic marking* technique operates by looking for interpretations which can potentially import relevant base structure into the target. How can the relevant part of the base be found? Suppose we have target item G as our goal. That is, we want to find how G might legitimately be inferred on the basis of other (perhaps new) items in the target. For concreteness, suppose our goal is:

(DETECTABLE (GIVES-OFF EFFLUENT RADIATION))

Consider the set of match hypotheses generated for a comparison. The interpretations we are interested in must include a match hypothesis MH_G involving G, since only they can provide the structural grounds for candidate inferences involving G. (If G is not involved in any match hypotheses, then it cannot be the subject of any candidate inferences and hence we immediately know the comparison is useless for this purpose.) This means that the interpretation must in turn include MH's for the corresponding arguments of MH_G, and possibly for some larger structure of which it is a part.

Now consider the projection of MH_G onto the base domain. Again viewing the base as a graph, any pmap which includes the subgraph rooted in MH_G could provide inferences. However, pmaps which do not include this subgraph can also contribute to the structural grounding of an inference, so we must carefully examine them as well. There is some subset of roots of the base which contain MH_G's projection. Any pmap whose base projection lies outside this subset of the graph can be ignored, since it does not include the projection of our goal onto the base. Furthermore, any pmap inside this subset of the graph can be ignored if it is inconsistent with the correspondences implied by MH_G, since it could not be part of a gmap with it.

This intuitive picture provides the basis for the pragmatic marking algorithm (Figure 5). It is slightly more complicated to take into account the fact that there can be more than one MH_G, but otherwise is straightforward. The information required for the functions $TargetItem$, $BaseItem$, $Roots$, $BaseRoots$, $Descendants$, and $Nogood$ is already computed in the process of generating pmaps. The complexity is thus $\mathcal{O}(|\{pmap\}| \times |\{MH_G\}|)$.

Figure 6 illustrates the results of two queries in our extended example. With the query about radiation detection, three out of the five pmaps are potentially relevant, and $GreedyMerge$ successfully combines them all. The inference which results may be paraphrased as "By finding something which is sensitive to radiation, like litmus paper is sensitive to alcohol vapor, and holding it close to

Figure 5: Pragmatic Marking Algorithm

We assume that the standard SME algorithm has been executed, independent of any query, through pmap construction.

1. Let $\{MH_G\} = \{M | TargetItem(M) = G\}$
2. RELEVANT $\leftarrow \{\}$
3. For each $MH_G \in \{MH_G\}$,
    3.1 For each pmap$_i \in$ pmaps
        3.1.1 If $Descendants(\text{pmap}_i) \cap Descendants(MH_G) \neq \{\}$ then go to 3.1.4
        3.1.2 If $BaseRoots(\text{pmap}_i) \cap Roots(BaseItem(MH_G)) = \{\}$ then skip.
        3.1.3 If $Nogood(\text{pmap}_i, MH_G)$ then skip.
        3.1.4 Otherwise, RELEVANT $\leftarrow$ RELEVANT $\cup$ pmap$_i$
4. $GreedyMerge$(RELEVANT)

Figure 6: Inferences generated in response to queries

G = (DETECTABLE (GIVES-OFF EFFLUENT RADIATION))

```
There are 1 relevant interpretations:
GM1: 4 correspondences, SES = 2.5
  Object mappings: COOLANT <-> EFFLUENT, ALCOHOL-VAPOR <-> RADIATION
  Candidate Inferences:
(IMPLIES (AND (SENSITIVE-TO (:SKOLEM LITMUS32) RADIATION) (INSIDE EFFLUENT (:SKOLEM SUMP))
       (HELD-CLOSE (:SKOLEM LITMUS32) (:SKOLEM SUMP)))
       (DETECTABLE (GIVES-OFF EFFLUENT RADIATION)))
```

G = (INCREASED (FLOW-RATE (FLOW EFFLUENT HEAT-SINK HEAT HX)))

```
There are 1 relevant interpretations:
GM5: 10 correspondences, SES = 4.375
  Object mappings: PIPE <-> HX, COOLANT <-> HEAT, STILL <-> EFFLUENT, SUMP <-> HEAT-SINK
  Candidate Inferences:
(CAUSE (GREATER (TEMPERATURE EFFLUENT) (TEMPERATURE HEAT-SINK)) (FLOW EFFLUENT HEAT-SINK HEAT HX))
(IMPLIES (INCREASED (AREA HX)) (INCREASED (FLOW-RATE (FLOW EFFLUENT HEAT-SINK HEAT HX))))
(IMPLIES (DECREASED (TEMPERATURE HEAT-SINK)) (INCREASED (FLOW-RATE (FLOW EFFLUENT HEAT-SINK HEAT HX))))
```

---

the effluent's container, one may detect when the effluent is giving off radiation." Notice that this interpretation is not the structurally best, which makes the flows correspond but is inconsistent with the mapping of COOLANT to EFFLUENT. The second question exploits the structurally larger interpretation, suggesting that in order to bring about an increase in the rate of heat removal, one can either increase the area of the heat exchanger HX or decrease the temperature of the heat sink. We have also successfully tested pragmatic marking on a variety of standard SME examples, with correct results in each case.

5 Discussion

We have seen how the SME algorithm can be modified to efficiently generate interpretations of analogies by using a greedy merging algorithm, and demonstrated that pragmatic marking can focus its efforts on just those interpretations likely to lead to relevant, novel candidate inferences. In moving from an exhaustive algorithm to a polynomial one we give up the guarentee of optimality, but as our empirical results indicate, we lose little by doing so.

There are several directions to explore next. For example, sometimes degrees of certainty or relevance can be estimated for items in a representation. It would be useful to exploit such information, as ACME does. Combining scores for certainty and relevance with the structural evaluation score used by $GreedyMerge$ could provide an increased sensitivity to relevance that might be useful on larger problems. We also plan to use these techniques to embed SME into a larger simulation of human problem-solving activity.

6 Acknowledgements

This paper benefited from discussions with Dedre Gentner, Brian Falkenhainer, and Lenny Pitt. Gordon Skorstad helped draw figures, and Janice Skorstad provided valuable assistance with the SME data. This research was supported by the Office of Naval Research, Contract No. N00014-85-K-0559, an NSF Presidential Young Investigator award, and an equipment grant from IBM.

References

[1] Aho, A., Hopcroft, J. and Ullman, J. *Data Structures and Algorithms*, Addison-Wesley, Reading, Massachusetts, 1985.

[2] Burstein, M. H. Incremental learning from multiple analogies. In A. Preiditis (Ed.), *Analogica: Proceedings of the First Workshop on Analogical Reasoning*, London, Pitman Publishing Co., 1988

[3] Falkenhainer, B., An examination of the third stage in the analogy process: Verification-Based Analogical Learning, Technical Report UIUCDCS-R-86-1302, Department of Computer Science, University of Illinois, October, 1986. A summary appears in *Proceedings of the Tenth International Joint Conference on Artificial Intelligence*, Milan, Italy, August, 1987.

[4] Falkenhainer, B., The SME user's manual, Technical Report UIUCDCS-R-88-1421, Department of Computer Science, University of Illinois, 1988.

[5] Falkenhainer, B. Contextual Structure Mapping. Unpublished manuscript.

[6] Falkenhainer, B., K.D. Forbus, D. Gentner, The Structure-Mapping Engine, *Proceedings of the Fifth National Conference on Artificial Intelligence*, August, 1986.

[7] Falkenhainer, B., Forbus, K., Gentner, D. The Structure-Mapping Engine: Algorithm and examples *Artificial Intelligence*, **41**, pp 1-63, 1989.

[8] Forbus, K. and Gentner, D. Structural evaluation of analogies: What counts? *Proceedings of the Cognitive Science Society*, August, 1989.

[9] Gentner, D., The structure of analogical models in science, BBN Tech. Report No. 4451, Cambridge, MA., Bolt Beranek and Newman Inc., 1980.

[10] Gentner, D., Structure-mapping: A theoretical framework for analogy, *Cognitive Science* **7**(2), 1983.

[11] Gentner, D., Mechanisms of analogical learning. To appear in S. Vosniadou and A. Ortony, (Eds.), *Similarity and analogical reasoning.* Presented in June, 1986.

[12] Holyoak, K. & Thagard, P. Analogical mapping by constraint satisfaction, *Cognitive Science* **13**, 295-355, 1989.

[13] Skorstad, J., Falkenhainer, B., Gentner, D., Analogical Processing: A simulation and empirical corroboration, in: *Proceedings of the Sixth National Conference on Artificial Intelligence*, Seattle, WA, August, 1987.

[14] D. Abstraction processes during concept learing: A structural view. In *Proceedings of the Tenth Annual Meeting of the Cognitive Science Society*, Montreal, August, 1988.

Analogical Interpretation in Context

Brian Falkenhainer

Xerox Palo Alto Research Center

3333 Coyote Hill Road, Palo Alto CA 94304

Abstract: This paper examines the principles underlying analogical similarity and describes three important limitations with traditional views. It describes *contextual structure-mapping*, a more knowledge intensive approach that addresses these limitations. The principle insight is that each element of an analogue description has an identifiable *role*, corresponding to the dependencies it satisfies or its relevant properties in the given context. Analyzing role information provides a powerful framework for characterizing analogical similarity, relaxing the one-to-one mapping restriction prevalent in computational treatments of analogy, and understanding how such similarities may be used to assist problem solving. Second, it provides a unifying view of some of the central intuitions behind a number of converging efforts in analogy research.

1 Introduction

The core of analogy is mapping: the identification of correspondences between two analogues and using them to adapt a prior experience to a new situation. To identify similarities, most approaches find matching patterns in the two analogue's representation form, seeking both isomorphic structures and features described by the same predicate.

One such system is SME [7], an analogical mapping program originally developed to study Gentner's (1983) Structure-Mapping theory. However, in using SME for complex problem solving tasks [4, 5], three fundamental problems were found with traditional views of analogy. First, the restriction that matching expressions must be represented by the same predicate is too strong, and existing solutions based on conceptual closeness (e.g., ISA hierarchies) are too weak. Second, the one-to-one mapping restriction is too strong whenever multiple functions are supported by a single element in one of the analogues (e.g., function sharing). Third, the correspondences cannot always be determined from the initial descriptions of each analogue since their descriptions may not contain all of the relevant objects or inferences. Thus, additional information may have to be inferred or retrieved during the mapping computation.

This paper describes *contextual structure-mapping* (CSM), an approach that relaxes these restrictions while ensuring meaningful similarity judgments and tractable computation. It was essential to the success of PHINEAS [4, 5], a program that constructs new causal models of observed phenomena based on their similarity to understood phenomena. The key idea is explicit consideration of the contextual factors affecting analogical interpretation. Specifically, each element of an analogue description has an identifiable *role*, corresponding to the dependencies it satisfies or its relevant properties in the given context. The notion of role makes two important contributions. First, it provides a powerful framework for characterizing predicate "similarity", relaxing the one-to-one mapping restriction, and focusing problem solving and memory retrieval aimed at elaborating analogue correspondences. Second, it provides a unifying view of some of the intuitions behind derivational replay [3, 11], tweaking [10], knowledge-based pattern matching [1].

We begin by briefly describing role information. We then describe how this information is used to compute similarity correspondences within SME and adapt a prior problem solving experience to a new case. Finally, we discuss how the concepts presented here unify and explain several aspects of related work.

69

2 The role of role

We assume that each analogue is described by a set of *expressions*, where an expression may be a predicate-calculus formula, a feature in a feature vector representation, or a node or link in a semantic network. Take $\mathcal{B}$ and $\mathcal{T}$ to denote the sets of expressions representing the base and target analogues, respectively. Take $\mathcal{K}$ to be one's complete body of knowledge, such that $\mathcal{B}, \mathcal{T} \subset \mathcal{K}$. In general, $\mathcal{K}$ will include or entail information about each analogue not explicit in $\mathcal{B}$ or $\mathcal{T}$. The general mapping goal is to find a set of correspondences between the elements of $\mathcal{B}$ and $\mathcal{T}$. Some correspondences may be directly identifiable from the base and target descriptions; others arise as a side effect of adapting base information to apply to the target case.

Most accounts of analogy and case-based reasoning establish similarity correspondences by testing for predicate or feature identicality, but this is too restrictive. The typical solution for allowing non-identical relations to match is to evaluate similarity by measuring conceptual closeness, using ISA hierarchies [13, 2] or a-priori similarity scores [9]. However, these approaches can produce unmotivated and incorrect similarity correspondences. They fail to recognize an important point: similarity is context sensitive. Having some aspects in common is not an explanation for why two predicates should be viewed as corresponding; only some of their properties are relevant for determining similarity in a given context.

For example, consider classifying a cylindrical tin cup with a handle as a `Hot-Cup` (adapted from [13, 11]). In general, a `Hot-Cup` is something that a person can lift and drink from while it holds a hot liquid. From a previous styrofoam cup (scup) example, the following sufficient conditions were found:

`Styrofoam(scup) ∧ Open-Conical(scup) ∧ ⋯ → Hot-Cup(scup)`

In classifying the tin cup via analogy to the styrofoam case, conceptual closeness measures might pair `Open-Conical` with the tin cup's `Open-Cylinder` (both open concavities) and `Styrofoam` to `Tin` (both materials). Yet, if the original dependencies satisfied by the `Styrofoam` condition are retrieved (or reconstructed), it becomes clear that this misses the point of the analogy: the aspect of styrofoam important in this context is its insulating characteristics, just as the tin cup's handle is important because it provides another form of insulation. In this context, the property styrofoam should map to the property of having a handle.

Most matchers require one-to-one mappings because allowing many-to-many mappings can dramatically increase the number of possibilities and lead to incoherence. However, in the styrofoam cup, styrofoam and conical shape provide insulation and a grasping area, respectively, while both functions are provided by the tin cup's handle. Here, an isomorphic mapping fails to fully capture the correspondence; a many-to-one mapping from { `Styrofoam`, `Open-Conical`} to { `Has-Handle`} is needed. Similarly, consider the dual murderer / victim roles of someone committing suicide. Due to function sharing, many-to-many mappings occur in many physical systems.

The key to relaxing these constraints and determining an expression's relevant aspects is an understanding of its *role* in the analogue description. In CSM, an expression's roles are identified by the dependencies it satisfies. Within each analogue, if $\mathcal{C}$ is some predication whose truth is dependent on predication $\mathcal{A}$, then the *role* of $\mathcal{A}$ is to satisfy the dependency relationship with $\mathcal{C}$. $\mathcal{A}$ may fill other roles as well, in as much as $\mathcal{A}$ satisfies other dependencies.

Correspondences between two analogues' expressions are determined by analyzing their roles in the context of their respective analogues. Thus, if the dependencies supported by an expression $\mathcal{E}_b$ may be satisfied in an alternate manner, say by expression $\mathcal{E}_t$, then $\mathcal{E}_b$ and $\mathcal{E}_t$ are considered *functionally analogous* and may be placed in correspondence. We may generalize this (and form a recursive definition) by saying that given two corresponding roles (i.e., not necessarily identical), their role fillers may be considered functionally analogous and eligible for being placed in correspondence, independent of predicate (or feature) identicality. Importantly, a fundamental component of analogy is knowing what aspects of a given relation are relevant and hence be able to recognize alternate ways to achieve similar functionality. For example, the property RAINFALL should map to the property IRRIGATION if the role of these conditions is to ensure that a given crop receives sufficient water. Note they are not analogous in other roles, such as washing a plant's leaves. Further, to the extent that knowledge of $\mathcal{E}_b$'s role is incomplete and $\mathcal{E}_t$ does not provide identical functionality, the functionally analogous relation is merely plausible (e.g., the humidity associated with rainfall may be relevant).

Roles take many forms. In design, the role of particular design decisions and artifact components is the satisfaction of particular design specifications and rationale. The role of an agent's actions (as in planning or a story) may be in support of certain outcomes. In physical systems, the role of a given component is typically the behavior it contributes to. In deductive proof, the role of an antecedent is to provide logical support for its consequent. There are several ways to determine and exploit the role an expression is servicing. We discuss two of these next.

2.1 Explicit dependencies

When an expression's role is explicit in a given analogue representation, role determination consists simply of consulting this information. This appears in two forms. First, the roles of b_i and t_j may be explicit in both base and target descriptions. For example, expressions P and R will be placed in correspondence when matching IMPLIES(P,Q) with IMPLIES(R,Q), since their respective roles are to deductively support Q.

Second, the role of b_i may be explicit in $\mathcal{B}$ but there is not enough information in $\mathcal{T}$ to identify its correspondent. In this case, the task is to take the unmapped b_i's role and search for a corresponding role and role filler applicable to the target setting. Since $\mathcal{T}$ is generally a subset of all available knowledge about the target, this case will require memory retrieval and inferencing to find the desired information. For example, mapping

$\mathcal{B}$: High-Rainfall(region₁) — Well-Watered(region₁)
to
$\mathcal{T}$: Irrigated(region₂), Arid(region₂), Northern-Hemisphere(region₂)

requires retrieval of

Irrigated(region₂) — Well-Watered(region₂)

in order to determine which expression in $\mathcal{T}$ corresponds to High-Rainfall in $\mathcal{B}$.

2.2 Compiled and abstracted knowledge

Representations that are adequate for traditional approaches to problem solving may not be suitable for performing analogical reasoning. AI systems tend to represent a minimalist approach to encoding knowledge, in which detailed descriptions or intermediate reasoning steps are avoided to promote efficiency of use. For example, a physical process may be modeled at some level of abstraction and a design plan may not contain the rationale behind the decisions it embodies. Indeed, knowledge compilation is a central goal of explanation-based generalization. While effective for accelerating reasoning, a great deal of information is intentionally removed. This poses a significant problem for adaptation of a given base analogue: these intermediate or second-order justifications are often needed to ascertain the requisite role information (Figure 1).

For example, consider the following schema used to explain why crops grow in region₁:

```
Cro p-Growing(region₁)
    PRECONDITIONS    High-Rainfall(region₁) ∧  Fertile-Soil(region₁) ∧
                     Sunny(region₁) ∧ ...
    EFFECTS          Growing-Crops(region₁)
```

71

Figure 1: Compiled knowledge problem. Intermediate reasoning steps removed to increase problem solving efficiency are often required when considering how to elaborate analogical correspondences and adapt a solution to unanticipated cases. The **BASE** representation depicts a macro compiled from the inferences to the right. A question mark indicates a relevant base expression having no known target correspondent without more information about its role in the base context.

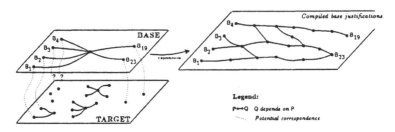

Why is the `High-Rainfall` precondition there? Suppose a deeper explanation is retrievable and reveals that this condition is important in this context because it ensures that the region is well watered. Without this deeper explanation, it would be impossible to justify why it is reasonable to place `High-Rainfall(region₁)` in correspondence with `Irrigated(region₂)`.

To address the compiled knowledge problem, we assume the availability of needed background knowledge, either cached or reconstructable. This background knowledge serves to decompose and elaborate the reasons underlying a particular dependency relationship. This information is consulted as needed during the mapping computation.[1] In the implementation, a `CACHE` field accompanies all compiled rules. For example, the crop growing schema should have an added `CACHE` field to store compiled reasoning steps like `High-Rainfall(region₁)` → `Well-Watered(region₁)`.

3 The Map and Analyze Process

The mapping process is traditionally depicted as a form of pattern matching between base and target descriptions. However, in realistic memories, mapping will be operating on a subset of all that is inferrably known about the base and target. Thus, the process of elaborating correspondences and adapting elements of the base to fit the target situation often requires inferring additional information during the mapping computation in response to mapping impasses. Rather than endow the mapping mechanism with unlimited inferencing power, we decompose the process to form a *map and analyze* cycle: use simple matching criteria to determine the best, initial mapping between the analogues, analyze the results and seek additional relevant information about unmatched areas, reexamine the mapping to determine the information's impact on the mapping (i.e., extensions or complete shifts), analyze the new results, etc.

The mapping phase is computed by SME [7] a general mapping tool which formulates mappings based on user-supplied *match rules*. Match rules specify which local, pairwise correspondences (called *match hypotheses*) between expressions and entities are possible, restrictions on how they may be combined, and preference criteria for scoring these combinations. Using the rules of contextual structure-mapping forms SME_{CSM}. Each time a mapping is computed, one out of the set of possible mappings is selected based on systematicity [8, 7] and relevance to the current problem solving goals [5, 6].

---

[1]Including all background knowledge in the original base and target descriptions would be too expensive. Additionally, which added details are needed cannot be identified until impasses arise during the mapping computation.

Figure 2: Categorizing a tin cup by analogy to a styrofoam cup.

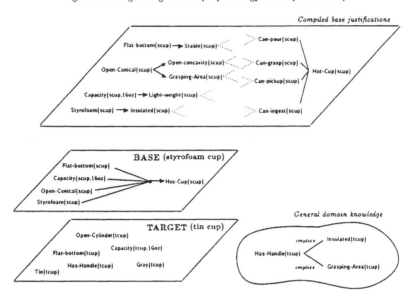

In the remainder of this section, we illustrate how role information is used to provide controlled relaxation of the same predicate and one-to-one mapping restrictions.

3.1 Relaxing identicality

Given base and target expressions, what criteria are used to propose a match between them? We start with the standard set taken from Gentner's structure-mapping theory [7]. The main rule pairs expressions that use the same predicate. Additional rules are used to support objects and commutative predicates. However, these rules suffer from a dependence on identicality to initiate matches. To motivate matches between expressions using different predicates, we add a rule to support the functionally analogous criterion:

Rule 1 (Functionally Analogous) *Two expressions are considered* functionally analogous *and may match if they fill corresponding roles in the context of the structures being matched.*

When role information is explicit in the base and target representations, SME$_{CSM}$ uses this rule to match functionally analogous expressions. When a relevant base expression has no discernible correspondent in the target case, its role is analyzed in greater depth.

To illustrate these match criteria, we use a simple example taken from [13, 11] and adapted to illustrate the key ideas. The task is to classify a given tin cup as an instance of Hot-Cup. The base exemplar is a previously classified styrofoam cup. Their descriptions are shown in Figure 2.

The process begins by comparing the initial descriptions of the two cases. SME finds that the relevant Flat-bottom and Capacity properties are shared by both cups. It also fails to find correspondents for the styrofoam cup's other important properties: Open-Conical and Styrofoam. During the analysis phase, more detail is retrieved about the roles of these two properties in

73

the styrofoam case's classification as a `Hot-Cup`. For example, its `Styrofoam` property provides insulation. The system then seeks aspects of the tin cup that fill these roles. For example, the tin cup's `Has-handle` property also provides insulation. When the mapping is reexamined, this added information now enables a complete match and successful classification of the tin cup as an instance of `Hot-Cup`.

3.2 Relaxing one-to-one

The notion of role provides exactly the right constraint for introducing many to many mappings while maintaining coherence and tractability. In CSM, the one-to-one restriction may be violated by a single base or target item filling multiple roles that are filled by multiple items in the other domain. In the cups example, Figure 2 shows the dependencies that motivate a many-to-one mapping from `Styrofoam(scup)` and `Open-Conical(scup)` to `Has-Handle(tcup)`.

The following three rules define *sanctioned* many-to-one mappings and enforce one-to-one mappings as the normal default by examining all cases of two base items mapping to a single target item.

Rule 2 (Direct role-filler) *Multiple base items b_1 and b_2, filling roles $\mathcal{R}_{b1}$ and $\mathcal{R}_{b2}$ respectively, may map to a single target item, t_i, filling roles $\mathcal{R}_{t1}$ and $\mathcal{R}_{t2}$, if role $\mathcal{R}_{b1}$ corresponds to role $\mathcal{R}_{t1}$ and role $\mathcal{R}_{b2}$ corresponds to role $\mathcal{R}_{t2}$.*

This rule sanctions match hypotheses that may violate the one-to-one restriction. In the cups example, it pairs the `Has-Handle` predicate in the tin cup description to both `Styrofoam` and `Open-Conical`. However, unless this sanctioning is propagated to their respective subexpressions (e.g., the predicates' arguments), a one-to-one restriction will still be in effect.

Rule 3 (Role-filler sub-expressions) *Multiple base items may map to a single target item if the base and target items are subexpressions of a sanctioned many-to-one mapping.*

In the cups example, because `Styrofoam` and `Open-Conical` apply to the same object, `scup`, only a one-to-one mapping from `scup` to `tcup` is needed and this rule does not apply.

With sanctioned violations of one-to-one identified, we are now ready to define when two match hypotheses are conflicting. Due to its non-monotonic nature, implicit in the following rule is the assumption that all sanctioned pairings are known at the time the rule is invoked.

Rule 4 (One-To-One) *Unless explicitly sanctioned, two match hypotheses are conflicting if they pair multiple base items to the same target item.*

Thus, the two match hypotheses (`Styrofoam, Has-Handle`) and (`Open-Conical, Has-Handle`) are compatible in the cups example. A symmetric set of three rules exist for multiple target items mapping to a single base item. Together, the six rules identify sanctioned many-to-many mappings and enforce one-to-one for all other, unsanctioned cases.

4 A Unifying View

The contextual structure-mapping framework provides a unifying view of the basic intuitions behind several recently developed methods for computing similarity. *Derivational replay* mechanisms make the observation that it is typically easier to reuse the problem solving process of a prior episode than the episode's final solution [3]. Taking a stored problem solving plan, a new problem is solved by replaying the plan top-down, resolving subgoals that no longer apply in the current situation. CSM's definition of *functionally analogous* explains the underlying intuition behind replay's appeal over mapping only a final solution: the root problem in reusing a prior solution is the need to understand the various roles or functions the solution fulfills. In problem solving, adapting a prior solution to a new problem instance is greatly simplified if decisions' rationale are known, so that their intent can be satisfied without necessarily adhering to the same decisions. Top-down replay achieves this by essentially reseeking each role filler in the new situation. An alternate method would start at the solution, and work backwards, analyzing role information at solution transfer impasses. The implicit assumption in replay mechanisms is that it is more efficient to work forward, replaying the entire decision-making process, than to work backward, reconsidering the decisions (alternate ways to achieve functionality) where needed. This tradeoff is influenced in part by the solution's modularity.

The Yale SWALE project [10], Kedar-Cabelli's PER [11], and PHINEAS (which uses CSM) [4, 5] are efforts to use analogy to reduce the cost and increase the creativity of explanation building. These systems demonstrate operations very closely related to the notions of role and derivational replay. For example, SWALE applies stored *explanation patterns* (schemas) to new situations, *tweaking* them as needed to adapt to the situation's novel aspects. Like Kedar-Cabelli's PER model, it attempts to rederive portions of a prior explanation that do not apply in the new situation. For the tweaking operation, SWALE uses a set of revision rules, such as *substitute alternate theme* or *substitute related action*. These suggest ways to repair inapplicable portions of a recalled schema. CSM offers a more general explanation of these tweaking operations: determine the anomalous item's role and seek elements of the current situation that could satisfy that role's dependencies. For example, if the current actor lacks a requisite theme, *substitute alternate theme* tries to find an alternate theme for the actor. In the CSM framework, this corresponds to an unsatisfied dependency (i.e., role) which either must be satisfied, assumed, or conjectured with new concepts.

PROTOS [1] performs diagnosis by relating a new case to a store of previously classified exemplars, performing classification by finding the exemplar that best matches the new instance. *Knowledge-based pattern matching* computes a match between an exemplar and a new instance by using the domain knowledge stored with each exemplar to explain the equivalence of non-identical features. For example, in comparing two chairs, LEGS and PEDESTAL are equivalent because they both provide SEAT-SUPPORT. In CSM terms, this process corresponds to showing that two features are functionally analogous. However, PROTOS limits the scope of a match to the explicitly given features of the two cases. It does not include the possibility that additional features may be derived or retrieved from memory in response to the needs of the match elaboration process. Furthermore, it uses a feature-vector representation (i.e., a set of attribute-value pairs) which is inadequate for representing a complex set of interrelationships between an analogue's parts.

5   Discussion

Analogical mapping for simple representations and tasks, particularly for within-domain comparisons, is a straightforward process. On the other hand, rich representations and complex problem solving tasks (both within and across domains) require a more sophisticated mechanism for computing similarities that is able to compare syntactically different analogues and select the best mapping when ambiguities arise. The utility of contextual structure-mapping for such settings has been demonstrated in PHINEAS [4, 5], a program that proposes qualitative causal explanations of observed, time-varying phenomena based on their similarity to understood phenomena. PHINEAS has been extensively tested on over a dozen examples, such as explaining evaporation by analogy to dissolving, heat flow and osmosis by analogy to liquid flow, and a variety of mechanical and electrical harmonic oscillators.

This paper has claimed that analogy requires role information to at least plausibly suggest the relevance and interrelatedness of each analogue's features. The ability to learn this relevance information is of fundamental importance. One approach is to use a developing analogy to motivate specific questions about the world and use directed experimentation to answer them and ascertain the requisite relevance information [5]. A second approach is to again use a developing analogy to motivate specific questions, but place the system in a learning apprentice setting and obtain requisite relevance information from the user [1]. We are currently investigating a third approach: use inductive methods to suggest which factors are relevant to the concept under study.

Acknowledgements

Ken Forbus, Dedre Gentner, Danny Bobrow, and Mark Shirley provided insightfull discussions and helpful comments on prior drafts of this paper. The foundation for this work is taken from the author's dissertation, which was supported by an IBM Graduate Fellowship and by the Office of Naval Research, Contract No. N00014-85-0559.

References

[1] Bareiss, R., Porter, B., & Wier, C. (1987). Protos: An exemplar-based learning apprentice. *Proceedings of the Fourth International Workshop on Machine Learning.*

[2] Burstein, M. (1986). Concept formation by incremental analogical reasoning and debugging. In R.S. Michalski, J. Carbonell, T. Mitchell (Eds.), *Machine Learning: An Artificial Intelligence Approach, Volume II.*

[3] Carbonell, J. (1986). Derivational analogy: A theory of reconstructive problem solving and expertise acquisition. In R.S. Michalski, J. Carbonell, T. Mitchell (Eds.), *Machine Learning: An Artificial Intelligence Approach, Volume II.*

[4] Falkenhainer, B. (1986). *An examination of the third stage in the analogy process: Verification-based analogical learning* (Technical Report UIUCDCS-R-86-1302). Department of Computer Science, University of Illinois. A summary appears in *IJCAI-87.*

[5] Falkenhainer, B. (1988). *Learning from physical analogies: A study in analogy and the explanation process.* PhD thesis, University of Illinois, 1988.

[6] Falkenhainer, B. (1990). Contextual structure-mapping. (*submitted for publication*).

[7] Falkenhainer, B., Forbus, K.D., & Gentner, D. (1989). The structure-mapping engine: Algorithm and examples. *Artificial Intelligence, 41,* 1-63.

[8] Gentner, D. (1983). Structure-mapping: A theoretical framework for analogy. *Cognitive Science, 7.*

[9] Holyoak, K. & Thagard, P. (1989). Analogical mapping by constraint satisfaction. *Cognitive Science, 13*(3).

[10] Kass, A., Leake, D., & Owens, C. (1986). SWALE, A program that explains. In R Schank (Ed.), *Explanation patterns: Understanding mechanically and creatively.* Lawrence Erlbaum Associates.

[11] Kedar-Cabelli, S. (1988). Formulating concepts and analogies according to purpose. PhD Thesis, Rutgers University.

[12] Kolodner, J., Simpson, R. & Sycara-Cyranski, K. (1985). A process model of cased-based reasoning in problem solving. *Proceedings of IJCAI-85.*

[13] Winston, P., Binford, T, Katz, B. & Lowry, M. (1980). Learning physical descriptions from functional definitions, examples, and precedents. *Proceedings AAAI-83.*

MULTIPLE ABSTRACTED REPRESENTATIONS IN PROBLEM SOLVING AND DISCOVERY IN PHYSICS

Nancy J. Nersessian
Program in History of Science
Princeton University

James G. Greeno
Stanford University and
Institute for Research on Learning

ABSTRACT

We discuss the process of mathematization in science, focussing on uses that theorists make of physical representations that we refer to as abstracted models. We review abstracted models constructed by Faraday and Maxwell in the mathematization of electromagnetic phenomena, including Maxwell's use of an analogy between continuum dynamics and electromagnetism. We discuss ways in which this example requires major modifications of current cognitive theories of analogical reasoning and scientific induction, especially in the need to understand the use of abstracted models containing theoretically meaningful objects that can be manipulated and modified in the development of new concepts and mathematized representations.

INTRODUCTION

Problem solving and discovery in physics involve the application of appropriate mathematical formalisms to specific configurations of physical phenomena. In the history of science, the process of figuring out the fit between mathematics and the physical world has been called "mathematization" (Koyre). That process consists of grasping the relational structure underlying phenomena; abstracting that structure; expressing the abstraction in mathematical formulae; and applying the formalism back to a wider class of phenomena. For example, "mathematization" of the motion of projectiles required formulating a relationship between the component forces acting on the body by abstracting the motion of an object in air to that of an idealized point mass in an empty three-dimensional, homogeneous, infinite space; and, as ultimately formulated in Newton's laws, this analysis showed the motions of projectiles, planets, and pendula to have the same formal structure.

Historically, the process of mathematization has often had as a central component the construction of a physical representation -- a model, a schematic representation, a diagram, etc. -- embodying tentative assumptions about the structural relationships under investigation. These representations are like equations and other descriptions that are physical objects in their own rights, enabling reflection and investigation of their properties separated from the phenomena they are meant to represent. We use the term "abstracted models" to refer to such models, schematic representations, diagrams, etc. Abstracted models allow scientists to manipulate familiar structures, observe consequences of adjusting relationships to satisfy domain constraints, and, ultimately, to generate equations that express the assumed relationships in formal terms. Because abstracted models reify the hypotheses of the investigator, he or she can reason with and about the abstraction rather than the represented phenomena.

One advantage of reasoning with a model is that reasoning about the represented phenomena in all their complexity can create a cognitive "overload," since what is or isn't relevant is often not evident. Another advantage is that the abstracted model provides support for productive situated reasoning about interactions among hypothesized properties and relations. The objects in a model representation that correspond to properties and relations in the phenomena can be examined in different arrangements to allow exploration of interactions that cannot be produced and observed as directly in the domain of the phenomena. (For a discussion, see Greeno, 1989.) This paper is particularly concerned with an example of discovery that came from formulating and modifying a causal model with objects corresponding to properties and relations in phenomena of electricity and magnetism.

MATHEMATIZING ELECTROMAGNETIC PHENOMENA

The history of science is replete with examples. The derivation of the electromagnetic field equations provides a particularly salient case study. The standard textbook account at both the undergraduate and graduate levels (e.g., Jackson, 1962; Feynman et al., 1963; Panofsky & Phillips, 1962) all present Maxwell as starting from a set of field equations for closed circuits plus the equation for continuity of charge shown in Table 1. Maxwell's problem is portrayed as that of reconciling these equations for the case of open circuits. According to this account, considerations of formal consistency required that he add a term to Ampere's Law to represent the contribution of electrostatic polarization to current.

Table 1 about here

Space limitations require that we present an exceedingly compressed version of the actual process through which the field equations were derived. Nersessian (1984, 1986, in press) has presented fuller analyses. What we hope to do here is to show how different the actual process was from that presented in textbooks and, in particular, to demonstrate how important various abstracted models were in the mathematization process.

Figure 1 about here

It was Maxwell who generated the field equations for electromagnetism, but his analysis of the problem began with specific abstracted models created by Faraday. In opposition to the mathematical representation of electric and magnetic actions as Newtonian actions at a distance by Ampère, Faraday hypothesized that the lines of force that form when iron filings are sprinkled around magnets and charged matter indicate that some real physical process is going on in the space surrounding these objects and that this process is part of the transmission of the actions. Figure 1(a) shows the actual lines as they form around a magnet and Figure 1(b) shows an abstracted representation of these lines in geometrical and dynamical form. That this abstraction played a central role in his reasoning about electric and magnetic phenomena can be seen in the many line-like features that he incorporated into his descriptions of the actions and that guided his attempts to detect them experimentally. For our purposes, it is most notable that the only quantitative measure he introduced is between the number of lines cut and the intensity of the induced force. This relationship is incorrect, because "number of" is an integer while "field intensity" is a continuous function. The "mistake" occurs because in the abstracted model the lines are taken as discrete objects, while they actually spiral indefinitely in a closed volume.

Figure 2 about here

Near the end of his research, Faraday introduced another abstracted model representing the dynamical balance between electricity and magnetism. Figure 2(a) is Faraday's actual abstracted model. Figure 2(b) shows how the picture of interlocking curves is abstracted from the earlier abstracted model involving lines of force. For example, a lateral repulsion of the magnetic lines (outer lines) has the same effect as a longitudinal expansion of the current lines (inner lines).

Maxwell used both of Faraday's abstracted models in his first attempt to mathematize electromagnetism (Maxwell, 1890, pp. 155-229). In this analysis he replaced Faraday's relationship between the number of lines cut and the intensity of the induced force with a continuous measure by representing the lines of force as the flow of an incompressible fluid through fine tubes of variable section, filling all space. The interlocking curves, called "mutually embracing curves" by Maxwell (p. 194), formed the basis of his reciprocal dynamics. The effect of this abstraction on his thinking can be seen most directly in his complicated use of two fields -- one for a longitudinal measure of force and one for a lateral measure -- where we would now only use one.

Figure 3 about here

The abstractions that Maxwell took from Faraday were useful primarily for Maxwell's kinematical analysis. A dynamical analysis of the underlying forces that could produce the lines required the construction of a quite different abstracted model: one that would embody the dynamical relations between electric and magnetic forces. The abstraction that Maxwell constructed is an analogy between electromagnetism and continuum mechanics (fluids, elastic media, etc.). Maxwell first constructed a primitive abstracted model, shown in Figure 3(a), consistent with a set of constraints: a fluid medium composed of elastic vortices and under stress. With this form of the abstraction he was able to provide a mathematical representation for various magnetic phenomena. Analyzing the relations between current and magnetism required alteration of this abstraction. In Figure 3(a) all the vortices are rotating in the same direction, which means that if they touch, they will stop. Mechanical consistency, thus, requires the introduction of "idle wheels" surrounding the vortices, and Maxwell argued that their translational motion could be used to represent electricity. Figure 3(b) shows a cross section of this altered abstracted model. For purposes of calculation, Maxwell had to make the elastic vortices into rigid pseudospheres. He next formulated the mathematical relations between currents and magnetism. It then took him nine months to figure out how to represent the final (and most critical) piece of the problem: electrostatic actions. He found that if he made the vortices elastic once again, and identified electrostatic polarization with elastic displacement, it was possible to calculate the wave of distortion produced by polarization. That is, adding elasticity to the abstraction enabled him to show that electromagnetic actions are propagated with a time delay, i.e., they are field actions and not Newtonian actions at a distance. At this point Maxwell had achieved a fully mathematized representation of the electromagnetic field.

DISCUSSION

The main point of this example is that it was through a process of embodying the structural relations between electric and magnetic actions in a series of abstracted models, reasoning with and about these, and manipulating them in various ways, that Maxwell generated the field equations for electromagnetism. Considerations of formal consistency, as presented in textbooks, played no significant role in this analysis. At the same time, the known mathematical structure of continuum dynamics motivated the analysis and provided the basis for achieving the goal of a mathematized representation of the dynamics of electromagnetic fields.

The analysis illustrates reasoning that is concretely situated, yet relies on a process of abstraction that is crucial to the success of the reasoning effort. The construction of an abstracted model removes a set of properties and relations from its initial context, creating objects in a new situation that can be analyzed and manipulated. Analysis of the properties of the abstracted model is situated in the context that the model provides. The effort to use that model as a representation for a different domain proceeds by considering various requirements that arise from features of the second domain that may be known or emerge in the problem-solving process. These requirements act as constraints on the model, as the theorist seeks a modified model that behaves in accordance with them. Modifications are sought with the condition that the modified model should have a mathematical structure that can be understood and expressed in formal terms.

The process of arriving at Maxwell's equations according to this analysis is significantly different from the processes of formula induction of the kind that Simon and his colleagues have studied (Langley, Simon, Bradshaw, & Zitkow, 1987). That process is situated in a context of numerical data and symbolic expressions that specify numerical operations between variables. The search takes place primarily in a space of formulas, with theoretical entities introduced as needed to account for invariant relations among numbers. In Nersessian's interpretation of Maxwell's discovery, the search is primarily a search for a model with a coherent causal structure that originates in one domain but is changed so that its behavior fits constraints that hold in a different domain. After the change, of course, it no longer provides an accurate representation of the phenomena in the domain from which it was abstracted.

Analogical reasoning of the kind identified in this analysis also differs significantly from the analyses that have been studied by cognitive psychologists such as Gentner (1983), by Gick and Holyoak (1983; 1980). In these analyses, an attempt is made to match the relational structures of two or more domains, with those analogies considered best that provide the closest match between patterns of relations. In contrast, the analogy between continuum dynamics and electromagnetic fields was productive because of the possibility of constructing an abstracted model of continuum dynamics that could be changed to fit the constraints of electromagnetism.

The success of the analogy depended upon having a representation that could be analyzed and manipulated as an object separate from its role as a representation of continuum dynamics. The representation included drawings, but clearly those notations were not sufficient to support Maxwell's reasoning. The model includes notations along with their interpretations as hypothetical objects that can be considered, combined, and modified to have different properties and interactions. Study of the abstracted model, including exploration of variations of its basic structure, was possible and necessary for it to provide the basis of Maxwell's theoretical achievement. Models in which analogical thinking depends only on a hypothesized cognitive representation of a mapping or schema that connects two domains have not addressed the role of the representation as providing an object of analysis and hypothesis construction. We expect to learn more about these issues from a thorough comparison of the Maxwell example and others like it with models of analogical reasoning by schemata and structure-mapping. Our analysis should also provide a deeper understanding of the reciprocal processes through which formal representations and abstracted models are constructed in scientific discovery. We hope additionally that this exploration will provide helpful suggestions about ways in which abstracted models can be used more productively in the practice of science education.

ACKNOWLEDGEMENTS

Preparation of this paper was supported in part by National Science Foundation Scholars Award SES-8821422 to Nersessian and by National Science Foundation Grant BNS-8718918 to Greeno.

REFERENCES

Faraday, M. (1835-55). *Experimental Researches in Electricity*. Reprinted, New York: Dover.
Feynman, R. P., Leighton, R. B., & Sands, M. (1964). *The Feynman Lectures on Physics*. Reading, MA: Addison-Wesley.

Gentner, D. (1983). Structure-mapping: A theoretical framework. *Cognitive Science, 7*, 155-170.

Gick, M. L., & Holyoak, K, J. (1980). Analogical problem solving. *Cognitive Psychology, 12*, 306-355.

Gick, M. L., & Holyoak, K. J. (1983). Schema induction and analogical transfer. *Cognitive Psychology, 15*, 1-38.

Greeno, J. G. (1989). Situations, mental models, and generative knowledge. In D. Klahr, & K. Kotovsky (Eds.), *Complex information processing: The impact of Herbert A. Simon* (pp. 285-318). Hillsdale, N.J.: Lawrence Erlbaum Associates.

Jackson, J. D. (1962). *Classical Electrodynamics.* New York: Wiley.

Langley, P., Simon, H. A., Bradshaw, G. L., & Zitkow, J. M. (1987). *Scientific discovery: Computational explorations of the creative processes.* Cambridge, MA: MIT Press.

Maxwell, J. C. (1890). *The Scientific Papers of James Clerk Maxwell,* W. D. Niven, ed. Cambridge: Cambridge University.

Nersessian, N. J. (1984). *Faraday to Maxwell: Constructing Meaning in Scientific Theories.* Dordrecht: Kluwer.

Nersessian, N. J. (1988). Reasoning from imagery and analogy in scientific concept formation. In A. Fine & J. Leplin, eds. *PSA 1988.* East Lansing, MI: PSA.

Nersessian, N. J. (in press). *Methods of conceptual change in science: Imagistic and analogical reasoning.* Philosophica.

Panofsky, W. & Phillips, M. (1962). *Classical Electricity and Magnetism.* Reading, MA: Addison-Wesley.

Coulomb's Law: $\text{div } \vec{D} = 4\pi\rho$

Ampère's Law: $\text{curl } \vec{H} = 4\pi \vec{J}$

Faraday's Law: $\text{curl } \vec{E} = -\partial\vec{B}/\partial t$

Absence of Free
Magnetic Poles: $\text{div } \vec{B} = 0$

Equation of Continuity: $\text{div } \vec{J} + \partial\rho/\partial t = 0$

TABLE 1: Equations Maxwell began with according to standard
textbook account

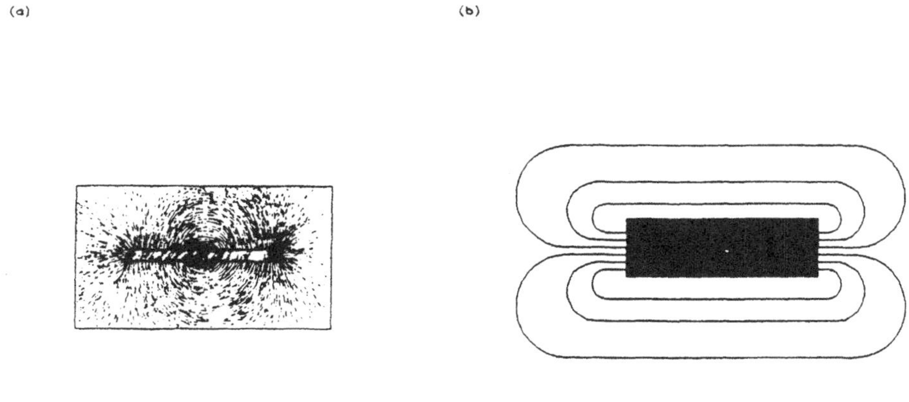

(a)   (b)

Figure 1: (a) Actual pattern of lines of force surrounding a bar magnet (from Faraday (1839-55). vol. 3); (b) Schematic representation of lines of force surrounding a bar magnet.

(a)

(b)

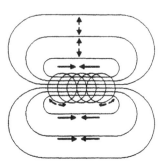

Figure 2: (a) Faraday's representation of the interconnectedness of electric currents and magnetic force (from Faraday (1839–55), vol. 3); (b) Schematic representation of the reciprocal relationship between magnetic lines of force and electric current lines.

(a)

(b)

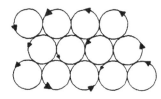
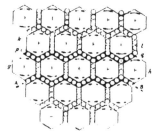

Figure 3: (a) Schematic representation of initial crude source retrieved by Maxwell; (b) Maxwell's representation of his fully elaborated "physical analogy" (from Maxwell (1861–2)).

Viewing Design as a Cooperative Task

Katia P. Sycara

The Robotics Institute
Carnegie Mellon University
Pittsburgh, PA 15213
katia@cs.cmu.edu

ABSTRACT

Design can be modeled as a multi-agent planning task where several agents that possess different expertise and evaluation criteria cooperate to produce a design. The differences may result in conflicts that have to be resolved during design. The process by which conflict resolution is achieved is negotiation. In this paper, we propose a model of group problem solving among cooperating experts that supports negotiation. The model incorporates accessing information from a case memory of existing designs, communication of design rationale, evaluation and critiquing of design decisions. Incremental design modifications are performed based on constraint relaxation and comparison of utilities.

INTRODUCTION

The design task can be described as taking a set of functional specifications and constraints, and producing an artifact representation whose behavior, when manufactured, conforms to the given specification description. Design constraints involve not only physical laws and domain principles that determine the behavior of the device but also restrictions and interactions arising from concerns such as cost, ease of manufacturing, ease of assembly and ease of maintaining the artifact. Taking these concerns into consideration in the initial design stages is known as concurrent engineering [DICE 89, Sriram 88][2]. Concurrent engineering is a team effort that requires the collaboration of teams of specialists representing relevant perspectives. Typically, each specialist has expertise in one area pertaining to the design, limited knowledge of the constraints and intentions of the other specialists and in general different evaluation criteria of the design. Hence, inconsistencies and conflicting views may occur. The specialists interact in a cooperative manner in order to effect tradeoffs and resolve inconsistencies. The final design is a compromise that has been agreed upon by all concerned agents[3]. Existing approaches to modeling concurrent design have primarily focused on investigating architectures for communication between various experts [DICE 89, Lander 88, Talukdar 88], or on conflict detection [Robinson 87, Sriram 88]. In this paper, we present a model of the group problem solving process of a team of concurrent engineering cooperating experts. The proposed team design model is inspired by our work in an adversarial domain, namely conflict resolution in labor management disputes [Sycara 87]. The model is currently being implemented in the CADET system that integrates Case-Based Reasoning, Qualitative Reasoning, and Constraint Propagation in the domain of mechanical design [Sycara 89a, Sycara 89b].

---

[1]This research has been supported by DARPA and AFOSR under contract number F49620-90-C-0003.

[2]It has been recently recognized that the practice of concurrent engineering is very advantageous in terms of reducing the time of a product from "concept to market". Industry is rapidly moving to adopt the paractice.

[3]We use the words "agent", "expert" and "specialist" interchangeably for the purposes of this paper.

The team design problem has the following characteristics:

- The global goal is to produce a design that is synthesized from contributions of different expertise, concerns and constraints

- During the design process, conflicts in the form of constraint violations could arise. If these conflicts are not resolved in a satisfactory manner, infeasible designs will occur.

- Disparate evaluations of (partial or complete) designs could surface as a result of different criteria used to evaluate designs from different perspectives. Typically, these criteria cannot be simultaneously and optimally satisfied. The design decisions that optimize one set of criteria could conflict with those that optimize another set. If these conflicts do not get resolved in a satisfactory fashion, design suboptimalities occur.

- The global goal is achieved by making the best tradeoffs on conflicting design goals and constraints.

- Because of the presence of conflicting constraints, goals and possibly evaluation criteria, it is impossible for each expert to optimize the overall design using only local information.

- Backtracking, resulting from infeasible designs, can be a major problem since it may result in invalidating design decisions that other agents have made.

As a result of the above characteristics, the final successful design can be viewed as a compromise[4]. that incorporates tradeoffs such as cost, ease of manufacturing and assembly, reliability and maintainability. The process through which design decisions are made by a team of experts is *negotiation*. Typically in manufacturing enterprises (e.g., [Bond 89]), after initial study of the design specifications, an initial design (called an initial cartoon) is created by the main designer. Subsequently, the specialists meet to negotiate proposed changes and tradeoffs with respect to the initial design. Compromises are suggested and discussed. The suggested compromises initiate further studies that necessitate additional meetings to reconcile continuing problem areas. This iterative process continues until all parties reach agreement[5]. Depending on particular decisions concerning tradeoffs, different designs will be produced. For example, the valve for a water tap could be a metallic threaded part or a plastic plug valve with a hole. There is a tradeoff between the low cost of the plastic valve and the high durability of the metal valve. Despite the difficulty of applying negotiation techniques, recorded conflicts and their resolution, namely previous similar design cases, provide a foundation for rationalizing designs.

Negotiation enters the design process at the following points:

- When the result of design decisions is an infeasible design (i.e. when constraint violations have been identified).

- When a design is feasible but suboptimal.

- When alternate approaches can achieve similar functional results.

---

[4]Pruitt [Pruitt 81] has identified two types of negotiation which are used by expert human negotiators to seek acceptable solutions and which may be applicable to machine agents: (a) compromise negotiation where each party makes concessions on its demands to facilitate agreement, and (b) integrative negotiation where the most important goals of each party are used to form innovative solutions, relinquishing, if necessary, secondary goals. In our view, both these negotiation types result in *compromise* solutions, in other words in partial goal satisfaction. Moreover, in typical negotiations a goal of secondary importance to one agent could be of primary importance to another because of different local evaluation functions. My use of the word "compromise" encompasses both these negotiation types.

[5]Throughout this process, time and cost determine the number of iterations allowed.

Negotiation is a process in which the parties iteratively exchange proposals and proposal justifications until an agreement is reached. During the negotiation process, the feasibility and desirability of proposed tradeoffs is evaluated and may result in incremental design adaptations. Thus, a negotiation model must be (a) iterative, (b) include mechanisms to incorporate feedback of the parties concerning evaluation of a proposal (partial design) from their point of view, (c) include criteria for judging whether progress in the negotiation is being made, and (d) incorporate negotiation protocols for the exchange of proposals, arguments and justifications of the proposed design decisions. The proposed model incorporates the above characteristics.

AN EXAMPLE OF EXPERT INTERACTION

Consider the process of designing a turbine blade. Some of the dominant specialties are aerodynamics, structural engineering, manufacturing and marketing. The blade design team operates within constraint ranges specified by the design team for the aircraft engine. The blade design team incorporates various concerns. The concern of aerodynamics is aerodynamic efficiency; for structural engineering it is reliability and safety; for manufacturing, it is ease and cost of manufacturing and testing; for marketing it is overall cost and customer satisfaction. The two variables of concern in a turbine blade that we consider are: (a) root radius, and (b) blade length. From the perspective of structural design, the bigger the root radius, the better since it decreases stress concentration. From the perspective of aerodynamics, the smaller the root radius, the better, since it increases aerodynamic efficiency. Concerning the length of the blade, from the point of view of structural design, the shorter the blade, the lower the tensile stresses; from the point of view of aerodynamics the longer the blade, the better the aerodynamics. On the other hand, if the blade is shorter, it makes for a lighter engine which is a desirable characteristic for aerodynamic efficiency. Thus, we see that the aerodynamics expert needs to make tradeoffs internal to its perspective. From the point of view of marketing, aerodynamic efficiency lowers the cost of operation of the aircraft, thus making it more attractive to customers. From the point of view of manufacturing, it is easier to manufacture shorter blades with bigger root radii.

The following is a simplified example dialogue of the various concerned perspectives in an attempt to arrive at a mutually satisfactory turbine blade design:

Aerodynamics (using case based reasoning) suggests particular values x and y for length and root radius of the blade. The suggested x and y values are within acceptable constraint ranges.

Structural engineering evaluates these values from its point of view and suggests values x' and y' where x'<x and y'>y (i.e., shortening the length and increasing the root radius) to increase safety.

Aerodynamics counters by saying that the values structural engineering suggested would considerably decrease aerodynamic efficiency.

Structural engineering counters that shorter blade makes engine lighter, thus also increasing efficiency.

Marketing says aerodynamic efficiency sells the product since it is less costly to operate.

Manufacturing supports structural by saying it is easier to manufacture short blades with big root radius.

Aerodynamics suggests that the materials engineering expert could try to investigate new materials that make the blade lighter, thus alleviating weight considerations.

Manufacturing says that new materials take lots of time to test and debug.

Structural engineering adds that new materials may introduce safety hazards that could go undetected.

This example illustrates the exchange of proposals for values of length and radius of the blade as well as the exchange of arguments and justifications in critiquing the proposed values. The nature of the resulting design will depend on (a) the ranges of various artifact constraints, (b) which constraints can be relaxed and in what ways, (c) the relative importance of various artifact-dependent goals (e.g., aerodynamic efficiency), (d) relative importance of various artifact-independent goals (e.g., safety), and (e) the way in which particular variable values contribute to the achievement of the goals.

THE MODEL

At the start of the team design process, an initial design is generated and presented to each expert, who evaluates it from its own point of view and registers its reactions (evaluations, objections and suggestions). At each negotiation iteration, the input is the set of conflicting concerns, violated constraints of the various design agents and the context of the design (e.g., constraints that have been handed to the design team from others). The final output is either a single agreed upon design or an indication of failure if the negotiating agents did not reach agreement within a particular number of iterations. The final output is reached through iterations of the following tasks: (a) proposal of an initial design, (b) arguments to support justification and critiquing of the design and (c) incremental modification and improvement. These tasks are performed using knowledge of existing designs and their characteristics, knowledge of physical laws and constraints, traces of design decisions made so far, and models of the expertise and concerns of the participating agents. The agents have access to a common case base of previous designs but because of their specialized knowledge each one accesses and evaluates a design from a particular *view*.

Negotiation, as seen in Figure 1, is performed through integration of Case-Based Reasoning (CBR) [Kolodner et al. 85, Sycara 87], use of multi-attribute utilities, called Preference Analysis, and constraint relaxation. These methods are employed in all negotiation tasks, namely in generation of an initial proposal, repair of a rejected proposal to formulate a counterproposal, and communication of justifications and objections. The process interleaves local computation and communication of computation results to other agents. One of the important concerns in distributed problem solving is minimization of communication overhead.

Use of previous design cases offers a reasoner (a) suggestions of how tradeoffs and resolutions have been made in the past, (b) failure avoidance advice (since failures are recorded in the design case), and (c) possible modifications and repairs to design suboptimalities. In addition, for group problem solving, having a memory of past problem solving experiences (successes and failures) has the following advantages [Sycara 89c]:

- Case-based inference minimizes the need for information exchange, thus minimizing communication overhead.

- Anticipating and avoiding problems through reasoning from past failures helps the agents minimize the exchange of proposals that will be rejected, thus minimizing backtracking.

- Reasoning from previous cases helps in recognizing problems or opportunities in a proposed design.

- If the repair of a past failure is also stored in memory, computation by each agent is

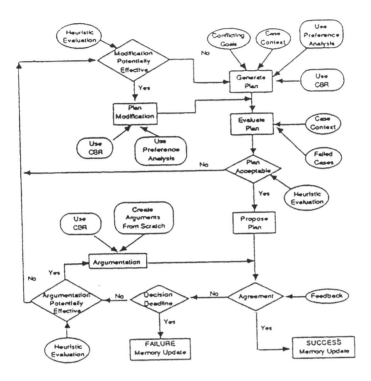

Figure 1: The Negotiation Process

minimized.

An integral part of the negotiation process is the ability of the agents to communicate their views and preferences as well as influence the decisions of other agents. Thus, a group problem solving model must have the ability to support (a) representing and maintaining belief models, (b) reasoning about agents' beliefs, and (c) influencing other agents' beliefs. The knowledge needed to perform these tasks is an agent's *belief* and *preference* structure. The belief structure of an agent, represented in a goal graph, consists of a collection of goals, goal importance and relationships among goals. The preference structure of an agent records its utilities associated with various potential decisions. The values in the goal graph are based on the constraints on the design and company policy. For example, after an airplane crash whose cause is traced to a defective engine, the importance of the safety goal increases for the marketing agent[6].

We represent an agent's belief structure as a directed acyclic graph where each node represents an agent's goal. Edges of the graph linking two goals represent the relationship between goals in terms of how one affects (positively or negatively) the achievement of the other. For example, aerodynamic efficiency positively affects lower operation costs. Associated with each node is:

---

[6]This has been observed in real situations, such as one of last year's airplane accidents involving an engine made by GE. The company gave increased important to testing procedures and design practices to increase engine reliability.

- a *sign* (+ or -) that denotes the desirability of an increase or decrease in that goal
- the *values* by which the attribute/goal should be increased or decreased
- the *importance* that the agent attaches to the goal
- the *feasibility* as perceived by the agent of achieving the goal

Directed edges connect subgoals to the higher level goals to which they contribute. A *contribution* value is associated with each directed edge denoting the contribution of the subgoal to the higher level goal. Contribution values range from -100% to +100%. A positive value means that the subgoal supports the achievement of the higher level goal by the denoted percentage. A negative contribution value has the interpretation that the subgoal is detrimental to the higher level goal. Sink nodes[7] are the highest level goals of an agent.

A path from node X to node Y in a goal graph constitutes a causal/justification chain that provides an explanation of the change in Y in terms of the change in X, assuming no other change has ocurred in the rest of the graph. For example, lengthening a turbine blade results in increasing aerodynamic efficiency, which in turn results in lower operating costs, thus resulting in increased marketability of the blade. By traversing goal graphs a reasoner can answer the following queries:
- Which goals are supported by a set of design decisions?
- Which design decisions are justified by a set of goals?

In addition to an agent's beliefs, the representation includes an estimate of its utilities for each attribute in the goal graph. Utilities express the *preference structure* of an agent [Sycara 88]. Moreover, utilities express the tradeoff structure among various attribute values associated with alternative designs. The (possibly nonlinear) utilities of individual attributes are combined to give an overall utility, the payoff, of an alternative. Being able to compare different alternatives enables a reasoner to choose the alternative that affords the maximum payoff. An integration algorithm traverses the belief structure to determine which way goal values should be moved to increase payoff and thus the acceptability of a resolution. Moreover, goal graph traversal allows an agent to discover alternative design decisions that support important goals thus leading to innovative designs.

THE NEGOTIATION PROTOCOL

The agents interact through message passing. The messages that the negotiating agents exchange contain the following information:
- The proposed design
- Justifications of design decisions
- Agreement or disagreement with the proposal
- Requests for additional information, such as with which issue in the proposed design the agent disagrees.
- Reasons for disagreement.
- Utilities/preferences of the agents associated with disagreed upon issues.

---

[7]Sink nodes have no out-going edges

We present in detail the communication protocol used in our system[8].

1. Agent1 communicates to agent2 a design proposal, as well as arguments and justifications in support of the proposal.

2. Agent2 uses the arguments and justifications communicated by agent1 to possibly modify its goal graph (e.g., change importance of goals, including possibly abandoning goals).

3. Agent2 evaluates the proposal from its point of view (using its constraints and utilities).

4. If the proposal satisfies agent2's local constraints and gives it payoff above a threshold, it communicates ACCEPT to agent1.

5. If not, agent2 generates a counterproposal by whatever problem solving means it has at its disposal (e.g., CBR, constraint relaxation).

6. Agent2 evaluates the counterproposal. If the counterproposal gives agent2 payoff above the threshold, agent2 communicates to agent1:
   - The PORTION/ISSUES of the proposal that have been modified
   - The REASON for modifying the previous proposal (e.g., value1 violates some of the agent2's hard constraints, a set of proposed values does not contribute enough to higher level goals of agent2).
   - The COUNTERPROPOSAL and its PAYOFF.
   - ARGUMENTS and JUSTIFICATIONS in favor of the counterproposal.

7. If the counterproposal does not give agent2 payoff above the threshold, agent2 goes to step 5.

8. If agent2 has exhausted all counterproposals it can generate through the methods of step 5, it traverses its goal graph to see whether there is another way to satisfy its higher level goals.
   - If there is, it generates a counterproposal and goes to step 6.
   - If there is not, it communicates FAILURE to agent1 (who now has to generate a modification and/or look for alternative ways in *its* goal graph).

CONCLUDING REMARKS

Design can be viewed as a multi-agent planning process involving multiple conjunctive and potentially conflicting goals. The agents have different expertise (e.g., mechanisms, hydraulics, assembly, testing) which results in viewing and evaluating designs using different, possibly conflicting criteria. The process of negotiation is used to propose and examine design decisions involving various tradeoffs. Negotiation is performed recursively at all stages of design and involves different design teams. We have proposed a model of group problem solving by cooperating experts that supports negotiation. The model is based on (a) knowledge of previous designs, (b) communication of design rationale, justifications and objections to proposed design decisions, (c) constraint propagation and relaxation, and (d) traversal of goal graphs.

---

[8]For simplicity, the protocol is presented for two agents, agent1, who initiates an initial design and agent2, who evaluates the design and possibly generates a counterproposal. The protocol generalizes to more than one agent that evaluates and suggests modifications.

REFERENCES

[Bond 89]   Bond, A.H., and Ricci, R.J., "Cooperation in Aircraft Design," *Proceedings of the MIT/JSME Workshop on Cooperative Product Development*, MIT, Cambridge, Mass., November 1989.

[DICE 89]   DICE: Initiative in Concurrent Engineering, "Red Book of Functional Specifications for the DICE Architecture," Tech. report, Concurrent Engineering Research Center, West Virginia University, February 1989.

[Kolodner et al. 85]   Kolodner, J.L., Simpson, R.L., and Sycara-Cyranski, K., "A Process Model of Case-Based Reasoning in Problem Solving," *Proceedings of IJCAI-85*, Los Angeles, CA, 1985, pp. 284-290.

[Lander 88]   Lander, S. and Lesser, V., "Negotiation to Resolve Conflicts Among Design Experts," *Proceedings of the AAAI-88 Workshop on AI in Design*, AAAI, St. Paul, MN., 1988.

[Pruitt 81]   Pruitt, D. G., *Negotiation Behavior*, Academic Press, New York, N.Y., 1981.

[Robinson 87]   Robinson, W., "Towards the formalization of specification design, Master's Thesis," Tech. report, University of Oregon, 1987.

[Sriram 88]   Sriram, D., Logcher, R., and Groleau, N., "Cooperative Engineering Design," *Proceedings of the AAAI-88 Workshop on AI in Design*, AAAI, St. Paul, MN., 1988.

[Sycara 87]   Sycara, K., *Resolving Adversarial Conflicts: An Approach Integrating Case-Based and Analytic Methods*, PhD dissertation, School of Information and Computer Science Georgia Institute of Technology, 1987.

[Sycara 88]   Sycara, K., "Utility Theory in Conflict Resolution," *Annals of Operations Research*, Vol. 12, 1988, pp. 65-84.

[Sycara 89a]   Sycara, K. and Navinchandra, D., "Integrating Case-Based Reasoning and Qualitative Reasoning in Engineering Design," in *Artificial Intelligence in Engineering Design*, J. Gero, ed., Computational Mechanics Publications, 1989.

[Sycara 89b]   Sycara, K. and Navinchandra D., "A Process Model of Experience-Based Design," *Proceedings of the Eleventh Annual Conference of the Cognitive Science Society*, Ann Arbor, MI., 1989.

[Sycara 89c]   Sycara, K., "Multi-Agent Compromise via Negotiation," in *Distributed Artificial Intelligence, Volume II*, M. Huhns and L. Gasser, ed., Pittman Publishing Ltd and Morgan Kaufmann, 1989.

[Talukdar 88]   Talukdar, S., Elfes, A., and Papanikolopoulos, N., "Concurrent design, simultaneous engineering and distributed problem solving," *Proceedings of the AAAI-88 Workshop on AI in Design*, AAAI, St. Paul, MN., 1988.

The Temporal nature of Scientific Discovery: The roles of Priming and Analogy

Kevin Dunbar & Christian D. Schunn
Department of Psychology, McGill University

Abstract: One of the most frequently mentioned sources of scientific hypotheses is analogy. Despite the attractiveness of this mechanism of discovery, there has been but a small success in demonstrating that people actually use analogies while solving problems. The study reported below attempted to foster analogical transfer in a scientific discovery task. Subjects worked on two problems that had the same type of underlying mechanism. On day 1, subjects discovered the mechanism that controls virus reproduction. On day 2, subjects returned to work on a problem in molecular genetics that had a similar underlying mechanism. The results showed that experience at discovering the virus mechanism did facilitate performance on the molecular genetics task. However, the verbal protocols do not indicate that subjects analogically mapped knowledge from the virus to the genetics domain. Rather, experience with the virus problem appeared to prime memory. It is argued that analogical mapping can be used flexibly in scientific discovery contexts and that primed knowledge structures can also provide access to relevant information when analogical mapping fails.

The origins of scientific hypotheses and theories have often been considered to be outside the purview of scientific investigation. Recently, however, a number of accounts of scientific discovery have appeared that provide detailed mechanisms of discovery (e.g., Holland, Holyoak, Nisbett and Thagard, 1986; Klahr & Dunbar, 1988; Langley, Bradshaw, Simon & Zytkow, 1987). One such account is the Scientific Discovery as Dual Search framework of Klahr and Dunbar (Klahr & Dunbar, 1988). Scientific Discovery as Dual Search (SDDS) is based upon the assumption that scientific reasoning consists of a search in two main problem spaces --an hypothesis and an experiment space. Using this framework, it has has been possible to explore the manner in which the current hypothesis guides experiment space search, and how experimental results in turn determine search of the hypothesis space. For example, Klahr & Dunbar (1988) have discovered that when subjects fail to find an hypothesis by searching the hypothesis space, they switch to searching the experiment space. Dunbar (1989) and Klahr, Dunbar, & Fay (1990) have discovered

a number of heuristics for experiment space search.

While we are now acquiring a more detailed picture of the heuristics that guide experiment space search, relatively little is known about the heuristics governing the search of the hypothesis space. Klahr and Dunbar (1988) have shown that when subjects attempt to make a discovery, they initially search memory for an hypothesis. When an hypothesis has been found, the subjects then conduct experiments to see if the hypothesis is correct. If the hypothesis is incorrect, the subjects then either modify the hypothesis, search memory for a new hypothesis, or switch to a search of the experiment space. However the actual mechanisms underlying this search of the hypothesis space are unclear. The purpose of the research reported here was to provide a more detailed account of Hypothesis space search.

Research in other laboratories suggests two main mechanisms for hypothesis space search; analogical mapping (Gentner, 1983; Holland, Holyoak, Nisbett & Thagard 1986), and Remindings (Ross; 1989). Holland, et al. (1986) have emphasized the central role of analogical mapping as a source of initial scientific hypotheses. Surprisingly, empirical research has demonstrated that subjects often fail to notice an analogical mapping when one is present. Most research that has demonstrated an inability of subjects to make use of analogies has been conducted using problems that demand little prior knowledge, and the subjects do not work on the problems for extensive amounts of time (e.g., Gick & Holyoak, 1983). When subjects are given more extensive training on a source domain there is a greater probability of analogical mapping occurring (e.g., Bassock & Holyoak, 1989). This suggests that the type of representation that subjects have of both the source and the target domain determines whether analogical mapping will occur. Gentner's (1983) structure mapping theory suggests that subjects will map from one domain to another only when they can abstract the relational structure of the source domain and the target domains. Both Gentner's theory and the goal oriented approach of Holyoak and Thagard (1989) suggest that subjects must have a detailed representation of the both the source and the target problems to make analogies.

Another mechanism that could be involved in mapping previously acquired knowledge on to a new problem is remindings; the use of an earlier example that the problem solver is reminded of while solving a problem. Remindings must be part of the analogical mapping process or could occur without being used in analogical mapping. Ross (1989) has proposed that when solving a problem there is a search of memory for related information. If the search is successful, the subject will be able to use the earlier example to solve the problem. If the earlier example has the same structural characteristics as the current problem the subject may be able to analogically map the earlier solution on to the current problem. If there is no structural overlap the subject could still use the reminding by fitting the previous solution to the current problem.

When applied to a scientific reasoning context, these views suggest that when a scientist has knowledge of a source domain,

analogical mapping will occur only when a representation of the target domain has the same structure or the same subgoals as the source problem. When working on a problem, the scientist will initially retrieve some knowledge thought to be relevant to the problem. Experiments are then conducted. The experiments lead to a more detailed representation. When a more detailed representation of the problem is acquired, a search of memory for a structure or solution that will map onto the target domain will occur. While working on a problem a scientist may retrieve many different analogies to formulate hypotheses until a satisfactory solution to the problem is reached.

In sum, previous research suggests that if an attempt to map from the base to the target domain is made when subjects begin working on a problem, subjects will have superficial information about the target domain. Subjects should use their superficial knowledge of that domain to search memory for hypotheses relevant to the problem. As a result of experimentation, subjects should learn that their initial hypotheses do not hold. Then, as they learn more about the relations among the elements of the target problem --through experimentation-- they should develop a more detailed representation of the problem. This should make it possible to search memory for a structurally similar solution, or solutions that have been used to solve similar problems.

The Molecular Biology domain

To investigate the temporal course of the development of hypotheses a task that fosters the development of changing representations of a problem is needed. Rather than invent an arbitrary problem, two problems from molecular biology that involve similar underlying mechanisms were used. The source problem was one of discovering why viruses are sometimes dormant (do not reproduce), and other times are active (reproduce rapidly). Molecular biologists have discovered that dormant viruses secrete enzymes that inhibit virus reproduction. This is a form of negative regulation. The target problem also involved negative regulation. The target problem was to discover how genes are controlled by other genes. The specific question addressed was why genes secrete beta-galactosidase only when there is lactose present. Again the mechanism underlying this is negative regulation (Jacob & Monod, 1961). Monod and Jacob were awarded the Nobel prize for discovering that the control mechanism in viruses and in lactose is negative regulation.

To investigate the time course of analogical mapping a paradigm developed by Dunbar (1989) was used. In the Dunbar (1989) study subjects were taught some elementary knowledge about molecular genetics. Then, subjects were taught how to conduct molecular genetics experiments on the computer. Then they were given the problem of discovering the way that genes control other genes. Subjects tended to use their knowledge of the genetics domain to formulate their initial hypotheses. Subsequent hypotheses were formed by inducing the concept of negative regulation from patterns of data or memory search.

In the current study, subjects were taught about viruses and genetics and were shown how to conduct simulated experiments on the computer. For both the virus and the genetics problem subjects were asked to discover the control mechanism. The tasks that the subjects were given and the potential analogical mappings will now be described in detail.

The Experiment

Subjects. Sixty McGill undergraduates were paid to participate in the experiment. All subjects had taken an introductory biology course and they were not familiar with gene regulation in bacteria or viruses. Their knowledge of molecular genetics consisted of knowing that DNA and RNA exist.

Procedure. There were three conditions. In the *No-Virus* condition, subjects participated only in the gene regulation problem. There were two experimental conditions --*Negative-Virus* and *Correlated-Virus*. In these conditions subjects attempted to discover why viruses are sometimes active

and sometimes dormant. The virus problem was presented on day 1, and the genetics problem was presented on day 2. Subjects conducted their experiments on a MacIntosh II computer. The display was highly interactive: subjects conducted experiments by using menus and selecting various options. Once the experiment was designed subjects could conduct the experiment and monitor the results. A permanent record of all experiments and results was available after each experiment was conducted.

Day 1. Virus Problem. The virus problem was carried out in three phases. First, the subjects were taught some basic facts about viruses and biochemistry, and were shown two methods of determining whether a chemical is involved in virus reproduction. One method was to view the amount of a chemical that is present in an active or dormant virus. By doing this the subject could see whether there was a relationship between the amount of a chemical and the number of viruses present. The second method was to add a chemical to an active or dormant virus and monitor its effect on the number of viruses present.

Second, the subjects were instructed on how to give a verbal protocol. Third, the virus problem was given to the subjects. They were told that viruses were sometimes active and sometimes dormant, and that biochemists thought that one of three chemicals that the virus can secrete was responsible for making the virus active or dormant. Subjects were asked to discover which of the three chemicals causes the virus to be active or dormant and what the control mechanism was.

For the *Negative-Virus* group the mechanism causing the virus to become dormant was negative regulation: The dormant viruses secrete a chemical that prevents generation of new viruses. For the *Correlated-Virus* group, there was a positive correlation between the amount of Q that was present and the number of viruses. In this case, Q was a by-product of the number of viruses present. There was no causal mechanism for this group; this was a control condition. Subjects worked on this problem until they felt that they had discovered the correct answer. Subjects were not told if they had discovered the correct mechanism. All subjects were asked to return for another problem the next day.

There were 12 possible experiments that could be conducted. in the virus problem. The small number of experiments made it extremely likely that subjects would conduct all possible experiments. In particular, in the *Negative-Virus* condition, subjects should conduct an experiment where Q is added to an active virus and the number of viruses decreases, (see Figure 1). This would suggest that Q inhibits virus reproduction. Due to the small size of the experiment space it was expected that most subjects would discover the correct mechanism.

FIGURE 1: NEGATIVE-VIRUS CONDITION

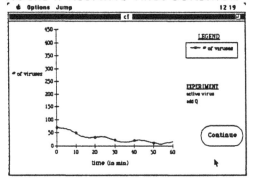

Day 2. Genetics problem. All three groups of subjects were given the genetics problem. There were three phases in the genetics problem. First, the subjects were taught some basic facts about molecular biology. They were told that certain genes control the activities of other genes by switching them on when there is a nutrient present. This is an example of positive regulation --the regulator gene senses that there is a nutrient present and then releases substances that instruct other genes to secrete enzymes that can utilize the nutrient. The example of positive regulation given to the subjects can be seen in Figure 2. Here, the A gene switches on the enzyme producing genes. When the A gene is absent and fructose is present no enzyme is produced

(FIG 2A). When the A gene is present in a diploid cell the cell secretes an enzyme that breaks down the fructose (FIG 2B).

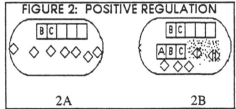

In the second phase of the genetics problem, subjects were shown how to give a verbal protocol. In the third phase, subjects were presented with two findings about a set of genes labelled I, O, and P: The enzyme producing genes secrete an enzyme when there is lactose present, and do not secrete the enzyme when there is no lactose. Subjects were asked to discover how the enzyme producing genes are controlled. The presentation of the I,P,O genes was identical to the A,B,C genes. The differences were (i) that there were different letters on the genes (ii) the nutrient was lactose rather than fructose, and (iii) the enzyme secreted was betagalactosidase rather than delta. Finally, unbeknownst to the subject, there was a different underlying mechanism --negative regulation rather than positive regulation. The subjects have to discover that the I and O genes negatively regulate (i.e., inhibit) the activity of the enzyme producing genes until a nutrient is present. Subjects must also learn that the I gene can be present on either the male or female chromosome, but that the O gene can only be on the O gene.

There are 120 possible experiments that can be conducted (6 amounts of nutrient x 20 genetic combinations). For a normal Ecoli, the amount of enzyme produced is half whatever the amount of nutrient is. The I gene mutants (designated I- mutants) produce an output of 876, and O- mutants produce an output of 527. The I- and O- mutants produce this amount of enzyme regardless of the amount of nutrient administered. Thus, I- and O- nutrients will produce enzymes even when no nutrient is administered. This is a strong clue for negative regulation being involved. In this study, the P gene plays no role at all.

Subjects were expected to make a number of different mappings from both the virus and the genetics domains during the course of the experiment. First, there should be a mapping from the positive regulation example given at the start of the genetics problem. The positive regulation example had a virtually identical structure to the target problem. There were three regulator genes, three enzyme producing genes, nutrients with similar names (lactose and fructose), and enzyme products that also have similar names (beta and delta). Thus, as in the Dunbar (1989) study, it was expected that initial hypotheses would be of positive regulation.

Once subjects discover that none of the genes work by positive regulation there should be a search of the hypothesis space for another mechanism. For the *Negative-Virus* group, it was expected that the presence of large amounts of enzyme when either the I or O genes were mutants would be equivalent to the situation of large numbers of virus being present when Q was absent. At this point, subjects should mention that the genetics problem is like the virus problem. The subjects should then map over the concept of negative regulation from the virus to the genetics domain.

If the virus problem is used to help solve the genetics problem, then it could occur in a number of stages. First, subjects would have to extract a representation such as *X inhibits Y* from *Q inhibits virus production*. Then they should apply this relation to the genetics problem. Second, even with this mapping, the problem is not solved; the *X inhibits Y* relation must be modified to include two genes (I and O), and the that the I and O genes inhibit in different ways. Thus, subjects should retrieve the *X inhibits Y* relation, and then modify it (by experimentation) to fit the current problem. The genetics problem not only involves a memory search for hypotheses, but also a modification of hypotheses to solve the problem.

Results

Day 1 (virus problem). All of the 20 subjects in the *Correlated-Virus* condition discovered that the positive non-causal relationship between the amount of Q and the number of viruses. Sixteen of the 20 subjects in the *Negative-Virus* group discovered that the dormant virus secretes a chemical that inhibits virus reproduction. The four subjects that did not discover negative regulation concluded that there was a complex interaction of chemicals that switch on reproduction.

Day 2 (genetics problem). As shown in Table 1, for the *No-virus* group, 7 out of 20 subjects discovered that the I and O genes inhibit and that the P gene plays no role. For the *correlated-virus* condition, the results were almost identical: 7 subjects discovered the roles of I, O, and P. This indicates that the experience with conducting virus experiments on day 1 had no beneficial effect on performance. Results for the *Negative-Virus* group were very different; 12 of the subjects discovered the mechanism of genetic control. This indicates that discovery of the negative regulation of viruses on day 1 did indeed benefit performance on the genetics problem.

Table 1
Subjects discovering genetics mechanism

Condition		
	No-Virus	7 (35%)
	Correlated virus	7 (35%)
	Negative virus	12 (60%)

As can be seen from Table 2, 12 of the subjects who discovered negative regulation in the virus problem also discovered negative regulation on the genetics problem. Four of the subjects who discovered negative regulation in the virus problem did not discover negative regulation in the genetics problem. These subjects did mention inhibition, but also proposed a positive regulation mechanism.

Table 2
Effects of discovering virus mechanism on discovering genetics mechanism

	discover genetics	miss genetics
discover virus	12	4
miss virus	0	4

97

Initial hypotheses. It is possible to determine whether subjects immediately saw if the mechanism that they learned in the virus problem was applicable to the genetics problem by examining initial hypotheses. None of the subjects in the *No-Virus* or the *Correlated-Virus* conditions initially proposed negative regulation as a potential mechanism. Only one of the subjects in the *Negative-Virus* condition proposed that negative regulation as an initial hypothesis. This indicates that subjects initial mappings were not from the virus domain. Instead, initial hypotheses were taken from the example demonstrating positive regulation at the beginning of the genetics problem.

Subsequent hypotheses. As mentioned above, previous research using this paradigm (Dunbar, 1989) has shown that subjects discover negative regulation using two main strategies. One is by searching memory for an appropriate mechanism and the other is by inducing the mechanism from a series of experimental results. If subjects were using the knowledge obtained from the virus experiment, then subjects should discover the concept of negative regulation by a memory search, rather than by inducing negative regulation from a series of experimental results

We were able to categorize performance as memory search by one of two criteria. One criterion was whether subjects stated that they were searching memory for hypotheses or that the genetics problem reminded them of the virus problem. None of the subjects in either the *Correlated-Virus* or the *Negative-Virus* groups mentioned the virus experiment while they were working on the genetics problem. The other criterion was if on the first experiment that was inconsistent with positive regulation, subjects proposed negative regulation. For example, when an I-experiment is conducted there is a very large output of betagalactosidase. This result is inconsistent with positive regulation. All three groups of subjects conducted an I- or an O- experiment as one of their first four experiments. In the *No-virus* condition, 4 subjects suggested negative regulation after their first I-

experiment. In the *Correlated Virus* condition 4 subjects proposed negative regulation. By contrast, 11 subjects in the *Negative-virus* condition proposed negative regulation .

Incorrect final hypotheses. It is also possible that the virus problem influenced the types of incorrect hypotheses proposed. In the *No-Virus* condition only 5 of the 13 subjects mentioned negative regulation. In the *Correlated-Virus* condition 4 of the 13 subjects mentioned negative regulation. In the *Negative-Virus* condition 8 subjects failed to propose the correct mechanism. The 4 subjects who missed both the virus and the genetics problem never mentioned inhibition. Three of the 4 subjects who solved the virus problem but did not solve the genetics problem mentioned negative regulation. Thus, all but one of the subjects who solved the virus problem proposed some form of negative regulation in the genetics problem.

One possible explanation for the better performance of the *Negative-Virus* group could be that these subjects learned various experimental skills while working on the virus problem. The performance of the *Correlated-Virus* group does not support this explanation. If subjects acquired knowledge of how to conduct experiments during the virus experiment, then both the *Correlated-Virus* and *Negative-virus* groups should have benefitted. As only the *Negative-virus* group showed improved performance, this explanation seems unlikely.

Discussion

The results of this study illustrate the dynamic nature of the scientific discovery process. Initial hypotheses were formed by analogically mapping from the same domain. When initial hypotheses were disconfirmed there was a search of memory for an hypothesis that could account for the discrepant results. This search was not based on superficial features of the problem. Subjects searched for a mechanism that could account for the current results. Once the mechanism of negative regulation had been retrieved it had to be modified to fit the current context.

Subjects in the *Negative-Virus* condition did not appear to discover negative regulation by analogical mapping from the virus domain. If subjects were mapping knowledge over from the virus domain, then there should have been a reference in the verbal protocols to the virus domain prior to proposing an inhibitory mechanism. None of the subjects made any reference to the virus domain. Furthermore, at the end of the experiment all subjects were asked whether they had thought of the virus experiment while working on the genetics problem. All the subjects claimed that they had not thought of the virus experiment. When asked if they thought that the virus problem had helped them on the genetics problem almost all subjects stated that the experience with the genetics problem helped them design better experiments. However, the fact that the performance of the subjects *No-Virus* condition was virtually identical to that of the subjects in the *Correlated-Virus* condition indicates that experience with the virus problem *per se.* had no effect on experimental strategies. In sum, these results appear to indicate that there is no direct mapping from the virus to the genetics problem.

The fact that subjects made no explicit mapping from the virus to the genetics problem was surprising. Most theories of analogical reasoning assume that when mapping occurs, it is a conscious activity that occurs by searching memory for a match between the target problem and other possibly relevant mappings. The results of this study suggest a different mechanism: The virus problem may have primed the concept of negative regulation. When the subjects discovered that the mechanism was not one of positive regulation, they engaged in a memory search. The memory search finds negative regulation because it has been primed by the virus problem. This priming mechanism would account for the fact that (a) subjects initial hypotheses were not concerned with negative regulation, and (b) no evidence of an explicit mapping from the virus to the genetics domain appeared in the protocols.

A number of mechanisms could have produced the results obtained in this study.

One is priming of a pre-existing knowledge structure. Cheng and Holyoak (1986), and Fong and Nisbett (1989) have proposed that there are a number of well ingrained concepts in memory that they have labelled 'pragmatic reasoning schemas.' A concept such as negative regulation could be one of these types of schemas. In the current study, solving the virus problem may have primed the concept of negative regulation, making it more likely to be retrieved while solving the genetics problem.

If the prior learning episode primes a concept that is already present in memory, then it suggests that this knowledge structure priming will occur only for concepts that are represented in memory prior to participation in the experiment. However, studies of implicit learning (cf. Reber, 1989) have discovered that when subjects observe a number of instances that follow a rule, they form an abstract representation of the rule that is not tied to the particular context under which the 'rule' was learned. A similar type of learning may have occurred in this study. By learning through experimentation, subjects may have acquired an abstract concept that is missing the contextual information about how the concept was acquired. When working on the genetics problem this abstract representation may have been accessed and used to solve the problem. As the concept had no contextual information associated with it, no remindings occurred. We are currently investigating this hypothesis..

Finally, we can now provide a more dynamic account of the heuristics governing hypothesis space search in SDDS. First there is a search for an hypothesis that can account for an instance that has similar features to the target problem. These initial hypotheses can be based upon the superficial features of the target problem and also upon what little is known about the deep structure features of the problem (cf..Faries & Reiser, 1988). Second, if this search is successful, then the hypothesis is tested. Third, if the hypothesis fails the test, then there is a search for other potential hypotheses, if none are found there is an attempt to modify the initial hypothesis to accommodate the data. This later search is qualatitively different from the first search; subjects now have more knowledge of the target problem and can search for an underlying mechanism rather than a match for superficial features. When a mechanism is being searched for, the current state of activation of all mechanisms in memory will determine which mechanisms will be retrieved. If, as in the current study, a mechanism has been primed by a prior problem, then it will be retrieved.

References

Bassock, M., & Holyoak, K.J. (1989).Interdomain transfer between isomorphic topics in algebra and physics. *Journal of Experimental Psychology: Learning, Memory, and Cognition, 15*, 153-1666.

Cheng, P, & Holyoak, K. (1985). Pragmatic reasoning schemas. *Cognitive Psychology, 17,* 391-416.

Dunbar, K. (1989). Scientific reasoning strategies in a simulated Molecular genetics environment. *In the proceedings of the 11th annual meeting of the Cognitive Science society, MI Ann Arbor,* 426-433.

Dunbar, K., & Klahr, D. (1989). Developmental differences in Scientific Discovery Strategies. In D. Klahr, & K. Kotovsky (Eds.). *Simon and Cognition: Proceedings of the 21st Carnegie-Mellon Symposium on Cognition.* Erlbaum: Hillsdale, New Jersey.

Faries, J.M., & Reiser, B.J. (1988) Access and use of previous solutions in a problem solving situation. *In the proceedings of the tenth annual meeting of the Cognitive Science Society. Montreal, Quebec.*

Fong, G.T., & Nisbett (1990). Immediate and delayed transfer of training effects in statistical reasoning. Manuscript submitted for publication.

Gentner, D. (1983). Structure-mapping: A theoretical framework for analogy. *Cognitive Science, 7 ,* 155-170.

Gentner, D. (1989). The mechanisms of analogical learning. In S. Vosniadou, & A. Ortony (Eds.), *Similarity and Analogical reasoning.* Cambridge, Cambridge University Press.

Gick, M.L., & Holyoak, K.J. (1983). Schema induction and analogical transfer. *Cognitive Psychology, 15,* 1-38.

Holland, J., Holyoak, K., Nisbett, R.E., & Thagard, P. (1986). *Induction: Processes of Inference, Learning, and Discovery .* Cambridge, MA: MIT Press.

Holyoak, K. J. & Thagard, P.J. (1989). A computational model of analogical problem solving. In S. Vosniadou, & A. Ortony (Eds.), *Similarity and Analogical reasoning.* Cambridge, Cambridge University Press.

Jacob, F., & Monod, J. (1961). Genetic regulatory mechanisms in the synthesis of proteins. *Journal of Molecular Biology, 3,* 318-356.

Klahr, D., & Dunbar, K. (1988). Dual space search during scientific reasoning. *Cognitive Science .* 12, 1-48.

Klahr, D., Dunbar, K, & Fay. (1990). Designing good experiments to test "bad" hypotheses. In J. Shrager, & P. Langley (Eds.), *Computational models of discovery and theory formation.* Ann Arbor, MI: Morgan Kaufmann.

Langley, P, Simon, H.A., Bradshaw, G.L., & Zytkow, J. (1987). *Scientific Discovery: Computational explorations of the creative processes.* Cambridge, MA: MIT press.

Reber, A. S. (1989) Implicit learning and tacit knowledge. *Journal of Experimental Psychology: General, 118,* 219-235.

Ross, B.H. (1989). Remindings in learning and instruction. In S. Vosniadou, & A. Ortony (Eds.), *Similarity and Analogical reasoning.* Cambridge, Cambridge University Press.

Notes

This research was supported by grant number OGP0037356 from the National Sciences and Engineering Council Canada to Kevin Dunbar and a summer NSERC research award to Christian D. Schunn.

Correspondence can be addressed to:Kevin Dunbar, Department of Psychology, McGill University, Montreal, Quebec, Canada H3A 1B1
Email: DUNBAR@HEBB.PSYCH.MCGILL.CA

Reasoning directly from cases in a case-based planner

Robert McCartney
Department of Computer Science and Engineering
University of Connecticut, U-155
Storrs. CT 06269-3155
robert@uconn.edu *

Abstract

A good deal of the reasoning done in a case-based planning system can be done directly from (episodic) cases. as opposed to specialized memory structures. In this paper, we examine the issues involved in such direct reasoning including how this representation can support multiple uses. and what role execution plays in such a framework. We illustrate our points using COOKIE. a direct case-based planner in the food preparation domain.

1 Introduction

In this paper, we examine the issues regarding the direct use of cases by a case-based planner. By direct use, we mean performing the underlying reasoning in a system by manipulating representations of episodes in memory, rather than an intermediate description or specialized structure. While these issues are shared by all case-based reasoners, we focus particularly on case-based planning. We examine case representation, how cases are used for different purposes, and the role of execution; these examinations are based on work with COOKIE. a case-based system that plans and monitors execution in the domain of meal planning and preparation.

What is case-based reasoning?

Case-based reasoning is the solving of problems through the reuse of experience—when faced with a problem situation, the problem solver retrieves a similar situation (with its solution) from memory, then adapts the previous solution to solve the current problem [Riesbeck and Schank. 1989]. This can be distinguished (in theory) from rule-based reasoning, since we reason from cases corresponding to real episodes rather than from rules which are distillations of experience. In fact, this separation is muddied in practice, as case-based systems include cases that are abstractions based on a number of real episodes, and rule-based systems include rules that are in fact grounded in a single experience. Case-based reasoning has been used in a variety of domains for a variety of tasks: it has showed the most promise in situations characterized by uncertainty, lack of a complete domain theory, and/or computational constraints, where more traditional approaches have had little success.

*This research has been supported by Booth Research Center grant BG-6. The author gratefully acknowledges the assistance of Kate Sanders, Mallory Selfridge, and Karl Wurst.

Desiderata for a case-based planner

Case-based planning (CBP) is an attempt to solve planning problems by reusing previous episodes. The planning problem is to find a sequence of primitive actions that leads to some specified results—goals to be accomplished and constraints to be satisfied. A case-based planner does this by remembering experiences. At essence, a case-based planner follows the principles given by Hammond [Hammond, 1988]:

> *If it worked, use it again,* and
>
> *If it didn't work, remember not to do it again.*

To these, we add a principle of our own:

> *If my plan fails, I should figure out why.*

These principles can be translated into the three basic functions that a case-based planning system should be able to accomplish.

First, a CBP system should be able to generate plans given it has succeeded in a similar situation. This process is one of retrieving the similar situation (case), then performing transformations on the case until it matches the description of the current problem. Once it matches, "use it again" becomes a simple reapplication of the sequence of steps. For this to be effective, the transformations applied should be equivalence preserving, at least in regard to the goals and constraints.

Second, a CBP system should be able to recognize that a particular approach failed before, so should not be used again. Simply not retrieving failures for adaptation is insufficient here—if we transform a (successful) plan into one that fails, we would like to avoid doing it in the future.

The third principle relates to the second—to avoid failure in the future, we need to understand why we failed. If we can anticipate failure, then we can either use a different plan or modify our plan to avoid the problem. The principle as given only works in a negative way, but sometimes plans have unexpected good results. A more general principle can be based on expectation failures [Schank, 1982] rather than plan failures:

> If something odd happens, figure out why and remember it.

Overview of COOKIE

COOKIE is a case-based system that plans and monitors the preparation of food. Previous work (notably CHEF [Hammond, 1986] and JULIA [Kolodner, 1987]) has demonstrated the benefits of doing planning research in this domain, which is both rich and unpredictable. COOKIE's input is a set of goals and constraints: it first produces a plan to satisfy the input; then monitors the execution of that plan (performing execution-time repairs of the plan, if necessary), then incorporates the results of that execution into its memory. Execution is done externally to the system by human cooks using real food; case-memory is comprised of these episodes and other real cookings taken from transcripts. There is no causal reasoner for analyzing failure, nor is there a simulator that can be used to execute cookings. Explanations of anomalous behavior are built from the assumptions used to predict the non-anomalous behavior and from adaptations of other explanations found in cooking transcripts. COOKIE is designed to reasoning directly from its cases as much as possible, and relies on few other mechanisms. Specific examples of COOKIE's behavior relating to this paper's topic are given in the next few sections.

The rest of this paper is arranged (in order) around the following questions:

- What is an episodic case representation?

- How can an episodic representation scheme support multiple uses in a planner (generation, projection, recognition, explanation, and failure recovery)?

- What is the role of execution in a direct case-based planner?

Finally, in the conclusions, we discuss possible roles for abstraction in a case-based planner.

2 Case representation

Episodic representation—what it is, what it involves

Informally, an episodic representation is one that allows reconstruction of an episode as a story—what happened, when the various things happened relative to each other, what the results were, and so forth. More concretely, an episodic representation is a reasonably complete statement of the facts that is neither simplified nor abstracted. For any domain, the representation includes all of the facts about an episode that are likely to be useful in any future reasoning task. In the food preparation domain, this includes all of the cook-food interactions, as well as seemingly unrelated cook actions that occur during the cooking. For example, if a cook answers the telephone during meal preparation and talks for five minutes to "Dialing for Dollars", that fact is part of the episode, not just that the cook was out of the kitchen for five minutes.

Reasoning directly from cases

In a case-based reasoning system (or more generally, any reasoning system where the rules are ultimately grounded in episodes), we have two options: reasoning by direct manipulation of episodes, or reasoning from abstractions and/or simplifications of episodes. There are advantages and disadvantages to each approach. On the one hand, an episodic representation is likely to contain a good deal of irrelevant information for a particular task; if we want to explain burned biscuits, the cook not monitoring the food for five minutes is enough information, and the facts that it was a phone call, the exact time, that it was from "Dialing for Dollars" and so forth are unnecessary and could have been simplified out of the case. On the other hand, a simplification or abstraction may not have retained the right information. Suppose the above dinner turns out to be poisoned, killing the cook, and his beneficiary happens to work for the television station broadcasting "Dialing for Dollars"—the simplification to "the cook not monitoring the food for five minutes" precludes the obvious explanation of said beneficiary arranging for the phone call so he could poison the meal while the cook was distracted. *The main advantage in reasoning from episodes is that the information used can be extracted when the reasoning task and its context are established, rather than at the time the episode is stored.* This does not rule out a memory where episodes are stored at multiple levels of abstraction, precomputing those that are likely to be useful, but unless we can be certain of precomputing all useful abstractions, the need for direct reasoning cannot be eliminated.

Representation scheme in COOKIE

The representation language used in COOKIE is a temporal propositional logic. For example, (occur ev3 (do chef1 (stir soup5 saucepan1 spoon23)) t1 t2) means that event ev3, chef1 stirring soup5 in saucepan1 with spoon23, occurred beginning at time t1 and ending at time t2. Cases describing cooking episodes are propositional, and contain goals, descriptions of input, output, and (possibly) intermediate states, actions, a critique, and (if applicable) problems encountered and their associated repairs. An example, broiled steak with fried onions, is given in Figure 1. Propositions that are true at the same (specific) times are grouped together here. This is purely a syntactic aid to

103

```
(cooking steak-and-onions1
  (initial (raw steak23)(raw onion24)(cold frypan1) (quantity steak23 1lb)
           (thickness steak23 1.5 in) (quantity onion24 1 medium) (quantity oil25 1 Tb)
  (goals  (cooked steak23) (cooked onion24) (shape onion24 rings)))
  (final  (cooked steak23) (cooked onion24) (shape onion24 rings)
          (rating steak-and-onions1 success)))
  (facts  (inst steak23 beefsteak) (inst onion24 onion) (inst oil25 corn-oil)
  (events (occur ev0 (do chef1 (slice onion24 thin knife2)) 0 1)
          (occur ev1 (do chef1 (heat burner2 high)) 4 8)
          (occur ev2 (do chef1 (heat broiler1 high)) 0 8)
          (occur ev3 (do chef1 (put oil25 frypan1)) 4 4)
          (occur ev4 (do chef1 (put frypan1 burner2)) 4 4)
          (occur ev5 (do chef1 (put steak23 b-pan1)) 1 1)
          (occur ev6 (do chef1 (put b-pan1 broiler1)) 1 1)
          (occur ev7 (do chef1 (flip steak23 b-pan1 fork8)) 5 5)
          (occur ev8 (do chef1 (put onion24 frypan1)) 5 5)
          (occur ev9 (do chef1 (occasional (stir onion24 frypan1 fork8))) 5 8)
          (occur ev10 (do chef1 (remove onion24 frypan1)) 8 8)
          (occur ev11 (do chef1 (remove steak23 b-pan1)) 8 8)))
```

Figure 1: Broiled steak and onion rings.

the user; internally, a case is a conjunction of propositions with individual temporal characteristics. This case is a relatively simple one: other cases include (among other things) termination tests for events, underlying assumptions used in planning the episode, and expectation failures with their associated real-time repairs.

3   Multiple purposes from a single representation scheme

One benefit claimed for an episodic representation is that it is *task-neutral*: the same representation should be useful for a variety of reasoning tasks [McCartney and Sanders, 1990]. In COOKIE, the episodic representation directly supports plan generation and projection, explanation, and failure recovery during execution, and interacts with low-level abstractions during plan recognition.

Plan generation and projection

Plan generation (coming up with a sequence of actions to perform a task) and projection (predicting the effects of a proposed set of actions) in COOKIE are done by performing transformations on cooking episodes. The transformed episode corresponds to the generated plan (actions and expectations) and is processed directly by the execution module (see Section 4).

Projection is based on the assumption that the objects in the transformed episode will behave as their counterparts did in the original episode, so any observed facts in the original episode become expected facts (that is, the projections) in the transformed episode. For a given situation, there is a set of permissible transformations whose application should lead to behavioral equivalence in the transformed case. Suppose, for example, we want a plan for broiled hamburger and onions, and can use the following transformations:

$(x \rightarrow y$: if (and (inst x z) (inst y z)(food z)))

$(x \rightarrow y$: if (and (inst y ground-beef)
         (inst x beefsteak)
         (shape y patty)))

These correspond to the assumptions that food is fungible and we can substitute hamburger for steak if the hamburger is in a patty shape. We generate the new plan by performing the constant-for-constant substitutions steak23→hamburger26, onion24→onion27, and oil27→oil25 in steak-and-onions1. Executing the new plan involves executing the events of the transformed episode at the prescribed times, corresponding to this "recipe":

> Slice an onion while heating the broiler for one minute. Put burger under broiler for 4 minutes. When burger has been in for 3 minutes, put frying pan on high heat, adding 1 T oil. Add onions to pan, and flip burger under broiler. Stir onions occasionally for 3 minutes, then remove from pan and remove burger from broiler. Serve together.

We project the facts that the hamburger and onions will be cooked, the onion will be in ring shapes, and the cooking will be a success.

Plan recognition

Part of case-based planning is the assimilation of experience into a usable memory structure. In the steak-cooking case, the relationships between the actions and goals are not explicit; ascribing actions to goals (making the relationships explicit) is the function of plan recognition— given a set of actions, determine the plan (and goals) that they serve. In COOKIE, this is done to a very limited degree, as this conflicts with the philosophy of reasoning from complete episodes. We allow the recognition of low-level action aggregates corresponding to subplans that express action groupings common to a variety of plans. These are expressed as subplan-schemas (corresponding to MOPs) which allow us to relate actions and goals within an episode. A subplan schema consists of goals, steps, and type and temporal constraints on the steps. We have, for example, a subplan schema for frying things; this schema has the goal of cooking some food item and these steps: preparing the food, heating a pan, oiling the pan, adding the food to the pan, interacting with the food in the pan, and removing the food from the pan. When COOKIE processes the steak-and-onions episode, the actions having to do with the onion and pan are used to recognize an instance of a general frying by mapping the actions in the episode to corresponding steps in the schema (and the "cooked onion" goal in the episode to the corresponding schema goal). Once we have recognized the frying subplan here, we allow these parts to be used as a separate episode (for subsequent reasoning) with the added assumption that using this episode is based on the assumption that the onion cooking does not interact with the rest of the cooking (which is recognized as a broiling). Since schemas are only used for recognition (not generation), we can afford to be fairly non-restrictive with the steps—describing them in a general way and allowing most to be optional. This recognition allows the frying and broiling to be used either together or separately; furthermore it gives us an instance of two subplans that can be coordinated in a single meal by one cook.

Explanation

Explanation in COOKIE is closely related to projection and generation, as explanations are only generated when an expected state fails to occur—a generated plan fails or a projection proves false

105

on execution. The generated explanations can come from two sources. One is the failure of any transformation or separability assumptions made. Suppose we generate a plan for cooking onions based on the onion-frying subplan of steak-and-onions. We explicitly know that this plan is based on underlying assumptions of ingredient fungibility and subplan independence, so if the plan fails, we can assign ingredient difference and subplan dependence as candidate explanations. The other source of explanations is the modification of explanations from other cases (as in SWALE [Kass and Leake, 1988]), which can be used to choose among or make more specific the candidate explanations. The explanation mechanism (i.e., attributing unexpected behavior to causes) in COOKIE is quite simple, but it allows explanation in the absence of a detailed causal theory. Although these explanations do not individually provide the predictive power of a causal explanation, combining evidence from multiple cases could lead to an effective set of predictive features without the need of deep understanding.

Failure recovery

Repair in COOKIE is case-based—execution-time repair is based on remembering and adapting repairs to similar problems problems in previous cases. Such repairs are necessary in planning unless we have either complete prescience or the luxury of being able to "undo" back to a choice point when something goes wrong. In COOKIE's domain, we have neither. and often are faced with problems. The steak-and-onions case had no repairs, but we can use two other cases to illustrate how repair works. The first case is fried-burger-and-onions; it is similar to the previous steak-and-onions, but both the burger and onions are fried in the same pan, the onions being added when the burger is flipped. Due to high fat content, the pan is not oiled for the burger, and the fat released in cooking the meat is enough to keep the onions from sticking. The other cooking is one of curried cauliflower, prepared by stir-frying the cauliflower in 1 T oil, then adding the curry spices for the last couple of minutes of cooking. When it was prepared, the addition of the spices soaked up all of the oil in the pan, causing everything to stick. This was repaired by adding 1 T oil and mixing.

Suppose we have frying onions as a goal; furthermore, we generate this recipe from the onion-frying subplan in fried-burger-and-onions— as in the other burger-and-onions, we separate this meal into a frying of a hamburger and a frying of onions (based on a non-interfering subgoals) with a number of shared steps that could be separated. The generated recipe is to slice onions, heat pan, add onions, stir, remove. When executed, however, the stir fails as the onions stick to the pan. We use the cauliflower case to repair the plan by adding oil, and note two possible explanations for the failure; some subgoal interaction in the original cooking (which is true here), and variation among onions. It doesn't matter that we cannot tell which is which; whenever we fry onions in the absence of meat, we will be prepared to add oil.

4   The role of execution in a CB planner

The purpose of planning is to produce instructions to be executed by some actor. The instructions are a sequence of primitive actions, including information about timing and how progress should be monitored. The information used in this process by a case-based planner is experiential; we get plans for new situations based on what we did in other situations. The subsequent execution of that plan adds an experience to our knowledge base, as well as providing information for evaluating and improving our ability to plan. In COOKIE, the plans given to the execution monitor are episodic representations of "doing it again"; the execution monitor controls execution, monitors expectations, and provides feedback useful in subsequent planning. In this context, plan generation and execution can be considered as mappings: from an episode to expected behavior for generation, and from expected behavior to a real episode for execution.

From episode to expected behavior

Plans are generated in a direct case-based planner by adapting episodes— transformations are performed on episodes until they match the goals and constraints specified. Basic assumptions in case-based reasoning are that performing the same actions on the same objects would produce identical results, and there exist transformations that are equivalence preserving in terms of those results—if we perform such transformations on these actions, objects, and results, then perform the actions on the objects, we get these results. The adapted episodes can be seen as "expected episodes", and describe the expected behavior of reproducing the described episode.

From expected behavior to episode

Knowing the expected behavior simplifies execution monitoring to a great degree. The actions and conditions in the expected behavior become observed actions and conditions in the episode when execution is done, as long as all expectations are met. If expectations are not met, the anomalies become part of the new episode, and the planner may be invoked to repair the plan. The role of the execution monitor, then, is to cause actions to be initiated at the expected times (if possible), monitor all of the conditions given in the episode, and signal expectation failures back to the planner for possible repair. Expectation failures are labeled as such in the new episode, which will also include any response to that failure.

Execution in COOKIE

Execution monitoring in COOKIE is provided by DEFARGE[1], a dedicated execution monitor that provides the mechanisms for executing plans, adds episodes to COOKIE's knowledge base, interacts with the real-time repair capabilities of COOKIE, and provides feedback to be used in further planning. DEFARGE provides the mapping from expected to real episodes: it causes plans to be executed by side-effect. Its input is the episodic representation of the plan—an adaptation of a real episode. It converts the propositions in the episode into a set of external actions to be directed; starting events, terminating events, and testing conditions, which are assigned expected times based on the times in the episode. In execution, DEFARGE gives instructions and receives information from the external cook. As events terminate and condition tests are reported, the appropriate propositions (with the actual time information) are added to the episode description. If a test results in an anomaly (any expectation failure), the information is forwarded to the planner which can prescribe repairs to be executed and associated with the anomaly.

Since DEFARGE can extract the appropriate tests and expectation from what it is given by the generator, the amount of reasoning done by the monitor is limited. This is by design—the role of the monitor is to extract the necessary information from the plan, interact with the user and planner, do the necessary accounting (keeping track of time, propagating constraints), and convert the execution trace to a usable episode. The relative simplicity is enabled by the detailed information in the episodic representation of the generated plan.

---

[1]Named for the notorious Mme. Defarge, who monitored quite a few executions [Dickens, 1859].

5 Conclusions

We do not claim that direct use is the only way to use experiential knowledge; it is, however, one that can be used with minimal domain knowledge and computational overhead. It provides a computational framework for reasoning in domains where we don't have detailed, well structured information and causal models. There is strong evidence that human memory is at least partially organized around episodes, and that experience can be used in the future in ways unimagined at the time.

We have only discussed one role for abstraction—in plan recognition we use subplan schemas to ascribe actions to particular goals and to separate out parts of episodes for later use. Most CBR systems, by contrast, have abstraction hierarchies as a central feature of the work. In HYPO, for example, legal cases are viewed at a number of different levels of abstraction [Ashley, 1988]. In CHEF (as in most CBR systems), allowable transformations are implicit in the abstraction hierarchy for objects (allowing transformation between objects that share an ancestor in the isa hierarchy). We do not dispute the usefulness of such abstractions; we simply claim that they are inadequate. Unless we have precomputed all useful abstractions, direct case manipulation is still necessary. Similarly, unless we can somehow encode transformations as a hierarchy that reflects the context-sensitivity of their applicability, we will need to deal with explicit transformation sets.

References

[Ashley, 1988] Ashley, Kevin D. (1988), Modeling legal argument: reasoning with cases and hypotheticals. Tech. Rept. 88-01, University of Massachusetts Department of Computer Science.

[Dickens, 1859] Dickens, Charles (1859). *A Tale of Two Cities*. Oxford University Press.

[Kolodner, 1987] Kolodner, Janet L. (1987). Capitalizing on failure through case-based inference. In *Proc. of the 9th Annual Conference of the Cognitive Science Society*, pp 691–696.

[McCartney and Sanders, 1990] McCartney, Robert, and Kathryn E. Sanders (1990). The case for cases: a call for purity in case-based reasoning. In *Proc. of the AAAI Spring Symposium on Case-based Reasoning*.

[Hammond, 1988] Hammond, Kristian J. (1988), Case-based planning. In *Proc. of a Workshop on Case-based Reasoning*, pp. 17–20.

[Hammond, 1986] Hammond, Kristian J. (1986), Case-based planning: and integrated theory of planning, learning, and memory. Tech. Rept. YALEU/CSD/RR 488. Yale University Department of Computer Science.

[Kass and Leake, 1988] Kass, Alex M. and David B. Leake (1988). Case-based reasoning applied to constructing explanations. In *Proc. of a Workshop on Case-based Reasoning*, pp. 190–208.

[Riesbeck and Schank, 1989] Riesbeck, Christopher K., and Roger C. Schank (1989). *Inside Case-based Reasoning*. Lawrence Erlbaum Associates. Hillsdale, NJ.

[Schank, 1982] Schank, Roger C. (1982). *Dynamic Memory: a Theory of Learning in Computers and People*. Cambridge University Press.

An Internal Contradiction of Case-Based Reasoning[1]

David B. Skalak[2]
Department of Computer and Information Science
University of Massachusetts
Amherst, MA 01003
SKALAK@cs.umass.edu

Abstract

In a case-based reasoning system, one simple approach to assessment of similarity of cases to a given problem situation is to create a linear ordering of the cases by similarity according to each relevant domain factor. Using Arrow's Impossibility Theorem, a result from social welfare economics, a paradox is uncovered in the attempt to find a consistent overall ordering of cases by similarity that satisfactorily reflects these individual rankings. The implications of the paradox for case-based reasoning are considered.

1. Introduction

1.1 Framework for this Paper

This paper attempts to demonstrate that one underlying model of case-based reasoning ("CBR") is internally contradictory. This model, called the "Simple Model" here, assumes that cases can be ranked in order of their similarity to a current problem situation. The conclusion to be drawn from this work is that the model of CBR used by a system must take care to avoid the assumptions that give rise to the contradiction, or must use an entirely different approach, such as one based on numeric weighting of cases, which has its own well-trodden pitfalls.

The path to this result is somewhat circuitous, for it involves translating a result, Arrow's Impossibility Theorem[3], from social welfare economics to CBR. But first as background, case-based reasoning is briefly reviewed, and the problematic model is then presented. An example of a possible CBR contradiction is given.

The first leg of this circuitous path is the presentation of Arrow's Theorem in its original form. In broad scope, the Theorem yields a contradiction that arises in the following circumstances. A group of people rank their preferences for some set of candidates or goods or some other resource. The goal is to derive an overall ranking for the group of individuals as a whole that consistently reflects the individual rankings. Certain apparently reasonable conditions are placed on the compromise ordering and how it should reflect the individual rankings. The Theorem's conclusion is that it is impossible within certain limitations to create a preference procedure to derive the "social" ordering from the individual rankings.

Arrow's original, surprising result is phrased in terms of an "individual" "preferring" one "social state" to another. To establish the contradiction for CBR, it

[1] This work was supported in part by the National Science Foundation, contract IRI-8908481, the Office of Naval Research under a University Research Initiative Grant, contract N00014-87-K-0238, and a grant from GTE Laboratories, Inc., Waltham, Mass.

[3] Arrow originally referred to the theorem as the General Possibility Theorem (Arrow 1963). Consistent with common usage, I have called it the "Impossibility" Theorem.

will remain to show that Arrow's Theorem can be duly translated to the realm of CBR and the Simple Model. The term "individual" in the Theorem is translated into "domain factor", "preference" into "ranks as more similar to the current problem case", and "social state" into "case". Translated in this way, the conditions of Arrow's Theorem are shown to apply. Thus the conclusion of the Theorem is yielded: that there exists no function to achieve a consistent overall ranking of cases by each individual factor that appropriately reflects the individual rankings. After this result is established, its implications for CBR are discussed.

1.2 Case-Based Reasoning

Case-Based Reasoning is using past problem-solving episodes to analyze or solve a new problem. If necessary, a previous analysis or solution will be adapted to reflect the differences between the new and old cases.

CBR involves several steps, including: (1) accept a new experience and analyze it in order to retrieve relevant cases from case memory; (2) order the retrieved cases to select a set of "best" cases from which to craft a solution or analysis of the problem case; (3) derive the solution by modifying that of the most similar case or formulate an analysis of the problem case in view of the most "on-point" cases; and (4) optionally, store the newly solved or interpreted case in case memory, adjusting indices into memory as appropriate.

1.3 The Relevance of this Result to CBR

When confronted with a situation where a variety of conflicting factors are at work, one may appeal to CBR. In this circumstance, it is difficult to assign blame or credit for the results of a case to a single factor or even to cluster of them. Cases may be viewed from conflicting vantage points that can point to different results (Ashley 1989b). When viewed from the perspective of one factor, one case may seem to be the most similar; another factor may point to another case as being more salient. Or, in a mixed paradigm system or blackboard architecture that uses a variety of knowledge sources to suggest lists of similar cases, those knowledge sources will probably yield different rankings of cases by similarity. *Cf.* (Rissland and Skalak 1989). According to Arrow's Theorem, duly translated, no collective ranking process that meets its preconditions can take the linear orderings of cases by the individual knowledge sources and combine them into a consistent collective similarity ordering.

In the variety of CBR sometimes called "problem-solving" CBR, one case is usually selected as the most similar, and its solution (plan, diagnosis, *etc.*) is modified to solve the original problem posed. If modifying that case turns into a dead end, the next most similar case may be processed and its solution modified. In the variety of CBR referred to as "interpretive" or "precedent-based" CBR, cases are usually presented in an ordering according to their similarity to the current problem case. Both varieties of CBR require that cases be ranked by similarity in some fashion. That different rankings are available to the system, either by virtue of distinct knowledge sources or contrasting factor vantage points, necessitates collecting these rankings into a single ranking. Applying Arrow's Theorem to a simple CBR model suggests that this attempt to construct an overall ordering may involve internal contradictions. Either no procedure will be able to create such a ranking, or we shall have to give up some of the requirements normally placed on the individual rankings and how the collective ranking is to reflect them.

2. The Simple CBR Model

2.1 Description of the Model

Consider the following simplified model of CBR, here called the "Simple Model" . We are given a set of cases, a set of relevant factors, and a problem case called the "current fact situation". The relevant factors have been pre-designated to determine case similarity and to serve as indices for retrieval of similar cases from the case knowledge base. In this model, the goal of CBR is to rank the cases in a linear ordering in view of their "overall similarity" to the current fact situation.

The Simple Model's apparent solution is to begin by linearly ordering the cases according to similarity with respect to each individual factor. "Ties" are permitted: two or more cases may be equally similar according to a factor. Once these factor-by-factor rankings are assembled, one could try to combine each factor's ranking of cases into a single ordering by overall similarity. I attempt to demonstrate that it is not possible to produce this overall ranking within certain apparently reasonable constraints.

The objection may be made that this Simple Model is unrealistic --- no current CBR system in practice employs it. Several responses to this objection may be made. (1) Elements of the Simple Model are present in some systems, as discussed in Section 5.2. (2) If the Simple Model is not used in its pure form, it may be useful to say why this obvious approach has been avoided. (3) The relevance of the Simple Model may be seen more realistically in the context of a blackboard implementation of CBR, where a number of knowledge sources are available to rank cases. It is likely that individual knowledge sources would suggest contrasting similarity rankings of cases. One would think therefore not in terms of factors ranking cases, but in terms of knowledge sources (that may themselves consider a variety of factors) ranking cases. (4) The factor-by-factor approach is found elsewhere in artificial intelligence. For a recent example see the analysis of the Independent Credit Assignment assumption by Subramanian and Feigenbaum (1986).

2.2 An Example of a Similarity Contradiction

Suppose we have the following three cases and a current fact situation ("CFS") dealing with whether the law permits a driver to overtake an automobile traveling in the same direction. Let us suppose also we have identified three factors as relevant:

1. type of pavement center line (with values none, dotted, single, and double),
2. visibility (poor, fair, good), and
3. distance from position of car to oncoming car in the opposite lane (in feet).

Case	Line	Visibility	Distance	Result
CFS	single	good	800	?
A	single	poor	900	No
B	dotted	good	1000	Yes
C	none	fair	850	Yes

Then, from the point of view of the --

line factor, case A is more similar to the CFS than case B, and case B is more similar to the CFS than case C (write: ApB & BpC, where the relation p may be thought of as "is preferred to");

visibility factor, case B is more similar than case C, and case C is more similar than case A (BpC & CpA);

distance factor, case C is more similar than case A, and case A is more similar than case B (CpA & ApB).

A majority of the factors --- two out of three in each instance --- indicate that case A is more similar than case B and that case B is more similar than case C (ApB & BpC). By transitivity of the preference relation, a majority of the factors

111

therefore would say that **case A** is more similar than **case** C (ApC). However, a majority of the factors (visibility and distance) actually rank **case C** as more similar than **case A** (CpA). This is a contradiction. This theoretical contradiction presents a practical quandary for a driver's selection of the most similar case in view of the opposite results of **case A** and **case C**. In **case A** passing is not permitted; in c a s e **C**, it is.

3. Arrow's Impossibility Theorem

The above case-based example is actually a reflection of a voting paradox known for over a century (Nanson 1882). Paradoxes like this one have given rise to research by Kenneth Arrow to investigate the conditions under which the ranking by individuals of preferences for "social choices" (for example, for political candidates) may fail to yield a satisfactory "social" (collective) ranking that reflects the individual preference orderings.

Two conditions are placed on the notion of a preference to ensure its accordance with its common meaning. A *preference* (a) must be transitive, and (b) must permit the comparison of any two choices; that is, for any two choices x and y, (x is preferred to y) or (y is preferred to x), or we are indifferent as between x and y (Arrow 1963).

Arrow's Impossibility Theorem on the collective ranking of social choices by individuals is stated in terms of five conditions that might reasonably be placed on a social preference ordering. These conditions are quoted below directly from (Mueller 1979) citing (Vickrey 1960) and are more transparent than Arrow's original renderings. The exception may be Condition IV, which is stated in a more plausible way by Arrow's original work and I have used that formulation[4] (Arrow 1963). The Theorem denies the existence of a *social welfare function*, defined as "a process or rule which, for each set of individual orderings $R_1,....R_n$ for alternative social states (one ordering for each individual), states a corresponding social ordering of alternative social states, R". (Arrow 1963, p.23). A *social state* is a catch-all term that would include such diverse persons and objects as political candidates, governmental forms, welfare entitlement schemes and access to certain goods.

The five Preconditions to Arrow's Impossibility Theorem:

I. Unanimity (The Pareto Postulate). If an individual preference is unopposed by any other contrary preference of any other individual, this preference is preserved in the social ordering.

II. Nondictatorship. No individual enjoys a position such that whenever he expresses a preference between any two alternatives and all other individuals express the opposite preference, his preference is always preserved in the social ordering.

III. Transitivity. The social welfare function gives a consistent ordering of all feasible alternatives. [That is, the social ranking must be transitive.]

IV. Range. (Unrestricted domain). Among all the alternatives there is a set S of three alternatives such that, for any set of individual orderings $T_1,....,$ T_n of the alternatives in S, there is an admissible set of individual orderings $R_1,...., R_n$ of all the alternatives such that, for each individual i, $x R_i y$ if and only if $x T_i y$ for x and y in S.

---

[4]Mueller's statement of Condition IV posits the existence of a "universal" alternative, which assumption he admits is not crucial (Mueller 1979, p.186).

V . Independence of Irrelevant Alternatives. The social choice between any two alternatives must depend on the orderings of the individuals over only these two alternatives, and not on their orderings over any other alternatives.

Arrow's Impossibility Theorem:
No social welfare function satisfies conditions I through V.

The reader is referred to (Arrow 1963) and (Mueller 1979) for proofs of the Theorem.

Arrow's original rendering of the Range Condition may benefit from a little explication. It requires that "every logically possible set of individual orderings of a certain set S of 3 alternatives can be obtained from some admissible[5] set of individual orderings of all alternatives." (Arrow 1963, p.24). The assumption assures that the collective, overall ranking process is not performed in a way that necessarily rules out some possible collective orderings (Mueller 1979). The purpose of the condition is to ensure that the social welfare function is not biased against certain rankings.

4. The Application of Arrow's Theorem to the Simple CBR Model
To establish the result of this paper, it remains to translate Arrow's Theorem from the realm of individual preferences for social states and social welfare functions into the language of CBR: the language of domain factors, similarity, and case ranking procedures.

Let CFS be a given problem case. Instead of saying that an individual prefers one social state to another, say that a *factor prefers* Case 1 to Case 2 if considering that factor alone would lead one to say that Case 1 is "more similar" than Case 2 to the problem CFS. A factor may rank two (or more) cases as equally similar -- in the language of public choice, the factor is *indifferent to* them. This definition of preference may be seen to satisfy the above two criteria placed on a preference. The translation of "social welfare function" is to the procedure that ranks cases by overall similarity from the factors' similarity orderings.

It can be seen that each of the five conditions is reasonably imposed in the translated setting provided by the Simple CBR Model.

For example, the translated Unanimity Condition would state: if a factor's preference between two cases (*i.e.*, that factor's favoring one case as being more similar than another case to a problem situation) is unopposed by any other contrary preference of any other factor, this preference is preserved in the overall ranking of cases. If each factor says that one case is more similar than another to a problem situation, then the collective ordering must preserve this similarity rating.

The Nondictatorship Condition ensures that no factor has so much importance attached to it that it alone can veto the similarity assessment of the remaining factors.

The Transitivity Condition requires that the collective ranking of cases by similarity be transitive. (This condition appears reasonable at first glance, but may be suspect in some applications.)

The Range Condition is perhaps the most opaque, but seems to provide the "twist" that makes the proofs of the Theorem work. In the CBR realm, it requires that there are three cases (A, B and C) that have the property that in the overall ranking any of the relative similarity rankings of those cases is possible for some conceivable

---

[5] An *admissible* set of orderings is a set that is in the domain of the social welfare function, the process that performs the collective ranking.

individual rankings of the cases. This condition requires that these three cases may be ordered in any way, as long as the individuals rankings require it. The upshot of the Range Condition is that the rankings are unbiased to the extent that they do not rule out the possibility of any relative ordering of the three cases. Any of case A, B or C may be the most on point; any may be the least on point. Their relative similarity depends solely on what the individual factors require.

The last condition, the Independence of Irrelevant Alternatives, can also be seen to reasonably apply to the CBR realm. The overall relative similarity of two cases depends only on each factor's ranking of those two cases and not the factor rankings of other cases. If case A is more similar overall than case B, that result does not depend on the individual factor rankings of any other case.

The power of the Arrow's result for public choice is partly due to the self-evident nature of its preconditions. The conditions retain their manifest attraction when translated to the CBR realm. Once one is assured that the five conditions are met, the Theorem's original proofs apply (duly translated), and we have the

Impossibility Result for Case-Based Reasoning: Under these assumptions, there is no process that performs the collective ranking of cases by similarity that satisfies Conditions I to V.

5.   Limitations and Implications of the Result

5.1 Arrow's Assumption of No Cardinal Utilities
There is a somewhat obscured assumption to Arrow's results that is not contained in his statement of the Theorem, but is referred to elsewhere in (Arrow 1963). In his own work on social welfare functions, Arrow has assumed that one does not rely on "cardinal, interpersonal comparisons of utility" to obtain the social ranking (Arrow 1963, p.9). In other words, Arrow posits that one may not assign numerical values to gauge the strength of the individual preferences, and use a numerical social welfare function to yield a collective preference ranking for all the individuals. This assumption is rooted in his expressed desire to avoid the difficulties created by assigning numerical values to personal preferences and the conceptual ambiguity of comparing degrees of preference across individuals.

The upshot of Arrow's assumption for the Simple CBR Model is that the Theorem assumes that we are not using cardinal assessments of case similarity for each factor, and then applying an evaluation function to combine these numerical assessments of similarity into an overall ranking. One such constraint is a proscription upon using cardinal numbers to gauge the degree of each factor's preferences. Only ordinal preferences are permitted by the Simple Model. That is, it can be said whether one case is more similar to than another to the current fact situation, but no numerical value can be used to quantify the relative similarities of the cases to the current problem. In particular, this model would not permit using a numerical evaluation function that weights each factor's cardinal preference for a case and sums those weighted preferences into a real number that reflects the collective preference for that case.

Following Arrow's interdiction against cardinal utilities is reasonable in many CBR domains. Numerical weighting schemes for credit assignment may be avoided in view of a litany of conceptual and pragmatic objections against their use. See, *e.g.*, (Ashley 1989a), (Ashley and Rissland 1988), (Kolodner 1988). A number of these objections are collected in (Ashley 1990): (1) lack of cognitive validity for many domains and domain experts; (2) uncertainty and arbitrariness in weight assignment and lack of an authoritative source of numerical weights, with the consequent disagreement among experts as to specific weights; (3) the failure of static weights to reflect the context-dependent importance of factors; (4) pitfalls of a premature commitment to a weighting scheme; and (5) reduction of information into a single number entails a representation that loses information that might otherwise be used to advantage.

5.2 Three Weighting Models

Ashley (1989a) identifies three models of factor weighting that underlie current CBR systems: numerical, precedent-based, and heuristic. The consequences for each of these models of the Impossibility Result are discussed below.

One way for a CBR system to avoid the paradox of the theorem is to use numerical functions to assess case similarity. See, *e.g.*, (Kibler and Aha 1987). Numerical weights may be appealed to in domains where an analytic or statistically-based model is accessible. See (Ashley 1989a). In domains where numeric weighting of factors is reasonable, the Nondictatorship Condition of the Theorem may be violated, however. A factor with a sufficiently large weight may determine the outcome of the similarity ranking, regardless of the rankings by lesser weighted factors. However, an evaluation function that is used merely for its ordinal, and not its cardinal, properties --- used just to rank cases by similarity in a total order --- may be subject to the strictures of the Theorem nonetheless.

In some areas of application, models of any sort are simply not available, and one must appeal to previous cases to assess the relative importance of factors (Ashley and Rissland 1988). The lack of some domain models is apparently a classical impetus for the use and development of case-based reasoning techniques in the first place. In such applications of CBR, one must rely merely on the patterns of combinations of factors that have appeared in previous cases to perform credit assignment. It is difficult to identify the factor(s) that determine the results in such instances, and one must avoid embracing a ranking scheme that reduces to a voting arrangement. In such precedent-based schemes where no numeric or heuristic weighting is available, special care must be taken to avoid the siren song of the Theorem. The scheme used must violate at least one of the Theorem's preconditions, explicit or implicit, or be potentially subject to the paradox. In the work of Rissland and Ashley, for example, (a) cases are ordered by clusters of factors and not by individual factors, (b) that ordering is partial and not total, and (c) the Range Condition may not be satisfied.

The appeal to an analytic model provides an intermediate point between numeric weights and the assessment of the importance of factors based on precedent. Where a causal or other analytic model is available, it may be used to rank goals and the features that influence their attainment (Koton 1988), (Bareiss 1987), (Kolodner 1985), (Hammond 1987). See generally (Ashley 1989a). Where factors can be ranked in a preference ordering according to their importance, the Theorem's paradox is circumvented through the violation of the Nondictatorship Condition. The similarity ranking may be dominated by the most important feature. For example, Kolodner's PARADYME system avoids the paradox by using an ordered set of preference heuristics to choose the most useful cases from those retrieved from a previous partial matching (Kolodner 1989). In general, systems that use a model to rank goals (and the factors that influence goal attainment) may avoid the potential for internal contradiction by avoiding the Theorem through the violation of the Nondictatorship Condition.

6. Conclusion

CBR is inherently subject to a dilemma. On one hand, it is problematic to assign numerical values and weights to similarity preferences, and thereby hide the resulting "value" judgements in trading off disparate and fundamentally

115

incommensurate factors. On the other hand, one must avoid embracing a symbolic or implicit weighting scheme that can be construed as a voting procedure of the sort here presented with its attendant paradoxes.

References

Arrow, K. J. (1963). Social Choice and Individual Values. Cowles Foundation for Research in Economics at Yale University. New Haven, Yale University Press.

Ashley, K. D. (1989a). "Assessing Similarities Among Cases." Proceedings of the Second DARPA Case-Based Reasoning Workshop, May 1989, Pensacola Beach, FL.

Ashley, K. D. (1989b). "Toward a Computational Theory of Arguing with Precedents: Accommodating Multiple Interpretations of Cases." In Proceedings of the Second Annual Conference on AI and Law, June 1989, Vancouver, B.C.

Ashley, K. D. (1990). Modelling Legal Argument: Reasoning with Cases and Hypotheticals. Cambridge, MA, MIT Press (in press).

Ashley, K. D. and Rissland, E.L. (1988). "Waiting on Weighting: A Symbolic Least Commitment Approach." Proceedings AAAI-88, American Association for Artificial Intelligence, August 1988, Minneapolis.

Bareiss, E. R., Porter, B.W., and Wier, C. C. (1987). "Protos: An Exemplar-Based Learning Apprentice." In Proceedings of the Fourth International Workshop on Machine Learning, pages 12--23, June 1987, University of California at Irvine.

Hammond, K. J. (1987). "Explaining and Repairing Plans that Fail". In Proceedings IJCAI-87, International Joint Conferences on Artificial Intelligence, Inc., August 1987, Milan.

Kibler, D. and Aha, D.W. (1987). "Learning Representative Exemplars of Concepts: An Initial Case Study." Proceedings of the Fourth International Workshop on Machine Learning, pages 24--30, June 1987, University of California at Irvine.

Kolodner, J. L. and Simpson, R. L., and Sycara-Cyranski, K. (1985). "A Process Model of Case-Based Reasoning in Problem Solving." In Proceedings IJCAI-85, International Joint Conferences on Artificial Intelligence, Inc., August 1985, Los Angeles.

Kolodner, J. L. (1988). "Retrieving Events from a Case Memory: A Parallel Implementation." Proceedings of the DARPA Case-Based Reasoning Workshop, May 1988, Clearwater Beach, FL.

Kolodner, J. L. (1989). "Judging Which is the `Best' Case for a Case-Based Reasoner." Proceedings of the DARPA Case-Based Reasoning Workshop, May 1989, Pensacola Beach, FL.

Koton, P. (1988). "Reasoning about Evidence in Causal Explanations." In Proceedings of the First DARPA Case-Based Reasoning Workshop, May 1988, Clearwater Beach, FL.

Mueller, D. C. (1979). Public Choice. Cambridge Surveys of Economic Literature. Cambridge, England, Cambridge University Press.

Nanson, E. J. (1882). Transaction and Proceedings of the Royal Society of Victoria. 19: 197-240.

Rissland, E. L. and Skalak, D. B. (1989). "Combining Case-Based and Rule-Based Reasoning: A Heuristic Approach." Proceedings IJCAI-89, International Joint Conferences on Artificial Intelligence, Inc., August 1989, Detroit.

Subramanian, D. and Feigenbaum, J. (1986). "Factorization in Experiment Generation." In Proceedings AAAI-86, American Association for Artificial Intelligence, August 1986, Philadelphia.

Vickrey, W. (1960). "Utility, Strategy, and Social Decision Rules." Quart. J. Econ. 74(Nov.): 507-35.

Qualitative Reasoning about the Geometry of Fluid Flow

Hyun-Kyung Kim

Qualitative Reasoning Group
Beckman Institute, University of Illinois

Abstract: Understanding the interaction between dynamics and geometry is crucial to capturing commonsense physics. This paper presents a qualitative analysis of the direction of fluid flow. This analysis is dependent on qualitative descriptions of the surface geometry of rigid bodies in contact with the fluid and a pressure change in fluid. The key problem in designing an intelligent system to reason about fluid motion is how to partition the fluid at an appropriate level of representation. The basic idea of our approach is to incrementally generate the qualitatively different parts of fluid. We do this by dynamically analyzing the interaction of geometry and pressure disturbance. Using this technique, we can derive all possible fluid flows.

1 Introduction

Understanding the interaction between dynamics and geometry is crucial to capturing commonsense physics. Without spatial reasoning, dynamics cannot fully explain the physical world. For example, applying the same force to different points on an object can cause dramatically different behaviors. Without geometric information, these behaviors would be difficult to predict.

Unfortunately, the general spatial reasoning problem is intractable. Thus, recent research has focused on more constrained problems such as motion in limited domains [2,3], mechanical mechanisms [7,8] and fluid ontologies [1,6]. The studies dealing with mechanical mechanisms and motion focus only on rigid objects, ignoring the motion of fluid. In addition, the fluid ontology research is insufficient to fully explain fluid behavior. Two basic approaches to fluid ontology are *contained-stuff* ontology and *piece-of-stuff* ontology [1,6]. Neither of these approaches suffices to explain the geometry of fluid motion. Suppose we want to explain the motion of the gas in a piston when the valve in the middle of the right side is open and the pressure inside the piston is greater than the pressure outside. Since *contained-stuff* ontology treats the gas in the piston as one object, it is impossible to reason about different flow directions in the various parts of the piston. Similarly, it appears to be impossible to consider the motion of every piece of the gas. People do not seem to use either ontology to explain this problem. However, people can reason about the gas near the top surface moving downward to the right and the gas near the bottom surface moving upward to the right, etc.

This paper presents a technique for reasoning about the direction of fluid flow in two-dimensions using incremental generation of the *places* in space. We extend the work of [5,8,3] on places—from the rigid body domain onto the fluid domain. Since fluid motion is determined by the pressure difference and the geometry of surface contact with the fluid, we assume qualitative descriptions of these two terms as input. The theory predicts an equivalence class of places that are created based on the qualitative behavior of the fluid. In addition, it describes the flow in each of these places.

Section 2 presents the theory for reasoning about flow direction in qualitative and geometric terms, given a pressure change and surface geometry. The fluid are partitionied so each part has the same qualitative fluid motion. Section 3 explains how envisionments qualitatively simulate the behaviors of fluid in each part. In section 4 we summarize our results and discuss possible extensions to our theory.

2 A Qualitative Theory of Fluid Motion

The key problem in commonsense reasoning about fluid motion is how to partition the fluid at an appropriate level of representation. Our approach partitions the fluid into a set of *places* by reasoning about pressure wave propagation and geometry. These two factors determine the flow direction. We show how to decompose space incrementally into places.

2.1 Qualitative Direction

In spatial reasoning, the concept of direction is essential in describing the position, force, and motion [8]. We assume a single global reference frame. This reference frame can be translated but not rotated. In our theory, direction is represented by a qualitative vector [8] and qualitative vector arithmetic is used to compute the directions. In our 2D space representation, the first and second components of a qualitative vector represent the qualitative direction along the x-axis and y-axis, respectively. To represent the x-axis direction, we use "+" for "right" and "−" for "left" and "0" for center. For the y-axis, "+" is used for "up" and "−" for "down" and "0" for center. For example, (−−) indicates the vector lies to the lower left of some reference frame.

Definition 1 (Inversion) *Inversion(v)* is the qualitative vector v rotated by 180 degrees.

Definition 2 (Open-Half-Plane) *Open-Half-Plane(v)* are the vectors whose vector dot product with v is "+".

2.2 Rigid Object Representation

Rigid objects are represented by their surfaces in contact with the fluid. In our 2D space, a surface is represented as a line segment. For each surface, we represent the direction of the line segment as the position of one end-point relative to the other. (We define end-points as the points where the line segment meets the neighbors.) In general, the relative position can be defined for any two points:

Definition 3 (Relative-Position) *Relative-Position(p1,p2)* is the qualitative vector which represents the direction from point p2 to point p1.

Consider a surface with end-points p1 and p2, which are connected to other adjacent surfaces. The direction of the surface is represented by Relative-Position(p2,p1).

Information about the relative position can be propagated using transitivity:

Law 1 (Transitivity of Relative-Position) For any points p1,p2, and p3, Relative-Position (p1,p3) is computed by adding given values Relative-Position(p1,p2) and Relative-Position (p2,p3).

The surface normal represents the direction which points from the surface into fluid.

Definition 4 (Surface Normal) *Surface-Normal(s)* is the qualitative vector which represents the surface normal of the surface s.

Definition 5 (Surf-Rel-Pos) For any two adjacent surfaces s1 and s2 whose end-points are (p1,p2) and (p2,p3), *Surf-Rel-Pos(s1,s2)* represents Relative-Position(p1,p3). This represents the relative direction of two adjacent surfaces.

2.3 Fluid

Unlike a solid, a fluid moves and deforms continuously as long as a pressure difference exists. Its shape is determined by the container. These properties of fluid make them difficult to individuate in a reasoning system. In general, people do not reason about the individual molecules of fluids, but rather they focus on the collection of molecules within fluids.

Pressure Wave Propagation (PWP): When a pressure disturbance occurs in a compressible fluid, the disturbance travels with a velocity of sound. For example, if we throw a stone into the pond in rest, we can see the circular wave-fronts on the surface are diverging from the source. If the disturbance is due to the lower pressure, then an *expansion* wave is propagated. If it is due to the higher pressure, then a *compression* wave occurs. The pressure wave moves from the source toward the wave-fronts and it is perpendicular to the wave-fronts. As the pressure wave is propagated through a still fluid, the fluid properties (i.e., pressure, temperature, and density and so on) change and it start to move. As a compression wave is propagated, the fluid molecules have a velocity which has the same direction as the wave propagation. On the other hand, when an expansion wave travels, the fluid has a velocity which has the opposite direction of the wave (i.e., toward the

118

source of the disturbance). The induced velocity of the fluid by wave propagation is much slower than the wave propagation.

Definition 6 (Prop-Constraint) Suppose a surface s is in contact with the fluid. *Prop-Constraint* (s,d) is *true* when PWP is prevented in direction d near s.

Law 2 (Surface-Constraint) Suppose s is in contact with the fluid and its surface normal is sn. Then the pressure wave cannot propagate from the surface to the fluid. Thus for every d which belongs to Open-Half-Plane(sn), Prop-Constraint(s,d) is *true*.

Continuous Change (CN): We assume the flow is smooth and steady (*laminar*). When flow is not laminar but fluctuating and agitated (*turbulent*), it is impossible to explain the behavior. Even in fluid mechanics, no general analysis of fluid motion in turbulence yet exists and there may never be. People also have difficulty explaining the direction of the turbulent flow. In laminar flow, the changes of properties are continuous. To support laminar flow, we assume the surface is smooth and the changes in surface are not abrupt.

2.4 Place Generation

In FROB [3], given a geometric description of the surface, the places needed to envision the possible motions of a ball are generated by the constraints of geometry of the surface and gravity. Since the gravity constraint is the same everywhere, space can be divided without regard to the neighbors. However, since a direction of PWP can keep changing by the surface geometry of rigid body as it propagates, the place cannot be generated without considering interaction between these two. Even though two given spaces have the same geometry, they can be partitioned in completely different ways with different directions of pressure wave.

In fluid motion, qualitatively different parts have different fluid directions since the pressure wave arrives from different directions. Thus *places* in our reasoning problem should be distinguished by difference of the direction of pressure wave in each part. Continuous interaction of pressure wave and geometry suggests our place generation should be incremental as the pressure wave propagates from the source of disturbance.

Definition 7 (Place) A *Place* is defined by its boundaries (i.e., left, right, up, and down) and the direction of the pressure wave and the direction of the induced velocity. Given a place P, *Pres-Wave*(P) returns the the direction of pressure wave in P. The boundaries represent the adjacent places or surfaces of a given place.

Definition 8 (Place) *Place*(s) maps from a surface s to the *place* in which s is a boundary.

Law 3 (Connectivity of Place) Given two adjacent surfaces s1 and s2, Place(s1) and Place(s2) are also adjacent. Furthermore, since the relative direction between the two surfaces is Surf-Rel-Pos (s1,s2), Place(s1) is oriented in the same direction.

As the law of *Connectivity of Place* shows, to represents the connectivity of places, the numeric information is not used. It is represented by the relative position between the places in qualitative terms. For example, in in Figure 1 Place(s5) is located to the right of and above Place(s3) since Surf-Rel-Pos(s5,s3) is (−+).

In our approach, places are generated incrementally from the initial pressure change to the direction of PWP. For example, in Figure 1, when portal becomes open, the expansion wave is propagated from the outside to s1 and s2 first since they are close to the outside. Then places are generated around these surfaces. After that, places near s3 and s4 are generated as the pressure wave keeps traveling. Figure 1 graphically shows this incremental generation.

Since the surfaces of a rigid body can be the only explicit boundaries of the fluid from the input, our approach first generates the places near the surfaces by propagating the pressure wave across the pairs of adjacent surfaces. The places of the space which are not bounded by the surface are not generated at first since it is impossible to trace every point and give the boundary of the place. But as places around the surfaces are generated, the whole space can be covered by the property of fluid, CC. For example, in Figure 1, when places near s1, s2, s3, s4, s5,and s6 are generated, by

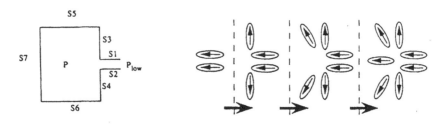

Figure 1: Incremental Place Generation in Piston-Cylinder

An oval represents the a place generated. The locations of ovals represent the connectivity of places.

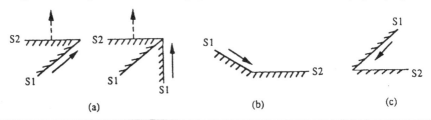

Figure 2: Examples of Forward Propagation when Surface-Normal(s2) = (0+)

(a)   (b)   (c)

CC, a place whose Pres-Wave is (−0) is generated between them .

To propagate a pressure wave across the pairs of adjacent surfaces, the first step is to determine the propagation order between the adjacent surfaces. Given a newly generated place, our system checks how the pressure wave can propagate toward adjacent surface.

Definition 9 (Forward-Propagation?) Suppose s1 and s2 are two adjacent surfaces and their end-points are (p1,p2) and (p2,p3). If the Pres-Wave(Place(s1)) belongs to Open-Half-Plane(Relative-Position(p2,p1)), then *Forward-Propagation?*(s2, s1) is *true*. Otherwise, it is *false*.

As Figure 2 shows, when Forward-Propagation?(s2, s1) is true, we can infer the source of disturbance is not closer to s2. Thus the following law is introduced.

Law 4 (Forward Propagation) Suppose Forward-Propagation?(s2, s1) is *true* and the end-points of s1 and s2 are (p1,p2) and (p2,p3). Then s2 belongs to *next wave front* of s1 if Pres-Wave(Place(s1)) belongs to Open-Half-Plane(Surface-Normal(s2)) (*blocked*) (Figure 2a) or if s2 is not blocked and Pres-Wave(Place(s1)) belongs to Open-Half-Plane(Relative-Position (p3,p2)) (*further*) (Figure 2b). s2 belongs to *same wave front* of s1 if s2 is not blocked and Pres-Wave(Place(s1)) belongs to Open-Half-Plane(Inverse(Relative-Position(p3,p2))) (Figure 2c).

Law 5 (Further Propagation) Suppose Forward-Propagation?(s2, s1) is *true*. If s2 is *further* than s1 from the source, then Pres-Wave(Place(s2)) from the source belongs to Open-Half-Plane (Pres-Wave(Place(s1))).

This law shows if PWP is not blocked, then it smoothly changes the direction across the adjacent surfaces.

A pressure wave travels from the source of disturbance to the all direction unless it is blocked by the surface of the rigid body. Unless the direction of PWP is changed by any surface, then Pres-Wave of any point can be simply inferred as direction from the source to that point. However, as the wave travels, a new source can be generated by geometry of the surfaces. Figure 3 shows how a

Figure 3: New Source

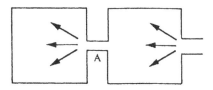

new source is generated when wave arrives at point A from the source.

We identify the cases to generate the new source.

Law 6 (New Source) Suppose Forward-Propagation?(s2, s1) is *true* and the end-points of s1 and s2 are (p1,p2) and (p2,p3). Then there are two cases to generate a new source: (1) *Blocking* -If s2 is *blocked*, then new source is generated around p2. (2) *First-Moving* - If s2 is *further* than s1 from the source, then new source might be generated in Place(s1). Since the fluid in Place(s1) starts to move earlier than that of s2, this may cause a pressure disturbance.

Once the next surface to be propagated is chosen and a new source is identified, Pres-Wave(Place (s2)) is determined by the relationship between s1 and s2, say, whether s2 is in the next wave front or the same wave front and a new source might be generated. In the case of *Blocking*, Relative-Position (p3,p2) becomes Pres-Wave(Place (s2)) since a new source of disturbance is generated near p2. In case of *First-Moving*, PWP by the original and the newly generated source should be considered. If a pressure wave can arrive at s2 without the blocking by surface, the relative direction from the source of disturbance to the surface s2 can be computed by adding that of s1(i.e., Pres-Wave(Place(s1))) and Relative-Position(p3,p2) by the law of *Transitivity of Relative-Position*. Since our approach is based on the qualitative information, every possible inference is made. Thus Relative-Position(p3,p2) and Pres-Wave(Place(s1)) + Relative-Position(p3,p2) are possible directions for Place(s2). In the case of *Same wave front*, at least the parts of s2 which are closer to s1 have the same Pres-Wave as s1. Thus places of s1 and s2 are *merged*. As we mentioned previously, during generation of the places based on this, new places may be generated by the CC.

2.5   Inferring Propagation in Backward Direction

Since our approach propagates the pressure wave across the connected surfaces and divides the space based on the places near the surface, it may not suffice given a more complicated geometry. For example, in Figure 4 when Place(s1) is generated, a new place cannot be generated any more since there is no surface adjacent to s1 in the forward direction of PWP. By the same reason, new place cannot be generated after Place(s4).

However, by the reverse inferencing of the forward PWP, this problem can be solved. As we can expect, this reverse inference may bring out ambiguities. Since our technique does not use any metric information, several possibilities can be introduced. But using some constraints due to the characteristics of fluid, we can eliminate many ambiguities.

Definition 10 (Backward-Propagation?) Suppose s1 and s2 are two adjacent surfaces and their end-points are (p1,p2) and (p2,p3). If the Pres-Wave(Place(s1)) belongs to Open-Half-Plane (Inverse(Relative-Position(p2,p1))), then *Backward-Propagation?*(s2,s1) is *true*.

If Backward-Propagation?(s2,s1) is *true*, then Forward-Propagation?(s1, s2) is *true*. Thus s1 belongs to the next wave front or the same wave front of s2. We identified how to infer whether s2 belongs to previous or same wave front of s1 from the geometric analysis for all possible cases.

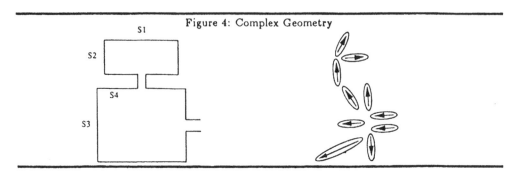

Figure 4: Complex Geometry

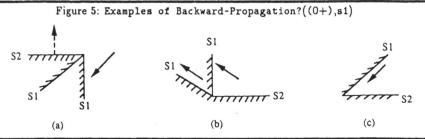

Figure 5: Examples of Backward-Propagation?((0+),s1)

(a)   (b)   (c)

Law 7 (Backward Propagation) If BackwardPropagation?(s2,s1) is *true*, the relationship between s1 and s2 in propagation of a pressure wave is: (1) *same wave front* - Pres-Wave(Place(s1)) belongs to Open-Half-Plane(Inverse(Surface-Normal(s2))); In addition, if Relative-Position (p1,p2) is equal to the Pres-Wave(Place(s1)), then this geometry can be the reverse of the *Blocking* in forwarding propagation (Figure 5a), (2) *previous wave front* - unless s2 is *same wave front* (Figure 5b).

In case of *same wave front*, Pres-Wave(Place(s2)) is computed by adding Pres-Wave(Place(s1)) and Relative-Position(p3,p2). For the reverse of the *Blocking*, Pres-Wave(Place(s2)) can be any d which belongs to Open-Half-Plane(Surface-Normal(s1)) and is not constrained can be Pres-Wave(Place(s2)). In the case of *previous wave front*, we cannot compute the possible directions but can give constraints which filter the illegal ones.

Law 8 (Source-Constraint) Suppose Backward-Propagation?(s2, s1) is *true* and the end-points of s1 and s2 are (p1,p2) and (p2,p3). Then, (1) pressure wave cannot propagate from p2 to s2. Thus for every d which belongs to Open-Half-Plane(Relative-Position(p3,p2)), Prop-Constraint(s2, d) is *true*. (2) pressure wave cannot propagate from s1 to s2. Thus by the law of *Further Propagation*, for every d which belongs to Open-Half-Plane(Inverse(Pres-Wave(Place(s1)))), Prop-Constraint (s2,d) is *true*.

By the inferring in reverse order, it is not easy to determine the direction of a possible pressure wave; there may be several possibilities. When there are several possibilities for one problem, people tend to eliminate inadequate ones by constraints to get the final solutions. By giving the *Surface* and *Source* constraints, we can filter out the illegal ones. For example, in Figure 5b, if we apply these two constraints, the only possible directions for Pres-Wave(Place(s2)) are (-0) and $(-+)$. In case of c, no direction is left after filtering out, which means Pres-Wave(Place(s1)) cannot have the direction of $(-+)$. Like in c, even if the illegal places generated by reverse inference by the lack of information, they can be filtered out later.

Figure 6: Flow and Surface Interaction

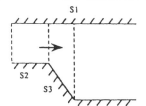

3 Envisioning Flow direction

Given an external disturbance of pressure, the space of interest is incrementally divided by connected places. Our system computes every possible combination of the places. Then the fluid in each place starts to move in the direction of a pressure wave if it is a compression wave or in the opposite direction of a pressure if it is an expansion wave. By the connectivity of the places, we can predict the next place where the fluid will go. For example, if the induced velocity of a place is (+−), then the fluid in that place will flow into the places where are located to the right or down from the place.

When the moving flow comes to the place, then the induced force by the interaction of the flow and surface of the rigid body may be applied to the flow. Figure 6 shows an example of this. Arrows represent the direction of the induced velocity. When the fluid in Place(s2) arrives at Place(s3) with the velocity (+0), it keeps going to that direction. However, the area near the surface s3 change and has less molecule of the fluid compared to the other parts of Place(s3).

Compared to the pressure disturbances in previous section, the influence of disturbance of flow and geometry is small and local since as soon as it happens the flow in that place changes the direction by the induced force. Thus its disturbance is diminished. But even if the induced force is applied to the moving flow, the flow does not immediately change the direction to the direction of the applied force since the flow already has the momentum. Since this effect is local to the flow in that place, it generates a *local* place inside the place. Its effect assumes to be limited inside of the place. Even though we can infer this region exists inside of the place, it seems to be impossible to explicitly give their boundary since its effect keeps diminishing and the interaction between the flow close to that region and that disturbance keeps changing.

Since the local place is also generated by pressure change, two kinds are possible:

Definition 11 (N-Local-Place) Suppose P represents Place(s). If the pressure adjacent to s is lower than the other part of inside of P, then *N-Local-Place*(P,s) is generated near s.

Definition 12 (P-Local-Place) Suppose P represents Place(s). If the pressure adjacent to s is higher than the other part of inside of P, then *P-Local-Place*(P,s) is generated near s.

We identified the interaction between flow and geometry as follows:

Law 9 (Pulling) Suppose P represents Place(s) and the flow with the velocity v is entering the place P. If Surface-Normal(s) belongs to Open-Half-Plane(v), then N-Local-Place(P,s) is formed. This N-Local-Place gives the force in direction of Inverse(Surface-Normal(s)) to the flow in P (i.e., it pulls the flow into the surface).

Law 10 (Pushing) Suppose P represents Place(s) and the flow with the velocity v is entering the place P. If Surface-Normal(s) belongs to Open-Half-Plane (Inverse(v)), then P-Local-Place(P,s) is formed. This P-Local-Place gives the force in direction of Surface-Normal(s) to the flow in P (i.e., it pushes the flow into the surface).

Pushing happens since the fluid molecules hits the wall and those collisions increase the pressure near the wall.

Thus fluid direction in each place can be envisioned by starting from its original place and traveling into the adjacent places with possible changing of its direction due to the surface interaction. The flow will be stop if it goes to equilibrium after moving.

4   Discussion

This paper presents a theory of geometry of fluid flow in two-dimensional space. Given qualitative descriptions of geometry and a pressure change in fluid, we can determine the possible directions of fluid motion. The interaction between the surface geometry of rigid body and pressure wave propagation is identified in our theory. This idea is being implemented.

We have only dealt with the velocity change of fluid here. We plan to expand our theory to have a complete theory for reasoning about fluid. Reasoning about the other important properties of fluid, such as pressure, temperature, and density so on is left as future work. What we hope to analyze eventually is a real system, such as internal combustion engine, which should be explained by tightly integrating dynamics and kinematic of rigid bodies and fluid. Our theory for analyzing the directions of fluid flow is one step towards that goal.

5   Acknowledgements

I would like to thank Ken Forbus for his guidance. Thanks to Janice Skorstad, John Collins, and Dennis DeCoste for proofreading and comments. This research was supported by the Office of Naval Research, Contract No. N00014-85-K-0225.

References

[1] Collins, J. "Reasoning About Fluids Via Molecular Collections", Proceedings of AAAI-87, July, 1987

[2] deKleer, J. "Qualitative and Quantitative Knowledge in Classical Mechanics", TR-352,MIT AI Lab, Cambridge,MA., 1975

[3] Forbus, K. "A Study of Qualitative and Geometric Knowledge in Reasoning about Motion", TR-615,MIT AI Lab, Cambridge,MA, 1981

[4] Forbus, K. "Qualitative Process Theory", *Artificial Intelligence*, **24**, 1984

[5] Forbus, K., Faltings, B., and Nielsen, P. "Qualitative Mechanics: A Framework", UIUCDCS-R-87-1352, University of Illinois, 1987

[6] Hayes, P. "Naive Physics 1: Ontology for Liquid" in Hobbs, J. and Moore, B. (Eds.), *Formal Theories of the Commonsense World*. Ablex Publishing Corporation, 1985

[7] Joskowicz, L. "Shape and Function in Mechanical Devices" Proceedings of AAAI-87, July, 1987

[8] Nielsen, P. "A Qualitative Approach to Mechanical Constraint" Proceedings of AAAI-88, August, 1988

[9] White, F. *Fluid Mechanics*, McGraw-Hill Book Co., 1979

Is There a Default Similarity Distance for Categories?

Yaakov Kareev and Judith Avrahami
The Goldie Rotman Center for
Cognitive Science in Education
School of Education
The Hebrew University of Jerusalem

Abstract

How do people decide whether or not an item belongs to a new category, the variability of which they do not know? We postulate that people have a default similarity distance (DSD) which they use when no other information about the variability of a category is available. To test our claim, subjects were asked to tell how they would instruct a being from another world to distinguish members of a category, by showing pictures. The categories were from different levels thus differing in variability. For highly variable categories subjects tended to present multiple positive instances (thus indicating their extraordinary variability), whereas for narrow categories they tended to present negative instances (thus explicitly delimiting them). These results indicated that a norm, relative to which additional information is supplied, lay in between. Indeed, there was a level at which subjects apparently relied on DSD, finding it sufficient to show but a single exemplar of the category. This happened with basic-level categories for 8th graders and adults and with subordinate categories for 2nd graders, thus demonstrating a developmental trend in what is considered a normal standard category.

Dealing with the classification of new items into categories, researchers have focused mainly on what it is that a new item is compared with to decide whether it belongs to a particular category or not. That entity is variously claimed to be a prototype (Rosch, 1973; Rosch & Mervis, 1975), a set of all properties of members of the category (Hayes-Roth & Hayes-Roth, 1977), or a collection of all exemplars of the category hitherto encountered (Medin & Shaffer, 1978). All theories agree, however, that the new item need not be identical to any of the above; it just has to be sufficiently similar or, in Medin and Barsalou's (1987) terms "above a certain threshold" of similarity.

It is clear that there is no single value which defines "sufficient similarity," since lower similarity is allowed between items of a higher level category than between items of a lower level category. Thus, an object has to

125

be more similar to other bulldogs to be considered a bulldog than to other animals to still be considered an animal. Indeed, Fried and Holyoak (1984) suggest that the representation of a category includes both a mean value of the category and an indication of the density of its exemplars in a feature space. This density can be viewed as the variability or similarity distance allowed and expected between exemplars of the category.

To better understand classification we still need some explanation for situations in which classification is based on a single item or in which categories are formed with no feedback. We suggest that people have a notion of a "proper" distance or "plausible" similarity which serves as the threshold mentioned above. It is a default similarity distance (DSD), used when no information about the variability of the category or about its neighboring categories is available. We expect it to be some middle value, close to the mean similarity distance of categories known to the subject. Whatever the initial similarity distance assumed, it is continuously updated following subsequent encounters with exemplars which are known to belong to the category in question and ones that do not.

To test our hypothesis that people have such a DSD we had our subjects tell how they would teach a creature from another world to identify members of a certain category by showing it pictures. If there is no DSD one would expect subjects to provide for any category not only a representative member of it but also some indication of its variability, or allowed similarity distance. If, on the other hand, subjects take DSD into account and assume others to share it, they would see a lesser need to indicate the variability of categories for which DSD is more appropriate; for those categories, they may consider it sufficient to present but one typical exemplar.

The argument, then, goes as follows: for categories whose similarity distance is close to that denoted by DSD, subjects will be more likely to be

126

satisfied with a single representative exemplar of the category than for categories where DSD is inadequate. In the latter case subjects will be more likely to provide additional information to indicate the variability of the category.

How can the variability of a category be indicated? To indicate that the variability of a category is greater than the expected value, multiple, various exemplars belonging to that category can be used. When the variability of a category is narrower than the expected value, negative exemplars can be used - items which do not belong to the category in question but would belong if it were a category with the default distance. To insure a wide range of variabilities, we included categories of different levels: basic-level, superordinate, and subordinate.

To find out whether DSD changes with age, we employed subjects of different ages.

Method

Design. The study had a two-way factorial design with the variables of age and level of category.

Subjects. The sample consisted of 122 2nd graders (aged 7(3) to 8(2)) and 187 8th graders (aged 13(3) to 14(2)) from middle-class neighborhoods and 110 undergraduate students attending an introductory course in statistics at the Hebrew University.

Materials. The following items were used in the study: a) Superordinate categories: animal, plant, means of transportation; b) Basic-level categories: dog, bird, tree, mushroom, car, boat; c) Subordinate categories: bulldog, dachshund, wagtail, oal, cypress, fir, sedan-car, sports-car, sailing-boat, pedal-boat. All items are well known to Israeli children of the ages included in the study. The number of subjects at the three levels were: 2nd graders -

127

20, 37, 65; 8th graders - 27, 62, 98; college students - 22, 38, 50.

Procedure. The task was administered in groups. Each subject was handed a sheet of paper with the following instructions:

"Imagine that creatures from another world, which are very much like human beings, have landed on Earth. You have to instruct them, through the use of pictures, to identify things (such as a chair, a carrot, a tool). Imagine that you have at your disposal a collection of pictures which can include any picture you wish.

Which pictures would you choose to show them, so that when they encounter an object they will know whether or not it is a _____ ?"

The blank line was completed with one of the 19 items mentioned above.

Results and Discussion

Classification of answers. For the purposes of the present paper each answer list was characterized by its values on two dimensions:

a) Mentioning of multiple positive instances of the category: A list either contained multiple positive instances of the category (MP+) or did not (MP-).

b) Mentioning of negative instances of the category: A list either contained one or more negative instance (N+) or did not contain any negative instance (N-). A list was regarded as N+ if it contained at least one item from a category which shares the same immediate superordinate category with the item in question (for example, for bird "I'll show a picture of a butterfly and cross it out"; for bulldog, "I'll show a picture of a German shepherd").

The answers were independently evaluated by two judges. Agreement was very high (over 98%). The four resulting patterns of answers are discussed below.

a) (MP-/N-): Absence of multiple positive instances and absence of negative instances. This pattern was understood to mean that the subject relied on the DSD to indicate the variability of the category in question.

128

b) (MP-/N+): Absence of multiple positive instances and presence of negative instances. This pattern was understood to mean that the variability of the category in question was smaller than what the subject considered to be the norm, and had to be explicitly delimited by presenting negative instances.

c) (MP+/N-): Presence of multiple positive instances and absence of negative instances. This pattern was understood to mean that the variability of the category in question was larger than what the subject considered to be the norm, and had to be explicilty expanded by presenting more than one positive instance.

d) (MP+/N+): Presence of both multiple positive instances and negative instances. Here nothing can be inferred concerning the variability of the category in question relative to DSD.

Analysis. A corrolary of the claim that there exists a DSD for categories, is that category variability is explicitly indicated when DSD is inappropriate. Since the higher the level of a category the larger its variability, we expected the incidence of the MP+/N- pattern to increase with level. The opposite was expected for the MP-/N+ pattern: We expected it to be more prevalent the lower the category level. The relationship between category level and the incidence of the two patterns is depicted in Figure 1.

Since support for these two predictions is a prerequisite for any further analysis we first tested the main effect of level for the two patterns of responses in question. The analyses revealed a highly significant main effect of level both for the MP+/N- pattern of answer ($F(2,410) = 23.93$ p < .001) and for the MP-/N+ pattern of answer ($F(2,410) = 16.00$, p < .001)).

These two results establish that subjects performing the task were sensitive to category variability: The greater the variability the more likely they were to use multiple positive instances; the smaller the variability the more likely they were to use negative instances.

129

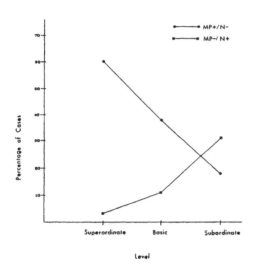

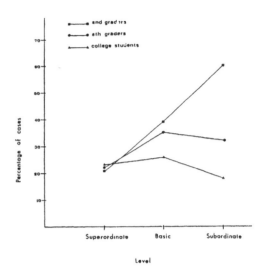

Figure 1: Incidence of MP+/N- and MP-/N+
Patterns of answers at the three levels.

Figure 2: Incidence of the MP-/N- pattern of answers
at the three category levels for each age group.

The results for the MP-/N- pattern of responses - the cases where subjects presumably relied on DSD - are presented in Figure 2. A two-way analysis of variance of the responses revealed significant effects of age ($F(2,410) = 3.79$, $p = .023$) and level ($F(2,410) = 3.19, p = .042$), as well as a significant interaction between the two variables ($F(4,410) = 2.42$, $p = .048$). The MP-/N- pattern was more prevalent the younger the subjects (its incidence was .39, .30, and .22 for the three age groups) and the lower the level (an incidence rate of .37, .33, and .22 for subordinate, basic-level and superordinate categories, respectively). Most interesting, the MP-/N- pattern was very common among 2nd graders teaching items from subordinate categories (60%), whereas for older subjects the mode was at the basic-level categories. This trend towards an increase in the size of DSD with age is also evidenced in the finding that for 8th graders the second most frequent MP-/N- cell was that of subordinate categories, while for the college students it was that of superordinate categories.

130

Our claim that people have a default similarity distance which they use and expect others to use when constructing a new category, provides a coherent and succinct explanation of the results. For each age group there was some category level for which a large proportion of the subjects found it unnecessary to indicate its variability. At the same time, subjects used multiple positive instances to indicate the greater than normal variability of more general categories and negative instances to indicate the relative narrowness of lower-level categories.

The results strongly imply that the size of DSD changes with age: For younger children the default variability was close to that of subordinate categories while for older children and adults the value was closer to the variability of basic-level categories. The evidence of the smaller size of children's default distance for categories is in line with findings of developmental studies of free categorization which indicate that younger children tend to create narrower categories than older ones (Nelson & Bonvillian, 1973, 1978; Saltz, Soller & Sigel, 1972).

The relationship between age and DSD has some implications for models of machine learning. Every model has to allow some similarity distance between items it classifies into the same category. Our findings imply that a model of human learning should initially use a steep generalization gradient and relax this requirement as more knowledge about the world accummulates. Thus, the present findings provide researchers in the field of machine learning with some idea of the size of the default similarity threshold to be installed for grouping stimuli into categories and the changes it should undergo with increased experience.

Bibliography

Fried, L. S. & Holyoak, K. J. (1984). Induction of category distributions: A framework for classification learning. Journal of Experimental Psychology: Learning, Memory and Cognition, 10, 234-257.

Hayes-Roth B. & Hayes-Roth, F. (1977). Concept learning and the recognition and classification of exemplars. Journal of Verbal Learning and Verbal Behavior, 16, 321-338.

Medin, D. L. & Barsalou, L. W. (1987). Categorization processes and categorical perception. In S. Harnad (Ed.) Categorical Perception. Cambridge, England: Cambridge University Press.

Medin, D. L. & Shaffer, M. M. (1978). A context theory of classification learning. Psychological Review, 85, 207-238.

Nelson K. E. & Bonvillian J. D. (1973). Concepts and words in the 18-month-old: Acquiring concept names under controlled conditions. Cognition, 2, 435-450.

Nelson K. E. & Bonvillian J. D. (1978). Early language development: Conceptual growth and related processes between 2 and 4.5 years of age. In K. E. Nelson (Ed.) Children's language (Vol. 1). New York: Gardner.

Rosch, E. (1973). On the internal structure of perceptual and semantic categories. In T. E. Moore (Ed.) Cognitive development and the acquisition of language. New York: Academic Press.

Rosch, E. & Mervis, C. B. (1975). Family resemblances: Studies in the internal structure of categories. Cognitive Development, 7, 573-605.

Saltz E., Soller, E. & Sigel I. E. (1972). The development of natural language concepts. Child Development, 43, 1191-1202.

Judgment, Graininess and Categories

Ilan Yaniv and Dean Foster
University of Chicago

Judgment plays a role in reasoning, decision making, and planning. An appraisal of a house's value may influence the seller's consideration of various bids, an estimate of a distance may influence a tourist's decision to walk or ride a bus, and the estimated arrival time of a guest may change the dinner schedule. Clearly optimal choice in such cases may hinge on having good judgmental estimates (Tversky & Kahneman, 1974; Dawes, Faust, & Meehl, 1989).

How good a judgmental estimate is, depends on how close it is to the "truth". However, this is not the whole story. People often communicate the "fineness of grain" of their judgmental estimates. For example, compare the following:

(a) John has promised to be at a meeting at "5:00 pm". John arrives at 5:15 pm.

(b) Bill has promised to be at a meeting around "fivish". Bill arrives at 5:15 pm.

Each of the estimates, 5:00 and fivish, conveys different graininess ("grain size"). The first estimate is fine-grain, whereas, the second is coarse-grain. Although the difference between the promised and actual arrival times is the same in both cases, John's late arrival appears to have been more significant because he has committed himself to greater precision by giving a fine-grain estimate. Intuitively, it seems from this example that the quality of a judgmental estimate depends on its graininess.

Communication of graininess in judgment seems ubiquitous. People have at their disposal alternative, parallel scales differing in graininess that allow them to pack efficiently grain size information in their estimates. For example, an hour and 60 minutes refer to identical durations, but differ in their graininess, thus people might pick one or the other depending on their intended precision. Whereas an hour represents a broad category (potentially including values such as 55, 59, and 64 min), the estimate 60 minutes conveys greater precision. Other pairs such as three weeks vs 21 days and 1/2 a year vs 183 days, to list but a few, involve similar contrasts.

What is the role of graininess in judgment? To begin with, we suggest that the psychological impact of a judgmental error depends on the ratio between the size of the error and the graininess of the judgment. This ratio is called grained error (for definitions see Yaniv & Foster, 1990). To illustrate this concept, consider two hypothetical opinions concerning the date the University of Chicago was founded: (a) Bill's opinion is "in the 1880s" (b) John's opinion is "1885". In light of the correct answer (1892), both opinions are wrong. But the graininess of Bill's estimate is a decade thus his estimate is about "one grain away" from the truth, whereas the graininess of John's estimate is one year, thus his estimate is several (more than one) grains away from the truth.

How do people select the appropriate "grain size" for their judgmental estimates? What role does graininess play in evaluating the accuracy of judgments made by other people? We briefly report here the results of two representative studies (see Yaniv & Foster for full report). In the following section, we outline the paradigm of the first study, our hypotheses and the results.

Grain-Scale study

Method. We asked a group of 44 University of Chicago students to estimate a variety of quantities, such as, "The US population in 1987," "Air distance between Chicago and New York," and " Number of American symphony orchestras." The sample question shown in Figure 1, "The date the University of Chicago was founded," illustrates the format of the questionnaire. Various scales were provided in increasing order of fineness of grain. The top scale was provided as an option in case the respondents didn't know anything about the subject of the question in which case they were supposed circle the whole range. However, if they felt they knew more, they could select finer grain scales. They could circle an interval representing a century on

134

the second scale (grain size = a century), or else, if they felt they knew the answer with more precision, they could circle an interval representing a fifty-year period on the third scale, etc. They were also given the option of writing down the exact year in the space provided above the sixth scale (grain size = 1 year). Thus, they were supposed to make only one grain-scale estimate per question by selecting an appropriate scale and an interval on that scale. This method jointly elicited their best guesses (approximately the midpoint of the selected interval) along with the graininess of their judgments (represented by the width of this interval).

As part of the analysis, we calculated the grained error of each estimate. For illustration, the grained error of the answer shown in Figure 1 is +2 because it is 2 units away from the interval containing the correct date. (In contrast, the grained error of the estimate 1900-1909 would have been -1, while the grained error of 1890-1899 would have been 0 because this interval contains the correct date.)

Hypotheses. One hypothesis is that in selecting grain sizes for their judgments, individuals signal to others the magnitude of judgmental error that they expect. Thus, individuals estimate historical dates in decades if they believe their best guess might be (on the average) 10 years off the truth, and they give estimates in centuries if they expect an average (absolute) error on the order of 100 years. A corollary of this hypothesis is that the mean absolute grained error across judgments should average one.

Another possible hypothesis is that grain size of a judgment is like a ˚confidence interval˚ -- an interval that includes the true answer with measured certainty, for example, with a probability of 95% or 99%. If this is true, then grain-scale judgments should include the correct answers with a high probability.

Results. The distribution of the grained errors across all grain-scale judgments is plotted in Figure 2. The most striking result is that only 46% of the grain-scale judgments actually contained the correct answer; 75% of the judgments had a grained error that was either -1, 0, or +1; and 95% of the judgments had a grained error that ranged from -5 to +5. Thus, grain-scale judgments do not appear to "behave" like confidence intervals that contain the correct answers with a high probability. These results are consistent with Alpert and Raiffa's (1982) who found that judgmental confidence intervals tend to be too narrow (see also Yates, 1990).

It is interesting that grain-scale judgments tend to be "too finely-grained" and hence exclude the truth so frequently. Clearly, giving coarsely-grained estimates can reduce grained error and increase the chances that the truth is included in the estimate. For instance, a coarse-grain estimate for the date the University of Chicago was founded "1700-1900" will generate a lower grained error than a fine-grain estimate such as "in the 1880s."

Grained Error vs Graininess: A Tradeoff

In everyday situations, however, giving excessively coarse judgments is discouraged by linguistic/social norms which imply that speakers should be truthful and appropriately informative (Grice, 1975). Judgmental estimates are expected to be truthful, that is, have low grained error. But, they are also expected to be informative, or finely-grained. For instance, the forecast that inflation rate in the US in 1990 will be between 1% and 55% appears vacuous although it is quite likely to be truthful. Consider for example two estimates of the age of a particular person: (a) "25 to 40 years" (b) "40 to 42 years." Suppose that the person's true age is 39 years. In retrospect, which estimate would we prefer to have had? The first estimate is coarser than the second and has a lower grained error. The second estimate is more informative, but it has a higher grained error. The evaluation of estimates appears to involve a tradeoff between grained error and graininess. A model which formalizes this tradeoff between the truthfulness (grained error) and informativeness (graininess) of a given judgment is presented in Yaniv and Foster (1990).

136

Evaluation Study

We briefly outline a study designed to test our model. We told our respondents to "imagine that you are a senator preparing an argument. You solicit quick judgmental estimates for some missing information from two of your aides. Later, you compare these estimates to the truth." We presented to them pairs of grain-scale estimates of the target questions along with the correct answer. For example:

Amount of money spent on education by the U.S. federal government in 1987?
_____ Aide A responds: $20 to   40 billion
_____ Aide B responds: $18   to   20 billion
The actual answer was: $22.5 billion. Which aide is more credible?

In each case, respondents were supposed to compare the estimates in terms of their quality, specifically, to indicate which of the two aides they would prefer to consult in the future.

Results. Our model provided a weighted measure of the "quality" of each estimate based on its grained error and graininess (width of the judgmental interval). We found that the preferences implied by our model predicted the preferences indicated by our respondents.

Final Comments

We have discussed two major ideas. First, judges seem to select grain sizes which estimate the expected error of their estimates. Second, the graininess of a given judgment depends on the tradeoff between the judge's pragmatic (and conflicting) needs to be truthful and informative at the same time (for further discussion see Yaniv & Foster).

It would be interesting to speculate on the representation that may give rise to grain-scale judgments. It is conceivable that grain-scale judgments rely on permanent hierarchical memory representations similar to those underlying natural language categories (e.g., Smith & Medin, 1981). Recent work (Huttenlocher et al., 1990) suggests that the dates of particular autobiographical events (e.g., the date we saw a particular movie) might be coded at multiple levels (e.g., "January 20", "January" and "Winter quarter".) It is possible that numerical information is generally coded in such structures. For example, historical events (e.g., the date the University of Chicago was founded) may be coded at multiple levels varying in fineness (similar to the levels represented in Figure 1) and with different degrees of certainty. Thus we may remember the target event was "definitely a 19th century event", "most likely in second half of the 19th century," "possibly in the 1880s," etc. Grain-scale judgments may result from the confluence of several such sources of information.

References

Alpert, M., & Raiffa, H. (1982). A progress report on the training of probability assessors. In D. Kahneman, P. Slovic, & A. Tversky, Judgment under uncertainty: Heuristics and biases. New York: Cambridge University Press.

Dawes, R.M., Faust, F., & Meehl, P.E. (1989). Clinical versus actuarial judgment. Science, 243, 1668-1674.

Grice, H.P. (1975). Logic and conversation. In P. Cole & J.L. Morgan (Eds.), Syntax and semantics: Vol. 3. Speech acts (pp.64-74). New York: Academic Press.

Huttenlocher, J., Hedges, L., & Bradburn, N. (1990). Reports of elapsed time: Bounding and rounding processes in estimation. Journal of Experimental Psychology: Learning, Memory, and Cognition, 16, 196-213.

Smith, E.E., & Medin, D.L. (1981). Categories and concepts. Cambridge, MA: Harvard University Press.

Tversky, A., & Kahneman, D. (1974). Judgment under uncertainty: Heuristics and biases. Science, 185, 1124-1131.

Yaniv, I., & Foster, D.P. (1990). Graininess of judgment. Center for Decision Research, University of Chicago.

Yates, J.F. (1990). Judgment and Decision Making (pp. 75-111). Englewood Cliffs, NJ: Prentice Hall.

Figure 1.

Date the University of Chicago founded?

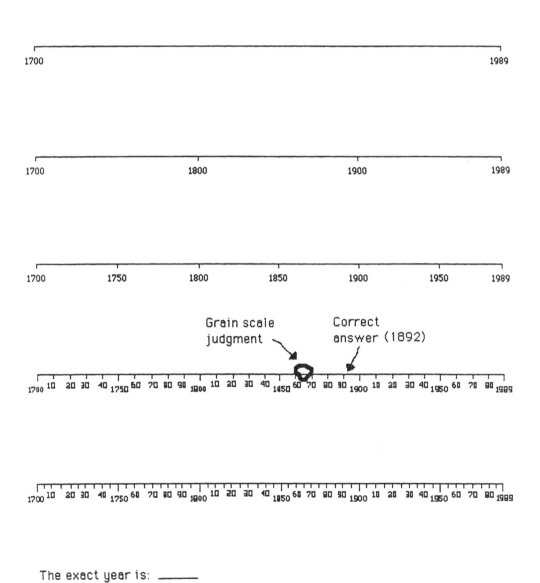

Figure 2.

Grain-Scale study: Distribution of Grained Errors

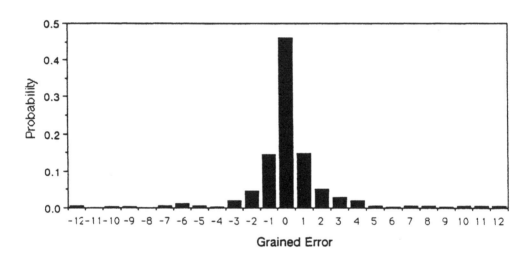

Learning Attribute Relevance in Context
in Instance-Based Learning Algorithms

David W. Aha
Dept. of Information & Computer Science
University of California, Irvine
Irvine, CA 92717
aha@ics.uci.edu

Robert L. Goldstone
Department of Psychology
University of Michigan
Ann Arbor, MI 48109
rob_goldstone@ub.cc.umich.edu

Abstract

There has been an upsurge of interest, in both artificial intelligence and cognitive psychology, in *exemplar-based* process models of categorization, which preserve specific instances instead of maintaining abstractions derived from them. Recent exemplar-based models provided accurate fits for subject results in a variety of experiments because, in accordance with Shepard's (1987) observations, they define similarity to degrade exponentially with the distance between instances in psychological space. Although several researchers have shown that an attribute's relevance in similarity calculations varies according to its *context* (i.e., the values of the other attributes in the instance and the target concept), previous exemplar models define attribute relevance to be invariant across all instances. This paper introduces the GCM-ISW model, an extension of Nosofsky's GCM model that uses *context-specific* attribute weights for categorization tasks. Since several researchers have reported that humans make context-sensitive classification decisions, our model will fit subject data more accurately when attribute relevance is context-sensitive. We also introduce a process component for GCM-ISW and show that its learning rate is significantly faster than the rates of previous exemplar-based process models when attribute relevance varies among instances. GCM-ISW is both computationally more efficient and more psychologically plausible than previous exemplar-based models.

1. Introduction

Several studies have shown that the Context Model (Medin & Schaffer, 1978) and the Generalized Context Model (GCM) (Nosofsky, 1986; 1987), two exemplar-based models of categorization, provide excellent fits for subject data from a wide variety of experiments. These models remove the assumption that attributes have equal relevance in similarity computations by introducing a parameter (attribute weight) for each attribute, whose value is determined by some exterior attention mechanism. Humans are hypothesized to selectively attend to attributes to optimize their classification behavior (Nosofsky, 1986). These models differ from previous exemplar models (e.g., Reed, 1972) in that they define similarity to decrease exponentially with psychological distance, in accordance with Shepard's (1987) numerous empirical observations on stimulus generalization. However, these models ignore evidence that attribute relevance varies depending on the context of the classification task (Tversky, 1977; Barsalou, 1982; Roth & Shoben, 1983; Medin & Edelson, 1988). Therefore, they cannot be expected to provide accurate fits when attribute relevance varies according to context, which occurs frequently in real-world classification tasks.

For example, consider the problem of predicting whether a pro-life politician will endorse proposed legislation on abortion rights. As with most real-world categorization tasks, some attributes should be given more attention than others. In this case, dimensions such as

141

"past voting record" should be weighted more than dimensions such as "height." Relative attribute relevance differs depending upon the prediction task (Aha & McNulty, 1989; Aha, 1989) (i.e., "past voting record" is far less relevant than "height" when predicting the ability to dunk a basketball). However, an attribute's relevance to a categorization task often also depends on its *context* – the values of the other attributes in an instance. For example, the relevance of the "past voting record" attribute will be low if the "percentage of pro-choice constituency" attribute has a high value (due to pressure from pro-choice political action groups). However, it will be high if the "seek re-election" attribute value is "false", which diminishes the influence of political action groups. Context sensitive attribute weights are required to derive an appropriate psychological space and satisfy the attention-optimization hypothesis when attribute relevance is context-dependent.

In this paper, we introduce the *GCM-ISW* (Instance-Specific **W**eights) model, an extension of the GCM that adds a set of attribute weight parameters for each instance for each target concept. Section 2 describes evidence that the GCM-ISW is more *computationally efficient* (i.e., records significantly faster learning rates) than previous exemplar-based process models when attribute relevance is context-dependent. Several researchers have reported evidence that humans make context-sensitive classification decisions when attribute relevance is dependent on context. In Section 3, we review this evidence and discuss alternative weighting schemes for exemplar-based models.

2. Instance-Based Learning Algorithms

This section describes a sequence of four, comprehensive *instance-based learning* (IBL) algorithms, which are exemplar-based process models. The attribute weights in the first (and simplest) model, named *GCM-NW* (**N**o **W**eights), are fixed to be equal. We describe evidence that a process model for the GCM, named *GCM-SW* (**S**ingle set of attribute **W**eights), learns significantly faster than the GCM-NW when the relevance to classification judgements varies among attributes. The third model, named *GCM-MW* (**M**ultiple sets of attribute **W**eights), employs a separate set of attribute weights per target concept and learns significantly faster than the GCM-SW when attribute relevance varies among target concepts. The final model, GCM-ISW, employs a separate set of attribute weights for each instance for each target concept. We present evidence that it learns significantly faster than GCM-MW when attribute relevance varies among instances.

2.1 GCM-SW: Learning Attribute Relevance

IBL algorithms input a sequence of training instances, drawn from an n-dimensional *instance space*, where n is the number of attributes used to describe each instance. A subset $p < n$ of these attributes, called *predictors*, are used to predict values for the remaining $(n - p)$ *targets*. In this paper, we assume that predictors have numeric values and target attributes have binary values: "positive" and "negative."[1] Positive target values are understood to be members of the *target concept*. For each target, IBL algorithms yield one *concept description* which contains the processed training instances and a set of attribute weight settings. Given an instance x and its similarity with each instance in target a's concept description, IBL algorithms can predict whether x is a member of concept a.

---

[1] Stanfill and Waltz (1986) describe an interesting IBL algorithm for symbolic-valued predictors. Kibler, Aha, and Albert (1989) address the issue of numeric-valued targets.

IBL algorithms use a *similarity function*, defined over the predictor attributes, to compute the similarity of the instance to be classified with the previously processed training instances. GCM-SW's similarity function is $\text{similarity}(x, y) = e^{-\text{distance}(x,y)}$, where

$$\text{distance}(x, y) = s\sqrt{\sum_{i=1}^{p} w_i(x_i - y_i)^2},$$

where parameter s (set to 10 in all our simulations) is GCM-SW's parameter that determines the slope of the exponential decay and w_i is GCM-SW's weight for attribute i. Values for attribute weights are always initialized to $\frac{1}{p}$, range in $[0, 1]$, and are normalized to sum to 1.

Given these similarities, a *memory updating function* modifies the attribute weights for the instances in a's concept description and, afterwards, always adds x to a's description.[2] The GCM-SW training algorithm is: (where cd_a is target a's concept description)

1. $cd_a \leftarrow \emptyset$
2. FOR EACH $x \in$ training set DO
   2.1 FOR EACH $y \in cd_a$: compute $\text{similarity}(x, y)$
   2.2 FOR EACH $y \in cd_a$: FOR EACH predictor attribute i: adjust_weight(i, x, y, a)
   2.3 $cd_a \leftarrow cd_a \cup \{x\}$

Attribute weights denote the estimated relevance of an attribute for a categorization task. Each predictor i's weight is computed using a function of the estimated conditional probability that two instances will have the same class, given that their similarity is high and the difference of their values for i is small. If we denote this probability at time t as $\text{Pr}_i(t)$, then the attribute weight for i after t training instances have been processed is $\text{Pr}_i(t) - (1 - \text{Pr}_i(t))$. Adjust_weight updates estimates of conditional probability as follows:

$$\text{Pr}_i(t+1) = \text{Pr}_i(t) + (r - \text{Pr}_i(t)) \times \text{similarity}(x, y) \times e^{-s|x_i - y_i|} \times \rho,$$

where Boolean variable r is 1 only if x_a equals y_a and ρ is a learning rate parameter, which is set to 0.01 for GCM-SW and GCM-MW in our simulations. The size of the update to i's conditional probability increases exponentially with linear decreases in both $\text{distance}(x, y)$ and $|x_i - y_i|$. Therefore, attribute i's weight is most strongly influenced by highly similar instances with similar values for i.

The classification accuracy of our IBL algorithms is measured using a *classification function*, which inputs the computed similarities for target a and generates a class prediction (i.e., "positive" or "negative"). The probability that instance x will be a member of concept a is estimated as follows:

$$\text{Pr}(x_a = \text{"positive"}) = \frac{\sum_{y \in cd_a} \text{similarity}(x, y) \times (y_a = \text{"positive"})}{\sum_{y \in cd_a} \text{similarity}(x, y)}$$

Instance x is predicted to be a member of concept a only if this value is above 0.5. All the IBL algorithms in this paper use the following testing algorithm (for each target attribute

---

[2] Aha, Kibler, and Albert (in press) analyze IBL algorithms that significantly reduce storage requirements.

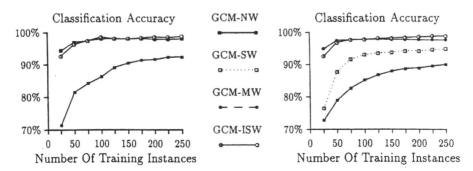

Figure 1: Learning curves for the four IBL algorithms. Left: GCM-NW learns slowly when attributes have different relevance. GCM-SW and GCM-MW behave identically in this simulation since there is only one target concept. Right: GCM-SW learns slowly when each attribute's relevance differs among target concepts. All our curves are averaged over 20 pairs of training and test sets with 250 and 100 instances respectively. Values for predictor attributes are selected randomly from $[0, 1]$ according to a uniform distribution.

a): (1) compute the current training instance x's similarity to the instances in a's concept description, (2) compute the probability that x_a is "positive", and (3) output "positive" for this classification if this probability is above 0.5 (otherwise, output "negative").

GCM-SW's attribute weights are useful when attribute relevance varies among predictors. To show this, we compared its performance with the performance of GCM-NW, whose weights remain fixed with value $\frac{1}{p}$. GCM-NW learns slowly when attribute relevance differs among the predictors. The graph in the left of Figure 1 shows the average learning curves for a simulation with one target concept and ten predictors, only one of which was relevant. Target concept members were defined to be those whose relevant attribute's value was greater than 0.5. As expected, GCM-SW's average accuracy (measured across the ten applications to the test set per trial) is significantly greater than GCM-NW's ($t(19) = 4.54, p < 0.001$). However, since the GCM-SW model uses the same setting of attribute weights for all targets, it performs relatively poorly when the relative relevance of attributes differs greatly among target concepts (Aha & McNulty, 1989) or when relative attribute relevance varies among instances. The right-hand graph in Figure 1 shows the average learning curves when the artificial domain is extended to contain an additional three target concepts, where each of the four target concepts have a single (different) relevant predictor. GCM-SW's learning curve rises slowly because it is unable to learn concept-dependent attribute relevances: its weights for the four relevant attributes each converge to 0.25. GCM-SW's average classification accuracy is significantly lower than GCM-MW's ($t(19) = 5.33, p < 0.001$).

2.2 GCM-MW: Learning Concept-Dependent Attribute Relevance

GCM-MW's concept-dependent similarity function is $\text{similarity}(a, x, y) = e^{-\text{distance}(a,x,y)}$, where w_{a_i} denotes the weight of attribute i for target concept a in

$$\text{distance}(a, x, y) = s\sqrt{\sum_{i=1}^{p} w_{a_i}(x_i - y_i)^2}.$$

144

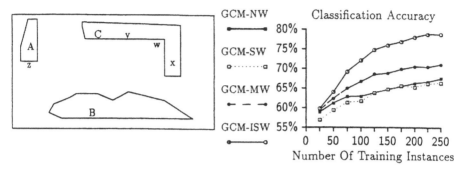

Figure 2: Left: Attribute relevance can vary among instances. Right: GCM-ISW works best in such situations.

The GCM-MW model will outperform the GCM-SW model when attribute relevance varies among target concepts. However, GCM-MW's assumption that an attribute's relevance is invariant across all instances is easily violated. For example, attribute relevance can vary among a concept's disjuncts. Furthermore, it can also vary *within* a disjunct. Figure 2 displays a two-dimensional domain containing three disjuncts of a single target concept. The horizontal attribute is more relevant than the vertical for disjunct A: small perturbations in the horizontal's values will more frequently change disjunct membership status than will perturbations in the vertical's values. The vertical attribute is more relevant for B while C's attributes are approximately equally relevant. However, attribute relevance differs greatly among instances. For example, although both attributes are relevant for classifications made by instance w, the horizontal attribute is more relevant for x and less relevant for y. Finally, z's vertical attribute is more relevant. GCM-MW's learning rate can be significantly reduced when attribute relevance varies among instances. Figure 2 displays the average learning curves when the learning task is changed so that each of the four concepts is defined by a set of five disjuncts. In this case, each disjunct is defined by a single relevant attribute and each attribute in the domain is relevant to exactly two disjuncts overall. The threshold values for inclusion in a disjunct were below 0.14 for the disjuncts of the first two target concepts and above 0.86 for the latter two target concepts. GCM-MW's average accuracy is significantly lower than GCM-ISW's $(t(19) = 3.85, p < 0.002)$.

2.3 Learning Context-Sensitive Attribute Relevance

GCM-ISW differs from GCM-MW in that it learns *instance-specific* attribute weights, one for each ⟨attribute,instance,target⟩ triplet. This provides greater flexibility than found in GCM-MW: GCM-ISW removes the assumption that attribute relevance is invariant among a target concept's saved instances.

GCM-ISW's instance-specific weights can be easily misapplied. For example, if the only relevant attribute for instance z in Figure 2 is the vertical attribute, then z will appear to be very similar to x, which is located far from z in this instance space. Therefore, instance-specific weights should be used only when the instance being classified is highly similar to the classifying instance. GCM-ISW solves this problem by learning both concept-dependent weights (as is done in GCM-MW) and a separate set of instance-specific weights. (Adjust_weight updates each saved instance's attribute weights when classifying each subsequently presented training instance.) GCM-ISW's similarity function then combines these two sets of weights to compute the *context*-specific similarity of two instances as follows:

$$\text{distance}(a, x, y) = s\sqrt{\sum_{i=1}^{p} \text{combine\_weights}(a, x, y, i) \times (x_i - y_i)^2}.$$

When computing the similarity of a new instance x to previously processed instance y, combine_weights calculates attribute i's *context-specific* weight as follows:

$$\text{combine\_weights}(a, x, y, i) = (w_{a_i}(y) \times \text{scale\_factor}) + (w_{a_i} \times (1 - \text{scale\_factor})),$$

where scale_factor $= (1 - |x_i - y_i|)^c$, $w_{a_i}(y)$ is i's attribute weight for saved instance y, and c is a combination parameter that determines the relative impact of the concept-dependent and instance-specific attribute weights in calculating the context-sensitive weight.[3] Combine_weights uses instance-specific weights more confidently when the difference of the values for i is small. This reduces the frequency with which instance-specific weights are used when the distance between instances is large. After GCM-ISW computes similarities, it updates the conditional probabilities and attribute weights for both its concept-dependent and its instance-specific weights. GCM-ISW performed significantly better than the other models in the third simulation and performed as well as GCM-SW and GCM-MW in the first and second simulations respectively.

3. Discussion: Supporting Evidence and Alternative Models

While formal psychological models involving context-specific weight learning do not exist, there is a plethora of psychological data suggesting the existence of such specific weighting systems. Nosofsky's (1986) GCM model treats attribute weights as parameters that can be assigned experimentally-derived values to accurately fit subject data. However, more flexible weighting systems, namely those that employ context-sensitive weights, are required to accurately fit subject data and increase learning rate when attribute relevance varies among instances. These weights can also be used to decrease storage requirements: attributes with low relevance can be discarded without sacrificing classification accuracy (Smith & Medin, 1981). Aha (1989) described simulations of IBL algorithms that drop both attributes *and* instances and, simultaneously, increase learning rates for real-world classification tasks.

Many researchers agree that models of categorization should be context-sensitive. Roth and Shoben (1983) and Barsalou (1982) argue that an instance's context influences its perceived typicality and determines which of its attributes receives attention. For example, Barsalou noted that, while some attributes of "basketball" (e.g., "round") are always salient, others (e.g., "floats") only become salient (i.e., quickly retrieved) in contexts involving water. This provides psychological support for the GCM-ISW model: people on a luxury liner attend more to the "floats" attribute when the ship is sinking (to judge whether objects are members of the "can support me in the water" category) than when it is in port. Goldstone, Medin,

---

[3]We used $c = 0.5$ for our simulations. We also set GCM-ISW's learning rate parameter to be higher (0.1) when it updates instance-specific weights. This is needed because, given any one training instance, few other training instances are highly similar to it. However, when updating concept-dependent weights, there will be several highly similar pairs of instances.

and Gentner (in press) argue that, when comparing instances, the influence that one attribute has depends on the other attributes that are shared by the instances. Medin and Edelson (1988) also suggested using context-specific attribute weights. When an instance is correctly classified, their proposed process model assigns high relative weights to the attributes shared by the classifying instance and the instance being classified. Misclassifications result in assigning higher weights to attributes that are *not* shared by these two instances.

Several alternative weighting schemes have been proposed for exemplar-based process models. Nosofsky, Clark, and Shin (1989) considered *value-specific* weighting algorithms. However, these are not as flexible as instance-specific weighting algorithms: value-specific weights for some attribute i will not work well when i's relevance varies over instances that have the same value for i. In another example, Medin and Shoben (1988) present examples that suggest an *instance-directed* attribute-weighting scheme, whereby the influence of one attribute depends on the other attributes that are present. For example, while "White" is more similar to "Gray" than is "Black" for the attribute "hair," exactly the opposite pattern emerges with the attribute "clouds." This suggests extending the instance-specific weighting method to distinguish between directions along attribute dimensions. For instances of hair, the gray-black distance is widened while the gray-white distance is reduced. In any case, a single predefined weight for the "color" dimension will not survive changes of context.

The GCM-ISW model adds an enormous number of parameters into the GCM model. Although GCM-ISW increases learning rate, its additional parameters are not needed when attribute relevance remains constant across the entire dimension. We are currently developing a more elaborate IBL algorithm that can learn which parameters should be permanently fixed without need for subsequent attention. The algorithm would initially assume that all dimensions are weighted equally for all categories. If this assumption does not yield sufficiently fast learning rates, then the system would relax its assumptions and allow an attribute's weight to vary across categories. The assumption that weights are fixed across instances could also be automatically relaxed. Shifts in the target concept description could lead to more or less specific weighting algorithms in attempts to maximize classification accuracy while minimizing the number of unique weights that are postulated.

IBL algorithms that learn context-specific attribute weights resemble rule-based learning algorithms. By weighting dimensions selectively on the basis of their category diagnosticity, the instance-based systems are qualitatively distinguished from the simple storage of instances in a "raw form." Although instance information is not discarded, it is selectively emphasized. This representation is similar to that used for rules. For example, consider the concept of legal-sized suitcases (i.e., those with lengths less than five feet). An instance-directed weighting algorithm could learn a high weight for $4'9''$ in the positive direction and a low weight in the negative direction for legal-sized suitcases. This is similar to the rule "if $4'9''$ or less, then legal-sized luggage, otherwise illegal."

4. Conclusion

Results from simulations suggest that previous exemplar models that selectively weight attribute dimensions, while better than no selective weighting at all, can be improved by representing context-sensitive attribute weights. We introduced GCM-ISW, an extension of Nosofsky's (1986) GCM model that learns context-sensitive weights by combining concept-dependent and instance-specific attribute weights. Our results with simulations using a process model for the GCM-ISW show that its learning rate is significantly faster than the learning rates of previous process models for exemplar-based models (Aha & McNulty, 1989). We plan to show that the GCM-ISW model will fit subject data more accurately than will a process model for the GCM when attribute relevance varies among instances.

Acknowledgements

We would like to thank Marc Albert, Dale McNulty, Douglas Medin, and Mike Pazzani for providing comments on an earlier draft of this paper.

References

Aha, D. W. (1989). Incremental, instance-based learning of independent and graded concept descriptions. In *Proceedings of the Sixth International Workshop on Machine Learning* (pp. 387–391). Ithaca, NY: Morgan Kaufmann.

Aha, D. W., Kibler, D., & Albert, M. K. (in press). Instance-based learning algorithms. *Machine Learning*.

Aha, D. W., & McNulty, D. (1989). Learning relative attribute weights for independent, instance-based concept descriptions. In *Proceedings of the Eleventh Annual Conference of the Cognitive Science Society* (pp. 530–537). Ann Arbor, MI: Lawrence Erlbaum Associates.

Barsalou, L. W. (1982). Context-independent and context-dependent information in concepts. *Memory & Cognition, 10*, 82–106.

Goldstone, R. L., Medin, D. L., & Gentner, D. (in press). Attributes, relations, and the non-independence of features in similarity judgments. *Cognitive Psychology*.

Kibler, D., Aha, D. W., & Albert, M. (1989). Instance-based prediction of real-valued attributes. *Computational Intelligence, 5*, 51–57.

Medin, D. L., & Edelson, S. M. (1988). Problem structure and the use of base rate information from experience. *Journal of Experimental Psychology: General, 117*, 68–85.

Medin, D. L., & Schaffer, M. M. (1978). Context theory of classification learning. *Psychological Review, 85*, 207–238.

Medin, D. L., & Shoben, E. J. (1988). Context and structure in conceptual combination. *Cognitive Psychology, 20*, 158–190.

Nosofsky, R. M. (1986). Attention, similarity, and the identification-categorization relationship. *Journal of Experimental Psychology: General, 15*, 39–57.

Nosofsky, R. M. (1987). Attention and learning processes in the identification and categorization of integral stimuli. *Journal of Experimental Psychology: Learning, Memory, and Cognition, 13*, 87–108.

Nosofsky, R. M., Clark, S. E., & Shin, H. S. (1989). Rules and exemplars in categorization, identification, and recognition. *Journal of Experimental Psychology: Learning, Memory, & Cognition, 15*, 282–304.

Reed, S. K. (1972). Pattern recognition and categorization. *Cognitive Psychology, 3*, 382–407.

Roth, E. M., & Shoben, E. J. (1983). The effect of context on the structure of categories. *Cognitive Psychology, 15*, 346–378.

Shepard, R. N. (1987). Toward a universal law of generalization for psychological science. *Science. 237*, 1317–1323.

Smith, E. E., & Medin, D. L. (1981). *Categories and concepts.* Cambridge, MA: Harvard University Press.

Stanfill, C., & Waltz, D. (1986). Toward memory-based reasoning. *Communications of the ACM, 29*, 1213–1228.

Tversky, A. (1977). Features of similarity. *Psychological Review, 84*, 327–352.

Effects of Background Knowledge on Family Resemblance Sorting

Woo-Kyoung Ahn
University of Michigan

Abstract

Previous studies on category construction have shown that people have a strong bias of creating categories based only on a single dimension. Ahn and Medin (1989) have developed a two-stage model of category construction to explain why we have categories structured on the basis of overall similarity of members in spite of this bias. The current study investigates effects of background knowledge on category construction. The results showed that people created family resemblance categories more frequently when they had a priori knowledge on prototypes of potential family resemblance categories. It was also found that people created family resemblance categories much more frequently when they had knowledge on underlying dimensions which integrated surface features of examples. How the two-stage model should be extended is discussed.

Introduction

Generally, it has been argued that natural categories lack defining features that are true to all members in the same category (Rosch & Mervis, 1975; Smith & Medin, 1981). Instead, natural categories are considered to have family resemblance (FR) structure: members in the same category are generally similar to each other but members in different categories are dissimilar to each other. Rosch (1975) argued that FR categories might be created because people would try to achieve a compromise between maximizing within-category similarity and minimizing between-category similarity. However, previous studies showed that people rarely sort unclassified examples based on their overall similarity (Ahn, 1990; Ahn & Medin, 1989; Imai & Garner, 1965, 1968; Medin, Wattenmaker, & Hampson, 1987). Subjects in these experiments showed a strong tendency to sort examples based on values on a single dimension (uni-dimensional sorting) to create categories with defining features.

Ahn and Medin (1989) developed a two-stage model to explain why we have FR structure in spite of this strong bias for uni-dimensional sorting. Although the two-stage model has so far been successful in describing when uni-dimensional sorting and when FR sorting will be observed, the model has only been applied to domains where people do not have any background knowledge on examples to be classified. The present work investigates the effects of various types of background information on creation of FR categories. Specifically, this study is concerned with how knowledge about prototypes and underlying dimensions affect people's sorting behavior.

The first part of the paper briefly reviews previous data from free sorting tasks in knowledge-poor domains, followed by the two-stage model's explanations of these data. The second part presents an experiment in which subjects were provided with either prototypes or theories underlying categories. The final section discusses how the two-stage model should be extended to handle the data obtained in the current experiment.

Previous Results

Medin et al.'s experiments (1987) are the first systematic study showing that people rarely created FR categories even when exemplars to be classified were developed around prototypes on the basis of overall similarity. Figure 1 shows the abstract notation of stimuli used in their experiments. In this figure, the first column (E1, E2, ...) indicates each examples and the next four columns indicate each example's values on 4 dimensions (D1, D2, D3, and D4). These exemplars had characteristic features in the resulting FR categories (i.e., features that are generally true to members in the same category but can also appear in contrasting categories). The exemplars are laid out in two categories, each of which indicate one of the potential FR categories.

	D1	D2	D3	D4		D1	D2	D3	D4
E1	0	0	0	0	E6	1	1	1	1
E2	0	0	0	1	E7	1	1	1	0
E3	0	0	1	0	E8	1	1	0	1
E4	0	1	0	0	E9	1	0	1	1
E5	1	0	0	0	E10	0	1	1	1

Figure 1. Abstract Notation of Stimuli Used in Medin, Wattenmaker, & Hampson(1987)

This set consists of two prototypes (E1 and E6) and four distortions of each prototype, which were developed by replacing a value of a prototype with the value of a contrastingg prototype. Subjects in Medin et al.'s experiments were asked to create two categories from these exemplars. According to similarity-based clustering models (see Anderberg, 1973; Massart & Kaufman, 1983, for reviews), and category construction models considering predictability of categories as a critical determinant of category construction (Anderson, in press; Fisher 1989), the two categories that the subjects would create should be FR categories (see Ahn, 1990; Ahn & Medin, 1989 for more details). However, almost all subjects in Medin et al.'s experiments sorted examples based on values on a single dimension. Then why do we have FR categories?

Two-Stage Model

To explain these results, Ahn and Medin (1989) proposed a two-stage model of category construction; the first stage involves sorting examples based on one dimension and the second stage involves assigning remaining examples based on their overall similarity to the initially created categories (see also Ahn, submitted; Ahn, 1990, for more details). Ahn and Medin argued that the reason why hardly any FR sorting was observed in Medin et al.'s experiments was because their examples had characteristic features in the resulting FR categories: after subjects carried out uni-dimensional sorting in the first stage, there existed no remaining examples to be classified in the second stage, resulting in uni-dimensional categories.

The two-stage model argues that FR categories can be created as a by-product of the two stages only when the resulting categories have sufficient features. Take an example of the set used in Ahn and Medin (1989) shown in Figure 2 under the

Sufficient set. The FR categories from this set consisted only of sufficient features (i.e., 0's and 2's). Suppose a task is to create two categories and the first dimension was chosen for the most salient dimension. In the first stage, the model categorizes E1, E2, E3, and E4 into one category and E6, E7, E8, and E9 into another category. In the second stage, one of the remaining examples, E5, is grouped with E1, E2, E3, and E4, and E10 is grouped with E6, E7, E8, and E9, based on their overall similarity. As a result, the final categories have a FR structure. On the other hand, when the resulting FR categories have characteristic features such as in the set used in Medin et al.'s experiments and the Characteristic set in Figure 2, the resulting categories are always uni-dimensional.

In Ahn and Medin's experiments, as predicted by the model, no subjects given the Characteristic set created FR categories whereas more than half of those given the Sufficient set created FR categories.

Sufficient Set		Characteristic Set	
E1 0 0 0 0	E6 2 2 2 2	E1 0 0 0 0	E6 2 2 2 2
E2 0 0 0 1	E7 2 2 2 1	E2 0 0 0 1	E7 2 2 2 0
E3 0 0 1 0	E8 2 2 1 2	E3 0 0 2 0	E8 2 2 1 2
E4 0 1 0 0	E9 2 1 2 2	E4 0 1 0 0	E9 2 0 2 2
E5 1 0 0 0	E10 1 2 2 2	E5 2 0 0 0	E10 1 2 2 2

Figure 2. Abstract notation of Sufficient and Characteristic Set

Sorting in Knowledge-Rich Domains

Although existence of sufficient features is shown to be an important determinant of sorting in knowledge-poor domains, it may not be the only one in knowledge-rich domains. Results from Medin et al.'s Experiments 5 and 6 suggest that knowing interproperty relations is an important determinant of creation of FR categories. They used personality descriptions, prototypes of which are descriptions of either an introvert or an extrovert person. When all four dimensions were developed in such a way that they could be related in terms of a single underlying dimension (i.e., introvert / extrovert dimension), most of the participants created FR categories. However, these experiments relied on the background knowledge that was pre-experimentally obtained by the subjects.

To better control the background knowledge, in the current experiment, knowledge on interproperty relationship is experimentally manipulated by providing participants with information on how dimensions could be related in terms of a deeper theory[1]. Take an example used in the current experiment. There were four dimensions which were descriptions of tribes: The first dimension was whether a tribe wore cotton clothes or leather clothes. The second dimension was whether they had monotheism or polytheism. The third dimension was whether they were ruled by hierarchical leaders or by a single leader. The fourth dimension was whether they

---

[1]There have been debates on what theories are. Although in this paper I used the term, theory, to refer to underlying dimensions and their relationship with surface features, it may be an inappropriate use of the term.

cremated the dead or buried the dead.

At first sight, these dimensions seem to be just a list of independent features, but they can be easily integrated in terms of an agricultural / nomadic dimension. That is, agricultural tribes wore cotton clothes obtained in their farms, were monotheists because they hardly had any chance to learn other types of religion, had hierarchically organized leaders to control farmers living in their areas, and buried the dead near their farms. Nomadic tribes wore leather clothes obtained from their hunting, were polytheists because they had contacted many types of religions while travelling, had a single leader to make flexible and quick decisions in their changing environments, and cremated the dead because they were always on the move.

The underlying theories can be also used to determine prototypes of categories (or ideals, Barsalou, 1985) of the potential FR categories, each of which consists of characteristic values of each category. Therefore, even if FR sorting is observed when interproperty relationships are known, it can be simply attributed to the advantage of knowing the prototypes of the FR categories. To investigate whether there is an additional advantage of knowing theories besides knowing prototypes, it is important to have a condition in which subjects learn prototypes without knowing about interproperty relations.

Previously, prototypes have been considered as a collection of average or the most frequent values on each dimension used to represent members in the same category. In these types of prototype representations, interproperty relations are not necessarily preserved. In the case of agricultural / nomadic examples, knowing that a prototype of one category have values of "monotheism, cotton clothes, burying the dead, hierarchical leaders" does not indicate how these values are related to each other. Therefore, if subjects who receive only prototype information can be compared to those who receive underlying theories, we can examine whether there is an additional advantage of knowing interproperty relations.

Another rationale for having the prototype condition is as follows. People may learn the most typical examples first and then construct categories around the prototypes. One can argue that in the previous experiments, people might have failed to produce FR categories simply because they could not find prototypes. According to this argument, subjects may be more likely to create FR categories if prototypes are given before free sorting tasks. Therefore, introducing the prototype condition allows us to investigate whether the failure to construct FR categories was simply due to failure to identify prototypes.

Method

Basically, subjects received a set of exemplars and were asked to sort them into two groups of any size. There were two groups of subjects depending on whether they received the Characteristic set or the Sufficient set in Figure 2. Half of the subjects in each group received the set instantiated in pictures of flowers and the other half received the set instantiated in descriptions of tribes.

For the flower stimuli, the four dimensions and the values corresponding to 0 and 2 for each dimension were as follows. The first dimension was color with 0 being bright color and 2 being dark color. The second dimension was whether flowers bloomed at night or during daytime. The third dimension was whether flowers bloomed on trees or on grass. The fourth dimension was whether flowers were located near water or distant from water. (Parts of these stimuli were taken from Nakamura, 1985.) The subjects who received the flower stimuli were explicitly instructed about the four dimensions and their values. For the tribe stimuli, the four dimensions and the values were described in the earlier section. For both types of stimuli, the value 1 was absence of any value on the dimension. The subjects were told that if a certain dimension was not shown in an example, it meant that the information on the dimension was not available.

Within each stimulus set and within each stimulus type, there were three groups depending on types of background knowledge they received before sorting. The types of background knowledge that the subjects received were either none (Control group), prototypes (Prototype group), or underlying theories (Theory group).

The control group who did not receive any information about prototypes was simply asked to sort ten cards in a way that seemed natural to them. There were 78 subjects in the control group who were evenly distributed across the Characteristic and the Sufficient set conditions and across the two types of stimuli.

The Prototype group received eight non-prototype examples and was asked to sort them into two categories in a way that seemed natural to them. With these instructions, they received two prototypes of the potential FR categories (i.e., 0 0 0 0 and 2 2 2 2 in both the Characteristic and Sufficient set) and were told that these were the most typical exemplars of the two categories that they were to create. There were 80 subjects in the prototype group who were also evenly distributed across the various conditions.

The theory group received only the eight non-prototype examples coupled with theories underlying each category they were to create. For the flower stimuli, they were told that one group of flowers attracted a hypothetical class of birds called "champin" and the other attracted a hypothetical class of bees called "trood." They were also told that the champin birds liked bright color, were active at night, flew high, and laid eggs near water and that the trood bees liked dark color, were active during daytime, hovered low, and laid eggs distant from water. For the tribe stimuli, they were told about the theories on the agricultural / nomadic distinction mentioned in the earlier section. Although they could presumably determine the prototypes of the potential FR categories based on the theories, they did not see the actual prototypes during the experiment. There were 77 subjects in the theory group who were evenly distributed to the various conditions.

Results
The results are summarized in Table 1. Numbers in the table indicate percentages of FR sorting within each group within each set. Responses other than creation of FR categories were mostly uni-dimensional sorting.

Comparison between the Characteristic and the Sufficient sets
As in Ahn and Medin (1989), across all groups and across both kinds of stimuli, the Sufficient set led to more FR sortings than the Characteristic set. Chi-square and Fisher's exact tests indicated all the differences between the Sufficient set and the Characteristic set within each group were significant at p=.05 except for the theory group with the tribe stimuli (i.e., the difference between 78.9% and 100%).

153

	Flower Stimuli		Tribe Stimuli		Total	
Group	Char	Suff	Char	Suff	Char	Suff
Control	0	25	11	68	5	47
Prototype	20	90	45	100	33	95
Theory	55	95	79	100	67	98

Table 1. Summary of Results

Comparison among groups within the Characteristic set

In the previous experiments using materials in knowledge-poor domains (Ahn, 1990; Ahn & Medin, 1989), the subjects never created FR categories from the Characteristic set. In this experiment, when the subjects received prototype information on the Characteristic set, subjects created more FR categories (33%) than the control group who did not receive any background information (5%). In the flower stimuli, the difference between the control group (0%) and the prototype group (20%) who received the Characteristic set was not significant but in the tribe stimuli, the difference between the control group (10.5%) and the prototype group (45%) was significant ($p < .001$).

More subjects who received information on underlying theories created FR categories from the Characteristic set (67%) than those who received either prototype information (33%, $p < .05$) or no information (5%, $p < .05$). Within each stimulus type, these differences were also significant.

Comparison among groups within the Sufficient set

For the Sufficient set, almost all subjects in both the prototype group (95%) and the theory group (98%) produced the FR categories. The differences between these two groups and the control group (47%) was significant ($p < .05$). Separate analyses within each type of stimuli also showed the same kind of results.

Discussion

The results of the present experiment can be summarized as follows.

First, results in knowledge-poor domains (Ahn & Medin, 1989) were replicated by the control group in the current experiment. The control group who did not have any background knowledge rarely produced FR categories when the structure of exemplars had characteristic features in the resulting FR categories but a fair amount of FR categories was produced when they had sufficient features. Therefore, the two-stage model's explanation of FR sorting in knowledge-poor domains was once again supported.

Secondly, even when the potential FR categories had characteristic features, the knowledge on the prototypes of the potential FR categories led to the creation of FR categories. However, the difference between the prototype group and the control group in producing FR categories from the Characteristic set was significant only when the tribe stimuli were used, and it was not significant when the flower stimuli were used. The reason for this difference between the two types of materials is unclear.

Third, when the examples to be classified had characteristic features in the resulting FR categories, the theory group produced much more FR categories than both the control group and the prototype group. The significant difference between the theory group and the prototype group clearly showed that knowing underlying theories is more than simply knowing prototypes that could be derived from the theories.

These results suggest two problems with the current version of the two-stage model. First, the model does not explain why knowing prototypes in advance help people create FR categories. Considering the subjects' protocols, the prototype group seemed to be able to get over the strong bias of uni-dimensional sorting and instead they seemed to try to maximize matches between members of a category and its prototype. If people learn the most typical examples first, then the two-stage model might not be an appropriate account for category construction process.

Secondly, the advantage of knowing interproperty relationships is not explained by the model in its current form. However, sorting based on an underlying theory can be considered as a type of uni-dimensional sorting and therefore, it is not inconsistent with the spirit of the two-stage model.

The current version of the two-stage model assumes that features used for sorting are only surface features used to describe examples. However, people's strong bias to create highly structured categories (i.e., categories with defining features) would make them rely on background knowledge if it can provide them with defining features of categories. In other words, if background information provide them with a way to create a new dimension which allows them to construct categories that meet the task demand and that have defining features, they would rather create the new dimension than using only the given surface dimensions. Therefore, the two-stage model should be extended to allow creation of new dimensions using background knowledge if the new dimensions are better than the surface features in creating categories with defining features.

Conclusion

Based on the series of free sorting experiments conducted so far, it can be concluded that there are at least three ways to obtain FR structure. First, FR categories can be obtained as a result of two stages in which the first stage involves uni-dimensional sorting and the second stage involves assigning exceptions based on overall similarity. Secondly, knowing prototypes of each category before category construction encourages creation of FR categories. Third, the most effective way of producing FR categories known so far is creating a new dimension which can integrate surface features and carry out uni-dimensional sorting based on this dimension.

Acknowledgement

I would like to thank Doug Medin for his helpful advice in developing the experiment. Also I thank Rob Goldstone and Doug Medin for their comments on earlier drafts. This work was supported by NSF grant BNS88-12913 given to Doug Medin.

References

Ahn, W. (submitted). A two-stage model of category construction.

Ahn, W. (1990). A two-stage model of category construction. Unpublished doctoral dissertation, University of Illinois, Urbana, IL.

Ahn, W., & Medin, D. L. (1989). A two-stage categorization model of family resemblance sorting, Proceedings of the 11th Annual Conference of The Cognitive Science Society, Ann Arbor, MI, 315-322.

Anderberg, M. R. (1973). Cluster analysis for applications. New York: Academic Press.

Anderson, J. R. (1988). The place of cognitive architectures in a rational analysis. Proceedings of the Tenth Annual Conference of The Cognitive Science Society.

Fisher, D. (1987). Knowledge acquisition via incremental conceptual clustering, Machine Learning, 2, 139-172.

Imai, S., & Garner, W. R. (1965). Discriminability and preference for attributes in free and constrained classification. Journal of Experimental Psychology, 69, 596-608.

Imai, S., & Garner, W. R. (1968). Structure in perceptual classification. Psychonomic Monograph Supplements, 2 (9, Whole No. 2).

Massart, D., & Kaufman, L. (1983). The interpretation of analytical chemical data by the use of cluster analysis. New York: John Wiley & Sons.

Medin, D. L., Wattenmaker, W. D., & Hampson, S. E. (1987). Family resemblance, conceptual cohesiveness, and category construction. Cognitive Psychology, 19, 242-279.

Nakamura, G. V. (1985). Knowledge-based classification of ill-defined categories. Memory & Cognition, 13, 377-384.

Rosch, E. (1975). Universals and cultural specifics. In R. Brislin, S. Bochner, & W. Lonner (Eds.), Cross-cultural perspectives on learning. New York: Halsted Press.

Rosch, E., & Mervis, C. B. (1975). Family resemblance: Studies in the internal structure of categories. Cognitive Psychology, 7, 573-605.

Smith, E. E., & Medin, D. L. (1981). Categories and concepts. Cambridge, MA: Harvard University.

Superordinate and Basic Level Categories in Discourse: Memory and Context

Sandra L. Peters and William J. Rapaport
Department of Computer Science
State University of New York at Buffalo
peters@cs.buffalo.edu, rapaport@cs.buffalo.edu

ABSTRACT

Representations for natural category systems and a retrieval-based framework are presented that provide the means for applying generic knowledge about the semantic relationships between entities in discourse and the relative salience of these entities imposed by the current context. An analysis of the use of basic and superordinate level categories in discourse is presented, and the use of our representations and processing in the task of discourse comprehension is demonstrated.

1. Introduction. We present representations for natural category systems based on a Roschian model of categories that has been extended to accommodate recent categorization research [Barsalou & Billman 1988; Keil 1989; Medin 1985, 1987; Murphy 1985, 1988, 1989]. We take issue with the assumption, implicit in most artificial intelligence (AI), natural language processing (NLP) systems, that generic concepts can be viewed as simple lists or collections of attributes. Richer representations of categories are needed to provide the intraconcept relations that structure categories and interconcept relations that provide connections to the rest of the knowledge base; these semantic relations provide some of the background or commonsense knowledge necessary for language interpretation. An analysis of the use of basic and superordinate level categories in discourse is presented, and the use of our representations and processing in the task of discourse comprehension is demonstrated. Published texts, the twenty English "Pear Story" oral narratives told by subjects after viewing a film [Chafe 1980], and forty unpublished narratives written by student subjects who were directed to retell the story of O. Henry's *A Retrieved Reformation* [unpublished data collected by Scott & Segal] provide the data analyzed in this paper.

2. Representations for Natural Category Systems. We have previously discussed the special status of the basic level in promoting inferences: the informativeness of the basic level arises from the large amount of information organized at this level and the perceptual grounding of basic level objects [Peters & Shapiro 1987ab; Peters, Shapiro, & Rapaport 1988]. In this paper we will discuss extensions to previously presented representations. Our implementation uses the SNePS knowledge representation and reasoning system, including a generalized ATN parser-generator [Shapiro 1978; Shapiro & Rapaport 1987]. Since the basic level has special status in our representations and processing, we will begin with this level.

3. Enhanced Representations for Basic Level Concepts. Default generalizations are used to represent facts about the typical members of a category in our system. Thus, a basic level category in our semantic network is, in part, a collection of default generalizations about part/whole structure, other image schematic structure, additional percepts, and functional and interactional properties [See Peters & Shapiro 1987ab, Peters, Shapiro, & Rapaport 1988 for a discussion of these structures]. Figure 1 shows a default rule that can be paraphrased as *for all x, if x is a car, then typically x has an engine*, or more simply as *typically cars have engines*. We build many such default generalizations about a basic level category such as *car*.

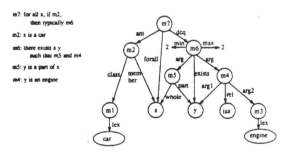

m7: for all x, if m2,
   then typically m6

m2: x is a car

m6: there exists a y
   such that m5 and m4

m5: y is a part of x

m4: y is an engine

The following defines a path to find all the parts of basic level objects
(def-path parts (compose arg2- arg1 part- whole forall- ant class))

Figure 1

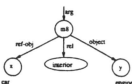

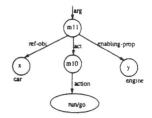

Figure 2: *Engines are interior parts of cars*   Figure 3: *Engines are mechanical parts of cars*   Figure 4: *Engines enable cars to run*

Many researchers have pointed out that as people's knowledge increases, they come to reject mere collections of surface attributes and other typical features as being adequate to specify concepts; categories become further structured by "deeper" conceptual relations [Barsalou & Billman 1988; Keil 1987, 1989; Medin & Wattenmaker 1987; Murphy & Medin 1985]. Additional default rules are built to capture these "deeper conceptual relations. Thus, in addition to part-whole relations (*m5* in Figure 1) and relations about other percepts, we structure basic level categories such as *car* with enabling, functional, and spatial relations, such as those shown in Figures 2-4. (We have not shown the entire default rules, just the additional conceptual relations that provide intraconcept connections. I.e, *m8*, *m9*, and *m11* would replace *m5*, the part-whole relation, in the default rule of Figure 1, creating three similar default rules.) Figure 2 shows a spatial relation that further structures (and clusters) the interior parts of *car*. We structure the external parts of *car* similarly. Figure 3 is used to further structure or cluster mechanical parts of *cars*, such as the *brakes* and *engine*; Figure 4 shows an enabling relation: *engines enable cars to run/go*. Thus, in our system, there will be many assertions linking *car* and *engine*: the knowledge associated with a basic level category such as *car* is highly interconnected and organized by spatial, temporal, casual, explanatory, and enabling relations. Basic level categories in our system are highly structured by intraconcept relations. Interconcept relations provide additional structure. E.g., *mortgage* is a thematic associate of *house*. Figure 5 shows the enabling relation that connects these two concepts.

3.1. Context-independent and Context-dependent Structure. Our representations and processing are also based on the view that the information activated after hearing or reading a category name varies widely across linguistic contexts. I.e., categorizing an entity at the basic level provides access to a large amount of information; however, only a small subset of the information associated with a category in long term memory (LTM) is incorporated in the temporary concept constructed in working memory (WM) in a particular context. Barsalou [1982] has proposed that there are two kinds of information associated with categories in LTM: context-independent (CI) properties are activated by the word for a category on all occasions, independent of context; context-dependent (CD) properties are activated only in relevant contexts.

We had originally decided that topographic structure, i.e., parts that define the overall shape of basic level objects, were context-independent attributes, i.e., automatically activated across all contexts. [Peters, Shapiro, & Rapaport 1988]. However, an examination of the normative data showing the properties listed by subjects for basic level objects in free articulation tasks [Ashcraft 1978; Rosch et al. 1976; Tversky & Hemenway 1984] disconfirms the hypothesis that all of the external parts that contribute to the overall shape are context-independent. Production frequency of properties is considered to be a measure of semantic relatedness between category names and their properties [Ashcraft 1978], and although some exterior parts of objects are always generated in these tasks, many are not. In addition, some interior (hidden) parts and some non-part attributes are always articulated. E.g., subjects generate *wheels, tires, seats, engine, steers,* and *transportation* for *car*. Here, only *wheels* and *tires* are exterior parts. *Tail, long ears, white fur, soft,* and *animal* are generated for *rabbit* (only *tail* and *long ears* are external parts), and *wings, beak, feathers, flies, eggs,* and *nests* for *bird*. We hypothesize that context-independence arises as additional causal and explanatory relations integrate or interconnect these attributes and the category name that evokes them. Thus, *engine* achieves context-independence because of its functional importance and because of the many conceptual relations that interconnect *engine* and *car*. Many interactional properties are also CI; e.g., *seats* and *steering wheel* achieve context-independence because we interact with cars by sitting on the *seats* and using the *steering wheel*. Thus, not all parts may achieve CI status, but rather, one could argue that only parts attended to get processed in a manner to produce CI status; in this case, causally relevant parts would have a distinct advantage [Barsalou 1989, personal communication].

158

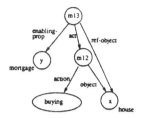

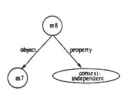

Figure 5: *Mortgages enable buying houses*   Figure 6: *Having an engine is a context-independent property of cars*

We currently create an assertion that marks CI properties, after a high degree of connectivity arises between properties and the category name. Figure 6 shows such an assertion, which we paraphrase as *having an engine is a CI property of cars*. CI properties, marked by such an assertion, are always activated when the category name is mentioned.

The category knowledge composed of the less strongly associated attributes (thematic associates and other non-centrally related entities) forms the context-dependent structure of basic level categories. We use the semantic relationships between verbs and nouns in discourse to evoke context-dependent entities, i.e., making the interrelated inferences normally made when particular verbs are used with particular nouns. E.g., *car* is associated with many different kinds of generalized actions: *driving, getting gas, washing, repairing, traveling, buying*. In our system, different knowledge associated with the category *car* is activated for each of these generalized actions. The demonstration runs in Appendix A show the activation of CI and CD entities in discourse comprehension, i.e., what interrelated inferences are made, and when they are made.

3.2. Examples of Contextual Fluctuations.   Two short examples illustrate the different entities highlighted in different contexts. In the first passage, parts of the car relevant to driving, starting, and stopping are referenced:

> As the *car* crept up the slope of the bridge, the inspector burst out laughing. He laughed so hard he could scarcely give his next direction. "Stop here," he said, wiping his eyes, "then start 'er up again."

> Marian pulled up beside the curb. She put the car in neutral, pulled on *the emergency*, waited a moment, and then put the car into gear again. Her face was set. As she released *the brake*, her foot slipped off *the clutch pedal* and *the engine* stalled (A. Gibbs, *The Test*, p. 255, italics added).

In the second passage, in which the car is stopped, and the characters get out and move around the outside of the car, exterior parts of the car are referenced:

> Lloyd brought the *car* to a screeching halt at the very edge of the boat launching ramp.

> Lloyd looked calm, cool, and loaded as he got out and swayed his way around to *the rear* of the car. I thought he was going to open *the trunk* and present me with my father's coat, but instead he hoisted himself up on *the back* of the car. He lit a cigarette and from his perch on *the roof* he seemed to be enjoying my fright over the near plunge into the water (P. Zindel, *Confessions of a Teenage Baboon*, pp. 106-113, italics added).

The next example shows the use of activated CI information. Since *fur* is automatically activated for Cyril, the cat, (fur has CI status, since it is an interactional property; i.e., people pet cats, stroking their fur), disambiguation of the reference *his fur* is easily handled. Disambiguation here does not involve choosing the most activated or highly focused entity, but rather choosing an activated entity with this activated property. Claws also has CI status for cats.

> When Jury (a detective) opened the door to Racer's (Jury's boss) sanctuary, Cyril (cat) slid between *his feet*, streaked snake-like across a carpet the color of *his fur*, and was scaling the bookcase set back against the wall to the left of Racer's large desk. *His claws* were like pinions digging into forensic science, ... (M. Grimes, *The Five Bells and Bladebone*, p. 188, italics added).

An example showing a reference to a CD entity follows. Here *the paw* is evoked in the context of the cat *striking* at the water:

> The cat walked out of the secluded garden and toward the bank of a stream farther on. Here it crouched and watched a wren having a dust bath. Before it could pounce, the wren was away, skimming across the water. Looking into the stream, as if the bird might have fallen there, the cat saw shadows deep inside darting, hanging suspended, darting forward again. The cat struck at the water, trying to fix the moving shadow. ... It yawned again, washed at *the paw*, stopped when it saw something skittering across the footbridge and followed. (M. Grimes, p. 11, italics added)

4. Superordinates and Basic Level Names in Discourse.   Since basic level categories carry the most information, they denote referents at their level of "usual" utility; i.e., at a level that is both sufficiently informative and cognitively efficient to manipulate. Thus the use of basic level terms to refer to entities in discourse follows the Gricean maxims of conversational quantity and manner, since basic level names usually carry sufficient information for an addressee/reader to be able to identify the individual or category being referred to. What constraints cause a speaker/writer to abandon basic level terms in categorizing a given entity at a given point? In particular, when are superordinate level names used in discourse, and how is the knowledge stored with superordinate level concepts used during discourse comprehension? The next sections will analyze the use of superordinate terms in written and oral narratives.

4.1. Discourse Analysis: Use of Superordinate Level Names. Basic level terms constituted 93% of the nominal references to concrete entities in the twenty "Pear Story" oral narratives; superordinate level terms were used very infrequently, constituting only 2% of the references [Downing, 1980]. Basic level terms again predominated in the Scott & Segal subjects' written narratives, constituting 75% of nominal references to concrete entities. Superordinates occurred much more frequently than in the oral "Pear Story" narratives, constituting 17% of the references in the Scott & Segal written narratives. In the next sections superordinate level references will be examined more carefully.

4.1.1. Groups, Collections, and Classes. It has been suggested [e.g., Murphy & Wisniewski 1989; Wisniewski & Murphy 1989] that superordinates are frequently used to refer to groups, collections, and classes. I.e., basic level names are frequently used to refer to individuals or single objects, while speakers use superordinate names such as *furniture*, *clothes* and *plants* to refer to groups of related objects simultaneously [Wisniewski & Murphy 1989]. Our text analysis confirmed this usage of superordinate names. The following passages from O. Henry's *A Retrieved Reformation* (with italics added to indicate the superordinate level term) illustrate this usage:

(1) Take him back, Cronin, smiled the warden, and fix him up with outgoing *clothes*.

(2) Pulling out from the wall a folding-bed, Jimmy slid back a panel in the wall and dragged out a dust-covered suitcase. He opened this and gazed fondly at the finest set of burglar's *tools* in the East.

(3) He was at much at home in the *family* of Mr. Adams and that of Annabel's married sister as if he were already a member.

In the following sections we discuss additional uses of superordinate labels that were found in the written and oral narratives examined.

4.1.2. Introductory Mentions of Entities. Frequently superordinate labels are used to introduce entities to the hearer/reader, i.e., an author/speaker uses a superordinate level term for the first mention of an entity, later switching to a basic level term [Downing, 1980]. This technique is typically used only with characters and other elements that are central to the narrative. Two examples of this technique follow:

It was on the Dover road that lay, on a Friday night late in November, before the first of the *persons* with whom this history has business. [Dickens, *A Tale of Two Cities*, p. 8]

About three hundred eighty-five thousand years ago, when the oceans and continents were in place as we know them to-day, the land bridge from Asia was open, and a huge ponderous *animal*, looking much like an oversized elephant but with enormous protruding tusks, slowly made his way eastward, followed by four females and their young. [Michener, *Alaska*, p. 15]

In both of these examples the reader has the expectation that she will soon find out more about the characters being introduced by the superordinate level terms, and the superordinate level names seem to contribute to the readers being gradually "drawn" into the story. Thus, the readers' attention becomes focused on entities introduced in this way.

4.1.3. References to Focused Discourse Entities. A superordinate label is also frequently used to refer to a discourse entity that is focused, but not so highly activated that a pronoun or zero is easy to understand, yet too highly activated for a basic level term to be used without sounding childish or redundant. I.e., the basic level term may give too much information, given the focus level of the referent. For example:

He took a train for three hours, got off and went to a cafe owned by Mike Dolan. Dolan gave Jimmy his key. Jimmy went to a room in the back of the *establishment*. [Scott & Segal unpublished data, subject's retelling of O. Henry's, *A Retrieved Reformation*]

At the end of this passage the key and the cafe are competing, focused discourse entities (both can be referred to using *it*). Since the key is more highly focused, a pronominal reference to the cafe (use of *it*) seems less suitable than the use of the superordinate term *the establishment*. The use of the basic level term *the cafe* also seems less suitable than *the establishment*, because it is redundant. An additional example follows:

The cab stopped in front of Lloyd's house and I got out. I think the driver thought I was going to run away without paying but my slacks were so tight I couldn't get my money out of my pocket without standing up. I gave him the fare, including a good tip, which left me with about a dollar and twenty-nine cents to my name. It was the absolute end of my savings from the last case my mother had, where her boss gave me a couple of dollars a day to walk his Yorkies. The driver just floored his junk heap and took off making so much noise I didn't hear the lilt of music until the taxi turned at the far corner. It had been quite a while since Helen and I had vacated the *place* and I couldn't believe the party was still going on. [P. Zindel, *Confessions of a Teenaged Baboon, p. 141]*

Here, a pronominal reference to the house (*it*) cannot be used, because there is too much distance between the first mention of the *house* and this reference. However, the superordinate, *the place*, is easily disambiguated. The next example again shows competing, focused discourse entities:

Anyway, this time it was a black cat reclining in the middle of this busy boulevard and it was positioned so it looked like it had been half run over by a car, squashing part of its body into a type of base like a buttress for a paper doll. It looked like I was staring at a stone statue of a cat with metallic eyes glazed with fire and that if I wanted to I could just take the *thing* home and use it as a garden ornament. The *animal* seemed dead except for its eyes, and I had the strangest feeling it might still be alive, . . . [P. Zindel, *Confessions of a Teenaged Baboon, p. 121]*

Here the superordinate label *the thing* refers to one discourse entity, the *stone statue of a cat*, while *the animal* refers to a second discourse entity, the *cat.*

4.1.4. Superordinates: Generality. Since superordinate labels are more general (less specific) than basic level terms, they can be used to communicate a sense of "vagueness". Thus, a superordinate name may be used to communicate that someone (a) doesn't know what something is, or what the name of something is (see example (1) below); (b) cannot see something very well (see example (2) below; (c) doesn't remember specifically what something was (see example (3) below); (d) doesn't want to call attention to irrelevant details or promote too many inferences (see example (3) again), or (e) wants to deliberately conceal information (e.g., in a mystery the detective may choose not to reveal the specific murder weapon used to commit the crime to a witness being questioned).

(1) Three boys came out, helped him pick himself up, pick up his bike, pick up the pears, one of them had a *toy*, which was like a clapper. And, I don't know what you call it except a paddle with a ball suspended on a string. [Chafe, 1980, transcript from English "Pear Film" narrative]

(2) Zoe squinted through a square of the lattice. Outside the crawl space it was lighter. She could see three *figures* standing beside a small truck. [Z. Oneal, *War Work, p. 133]*

(3) He [Jimmy] jumps on a train heading for the state boarder [sic] after he has some *food* and wine not of prison origin. [Scott & Segal unpublished data, subject's retelling of O. Henry's, *A Retrieved Reformation*]

In (1) the speaker telling the story of the "Pear Film" didn't know a name for the toy that a character in the film was playing with. In (2) Zoe cannot see the characters she is describing very well. In (3) the subject retelling the story either didn't remember that the food Jimmy Valentine had eaten was broiled chicken, or chose to be less specific when recounting this event, using a superordinate label rather than a more specific, basic level one.

4.2. Non-taxonomic Superordinates. In general, superordinates convey much less information than basic level terms. However, non-taxonomic superordinates (e.g., friend, enemy, jerk) frequently add information, communicating an attitude toward the referent(s):

I'm fifty and for half of those years I had worked for a Chicago newspaper I would rather not identify because it no longer exists. Its name exists, but it is a vulgar *rag* filled with sex and crime, edited by a gang of *creeps*, and owned by a right wing egomaniac who bought it for a song from the childish, idiotic woman who inherited it. [D. Kiker, *Murder on Clam Pond, p. 22]*

Non-taxonomic superordinates also frequently focus attention on particular attributes. In the following example, *enemy* evokes or activates entities such as *claws, tusks, teeth* as well as external body parts. All of these are relevant in the context of the struggle between these two enemies.

. . . he [Mastodon] heard a rustle that disturbed him. Prudently, he withdrew lest some enemy leap upon him from a hiding place high in the trees, and he was not a moment too soon, for as he turned away from the willow, he saw emerging from the protection of a nearby copse *his most fearsome enemy.*

It was a kind of tiger with powerful *claws* and a pair of frightful upper *teeth* almost three feet long and incredibly sharp. Mastodon knew that though this saber-tooth could not drive *those fearsome teeth* through *the heavy skin of his protected rear or sides*, it could if it obtained a secure foothold on *his back*, sink them into *the softer skin at the base of his neck.*
. . . Mastodon had *his long tusks*, of course, but he could not lunge forward and expect to impale his adversary on them, they were not intended for this purpose. [J. Michener, *Alaska*, p. 17, italics added]

4.3. Superordinates: Theories and Causal Reasoning. A number of researchers [e.g., Keil 1987, 1989; Murphy & Medin 1985; Barsalou & Billman 1988] have pointed out that our deep, rich theories about objects are linked to superordinate level concepts: theories that take us beyond categorization based on perceptual or surface similarity. In

161

order to appropriately categorize a whale as a mammal, we are required to move beyond using surface similarity as a basis for categorization: we need to recognize that hidden features and elaborated theories about origins are more important than perceptual features in categorizing biological kinds at a superordinate level. Theoretical knowledge also helps us to deduce reasons for correlations among basic level features: e.g., wings, hollow bones, small, and flies are correlated because they are causally linked. Our scientific knowledge organized at the superordinate level helps us understand these linkages. Taxonomic superordinates enrich basic level concepts, providing access to deep causal and explanatory relations.

4.4. Causal Reasoning in Discourse Understanding. Even when superordinates are not explicitly mentioned in discourse, they may provide the causal and explanatory relations necessary to our understanding of discourse. Our understanding of humor frequently depends on our use of superordinate level knowledge. E.g., in a short monologue about coffee, Garrison Keillor stated that although people said that decaffeinated coffee was dangerous and that a chemical used to decaffeinate coffee caused cancer in rats, his feeling was that the more rats that get cancer the better [*Garrison Keillor's American Radio Company of the Air*, February 16, 1990, WNED-FM]. This joke like many others is amusing because we recognize that an inappropriate conclusion has been drawn: the reasoning has been ineffectual. I.e., we know that rats, like people, are animals (in fact we know that both are mammals); that animal models are used to screen carcinogenic agents (with rats frequently being used as test animals); that if a chemical causes cancer in one kind of animal, there is a great likelihood that it will cause cancer in other animals (especially closely related animals). The knowledge used in this reasoning is superordinate level knowledge.

5. Discourse Processing: Inferences. The processing performed by our system will be illustrated by considering the problem of comprehending references to implicitly evoked CI and CD entities in discourse. As stated previously, basic level categories evoke a rich set of entities which may be referred to later in discourse. Superordinates, in contrast, evoke few discourse entities directly associated with the superordinate category itself, but frequently influence what is activated

The inferences made at the basic level seem to involve automatic processing: i.e., they are initiated by well-established memory structures, rely on connectivity between concepts, are computationally "cheap", and are plausible inferences rather than logically derived assertions which necessarily follow from the text. Superordinates, in contrast, do not seem to promote many inferences [Rosch 1981; Tversky & Hemenway 1984; Gelman 1989]: subjects frequently list few or no attributes for superordinate level concepts. Thus, our knowledge about superordinate concepts is a deeper and less easily verbalized knowledge, involving underlying principles and theories about the world. Inferencing at this level is not computationally "cheap" and effortless, but instead seems to require substantial attentional resources. The inferences made involve causal knowledge and explanatory relations (theoretically-oriented knowledge), and are deducible from the text and the knowledge base. We use a "spreading activation" form of inference similar to marker passing to activate the relevant basic level information, and deductive inference to reason about theory-laden superordinate level knowledge, forming assertions which follow logically or necessarily from the text.

5.1. Path-Based Inference. The SNePS path-based inference package provides the subconscious reasoning required for the automatic activation of CI and relevant CD entities: the definition of appropriate paths in the network enables the automatic retrieval of the relevant satellite concepts of basic level concepts. The context-independent entities can be retrieved by defining a path of arcs from a node representing a basic level category, e.g., *car*, to its context-independent properties: *wheels, tires, engine, seats, steering wheel*. The following path is used to retrieve all context-independent properties of basic level categories:

(find (compose arg2- arg- deq- object- (domain-restrict (property context-independent)) object ant class)(find lex *basic-level-category-name*))

Our current implementation activates context-dependent information in response to discourse comprehension of events containing generalized actions such as *buying/selling a house, driving/stopping/repairing/washing a car, seeing/walking/washing a dog*. Additional paths are defined to retrieve these entities. Parts can be retrieved by defining a path of arcs from a node representing a basic level category, e.g., *car*, to its parts: *engine, roof, hood, trunk, wheels, brakes*, etc. Figure 1 in section 3 shows a defined path called *parts* which is used to activate these entities. The "parts" path is never used alone, rather it's used in conjunction with additional paths specified through default rules such as those shown in part in Figures 2-4, i.e., paths through the spatial, enabling, and other intraconcept and interconcept relations described earlier. E.g., we use an "exterior or surface parts path" to retrieve only exterior parts following generalized actions such as *washing a car* or *watching a bird*, and interior, mechanical parts following generalized actions such as *repairing a car*. Causal and enabling relations are considered to be more important than other relations in this system, and satellite associates that enable actions are activated by using "paths to enablers" to retrieve these associates in the relevant contexts. E.g., *mortgage* is retrieved following the generalized action, *buying a house*. An ATN grammar then makes use of the defined paths to activate, i.e., implicitly focus, the context-

162

independent and relevant context-dependent satellite entities of a basic level category (that has been either encountered in input or activated by a subordinate level concept): returning all the nodes that are found at the end of the defined paths of arcs emanating from the basic level categories and placing them in the system's working memory. (It is well established that categories automatically activate their superiors [Rosch 1978; Barsalou 1982].)

6. Demonstration of Discourse Processing. Appendix A shows four sample runs of SNePS/CASSIE illustrating some of our current capabilities. User input is on lines with the :-prompt; the systems' output and timing information are on the following lines. After a few of the sentences, a list of the activated context-independent (CI) and context-dependent (CD) entities or nodes (labeled CI evoked and CD evoked respectively) associated with the basic level category *car* is shown. (A complete listing of the associates of *car* activated in these sample runs is also found in Appendix A. See *Nodes Evoked in Demos 1, 2, & 3.*)

In sentence (1abc), comprehension of the basic level category *car* implicitly evokes many entities, including the following CI entities: the *engine, seats, steering wheel, wheels,* and *tires*.[1] In addition, the verb *bought* in conjunction with *car* activates a CD entity: the *price* of the car. Sentence (2a) of Demo 1 contains a reference to an implicitly focused CI item, *the engine;* sentence (3a), a reference to an implicitly focused CD item, *the price.* The verb *fixed* in conjunction with *car* in sentence (4a) of Demo 1 causes the activation of many CD associates of *car*, e.g., the *carburetor, distributor, spark plugs, battery,* and *brakes*.[2] Sentences (5a) - (7a) contain references to previously activated CI and CD entities.

In sentence (2b) of Demo 2, the generalized action *washing the car* causes activation of many CD entities: exterior parts of cars (the *bumper, grill, trunk, hood, roof, tires, wheels, windshield, finish,* and the *exterior*). Many of these activated entities are referenced in sentences (3b) - (7b).

In sentence (4c) of Demo 3, the mention of *starting the car* evokes many CD entities, e.g., the *ignition, key, battery, accelerator, brakes,* and a CI entity, the *engine.* Sentences (5c) - (12c) contain references to these activated entities.

In sentence (1d) of Demo 4 comprehension of the basic level category *house* implicitly activates many CI entities (e.g., *windows, doors, roof, shelter*). In addition, the verb *bought* in conjunction with *house,* activates such CD entities as the *mortgage* and *price.* Thus, the concept *house* constructed in WM has been tailored to the current context. Sentence (2d) contains a reference to the *mortgage* which was activated in (1d). Sentence (4d) contains a reference to *the butler,* an entity that has not been activated, since it is not a CI associate of *house,* and was not activated in the context of *buying a house.* Thus, comprehension of *the butler* requires inferencing using the total knowledge base. A comparison of the timing information for sentences (2d) and (4d) illustrates that in our system the comprehension time for a non-activated entity (*the butler*) is longer than that for an activated entity (*the mortgage*). Sentence (5d) contains a reference to the subordinate level category *collie,* which activates its immediate superior, the basic level category *dog.* The usual inferences about *dogs* are then drawn, and many CI entities (e.g., *tail, barking, animal*) are activated. It also contains the generalized action of *buying a dog,* so *cost* is activated. In sentence (6d), resolution of the definite anaphor *her barking* cannot be based on the normal mechanism of finding the most highly focused antecedent that matches the semantic features of the possessive pronoun *her.* It was not Lucy's barking! Rather, it requires a search of WM for the concept of *barking,* returning its evoking concept *collie.* Sentences (12d) and (13d) also illustrate the need for using a focusing mechanism based on more than activatedness, recency, and matching semantic features. I.e., *tail* was evoked as part of the basic level category *cat* in (7d), but not as part of either the subordinate level category *canary* or its immediate superior *bird;* whereas *chirp* was evoked as associated with *bird/canary* in (9d), but not with *cat.* Our processing of *his tail* and *his chirp* simply involves searching WM for these previously activated entities and their evoking concepts, not a search of the whole knowledge base. Thus, integration of implicitly evoked associates (e.g., *chirp*) with the previously mentioned evoking concept (e.g., *bird/canary/Tweety*) is quite simple and comprehension time quite fast.

---

[1] The CI entities that are always automatically activated in our system are those associates that have many causal and explanatory relations integrating them with the basic level category name that evokes them. They also are taken from property-norm data of Ashcraft, Rosch, and Tversky & Hemenway referenced earlier in this paper.

[2] Because of space limitations for these sample runs, only a few CD entities are shown as being evoked. Many more nodes are actually activated.

7. Future Research. Many problems remain to be solved. In particular, further work is needed in developing representations for and using superordinate level knowledge, in deciding which properties associated with a category have context-independent status, and in extending our work to consider context effects arising from the topic area, the task at hand, goals and discourse purposes.

REFERENCES

(1) Ashcraft, M. (1978), "Property Norms for Typical and Atypical Items from 17 Categories: A Description and Discussion," *Memory & Cognition*, vol 6, no. 3, pp. 227-232.

(2) Barsalou, L. W. (1982), "Context-independent and context-dependent information in concepts," *Memory & Cognition*, vol 10, pp. 82-93.

(3) Barsalou, L. W. (1987), "The Instability of Graded Structure," In U. Neisser (ed.), *Concepts and Conceptual Development* (Cambridge: Cambridge University Press).

(4) Barsalou, L. W., & Billman, D. (1988), "Systematicity and Semantic Ambiguity," In D. S. Gorfein (ed.), *Resolving Semantic Ambiguity* (New York: Springer-Verlag).

(5) Downing, P. (1980), "Factors Influencing Lexical Choice in Narrative," in W. Chafe, (ed.), *The Pear Stories* (New Jersey: ABLEX Publishing Company)

(6) Keil, F. (1987), "Conceptual Development and Category Structure," In U. Neisser, (ed.), *Concepts and Conceptual Development* (Cambridge: Cambridge University Press).

(7) Keil, F. (1989), *Concepts, Kinds, and Cognitive Development* (Cambridge: MIT Press)

(8) Mervis, C. B., & Rosch, E. (1981), "Categorization of Natural Objects," Ann. Rev. Psychol., vol. 32, pp. 89-115.

(9) Medin, D., & Wattenmaker, W. (1987), "Category Cohesiveness, Theories, and Cognitive Archeology," In U. Neisser, (ed.), *Concepts and Conceptual Development* (Cambridge: Cambridge University Press).

(10) Murphy, G., & Medin, D. (1985), "The Role of Theories in Conceptual Coherence," *Psychological Review*, vol. 92, pp. 289-316.

(11) Murphy, G. L., & Wisniewski, E. J. (1989), "Categorizing Objects in Isolation and in Scenes: What a Superordinate is Good For," *Journal of Experimental Psychology: Learning, Memory, and Cognition*, 15, 572-586.

(12) Peters, S. L., & Shapiro, S. C. (1987a), "A Representation for Natural Category Systems I," *Proceedings of the Ninth Annual Conference of the Cognitive Science Society*, Seattle, WA, pp. 379-390,

(13) Peters, S. L., & Shapiro, S. C. (1987b), "A Representation for Natural Category Systems II," *Proceedings of the Tenth International Joint Conference on Artificial Intelligence*, Milan, pp. 140-146.

(14) Peters, S. L., & Shapiro, S. C. (1988), "Flexible Natural Language Processing and Roschian Category Theory," *Proceedings of the Tenth Annual Conference of the Cognitive Science Society*, Montreal, Quebec, Canada, pp.

(15) Rosch, E., Mervis, C. B., Gray, W. D., Johnson, D. M., & Boyes-Braem, P. (1976), "Basic Objects in Natural Categories," *Cognitive Psychology*, vol. 8, pp. 382-439.

(16) Rosch, E., & Lloyd, B. B., (eds.), (1978), *Cognition and Categorization* (Hillsdale, NJ: Lawrence Erlbaum Associates).

(17) Shapiro, S. C. (1978), "Path-Based and Node-Based Inference in Semantic Networks," In D. Waltz, (ed.), *Theoretical Issues in Natural Language Processing-2* (Urbana, Illinois) pp. 219-225.

(18) Shapiro, S. C., & Rapaport, W. J. (1987), "SNePS Considered as a Fully Intensional Propositional Semantic Network," In G. McCalla & N. Cercone, (eds.), *The Knowledge Frontier: Essays in the Representation of Knowledge* (New York: Springer-Verlag), pp. 262-315.

(19) Tversky, B., & Hemenway, K. (1984), "Objects, Parts, and Categories," *Journal Of Experimental Psychology: General*, vol. 113, pp. 169-93.

(20) Wisniewski, E. J., & Murphy, G. L. (1989) "Superordinate and Basic Category Names in Discourse: A Textual Analysis," *Discourse Processes*, 12, 245-261.

CITED TEXTS

(1) Dickens, C., *A Tale of Two Cities* (New York: Colonial Press)

(2) Gibbs, A., (1940), "The Test," in *Short Stories from the New Yorker* (New York: Simon and Schuster), 252-256.

(3) Grimes, M., (1987), *The Five Bells and Bladebone* (New York: Dell).

(4) Kiker, D. (1986), *Murder on Clam Pond* (New York: Ballantine Books).

(5) Michener, J., (1988), *Alaska* (New York: Random House).

(6) North, S., (1963), *Rascal* (New York: E.P. Dutton & Co.).

(7) Scott, P., & Segal, E., Unpublished Narratives, Retellings of O. Henry's, "A Retrieved Reformation".

(8) Zindel, P., (1977), *Confessions of a Teenage Baboon* (New York: Harper and Row).

Appendix A

Demo 1: *Repairing the Car*

(1a) : Lucy bought an old car.
I understand that Lucy bought an old car
CI evoked: (m138 m51 m20 m12 m3 m317)
CD evoked: (m94)
( ) exec: 12.41 sec   gc: 4.71 sec

(2a) : the engine was rebuilt.
I understand that the engine of the old car is
rebuilt
( ) exec: 9.28 sec   gc: 2.35 sec

(3a) : the price was low.
I understand that the price of the old car is
low
( ) exec: 9.21 sec   gc: 2.33 sec

(4a) : A mechanic fixed the car.
I understand that a mechanic fixed the old car
CD evoked: (m245 m224 m217 m153 m35
m3)
( ) exec: 13.08 sec   gc: 2.43 sec

(5a) : He tuned the engine.
I understand that the mechanic tuned the engine of the old car
( ) exec: 11.86 sec   gc: 4.85 sec

(6a) : He replaced the carburetor.
I understand that the mechanic replaced the
carburetor of the old car
( ) exec: 11.81 sec   gc: 2.38 sec

(7a) : He fixed the distributor.
I understand that the mechanic fixed the distributor of the old car
( ) exec: 11.86 sec   gc: 2.40 sec

Demo 2: *Washing the Car*

(1b) :Lucy bought a red car
I understand that Lucy bought a red car
CI evoked: (m138 m51 m20 m12 m3 m317)
CD evoked: (m94)
( ) exec: 12.38 sec   gc: 4.83 sec

(2b) : She washed the car.
I understand that Lucy washed the red car
CD evoked: (m278 m265 m131 m87 m80
m73 m66 m59 m28 m20 m12)
( ) exec: 11.88 sec   gc: 2.35 sec

(3b) : She cleaned the windshield.
I understand that Lucy cleaned the windshield
of the red car
( ) exec: 11.98 sec   gc: 4.83 sec

(4b) : She washed the grill.
I understand that Lucy washed the grill of the
red car
( ) exec: 11.75 sec   gc: 4.81 sec

(5b) : She scrubbed the front bumper..
I understand that Lucy scrubbed the front
bumper of the red car
( ) exec: 12.36 sec   gc: 4.98 sec

(6b) : She waxed the hood.
I understand that Lucy waxed the hood of the
red car
( ) exec: 12.21 sec   gc: 2.63 sec

(7b) : The exterior is sparkling.
I understand that the exterior of the red car
is sparkling
( ) exec: 10.55 sec   gc: 2.48 sec

Demo 3: *Driving the Car*

(1c) : Lucy bought an old car.
I understand that Lucy bought an old car
CI evoked: (m138 m51 m20 m12 m3 m317)
CD evoked: (m94)
( ) exec: 12.73 sec   gc: 4.80 sec

(2c) : she took a driving test.
I understand that Lucy took a driving test
( ) exec: 10.36 sec   gc: 4.73 sec

(3c) : She was nervous.
I understand that Lucy is nervous
( ) exec: 6.18 sec   gc: 2.40 sec

(4c) : she started the car.
I understand that nervous Lucy started the old
car
CD evoked: (m224 m160 m147 m43 m35 m3)
( ) exec: 12.51 sec   gc: 2.41 sec

(5c) : she flooded the engine.
I understand that nervous Lucy flooded the engine of the old car ( )
exec: 13.01 sec   gc: 4.85 sec

(6c) : she restarted the car.
I understand that nervous Lucy restarted the old
car
( ) exec: 11.33 sec   gc: 2.41 sec

(7c) : she tapped the accelerator.
I understand that nervous Lucy tapped the accelerator of the old car ( )
exec: 12.90 sec   gc: 4.95 sec

(8c) : she entered a busy street.
I understand that nervous Lucy entered a busy
street
( ) exec: 12.30 sec   gc: 4.86 sec

(9c) : she approached an intersection.
I understand that nervous Lucy approached an
intersection
( ) exec: 10.25 sec   gc: 2.48 sec

(10c) :she stopped the car.
I understand that nervous Lucy stopped the old
car
( ) exec: 13.15 sec   gc: 2.58 sec

(11c) : the brakes were squeaky.
I understand that the brakes of the old car are
squeaky
( ) exec: 8.25 sec   gc: 0.00 sec

(12c) : she failed the test.
I understand that nervous Lucy failed the driving
test
( ) exec: 11.03 sec   gc: 2.58 sec

Nodes evoked in Demos 1, 2, & 3:

(m3 (lex (engine)))
(m12 (lex (tire)))
(m20 (lex (wheel)))   (m28 (lex (windshield)))
(m35 (lex (brake)))   (m43 (lex (accelerator)))
(m51 (lex (seat)))   (m59 (lex (trunk)))
(m66 (lex (roof)))   (m73 (lex (hood)))
(m80 (lex (exterior)))
(m87 (lex (finish)))   (m94 (lex (price)))
(m131 (lex (door)))
(m138 (lex (steeringwheel)))
(m147 (lex (ignition)))
(m153 (lex (carburetor)))
(m160 (lex (key)))
(m217 (lex (sparkplugs)))
(m224 (lex (battery)))
(m245 (lex (distributor)))
(m265 (lex (grill)))
(m278 (lex (bumper)))
(m317 (lex (vehicle)))

Demo 4: General Demo

(1d) : Lucy bought a Victorian house.
I understand that Lucy bought a Victorian
house
( ) exec: 11.28 sec   gc: 4.83 sec

(2d) : The mortgage is huge.
I understand that the mortgage of the Victorian house is huge
( ) exec: 9.28 sec   gc: 2.35 sec

(3d) : John visited her.
I understand that John visited Lucy
( ) exec: 8.48 sec   gc: 2.48 sec

(4d) : The butler opened the door.
I understand that a butler opened the door of
the Victorian house ( )
exec: 20.83 sec   gc: 7.45 sec

(5d) : Lucy bought a collie.
I understand that Lucy bought a collie
( ) exec: 11.83 sec   gc: 2.61 sec

(6d) : Her bark wakes Lucy.
I understand that the bark of the collie is waking Lucy
( ) exec: 13.98 sec   gc: 5.16 sec

(7d) : John owns a cat
I understand that John owns a cat
( ) exec: 10.20 sec   gc: 2.46 sec

Demo 4 Continued

(8d) : The cat is named Sylvester.
I understand that Sylvester is the cat
( ) exec: 8.05 sec   gc: 0.00 sec

(9d) : He bought a canary.
I understand that John bought a canary
( ) exec: 10.66 sec   gc: 2.48 sec

(10d) : The bird is named Tweety.
I understand that Tweety is the bird
( ) exec: 8.60 sec   gc: 0.00 sec

(11d) : The cat stalks Tweety.
I understand that Sylvester is stalking Tweety
( ) exec: 11.86 sec   gc: 2.36 sec

(12d) : His tail is swishing.
I understand that the tail of Sylvester is swishing
( ) exec: 10.63 sec   gc: 2.53 sec

(13d) : The chirp alerted John.
I understand that the chirp of Tweety alerted
John
( ) exec: 13.46 sec   gc: 2.58 sec

165

Learning Overlapping Categories*

Joel D. Martin
School of Information and Computer Science
Georgia Institute of Technology
Atlanta, Georgia 30332
joel@gatech.edu

Abstract

Models of human category learning have predominately assumed that both the structure in the world and the analogous structure of the internal cognitive representations are best modeled by hierarchies of disjoint categories. Strict taxonomies do, in fact, capture important structure of the world. However, there are realistic situations in which systems of overlapping categories can engender more accurate inferences than can taxonomies. Two preliminary models for learning overlapping categories are presented and their benefit is illustrated. The models are discussed with respect to their potential implications for theory-based category learning and conceptual combination.

1 Introduction

The natural world can be neatly organized into a hierarchy of disjoint categories. A platypus is a mammal, not a bird; and mammals are animals, not plants. Artificial categories can also be placed in a strict hierarchy. Something that is a balpeen hammer is not a claw hammer. Similarly, it is a hammer, not a saw; and a hand tool, not a power tool. Each category, whether natural or artificial, can be distinguished from its alternatives by its distinct intensional description, which might be represented as lists of feature frequencies or a list of instances. Taxonomies such as these are elegant, economical, and seem to be the most suitable representation for many natural and artificial categories.

Presumably, if humans learn and use taxonomic structures, they would efficiently and accurately characterize the regularities in the world. The assumption that they do so has been an extremely fruitful seed for generating models of human category learning. So fruitful, in fact, that alternate structures of categories have been neglected until recently. Structures of overlapping categories can actually be superior to taxonomies when there are multiple equally good ways to partition a set of experiences. In these circumstances, non-disjoint categories permit faster learning and more economical storage than is possible with disjoint categories.

If one assumes the world contains such domains and that humans are optimally adapted to their environment as suggested by Anderson (1988), then overlapping category structures should motivate better models of human behavior. Indeed, some structures of overlapping categories suggest preliminary methods for modeling theory-based concept learning (Murphy & Medin, 1985) and conceptual combination (Smith & Osherson, 1984).

*This research was supported in part by a Georgia Institute of Technology Stelson grant and NIH grant 7R23HD20522-03.

2 Taxonomies

The purpose of taxonomies is to maximize the probability of correct inference without requiring the retrieval of large sets of past experiences for every prediction. They compactly summarize predictive relationships. However, there are domains for which taxonomies not only do not maximize the probability of correct inferences, but also do not compactly represent the regularities. These are domains that permit multiple different, but equally predictive taxonomies. Each of these taxonomies allows roughly the same number of correct inferences, but they differ with respect to which attributes or aspects of experiences about which they are most informative.

2.1 Disjoint categories

A set of objects or events can be split into disjoint subsets in many ways. Given a collection of a dog, a cat, a goldfish, and a whale, one split may group the dog with the fish and the cat with the whale. Another may assign each individual to a separate subset, and yet another may divide the mammals from the fish. Of these many possibilities the one that permits the most correct inferences is preferred. Any collection of categories is only useful to the extent that category membership permits accurate predictions. For instance, knowing that a particular object is a bird allows probable predictions about body covering, food, and habitat.

This notion has been formalized for a single set of disjunctive categories by both Gluck and Corter (1985) and Anderson (1990). For example, Gluck and Corter derive that the probability of making correct inferences is equal to the sum, over all categories, of the probability of the category multiplied by the square of the probability of a particular value given the category:

$$P(correct) = \sum_k P(C_k) \sum_j \sum_i P(A_j = V_{ij} \mid C_k)^2 \qquad (1)$$

This measure could be applied by performing every possible partitioning and choosing the one with the largest $P(correct)$. This would be horrendously expensive, though, because the number of possible partitionings grows exponentially with the number of categories. A more practical approach accepts a set of experiences in a particular order and deals with each instance in turn. Each instance can be used to update the intension of a category. It is added to the category that allows the greatest rise in the probability of correct inference. This is a hill-climbing search toward the optimal partitioning (Fisher, 1987).

Gluck and Corter (1985) originally intended their measure to be a predictor of the basic level in a taxonomy (eg. Rosch et al., 1976). However, it or a similar measure can be used recursively to form complete taxonomies, as was suggested by Fisher (1987) and Anderson (1990).

Gluck and Corter's measure will be used below as a paradigmatic example of a model for learning disjoint categories. As well, Fisher's (1987) method for generating hierarchies will be assumed. The generated hierarchies, unlike the disjoint category measure, are not necessarily close to optimal. The technique produces performance that is below the theoretical maximum in some situations because it attempts to maximize the predictive work done at each layer. However, there are no formal theories for acquiring optimally predictive hierarchies, so this heuristic method will suffice.

2.2 The trouble with taxonomies

Fisher's (1987) COBWEB system, which is rooted in Gluck and Corter's (1985) measure, has been quite successful at acquiring taxonomies that allow accurate inferences. COBWEB has been applied to both real and artificial domains. Given this success, it is valuable to identify what shortcomings COBWEB and related models might have, if any. As well, if shortcomings are found, it is essential to demonstrate that the conditions in which taxonomies fail occur frequently in human experience. However, if such conditions are very rare, humans would do well enough with taxonomies and not require any alternative model.

2.2.1 The problems

All of the difficulties with taxonomies that will be discussed here occur when the domain to be learned allows many different, but equally useful taxonomies. These domains will be referred to as *cross-classification* domains. For example, a list of athletes may specify their height, weight, eye color, and hair color. For these athletes, the values for height and weight are mutually predictive, as are the values for eye and hair color. Height though, is only randomly related to eye and hair color, and similarly for weight. Taller athletes are heavier and blue-eyed ones tend to be blond, but tall athletes do not have a characteristic hair color.

A system that learns disjoint categories in this domain has several choices. First, it could choose to partition the instances on the basis of height and weight or on the basis of eye and hair color. This, however, limits the probability of correct inferences by completely ignoring one of the predictive relationships. Alternatively, it could try to balance the two relationships without storing every instance. This again loses some predictive information. In order for the categories to capture one relationship, it must jeopardize the accuracy of the other.

A third possibility is that the system could simply create a category for each combination of values for the domain. This results in no timing or storage benefit for categories over individual instances, but does achieve better prediction than the above proposals. This method will be generally inefficient for domains in which there are multiple clusters of mutually predictive values, because there is potentially an exponential number of categories that must be stored. More importantly, though, each of these categories must be separately learned. This requires that every combination must be seen before the domain is well learned. This is likely too restrictive, because humans, at least, do not have to have seen a striped apple to be able to make inferences about it.

A final possibility is that the system could choose one relationship for each level of the hierarchy, such that, for example, height and weight would initially classify the instance, and then hair and eye color would classify it further. This possibility shares the criticisms above, but is somewhat more economical. Instead of storing every combination of values as a separate category, this possibility allows each partitioning to be a decision about the values of some set of correlated attributes, thereby apparently reducing the order of the number of categories. However, each decision except the one at the top of the tree must be replicated many times throughout the hierarchy. This requires excessive storage and, as in the last section, learning rate and accuracy will be adversely affected. One additional difficulty with this approach is that it fixes the order of the decisions. If some instance is encountered that happens not to have values for the decision that is highest in the tree, then the information in the hierarchy may be inaccessible.

A single set of disjoint categories or a strict hierarchy, when applied in cross-classification domains, will either require excessive storage, extended learning, or will produce less than optimal prediction behavior.

2.2.2 Cross-classification domains

These difficulties are hardly significant if humans only rarely encounter cross-classification domains. On the other hand, if cross-classification domains are common and humans are optimally adapted to their world(Anderson, 1988), then humans must learn overlapping categories.

Linnaeus' taxonomy of the plant and animal kingdom was one of the most significant early indications that hierarchies of disjoint categories reflect the structure of the world. An important source suggesting the existence of overlapping categories in the world is artificial intelligence and cognitive science work in knowledge representation. As structured representations for knowledge appeared, it was acknowledged that the same event or object would need to be multiply classified (Minsky, 1975). Minsky argued that a generator from a car is an instance of both a mechanical system and an electrical one. These different points of view would likely be useful for different tasks. Most proposals for generic knowledge representation languages include the ability to identify multiple classes for an instance (eg. *ConjGeneric* in KRYPTON, Brachman, Fikes, & Levesque, 1983). A particular person can be classified as both a male and a parent and can inherit inferences from each.

The primary reason cited in the representation literature for the use of multiple inheritance is that it limits duplication of information and eliminates unnecessary subclasses (Touretzky, 1986). For example, different animals can have different roles in human life, some are pets, some are circus performers, and some are work animals. A strict hierarchy might require a node for each animal-role pair. With ten different animals and ten different roles, the hierarchy would have at most 100 nodes. The memory requirements could be greatly reduced if circus elephants, for example, could inherit properties from both *circus-performer* and *elephant*. If such overlapping categories were permitted, memory would only require 20 nodes to represent most of the same information.

The world does seem to present cross-classification domains. There are many simple examples of combined concepts, such as pet fish or striped apple (see Osherson & Smith, 1982). Additionally, as mentioned above, researchers concerned with representing knowledge are able to adopt overlapping categories to simplify their task, suggesting that the structure is available. Both of these pieces of evidence argue that because English words express overlapping categories, there must be such structure in the world. Anderson (1990), however, cautions against assuming that category labels correspond to the actual category structure of a domain. The labels may be merely attributes like any other. Two categories may or may not share a particular label. Therefore, the apparent existence of overlapping categories might be the result of some name or label attributes that overlap across categories, just as the extension of *red thing* and the extension of *round thing* overlap.

A category label, however, is assumed to be something special, in that it is extraordinarily useful for predicting other attributes. This is true for the above examples. The category, *circus performer*, indicates much about the lifestyle of the creature, and *elephant* indicates much about the size and shape of the creature. Hence, even if the categories are only labels, there are important predictive relations between the label and other attributes. A strict hierarchy would require that the predictive relations about, for example, circus performers would be duplicated for all types of circus performer. Overlapping categories could permit the clusters of predictive relations to be encapsulated and reused, rather than duplicated. Again, systems of disjoint categories produce inferior performance when compared with systems of overlapping categories.

3 Models of Overlapping Categories

Overlapping categories, by encapsulating predictive relationships, produce more accurate inferences and reduce duplication of information. For this to be true, the various categories must complement each other. In particular, different categories that apply to the same object must differ with respect to the attributes that they are best able to predict. If something is a *beanbag* and a *chair*, the *beanbag* category is best for predicting shape, whereas the *chair* category is best

169

for predicting size and function.

There are two general approaches to learning sets of complementary, overlapping categories. They be learned either one at a time or simultaneously. Suppose the task is to learn, among other things, the concepts *young* and *mallard*. A learner might at one time hear about a young mallard and only care about predicting body covering and means of locomotion. It would then begin to learn the category, *mallard*. At another time, it might care about predicting degree of coordination or source of food and hence will begin to learn the category *young* for animals. Over time, the two overlapping categories would become more entrenched as young and mallard occurred in other contexts. Both *young* and *mallard* will still participate in sets of disjoint categories. For instance, young things contrasts with old things and mallard contrasts with geese. The resulting structure for the example can then be viewed as an interwoven set of alternate hierarchies.

A simultaneous strategy for learning overlapping categories would produce a similar structure, but would do it with fewer instances. Instead of starting with particular prediction goals, the simultaneous strategy begins with the general goal of extracting as much predictive structure as possible. With each instance, it attempts to maximize its ability to predict all attributes. It would begin to learn about both *young* and *mallard* simultaneously.

3.1 Model 1: Learning overlapping categories across presentation

One possible model for learning overlapping categories across instance presentations uses a single set of categories that at any one time are considered disjoint. An instance, however, can be classified into different categories depending on what the prediction goal is. In this model, an instance is learned by first highlighting which attribute or attributes will be most useful to predict. Then, with this in mind, the instance is incorporated into the best category just as in Fisher's (1987) model. Prediction proceeds in the same manner and results in prediction of the most probable values for the goal attributes.

To actually implement this idea, Fisher's basic algorithm was adopted. However, the Gluck and Corter (1985) measure was inadequate, because it always assumed that all attributes are equally important to predict. Their measure was modified (see Martin & Billman, 1990) to produce the following:

$$Q = \sum_k \sum_l \frac{1}{N_I} P(C_k \mid matchfnc \wedge I_l) \sum_j \sum_i P(a_{A_j}) P(A_j = V_{ij} \mid C_k)^2 \qquad (2)$$

This metric is fairly complicated, but is based directly on Gluck and Corter's simple result. It was modified to allow some attributes to be ignored when learning categories. The term $P(a_{A_j})$ differentiates goal attributes from others. It is 1 if A_j is a goal attribute and 0 otherwise. The term N_I is the number of instances observed, $matchfnc$ is the procedure used for matching, and I is a particular instance that is matched. The match function may be any metric that assigns a degree of match between a particular instance and each disjoint category. Simple possibilities are an arithmetic or geometric average.

3.2 Model 2: Learning overlapping categories simultaneously

The major difference between this model and the last is that this model attempts to pull as much predictive structure out of the instances as it can. It allows simultaneous multiple classification. During prediction, an instance is multiply classified and predictive information is combined from the recognized categories to make a prediction. As an illustration of the idea, imagine that each of several guards has a limited view of the outer wall of a fortress, and that they each report to a commander, who collects the separate pieces of information. The commander can compose the different fragments to permit informed predictions.

Learning in this model consists of adding new categories, modifying the descriptions of categories, and modifying parameters of the composition function. The system can concurrently learn new categories and learn how to combine the information provided by the categories. If the size of a pet fish is not well predicted from information about pets and fish, either a new pet-fish category would be added or parameters of the composition function would be altered to handle this exception.

More specifically, the model assumes that there are several *non-disjoint* sets of two or more *disjoint* categories. The simplest case is when each set has two possibilities. For example, one category may split plants into those that live underwater and those that do not. Another may split plants into those that are large and those that are small. One category from each the non-disjoint sets could be accessed by an instance. Both learning and prediction use Equation 2 to classify instances into each set in the same manner as in Model 1.

Composition is achieved by assuming that the non-disjoint sets and their activated members are attributes and values of instances that can be categorized by another set of disjoint categories. For each attribute, Equation 2 and the accessed categories are used to select a category from which to generate predictions.

3.3 Empirical illustration

The above models were compared to COBWEB using a cross-classification domain. The domain had twelve binary attributes grouped into four clusters of three mutually predictive attributes. In each cluster, each attribute's values were consistently paired with values on the other two attributes.

Testing was divided into 5 runs for each model. For each run, the domain of 16 instances was randomly ordered and split into a 12 instance training set and a 4 instance test set. After each instance in the training set was presented, the model's ability to make correct predictions about the test instances was determined.

The averaged results demonstrate the predicted benefit of overlapping categories. Both of the overlapping category models achieved a maximum score of approximately 70% correct after all training instances had been seen (67.5% for the first model and 72.5% for the second). COBWEB, on the other hand, achieved only 48.5% correct. One interesting result is that COBWEB only required one instance to achieve a prediction accuracy of $50\% \pm 2\%$. In contrast, the overlapping category models required four and three instances respectively. This suggests that the improved accuracy might be associated with slower initial learning.

4 Discussion

Disjoint categories divide the world at its joints (Rosch, 1978). The different levels of a taxonomy divide the world into either coarse or fine pieces. In these terms, overlapping categories allow the system to identify and consolidate pieces that recur often. Instead of repeatedly defining categories that extract the same piece, that piece is learned once and made generally available.

4.1 Theory-based concept learning

The above statement implies that general predictive rules could be learned and used in a system that permits overlapping categories. These general rules may constitute a theory that can then influence later learning. A simple way this might happen is if previous learning had established a set of interpredictive values, and future learning assumed that the set of values remained interpredictive. When learning in a new domain, past learning can transfer, possibly permitting faster learning.

Murphy and Medin (1985) argue that general theories do not simply coexist with categories; they interact in many ways. Most importantly, a background theory can provide an explanatory principle for category membership. Although the current representation for theories includes no relationships aside from cooccurrence, conceptual coherence can be simulated with overlapping categories.

There may, for example, already be categories that predict weight from height, and that predict height from gender. Now the learner must learn to partition individuals based on their weight, but they are not given either the weight or the height. All of the information necessary to reason that women are generally lighter than men is available. The background theory permits the identification of important attributes, such as gender, and provides a weak theory to explain why the lighter category contains mostly women.

To fully develop the use of overlapping categories as theories, a more complex representation is needed, including causal and other relations between attributes.

4.2 Conceptual combination

Several overlapping categories can be learned and can be recombined into novel configurations about which the system will have inferential commitments. Someone might, for example, expect a toy elephant to be gray because all elephants they knew were gray and toys have no characteristic color. This general notion is almost identical to the intuition behind conceptual combination (Osherson & Smith, 1982). People are assumed to have separate meaning representations for various nouns and adjectives that can be combined. The major goal of the conceptual combination research is to determine how inferences from separate representations are combined, especially when they are competing. That is also a major issue for models of overlapping categories. The first model presented above makes no commitments about how it might combine two or more categories

The second model, however, adopts a relatively novel perspective on conceptual combination. It does assume a simple multiplicative combination rule, but unlike existing models of combination (Osherson & Smith, 1982), it can modify how the combination is achieved as it learns. So in contrast to earlier approaches, there is not a simple fixed mechanism, but rather a more flexible adaptive method.

4.3 Summary

Although taxonomies have long been the standard model for human categories, they do not always provide the most economical storage nor the best predictions. In particular, in cross classification domains, structures that permit overlapping categories are superior. Two models were presented that learned overlapping category structure, and they were demonstrated to be superior to a method that relies on non-overlapping structure.

5 Acknowledgements

I would like to thank Dorrit Billman for her advice, and I would like to thank Nancy Smith Martin and Tom Hinrichs for assistance with earlier drafts of this paper.

References

Anderson, J. R. (1988). The place of cognitive architectures in a rational analysis. In *Proceedings of Tenth Annual Conference of the Cognitive Science Society*, Montreal, Canada.

Anderson, J. R. (1990). *Adaptive Character of Thought*. Erlbaum, Hillsdale, NJ.

Brachman, R. J., Fikes, R. E., and Levesque, H. J. (1983). Krypton: A functional approach to knowledge acquistion. *IEEE Computer*, 16:67–73.

Bruner, J. S., Goodnow, J. J., and Austin, G. A. (1956). *A Study of Thinking*. Wiley, New York.

Fisher, D. (1987). Knowledge acquisition via incremental conceptual clustering. *Machine Learning*.

Gluck, M. and Corter, J. (1985). Information, uncertainty, and the utility of categories. In *Proceedings of the Seventh Annual Conference of the Cognitive Science Society*, Irvine, CA.

Gluck, M. A. and Bower, G. H. (1988). Evaluating an adaptive network model of human learning. *Journal of Memory and Language*, 27:166–195.

Martin, J. D. (1989). Reducing redundant learning. In *Proceedings of Sixth International Workshop on Machine Learning*, Ithaca, NY.

McClelland, J. L. and Rumelhart, D. E. (1986). *Parallel Distributed Processing: Explorations in the Microstructure of Cognition, Vol I*. MIT Press, Cambridge, MA.

Medin, D. L. and Shoben, E. J. (1988). Context and structure in conceptual combination. *Cognitive Psychology*, 20:158–190.

Minsky, M. (1975). A framework for representing knowledge. In Winston, P. II., editor, *The Psychology of Computer Vision*. McGraw-IIill, New York.

Murphy, G. L. and Medin, D. L. (1985). The role of theories in conceptual coherence. *Psychological Review*, 92:289–316.

Osherson, D. N. and Smith, E. E. (1982). Gradedness and conceptual combination. *Cognition*, 12:299–318.

Rosch, E., Mervis, C. B., Gray, W. D., Johnson, D. M., and Boyes-Braem, P. (1976). Basic objects in natural categories. *Cognitive Psychology*, 8:382–439.

Touretsky, D. S. (1986). *The Mathematics of Inheritance Systems*. Pitman Publishing, London.

The Right Concept at the Right Time: How Concepts Emerge as Relevant in Response to Context-Dependent Pressures

Melanie Mitchell and Douglas R. Hofstadter
Center for Research on Concepts and Cognition
Indiana University

Abstract

A central question about cognition is how, faced with a situation, one explores possible ways of understanding and responding to it. In particular, how do concepts initially considered irrelevant, or not even considered at all, *become* relevant in response to pressures evoked by the understanding process itself? We describe a model of concepts and high-level perception in which concepts consist of a central region surrounded by a dynamic nondeterministic "halo" of potential associations, in which relevance and degree of association change as processing proceeds. As the representation of a situation is built, associations arise and are considered in a probabilistic fashion according to a *parallel terraced scan*, in which many routes toward understanding the situation are tested in parallel, each at a rate and to a depth reflecting ongoing evaluations of its promise. We describe a computer program that implements this model in the context of analogy-making, and illustrate, using screen dumps from a run, how the program's ability to flexibly bring in appropriate concepts for a given situation emerges from the mechanisms we are proposing.

Suppose you invite your friend Greg to dinner, and he doesn't show up on time. What do you do? At first, simple, standard explanations and actions come to mind: he was briefly delayed; he ran into traffic; he had trouble parking. But as half an hour passes, then an hour, then two, the explanations and actions you think of become more and more out of the ordinary. The following might come to mind: call his office (no answer); call his apartment (no answer); check your calendar to make sure the dinner date *is* tonight (it is); rack your brains trying to remember if he warned you he might be late (no such memory); call friends of his to see if they know where he is (they don't); call his parents in Philadelphia (haven't heard from him in weeks); call the police (they suggest checking the hospital); call the hospital (not there); go to his apartment (not there); ask his neighbors if they've seen him lately (last saw him this morning); drive along routes he would likely have taken (he's nowhere to be seen); buy a megaphone and call out his name as you drive along; call several airlines to see if he's on a plane leaving town tonight; turn on the TV to see if you can spot him sitting in the audience of his favorite talkshow; and so on. Though the last few are outlandish, most of these thoughts *did* occur to the authors when they were in such a situation. The point is: as time goes by and pressure builds up, one's thoughts go farther and farther out on a limb. One considers things one never would have considered initially, letting seemingly unquestionable aspects of the situation "slip" under mounting pressure (e.g., Did I dream I invited him? Did we have a falling-out I forgot about? Did he leave town and not tell me?).

This example illustrates some critical issues in cognition: Faced with a situation, how does one explore possible ways of understanding it, explaining it, or acting in response to it? How do concepts initially considered irrelevant, or not even considered at all, *become* relevant in response to pressure? How does one let go of notions that *looked* relevant but turn out not to be of help after all?

We are studying these issues by developing a model of concepts and high-level perception in which a concept consists of a central region surrounded by a dynamic, probabilistic "halo" of potential associations (Hofstadter, 1988). In its halo, "driving" has such concepts as "parking", "getting stuck in traffic", "having an accident", etc., each with a degree of association that changes in response to context (a phenomenon often discussed by psychologists, e.g., Tversky, 1977; Barsalou, 1989). The halo has no fixed boundary; it cannot be said absolutely that a given concept *is* or *is not* associated with "driving". Instead, different degrees of association reflect probabilities that once a concept is seen as relevant, various associated concepts will also become relevant. The dynamic nature of relevance and conceptual distance imbues human concepts with flexibility and adaptability.

Not only are certain concepts *explicitly* present in one's mental representation of a situation (you consciously believe Greg is *driving*); there are also *implicit* associations with those concepts, most of which stay well below the level of awareness. Given Greg's lateness, the thought that he's driving might easily evoke an image of his having trouble parking (a strong association). However, it is less likely that, early on, you will imagine him in a car accident. This weaker association is *potentially* there, but will not be brought into the picture without pressure (he is quite late, it is dark outside, etc.) This illustrates a general point: far-out ideas (or even ideas slightly past one's defaults) cannot continually occur to people for no good reason; a person to whom this happens is classified as crazy or crackpot. Time and cognitive resources being limited, it is vital to resist nonstandard ways of looking at situations without strong pressure to do so. As an extreme example, had the Michelson–Morley experiment come out the other way (i.e., it had proved there *is* an "ether") and had Einstein *still* proposed special relativity, with all its deeply counterintuitive notions, it would have been seen as just a fascinating crackpot theory, not a great scientific advance. Not only is pressure needed for one to bring in previously uninvolved concepts in trying to make sense of a situation, but the concepts brought in are related to the *source* of the pressure; they are a function of the pressure. (These ideas overlap with Kahneman & Miller's 1986 treatment of counterfactuals.)

One aim in our model is to avoid two opposite strategies, both psychologically implausible, for searching through concepts to be used in understanding a given situation: (1) All concepts are *explicitly* and *equally* available from the start (e.g., you have a preconstructed list of concepts relevant to "late-dinner-guest" situations — you may not need to try them all out, since Number 4 on the list might fill the bill, but they are spelled out nonetheless. An equally implausible variant of this would be that the possibilities are not spelled out explicitly, but it is easy to generate the next one on the list if a given entry fails); and (2) Certain concepts are definitively excluded from the start, and can *never* be brought in as relevant. A premise of our model is that in humans, the presence or absence of a concept in a situation is not black-and-white; rather, all one's concepts should have the *potential* to become relevant in any situation, but due to the necessity for cognitive economy, they can't all be made available all the time or to the same degree. People resist even *generating* less standard views, not to mention *exploring* them; the less standard a view, the more it is resisted.

In our model, every concept possessed by the system has *some* probability of becoming relevant in every context, but different concepts have vastly different probabilities, and these vary with context. There are many possible explanations (you could have written down the wrong date or given Greg the wrong address; your street's name could even have been secretly changed), so it is important not to *absolutely* exclude any particular pathway ahead of time. All must be potentially open, but there is not enough time to explore all equally, or even to generate all. Allocation of cognitive resources to different pathways must be a *dynamic* function of context-dependent pressures, because those pressures might change as exploration proceeds (when you try to call Greg, you find your phone is out of order and no one can call in; this will tend to make the "car accident" pathway less plausible). Our model proposes that many potential pathways are being tested out all the time, but at different speeds and to different levels of depth: due to context-dependent pressures, not all pathways are tested equally. Some may not be considered at all, but that's the luck of the (biased) draw; the point is that they are *potentially* open for exploration. We term this non-egalitarian style of exploration a *parallel terraced scan*: many different pathways are explored in parallel, but not equally; each pathway is explored at a rate and to a depth proportional to moment-to-moment estimates of its promise.

Our model thus has two interrelated aspects: The first is the existence of a probabilistic halo of potential associations around the central region of each concept. Like an electron orbit in an atom, a concept is blurry and distributed in "semantic space", with various probabilities that it will "be" at a given spot. For concepts, as for electrons, the probability distribution changes in a context-dependent way. The second aspect is the notion of a parallel terraced scan. These ideas are implemented in Copycat, a computer model of concepts and high-level perception in analogy-making.

To isolate many issues of general psychological import, we use an idealized microworld in which these issues emerge very clearly. Our methodology resembles that of physics, where problems are *idealized* in order to isolate what is interesting about them and to allow them to be studied more precisely. In this spirit, Copycat operates in a "frictionless" world consisting of analogy problems involving letter strings; despite their apparent simplicity, these problems capture many of the broad issues we are investigating. Four sample problems in Copycat's microworld are:

1. **abc** ⟹ **abd**; **ijk** ⟹ ?
2. **abc** ⟹ **abd**; **iijjkk** ⟹ ?
3. **abc** ⟹ **abd**; **kji** ⟹ ?
4. **abc** ⟹ **abd**; **xyz** ⟹ ?

Solving such problems requires many abilities necessary for high-level perception and analogy-making in general: mentally building a coherently structured whole from initially unconnected parts; describing objects, relations, and events at an "appropriate" level of abstraction; paying attention to relevant aspects and ignoring irrelevant and superficial aspects of situations; deciding which elements of a situation to chunk and which to view individually; deciding which descriptions to take literally and which to let slip when perceiving correspondences between aspects of two situations; and allowing competition among various ways of interpreting and mapping the situations. Discussions of how problems 1–4 require these abilities and how Copycat solves 1–4 are given in Hofstadter & Mitchell (1988) and Mitchell & Hofstadter (1990). Our goal is not to study the domain-specific mechanisms people use in solving letter-string analogies, but to develop a computer model of human flexibility and insight in general; we use this microworld because it cleanly isolates many of the abilities we are investigating.

175

The central issue of this paper — how dormant concepts "bubble up" in response to pressure and become relevant — arises somewhat in problems 1–4, but is manifested most clearly in this one:

5. abc ⇒ abd; mrrjjj ⇒ ?

This problem has a seemingly reasonable, straightforward solution: mrrkkk. Most people give this answer, reasoning that since abc's rightmost letter was replaced by its successor, and since mrrjjj's rightmost "letter" is actually a *group* of 'j's, one should replace all the 'j's by 'k's. Another possibility is to take "rightmost letter" literally, thus to replace only the rightmost 'j' by 'k', giving mrrjjk. However, neither answer is very satisfying, since neither takes into account the salient fact that abc is an alphabetically increasing sequence. This internal "fabric" of abc is a very appealing and seemingly *explanatory* aspect of the string, so you want to use it in making the analogy, but how? No such fabric seems to weave mrrjjj together. So either (like most people) you settle for mrrkkk (or possibly mrrjjk), or you look more deeply. But where to look when there are so many possibilities?

The interest of this problem is that there happens to be an aspect of mrrjjj lurking beneath the surface that, once recognized, yields what many people feel is a more satisfying answer. If you ignore the *letters* in mrrjjj and look instead at *group lengths*, the desired successorship fabric is found: the lengths of groups increase as "1-2-3". Once this hidden connection between abc and mrrjjj is discovered, the rule describing abc ⇒ abd can be adapted to mrrjjj as "Replace the length of the rightmost group by its successor", yielding "1-2-4" at the abstract level, or, more concretely, mrrjjjj. Thus this problem demonstrates how a previously irrelevant, unnoticed aspect of a situation emerges as relevant in response to pressures (e.g., the unsatisfied desire for a common fabric, among others).

How can the notion of group length, which in most problems remains essentially dormant, come to be seen as relevant by Copycat? *Length* is certainly in the halo of the concept *group*, as are concepts such as *letter-category* (e.g., 'j' for the group 'jjj'), *string-position* (e.g., *rightmost*), and *group-fabric* (e.g., *sameness between letters*). Some are more closely associated with *group* than others; in the absence of pressure, the notion of *length* tends to be fairly far away in conceptual space. Thus in perceiving a group such as 'rr', one is virtually certain to notice the letter-category ('r'), but not very likely to notice, or at least attach importance to, the length. However, since *length* is in *group*'s halo, there is *some* possibility that lengths will be noticed and used in trying to make sense of the problem. One might consciously notice a group's length at some point, but if this doesn't turn out to be useful, *length*'s relevance diminishes after a while. (For example, this might happen in the variant problem abc ⇒ abd, mrrrrjj ⇒ ?.) This *dynamic* aspect of relevance is very important: even if a new concept is at some point brought in as relevant, it is counterproductive to continue spending much of one's time exploring avenues involving that concept if none seems promising.

Since Copycat is nondeterministic, it follows different paths on different runs; thus not only does it come up with a variety of answers, but it can reach each answer in myriad ways. Indeed, Copycat's flexibility depends on the fact that all pathways involving any of its concepts are potentially open; despite this, the program generally manages to avoid exploring unpromising pathways, except fleetingly. Below is a chart showing the results of running Copycat some 650 times on problem 5. Its answers, ordered by frequency, range from the superficially alluring mrrkkk to the downright bizarre mrrjkk (in which the two rightmost 'j's were perceived as a chunk), nrrjjj (in which abc's *rightmost* letter was equated with mrrjjj's *leftmost* letter), mrrjjj (using the rule "Replace all 'c's by 'd's"), and drrjjj.

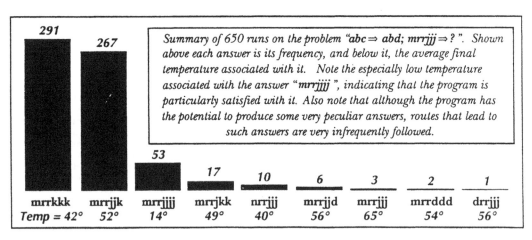

291	267							

Summary of 650 runs on the problem "abc ⇒ abd; mrrjjj ⇒ ?". Shown above each answer is its frequency, and below it, the average final temperature associated with it. Note the especially low temperature associated with the answer "mrrjjjj", indicating that the program is particularly satisfied with it. Also note that although the program has the potential to produce some very peculiar answers, routes that lead to such answers are very infrequently followed.

		53						
			17	10	6	3	2	1
mrrkkk	mrrjjk	mrrjjjj	mrrjkk	nrrjjj	mrrjjd	mrrjjj	mrrddd	drrjjj
Temp = 42°	52°	14°	49°	40°	56°	65°	54°	56°

Although there are only nine distinct answers, each run was unique on a fine-grained level. Under each answer is the *final temperature* averaged over all runs yielding that answer. Temperature is explained later; for the time being, think of a run's final temperature as a measure of Copycat's "happiness" with the answer produced, with high temperature corresponding to low happiness and vice versa. Thus Copycat is by far the happiest with **mrrjjjj**. Note the lack of correlation of frequency with final temperature — meaning, roughly, that obviousness and elegance are independent.

The frequencies shown in the chart are not meant to be strictly compared with the frequencies of various answers given by people to this problem, since, as we said earlier, the program is not meant to model the domain-specific mechanisms people use in solving these letter-string problems. Rather, what is interesting here is that the program *does* have the potential to arrive at very strange answers (such as **mrrjkk** and **drrjjj**), yet manages to steer clear of them almost all the time; most always, it gets answers that people find reasonable and, sometimes, even insightful.

In a complex world (even one with the limited complexity of Copycat's microworld), one never knows in advance what concepts may turn out relevant in a given situation. It is thus imperative not only to avoid dogmatically *open-minded* search strategies, which entertain all possibilities equally seriously, but also to avoid dogmatically *closed-minded* search strategies, which in an ironclad way rule out certain possibilities *a priori*. Copycat opts for a middle way, which of course leaves open the potential for disaster — and indeed, disaster occurs once in a while. This is the price that must be paid for flexibility. People, too, occasionally explore and even favor peculiar routes. Our program, like us, has to have the potential to concoct far-out solutions in order to be able to discover subtle and elegant ones like **mrrjjjj**. (In fact, Copycat still lacks important mechanisms that would allow it to pursue yet stranger pathways!) To rigidly close off any routes *a priori* would necessarily remove critical aspects of Copycat's flexibility. On the other hand, the fact that Copycat so rarely produces weird answers demonstrates that its mechanisms manage to strike a pretty effective balance between open-mindedness and closed-mindedness, imbuing it with both flexibility and robustness.

We now sketch one way Copycat arrives at **mrrjjjj** (more details given below). The input consists of three "raw" strings (here, **abc**, **abd**, **mrrjjj**) with no preattached relations or preformed groups; it is thus left entirely to the program to build up perceptual structures constituting its understanding of the problem in terms of concepts it deems relevant. On most runs, the groups 'rr' and 'jjj' are constructed (the program is able to perceive copy-groups — groups consisting of repeated copies of a given letter — quite readily). Each group's letter-category ('r' and 'j' respectively) is explicitly noted, since *letter-category* is relevant by default. There is some probability for lengths to be noticed at the time the groups are made, but it is low, since *length* is not strongly associated with *group*. Once 'rr' and 'jjj' are made, *copy-group* becomes very relevant. This creates top-down pressure for the system to describe other objects — especially in the same string — as copy-groups if possible. The only way to do this here is to describe the 'm' as a copy-group with just one letter. This is strongly resisted by an opposing pressure: a single-letter group is an intrinsically weak and far-fetched construct. However, the existence of two other copy-groups in the string, coupled with the system's "unhappiness" at its failure to incorporate the lone 'm' into any large, coherent structure, pushes against this resistance.

These opposing pressures fight; the outcome is decided probabilistically. If the 'm' is perceived as a single-letter group, its length will very likely be noticed (single-letter groups are noteworthy precisely because of their abnormal length), making *length* more relevant in general, and thus increasing the probability of noticing the other two groups' lengths. Moreover, *length*, once brought into the picture, has a good chance of staying relevant, since descriptions based on it turn out to be useful. (Note that had the string been **mrrrrjj**, *length* might be brought in, but it would not turn out useful, so it would likely fade back into obscurity.) In **mrrjjj**, once lengths are noticed, the successor relations among them are quickly constructed by relation-detectors continually seeking new relations. There is also an independent top-down pressure to see successor relations in **mrrjjj**, coming from the already-seen successor relations in **abc**. As this satisfying new view of **mrrjjj** begins to emerge, the importance of the groups' letter-categories fades and *length* becomes their most salient aspect. Thus the crux of discovering this solution lies in the triggering of the concept *length*.

In summary, Copycat's solution of **abc** ⇒ **abd**, **mrrjjj** ⇒ **mrrjjjj** requires the interaction of:

- *concepts consisting of a central region surrounded by a halo of potential associations;*
- *a mechanism for probabilistically bringing in new associations related to the current situation;*
- *a mechanism by which concepts' activations decay over time, unless reinforced;*
- *agents that continually seek new relations, groups, and correspondences;*
- *mechanisms for applying top-down pressures from concepts already brought in;*
- *mechanisms allowing competition among pressures;*
- *the parallel terraced scan, allowing rival views to develop at different speeds.*

We now describe and illustrate how these mechanisms are implemented. (For more details, see Mitchell & Hofstadter, 1990.) Copycat's concepts reside in a network of nodes and links called the *Slipnet*. A concept's central region is a node, and its associative halo corresponds to other nodes linked to the central node. A node (such as *copy-group* or *successor*) becomes activated when instances of it are perceived (by *codelets*, as described below), and loses activation unless its instances remain salient. A node spreads activation to nearby nodes as a function of their proximity. Activation levels are not binary, but can vary continuously. The probability a node will be brought in or be considered further at any given time as a possible organizing concept is a function of the node's current activation level. Thus there is no black-and-white answer to the question of whether a given concept is "present" at a given time; continuous activation levels and probabilities allow different concepts to be present to different degrees. All concepts have the potential to be brought in and used; which ones become relevant and to what degree depends on the situation the program is facing, as will be seen below.

In addition to the Slipnet, where long-term concepts reside, Copycat has a working area in which perceptual structures (e.g., descriptions, relations, groups, and correspondences) are built hierarchically on top of the "raw" input (the three letter-strings). This building process is carried out by large numbers of simple agents called *codelets*. A codelet is a small piece of code that carries out some small, local task that is part of the process of building a structure (e.g., one codelet might notice that the two 'r's in mrrjjj are the same letter; another codelet might estimate how well that proposed relation fits in with already-existing relations; another codelet might build the relation). *Bottom-up* codelets work toward building structures based on whatever they happen to find, without being prompted to look for instances of specific concepts; *top-down* codelets look for instances of particular active nodes, such as *successor* or *copy-group*. The probability at a given time that a node in the Slipnet will add a top-down codelet to the current codelet population is a function of the node's activation level. Any structure is built by a series of codelets running in turn, each deciding probabilistically on the basis of its estimation of some aspect of the structure's strength whether to continue, by generating one or more follow-up codelets, or to abandon the effort at that point. If the decision is made to continue, the running codelet assigns an *urgency* value (based on its estimate of the structure's promise) to each follow-up codelet. This value helps to determine how long each follow-up codelet will have to wait before it can run and continue the evaluation of that particular structure.

Any run starts with a standard initial population of bottom-up codelets with preset urgencies; at each time step, one codelet is chosen to run and is removed from the current codelet population. The choice is probabilistic, based on relative urgencies in the current population. As the run proceeds, new codelets are added to the population either as follow-ups to previously-run codelets, or as top-down scouts for active nodes. A new codelet's urgency is assigned by its creator as a function of the estimated promise of the task it is to work on. Thus the codelet population changes as the run proceeds, in response to the system's needs as judged by previously-run codelets and by activation patterns in the Slipnet, which themselves depend on what structures are built. There is no top-level executive directing the system's activity; all processing is carried out by codelets.

The fine-grained breakup of structure-building processes serves two purposes: (1) it allows many such processes to be carried out in parallel, by having their components interleaved; and (2) it allows the computational resources allocated to each such process to be dynamically regulated by moment-to-moment estimates of the promise of the pathway being followed. A process is not a predetermined macroscopic act that is then broken up into convenient chunks; rather, any sequence of codelets that amounts to a coherent macroscopic act can *a posteriori* be labeled a process — thus processes are *emergent*. The speed of any process emerges dynamically from the urgencies of its component codelets. The upshot is a parallel terraced scan — more promising views tend to be explored faster than less promising ones.

A final mechanism, *temperature*, both measures the degree of perceptual disorganization in the system (its value at any moment is a function of the amount and quality of structure built so far), and controls the degree of randomness used in making decisions (e.g., which codelet should run next, which structure should win a competition, etc.). Higher temperatures reflect the fact that there is little information on which to base decisions; lower temperatures reflect the fact that there is greater certainty about the basis for decisions. Temperature in Copycat is described in detail in Mitchell & Hofstadter (1990). All these mechanisms are illustrated in the set of screen dumps from a run of the program, given below.

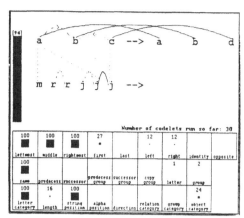

1. The problem is presented. Temperature, shown on a "thermometer" (left), is at its maximum of 100 (no structures yet built). At the bottom, some Slipnet nodes are displayed (links not shown). (Due to limited space, many nodes are not shown, e.g., those for 'a', 'b', etc.) A black square represents a node's current activation level (the actual value, from 0 to 100, is shown above). Nodes here displayed include *string-positions* of objects (*leftmost*, *middle*, and *rightmost*); *alphabetic-positions* of letters (*first*, filled by 'a', and *last*, by 'z'); *directions* for relations and groups (*left* and *right*); *identity* and *opposite* (some of the possible relations between concepts); *relation-categories* for relations between letters and groups (*same*, *predecessor*, and *successor*); *group-categories* (*predecessor-group*, *successor-group*, and *copy-group*); *object-categories* (*letter* and *group*); and in row 3, nodes representing these various categories of descriptions, including *length*. Every letter has some preattached descriptions: *letter-category* (e.g., 'm'), *object-category* (*letter*, as opposed to *group*) and *string-position* (*leftmost*, *middle*, *rightmost*, or none — e.g., the fourth letter in mrrjjj has no string-position description). These nodes start out highly activated.

2. The 30 codelets so far run have begun exploring many possible structures. Dashed lines and arcs are structures in various stages of consideration; solid ones are structures actually *built*, which can thus influence temperature, and the building of other structures. Relations and correspondences between letters are being considered (the 'a'–'j' potential mapping is based on the weak *leftmost–rightmost* Slipnet link; being implausible, it won't be pursued much further). The abc/abd correspondences and the rightmost 'j'–'j' sameness relation have been built by bottom-up codelets; this activated *same*, resulting in top-down pressure (new codelets) to seek sameness elsewhere. Some nodes have become lightly activated via spreading activation (e.g., the node *first*, from 'a' [not shown]). *Length*'s activation comes from its weak association with *letter-category* (letters and numbers are increasing sequences and thus similar; numbers are associated with length). Temperature has fallen in response to structures so far built. Many non-displayed fleeting explorations are occurring (e.g., "Any relation between the 'm' and its neighbor 'r'?").

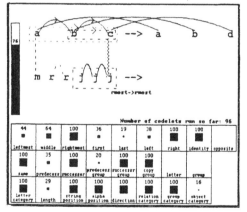

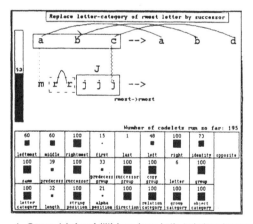

3. The successorship fabric of **abc** has been seen, and two mutually competing groups based on it are being considered: 'bc' and 'abc'. The latter is much stronger than the former, thus has a much higher chance. Exploration of the diagonal 'a'–'j' correspondence was aborted. A 'c'–'j' correspondence has been built (jagged vertical line); its reason for existence (both letters are rightmost) is given beneath it. A 'jjj' group is being considered. Since *successor* and *sameness* relations have been built, these nodes are highly active; they in turn have spread activation to *successor-group* and *copy-group*, which creates top-down pressure to look for such groups. Also, since *first* was active, *alphabetic-position* became highly active (a probabilistic event), making alphabetic-position descriptions likely to be considered.

4. Groups 'abc' and 'jjj' have been built (relations between letters are no longer being displayed). An 'rr' group is being considered (the group 'jjj' strongly supports it, so its construction is accelerated). Meanwhile, a *rule* (at top) has been constructed to describe how **abc** changed. The current version of Copycat assumes the example change involves replacing exactly one letter, so rule-building codelets fill in the template "Replace ___ by ___", choosing probabilistically from descriptions the program has given to the changed letter and its replacement, with a default bias toward more abstract descriptions (e.g., usually preferring "rightmost letter" to 'c'). Nodes *first* and *alphabetic-position* didn't turn out useful and thus have faded. Also, *length* received additional activation from *group* but is still not very activated, so noticing lengths is still unlikely.

179

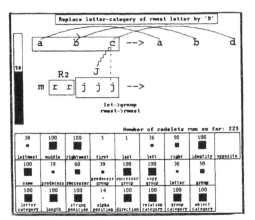

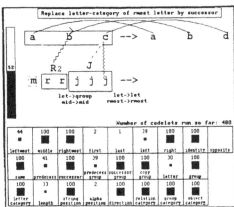

5. Now, 225 codelets into the run, the letter-to-*letter* 'c'–'j' correspondence was defeated by a stronger letter-to-*group* 'c'–'J' correspondence, though the former possibility still lurks in the background. Meanwhile, an 'rr' group was built whose length was noticed (a probabilistic event) and is displayed at the top of the group. *Length* is now fully active.

A new rule, "Replace the letter-category of the rightmost letter by 'D'", appears at the top of the screen; although it is weaker than the old rule, fights are decided probabilistically, and it won. However, its weakness caused temperature to go up. If the program were to stop now (unlikely, as temperature is still fairly high; the program decides probabilistically when to stop, based on temperature), the rule would be adapted for **mrrjjj** as "Replace the letter-category of the rightmost *group* by 'D'" (the 'c'–'J' correspondence establishes that the role of *letter* in abc is played by *group* in **mrrjjj**), yielding **mrrddd** (and Copycat does get this answer on occasion).

6. The previous, stronger rule has been restored (again the result of a fight having a probabilistic outcome), but the 'c'–'J' correspondence has been defeated by a 'c'–'j' correspondence. The activation of *length* has decayed a good deal, since the length description given to 'rr' hasn't been found to be useful. (This is graphically indicated by the fact that the '2' is no longer in boldface.) The temperature is still fairly high, since the program is having a hard time making a single, coherent structure out of **mrrjjj**, as it did with abc. That fact, combined with strong top-down pressure from the two copy-groups in **mrrjjj**, makes it somewhat plausible for the system to flirt with the idea of a single-letter group (dashed rectangle around the 'm').

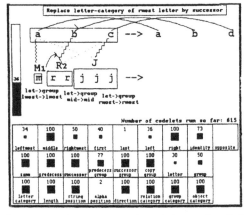

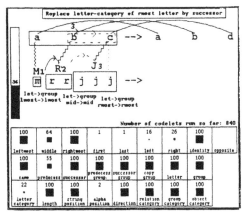

7. As a result of these pressures, the *a priori* extremely unlikely single-letter copy-group 'm' has been built, and its length of 1, being very noteworthy, has been attached as a description. The relation between the 1 and the 2 has been built; all of this is helping *length* to stay active. A complete set of *letter* ⇒ *group* correspondences has now been made, and as a result of these promising new structures, the temperature has fallen to 36, which in return helps to lock in this emerging view.

8. As a result of *length*'s continued activity, length descriptions have been attached to the other two groups in the problem ('jjj' and 'abc'), and a relation between the 2 and the 3 (for which there is much top-down pressure coming from both abc and the emerging view of **mrrjjj**) is being considered. *Letter-category* has decayed, indicating that it hasn't lately been of use in building structures.

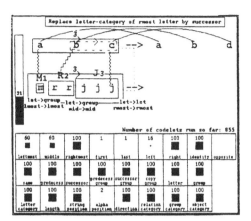

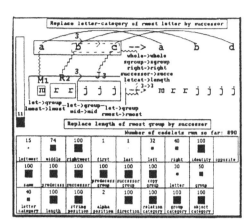

9. The 2–3 relation was built and a successor-group was built out of the group-lengths in mrrjjj (large rectangle surrounding the three copy-groups). Also, a correspondence (dashed vertical line to the right of the two strings) is being considered between abc and mrrjjj in their entireties.

10. A correspondence has been built between the two strings as wholes, and its concept-mappings (e.g., *letter-category* ⟹ *length*) are listed to its right. The original rule has been translated, using these concept-mappings; the translated rule appears just above the Slipnet, and the answer mrrjjjj at the right. The low temperature reflects the program's satisfaction with this answer.

In summary, Copycat is a model of concepts and perceptual mechanisms flexible enough to deal with a range of problems in its microdomain, reflecting many central psychological issues. It differs from other computer approaches to analogy-making in that it models not only how situations are mapped onto each other, but also the mechanisms by which initially uninterpreted situations are mentally structured. Models such as SME (Falkenhainer et al., 1986), and ACME (Holyoak & Thagard, 1989), are concerned with just the mapping process; all relations and other perceptual structures are precoded into predicate-logic representations that serve as input. A detailed comparison of Copycat with these models is given in Mitchell (1988). Copycat starts on any problem from a standard initial state; however, it quickly senses unique aspects of the problem, bringing out certain associations while downplaying others, allowing it (usually) to home in on a suitable set of relevant concepts and avenues of approach. Copycat achieves, through mechanisms we believe are psychologically plausible, a delicate balance between being too open-minded (exploring every avenue indiscriminately, thus grossly wasting computational resources) and being too closed-minded (rigidly cutting out certain avenues *a priori*, thus preventing many creative pathways from ever being looked at). Walking this fine line imbues Copycat with its robustness and flexibility.

Acknowledgments

We thank Robert French for contributions to the Copycat Project, and Liane Gabora for writing the statistics-gathering program. Thanks also to David Chalmers and David Moser for helpful comments on this paper, and to Greg Huber for a "late" inspiration. This research has been supported by grants from Indiana University, the University of Michigan, and Apple Computer, Inc., as well as a grant from Mitchell Kapor, Ellen Poss, and the Lotus Development Corporation, and grant DCR 8410409 from the National Science Foundation.

References

[1] Barsalou, L. W. (1989). Intraconcept similarity and its implications for interconcept similarity. In Vosniadou, S. and A. Ortony, *Similarity and analogical reasoning*, 76–121. Cambridge, England: Cambridge University Press.

[2] Falkenhainer, B., K. D. Forbus, and D. Gentner (1986). The Structure-Mapping Engine. In *Proceedings of the American Association for Artificial Intelligence, AAAI-86*. Los Altos, CA: Morgan Kaufmann.

[3] Hofstadter, D. R. (1988). Common sense and conceptual halos. *Behavioral and Brain Sciences, 11* (1), 35–37.

[4] Hofstadter, D. R. and M. Mitchell (1988). Conceptual slippage and analogy-making: A report on the Copycat project. *Proceedings, Tenth Annual Cognitive Science Society Conference*. Hillsdale, NJ: Lawrence Erlbaum Associates.

[5] Holyoak, K. and P. Thagard (1989). Analogical mapping by constraint satisfaction. *Cognitive Science, 13* (3), 295–355.

[6] Kahneman, D. and D. T. Miller (1986). Norm theory: Comparing reality to its alternatives. *Psychological Review, 93* (2), 136–153.

[7] Mitchell, M. (1988). A computer model of analogical thought. Unpublished thesis proposal. University of Michigan, Ann Arbor, MI.

[8] Mitchell, M. and D. R. Hofstadter (1990). The emergence of understanding in a computer model of concepts and analogy-making. *Physica D*, in press.

[9] Tversky, A. (1977). Features of similarity. *Psychological Review, 84*, 327–352.

Classification of Dot Patterns with Competitive Chunking

Emile Servan-Schreiber

Department of Psychology, Carnegie Mellon University

Abstract

Chunking, a familiar idea in cognitive science, has recently been formalized by Servan-Schreiber and Anderson (in press) into a theory of perception and learning, and it successfully simulated the human acquisition of an artificial grammar through the simple memorization of exemplar sentences. In this article I briefly present the theory, called Competitive Chunking, or CC, as it has been extended to deal with the task of encoding random dot patterns. I explain how CC can be applied to the classic task of classifying such patterns into multiple categories, and report a successful simulation of data collected by Knapp and Anderson (1984). The tentative conclusion is that people seem to process dot patterns and artificial grammars in the same way, and that chunking is an important part of that process.

Introduction

Chunking, our natural tendency to process stimuli by parts, is one of the most familiar and powerful ideas of cognitive science. Strangely, apart from Laird, Newell, and Rosenbloom's recent *Soar* theory (Newell, in press), there have been no serious attempts to formalize chunking since its discovery by Miller 34 years ago (Miller, 1956). Recently, Servan-Schreiber and Anderson (in press) have demonstrated how a chunking program can simulate human subjects learning an artificial grammar through mere memorization of exemplar sentences. That program was based on a theory called *competitive chunking*, or *CC*. In this paper, I demonstrate how *CC* can be applied to the classic problem of classifying random dot patterns.

Competitive Chunking of Dot Patterns

Representation: what is a chunk?

A chunk is a long term memory hierarchical structure whose constituents are chunks also. Every chunk has an associated *strength* which is a composite score reflecting how often and recently it has been used in the past. A newly created chunk has a strength of one unit. Its strength is increased by an additional unit every time it is used, or re-created. Strength also decays with time. At any point in time, the strength of a chunk is the sum of its successive, individually decaying, strengthenings:

$$\text{Strength} = \sum_i T_i^{-d} \tag{1}$$

where T_i is the time elapsed since the ith strengthening, and $\underline{d}$, the decay parameter, determines the severity of strength decay ($0 < \underline{d} < 1$). Once a chunk is created, it exists for ever, and there is no limit on how much strength it can accumulate. This strength construct is identical to that of ACT* for declarative memory traces (Anderson, 1983).

When the stimuli are dot patterns, two kinds of chunks are assumed: dot-chunks, and complex-chunks. Dot-chunks encode a single stimulus dot, whereas complex-chunks encode a pair of chunks. For example, the dot-chunk ((35 22)) encodes a dot located at cartesian coordinates (35 22) on the stimulus matrix. Examples of complex chunks are: (((35 22)) ((100 75))) which encodes two dot-chunks, and ((((35 22)) ((100 75))) ((125 200))) which encodes a complex-chunk and a dot-chunk.

Processes: What are chunks for?

Chunks are used to perceive stimuli. In the case of dot patterns, a percept is a collection of stimulus dots and chunks. Perception consists of multiple passes through a percept elaboration cycle, where the elementary (pre-elaboration) percept is simply the set of stimulus dots present in the pattern: chunks are retrieved as competing candidates to build upon the current percept, and some are selected. The selected chunks are used to elaborate on the percept, yielding a new percept as a basis for another cycle. The cycle repeats until no chunks are retrieved for further elaboration.

To be retrieved as a candidate for elaboration, a chunk must *match* some part of the current percept. Matching is defined slightly differently for dot-chunks and complex-chunks. A dot-chunk has a certain probability of matching any dot that is present within its immediate surroundings. This probability is 1 for the dot that is encoded by the dot-chunk, and decreases exponentially with the distance between the encoded dot and the target dot:

$$\text{Probability of match} = e^{-m \cdot \text{distance}} \qquad (2)$$

where m, the match parameter, determines how steep the exponential is ($m > 0$). The larger m is, the harder it is for a dot-chunk to match distant dots. Figure 1 plots this function for $m = .05$.

A complex-chunk matches some part of the percept if and only if both of its subchunks are equivalent to chunks in the percept. Chunk equivalence is defined recursively: The equivalence between two dot-chunks is probabilistic, depending on the distance between their encoded dots, following Equation (2). Then, two complex-chunks are equivalent if and only if (a) they have the same hierarchical structure, and (b) they have equivalent terminal dot-chunks at the bases of their hierarchies.

Still, it isn't enough that a chunk matches some part of the percept for it to be retrieved as a candidate for elaboration. The match must also have enough *support*. The support for a complex-chunk match is defined as the summed strength of the matched chunks. But the support for a dot-chunk match is infinite. The probability that a chunk match is retrieved is then a negatively accelerated increasing function of its support:

$$\text{Probability of retrieval} = \frac{1 - e^{-c \, \text{support}}}{1 + e^{-c \, \text{support}}} \qquad (3)$$

where c, the competition parameter, determines the steepness of the probability curve ($c > 0$). The larger c is, the easier it is to retrieve chunks, at all levels of support. Figure 2 plots this function for $c = .5$.

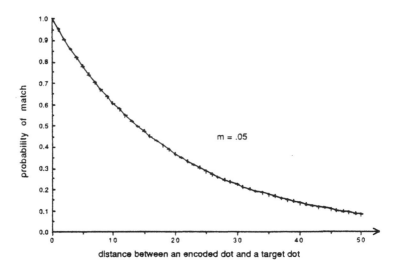

Figure 1. Plot of the probability that a dot-chunk matches a stimulus (target) dot. It decreases exponentially as the distance between the dot that is encoded by the dot-chunk and the target dot increases, following Equation (2). The value of m that is shown is the one I used in the simulation I describe later.

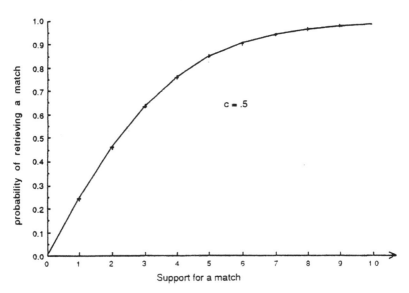

Figure 2. Plot of the probability that a chunk match is retrieved as a candidate for elaboration. It increases as its support increases, following Equation (3). The value of c that is shown is the one I used in the simulation I describe later.

Once chunk matches have been retrieved, they are organized into sets of compatible matches. Two matches are compatible if they match different parts of the percept. The alternative sets then compete against each other for the privilege of elaborating on the percept. For each set, the sum of the strengths of its constituent chunks is computed, and the set of matches with the highest score is selected as the winner. Elaboration then consist of replacing the parts of the percept that were matched by the chunks in the selected set of matches.[1] Every elaborating chunk is strengthened, while their losing competitors are left to decay. Note that this selection process, based on compatibility and strength, favorises sets of many matches over sets of fewer matches. It also encourages the participation of weaker chunks as long as they are compatible with a number of stronger chunks. This, in turn, allows them to gain strength.

It is interesting to note the dual role that strength plays in the elaboration process: The probability that a matching chunk is retrieved depends on the strength of the chunks that it matches , its support, while the probability that it is selected among the retrieved chunks depends on its own strength. Thus, a chunk's strength is a critical parameter for both itself and the chunks that may match it. When a chunk is strengthened, both itself and the chunks that may match it are being learned. Conversely, when a chunk's strength is left to decay, both itself and the chunks that may match it are being forgotten. A chunk is being learned the fastest, then, when its subchunks tend to be equivalent to chunks that co-occur frequently in the environment.

Stimulus Familiarity.

Given that chunks are, by definition, familiar units of knowledge, it follows that the more chunks participate in the percept elaboration process, the more familiar the stimulus is perceived to be. The notion of familiarity can easily be formalized in CC. Note that every time that a complex-chunk elaborates on the current percept, two of the percept's chunks are replaced by a single chunk in the next percept. Thus, elaborating on the percept with complex-chunks has the effect of reducing the number of parts at the top level of the percept. The implication is that the more chunks participated in the elaboration process, the less parts there are in the final percept. Therefore, the relationship between familiarity and the number of parts in the final percept, call it nchunks, can be characterized as follows: the larger nchunks is, the less familiar the stimulus is perceived to be. Conversely, the smaller nchunks is (its minimum value is 1), the more familiar the stimulus is perceived to be. To formalize further, Servan-Schreiber and Anderson (in press) assumed that familiarity can take values from 1 (maximum) to an asymptotic 0 (minimum), and that it is a rapidly decreasing function of nchunks:

$$\text{Familiarity of stimulus } = e^{1 - \text{nchunks}} \tag{4}$$

This formula captures the notion that if a stimulus can be sufficiently elaborated upon so that the final percept consists of a single chunk, then it is perceived as maximally familiar.

---

[1] Making the elaboration process set-based is a departure from its earlier specification in Servan-Schreiber and Anderson (in press). In that earlier verion of the theory, matches competed individually for elaboration, and a single match, that with the strongest chunk, was selected at each cycle.

Chunk Creation.

Learning in CC is two-fold. As discussed above, existing chunks are learned when they are strengthened. Strengthening and strength decay allow for the tuning of the existing knowledge base. But CC also has a process for chunk creation.

The creation process is a direct extension of the perception process, and shares many of its characteristics. The input to the creation process is the final percept, and its output is a collection of new chunks. The goal of that process is to create chunks that will have a good chance of participating in the perception process should the same or a similar stimulus be presented, thus increasing its familiarity by reducing nchunks. To that end, the proposed new chunks are those that would have enough support to be retrieved. Because stimulus dots provide infinite support to dot-chunks that encode them, if the final percept contains some stimulus dots that were not matched by any dot-chunk, then new dot-chunks are created to encode them. If the final percept contains two or more chunks, then a new complex-chunk is proposed that encodes the pair of chunks, in the percept, with the largest summed strength. Because that measure is akin to the proposed new chunk's support, Equation (3) is used to compute the probability that it is created. A newly created chunks is given a strength of one unit. If it already exists then it is simply strengthened. CC does not keep multiple copies of a chunk.

Applying CC to the Classification Task

General Principles.

A classic design of dot-pattern classification experiments includes a training phase and a testing phase. In the training phase, subjects are shown distortions of three prototype patterns and are instructed to classify them into three categories. When they make an incorrect classification, they are given feedback on the correct response. In the testing phase, the feedback is suppressed and the patterns that must be classified are of at least three kinds: distortions of the prototypes that were shown during the training (OLD), distortions of the prototypes that were not shown during training (NEW), and the prototypes themselves (PRO). The dependent variables of interest are then the percentages of correct classifications of each kind of pattern.

When CC is presented with a dot pattern, it builds as compact a percept as it can. The output of the perception process is then nchunks, a measure of how familiar the stimulus is perceived to be. When its task is to classify, CC keeps multiple separate sets of chunks, one per category. Then, when a pattern is presented, CC can compute multiple values of nchunks, one per chunk set, and select the category that is associated with the set of chunks that yielded the smallest value of nchunks, the most familiar percept. If feedback on the correct classification is given, as in the training phase, then it can be used to guide the creation of new chunks. Chunks are created only from the percept associated with the correct category, and the new chunks become part of the set of chunks associated with that category. The next time that a pattern from that category is presented, CC has thus increased its chance of building a compact percept with the chunks from

186

the correct category.

To make the selection of a response, on each trial, more dependent on the context provided by the previous trials, I decided to transform the values of nchunks into relative familiarity scores, or f-scores. Given a particular set of chunks, an *f-score* is simply the ratio of the average value of nchunks for all previous stimuli to the value of nchunks for the current stimulus. Therefore the smaller the value of nchunks for the current stimulus is, compared to its average value for previous stimuli, the larger its f-score is. An f-score that is less than 1 indicates that the current stimulus appears less familiar than previous stimuli have (on average). An f-score that is larger than 1 indicates the converse. The response selection rule is then to select the category that is associated with the set of chunks that yields the largest f-score.

Experimental Test of the Theory.

To test CC's ability to classify random dot patterns, I selected the experimental design of Knapp and Anderson (1984). There are 3 categories. During training, a single distortion of category A's prototype is presented 24 times, 6 distortions of category B's prototype are presented 4 times each, and 24 distortions of category C's prototype are presented once each, for a total of 72 training patterns, 24 per category. The 3 prototypes are generated by placing 9 dots at random locations in a 300 by 300 array, and the distortions are generated by moving each dot in a prototype exactly 25 array units from its original location, in a randomly chosen direction. (Three prototypes are randomly generated for each subject.) At test, OLD, NEW, and PRO patterns are presented from each category, 8 patterns representing each of the 9 possible combinations of pattern kind and category, yielding 72 testing trials.

Knapp and Anderson found (a) that the correct classification of OLD patterns decreased as the number of different exemplars seen during training increased, (b) that the correct classification of NEW and PRO patterns, on the contrary, increased with the number of different exemplars seen during training, and (c) that the PRO patterns were always more correctly classified than the NEW patterns.

There are three parameters to be set in CC: the decay parameter d, the competition parameter, c, and the match parameter, m. Due to the high computational cost of running simulated subjects, I did not try many different combinations of values for these parameters, but, rather, relied on past experience with CC to select reasonable values. The values of c and d that Servan-Schreiber and Anderson (in press) found appropriate in simulating the acquisition of an artificial grammar were .5 and .5. I used those. For m, which is a new parameter for CC, I relied on Knapp and Anderson's (1984) experience with their own theory that contained a dot matching function very similar to Equation (2). Their experience points to a value of m of about .05. I used that. To reduce the computational cost further, without sacrificing psychological plausibility, CC was allowed to create new chunks only on those training trials when it made an incorrect classification. On testing trials, the chunk creation process was completely turned off, although the strengthening and strength decay processes continued to operate. Time was increased by one unit with every trial.

187

Figure 3 plots the average classification performance of 50 simulated subjects. Clearly, the qualitative pattern of results reported by Knapp and Anderson (1984) is reproduced. As the number of different exemplars of a category seen during training increases, the classification of OLD patterns suffers, while that of NEW and PRO patterns is enhanced. At the same time, the PRO patterns are always more easily classified than the NEW patterns.

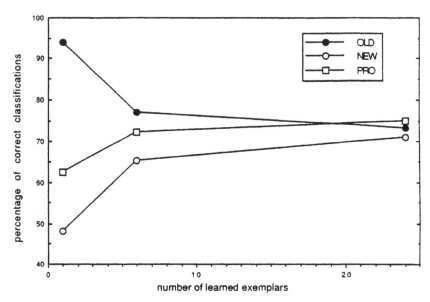

Figure 3. Percentages of correct classifications of OLD, NEW, and PRO patterns in each of the three categories A (1 learned exemplar), B (6 learned exemplars), and C (24 learned exemplars). The values of CC's parameters c, d, and m, in this experiment, were .5, .5, and .05 respectively.

Conclusion

CC already offers a precise and comprehensive theory of how subjects acquire artificial grammars, in the laboratory, through the simple memorization of exemplar sentences. The research I report here is CC's first foray into the classic problem of abstracting visual categories from exemplars. The results of a limited experiment are encouraging, and call for more experimentation with the theory. There is also independent evidence that the classification of dot patterns is likely a fertile ground for a theory of perception and learning based on chunking. Hock, Tromley, and Polmann (1988) report that, in the process of encoding dot patterns, people are very sensitive to configurational cues encoded into what they call "perceptual units". Evidently a synonym for "chunk". CC has the potential to provide a unified explanation of how people abstract category information, through the chunking of exemplars, in both verbal and visual domains.

Acknowledgments

This research was supported by contract N00014-86-K-0678 from the Office of Naval Research. I thank John Anderson for his intellectual support and encouragement. Correspondence regarding this article should be addressed to Emile Servan-Schreiber, Department of Psychology, Carnegie Mellon University, Pittsburgh, Pennsylvania, 15213-3890.

References

Anderson, J. R. (1983). *The Architecture of Cognition*. Cambridge, MA: Harvard University Press.

Knapp, A. G., & Anderson, J. A. (1984). Theory of categorization based on distributed memory storage. *Journal of Experimental Psychology: Learning, Memory, and Cognition, 10*, 616-637.

Hock, H. S., Tromley, C., & Polmann, L. (1988). Perceptual units in the acquisition of visual categories. *Journal of Experimental Psychology: Learning, Memory, and Cognition, 14*, 75-84.

Miller, G. A. (1956). The magical number seven, plus or minus two: some limits on our capacity for processing information. *Psychological Review, 63*, 81-97.

Newell, A. (in press). *Unified Theories of Cognition*. Cambridge, MA: Harvard University Press.

Servan-Schreiber, E., & Anderson, J. R. (in press). Learning artificial grammars with competitive chunking. *Journal of Experimental Psychology: Learning, Memory, and Cognition.*

Can Causal Induction Be Reduced to Associative Learning?

Michael R. Waldmann
University of Frankfurt

Keith J. Holyoak
University of California, Los Angeles

ABSTRACT

A number of researchers have recently claimed that higher-order human learning, such as categorization and causal induction, can be explained by the same principles as govern lower-order learning, such as classical conditioning in animals. An alternative view is that people often impose abstract causal models on observations, rather than simply associating inputs with outputs. We report three experiments using a multiple-cue learning paradigm in which models based on associative learning versus abstract causal models make opposing predictions. We show that different causal models can yield radically different learning from identical observations. In particular, we compared people's abilities to learn when the positive cases were defined by a linear cue-combination rule versus a rule involving a within-category correlation between cues. The linear structure was more readily learned when the cues were interpreted as possible causes of an effect to be predicted, whereas the correlated structure was more readily learned when the cues were interpreted as the effects of a cause to be diagnosed. The results disconfirm all associative models of causal induction in which inputs are associated with outputs without regard for causal directionality.

Introduction

The Associative View of Multiple-Cue Learning

Tasks as different as classification learning, causal induction, and classical conditioning can be viewed as examples of multiple-cue learning. In each of these tasks, a number of cues, which might be features, causes, or conditional stimuli, are combined to trigger a response. This response might be a classification decision, a prediction of an effect, or a conditioned response. Because of the apparent similarity between different types of multiple-cue learning situations, it is tempting to postulate common underlying learning mechanisms for them. A currently popular view of multiple-cue learning treats it as a bottom-up process that is fundamentally associative in nature. Thus higher-order types of learning in humans, such as classification learning, and lower-order types of learning in animals, such as classical conditioning, are seen as examples of similar learning processes.

A number of researchers have recently claimed that higher-order types of human learning, such as categorization and causal induction, can be explained by principles that govern lower-order learning in animals, such as classical conditioning (e.g., Gluck & Bower, 1988a, b; Shanks & Dickinson, 1987). In particular, Gluck and Bower (1988a, b) have suggested that adaptive associative networks can provide powerful models of human categorization as well as of classical conditioning. These connectionist models consist of an input layer that represents potential cues, such as symptoms of possible diseases observed in a patient, and an output layer that might represent classification responses, such as diagnoses of alternative diseases. The responses are computed by a linear function of the weighted cues. The weights are learned in a competitive fashion using the least mean squares (LMS) learning rule (Widrow & Hoff, 1960), in which the weights are incrementally updated in proportion to the response error they produce. Gluck and Bower have shown that a simple model of this sort compares favorably with other models of human categorization (also see Estes, Campbell, Hatsopoulos, & Hurwitz, 1989; for a critique see Shanks, 1990). Since the LMS rule is formally equivalent to

---

This research was supported by NSF Grant BNS 87-10305 to Patricia Cheng. Michael Waldmann was sponsored by a grant from the German Research Foundation. We thank Patricia Cheng for helpful advice and discussions.

190

Rescorla and Wagner's (1972) theory of classical conditioning (Sutton & Barto, 1981), these findings suggest that important commonalities link higher-order learning such as categorization and lower-order classical conditioning. Thus Gluck and Bower basically claim that categorization can be modelled as simple associative learning. Similarly, Shanks and Dickinson (1987) argue that causal induction can be reduced to associative learning.

As pointed out by Minsky and Papert (1969), simple one-layer networks can only learn linearly-separable learning tasks. To deal with this major limitation, various extensions of associative network models have been suggested in the connectionist literature. Gluck, Hee, and Bower (1989) proposed a configural-cue network in which pairwise conjunctions of simple cues are coded using configural cues added to the input layer (see also Gluck & Bower, 1988b). Alternatively, the standard connectionist approach to nonlinear learning tasks is to add intermediate layers of hidden nodes between the input and the output layers, which can be used to code cue combinations (Rumelhart, Hinton, & Williams, 1986). Using backpropagation of error signals, which conceptually is an extension of the LMS learning rule to multiple-layer networks, these hidden units can be trained to code interactions in the input. Despite the differences among the various alternative network models, each of these connectionist learning schemes shares a fundamental associationistic assumption: The network simply tries to learn statistical associations between the nodes coded on the input level and the desired output.

Learning Within Abstract Causal Models

The associative view of learning can be contrasted with a more mentalistic approach, which can be traced back to Gestalt psychology. In this tradition, it is claimed that people use abstract, meaningful world knowledge to guide their learning about new domains. Higher-order learning and lower-order associative learning are seen as different in important ways. In particular, one view of human learning is that people impose abstract causal models on observations. Wattenmaker, Dewey, Murphy, and Medin (1986) have shown that people profit from specific world knowledge. People become more sensitive to structural relations between the input cues during learning when they can relate the learning material to previously acquired knowledge. We will argue here that even in situations in which people cannot bring to bear specific world knowledge, they nonetheless might use abstract knowledge about central properties of the world -- in particular, abstract knowledge about causal relations. We have set up an experimental situation in which associative learning and learning based on abstract causal models can be pitted against each other. We will show that different causal models can yield radically different learning from identical observations, a finding that cannot be explained by associative learning models.

Figure 1 illustrates how we decouple higher-order causal learning from associative learning in our experiments. The arrows represent temporal precedence, either in order of presentation of the information, or in order of cause and effect.

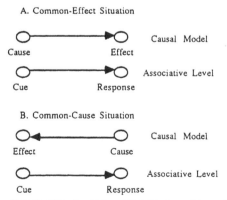

Figure 1. (A) Common-effect situation, in which causal cues are used to predict a potential effect; (B) Common-cause situation, in which presented effects serve as cues to diagnose a potential cause.

The lower halves of both Figure 1A and B show an associationistic representation of the learning situations: Cues are presented first, and the task is to learn to associate them with the correct responses. The corresponding upper halves show how the tasks map to a causal account. In a "common-effect" situation (Figure 1A), the cues represent causes and the responses represent decisions about a predicted effect. Since according to our world knowledge causes always precede effects, the temporal orderings are isomorphic between the causal and associationistic representations of the task. In a "common-cause" situation (Figure 1B), the cues represent effects, and the responses represent decisions about a cause to be diagnosed. The temporal ordering is reversed relative to a common-effect situation, and the mapping to the associationistic description is also reversed. By comparing learning in these two types of situations, this design allows us to disentangle predictions based on associative accounts from those derived from assumptions about causal models for induction. In both tasks, cues have to be associated with the required responses. Thus if subjects treat both tasks as associative multiple-cue learning, then both should yield identical patterns of learning. If, however, subjects represent the two situations in terms of causal models, the two tasks will differ in psychologically important ways, and the learning patterns should reflect these differences.

Experiment 1

Method

A multiple-cue learning task was used in this experiment. Subjects were handed index cards one at a time, with each giving a description of a fictitious person. Subjects were asked to give a "yes-no" response, classifying the cards either as positive or as negative cases. Immediately after every response subjects were told if their judgment was correct or incorrrect. The subjects were trained until they reached a learning criterion (two cycles through the eight basic cases without error) or until they received an upper limit of learning trials.

The descriptions on the index cards consisted of three binary values of dimensional features: weight, pallor, and perspiration. The fictitious persons had either high (e.g., anorexic) or low (e.g., underweight) intensity values on each of these dimensions. The eight possible cases were arranged either in a linearly separable or in a non-linearly separable, correlated fashion (see Figure 2). Similar structures have previously been investigated by Wattenmaker et al. (1986) and by Shepard, Hovland, and Jenkins (1961).

		+				-		
	Case	Dimensions			Case	Dimensions		
		1	2	3		1	2	3
	1.	H	H	H	5.	H	L	L
	2.	H	H	L	6.	L	L	H
Linearly Separable	3.	H	L	H	7.	L	H	L
	4.	L	H	H	8.	L	L	L
	1.	H	H	H	5.	L	H	H
	2.	H	L	H	6.	H	L	L
Correlated	3.	L	H	L	7.	L	L	H
	4.	L	L	L	8.	H	H	L

Figure 2: Structure of item sets used in Experiment 1

The positive set corresponds to a correct "yes" response, and the negative set to a correct "no" response. In the linearly separable arrangement high values of the dimensions are more typical for the positive set, and low values for the negative set. For both sets, each dimension has one exceptional value so that the dimensional values are only probabilistically related to the sets. However, a simple linear rule distinguishes the two sets. If a person has at least two out of three high values on the three dimensions, then this person belongs to the positive set. This structure does not require hidden layers or configural nodes in a connectionist learning network.

In the correlated, non-linearly separable condition, neither high nor low values are more or less typical for the positive or negative set. For each dimension, there are two persons with high values and two with low values in each set. There is therefore no linear rule to separate the two sets. The only way to distinguish the two sets is to notice the positive correlation between the first and the third dimension in the positive set, and the negative correlation in the negative set. The middle dimension is irrelevant for the classification. This task, which is formally equivalent to learning an "exclusive-or" structure, requires configural nodes or hidden layers in connectionist networks.

This linear-separability factor was crossed with a second factor involving manipulation of the causal structure imposed on the learning task. In the "common-cause" condition, subjects were told that they are going to learn about a disease that is caused by a virus, which could be more or less intense. In this condition the virus plays the role of a common cause that simultaneously affects the symptoms. The cues that subjects saw on the index cards thus correspond to effects of a common cause. This causal model naturally predicts a "spurious correlation" between the effects: A high-intensity virus should yield high-intensity effects, whereas a low-intensity virus should yield low-intensity effects. This situation in fact corresponds to the correlated condition; accordingly, we predicted that this condition should be particularly easy for subjects who received a cover story consistent with the common-cause model.

In a second causal context, the "common-effect" condition, the causal directions were reversed. Now the subjects were told that an experiment on social cognition had been conducted. In this experiment it was found that the appearance of some people produces a new emotional response in their observers. Here the cues on the index cards correspond to potential causes of a common effect. The subjects' task was to learn to predict which person elicits an emotional response in an observer. This emotional response might vary in intensity. Common-effect structures do not imply correlations among the causes. Learning correlated causes amounts to learning a disordinal interaction, whereas the linear condition corresponds to a causal model with three main effects. Given the preference people have for linear as opposed to configural causal structures, the linearly separable task should be relatively easy to learn (see Dawes, 1982).

It is important to note that although subjects were informed that the cause (common-cause condition) or effect (common-effect condition) could vary in intensity, no feedback about the intensity level of the outcome factor was ever provided. Rather, subjects were only told whether the outcome was obtained, regardless of its intensity.

To summarize, if subjects learn according to the accounts of associative learning theories (e.g., connectionist models with hidden layers or configural nodes), the different causal structures imposed on the task should not matter. Subjects across the two causal conditions see identical cues, and are required to learn identical cue-response mappings. However, if subjects are sensitive to the different structural implications of the two causal models, their learning rates for the linear and correlated condition should vary across the two causal cover stories.

Results

Figure 3 shows the results based on 40 UCLA undergraduates who served as subjects. The mean number of errors made prior to the subject reaching the learning criterion was used as an indicator of learning difficulty. As predicted, the causal cover story interacted with the structure of the item set, $F(1, 36) = 7.48, p < .025$. The correlated condition was easier to learn in the disease context, in which a correlation naturally falls out of a common-cause structure. In contrast, in the emotional-response condition the linearly-separable item set was easier to learn than the correlated set, as would be expected if people find main-effect models simpler to learn than causal interactions. Overall, the linear condition was learned with fewer errors than was the correlated condition, $F(1,36) = 5.78, p < .025$. The results of Experiment 1 thus clearly support the claim that subjects were using causal models during learning, rather than simply trying to associate the presented cues with the correct responses.

Mean Errors

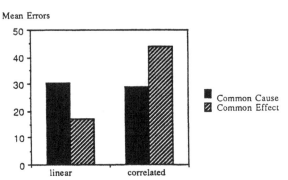

Figure 3. Mean errors prior to reaching criterion as a function of the causal model (common cause vs. common effect) and structure of the item set (linearly separable vs. correlated) in Experiment 1.

Experiment 2

Method

In a second experiment we focused on the correlated condition. In order to better approximate correlations with continuous variables, we used two variables with four intensity levels each in this experiment. We again used weight and pallor as dimensions. The levels of weight were "slightly underweight", "underweight", "seriously underweight", and "anorexic body"; analogous levels were used for pallor. In the positive set these two variables were perfectly positively correlated (values 4 4, 3 3, 2 2, and 1 1, for the four positive items), whereas in the negative set they were negatively correlated (values 4 1, 3 2, 2 3, and 1 4). Note that models like the configural-cue model of Gluck et al. (1989), which introduce separate configural cues for each pairwise feature-value combination, do not capture the monotonicity involved in a correlation of continuous variables. In addition, the number of configural cues required by such models grows exponentially with the number of levels.

In addition to examining learning with more clearly continuous variables, Experiment 2 addressed the question of whether subjects really need explicit information about the fact that the virus (the common cause) may vary in intensity. Even though capturing the positive correlation within the positive set requires the assumption of a continuous common cause, subjects might be able to infer this property of the cause by observing the learning patterns. If the effects are clearly continuous (as was the case for our materials), this may encourage the assumption that the underlying cause is also continuous. Accordingly, half of the subjects received the hint that the common cause might vary in intensity, as in Experiment 1, whereas the other half did not. This hint factor was crossed with the causal context factor, which again consisted of a common-cause and a common-effect condition. Ten subjects served in each of the four conditions.

Results

The results, displayed in Figure 4, replicated the finding that the correlated item set is learned more readily in the common-effect than in the common-cause condition, $F(1,36) = 7.38$, $p < .025$. Omitting the hint that the cause (virus) could vary in intensity did not significantly impair subjects' performance. The impact of causal models on learning correlated item sets thus generalizes to more continuous dimensions.

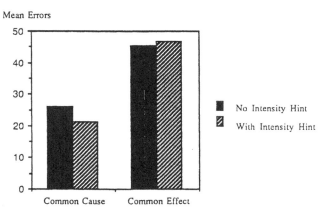

Mean Errors

Figure 4. Mean errors prior to reaching criterion as a function of the causal model (common cause vs. common effect) and provision of an intensity hint for a correlated item set in Experiment 2.

Experiment 3

Method

Experiment 3 addresses a restriction that Gluck et al. (1989) imposed on their configural-cue network model. The major advantage of configural-cue networks is that they can learn interactions using simple linear networks with the standard LMS-rule, without requiring backpropagation. Their major problem is that the potential number of configural cues grows exponentially with the number of input cues. Gluck and Bower (1988b) therefore suggest restricting configural cues to pairwise conjunctions. An obvious drawback of this restriction is that such a network is unable to handle problems for which the correct decision requires learning an interaction among three (or more) cues.

		+						-		
Case	Dimensions				Case	Dimensions				
	1	2	3	4		1	2	3	4	
1.	H	H	H	H	5.	H	H	L	H	(L)
2.	H	H	H	L	6.	H	L	H	L	(H)
3.	L	L	L	H	7.	L	H	H	H	(L)
4.	L	L	L	L	8.	L	H	L	L	(H)
					9.	L	L	H	H	(L)
					10.	H	L	L	L	(H)

Figure 5. Structure of item set used in Experiment 3.

In contrast, certain three-way interactions should be learned fairly easily within the context of a common-cause model. Figure 5 shows the structure of the material used in Experiment 3. The positive set was characterized by three correlated dimensions (H H H, or L L L), while the fourth dimension is irrelevant. This type of three-way interaction, like the pairwise interactions used in the correlated conditions in previous experiments, is consistent with a common-cause model in which the cause can vary in intensity. The negative set consisted of the full contrast set with respect to the first three dimensions, so that the subjects indeed had to learn the three-way interaction and could not use

195

two-way correlations to predict the correct response. In order to keep the negative set small, half of the subjects received the negative cases in which every uneven case has an L-value on the fourth irrelevant dimension, while for the other half these values were reversed. The dimensions and values were the same as those used in Experiment 1, with the addition of two levels of posture as the irrelevant dimension. As in the previous experiment, no hint was given regarding potential intensity variations of the virus. Two groups of subjects differed solely in the causal cover story they received: the disease story (common cause) or the emotional-response story (common effect). Twelve subjects served in each cover-story condition.

Results

The results presented in Figure 6 indicate that the three-way interaction was considerably more difficult to learn than were the correlated item sets within the earlier experiments with pairwise interactions (compare errors for the correlated conditions in Figures 3 and 4). Nonetheless, many subjects were able to attain the criterion of two passes through the items without an error, thus contradicting the implication of Gluck et al.'s (1989) configural-cue model, according to which the task should be unlearnable. In addition, and as in the previous experiments, the common-cause condition yielded a considerably lower error rate than did the common-effect condition, $F(1,22) = 5.40, p < .05$.

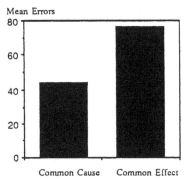

Figure 6. Mean errors prior to reaching criterion as a function of the causal model (common cause vs. common effect) for a correlated item set based on a three-way interaction in Experiment 3.

Discussion

Taken together, the three presented experiments clearly demonstrate the inadequacy of associationistic learning accounts of causal induction as they are embodied in recent connectionist models. Even though the cues and the required responses were identical across the two causal contexts, subjects proved sensitive to the structural implications of the different causal directions implied by the cover stories. Networks that simply code cues on the input layers and responses on the output layer cannot explain such reversal in the relative difficulty of linearly-separable versus correlated item sets, regardless of how they are internally configured.

Our results also demonstrate that causal induction cannot be reduced to associative learning. Associative accounts do not capture the fundamental differences between predictive and diagnostic reasoning (Pearl, 1988). Predictive reasoning requires learning the causal strengths between given causes and potential predicted effects. Once the causal links are learned, information about the presence of a cause allows probabilistic conclusions regarding its likely effects. In diagnostic reasoning, in which causes are inferred from effects, the situation is different. Even with perfect knowledge about cause-effect relationships, effect information is ambiguous with respect to its causes whenever there exists more than one potential cause. Reasoning in this situation requires an inference to the best explanation (Harman, 1986; Thagard, 1989). Different possible theories have to be weighed against each other, and a decision in favor of one or the other theory is based on the fit between the predictions of different theories and the evidence. An analogous approach is taken in research on statistical causal models as they are embodied in linear structural equations (Bollen, 1989). We are currently modelling the differences between predictive and diagnostic reasoning within a symbolic-connectionist framework, exploring models in which units are interpreted as causes and effects and core links are viewed as causal connections.

Finally, our results are in agreement with many findings demonstrating an overall preference for linear models (e.g., Dawes, 1982; Trabasso & Bower, 1968). Learning linear models puts less strain on information processing because the impact of individual causes is not moderated by the presence of other causes. A number of philosophers have argued that common-cause structures are prevalent in scientific reasoning. Salmon (1984), in particular, argued that theoretical concepts play the role of common causes. Psychologists and philosophers have asked many times what we gain from inferring invisible entities. A possible answer, suggested by the present results, might be that inferred common causes help people to re-represent nonlinear observable structures within a basically linear mental model.

References

Bollen, K. A. (1989). *Structural equations with latent variables*. New York: Wiley.

Dawes, R. M. (1982). The robust beauty of improper linear models in decision making. In D. Kahneman, P. Slovic & A. Tversky (Eds.), *Judgment under uncertainty: Heuristics and biases* (pp. 391-407). Cambridge: Cambridge University Press.

Estes, W. K., Campbell, J. A., Hatsopoulos, N., & Hurwitz, J. B. (1989). Base-rate effects in category learning: A comparison of parallel network and memory storage-retrieval models. *Journal of Experimental Psychology: Learning, Memory, and Cognition, 15,* 556-571.

Gluck, M. A., & Bower, G. H. (1988a). Evaluating an adaptive network model of human learning. *Journal of Memory and Language, 27,* 166-195.

Gluck, M. A., & Bower, G. H. (1988b). From conditioning to category learning: An adaptive network model. *Journal of Experimental Psychology: General, 117,* 227-247.

Gluck, M. A., Hee, M. R., & Bower, G. H. (1989). A configural-cue network model of animal and human associative learning. In *Proceedings of the Eleventh Annual Conference of the Cognitive Science Society*. Hillsdale, NJ: Erlbaum.

Harman, G. (1986). *Change in view*. Cambridge, MA: MIT Press.

Minsky, M., & Papert, S. (1969). *Perceptrons: An introduction to computational geometry*. Cambridge, MA: MIT Press.

Pearl, J. (1988). *Probabilistic reasoning in intelligent systems: Networks of plausible inference*. San Mateo, CA: Morgan Kaufmann.

Rescorla, R. A., & Wagner, A. R. (1972). A theory of Pavlovian conditioning: Variations in the effectiveness of reinforcement and non-reinforcement. In A. H. Black & W. F. Prokasy (Eds.), *Classical conditioning II. Current research and theory*. New York: Appleton-Century-Crofts.

Rumelhart, D. E., Hinton, G. E., & Williams, R. J. (1986). Learning internal representations by error propagation. In D. E. Rumelhart, J. L. McClelland, & the PDP Research Group (Eds.), *Parallel distributed processing* (Vol. 1, pp. 318-362). Cambridge, MA: MIT Press.

Salmon, W. C. (1984). *Scientific explanation and the causal structure of the world*. Princeton, NJ: Princeton University Press.

Shanks, D. R. (1990). Connectionism and human learning: Critique of Gluck and Bower (1988). *Journal of Experimental Psychology: General, 119,* 101-104.

Shanks, D. R., & Dickinson, A. (1987). Associative accounts of causality judgment. In G. Bower (Ed.), *The psychology of learning and motivation: Advances in research and theory, 21.* New York: Academic Press.

Shepard, R. N., Hovland, C. I., & Jenkins, H. M. (1961). Learning and memorization of classifications. *Psychological Monographs, 75,* 1-42.

Sutton, R. S., & Barto, A. G. (1981). Toward a modern theory of adaptive networks: Expectation and prediction. *Psychological Review, 88,* 135-170.

Thagard, P. (1989). Explanatory coherence. *Behavioral and Brain Sciences, 12,* 435-467.

Trabasso, T., & Bower, G. (1968). *Attention in learning: Theory and research*. New York: Wiley.

Wattenmaker, W. D., Dewey, G. I., Murphy, T. D., & Medin, D. L. (1986). Linear separability and concept learning: Context, relational properties, and concept naturalness. *Cognitive Psychology, 18,* 158-194.

Widrow, G., & Hoff, M. E. (1960). Adaptive switching circuits. *Institute of Radio Engineers, Western Electronic Show and Convention, Convention Record, 4,* 96-194.

Decision Models: A Theory of Volitional Explanation*

Ashwin Ram

Georgia Institute of Technology
School of Information and Computer Science
Atlanta, Georgia 30332-0280
(404) 853-9372
E-mail: ashwin@ics.gatech.edu

Abstract

This paper presents a theory of motivational analysis, the construction of volitional explanations to describe the planning behavior of agents. We discuss both the content of such explanations, as well as the process by which an understander builds the explanations. Explanations are constructed from *decision models*, which describe the planning process that an agent goes through when considering whether to perform an action. Decision models are represented as *explanation patterns*, which are standard patterns of causality based on previous experiences of the understander. We discuss the nature of explanation patterns, their use in representing decision models, and the process by which they are retrieved, used and evaluated.

1   Issues in explanation

In order to learn from experience, a reasoner must be able to *explain* what it does not understand. When a novel or poorly understood situation is processed, it is interpreted in terms of knowledge structures already in memory. As long as these structures provide expectations that allow the reasoner to function effectively in the new situation, there is no problem. However, if these expectations fail, the reasoner is faced with an *anomaly*. The world is different from its expectations. In order to learn from this experience, the reasoner needs to know *why* it made those predictions. It also needs to explain *why* the failure occurred, i.e., to identify the knowledge structures that gave rise to the faulty expectations, and to understand why its domain model was violated in this situation. Finally, it must store the new experience in memory for future use. Explanation is a central issue in this process of understanding and learning.

The construction of explanations is also known as *abduction*, or *inference to the best explanation*. This process is usually viewed as the chaining together of causal inference rules in order to create a causal chain, in which a proposed set of premises is shown to be causally responsible for the event or fact being explained. However, there are two problems with this view.

The first problem is the familiar one of combinatorial explosion of inferences. Most explanation programs create explanations by chaining together inference rules that describe the causality of the domain. For example, PAM [Wilensky, 1978] used a set of planning rules connecting together typical goals and plans of people, and chained them together to form motivational explanations for actions observed in a story. However, this process is very inefficient in complex domains, where the causal chains may be several steps long.

The second problem is the evaluation of explanations. Since the chaining process is seeking a connection between two concepts, most theories use an evaluation criterion based on the structural properties of this connection. For example, marker passing and spreading activation techniques (which are often proposed as a solution to the combinatorial explosion problem) usually judge the goodness of an explanation by the length of the causal chain. The shortest correct explanation is assumed to be the "best" one. However, the definition of "best" is dependent on the *goals* of the reasoner in forming the explanation and not just on the length or correctness of the causal chain underlying the explanation. In situations where there is no one "right" explanation, the "best" explanation must be more than a causal chain that describes the events in the domain; it must also address the reason that an explanation was required in the first place. This in turn determines what the reasoner can learn from the explanation.

---

*The research described was conducted while the author was at Yale University, and supported by the Defense Advanced Research Projects Agency and the Office of Naval Research under contract N00014-85-K-0108, and by the Air Force Office of Scientific Research under contracts F49620-88-C-0058 and AFOSR-85-0343.

In addition to processing issues, a theory of explanation must also address the content issues of the nature and representation of explanations. What is an explanation, and what kinds of knowledge does it provide? What is the nature of the causal knowledge that underlies volitional explanations? The answers to these questions depend both on the explanations that we desire to build, as well as on the process that is used to build them.

This paper presents a theory of explanation based on the claim that new explanations are built, not by chaining inference rules together, but rather by reusing explanations that have been encountered in previous situations and are already known to the system [Schank, 1986]. Our view raises several questions:

- *Content and representation:* What kinds of knowledge must an explanation provide? How do we represent this knowledge? What kinds of structures are used to represent explanations in memory? What is the vocabulary out of which these structures are built?

- *Retrieval:* How do we find pre-stored explanations in memory without having to try each one?

- *Evaluation:* How do we determine what kind of explanation is needed, and which explanation is the "best" one in a particular situation?

- *Learning:* How are explanations learned so that they can be reused in the future? What happens when pre-stored explanations don't apply to the current situation?[1]

The theory presented here has been implemented in the AQUA program, a story understanding program which learns about terrorism by reading newspaper stories about unusual terrorist incidents in the Middle East. We will illustrate our ideas with examples taken from this program. Further details may be found in [Ram, 1987; Schank and Ram, 1988; Ram, 1989].

2 What is an explanation?

The need for an explanation arises when some observed fact doesn't quite fit into the reasoner's world model, i.e., the reasoner detects an *anomaly*. An explanation is a knowledge structure that makes the anomaly go away. To illustrate the nature of such a structure, let us consider some candidate explanations for the following story (New York Times, Nov 27, 1985, page A9) from the domain of the AQUA program:

S-1: Suicide bomber strikes Israeli post in Lebanon.
SIDON, Lebanon, November 26 — A teenage girl exploded a car bomb at a joint post of Israeli troops and pro-Israeli militiamen in southern

Lebanon today, killing herself and causing a number of casualties, Lebanese security sources said.
...
A statement by the pro-Syrian Arab Baath Part named the bomber as Hamida Mustafa al-Taher, born in Syria in 1968. The statement said she had detonated a car rigged with 660 points of explosives in a military base for 50 South Lebanon Army men and Israeli intelligence and their vehicles.

Why did Hamida go on the bombing mission?
(1) Because Lebanon is a Middle Eastern country.
(2) To destroy the Israeli military base.
(3) Because she was a religious fanatic.
(4) Because she didn't realize she was going to die during the mission.

Consider (1). This does not seem like an explanation for S-1. The reason isn't that (1) is false, but rather that there seems to be no causal connection between (1) and S-1. Thus it is not sufficient for a proposed explanation to be true; *an explanation must be causally connected to the anomaly.* It must contain a set of premises and a causal chain linking those premises to the anomalous proposition. If the reasoner believes the premises, the proposition ceases to be anomalous since the causal interactions underlying the situation can now be understood.

However, not all causal structures are explanations. For example, (2) is causally relevant to S-1, but it still doesn't feel like an explanation. To understand why, let us make the anomaly in S-1 explicit. The real question isn't "Why did Hamida go on the bombing mission?", but rather one of the following:

S-2: Why was Hamida willing to sacrifice her life in order to destroy the Israeli military base?

S-3: Why did Hamida go on a mission that would result in her own death?

The reason that explanation (2) feels strange is that it misses the point of the question. If the point is made explicit as in S-2, (3) is a possible explanation for the anomaly. Alternatively, if the real question is intended to be S-3, (4) is a possible explanation. The point is that, in order to qualify as an explanation, a causal description must address the underlying anomaly.

To state this another way, *an explanation must address the failure of the reasoner to model the situation correctly.* In addition to resolving the incorrect predictions, it must also point to the erroneous aspect of the chain of reasoning that led to the incorrect predictions. An explanation is *useful* if it allows the reasoner to learn and to improve its performance at its task; the claim here is that *an explanation must be both causal and relevant in order to be useful.* This is important in evaluating explanations to determine the best one for a particular situation.

---

[1] These issues are beyond the scope of this paper.

3 Explanation patterns

An explanation is a causal chain that demonstrates why the anomalous proposition might have occurred by introducing a set of premises that causally lead up to that proposition. There may be more than one explanation for a situation, depending on the question that the reasoner is interested in. For example, if the system needs to explain the motivations behind the girl's actions in story S-1, it may build what we think of as the *religious fanatic explanation*: The girl was a Moslem fanatic; she was so determined to further the cause of her religion that she was willing to die for it; and she believed that destroying the military base would help her religious cause.

The premise of this explanation is that the girl was a religious fanatic. If the reasoner believes or can verify the premises of an explanation, the conclusion is said to be explained. Explanations are often verbalized using their premises. Thus in normal conversation this explanation would be stated succinctly as "Because she was a religious fanatic." However, the real explanation includes the premises, the causal chain, and any intermediate assertions (such as the girl's belief that the bombing would help her religious cause) that are part of the causal chain.

How might a reasoner construct such an explanation? PAM [Wilensky, 1978] used a set of planning rules connecting typical goals and plans of people, and chained them together to form explanations such as the above. However, this is too inefficient in complicated situations, where the causal chains could be several steps long. To get around this problem, AQUA uses pre-stored explanations for stereotypical situations. These explanations represent standard patterns that are observed in these situations, and hence are called *explanation patterns* [Schank, 1986].

An explanation pattern (XP) is a stock explanation for a stereotypical situation. For example, *religious fanatic does terrorist act* is a standard XP many people have about the Middle East terrorism problem. One might think of them as the "scripts" of the explanation domain.[2] When a reasoner encounters a situation for which it has a canned XP, it tries to apply the XP to avoid detailed analysis of the situation from scratch.

This approach is known as *case-based explanation*, since previous cases or explanations known to the reasoner are used to help in the construction

of new explanations. Explanatory cases in AQUA are based on the theory of explanation patterns described by [Schank, 1986], to which we add a theory of the representational structure and content of the XPs used in story understanding.

Explanations can be divided into two broad categories, physical and volitional.

3.1 Physical explanations

Physical explanations link events with the states that result from them, and further events that they enable, using causal chains similar to those of [Rieger, 1975] and [Schank and Abelson, 1977]. Physical explanations answer questions about the physical causality of the domain. For example, if the system had never read a story about a car bombing before, it might encounter an anomaly: "How can a car be used to blow up a building?" The answer to this question is a physical explanation:

(1) A car is a physical object.

(2) A car can contain explosives.

(3) A car can be propelled by driving it.

(4) Explosives can be blown up by the sudden impact of a car colliding with a building.

(5) A building can be blown up by blowing up explosives in its immediate vicinity.

Thus the explanation is that the bomber drove an explosive-laden car into the building, the impact caused the explosives to detonate, which caused the building to blow up.

3.2 Volitional explanations

Volitional explanations link actions that people perform to their goals and beliefs, yielding an understanding of the *motivations* of the characters. For example, the system might detect a different anomaly on reading story S-1, such as "Why would someone commit suicide if they are not depressed?" An explanation for this question, such as the religious fanatic explanation, must provide a motivational analysis of the reasons for committing suicide. For this reason, volitional explanations are also called motivational explanations. Although the basic structure of volitional explanations is the same as that of physical explanations, the vocabulary used to represent the causal chain is very different.

Volitional explanations fall into two broad categories:

1. **Abstract explanation patterns** for why people do things. These are standard high-level explanations for actions, such as "Actor does action because the outcome of action satisfies a goal of the actor."

2. **Stereotypical explanation patterns.** These are specific explanations for particular situation, such as "Shiite Moslem religious fanatic goes on suicide bombing mission."

---

[2] Unlike scripts, however, XPs are flexible since they contain a description of the *causality* underlying a situation in addition to a description of the situation itself. This allows XPs to be useful in novel situations, while retaining the advantages of pre-stored structures in stereotypical situations. The incremental elaboration of XPs in novel situations is discussed in [Ram, 1989; Ram, 1990b].

For example, an explanation of type 1 for the suicide bombing story could be "Because she wanted to destroy the Israeli base more than she wanted to stay alive." An explanation of type 2 would be simply "Because she was a religious fanatic." The internal causal structure of the latter explanation could then be elaborated to provide a detailed motivational analysis in terms of explanations of the first type if necessary.

Volitional explanations thus correspond to the filling out of the "belief-goal-plan-action" chain [Schank and Abelson, 1977; Wilks, 1977; Wilensky, 1978; Schank, 1986], although we need to expand the vocabulary of this chain in order to model such explanations adequately [Ram, 1989]. A volitional explanation relates the actions in which the characters in the story are involved to the *outcomes* that those actions had for them, the *goals, beliefs, emotional states* and *social states* of the characters as well as priorities or *orderings* among the goals, and the *decision process* that the characters go through in *considering* their goals, goal-orderings and likely outcomes of the actions before deciding whether to do those actions. A detailed volitional explanation involving the planning decisions of a character is called a *decision model*, and is illustrated in figure 1.

Decision models provide a theory of motivational coherence for stories involving volitional agents. When a decision model is applied to the actions of a given character in a story, it focusses attention on faulty assumptions or inconsistencies identified in the application of the decision model to the story. These inconsistencies signal anomalies, which must be explained by determining whether different parts of the decision model (e.g., the goals of the agent, his beliefs about the outcome, or his volition in deciding to perform the action) are actually present as assumed.

For example, the religious fanatic explanation is based on the following decision model:[3]

1. **Explains:** Why volitional-agent A did a suicide-bombing M, with results =

   (1) death-state of A
   (2) destroyed-state of target, a physical-object whose owner is an opponent religious group.

2. **Premises:**

   (1) A believes in the religion R.
   (2) A is a religious-fanatic, i.e., A has high-religious-zeal.

3. **Internals:**

   (1) A is religious and believes in the religion R (an emotional-state, perhaps caused by a social-state, such as upbringing).

[3]Typewriter font represents actual vocabulary items used by the AQUA program. Further details of the representation may be found in [Ram, 1989].

   (2) A is strongly zealous about R (an emotional-state).
   (3) A wants to spread his religion R (a goal, initiated by (1) and (2)).
   (4) A places a high priority on his goal in (3), and is willing to sacrifice other goals which we would normally place above the religion goal (a goal-ordering, initiated by (1) and (2)).
   (5) A believes that performing a suicide bombing against opponent religious groups will help him achieve his goal in (3) (a belief or expected-outcome).
   (6) A knows that the performance of a suicide bombing may result in a negative outcome for him (an expected-outcome).
   (7) A weighs his goals (3), goal-orderings (4), and likely outcomes (5) and (6) (a consideration).
   (8) A decides to do the suicide bombing M (a decision, based on the considerations in (7)).
   (9) A does the suicide bombing M (an action or mop, whose actor is A).
   (10) The suicide bombing has some outcome for A, which is either positive or negative as viewed from the point of view of A's goals and goal-orderings (a self-outcome).

The representation of the religious fanatic explanation is shown in figure 2. The decision model has the following components:

The outcome of an action: Every action results in some set of states that may or may not be beneficial to the people involved in that action, depending on their goals at that time. The outcome of an action, therefore, must be modelled *from the point of view of a particular volitional agent* involved in that action. The most common volitional participants are **actor** and **planner**, but any role involving a volitional agent must potentially be explained.

The decision process: Every agent involved in an action makes a *decision* about whether to participate in that particular volitional role (**actor**, **planner**, **object**, etc.) in the action. Such decisions represent the *planning* process that the agent underwent prior to the action. A complete model of this process requires a sophisticated vocabulary of goals, goal interactions, and plans, such as that of [Wilensky, 1983] or [Hammond, 1986]. There are three basic kinds of decisions:

1. **Choice:** The agent *chooses* to participate or not to participate in a given volitional role in some action. The explanation must describe why he made this choice.

2. **Agency:** The agent is *induced* to participate or not to participate in a given volitional role in an action. This is similar to the previous case in that the agent "enters" the action of his own volition. The difference is that here the agent is acting under the agency of another agent. Thus the

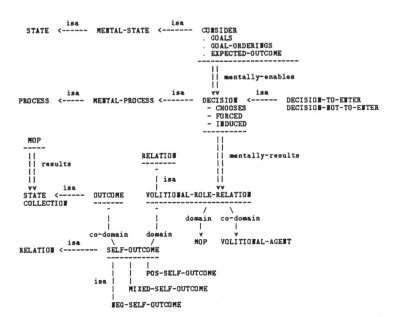

Figure 1: The structure of volitional explanations. A volitional-agent participates in some volitional-role in a mop, which then results in an outcome (a collection of states). Prior to this, the volitional-agent undergoes a decision process in which he considers his goals, goal-orderings and expected-outcome, which then mentally-results in the volitional-role-relation being considered being true (in) or false (out) depending on the outcome of the decision.

explainer must be able to model inter-agent interactions [Schank and Abelson, 1977; Wilensky, 1983; Ram, 1984].

3. **Coercion:** The agent is *forced* to participate or not to participate in a given volitional role in an action. This case arises when an agent is physically coerced into participation or non-participation.

Considerations in decisions: The system also needs to reason about what an agent was considering as he made a particular decision. Considerations model the goals and beliefs of an agent, along with orderings among these goals and expected outcome of the action being considered. Considerations are composed of three constituents: (1) `goals` considered by the agent while deciding whether or not to participate in an action, (2) `goal-orderings`, the agent's prioritization of these goals, and (3) the `expected-outcome`: the agent's beliefs about what the outcome of the action is likely to be. This is represented by the `consider` node in figure 1.

Each of these constituents may itself need to be explained further. For example, the system might question the social or mental (e.g., emotional) states that initiated a particular goal or goal-ordering in an agent, or how a particular belief about the outcome of an action came about. Explanations, therefore, may need to be *elaborated* according to the demands of the story and the goals of the system.

4 Structure of explanation patterns

AQUA has several XPs indexed in memory, representing its causal knowledge of the terrorism domain. These XPs are represented as graph structures (as illustrated above) with four main components:

1. **PRE-XP-NODES:** Nodes that represent what is known before the XP is applied. One of these nodes, the EXPLAINS node, represents the particular action being explained.

2. **XP-ASSERTED-NODES:** Nodes asserted by the XP as the explanation for the EXPLAINS node. These comprise the premises of the explanation.

3. **INTERNAL-XP-NODES:** Internal nodes as-

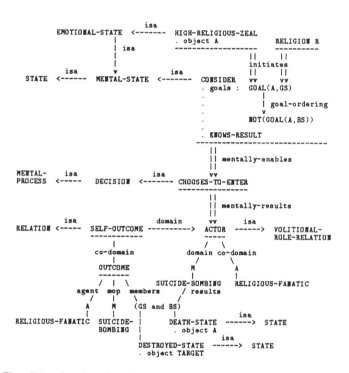

```
                                isa
      EMOTIONAL-STATE  <------- HIGH-RELIGIOUS-ZEAL
            |                    . object A              RELIGION R
            | isa               --------------------     ----------
            |                         ||    ||
            |                       initiates
            |                         ||    ||
            v                 isa     vv    vv
  STATE <------ MENTAL-STATE <------ CONSIDER  GOAL(A,GS)
                                      . goals :    |
                                      .            | goal-ordering
                                      .            v
                                      .          NOT(GOAL(A,BS))
                                      .
                                      . KNOWS-RESULT
                                      -------------------------------
                                            ||
                                            || mentally-enables
                                            ||
  MENTAL-     isa                   isa     vv
  PROCESS <----- DECISION <------ CHOOSES-TO-ENTER
                                      -----------------
                                            ||
                                            || mentally-results
                                            ||
                           domain           vv      isa
  RELATION <----- SELF-OUTCOME ---------> ACTOR ------>  VOLITIONAL-
                  -----------            -----              ROLE-RELATION
                      |                  /  \
                 co-domain           domain co-domain
                      |                /        \
                  OUTCOME            M          A
                  -------            |          |
                 / | \           SUICIDE-BOMBING  RELIGIOUS-FANATIC
            agent mop members     / results
              /   |    \     (GS and BS)
             A    M     |              |       isa
  RELIGIOUS-FANATIC SUICIDE- |    DEATH-STATE ------>  STATE
                   BOMBING   |     . object A
                             |              isa
                   DESTROYED-STATE ------>  STATE
                    . object TARGET
```

Figure 2: The religious fanatic explanation pattern. A is the agent, R his religion, M the action he chooses to do, and GS and BS the good and bad outcomes for A as a result of doing that action. A volitionally chooses to perform M knowing both outcomes, the **death-state** of A and the **destroyed-state** of the target.

---

serted by the XP in order to link the XP-ASSERTED-NODES to the EXPLAINS node.

4. LINKS: Causal links asserted by the XP. These taken together with the INTERNAL-XP-NODES are also called the internals of the XP.

An explanation pattern states that the XP-ASSERTED-NODES lead to the EXPLAINS node (which is part of a particular configuration of PRE-XP-NODES) via a set of INTERNAL-XP-NODES, the nodes being causally linked together via the LINKS (which in turn could invoke further XPs). In other words, an XP represents a causal chain composed of a set of nodes connected together using a set of LINKS (causal rules or XPs). The "antecedent" (or premise) of this causal chain is the set of XP-ASSERTED-NODES, the "internal nodes" of the causal chain are the INTERNAL-XP-NODES of the XP, and the "consequent" is the EXPLAINS node. The difference between XP-ASSERTED-NODES and INTERNAL-XP-NODES is that the former are merely asserted by the XP

without further explanation, whereas the latter have causal antecedents within the XP itself.

5 The explanation cycle

An explanation-based understander must be able to detect anomalies in the input, and resolve them by building motivational and causal explanations for the events in the story in order to understand why the characters acted as they did, or why certain events occurred or did not occur. This process characterizes both "story understanders" that try to achieve a deep understanding of the stories that they read, as well as programs that need to understand their domains in service of other problem-solving tasks. Explanations are constructed by retrieving XPs from memory, applying them to the situation at hand, and verifying or evaluating the resulting hypotheses.

5.1 Anomaly detection

Anomaly detection refers to the process of identifying an unusual fact that needs explanation. The anomalous fact may be unusual in the sense that it violates or contradicts some piece of information in memory. Alternatively, the fact may be unusual because, while there is no explicit contradiction, the reasoner fails to integrate the fact satisfactorily in its memory.

5.2 Explanation pattern retrieval

When faced with an anomalous situation, the reasoner tries to retrieve one or more explanation patterns that would explain the situation. Ideally, an XP should be indexed in memory such that it is retrieved only in those situations in which it is applicable. But this is impossible in practice. For example, consider the applicability conditions for "blackmail." In general, blackmail is a possible explanation whenever "someone does something he doesn't want to do because not doing it results in something worse for him." But trying to show this in general is very hard. Thus, in addition to general applicability conditions, a reasoner must learn specific, sometimes superficial, features that suggest possibly relevant XPs even though they may not completely determine the applicability of the XP to the situation. For example, a classic blackmail situation is one where a rich businessman who is cheating on his wife is blackmailed for money using the threat of exposure. If one read about a rich businessman who suddenly began to withdraw large sums of money from his bank account, one would expect to think of the possibility of blackmail. However, one does not normally think of blackmail when one reads a story about suicide bombing, although theoretically it is a possible explanation.

AQUA indexes motivational XPs in memory using typical contexts in which the XPs might be encountered (*situation indices*), as well as character stereotypes representing typical categories of people to whom the XPs might be applicable (*stereotype indices*) [Ram, 1989]. The third type of index is known as the *anomaly index* or *category index*. Recall that in addition to explaining the occurrence of the event, it is important for the XP to address the anomaly which arose from the failure of the reasoner to model the situation correctly. Thus the type of the anomaly provides an index to the type of XP required to build an explanation. For example, if the anomaly was one where an actor performed an action that violated one of the actor's own goals, the reasoner might look for a "goal sacrifice" XP (such as a religious fanatic sacrificing her life for the cause of her religion), or an "actor didn't know outcome" XP (such as a gullible teenager not realizing what the outcome of her action was going to be). However, the category of goal sacrifice XPs would be inappropriate for an anomaly in which the actor failed to perform an action which only had a good outcome for the actor; in this case, a "missed opportunity" XP might be chosen.

5.3 Explanation pattern application

Once a set of potentially applicable XPs is retrieved, the reasoner tries to use them to resolve the anomaly. This involves instantiating the XPs, filling in the details through elaboration and specification, and checking the validity of the final explanations. An XP is instantiated by unifying the EXPLAINS node of the XP with the description of the situation being explained, and instantiating the INTERNAL-XP-NODES and LINKS. If all the PRE-XP-NODES and INTERNAL-XP-NODES of the XP fit the situation, the hypothesis is applicable. If the unification fails, the hypothesis is rejected.[4]

5.4 Hypothesis verification and evaluation

The final step in the explanation process is the confirmation or refutation of possible explanations, or, if there is more than one hypothesis, discrimination between the alternatives. A hypothesis is a causal graph that connects the premises of the explanation to the conclusions via a set of intermediate assertions. At the end of this step, the reasoner is left with one or more alternative hypotheses. Partially confirmed hypotheses are maintained in a data dependency network called a *hypothesis tree*, along with questions (unconfirmed XP-ASSERTED-NODES) representing what is required to verify these hypotheses.

There are five criteria for evaluating the goodness of an explanation:

1. **Believability:** Does the system believe the XP from which the hypothesis was derived? This is not an issue when all XPs in memory are believed, but for a program that learns new XPs, some of which may be incomplete, the believability of the XP is an important criterion in deciding whether to believe the resulting hypothesis.

2. **Applicability:** How well does the XP apply to this situation? Did it fit the situation without any modifications?

3. **Relevance:** Does the XP address the underlying anomaly? Does it address the knowledge goals of the reasoner (i.e., does it allow the reasoner to learn)?

4. **Verification:** How definitely was the explanation confirmed or refuted?

5. **Specificity:** How specific is the XP? Is it abstract and very general (e.g., a proverb), or is it detailed and specific?

Intuitively, a "good" explanation is not necessarily one that can be proven to be "true" (criterion

---

[4]There is also the possibility of modifying the hypothesis to fit the situation [Schank, 1986; Kass *et al.*, 1986].

4), but also one that seems plausible (**1** and **2**), fits the situation well (**2** and **5**), and is relevant to the goals of the reasoner (criterion **3**).

The relevance criterion is important if the explanation is created for some purpose (and not as an end in itself). The fact that the reasoner encountered an anomaly indicates a need to learn, which could arise in several ways. The reasoner may not have the knowledge structures to deal with a novel situation, or the knowledge structures that the reasoner applies to the situation may be incomplete or incorrect. The domain knowledge may be misindexed in memory, i.e., the reasoner may have the knowledge structures to deal with the situation, but it may be unable to retrieve them since they are not indexed under the cues that the situation provides.

When an explanation is built, the reasoner needs to be able to identify the kind of processing error that occurred and invoke the appropriate learning strategy. For example, if an incomplete knowledge structure is applied to a situation, the resulting processing error represents both the knowledge that is missing, as well as the fact that this piece of knowledge, when it comes in, should be used to fill in the gap in the original knowledge structure. Similarly, if an error arose due to a mis-indexed knowledge structure, the explanation, when available, should be used to re-index the knowledge structure appropriately. The explanation is therefore constrained by the needs of the learning process [Ram, 1990a].

6   Conclusion

Abduction, or inference to the best explanation, is a central component of the reasoning process. Abduction is viewed, not as a process of chaining together inference rules to produce causal chains, but rather one of case-based reasoning from pre-stored causal chains, known as explanation patterns, associated with prior experiences in memory. This provides a way to control the combinatorial explosion of inferences, but introduces a new set of issues: the content and representation of explanation patterns, the types of indices used to retrieve XPs from memory, the evaluation of candidate hypotheses, and the learning of new XPs.

Evaluation is facilitated by using anomaly characterizations as retrieval indices for XPs. The "best" explanation is not one that is the most "correct," if correctness is even measurable in the domain of interest, but one that is most useful to the process that is seeking the explanation. The anomaly detection process provides retrieval cues that are used to find explanation patterns that are likely to be relevant to the anomaly.

These ideas have been explored in the AQUA program, a computer model of the theory of question-driven understanding. AQUA learns about terrorism by reading newspaper stories about terrorist incidents in the Middle East. The requirements of this task provided constraints on the theory of explanation presented here.

References

[Hammond, 1986] K. J. Hammond. *Case-Based Planning: An Integrated Theory of Planning, Learning and Memory*. Ph.D. thesis, Yale University, Department of Computer Science, New Haven, CT, October 1986. Research Report #488.

[Kass *et al.*, 1986] A. Kass, D. Leake, and C. Owens. *SWALE: A Program That Explains*, pages 232–254. Lawrence Erlbaum Associates, Hillsdale, NJ, 1986.

[Ram, 1984] A. Ram. Modelling Characters and their Decisions: A Theory of Compliance Decisions. Master's thesis, University of Illinois at Urbana-Champaign, Urbana, IL, August 1984. Technical Report T-145.

[Ram, 1987] A. Ram. AQUA: Asking Questions and Understanding Answers. In *Proceedings of the Sixth Annual National Conference on Artificial Intelligence*, pages 312–316, Seattle, WA, July 1987. American Association for Artificial Intelligence, Morgan Kaufman Publishers, Inc.

[Ram, 1989] A. Ram. *Question-driven understanding: An integrated theory of story understanding, memory and learning*. Ph.D. thesis, Yale University, New Haven, CT, May 1989. Research Report #710.

[Ram, 1990a] A. Ram. Goal-Based Explanation. In *Proceedings of the AAAI Spring Symposium on Automated Abduction*, Palo Alto, CA, March 1990.

[Ram, 1990b] A. Ram. Incremental Learning of Explanation Patterns and their Indices. In *Proceedings of the Seventh International Conference on Machine Learning*, Austin, TX, June 1990.

[Rieger, 1975] C. Rieger. Conceptual Memory and Inference. In R. C. Schank, editor, *Conceptual Information Processing*. North-Holland, Amsterdam, 1975.

[Schank and Abelson, 1977] R. C. Schank and R. Abelson. *Scripts, Plans, Goals and Understanding: An Inquiry into Human Knowledge Structures*. Lawrence Erlbaum Associates, Hillsdale, NJ, 1977.

[Schank and Ram, 1988] R. C. Schank and A. Ram. Question-driven Parsing: A New Approach to Natural Language Understanding. *Journal of Japanese Society for Artificial Intelligence*, 3(3):260–270, May 1988.

[Schank, 1986] R. C. Schank. *Explanation Patterns: Understanding Mechanically and Creatively*. Lawrence Erlbaum Associates, Hillsdale, NJ, 1986.

[Wilensky, 1978] R. Wilensky. *Understanding Goal-Based Stories*. Ph.D. thesis, Yale University, Department of Computer Science, New Haven, CT, 1978.

[Wilensky, 1983] R. Wilensky. *Planning and Understanding*. Addison-Wesley, Reading, MA, 1983.

[Wilks, 1977] Y. Wilks. What Sort of Taxonomy of Causation Do We Need for Language Understanding. *Cognitive Science*, 1:235, 1977.

Knowledge Goals: A Theory of Interestingness*

Ashwin Ram

Georgia Institute of Technology
School of Information and Computer Science
Atlanta, Georgia 30332-0280
(404) 853-9372
E-mail: ashwin@ics.gatech.edu

Abstract

Combinatorial explosion of inferences has always been one of the classic problems in AI. Resources are limited, and inferences potentially infinite; a reasoner needs to be able to determine which inferences are useful to draw from a given piece of text. But unless one considers the goals of the reasoner, it is very difficult to give a principled definition of what it means for an inference to be "useful."

This paper presents a theory of inference control based on the notion of interestingness. We introduce *knowledge goals*, the goals of a reasoner to acquire some piece of knowledge required for a reasoning task, as the focussing criteria for inference control. We argue that knowledge goals correspond to the *interests* of the reasoner, and present a theory of interestingness that is functionally motivated by consideration of the needs of the reasoner. Although we use story understanding as the reasoning task, many of the arguments carry over to other cognitive tasks as well.

1 Cognitive motivations: Knowledge goals as a basis for interestingness

When we compare the way people read newspaper stories with how computer programs typically read them, we notice the following differences:

Subjectivity: People are biased. They interpret stories in a manner that suits them. They jump to conclusions. Computer programs, on the other hand, are usually designed to read stories in an objective manner, and to extract the "correct" or "true" interpretation of a story to the extent that they can.

Variable depth parsing: People don't read everything in great detail. They concentrate on details that they find relevant or interesting, and skim over the rest. In contrast, computer programs are

*The research described was conducted while the author was at Yale University, and supported by the Defense Advanced Research Projects Agency and the Office of Naval Research under contract N00014-85-K-0108, and by the Air Force Office of Scientific Research under contracts F49620-88-C-0058 and AFOSR-85-0343.

designed to attend to every aspect of a story that is within the scope of their knowledge structures. Consequently, they either process the entire story in great depth, or else they skim everything in the story. They can not decide which aspects to process in detail and which ones to ignore.

Learning and change: People change as they read. They never read the same story twice in the same way. They notice different things the second time around, or they simply get bored. After reading a story, they interpret other similar stories differently. Computer programs, in contrast, are not adaptive; they always read a given story the same way.

What makes people different from computer programs? What is the missing element that our theories don't yet account for? The answer is simple: *People read newspaper stories for a reason: to learn more about what they are interested in.* Computers, on the other hand, don't. In fact, computers don't even have interests; there is nothing in particular that they are trying to find out when they read. If a computer program is to be a model of story understanding, it should also read for a "purpose."

Of course, people have several goals that do not make sense to attribute to computers. One might read a restaurant guide in order to satisfy hunger or entertainment goals, or to find a good place to go for a business lunch. Computers do not get hungry, and computers do not have business lunches.

However, these *physiological* and *social goals* give rise to several *intellectual* or *cognitive goals*. A goal to satisfy hunger gives rise to goals to find information: the name of a restaurant which serves the desired type of food, how expensive the restaurant is, the location of the restaurant, etc. These are goals to acquire information or knowledge, and are called *knowledge goals*. These goals can be held by computers too; a computer might "want" to find out the location of a restaurant, and read a guide in order to do so in the same way as a person might. While such a goal would not arise out of hunger in the case of the computer, it might well arise out of the "goal" to learn more about restaurants.

In other words, knowledge goals also arise from

the desire to learn, to pursue one's intellectual interests, to improve one's model of the world. These goals can be viewed as *questions* about the domain of interest. To be interested in terrorism, for example, is to have a lot of questions about various aspects of terrorism, and to think about these questions in the context of input data about terrorism, such as newspaper stories about terrorist incidents. The point of reading these stories is to answer one's questions, as well as to reveal flaws or gaps in one's model of terrorism in order to try to improve this model. These gaps give rise to new questions which in turn stimulate further interest in terrorism. Both computers and people can be "interested" in terrorism in this sense.

In contrast with people, therefore, a computer has only one underlying goal: to learn and improve its world model.[1] However, this (and, in the case of people, other physical and social goals) gives rise to knowledge goals that then drive the understanding process.

2 Computational motivations: What are the knowledge goals of an understanding program?

Understanding, then, can be viewed as the pursuit of one's interests or questions. However, it would defeat the purpose to build a "question-asking" or "interest-pursuing" program per se. Instead, these questions and interests should arise naturally as *cognitive goals* of the program during various stages of the reasoning process. This means that the program should ask a question only when it has a need to acquire that piece of knowledge. For example, in the case of a story understanding system, a knowledge goal should be formulated only when the system needs to know the answer for the purposes of understanding the story. In other words, knowledge goals should be *functionally useful* to the overall goals of the system.

The theory of knowledge goals presented in this paper depends on a theory of *understanding tasks*, the basic tasks of an understander. In addition to parser-level tasks such as noun group connection, pronoun reference, etc., these tasks include the integration of facts with what the understander already knows, the detection of anomalies in the text which identify flaws or gaps in the understander's model of the domain, the formulation of explanations to resolve those anomalies, the confirmation and refutation of potential explanations, the learning of new explanations for use in understanding future situations. These are the basic tasks that an understander needs to be able to perform.

In order to carry out these tasks, the understander needs to integrate the text, which is of-

ten ambiguous, elliptic and vague, with its world knowledge, which is often incomplete. In formulating an explanation, for example, the understander may need to know more about the situation than is explicitly stated before it can decide which is the best explanation. However, it is impossible to anticipate when a particular piece of knowledge will be available to the understander, since the real world (in the case of a story understanding program, the story) will not always provide exactly that piece of knowledge at exactly the time that the understander requires it. *Thus the understander must be able to suspend questions in memory, and reactivate them at the right time when the information it needs becomes available.* In other words, the understander must be able to remember what it needs to know, and why.

Furthermore, the system's understanding of any real world domain can never be quite complete. Conventional script, frame or schema-based theories assume that understanding means finding an appropriate script, frame or schema in memory and fitting it to the story. Schemas in memory are assumed to be "correct;" if an applicable schema is found, the story is understood. However, this model is inadequate since an understander's memory is always incomplete. Knowledge structures often have gaps in them, especially in poorly understood domains. These gaps correspond to what the understander has not yet understood about the domain. Even if a schema appears to be correct, novel experiences or stories may reveal flaws in the schema or a mismatch with the real world. Furthermore, the schema may not be indexed correctly in memory.

Understanding tasks, therefore, generate information subgoals or questions, representing what the understander needs to know in order to carry out the current task, be it explanation, learning, or any other cognitive task. These questions constitute the specific knowledge goals of the system, and are used to focus the understanding process.

Our theory of knowledge goals is motivated by these functional considerations, and corresponds well with a theory of interestingness motivated by the above cognitive considerations. The theory has been implemented in a computer program called AQUA (Asking Questions and Understanding Answers), which learns about terrorism by reading newspaper stories about unusual terrorist incidents in the Middle East [Ram, 1987; Schank and Ram, 1988; Ram, 1989]. AQUA uses its knowledge goals to direct the understanding process. We will illustrate our ideas with examples taken from this program.

3 A taxonomy of knowledge goals

Knowledge goals can be characterized according to the type of understanding task that they arise from.

Text goals: Knowledge goals of a text analysis program, arising from text-level tasks. These are the questions that arise from basic syntactic and semantic analysis that needs to be done on the input

---

[1] Since computers will eventually be expected to interact with the physical world (e.g., robots) and the social world (e.g., employees), they will also be expected to have some of the physical or social goals that we currently attribute only to people.

text, such as noun group attachment or pronoun reference.

Memory goals: Knowledge goals of a dynamic memory program, arising from memory-level tasks. A dynamic memory must be able to notice similarities, match incoming concepts to stereotypes in memory, form generalizations, and so on.

Explanation goals: Goals of an explainer that arise from explanation-level tasks, including the detection and resolution of anomalies, and the building of motivational and causal explanations for the events in the story in order to understand why the characters acted as they did, or why certain events occurred or did not occur.

Relevance goals: Goals of any intelligent system in the real world, concerning the identification of aspects of the current situation that are "interesting" or relevant to its own goals.

AQUA is an implementation of a integrated theory of story understanding, memory and learning, called *question-driven understanding*, which addresses the above issues. In addition to their theoretical role in our model of inference control and interestingness, knowledge goals have also played an implementational role in our research by providing a uniform mechanism for the integration of various cognitive processes. For example, knowledge goals arising from, say, memory tasks are indexed in memory and used in the same way as knowledge goals arising from explanation tasks. A knowledge goal generated from one task may be suspended, and satisfied opportunistically during the pursuit of some other task at a later stage or even during the processing of a different story. Implementational details may be found in [Ram, 1989].

4 Using knowledge goals to guide processing

A program that uses knowledge goals to guide understanding is an improvement over one that processes everything in equal detail, i.e., one that is completely text-driven. An understander that is completely text-driven would process everything in detail in the hope that it might turn out to be relevant. To avoid this, the understander should draw only those inferences which would help it find out what it needs to know. In other words, the understander should use its knowledge goals to focus its attention on the interesting aspects of the story, where "interesting" can be defined as "relating to something the understander wants to find out about."

Why would an understander need to find something out in the first place? Ultimately, the point of reading is to learn more about the world. Questions arise when reading a story reveals gaps or inconsistencies in the world model. It is useful to focus attention on such questions because they arise from a "need to learn." For example, questions arising from anomalous facts are more useful than those arising from routine stereotypical facts, since in the

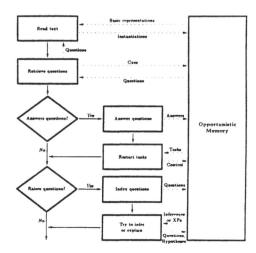

Figure 1: Control structure: The understanding cycle. A fact is interesting if it satisfies a knowledge goal pending in memory, or if it gives rise to new knowledge goals. Uninteresting facts pass vertically down with minimal processing; interesting facts cause suspended understanding tasks to be restarted, or new tasks to be created. New tasks can give rise to new knowledge goals, which are suspended along with the tasks if answers are not yet known and cannot be inferred.

former case the understander may learn something new about the world.

There are two basic ways in which a fact can turn out to be worth processing:

Top-down: A fact that answers a question is worth focussing on since it helps to achieve a knowledge goal of the understander, which in turn allows the understander to continue the reasoning task that was awaiting the answer.

Bottom-up: A fact that raises new questions is worth focussing if the questions arise from a gap or inconsistency in the understander's knowledge base, since the understander may be able to improve its knowledge base by learning something new about the world.

These correspond to the two diamonds in figure 1. These diamonds attempt to determine which facts the understander should focus on. To improve on this even further, the understander needs a way of determining which knowledge goals worth pursuing and which ones are not. Not all questions are equally important, nor are all answers equally valuable. The understander needs to be able to determine the priorities of its knowledge goals, depending on how likely the understander is to learn something by thinking about these knowledge goals. These decisions are made using a set of heuristics that will be described below.

The decision to focus attention corresponds closely with the notion of "interestingness." When an understander focuses on a particular fact and processes it in greater detail, it can be said to be "interested" in that fact.[2] For this reason, focus of attention heuristics can also be thought of as *interestingness heuristics*. These heuristics provide a functional definition of "interestingness" as a criterion for focussing attention: *Interestingness is a guess at what one thinks one might learn from paying attention to a fact or a question*. The guess must be made without processing the fact or question in detail, because otherwise the purpose of focussing attention to control inferences would be defeated. Thus the interestingness heuristics described below are indeed *heuristics* rather than precise measures of the value of thinking about a fact or a question.

5 Interestingness heuristics

In order to use questions to control inferences, an understander must be able to determine the interestingness of questions based on their content, as well as the task that they arose from. It must also be able to identify facts in the story that are interesting by virtue of being relevant to questions that the understander is interested in.

There are two types of heuristics for determining interestingness:[3]

Content-based: The interestingness of some input depends on its content or domain (more specifically, on the relationship between its content and the system's goals). In other words, some things are more interesting than others, depending on their relationship to the system's goals. For example, if one is intending to fly KLM in the near future, a story about a KLM flight being hijacked would be very interesting even if it were a stereotypical hijacking story. The understander would try to draw those inferences that were relevant to its goal of flying KLM. Similarly, stories about people one personally knows are more interesting than stories about strangers.

These heuristics use the content of the fact or question to determine its interestingness. The issue here is, which particular facts should the understander focus on? Which particular facts does the understander need to learn about?

Structure- or Configuration-based: Some kinds of situations are more interesting than others. For example, expectation failures are interesting, regardless of the content of the particular expectation that failed. These heuristics use the structure of the knowledge to determine interestingness. The issue here is, can the structure of the situation be used to determine which aspects of the situation are worth focussing on? Which configurations of knowledge structures signal gaps that the understander needs to learn about?

Of course, in any particular situation, the two conditions need to be combined in order to determine the overall interestingness of the input. For example, an expectation failure that relates to a goal of the system would have a higher priority than one that does not, and so the system would be more interested in the former.

Both types of heuristics identify situations in which the understander might be able to learn something useful. In the first case, the understander might learn more about a person it knows, or it might learn a new way to achieve a goal that it has. In the second case, the understander might be able to update its world model by identifying gaps in its model.

An example of the first type of heuristic is the principle of goal identification used by the POLITICS program [Carbonell, 1979]:

If the understander of an event identifies with the goals of one of the actors, he will focus attention on inferences that lead to the fulfillment of these goals.

This is a content-based heuristic since it relies on the actual type of goal, not merely on the fact that there is a goal being pursued. A configuration-based heuristic, on the other hand, relies on particular relationships between concepts in memory, not specifically on what those concepts are. For example, POLITICS used the following configuration-based heuristic to focus its attention:

Objective/Means distinction: If there are two or more actions in an event, and some actions are instrumental to stated or implicit objectives of one of the actors, the understander should focus attention on the objectives and non-instrumental actions.

In other words, an instrumental action is less likely to be significant than a larger action that it is part of, regardless of what the particular actions are. The reason this is a good strategy for an understander, according to the definition of interestingness proposed earlier, is that the understander is more likely to learn something by thinking about the larger action than it is by thinking about the instrumental action.

AQUA uses several heuristics to judge interestingness. These heuristics can be categorized according to the type of understanding goals that they pertain to. Let us start with relevance goals.

[2]Since interestingness depends on one's goals, the heuristics presented here do not cover interests that arise from goals that lie outside the scope of the basic understanding and learning tasks that AQUA performs. For example, a parent would be interested in the report card of his child. Since AQUA's goals do not include caring for children, it would not have any reason to be interested in a report card, unless the report card was anomalous with respect to AQUA's beliefs.

[3]This is orthogonal to the top-down/bottom-up distinction made earlier.

5.1 Interestingness from relevance goals

Interestingness arising from personal relevance usually falls into the class of content-based interestingness, since particular goals, people, locations, etc. are identified as being interesting to the understander. Questions and facts involving these goals, people, locations, etc. are worth pursuing since the understander might learn something relevant to it by doing so.

5.1.1 What could be relevant to a program?
In order for something to be personally relevant to a program, the program must have a personality in the real world. There must be goals it wants to achieve, people it knows or has heard of, places it knows about or has grown up in, and so on. Stories relevant to this personality are interesting even if they do not involve anomalies or novel explanations.

For example, two of the focus of attention criteria used by POLITICS fall into this category: "goal identification" and "interest in VIP activities." Since POLITICS had a political ideology, it could be said to have a personality in the sense used here. Thus it could focus its attention on those aspects of a situation that were relevant to its goals.

Since AQUA does not have any real experiences outside of reading stories, its "personality" consists of its knowledge goals, i.e., the questions that it is interested in finding answers to. The people, institutions, objects and locations that it is interested in learning about are the people, institutions, objects and locations that are involved in these questions. The goals that are interesting to AQUA are goals of characters in these stories that it has questions about.

One could say that AQUA has "adopted" the goals that it has questions about, in the sense that it is interested in stories (or aspects of stories) about such goals as if they were its own (an example follows later). An alternative approach to the problem of where a program might get its goals is to "give" goals to the program, for example, by programming particular ideologies into the program as in POLITICS. In AQUA, this would be analogous to tagging particular goals or people as being "personally relevant" or "interesting" to the program.

In contrast, the approach used in AQUA is to allow the program to evolve its own set of interests that are functional to the purpose of the program (learning about terrorism), by letting the questions that arise from this purpose *be* its goals. These interests can be used to focus attention on those aspects of the story that would help it achieve its purpose.

Let us now discuss interestingness heuristics based on this notion of personal relevance.

5.1.2 Goal relevance.
This is similar to the "goal identification" criterion used by POLITICS.

H-1: Goal relevance
A fact that could be instrumental to or could hinder a goal of the understander is more interesting than one that has no relevance to the understander's goals. A fact that directly matches or conflicts with a goal of the understander is very interesting.

5.1.3
Vicarious goals. Vicarious interests arise from goal configurations that are similar to one's own, or to those one is likely to have at some point. Stories about crisis goals or sudden goal changes, for example, are usually interesting from a vicarious point of view since the understander is likely to experience similar crisis goals or goal changes.

These heuristics are configuration-based, as opposed to content-based, since all goal changes are inherently interesting regardless of the particular goals involved. However, goal changes involving goals of personal relevance to the understander would be more interesting than those involving other goals.

H-2: Vicarious goal change
An action that drastically changes the goals of the planner or actor of the action is interesting.

H-3: Vicarious crisis goal
An action that initiates a crisis goal of the planner or actor of the action is interesting.

An example of a vicarious crisis goal is the self-preservation goal arising from acts of violence. Schank calls violence an "absolute interest" [Schank, 1979] since people universally seem to be interested in violence. This follows from the application of heuristic H-3 to the thematic goal of self-preservation which is universal among people.

5.1.4 Actor relevance.
There are four degrees to which a particular person or institution can be relevant to an understander, each of which produces more interest than the previous one:

H-4: Actor relevance
Stories involving people that are completely unknown are the least interesting. More interesting than these are stories involving people who the understander has heard of. Still more interesting are stories involving people who are famous, such as celebrities. Stories involving people who the understander personally knows are the most interesting.

This heuristic is similar to the "actor relevance" and "interest in VIP activities" criteria of POLITICS. AQUA uses similar heuristics for object and location relevance, omitted here due to space limitations.

5.2 Interestingness from explanation goals

So far, we have seen interestingness heuristics that tried to identify situations involving goals, people, objects or places that are personally relevant to the understander. Such situations provide an opportunity to learn something of personal relevance, e.g., to learn something more about a person the understander is interested in, or to learn a new plan to achieve a goal that the understander has. There is another class of heuristics which identify potential gaps in the understander's knowledge, in order to determine what the understander might learn from processing the given situation. Situations that are interesting according to these heuristics are those that allow the understander to improve its world model. These heuristics are based on explanation and memory goals of the understander.[4] Let us start with explanation goals.

5.2.1 Anomaly detection. Anomalies arise when incoming facts do not fit in with what the understander expected to see. Anomalies are interesting because there is a possibility that the world model that underlies the failed expectations is incorrect, which signals a need to learn more about the domain.

H-5: Anomaly detection
All anomalies are interesting, and therefore all knowledge goals that arise during the anomaly detection process are interesting. These goals are always pursued in an attempt to form explanations to resolve the anomalies.

Knowledge goals that seek explanations in order to resolve anomalies are less interesting if explanations are easily available. If no explanation is found, there is a gap in memory corresponding to an unexplainable anomaly. A knowledge goal that seeks to fill in this gap is interesting for an understander that is trying to learn about this domain.

H-6: Explanation availability
An explanation retrieval goal that fails to find an explanation in memory is more interesting than one where an explanation can be easily found.

Thus stories that have standard explanations are less interesting than novel and unusual stories.

Of course, this and any other heuristic might be overruled if other interestingness heuristics came into play. Heuristics like these encode rules that represent guesses at interestingness, *other things being equal.* Counter-examples can easily be found by playing up interestingness factors represented by other heuristics. The final interestingness measure is a combination of all these factors, not any single factor taken by itself. For example, a stereotypical explanation for the motivations of a person who one knows personally might be more interesting than an unusual explanation for the motivations of a person one doesn't know. This also depends on the goals of the system, since a reasoner might be particularly interested in the motivations of a particular person for some other reason.

The interestingness of an explanation goal also depends on the kind of explanation that the goal is seeking. Knowledge goals seeking explanations for the motivations of individuals arise from *human interest stories,* and are usually more interesting, from the human interest point of view, than those that seek explanations for the motivations of institutions.

H-7: Human interest
Knowledge goals involving motivations of individuals are more interesting than those involving motivations of institutions.

Note that heuristic H-7 judges interestingness from a human interest point of view. Human interest stories focus on the goals, motivations and emotions of particular individuals. From the point of view of politics or counter-planning, however, the motivations of the institution might be more interesting than those of an individual, unless the individual was an important political figure in that institution.

When searching for explanations for actions, instrumental actions are less interesting than the actions that they are instrumental to. This is similar to the objective/means criterion of POLITICS that was described earlier.

H-8: Instrumentality
If an action is instrumental to or part of another action, the former action is less interesting than the latter. If an action has more than one action instrumental to it, or a MOP has more than one scene, the most interesting of the instrumental actions is that which is the goal scene of the MOP (or the "maincons" of a script).

Similarly, habitual or commonly performed actions are uninteresting by the following heuristic:

H-9: Thematic or stereotypical action
If the actor, or a group that the actor belongs to, is known to perform such actions or select such plans in service of a known thematic goal, the action is not interesting. Thus common plans for goals and routine thematic or occupation-related actions are uninteresting.

These heuristics are used to focus the understander's attention on the most interesting actions. Other actions are "explained away" by building simple explanations. For example, AQUA does not explain stereotypical actions in detail. The explanation it builds is simply "Because the actor often performs such actions in service of his goals," unless it has been unable to explain such actions in the past in which case it would have a pending question which would make this action interesting. Such heuristics allow AQUA to spend its time processing the more interesting aspects of the story. If these heuristics are absent, AQUA will still process the interesting aspects of the story, of course, but it will spend a lot more time processing uninteresting details as well.

5.2.2 Hypothesis formation. When a possible explanation is found, it is applied to the anomalous situation in order to construct a hypothesis that

---

[4]Since AQUA does not perform any text-level learning, text-level goals are not interesting to AQUA according to the learning criterion for interestingness.

211

might explain the anomaly. If a stereotypical explanation is available that applies easily and directly, the story conforms to the explanation that the understander already knows about, and is therefore not very interesting. On the other hand, if existing explanations do not apply to the situation, the story is novel and therefore interesting.

H-10: Hypothesis formation
If an available explanation applies easily and directly to the story, the story is not very interesting. More interesting is the case when a known explanation applies but leaves gaps which need to be filled in before the hypothesis is verified. The most interesting story is one in which known explanations do not fit the situation and need to be modified.

This heuristic follows from the claim that interestingness is a measure of what the understander might learn from processing the situation. Stories that identify gaps in the understander's memory are more interesting than those that fit into stereotypical molds that the understander already knows about, since the understander is unlikely to learn anything from processing the latter kind of stories.

5.2.3 Hypothesis verification. The final step in the explanation process is the verification of hypotheses. Facts in the story that are relevant to existing hypotheses are more interesting than facts that have no bearing on hypotheses currently in memory:

H-11: Hypothesis verification
An input fact is interesting if it helps to verify or refute a hypothesis that might explain an anomaly.

It is worth noting that these heuristics are dynamic and therefore a considerable improvement over static heuristics that select interesting features or facts on some arbitrary basis. For example, the color of an agent's hair is usually irrelevant in most stories. However, if this feature were statically marked as being uninteresting, an understander would be unable to correctly process a story in which this feature turned out to be interesting for some unforeseen reason.

5.3 Interestingness from memory goals

For an explanation-based program such as AQUA, explanation goals are more interesting than memory or text-level goals. However, memory-level tasks also give rise to heuristics for interestingness which, as before, are based on trying to identify gaps in memory which give the understander an opportunity to learn. For example, the basic learning mechanism in a program such as IPP [Lebowitz, 1980] is that of similarity-based generalization, a process that builds categories in memory by noticing similarities between instances or sub-categories and building generalizations based on these similarities. This theory of learning suggests the following heuristics:

H-12: Uniqueness
A category with a unique example or specialization is more interesting than one with several examples. If two categories have unique examples, the category higher in the type hierarchy is more interesting than the one that is lower down.

H-13: Symmetry
A category which lacks a symmetric category is more interesting than one for symmetric categories are known.

The symmetry can be along any of the dimensions used for similarity-based generalization in memory. For example, if the understander builds categories of occupations based on the gender of the actor, occupations in which both male and female actors are seen would be less interesting than those in which only males or only females are seen. This assumes, of course, that these categories play some functional role in achieving the overall goals of the understander, otherwise there would be no principled reason for either building the categories or judging their interestingness.

6 Computing interestingness by combining heuristics

We have presented a set of content- and structure-based heuristics for judging interestingness based on different types of understander goals. This set is not exhaustive, of course, but it illustrates the type of heuristics that an understander would use to determine interestingness and focus its attention. This allows the understanding process to be sensitive to the knowledge goals of the system.

The final measure of interestingness is derived by combining the recommendations of all the applicable heuristics. This is used to judge the interestingness of the system's knowledge goals, as well as the interestingness of facts that might be relevant to these knowledge goals.

H-14: To determine the interestingness of a fact or a knowledge goal, apply all the interestingness heuristics to the fact or knowledge goal and combine the interestingness recommendations of each heuristic.

There is a potential problem here since the heuristics given above don't recommend specific interestingness values. For example, is an anomaly involving an uninteresting goal more interesting than a stereotypical way of achieving a highly interesting goal? This problem has not yet been addressed. The current implementation of AQUA pursues every knowledge goal that is judged to be interesting by one or more heuristics.

7 Examples

In conclusion, let us illustrate the above interestingness heuristics by using them to determine the interestingness of some example stories from the terrorism domain. Consider the following story (New York Times, April 14, 1985):

S-1: Boy Says Lebanese Recruited Him as Car Bomber.

JERUSALEM, April 13 — A 16-year-old Lebanese was captured by Israeli troops hours before he was supposed to get into an explosive-laden car and go on a suicide bombing mission to blow up the Israeli Army headquarters in Lebanon. ...

What seems most striking about [Mohammed] Burro's account is that although he is a Shiite Moslem, he comes from a secular family background. He spent his free time not in prayer, he said, but riding his motorcycle and playing pinball. According to his account, he was not a fanatic who wanted to kill himself in the cause of Islam or anti-Zionism, but was recruited [by the Islamic Jihad] through another means: blackmail.

We can use the above heuristics to judge the interestingness of this story.

H-8 **Instrumentality:** The suicide bombing is not instrumental to a known larger plan.

H-3 **Vicarious crisis goal:** The boy's action affects his **preserve-life** goal.

H-6 **XP availability and applicability:** A
H-10 stereotypical XP is available (religious fanatic) but inapplicable. Another stereotypical XP (blackmail) is applied in a novel context.

H-11 **Hypothesis verification:** The religious fanatic hypothesis is refuted. The blackmail explanation applies, but raises new questions such as "What could the boy want more than his own life?" which must be answered before the hypothesis is completely filled out.

H-7 **Human interest:** The explanation discusses personal motivation.

H-12 **Uniqueness:** The blackmail explanation has never been applied to a suicide bombing story before.

H-4 **Actor relevance:** The actor and planner are unknown to the understander.
Object relevance: The objects involved are unknown to the understander.

H-1 **Goal relevance:** No personal goals are achieved or violated.
Location relevance: Lebanon is not personally relevant to the understander.

This story, although not personally relevant, is interesting from the point of view of human interest. The story discusses novel explanations for the motivations behind the actions involving the violation of a shared thematic goal, **preserve-life**. Suppose AQUA has read several religious fanaticism stories, but has not encountered any coercion stories so far. After reading the above story, AQUA will be left with several questions, including:

- What did Mohammed value more than his own life?

- Why did the Islamic Jihad plan this mission?

- Why did the Islamic Jihad choose a teenager for the mission?

These questions are represented as knowledge goals in AQUA's memory. On the basis of these knowledge goals, AQUA will now be interested in stories involving the people or institutions it has questions about, such as:

- Another story about Mohammed Burro (relevance to known person)

- Another story about the Islamic Jihad (relevance to known institution)

AQUA will also be interested in stories involving the newly learned blackmail explanation, such as:

- Another story about someone being blackmailed into a suicide bombing mission (relevance to novel explanation)

AQUA will also be interested in a story involving goals or goal priorities that it has questions about, such as:

- Another story about someone valuing something over their own life (relevance to goal)

In contrast, consider the following more stereotypical story:

S-2: Suicide bomber strikes U.S. embassy in Beirut.

A teenage girl exploded a car bomb at the U.S. embassy in Beirut today, killing herself and causing a number of casualties, security sources said. A statement by an unidentified terrorist group claimed responsibility for the attack, adding that the girl was a martyr for the cause of Islam.

This story is relatively uninteresting. It is interesting only to the extent that it is about the U.S. embassy (personal relevance of object to an American understander), and that it discusses the motivations behind the violation of a vicarious crisis goal (heuristic H-3). However, since these motivations have a standard explanation that has been seen many times before (religious fanaticism), this story is not interesting even from the point of view of explanation (H-6, H-10).

8 Conclusion: Interest-producing conditions

We define interestingness as a criterion for inference control. Since the understander needs to focus its attention on those inferences likely to help it achieve its overall goals, it must devote its resources pursuing inferences that are most likely to be useful towards achieving these goals. Thus interestingness is a heuristic measure of the relevance of the input to the understander's knowledge goals. Since the point of satisfying knowledge goals is to improve one's understanding of the domain, interestingness can also be thought of as a measure of the likelihood of learning something from the story if one processes it in detail.

Interestingness is neither inherent in the information nor in the system, but rather arises from the interaction between the two. It arises from the interaction between the stimulus and the goals of the system. A system with no goals would have no reason to find any input more interesting than any other, nor would any particular piece of information be universally interesting for all systems unless they shared the same goals.

This is a functional approach to the problem of interestingness [Hidi and Baird, 1986; Schank, 1979] from the perspective of the theory of question-driven understanding. A similar approach can be used for systems performing other cognitive tasks, such as planning, since these systems would also need to focus their attention on inferences that were relevant to goals arising from their tasks.

In AQUA, interest in a concept is triggered by its likely relevance to questions or knowledge goals, and continuing interest is determined by its continuing significance to these goals. This is related to the "goal satisfaction principle" of [Hayes-Roth and Lesser, 1976], which states that more processing should be given to knowledge sources whose responses are most likely to satisfy processing goals, and to the "relevance principle" of [Sperber and Wilson, 1986], which states that humans pay attention only to information that seems relevant to them. These principles make sense because cognitive processes are geared to achieving a large cognitive effect for a small effort. To achieve this, the understander must focus its attention on what seems to it to be the most relevant information available [Sperber and Wilson, 1986].

Once the interestingness of a question or piece of input has been determined, AQUA uses it to guide processing by focussing its resources on the more interesting aspects of the story. Since the heuristics are geared towards learning, this ensures that AQUA spends its time on those aspects of the story that are most likely to result in something useful being learned. Without its interestingness heuristics, AQUA would still learn the same things, but it would spend a lot more time drawing inferences that ultimately turn out to be irrelevant.

References

[Carbonell, 1979] J. G. Carbonell. *Subjective Understanding: Computer Models of Belief Systems*. Ph.D. thesis, Yale Universtiy, New Haven, CT, January 1979. Research Report #150.

[Hayes-Roth and Lesser, 1976] F. Hayes-Roth and V. Lesser. Focus of attention in a distributed logic speech understanding system. In *Proceedings of the IEEE International Conference on ASSP*, Philadephia, PA, 1976.

[Hidi and Baird, 1986] S. Hidi and W. Baird. Interestingness — A Neglected Variable in Discourse Processing. *Cognitive Science*, 10:179–194, 1986.

[Lebowitz, 1980] M. Lebowitz. *Generalization and Memory in an Integrated Understanding System*. Ph.D. thesis, Yale University, Department of Computer Science, New Haven, CT, October 1980. Research Report #186.

[Ram, 1987] A. Ram. AQUA: Asking Questions and Understanding Answers. In *Proceedings of the Sixth Annual National Conference on Artificial Intelligence*, pages 312–316, Seattle, WA, July 1987. American Association for Artificial Intelligence, Morgan Kaufman Publishers, Inc.

[Ram, 1989] A. Ram. *Question-driven understanding: An integrated theory of story understanding, memory and learning*. Ph.D. thesis, Yale University, New Haven, CT, May 1989. Research Report #710.

[Schank and Ram, 1988] R. C. Schank and A. Ram. Question-driven Parsing: A New Approach to Natural Language Understanding. *Journal of Japanese Society for Artificial Intelligence*, 3(3):260–270, May 1988.

[Schank, 1979] R. C. Schank. Interestingness: Controlling Inferences. *Artificial Intelligence*, 12:273–297, 1979.

[Sperber and Wilson, 1986] D. Sperber and D. Wilson. *Relevance: Communication and Cognition*. Language and Thought Series. Harvard University Press, Cambridge, MA, 1986.

The Dempster-Shafer Theory of Evidence as a Model of Human Decision Making

Donald H. Mitchell
Amoco Production Company
Tulsa Research Center
P.O. Box 3385
Tulsa, OK 74102*

Abstract

Many psychology researchers have shown that humans do not process probabilistic information in a manner consistent with Bayes' theory [9, 10, 16, 24, 23, 27]. Robinson and Hastie [24, 23] showed that humans made non-compensatory probability updates, produced super-additive distributions, and resuscitated zero probability possibilities. While most researchers have classified these behaviors as nonnormative, we found that the Dempster-Shafer theory could model each of these behaviors in a normative and theoretically sound fashion. While not claiming that the theory models human processes, we claim that the similarities should aid user acceptance of Dempster-Shafer based decision systems.

1 Introduction

Due to the inherent uncertainty of evidence and conclusions in the world, decision support systems (including artificial intelligence systems) must often use methods for representing and reasoning under uncertainty. There are a number of possible methods. Each method has a different effect on the three major expert system stages: 1) acquisition, 2) inferencing, and 3) user interpretation of the results. While many products and papers downplay the importance, the choice is difficult and important. The chosen paradigm can mitigate or exacerbate errors in any of the stages thus making the system's results meaningless.

There are a number of results supporting each reasoning method. One attribute of comparison is theoretical soundness [6, 17, 18, 19, 2]. Most of these comparisons uphold the theoretical foundation of probability theory and particularly of Bayes' theorem. Another attribute is empirical performance

[8, 1, 29, 22, 17, 20, 21]. These studies support a variety of conclusions. Dawes [8], for example, shows that using a simple, yet incorrect, linear model is often better than a theoretically sound probabilistic model when they are both based on the same error-prone human estimates. In this paper, we argue for a third attribute—user interpretation and acceptance.

When consulting a decision support system, a human's ability to understand the computer's beliefs and decisions is important. Early research on automated tools showed that users more readily accept systems if they understand the systems' behaviors [4, 5, 11, 14, 25]. This understanding can result from any of three processes: 1) training the human to understand the theoretical correctness of the reasoning processes, 2) using a reasoning process that directly corresponds to the human's or 3) using a process whose observable behavior corresponds to the human's. The first process is apt to meet with resistance and makes general distribution and acceptance difficult. The second process, while of great potential, is difficult to accomplish due to the hidden nature of human decision-making processes. The third process corresponds directly to the way that most collaborative human decision-making works: when humans defend their reasoning, they refer to the evidence that caused them to increase or decrease their belief and not to their reasoning mechanisms.

This paper uses experimentally observed similarities between the Dempster-Shafer theory of evidence [26] and humans solving a probabilistic updating task to argue that humans may more readily understand Dempster-Shafer based systems. The paper does not directly address user acceptance in that it does not involve actual users of a system, but it indirectly addresses acceptance through the ability of humans to empathize with the behavior.

*(918) 660–4270, dmitchell@trc.amoco.com

2 The task and human data

This paper reports an experiment that compared the behavior of an automated Dempster-Shafer evidence accumulation system with the behavior of humans performing the same evidence accumulation task. The task and human experimental results come from a study by Robinson and Hastie [24, 23].

In an effort to find out whether humans followed Bayesian probabilistic reasoning principles, Robinson and Hastie asked human subjects to solve a murder mystery. The subjects saw a series of clues. After each clue, the subjects stated their beliefs about the guilt of each suspect in terms of probability. Robinson and Hastie found that the humans did not follow probabilistic principles. We will explain the exact form of the discrepancy when we describe the behavior of the Dempster-Shafer system.

Before describing the Dempster-Shafer system, we will address two concerns with the Robinson and Hastie data. Some may argue that Robinson and Hastie's subjects did not have adequate training in the probabilistic concepts. To test this hypothesis, Robinson and Hastie explicitly taught the fundamentals of probability to some of the subjects. Depending on the subject, the training led to either the same behavior as those without training or a behavior that did not reflect any evidence accumulation. Robinson and Hastie conjectured that the cognitive overhead prevented the subjects from applying the learning.

Another objection may be that one study makes an insufficient basis for concluding that humans are not Bayesian decision makers. Robinson and Hastie, however, are not the only researchers to show that humans make poor Bayesian probabilistic information processors. Many other psychology researchers have shown the non-Bayesian character of human information processing [9, 10, 16, 24, 23, 27].

3 Dempster-Shafer predictions

To test the predictions of the Dempster-Shafer [26] theory, we developed a straight-forward implementation of the theory [20] and then submitted the clues to it as a series of consonant belief functions. Although many artificial intelligence researchers [3, 7, 13, 12] have restricted their Dempster-Shafer representations to simple and dichotomous belief functions, we chose consonant belief functions because they are the form that Shafer says most naturally represent inferential evidence [26, pp. 223–229]. The reason other artificial intelligence researchers have ignored this repre-

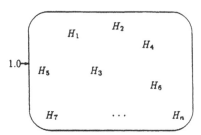

Figure 1: Venn graph of the vacuous function: there has been no evidence.

sentation is that it can result in exponential computational time requirements. For the sake of this study, computational time was not of direct concern.[1]

While it is not the intent of this paper to fully introduce the Dempster-Shafer theory, we will briefly describe belief functions. A belief function is the assignment of probabilities to sets of conclusions. This assignment differs from standard probabilistic theories in that it uses sets rather than single hypotheses. All probability theories can use sets to represent multiple simultaneously true hypotheses; however, the Dempster-Shafer system uses sets to indicate lack of differentiation in the evidence for mutually exclusive hypotheses. The interpretation of this assignment is that some element of the set is true but the evidence does not provide fine enough granularity to directly point to one hypothesis.

A consequence of this representation for belief is that there is a clear distinction between the inability to decide due to lack of evidence and the inability to decide due to too much conflicting evidence. In the Dempster-Shafer theory, a believer represents the lack of evidence as the assignment of all probability to the undifferentiated set of all possible hypotheses (e.g. figure 1), whereas the representation for conflicting evidence is the assignment of roughly equal amounts of probability to many separate singleton sets of hypotheses (e.g. figure 2). For example, in a well-matched musical competition, the judge's initial belief should be no one has evidence in their favor and all contestants can fight for the prize like a pie ready to be divided: there is no conflicting beliefs concerning the outcome. After listening to everyone perform

---

[1]Note, however, that [20, 15] both show linear complexity when applying the theory to naturally constrained problems.

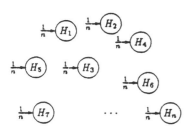

Figure 2: Venn graph of a maximally conflicting belief function: there has been evidence supporting each hypothesis equally.

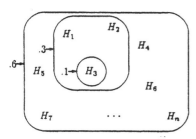

Figure 3: Venn graph of the consonant belief function: $\Pr(H_3) = .1$, $\Pr(H_1 \vee H_2 \vee H_3) = .3$, and $\Pr(H_1 \vee \cdots H_n) = .6$.

well, the judge should have belief in each contestant individually with little or no residual belief: each contestant has claims to more pie than is available. The evidence causes conflicting beliefs.

More generally, assigning non-zero probabilities to sets of hypotheses that don't subsume one-another represents conflicting belief. The common Dempster-Shafer representation used in artificial intelligence of assigning belief to a hypothesis and its negation, thus, directly encodes conflict. Individual pieces of evidence, however, should not show any conflict with themselves, and, therefore, this dichotomous representation is usually inaccurate. The consonant belief function is the non-conflicting alternative.

Figure 3 depicts a consonant belief function. In this example, some evidence supports hypothesis H_3. The same evidence has less direct support for hypotheses H_1 and H_2 and also has some residual uncertainty. This belief function is represented by assigning non-zero probabilities to the sets H_3, H_1, H_2, H_3, and finally to $H_1 \ldots H_n$. This gradual focusing of probabilities on progressive subsets is the definition of a consonant belief function. A consonant belief function is consonant with itself: that is, it shows no conflict with itself.

The consonance of an individual piece of evidence with itself implies nothing about consonance between pieces of evidence. Different pieces of evidence can conflict with each other. The detective story used in this experiment, for example, shows considerable conflict between clues. While each clue might be self-consistent and therefore consonant, that does not imply that all clues agree. The result of combining these disagreeing but self-consonant belief functions will not be consonant.

To make a choice among the hypotheses requires comparing the beliefs assigned to each hypothesis. In the Dempster-Shafer theory, there is not a single measure of belief for individual hypotheses. Shafer provides several measures. The most important ones are the Bel function that indicates the lower bound of belief and the Pl plausibility function that indicates the upper bound. This experiment uses both of these to compare the Dempster-Shafer system's results with the human subjects' guilt estimates.

4 Comparisons of behavior

One way in which the humans did not follow probabilistic principles was that they usually changed only the probability of the suspect directly impugned by the clue without making compensatory changes to the other suspects. Because probability requires that the sum of the probabilities over suspects equals 1.0, each change must be balanced with an equal change in the opposite direction for the other suspects. Bayesian probability requires proportionately equal changes in the non-impugned hypotheses. Robinson and Hastie termed their subjects' omission of this required compensation "non-compensatory probability updating."

Although subjects in general did not compensate, there were two conditions under which they did, at least partially: 1) when a clue had an extreme impact on the guilt of one suspect, and 2) after a large number of clues had already been processed. In the first case—extreme impact—the clue often contradicted prior belief: that is, it indicated that a subject's favorite suspect was actually innocent or that

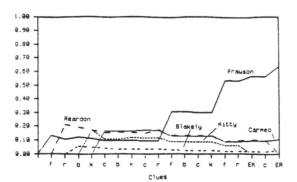

Figure 4: Dempster-Shafer Bel score guilt ratings for each suspect after each clue.

a long-shot was guilty.

Figure 4 shows the Dempster-Shafer system's Bel function assignment of guilt to each suspect after each clue. Each point on the abscissa is a separate clue. The first initial of the suspect mentioned by the clue marks each point. Some of the clues indicate guilt, some indicate innocence, and some are neutral. Like the human subjects, most of the Dempster-Shafer system's belief changes were non-compensatory. The only strong demonstration of compensation occurred in reaction to the two strong clues regarding Frawson and the clues eliminating Reardon and Kitty. This behavior corresponds exactly with Robinson and Hastie's descriptions of their subjects.

As an explanation for the humans' behavior, this result suggests that the humans may not fully partition their belief before collecting evidence. The humans may take an approach that is analogous to the Dempster-Shafer system's approach: that is, slowly portion out belief and only when there is a preponderance of evidence for one hypothesis do they take back belief from other hypotheses. We are not, however, claiming that the Dempster-Shafer system literally models the individual subjects. There was far too much variance between subjects to even attempt to analyze the system's ability to model the individuals.

Robinson and Hastie found two other aspects of the human data that conflicted with probability: probabilities usually added to over one—"super-additivity"—and some humans sometimes gave nonzero probability ratings to suspects after giving them zero ratings—"resuscitation."

If the Dempster-Shafer upper-bound probability measure Pl is used, then most of the probabilities add to over one thus qualitatively modeling the super-additivity. The interpretation in this case is that the subjects were sensitive to their residual uncertainty about the suspects and felt that the lower-bound estimates made them look overly convinced of the suspect's innocence. Assigning probabilities as low as the Bel scores in figure 4 might look like an admission of implausibility that did not correspond to the subjects' beliefs. The scoring mechanism did not give the subjects any way to indicate the suspects' potential guilt, and, therefore, the subjects may have blended the plausibility score with the actual belief.

Because the Bel measure naturally increases from zero to some non-zero value as evidence is collected, the Bel score could model the resuscitation. To use this explanation in conjunction with the super-additivity explanation requires the assumption that the subjects were somehow sensitive to both the Bel and Pl and chose to respond in some hybrid manner that sometimes allowed the Bel score to override the Pl score.

Simultaneously using the Bel and Pl measures to explain the human behavior is not adequately convincing especially because there are other possible explanations for the super-additivity and resuscitation. Explanations based on the input scale and human understanding seem more appealing than an explanation based on the Dempster-Shafer theory. For example, there are some problems with Robinson and Hastie's method of soliciting probability ratings. They used a scale marked into 0.05 probability intervals. The subjects may not have realized that position within an interval was significant. This explanation could explain the resuscitation effect because no suspect resuscitated to more than a probability of 0.1.

While the Dempster-Shafer system does provide an explanation of these anomalies, we feel that the major contribution of this work is to propose a behavior with which decision system users could empathize. The similarity is especially strong for the non-compensatory behavior. Because the Dempster-Shafer system is theoretically sound, system developers can feel secure using it.

5 Conclusion

If, as previous work has suggested [4, 11, 14, 28, 25], user acceptance depends on the ability of the user to empathize with system behavior, and if humans are particularly poor at understanding Bayesian probabilistic notions, then this result showing the similarity between human and Dempster-Shafer updating behaviors encourages further exploration of the

218

use of the Dempster-Shafer theory in automated reasoning. These results combined with the Dempster-Shafer theory's theoretical soundness and Mitchell's results [20, 21] concerning acquisition and computational requirements are a strong argument in favor of the Dempster-Shafer theory.

References

[1] Tversky A. and D. Kahneman. Causal schemas in judgments under uncertainty. In M. Fishbein, editor, *Progress in Social Psychology*, volume 1, pages 49–72. Lawrence Erlebaum, Hillsdale, NJ, 1980.

[2] AAAI. *Uncertainty in Artificial Intelligence*, 1987.

[3] J. A. Barnett. Computational methods for a mathematical theory of evidence. In *International Joint Conference on Artificial Intelligence*, pages 868–875, Vancouver, British Columbia, Canada, 1981.

[4] H. L. Bleich. The computer as a consultant. *New England Journal of Medicine*, 284(3):141–147, 1971.

[5] B. G. Buchanan and E. H. Shortliffe. *Rule-Based Expert Systems: The MYCIN Experiments of the Stanford Heuristic Programming Project*. Addison-Wesley, Reading, MA, 1984.

[6] P. Cheeseman. In defense of probability. In *International Joint Conference on Artificial Intelligence*, pages 1002–1009, 1985.

[7] Bruce D'Ambrosio. A hybrid approach to reasoning under uncertainty. *International Journal of Approximate Reasoning*, 2:29–45, 1988.

[8] R. Dawes. The robust beauty of improper linear models in decision making. *American Psychologist*, 34:571–582, 1979.

[9] Ward Edwards. Conservatism in human information processing. *Nature*, 32:414–416, 1971.

[10] B. Fischhoff and R. Beyth-Marom. Hypothesis evaluation from a Bayesian perspective. *Psychological Review*, 90(3):239–260, 1983.

[11] R. B. Friedman and D. H. Gustafson. Computers in clinical medicine, a critical review. *Computers and Biomedical Research*, 10:199–204, 1977.

[12] J. Gordon and E. Shortliffe. A method for managing evidential reasoning in a hierarchical hypothesis space. *Artificial Intelligence*, 26:323–357, 1985.

[13] J. Gordon and E. H. Shortliffe. The Dempster-Shafer theory of evidence. In B. G. Buchanan and E. H. Shortliffe, editors, *Rule-Based Expert Systems: The MYCIN Experiments of the Stanford Heuristic Programming Project*, pages 272–292. Addison-Wesley, Reading, MA, 1984.

[14] G. A. Gorry. Computer-assisted clinical decision-making. *Meth. Inform. Med.*, 12(1):45–51, 1973.

[15] R. C. Hughes and J. N. Maksym. Acoustic signal interpretations: Reasoning with non-specific and uncertain information. *Pattern Recognition*, 18(6):475–483, 1985.

[16] Daniel Kahneman, Paul Slovic, and Amos Tversky, editors. *Judgment Under Uncertainty: Heuristics and Biases*. Cambridge University Press, New York, 1982.

[17] Jin H. Kim and J. Pearl. A computational model for causal and diagnostic reasoning in inference systems. In *International Joint Conference on Artificial Intelligence*, pages 190–193, 1983.

[18] Lemmer and Kanal, editors. *Uncertainty in Artificial Intelligence: the 1985 workshop*. AAAI, North-Holland, 1985.

[19] Lemmer and Kanal, editors. *Uncertainty in Artificial Intelligence: the 1986 workshop*. AAAI, North-Holland, 1986.

[20] Donald H. Mitchell. *Automated Decision Support Using Variations on the Dempster-Shafer Theory*. PhD thesis, Northwestern University, 1987.

[21] Donald H. Mitchell, Steven A. Harp, and David K. Simkin. A knowledge-engineer's comparison of three evidence aggregation methods. In *Second Workshop on Uncertainty in AI*, pages 297–304. AAAI, Morgan Kauffman, 1987.

[22] J. Pearl. On evidential reasoning in a hierarchy of hypotheses. *Artificial Intelligence*, 28:9–15, 1986.

[23] L. B. Robinson. *In the Footsteps of Sherlock Holmes: Information Search and Hypothesis Testing*. PhD thesis, Northwestern University, 1986.

[24] L. B. Robinson and R. Hastie. Revision of beliefs when a hypothesis is eliminated from consideration. *Journal of Experimental Psychology: Human Perception and Performance*, 11(4):443–456, 1985.

[25] William B. Rouse and Nancy M. Morris. Understanding and enhancing user acceptance o computer technology. *IEEE Transactions on Systems, Man, and Cybernetics*, 16(6):965–973, 1986.

[26] Glenn Shafer. *A Mathematical Theory of Evidence*. Princeton University Press, 1976.

[27] P. Slovic and S. Lichtenstein. Comparison of Bayesian and regression approaches to the study of information processing judgement. *Organizational Behavior and Human Performance*, 6:649–744, 1971.

[28] T. S. Startsman and R. E. Robinson. The attitudes of medical and paramedical personnel toward computers. *Computers and Biomedical Research*, 5:218–227, 1972.

[29] A. Tversky and D. Kahneman. Causal schemas in judgments under uncertainty. In Kahneman, Slovic, and Tversky, editors, *Judgment Under Uncertainty: Heuristics and Biases*, pages 117–128. Cambridge University Press, 1982.

Feature Selection and Hypothesis Selection Models of Induction

Michael J. Pazzani & Glenn Silverstein
Department of Information and Computer Science
University of California
Irvine, CA 92717

Abstract

Recent research has shown that the prior knowledge of the learner influences both how quickly a concept is learned and the types of generalizations that a learner produces. We investigate two learning frameworks that have been proposed to account for these findings. Here, we contrast *feature selection* models of learning with *hypothesis selection* models. We report on an experiment that suggests that human learners use prior knowledge both to indicate what features may be relevant and to influence how the features are combined to form hypotheses. We present an extension to the POSTHOC system, a hypothesis selection model of concept learning, that is able to account for differences in learning rates observed in the experiment.

Introduction

There is a growing body of evidence that the prior knowledge of the learner influences the speed or accuracy of learning (e.g., Ahn, Mooney, Brewer, & DeJong, 1987; Ausubel & Schiff, 1954; Chapman & Chapman, 1967; Murphy & Medin, 1985; Nakamura, G, 1985; Pazzani, 1990; Schank, Collins, & Hunter, 1986; Wattenmaker, Dewey, Murphy, & Medin, 1986; Wisniewski,1989). In this paper, we contrast two learning frameworks that have been proposed to account for these findings. *Feature selection* models, such as that proposed by Lien & Cheng (1989), claim that prior knowledge influences learning by selecting a subset of the available features as potentially relevant. In the feature selection model, induction is accomplished by detection of covariation (Kelley, 1971; 1983) among the relevant features. In contrast, *hypothesis selection* models, exemplified by POSTHOC (Pazzani & Schulenburg,1989), claim that, in addition to selecting relevant features, prior knowledge influences how the relevant features are combined to form hypotheses and how hypotheses are revised when new data are encountered.

In this paper, we first present an experiment in which the feature selection and hypothesis selection frameworks make different predictions on learning rates. Next, we report on an extension to POSTHOC that provides it with the capability to reason about both positive and negative causal influences (i.e., factors that make an action more likely or less likely). Finally, we report on a simulation that indicates that POSTHOC can account for the learning rates observed in the experiment.

Drug Interactions: An Experiment

In order to differentiate between these two frameworks, we designed an experiment in which the their predictions differed. The experiment followed a 2x2 factorial design in which the factors were the type of concept acquired (internal or external disjunction) and the type of background information in the instructions. It has been reported (Wells, 1963), that in the absence of relevant prior knowledge, exclusive disjunctions concepts are more difficult for subjects to learn that inclusive disjunctive concepts. The feature selection model would predict that an exclusive disjunction of relevant features would take more trials to learn than an inclusive disjunction of the same relevant features. The reason for this prediction is that the feature selection model predicts that prior knowledge will influence only the selection of features. After this selection is made, one would expect the same degree of difficulty as in the case in which subjects have no relevant prior knowledge. In contrast, the hypothesis selection model predicts that an exclusive disjunction may be easier for subjects to learn than an inclusive disjunction, if the exclusive disjunction of relevant features is consistent with the subjects prior knowledge, but the inclusive disjunction of these same features is not consistent.

In the experiment, subjects were told that they were to review records of patients brought to the emergency room of a hospital because of an overdose of sleeping pills and that the effect of the sleeping pills was to lower the patients heart rate. The patient records were described by the following five features and that each feature had one of two values:

- Gender: The gender of the patient.   (Female or Male)
- Time: The time of day.   (AM or PM)
- Oral: Each patient is given a capsule to swallow.   (Drug-o or Sugar)
- Intravenous: Each patient is given an injection.   (Drug-i or Saline)
- Doctor: The attending physician.   (Ramsey or Jankins)

The subjects had to learn a way to predict whether or not the patient's heart rate will increase. Subjects had to learn either an inclusive or an exclusive disjunction of Drug-o and Drug-i (i.e., some subjects were presented with data that indicated that a patient's heart rate would increase only if a patient was given either Drug-i or Drug-o; other subjects were presented with data that indicated that the heart rate would increase only if a patient was given Drug-i or Drug-o, but not both).

The instructions also included background information. Two sets of instructions were prepared. The only difference between them is that one set of instructions omitted the item underlined below:

- The nurses in the PM shift receive a 10% higher salary than those in the AM shift.
- Female patients typically weigh less than male patients.
- Drug-o has been used by truck drivers to stay alert.
- Drug-i has been shown to increase aggressiveness in primate studies.
- When both Drug-o and Drug-i are given to laboratory animals, they result in a coma.
- Dr. Ramsey received his degree from Rutgers University in 1959.
- Dr. Jankins received his degree from Yale University in 1988.

Note that the background information contained items irrelevant to this particular task and that the relevant background information required plausible reasoning rather than purely deductive reasoning.

The hypothesis selection model makes several predictions about the outcome of the experiment. The predictions all follow from the thesis that concepts consistent with prior knowledge take fewer trials to learn than concepts that are not consistent with prior knowledge:

- Subjects learning the exclusive disjunction who were shown information on the drug interaction would learn more rapidly than subjects learning this concept without this information.

- Subjects learning the exclusive disjunction who were shown information on the drug interaction would learn more rapidly than subjects learning an inclusive disjunction with this information.

- Subjects learning the inclusive disjunction who were not shown information on the drug interaction would learn more rapidly than subjects learning this concept who were shown this information.

In contrast, the feature selection model would predict that including or omitting the information on the interaction between Drug-i and Drug-o would not affect the learning rate. It assumes that prior knowledge only focuses attention on features and covariation alone indicates how the features are combined.

Subjects. The subjects were 52 male and female undergraduates attending the University of California, Irvine who participated in this experiment to receive extra credit in an introductory psychology course. Subjects were randomly assigned to one of the four conditions. Subjects were tested in two groups of 26.

Stimuli. The stimuli consisted of patient records that were displayed on the monitor of a Macintosh computer. Since there are five two-valued features, a total of 32 records were constructed.

Procedures. Each subject was shown a patient record on the computer screen and asked to predict whether or not the heart rate would increase by clicking on a box containing the word Yes or a box containing the word No (i.e., using a mouse to move a pointer to the box and pressing a button on the mouse). While still displaying the patient record, the computer indicated the correct answer by displaying the word Increase or Decrease. Next, the subject clicked on a box labeled Continue and the next patient record was shown. This process was repeated until the subjects were able to predict or classify correctly on 7 consecutive trials. The subjects were allowed as much time as they wanted to make their prediction and to view the record after the correct answer was shown. We recorded the number of the last trial on which the subject made an error. The records were presented in a random order. If the subject did not obtain the correct answer after 60 trials, we recorded that the last error was made on trial 60. The subjects were permitted to consult the instructions, containing information on operating the computer and background information at any time during the experiment.

Results. Table 1 displays the results of the four conditions. The results of this experiment confirmed the predictions of the hypothesis selection model ($p < .05$, level $F(1, 48) = 4.48$). A Tukey HSD finds a significant difference ($p < .05$) on the the following comparisons:

- Subjects learning an exclusive disjunction and provided with information on the drug interaction did learn more rapidly than subjects learning the same concept without this background knowledge (7.3 vs. 28.2). This difference suggests that the knowledge of the interaction between the drugs facilitates learning this concept.

- Subjects learning an exclusive disjunction and provided with information on the drug interaction would learn more rapidly than subjects learning an inclusive disjunction and provided with information on drug interaction. (7.3 vs. 16.2). In this case, the knowledge of the interaction interferes with learning an inclusive disjunction since this hypothesis is not consistent with the prior knowledge.

Although not statistically significant, the data do not contradict the third prediction of the hypothesis selection framework:

- Subjects learning an inclusive disjunction and provided with information on the drug interaction would learn less rapidly than subjects learning an inclusive disjunction without this extra misleading knowledge (14.9 vs. 16.2). If we ignore the score of a subject who failed to complete the experiment, this result is more in line with our expectations (11.3 vs. 16.2).

Table 1. Mean number of trials required by human subjects

	Inclusive	Exclusive
With knowledge of interaction	16.2	7.3
Without knowledge of interaction	14.9	28.2

The results of this experiment provide support for hypothesis selection models of concept learning. In this framework, the hypothesis space is reduced by eliminating those hypotheses that are not consistent with the prior knowledge of the learner. In contrast, feature selection models restrict the hypothesis space less than hypothesis selection models. All hypotheses composed of potential relevant features are considered consistent with prior knowledge. As a consequence, the feature selection framework does not account for the differences in learning rates observed in this experiment.

POSTHOC: A hypothesis selection model

POSTHOC (Pazzani & Schulenburg, 1989) is a hypothesis selection model of concept learning. Through the use of a set of productions and a background theory that represents prior knowledge, POSTHOC maintains a single hypothesis that summarizes the examples seen and classifies new examples. The productions are used to suggest hypotheses and to revise hypotheses that misclassify examples. Because some of the productions do not make use of background knowledge, the system has the ability to create hypotheses that are not consistent with its background knowledge (e.g., if the background knowledge is incomplete or incorrect). In this paper, we discuss an extension to the system that allows it to make use of negative as well as positive influences. Note that POSTHOC was not modified in anyway to make it learn exclusive disjunctions. Rather, hypotheses representing exclusive disjunctions are formed using background knowledge when there are two separate features that positively influence a result, but the combination of the features negatively influence the result. Without the background knowledge of the specific drug interaction, POSTHOC would create an initial hypothesis consistent with its theory and latter be forced to revise them using productions that ignore the background knowledge. If POSTHOC has no background theory at all, then it would create its hypotheses using only productions that ignore background knowledge.

In POSTHOC, examples are expressed as set of feature-value pairs and an outcome. For example, in the medical experiments described in the previous section, a patient record describing a male patient who was administered Drug-o orally and a saline solution intravenously after noon and whose heart rate increased would be represented as follows:

```
[gender male] [time pm] [oral drug-o] [intravenous saline] ∈ increase
```

POSTHOC maintains a single hypothesis that consists of a DNF description (i.e., disjunction of conjunctions) of the concept being learned. One hypothesis that is consistent with the above example states that the heart rate will increase if Drug-o is given orally in the afternoon.

```
[oral drug-o] ∧ [time pm] → increase
```

Of course, there are numerous other hypotheses consistent with this example that may or may not be consistent with future examples or with the prior knowledge of the learner.

The influence theory which comprises POSTHOC's prior knowledge consists of two components: a set of influences which describe tendencies that either facilitate or hinder the desired outcome (e.g. increasing the heart rate) and a set of inferences rules that indicate when these influences are present. The influence theory of POSTHOC for the medical experiment described in the previous section includes the following influences and inferences:

224

Influences:
```
(easier more-alert  increase)
(easier more-aggressive  increase)
```
Inferences:
```
(implies [oral drug-o]  more-alert)
(implies [intravenous drug-i] more-aggressive)
```

These influences and associated inferences suggest that making a person more alert or more aggressive can facilitate increasing that persons heart rate and taking Drug-o orally tends to make a person more alert and taking Drug-i intravenously tends to make a person more aggressive.

The influence theory described above includes only positive influences. However, some influences can only be expressed naturally as negative influences. One such example the knowledge of drug interactions which arises in the medical experiment described in the previous section. For instance, if we wished to include the knowledge that Drug-i and Drug-o tend to interact negatively in the patient to produce a coma (thus lowering the heart rate), then this knowledge is represented as the following influence and associated inference:

Influences:
```
(harder coma  increase)
```
Inference
```
(implies ([oral drug-o] ∧ [intravenous drug-i]) coma)
```

Adding negative influences to POSTHOC required extending the productions presented in Pazzani & Schulenburg (1989). There are three types of productions. One set deals with errors of commission in which a positive example is falsely classified as a negative example. These productions makes the hypothesis more general. The second set deals with errors of omission in which a negative example is falsely classified as a positive example. These productions makes the hypothesis more specific. The final set creates an initial hypothesis when the first positive example is encountered. For brevity only those productions which utilize the negative influences will be described. For a description of the remaining productions, the reader is referred to Pazzani & Schulenburg (1989):

Initializing Hypothesis.
```
IF there are features of the example that are indicative of the
inverse of a negative influence
THEN initialize the hypothesis to the negation of the conditions
indicative of the negative influence.
```

Errors of Omission.
```
IF the hypothesis is consistent with the influence theory
AND there are features that are indicative of the inverse of a
negative influence
THEN create a conjunction of the current hypothesis and the negation
of the conditions indicative of the negative influence.
```

Errors of Commission.
```
IF the  hypothesis is consistent with the background theory
AND for each true conjunction there are features not present in the
current example that would be necessary for the inverse of a negative
influence
THEN modify the conjunct by conjoining the negation of the conditions
indicative of the negative influence.
```

225

To illustrate the use of these productions, a trace of POSTHOC learning an exclusive disjunction is provided below. For brevity, we omit the "doctor" attribute from the examples. The first example that POSTHOC is presented with is an example of a treatment that successfully increases the patient's heart rate where a male patient is administered a sugar pill orally and Drug-i intravenously in the PM by Dr. Ramsey:

    [gender male] [time pm] [oral sugar] [intravenous drug-i] ∈ increase

Since there is no initial hypothesis, POSTHOC uses an initialization production to create a hypothesis that accounts for the outcome of this example. A positive influence more-aggressive is present and POSTHOC creates the hypothesis that Drug-i leads to the increased heart rate:

    [intravenous drug-i] → increase

This hypothesis is consistent with several more examples. Next, an example is presented where a patient is administered Drug-o orally and a saline solution intravenously. Here an error of omission occurs since POSTHOC predicts that the patient's heart rate will not increase but it does increase. The example encountered is:

    [gender male] [time am] [oral drug-o] [intravenous saline] ∈ increase

The hypothesis is revised by an Error of Omission production for positive influences a multiple sufficient hypothesis is produced:

    [intravenous drug-i] ∨ [oral drug-o] → increase

Again this hypothesis is consistent with several more examples. However, POSTHOC makes the wrong prediction when it encounters an example where the patient is administered both Drug-i intravenously and Drug-o orally. POSTHOC predicts that the patient's heart rate will increase, but the patients heart rate does not increase. This results in an error of commission. The example presented to POSTHOC is:

[gender male] [time am] [oral drug-o] [intravenous drug-i] ∉ increase

To correct its hypothesis, POSTHOC uses the Error of Commission production for negative influences. For the each disjunct, [oral drug-o] and [intravenous drug-i], the negation of the features indicative of the negative influence is conjoined with each conjunct, the results hypothesis is:

    [intravenous drug-i] ∧ not ([oral drug-o] ∧ [intravenous drug-i]) ∨
    [oral drug-o] ∧ not ([oral drug-o] ∧ [intravenous drug-i]) → increase

This hypothesis can be simplified to:

    [intravenous drug-i] ∧ not ([oral drug-o]) ∨
    [oral drug-o] ∧ not ([intravenous drug-i]) → increase
which is consistent with the remaining examples and represents the exclusive disjunction.

Simulation Results

We ran POSTHOC on 200 random orderings of the data on each of the same four conditions used in the experiment on human subjects. The results are shown in Table 2. The negative influence (i.e., the drug interaction) was not used to simulate the condition in which this item was not included in the instructions. The data show the same trends as the human experimental data: learning the exclusive disjunction of administering Drug-i intravenously and Drug-o orally was facilitated by the knowledge that Drug-i and Drug-o interact to put the patient in a coma (8.3 vs. 45.7) ; when provided with information on the drug interaction, learning the exclusive disjunction of the drugs was easier than learning the inclusive disjunction (6.0 vs. 8.3); learning an inclusive disjunction of the drugs when provided with misleading information on the drug interaction required more trials than the same concept without this extra misleading knowledge (6.0 vs. 3.7).

Table 2. Mean number of trials required by POSTHOC

	Inclusive	Exclusive
With knowledge of interaction	6.0	8.3
Without knowledge of interaction	3.7	45.7

In POSTHOC, we have focused on how prior knowledge influences learning rates and we have so far ignored other information used by human learners (e.g., perceptual salience of features, Bower & Trabasso, 1968). As a consequence, POSTHOC is not intended to make quantitative predictions on the number of training examples but rather predicts the relative difficulty of learning.

Future Directions
There are three possible direction in which we plan to extend the hypothesis selection model. First, we would like to be able to use the prior knowledge of the learner to influence the interpretation of ambiguous feature (Medin & Wisniewski, 1990). Second, we would like POSTHOC to be able to use more abstract knowledge. Currently, POSTHOC can represent the information that there there is a specific interaction between two drugs or that there is no drug interaction. In contrast, our subjects also appeared to have more general knowledge that indicates such things as drugs may interact and can use this knowledge to explain the specific interaction seen in the experiment in terms of the general knowledge of drug interactions. Finally, we plan to extend POSTHOC so that when it learns accurate hypotheses that are not consistent with its background knowledge, the background knowledge is revised to accommodate the new findings.

Conclusions
We have presented experimental evidence that provides support for hypothesis selection models of concept learning. We have extended POSTHOC to include negative influences and shown that with this extension alone, it is able to predict the relative order of difficulty of trials on inclusive and exclusive disjunctions. Recent work on the analysis of the limitations of inductive learning algorithms (Valiant, 1984; Dietterich, 1989) is in sharp contrast to the versatility demonstrated by human learners. We believe that approaches that make use of background knowledge to focus all aspects of learning are central to accounting for the generality of human learning.

Acknowledgements
The software used to run the experiment was designed by Francis Nguyen and Takeshi Tsubota. We would like to thank Kamal Ali, Cliff Brunk, David Foster, and Scott Truesdel for assistance in running the experiment and Gupi Silverstein and Caroline Ehrlich for commenting on an earlier draft of the paper. This research is supported in part by National Science Foundation Grant IRI-8908260.

Bibliography
Ahn, W., Mooney, R., Brewer, W., & DeJong, G. (1987). Schema acquisition from one example: Psychological evidence for explanation-based learning. *Proceedings of the Ninth Annual Conference of the Cognitive Science Society*. Seattle, WA: Lawrence Erlbaum Associates.

Ausubel, D. M., & Schiff, H. M. (1954). The effect of incidental and experimentally induced experience on the learning of relevant and irrelevant causal relationships by children. *Journal of Genetic Psychology, 84*, 109-123.

Bower, G., & Trabasso, T. (1968). *Attention in learning: Theory and research*. New York: John Wiley and Sons.

Chapman, L. J., & Chapman, J. P. (1967). Genesis of popular but erroneous diagnostic observations. *Journal of Abnormal Psychology, 72*, 193-204.

Dietterich, T. (1989). Limitations on inductive learning. *Proceedings of the Sixth International Workshop on Machine Learning* (pp. 124-128). Ithaca, NY: Morgan Kaufmann.

Kelley, H. (1971). Causal schemata and the attribution process. In E. Jones, D. Kanouse, H. Kelley, N. Nisbett, S. Valins & B. Weiner (Eds.), *Attribution: Perceiving the causes of behavior*. Morristown, NJ: General Learning Press.

Kelley, H. (1983). The process of causal attribution. *America Psychologist*, 107-128.

Lien, Y., & Cheng, P. (1989). A framework for psychological induction: Integrating the power law and covariation views. *The Eleventh Annual Conference of the Cognitive Science Society*. (pp. 729-733).Ann Arbor, MI: Lawrence Erlbaum Associates, Inc.

Medin, D., & Wisniewski, E. (1990). Paper presented at the Symposium on Computational Approaches to Concept Formation, Stanford, CA.

Murphy, G., & Medin, D. (1985). The role of theories in conceptual coherence. *Psychology Review, 92*, 289-316.

Nakamura, G. (1985). Knowledge-based classification of ill-defined categories. *Memory & Cognition. 13*, 377-384.

Pazzani, M. & Schulenburg, D. (1989). The influence of prior theories on the ease on concept acquisition. *The Eleventh Annual Conference of the Cognitive Science Society*. (pp. 812-819).Ann Arbor, MI: Lawrence Erlbaum Associates, Inc.

Pazzani, M. (1990). *Creating a memory of causal relationships: An integration of empirical and explanation-based learning methods*. Hillsdale, NJ : Lawrence Erlbaum Associates.

Schank, R., Collins, G., & Hunter, L. (1986). Transcending inductive category formation in learning. *Behavioral and Brain Sciences, 9*, 639-686.

Valiant, L. (1984). A theory of the learnable. *Communications of the Association of Computing Machinery, 27*, 1134-1142.

Wattenmaker, W., Dewey, G., Murphy, T., & Medin, D. (1986). Linear severability and concept learning: Context, Relational properties and concept naturalness. *Cognitive Psychology, 18*, 158-194.

Wells, H. (1963). Effects of transfer and problem structure in disjunctive concept formation. *Journal of Experimental Psychology, 65*, 63-69.

Wisniewski, E. (1989). Learning from examples: The effect of different conceptual roles. *The Eleventh Annual Conference of the Cognitive Science Society*. (pp. 980-986).Ann Arbor, MI: Lawrence Erlbaum Associates, Inc.

A Rule Based Model of Judging Harm-doing[1]

Thomas R. Shultz

McGill University

ABSTRACT

A rule based computational model of the judgment of harm-doing is presented that qualitatively simulates the major principles of an emerging psychological theory of common sense moral reasoning. Simulation results indicate that the model, called MR for Moral Reasoner, generates verdicts in substantial agreement with those reached in somewhat difficult court cases. A higher rate of agreement with outcomes produced in simpler cases from traditional cultures suggests that the model possesses a good deal of cultural universality. Systematic damaging of the rules in the model indicated that most of the rules are essential in producing a high rate of agreement with court decisions and identified some rules regarding the mental state of the accused that, individually, are less essential because they compensate for each other.

A PSYCHOLGICAL THEORY OF JUDGING HARM-DOING

This project concerns the common sense evaluation of harm-doing. Whenever a person may have been harmed by someone else, a number of issues naturally arise. How was the harm caused, is anyone responsible for the harm, is that person blameworthy, and how much should he be punished? People encounter such cases of harm-doing frequently, either directly or through secondary accounts.

Shultz and Schleifer (1983) have developed a psychological theory of reasoning about harm-doing that was inspired principally by conceptual analyses in jurisprudence and moral philosophy. A brief synopsis of this theory is presented here, minus the philosophical motivation and supporting psychological evidence, much of which is reviewed in Darley and Shultz (1990). The main concepts and decisions in the theory are illustrated in Figure 1. For a case in which a person may have done something to harm someone else, major decisions focus on causation, morally responsibility, blame, and punishment. Each of these major decisions presupposes and uses information from previous major decisions.

Judgments of moral responsibility, for example, presuppose those of causation. If the accused is judged not to have caused the harm, then there is no need to consider whether he is morally responsible for it. Similarly, judgments of blame presuppose those of moral responsibility, and decisions about punishment presuppose those about blame. A person is responsible for harm that he caused if the harm cannot be excused. Blame refers to a decision that a person is at fault, given that he has caused and is responsible for the harm. Without responsibility, there is no need to consider blame. Punishment refers to a decision about what consequences should befall the person as a result of being blameworthy. If the person is blameless, then no decision needs to be taken about punishment.

---

[1] I am grateful to John Darley and Kevin Dunbar for helpful comments on this research. This research is supported by a grant from the Social Sciences and Humanities Research Council of Canada. Address correspondence to Thomas R. Shultz, Department of Psychology, McGill University, 1205 Penfield Avenue, Montréal, Québec, Canada H3A 1B1. E-mail: ints@musicb.mcgill.ca

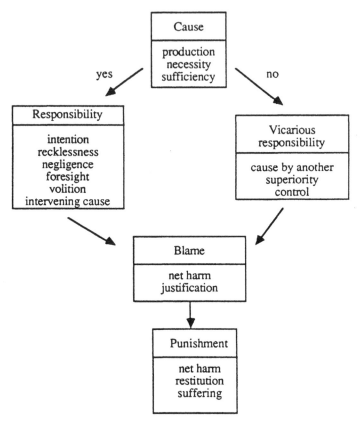

Figure 1. Major decisions and concepts in a theory of judging harm-doing

The first major judgment to be made concerns the causation of the harm. Causation is determined by a combination of generative and conditional information. On the generative view of causation, an effect is considered to be produced by some sort of transmission from the cause. Supplementing this approach is the *but for* (or sine qua non) test, which is widely used in jurisprudence. The *but for* test holds that a person's behavior is a cause of harm if and only if the harm would not have occurred without the person's behavior, thus focusing on the necessary conditions for harm. Some have argued for the use of sufficient conditions in judging causation: does the person's action distinguish the current harm-producing situation from some appropriate standard in which harm did not result?

The next major decision, responsibility, is determined by joint consideration of causation and excuses. One is held morally responsible for harm that he caused unless the harm was done accidentally (i.e., without intention, recklessness, or negligence), involuntarily (i.e., under external force), or without being able to foresee the resulting harm. Moreover, the causal chain leading from the action to the harm cannot be broken by some unforeseen event which exacerbated the harm.

230

The preferred way of judging intention is to match the accused's plan against the outcome. If his plan is known and the harm is included in the plan, then it is concluded that the harm was intended unless the harm was not caused as planned. If the actor's plan is unknown, then one falls back to objective heuristics such as valence, monitoring, and discounting. Did the harmful outcome have positive consequences for the actor, did he monitor his actions, or can intentionality be discounted because of alternate external causes? Recklessness is acting without due care coupled with high foreseeability of harm, unless the harm was intended. Negligence is acting without due care, but with a lower foreseeability of harm, unless the harm was intended or done recklessly.

Blame is a joint function of moral responsibility, the presence of some degree of net harm, and justification for the harm. If the accused is morally responsible for the harm and there is some net harm (i.e., more harm than benefit to the victim) then the accused is blameworthy, unless the harm can be justified. The distinction between moral responsibility and blame is somewhat subtle, but relies on the difference between excuses and justifications. Excuses, reflecting the concepts in the responsibility box in Figure 1, are offered when one admits to having caused harm, but does not accept responsibility for it. If such an excuse is accepted, then the issue of blame does not arise. Justifications come into play when one accepts responsibility for having caused harm, but denies that it was bad thing to have done, thereby avoiding blame, and perhaps earning credit.

In order to be justified, harm must achieve some goal, that goal must be more highly valued than not doing the harm, and the goal must be achievable in no less harmful way. These conditions are evaluated in sequence since a consideration of each one presupposes an appropriate decision on the preceding one. For example, if the harm achieves no goal, then there is no reason to consider whether any goal is more highly valued than not doing the harm.

The discussion has so far focussed on holding someone blameworthy for harm that he has directly caused. However, it is possible for blame to be assigned without direct causation. Such cases are typically understood as involving vicarious responsibility. A person is held vicariously responsible only when that person is in a superior position to the perpetrator or could have prevented the perpetrator from causing harm.

If the accused is blameworthy, then punishment can be assigned. Consistent with the retribution theory of punishment, punishment is directly proportional to the net amount of harm, scaled down by restitution the perpetrator has made, and the degree to which the perpetrator has suffered as a result of having caused the harm.

COMPUTATIONAL MODEL

A computer program was developed to simulate how the ordinary person (down to about 5-years-old) reasons about harm-doing. The program is called MR, for Moral Reasoner. MR provides a convenient way of rigorously specifying the psychological theory reviewed above and a technique for having the theory generate conclusions that can be compared with those produced by human subjects.

The version of MR used here is written in Lisp with rules implemented as boolean procedures, returning either *true* or *false*.[2] An English version of the rule dealing with moral responsibility is given as an example:

---

[2] A more conventional way to write this program would be as production rules in a production system interpreter. Several versions of MR have been done in just that way.

If & the accused produced the harm
    the accused's action was not accidental
    the accused's action was voluntary
    the harm was a foreseeable consequence of the accused's action
    there was no intervening cause of the harm
Then the accused is morally responsible for the harm
Else the accused is not morally responsible for the harm

The MR program accepts a case described in terms of categorical values on a number of features (e.g., foreseeability of the harm is high) and produces a series of conclusions on any of the other critical concepts in the model needed or requested.

EXAMPLE TRACE FOR A SINGLE CASE

The following illustrates how the MR program deals with a particular case. The case of Lynch vs. Fisher was tried in Louisiana in 1947 (Hart & Honoré, 1959):

A highway collision occurred through the negligence of accused, whereby a third party was trapped in his car and injured. The plaintiff, seeing the collision, went to help and finding a pistol on the floor, handed it to the injured man, who in a state of delirium through the shock of the accident, fired at plaintiff and wounded him.

A case is described to the MR program as a set of attribute-value pairs. The particular values for Lynch vs. Fisher[3] were:

((case-name lynch v fisher) (produce-harm ?) (necessary-for-harm y) (sufficient-for-harm n) (mental-state negligent) (careful n) (plan-known n) (plan-include-harm ?) (harm-caused-as-planned ?) (monitor y) (benefit-accused n) (foreseeability low) (external-cause n) (external-force n) (intervening-contribution y) (foresee-intervention n) (severity-harm 0.5) (benefit-victim 0) (achieve-goal n) (goal-outweigh-harm ?) (goal-achieveable-less-harmful ?) (restitution 0) (accused-suffer 0) (verdict g))

The output from the MR program is presented as a series of inferences. For Lynch vs. Fisher, the output was as follows: Case of Lynch v Fisher; accused caused the harm; no direct evidence that accused intended the harm; accused's intention to harm cannot be discounted; accused was not reckless; accused was negligent; no indirect evidence that accused intended the harm; accused did not intend the harm; the harm was not accidental; accused's action was voluntary; the harm was foreseeable; there was an intervening cause of the harm; accused is not morally responsible for the harm; accused is not blameworthy; disagree.

The accused caused the accident negligently, thus ruling out a pure accident. Also, the accused's actions were voluntary (i. e., not forced) and some kind of serious harm was

---

However, the Lisp version described here was found to be especially convenient for simulating large numbers of cases with damaged rules (see DAMAGING THE MODEL, below). The Lisp version of MR functions much like a backward chaining production rule interpreter.

[3] The symbols y, n, and ? refer to yes, no, and undecided, respectively. The symbol g refers to guilty, the verdict being used only to tabulate the rate of agreement between the program and the court.

foreseeable from negligent driving. However, because there was an intervening contribution to the harm, which was not foreseeable, MR decides that there was an intervening cause of the harm that mitigates responsibility and, thus, blame. In contrast, the court found the accused guilty.

EVALUATING THE COMPUTATIONAL MODEL

The model was tested on two large sets of actual cases of harm-doing. One set was based on legal cases in English and American law; the other set on cases recorded among traditional cultures that possess no codified legal system.

The first set consisted of the 95 most fully described legal cases in Hart and Honoré (1959), spanning the last five centuries of Anglo-American law. The overall proportion of agreement on MR's decision of blameworthy with a judicial decision of guilty was .84, X^2 = 44.47, $p < .001$.[4] This rate of agreement is gratifyingly high considering the difficulty of this set of cases, as indicated by the relatively low proportion of unsuccessful appeals, .61. The model agreed more with the final judicial decision than did the initial judicial decision, X^2 = 12.15, $p < .05$.

The second set contained 58 cases of harm-doing reported by anthropologists working in traditional, non-literate cultures around the world. The largest, single source was Pospisil (1958). The proportion of agreement was higher here (.97) than with the Hart and Honoré cases, X^2 = 4.61, $p < .05$, reflecting the fact that these cases were conceptually quite simple. This result suggests that the model implemented in MR does have some claim to cultural universality.

These above simulations, initially conducted blind with regard to the real life decisions, were useful in fine tuning the rule base, chiefly by repairing inconsistencies and anomalies in the rules.

DAMAGING THE MODEL

In order to determine whether each of the rules in the model is critical to matching real-life decisions, the cases were run again under conditions in which each rule was damaged. A rule was damaged by reversing the boolean value it returned: *true* if it was supposed to return *false*, *false* if it was supposed to return *true*. Only those rules leading up to the critical decision of blameworthy were damaged in this way.

The results for the 95 Hart and Honoré cases are presented as solid bars in Figure 2 in terms of proportion agreement with the final judicial decision. The proportion agreement produced by each type of damage was contrasted with that produced by the fully intact model using log-linear analysis. Damage to each rule did significantly lower the agreement rate (mean = .35, all ps < .001), except for those rules dealing with the mental state of the accused (mean = .83, all ps > .5). This revealed that for decisions of blame in cases of non-accidental harm (virtually all of the Hart and Honoré cases), it does not matter whether the accused acts intentionally, recklessly, or negligently. This seemed quite surprising until it was realized that these mental state concepts compensate for each other so that, even if one is damaged, another fills the gap.

---

[4] All of the statistics reported in this paper are based on log-linear analysis. Each result is reported as a 1 *df* Wald chi-square value.

Two rules are critical to understanding this compensation. One rule deals with accident, the other with intention:

If the protagonist's action was intentional, reckless, or negligent
Then the harm was not accidental
Else the harm was accidental

If there is direct or indirect evidence that the protagonist intended the harm
Then the harm was intended
Else the harm was not intended

As an example of compensation, even if the *intend* rule is damaged, the *reckless* or *negligent* rule may still prevent the harm from being viewed as accidental. As another example, even if the *strong-intend* rule (providing direct evidence of intention) is damaged, the *weak-intend* rule (providing indirect evidence of intention) may still lead to the conclusion that the harm was intended.

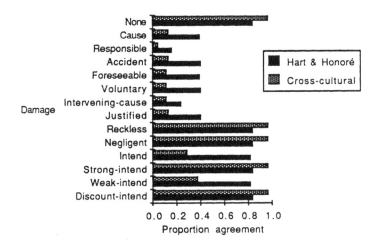

Figure 2. Proportion agreement with judicial decisions after rule damage.

The results for the 58 cross-cultural cases are likewise presented in hatched bars in Figure 2 in terms of proportion agreement with the actual decision. The proportion agreement produced by each type of damage was again contrasted with that produced by the fully intact model using log-linear analysis. The results were similar to those for the Hart and Honoré cases with two striking exceptions -- intend and weak-intend. The *intend* rule concludes that the harm was intended only if there is either strong or weak evidence of intention. The *weak-intend* rule concludes that there is weak evidence of intention if the accused's actions were neither reckless nor negligent, and one or more of the following is true: the accused's intending the harm cannot be discounted, the accused monitored his actions, or the harm benefitted the accused. A *strong-intend* rule concludes that there is strong evidence for intention if either the harm was described as intentional or the following all hold: the accused's plan was known, the accused's plan included the harm, and the harm was caused as planned.

Damage to the *intend* rule produced a proportion agreement of .82 in the Hart and Honoré cases, but only .29 for the cross-cultural cases, $X^2 = 37.32$, $p < .001$. Analogously, damage to the *weak-intend* rule produced a proportion agreement of .82 in the Hart and Honoré cases, but only .38 for the cross-cultural cases, $X^2 = 28.05$, $p < .001$. For the cross-cultural cases, damage to each rule did significantly lower the agreement rate as compared to the intact model (mean = .17, all ps < .001), except for the *reckless*, *negligent*, *strong-intend*, and *discount-intend* rules (mean = .97, all ps > .5).

This initially surprising discrepancy between the western and traditional cases can be explained by recalling that the latter cases are conceptually much simpler than the former. The Hart and Honoré cases were typically subtle and complex, turning on issues such as causation, intervening causation, negligence, or recklessness. In contrast, the cross-cultural cases were extremely straightforward, typically involving weak evidence for intention of the accused and not hinging on difficult issues such as causation, intervening causation, or alternative mental states such as negligence or recklessness. A typical cross-cultural case involved, for example, one person stealing another person's pig, and either making or not making restitution for it. Because there was no alternative mental state to compensate for damage to the *weak-intend* and *intend* rules in these latter cases, this type of rule-damage was fatal to proportion of agreement. In contrast, damage to the other mental state rules had little effect on proportion agreement since these other rules were rarely relevant to the cases.

CONCLUSIONS AND DISCUSSION

The simulations show that the MR program is computationally sufficient to qualitatively match human reasoning about harm-doing. They further suggest that the MR model and the psychological theory on which it is based have a large degree of cultural universality. Cultures undoubtedly vary in their value judgments about what constitutes what degree of harm and what sorts of justifications outweigh harms, but they do not appear to differ in the rules they apply to moral judgments about harm-doing. This universality could have important implications for explaining the development of these moral judgment rules.

The construction of the MR program was extremely useful in forcing a rigorous specification of an increasingly complex psychological theory. This was particularly true in terms of specifying how different parts of the theory ought to interact. Early simulations identified a number of inconsistencies and anomalies in the rule base. Corrections of these problems were then tested in subsequent simulations. It would have been extremely difficult to identify and test these issues without the benefit of a working computational model.

One unanticipated sort of interaction among of parts of the model was the degree to which mental state rules compensate for each other. Moreover, the extent of this compensation was found to interact with the subtlety of the case. For the relatively difficult cases found in books on western jurisprudence, the mutual compensation of mental state rules was extensive since many of the mental state rules were relevant to many of these cases. But for the relatively simple cases found in anthropological reports from traditional cultures, this mutual compensation disappeared since only a few of the mental state rules were relevant.

LIMITATIONS OF THE CURRENT MODEL AND SUGGESTIONS FOR FUTURE WORK

Although encouraging, these simulations do not constitute a very complete test of MR. They compare only one decision, blameworthiness, a decision that can be reached by a number of different paths through the rule base. More refined and more complete tests of

MR could be made by examining the intermediate decisions of ordinary subjects reading vignettes of legal cases.

Much more work is needed on the process of encoding the initial description of the case. Currently, the programmer translates the English version of the case into an attribute-value frame that the rules can use to make further inferences. It is likely, however, that subjects differ substantially in how they encode and interpret at least some cases. Such encoding differences would undoubtedly lead to differing conclusions about the case.

RELATED WORK

Pennington and Hastie (1988) investigated decision processes in simulations of trials by jury and constructed a theory of how jurors organize the information emerging during a trial. It is their view that the juror's main task is to construct a causal explanation of how the harm was produced and that the judge, through final instructions to the jury, often provides the responsibility and blame rules necessary to reach a decision on guilt or innocence. The emphasis of the present project is on explicating these rules as used implicitly by ordinary reasoners.

Thagard (1989) applied a connectionist model of explanatory coherence, ECHO, to two legal cases in which the prosecution and the defense advocated incompatible ways of explaining the evidence. Given a network of coherence and incoherence relations among propositions describing the evidence and competing claims of the case, ECHO propagated activation across the network to maximize the coherence of the network. ECHO focuses only on the issue of how the harm was caused.

Bain's JUDGE (in Riesbeck & Schank, 1989) is a case based reasoning program in the area of criminal sentencing. It uses rules to build up its case library. It has been our experience (via think aloud protocols and pointed questions) that, perhaps unlike judges, ordinary people have no extensive case libraries to draw on.

REFERENCES

Darley, J. M., & Shultz, T. R. (1990). Moral rules: Their content and acquisition. *Annual Reviews of Psychology*, **41**, 525-556.

Hart, H. L. A., & Honoré, A. M. (1959). *Causation in the law*. Oxford: Clarendon Press.

Pennington, N., & Hastie, R. (1988). Explanation-based decision making: Effects of memory structure on judgment. *Journal of Experimental Psychology: Learning, Memory, and Cognition*, **14**, 521-533.

Pospisil, L. (1958). *Kapauku Papuans and their law*. New Haven: Yale University Press.

Riesbeck, C. K., & Schank, R. C. (1989). *Inside case-based reasoning*. Hillsdale, NJ: Lawrence Erlbaum Associates.

Shultz, T. R., & Schleifer, M. (1983). Towards a refinement of attribution concepts. In J. Jaspars, F.D. Fincham, & M. Hewstone (Eds.), *Attribution theory and research: Conceptual, developmental and social dimensions* (pp. 37-62). London: Academic Press.

Thagard, P. (1989). Explanatory coherence. *Behavioral and Brain Sciences*, **12**, 435-467.

The Mechanism of Restructuring in Geometry

Stellan Ohlsson

Learning Research and Development Center
University of Pittsburgh, Pittsburgh, PA 15260
stellan@vms.cis.pitt.edu

Abstract. Restructuring consists of a change in the representation of the current search state, a process which breaks an impasse during problem solving by opening up new search paths. A corpus of 52 think-aloud protocols from the domain of geometry was scanned for evidence of restructuring. The data suggest that restructuring is accomplished by re-parsing the geometric diagram.

Introduction. A wide variety of problem solving processes have been analyzed in terms of heuristic search (Newell & Simon, 1972). For example, in geometry proofs the geometric theorems (operators) are applied to the mental representation of the diagram (the knowledge state) until the desired proposition (the goal state) has been attained (Anderson, 1981). The stepwise character of heuristic search contrasts with the Gestalt hypothesis that problem solving proceeds through (a) an initial, unsuccessful, attack on the problem, (b) a more or less protracted impasse, and (c) a restructuring of the problem, which is typically, but not necessarily, followed by insight (Ohlsson, 1984a).

Several attempts have been made to reconcile the information processing and Gestalt hypotheses. Simon (1966) proposed that it helps to sleep on a problem, because goal tree information is forgotten faster than problem information. After a pause, a new goal tree is built on the basis of more knowledge about the problem. Langley and Jones (1988) interpret an impasse as a failure to retrieve the relevant problem solving operator. Insight occurs when some *external* stimulus causes enough activation to spread to that operator to allow its retrieval. A related hypothesis claims that insight occurs when an appropriate analogy is retrieved (Keane, 1988). Both the differential rate of forgetting hypothesis and the spread of activation hypothesis require that the problem solver moves attention away from the problem, and so cannot explain insight during *ongoing* problem solving. Several researchers have proposed that problem representations can be improved by the construction of macro-operators (Amarel, 1968; Korf, 1985). Koedinger and Anderson (in press) have proposed the related idea that geometry experts combine geometric theorems into larger inference schemas, called *diagram configuration schemas*, which allow them to find a proof without step-by-step search of the proof space. The macro-operator and diagram configuration hypotheses explain expert performance, but they do not explain insights by novices. All of these hypotheses locate restructuring in the *processes* of problem solving.

In contrast, I have proposed that restructuring involves a change in *the mental representation of the current search state* (Ohlsson, 1984b). A change in the representation implies that objects, relations, and properties which initially are seen as instances of certain concepts are being re-encoded as instances of other concepts. For example, an object which is initially encoded as a *hammer* might in the course of problem solving become re-encoded as a *pendulum weight*, a *line* may be re-encoded as a *triangle side*, and so on. Re-encoding a search state changes the set of operators which are applicable in that state, and thus breaks an impasse by opening up new search paths. A similar theory has been proposed by Kaplan and Simon (in press) to explain restructuring in the Mutilated Checker Board Problem. The critique by Montgomery (1988) does not touch those aspects of the theory that are of main concern in this paper. The purpose of the present paper is to provide evidence for re-encoding from the domain of geometry, and to propose a mechanism for re-encoding in that domain.

Table 1. Geometric theorems acquired by the subjects.

Theorem 1. Supplementary angles are congruent.

Theorem 2. Vertical angles are congruent.

Theorem 3. The supplementary angle of a right angle is a right angle.

Theorem 4. If two angles and their common side in one triangle are congruent to the corresponding angles and their common side in another triangle, then the two triangles are congruent.

Theorem 5. If two sides in a triangle are congruent, then their opposite angles are congruent; and vice versa.

Method. Three undergraduate psychology students participated in an experimental course in elementary geometry. The experimenter saw each subject individually in sessions that lasted approximately one hour each. The subjects learned basic theorems of plane geometry, the first five of which are shown in Table 1. A typical session began with free recall of previously learned theorems, continued with the introduction of new theorems, and ended with problem solving practice. The subjects had the theorems available during problem solving, and they were instructed to think aloud. The data consist of 52 think-aloud protocols, representing a total of approximately nine hours of problem solving effort. The protocols were scanned for the occurrence of restructuring events. Ten such events were found. The three most informative events will be analyzed below. They illustrate deliberate restructuring, goal driven restructuring, and restructuring in response to a hint.

Case 1: Deliberate restructuring. Subject S3 was given the problem in Figure 1 after she had studied Theorems 1-5 (see Table 1). She began by proving that triangles

AED and BEC are congruent, and then entered an impasse. In fragments F65-F67 (see Table 2) she deliberately sets out to *see* the problem from *many viewpoints*. The process of restructuring proceeds through three steps. First, she mentally cuts the figure along the diagonal CA, forming the triangles CDA and CBA (F68-F70). She then mentally cuts the figure along the other diagonal, forming the triangles DCB and DBA (F71-F74). Finally, she keeps one triangle from each pair, as it were, and sets herself the task of proving them congruent (F75-F77). Figure 2 gives a diagrammatic analysis of the process. The geometric objects perceived by the subject are drawn in bold lines, while the rest of the diagram is drawn in broken lines. Restructuring was not followed by insight in this case. The subject worked on the problem for twelve minutes without solving it.

Table 2. Protocol excerpt from Subject S3.

F65. but perhaps one can see this in some other way also
F66. one can perhaps see this from many viewpoints here
F67. now we shall see
F68. one can see it as
F69. CDA and CBA
F70. triangles
F71. one can see it on
F72. DCB and DBA instead
F73. yes exactly yes
F74. those two
F75. well
F76. now I can see this in another way
F77. CDB and CAD ought to be congruent here in some way

Case 2: Goal-driven restructuring. S1 was given the problem in Figure 1 as his first problem after studying Theorems 1-5 (see Table 1). S1 misunderstood the goal of the problem to be to prove that angle ADC is congruent to angle BCD. When the protocol excerpt in Table 3 begins, he has proved that angles EDA and ECB are congruent by proving them corresponding parts of the congruent triangles EDA and ECB. He then sets himself the goal of proving that the *remaining parts*, i. e., angles EDC and ECD, are equal (F43). His plan is to prove that they are equal by proving that the *sides* of the triangle EDC are equal (F42-F45). This goal is reformulated as proving that the triangle EDC is *isosceles* (F46-F47). This view of the problem leads to an impasse (F48-F49). Prompted by the experimenter to continue to think-aloud, he states that he is thinking about *the same problem* but from *another angle* (F50-F52): he has re-encoded ED and EC as *lines* (F54). The goal is still to prove them congruent (F53-F55). He suddenly realizes that ED and EC are corresponding *sides* of the two triangles EDA and ECB, which he has already proved congruent (F56-F61). Figure 3 shows a diagrammatic analysis of the process with perceived geometric objects in bold lines and the rest of the diagram--the background--in broken lines. The subject quickly completed the correct solution.

Table 3. Protocol excerpt from Subject S1.

F42. yes now I am thinking about whether one can prove that these two sides [DE, EC] are equally long

F43. because if they are then those two angles [EDC, ECD] which are just the remaining parts of those angles which I want to get [ADE, BCD] must be equally long

F44. so then this and that angle [ADE, BCD] must be equally big

F45. and then the problem is solved

F46. so it is now a question of proving that it is isosceles

F47. that triangle [EDC]

F48. and that I cannot

F49. but perhaps one can do it in some other way

(What are you thinking?)

F50. well now I am thinking

F51. well it is the same problem

F52. but from another angle

F53. yes if this one

F54. is those two lines [ED, EC] are equally long

F55. I am thinking

F56. yes but they must be

F57. since they are parts of

F58. it is congruent

F59. these two here are congruent [triangles EDA, ECB]

F60. and it is [ED, EC] corresponding sides in the triangles [EDA, ECB]

F61. therefore these two sides [ED, EC] are equally long

Case 3: Hint-driven restructuring. S2 attempted Problem 2 (see Figure 4) after having learned the five theorems in Table 1, plus four others. She decided to prove triangles AED and BEG congruent and quickly reached an impasse. The protocol excerpt in Table 4 begins when the experimenter gives her the hint that there are other pairs of triangles in the figure that might be congruent. She first rejects this suggestion (F113-F115). She then runs through the triangles in the figure (F113-F121), and concludes that there are no other congruent triangles in the figure (F121). She then suddenly sees the triangles AEG and BDA (F123-F124). Figure 5 shows a diagrammatic analysis of the process with perceived geometric objects drawn in bold lines and the rest of the diagram drawn in broken lines. In spite of this restructuring, the subject failed to solve the problem.

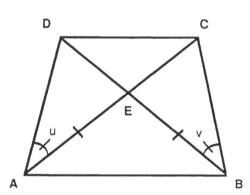

Prove angles ECD and CDE congruent.

Figure 1. Problem 1.

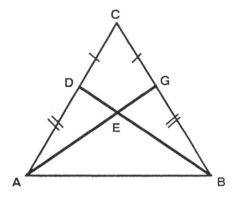

Prove line segments AG and BD congruent.

Figure 4. Problem 2.

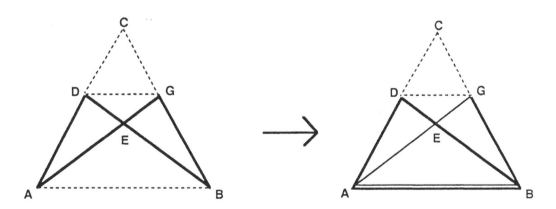

Figure 5. Analysis of S2's re-encoding process. Perceived geometric figures are drawn in bold lines, the rest of the figures in broken lines.

Table 4. Protocol excerpt from S2.

(What other triangles could be congruent?)

F109. what others

F110 could there be others which are congruent

F111. huh

(That could be. You have now been working the hypothesis that the whole point is to prove that those two triangles [AED, BEG] are congruent.)

F112. yes

(And just now you reached the conclusion that you cannot do that with the information you have. Can you find two other triangles which one can find which one could believe could be congruent?)

F113. congruent exactly alike

F114. no that is impossible there are no others

F115. it cannot be

F116. there are only one other

F117. also hypothetically then this line here

F118. then there are two here

F119. and those two here can surely never be congruent

F120. these two here can surely never be congruent

F121. no I do not understand that

F122. but

F123. now I see it

F124. I have forgotten this one here [AGB or BDA]

Discussion. The restructuring process revealed in these three protocol excerpts consists in *re-encoding the given figure*. The diagram--the set of lines on the paper--contains within it a large number of different geometric objects (angles, sides, triangles, etc.). Only some of those geometric objects are perceived at any one time. The others recede into the background. In particular, if a line configuration is perceived in one way, then alternative encodings of that same line configuration recede into the background. Restructuring consists of switching to one of the alternative encodings. How does the switching mechanism work? The data suggest that re-encoding is done by *re-parsing* the diagram. During initial problem perception complex objects (e. g., triangles) are constructed out of simpler objects (e. g., lines). This process is a search through a *description space* (Ohlsson, 1984b). Alternative interpretations of the perceptual information are possible, so some choices are made, resulting in a particular encoding of the given diagram. When an impasse forces the problem solver to re-encode the problem, he/she backs up in the description space, dismantles his/her previous encoding, and traverses another path through the description space. This process breaks an impasse by allowing other operators (geometric theorems) to apply to the current state. Restructuring is a rare

242

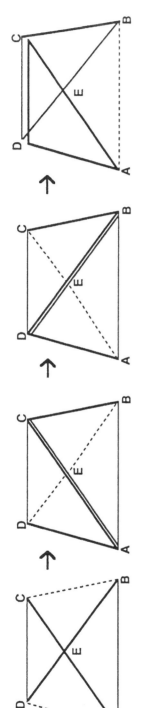

Figure 2. Analysis of S3's re-encoding process. Perceived geometric objects are drawn in bold lines, the rest of the figures in broken lines.

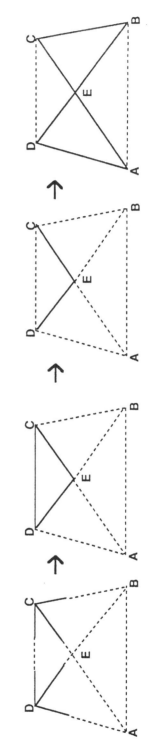

Figure 3. Analysis of S1's re-encoding process. Perceived geometric figures are drawn in bold lines, the rest of the figures in broken lines.

event: There was approximately one restructuring event per hour of problem solving effort in the present study. Restructuring does not necessarily lead to insight: In two of the three excerpts presented above, the subject failed to solve the problem. This study supports the idea that diagram parsing is central in geometry (Koedinger & Anderson, in press), but the validity of the re-parsing mechanism for other domains than geometry remains an open question. For example, a different mechanism seems to be responsible for re-encoding of the Mutilated Checker Board Problem (Kaplan & Simon, in press).

Acknowledgement. Preparation of this paper was supported, in part, by ONR grant N00014-89-J-1681. No endorsement should be inferred.

References

Amarel, S. (1968). On representations of problems of reasoning about actions. In D. Michie (Ed.), *Machine intelligence. Vol 3.* (pp. 131-171). Edinburgh, UK: Edinburgh University Press.

Anderson, J. R. (1981). Tuning of search of the problem space for geometry proofs. *Proceedings of the Seventh International Joint Conference on Artificial Intelligence* (pp. 165-170). Vancouver, Canada: University of British Columbia.

Kaplan, C. A. & Simon, H. A. (in press). In search of insight. *Cognitive Psychology.*

Keane, M. (1988). *Analogical problem solving.* New York, NY: Wiley.

Koedinger, K. R. & Anderson, J. R. (in press). Abstract planning and perceptual chunks: Elements of expertise in geometry. *Cognitive Science.*

Korf, R. E. (1985). *Learning to solve problems by searching for macro-operators.* Marshfield, MA: Pittman.

Langley, P. & Jones, R. (1988). A computational model of scientific insight. In R. J. Sternberg (Ed.), *The nature of creativity. Contemporary psychological perspectives* (pp. 177-201). Cambridge, MA: Cambridge University Press.

Montgomery, H. (1988). Mental models and problem solving: Three challenges to a theory of restructuring and insight. *Scandinavian Journal of Psychology, 29,* 85-94.

Newell, A. & Simon, H. A. (1972). *Human problem solving.* Englewood Cliffs, NJ: Prentice-Hall.

Ohlsson, S. (1984a). Restructuring revisisted. I. Summary and critique of the Gestalt theory of problem solving. *Scandinavian Journal of Psychology, 25,* 65-78.

Ohlsson, S. (1984b). Restructuring revisited. II. An information processing theory of restructuring and insight. *Scandinavian Journal of Psychology, 25,* 117-129.

Simon, H. A. (1966). Scientific discovery and the psychology of problem solving. In *Mind and cosmos: Essays in contemporary science and philosophy. Vol. III.* (pp. 22-40). Pittsburgh, PA: University of Pittsburgh.

Noticing Opportunities in a Rich Environment

Matthew Brand and Lawrence Birnbaum

Northwestern University
The Institute for the Learning Sciences and
Department of Electrical Engineering and Computer Science
Evanston, Illinois

Abstract

Opportunistic planning requires a talent for noticing plans' conditions of applicability in the world. In a reasonably complex environment, there is a great proliferation of features, and their relations to useful plans are very intricate. Thus, "noticing" is a very complicated affair. To compound difficulties, the need to efficiently perceive conditions of applicability is simultaneously true for the thousands of possible plans an agent might use. We examine the implications of this problem for memory and planning behavior, and present an architecture developed to address it. Tools from signal detection theory and numerical optimization provide the model with a form of learning.

1   The Problem

An agent operating in a rich and rapidly changing environment must constantly monitor the environment as it acts, and be prepared to deal with the opportunities and obstacles as they come up. The need to interact with rather than simply act upon the world presents a large variety of constraints on the computational behavior of a planner. We have tried to use these as guidelines for the design of an architecture for the pusuit of multiple goals and plans in a realtime environment.

A convenient route to the issues involved in realtime multiplanning lies in the colloquial language of opportunism. Our daily life is filled with myriad chances to satisfy or advance our goals. How we fare in the world has much to do with our ability to "notice" opportunities, "seize" them, and make use of them before the "window" of opportunity closes. Each of these idioms points to some of the many constraints that bear upon the design of a realtime multiplanner.

In particular, "noticing" means recognizing useful resources in the complexes of low-level, noisy sensory features available to the planner. Not all resources are worth attention; only those that enable plans which serve active goals. Thus, although "noticing" appears to be a perceptual process, its operation depends on decisions that must be informed by the high level goals of the agent. "Seizing" refers to the overhead of selecting a plan and executing it: choosing amongst competing plans and goals, verifying the opportunity, and assigning additional resources to the plan execution. "Window of opportunity" refers to the transience of opportunities: they have to be discovered and acted upon as suddenly as they appear and the agent may have to deal with their disappearing just as suddenly.

In short, realtime multiplanning presents three general constraints:

- The agent must incorporate an opportunity oriented planner, rather than a one-shot or agenda-oriented planners. However, being opportunity-driven does not mean that its behavior is determined bottom-up from perception: actions and indeed perceptions need to be goal-motivated. This is the *integration* constraint: The planner needs to adjudicate between bottom-up opportunities and top-down desires and expectations (see, e.g. [Birnbaum 86]).

- The agent must perform a quick and efficient mapping from surface features to applicable plans. This is the *time* constraint: The agent must have a fast and fairly constant reaction time in any situation.

- The agent must be constantly replanning as external conditions and internal goals change. This is the *flexibility* constraint: The agent must be prepared at any time to execute, suspend, resume, or abandon a plan in the face of novel circumstances.

These constraints have guide the design decisions that form the system described below.

2 Real-World Constraints

Most compelling in the design of a realtime planner are issues of computational efficiency. The environment will tolerate only a narrow range of reaction times on the part of the agent, and the shorter the better. The agent must move from low-level perceptual features to high-level decision processes in as few steps as possible. Traditional planning tools, especially those based on search, are undesirable because they require indeterminate and exponential time to find or construct applicable plans. An animal does not stop to think how it can relate the sighting of prey to the get-nourishment goal. An efficient alternative to search is matching against rich libraries of planning information. Making this work, however, necessitates unusual commitments vis-à-vis memory, processing, and architecture.

2.1 Memory Issues

In order to be able to recognize which circumstances constitute an opportunity for the inception or resumption of a plan, that plan must already be available–and quite some detail–in the agent's memory. At the very least, it must be present in enough detail for its conditions of applicability to be quickly consulted and compared to the world. This is especially important because of the large number of potentially useful plans. The typical range of activities in an agent's "everyday" behavior will likely require hundreds or thousands of precompiled plans. We call the need to have plans easily consulted the *accessibility* constraint.

Given that we want plans to be tightly coordinated with the perceptual apparatus that cues them, it will prove useful to think of a plan coupled with the computing elements that recognize its conditions of applicability as a unit: a *behavior*. When we talk of a planner endowed with sensors and effectors, we talk of a collection of behaviors which we want

to combine in ways salutary to the planner's goals. As with [Agre 88, Agre & Chapman 87, Firby 89, Maes 89] we are interested in the consequences of reinterpreting the planning task as a matter of *coordination of behaviors* rather then the *synthesis of plans*.

How specific should behaviors be? In any complex environment, behaviors do not have unique conditions of applicability; there is always some generality which cannot be captured in simple lists of features. An animal in a forest need not have one behavior for picking up edibles and another for picking up nesting materials. Having both in memory simply adds computational cost to the task of plan selection, probably more than is saved by simple feature matching. The plans in the agent's repertoire should be flexible, even though this makes recognizing each plan's conditions of applicability in the environment more expensive. There is a tradeoff between ease of opportunity recognition and generality of behaviors.

Schemes for flexible plans come with a number of extra burdens: plan synthesis requires search, plan modification requires extensive knowledge about planning, and abstract plan roles require complicated type checking. All three, however, violate the accessibility constraint. Consequently the planner's memory is strongly biased for ease of matching and against "abstract" or "universal" planning methods.

2.2 Attention Issues

Plans exist for many different time scales. Few are executed *en tous* and without interruption. Many cover spans of time so large that an agent cannot afford to execute them without interruption. For example, one cannot follow the house-building plan without breaks to entertain the eat-and-be-refreshed plan. Some plans are so long-term, such as write-thesis, or of such low priority, such as pick-up-money-from-sidewalk, that more time passes during interruptions than during execution.

Proverbially, we want an agent to be able to "walk and chew gum at the same time." This means dividing attention between many plans that are concurrently being executed, some in parallel, some in dovetailed sequence.

The idea of precompiled plans is helpful here too. If a plan may not be executed *en tous*, then conditions of applicability need be computed not only for its beginning, but at any point where it may be interrupted and later resumed. The more concrete the description of the plan, the less costly this calculation is.

The possibility of interruption also argues for plans that are as short as possible. Rather than try to execute a full plan for building a shelter, a agent will find it easier to have a building plan broken down into its component behaviors, which it can splice together as their conditions of applicability become true in the environment. This has a number of advantages for the planner. Breaking a plan into fragments provides convenient interruption points with precomputed requirements for resumption. Plan fragments can be recombined and reordered according to the vagaries of environmental change.[1]

3   Architecture

In perceiving the world, the agent should calculate an optimal set of features for its purposes–meaning it should compute as few features as possible to identify applicable plans and choose between them. Features should only be computed when necessary *vis-à-vis* likely plans, and when necessary to many plans, a feature should only be computed once.

An efficient architecture which addresses the two priorities of shared computation of features and arbitrary mappings is a feed-forward network. Low-level features pass their information up to increasingly complex features which in turn cue and re-cue candidate plans. This opens the door to parallelism. However, we cannot assume that the "magic" of massive parallelization will somehow make this network tractable. Limited resources mean that a limited number of features can be computed at any given time.

Optimization in this context means making choices about which nodes in the network will receive computational resources, and which will have to remain dormant. Dormancy means that the feature retains its old value, and is increasingly likely to become incorrect as the environment changes. We wish to construct a description of how efficiently the network is using its features (and thus retrieving appropriate plans). Any network control strategy that

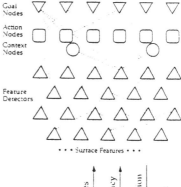

Schematic of Network Architecture

Goal Nodes

Action Nodes

Context Nodes

Feature Detectors

• • • Surface Features • • •

Information flow: Values Accuracy Activation Cost

Figure 1: Connectivity and information flow in the planning network.

optimizes that function will thus provide a means for intelligent attention focusing.

We have arranged the knowledge sources of our planner in a network for this purpose (see figure 1). Each node represents a kind of computation the planner can do: either computing a feature of executing a plan step. The links between nodes are pathways through which nodes interact, passing information and competing and cooperating to control the effectors and computational resources of the agent.

4   Representation

There are four basic types of knowledge in the agent: goals, action sequences, feature detectors, and memory pools. Between them pass three kinds of information: values, accuracy estimates, and activation.

4.1   Information Flow in the Planner

Values are scalars that are passed up from lower-level nodes to higher-level nodes. They indicate whether the feature computed by some node was present in the world last time the node was computed.

Accuracy estimates are scalars indicating how likely it is that a feature has been computed using obsolete information. Features can be inaccurate because subfeatures they depend upon may have been dormant while something in the world has changed. Accuracy estimates flow up the network along with values, and are reduced as they pass through each obsolete node.

Activation, also a scalar, flows down through the network over weighted connections. It is used to determine what parts of the network should be computed. Essentially, the activation at a node is an indicator of how interested the planner is in committing computational resources to it.

4.2 Knowledge Structures in the Planner

At the top of the network, goals provide the impetus behind the agent's choices. They are not predicates describing world states, as is the tradition in planning. Rather they are generators that supply activity to the action sequences which satisfy them and the features which recognize conditions in which they are satisfied.

Feature detectors are arbitrary functions which read in sensory data and/or other feature values and output a value indicating some state of affairs in the environment and the planner.

Action nodes encapsulate planning knowledge. Moving upwards, they signal their execution status to the goals that they serve, inhibiting or satisfying them. Moving downwards, they pass activation on to the feature detectors that correspond to their preconditions, priming them. From goal nodes they receive activation, and from feature detectors they receive information about their applicability. As the agent monitors the world, each action node jockeys for the right to determine the next action.

There is no basic unit of plan representation inside an action node node. Instead, these nodes hold plan fragments, single operators, and occasionally even entire canned plans.

Plans and plan fragments are expressed wholly in terms of effector instructions. There is no explicit representation of subgoals, else the planner would have to resort to search. Although this would seem to severely limit the potential sophistication of the plans the agent can express, we are take hope from two hypotheses. The first is that a large range of interesting and useful behaviors *can* be achieved under this limitation—perhaps even enough for a reasonable simulation of animal behavior.

The second is that where subgoaling really is necessary, we may expect subgoaling-like behavior in the way the agent sequences its behaviors. The reason why is that, should action node A need a precondition achieved, it will prime the feature detectors that are looking for satisfying conditions in the world. If action node B has those feature detectors as a description of what it achieves, and they are partially true, node B is likely to be executed opportunistically. Once this has happened, node A's preconditions have been satisfied, and it will be executed. Though not dependable, this scenario points a way to rudimentary subgoaling.

Memory pools are frozen contexts. Each name a plan in execution, the goal it serves, and the resources that are tied to the various roles in the plan. They point to the feature detectors that recognize their role fillers. In a carpenter's attach plan, for example, roles might be Object1, Object2, SupportingSurface, MeansOfAttachment, ClampingDevice, and Tool. Their fillers could be, respectively, a broken chair, its leg, a clear space of floor, wood glue, rope, and the right hand.

Memory pools are used to ensure that a plan can be continued. They are quite expensive, and tend to evaporate after time. This is because an agent must have a means of forgetting thwarted plans after some passage of time, in order to be reasonably free to exploit new opportunities.

5 Process Model

The steps of a typical planning cycle are:

- Choose the features to be recomputed.
- Recompute features.
- Propogate information throught the network.
- Choose an action node to control effectors.
- Execute one instruction from the node's plan fragment.
- Construction, update, or activate a memory pool to hold the current context.

The important steps in this cycle are the selection steps. These choices govern the agent's external and internal attention, and are governed by the parameters which flow through the network.

In addition to the three parameters described above—value, activation and accuracy—each node has a stationary parameter: cost. It represents the computation expense associated with that node, and is used to determine when the feature is worth recomputing. Low-level features, which are worth computing often because they are close to sensory information and are the basis for all other computation, are assigned low costs. High-level features, which are in a sense more speculative, are assigned high costs. In this way the network is biased to pay close attention to the environment.

How is the distribution of computation question decided? In the case of feature detector nodes, the feature is recomputed if

$$f(n) = \frac{activation_n - cost_n}{1 - accuracy_n} > T_F$$

where T_F is a global threshhold.[2] This equation expresses the main economy of feature computation. It simply ensures that the features are recomputed when they receive large amounts of activation or are very likely to be obsolete. A similar function $F(n)$, governs action nodes and memory nodes.

The purpose behind these parameters, besides providing the basis for interaction between knowledge sources, is to allow the planner to judge what is worth computing. The basic premise is that some kinds of computation are more expensive than others. Passing the parameters around the network and calculating $f(n)$ and $F(n)$ are cheap; we pretend that they are properties of some imaginary computational substrate. More importantly, they happen in constant time, regardless of the agent's circumstances. Actually computing the features also takes constant time, because a fixed fraction of the network is considered.

Computing the features is held to be more expensive than propagating information, and thus we limit the number that are computed each cycle. This is not just to conserve computation: if too many feature nodes are active, too many action nodes that will merit consideration. Thus as features receive inadequate activation they report increasingly obsolete information, and decay to an off-state, in which they are incapable of supporting any action node's bid for execution.

An action node is queued for evaluation if $F(n) = f(n) + K \cdot s(n) > T_A$, where K is a global coefficient,[3]

[2]T_F controls what fraction of the network's features are recomputed in any given cycle. A higher threshhold makes the agent like a panicked animal; it needs to respond very quickly and thus can only attend to its most immediate goals and sensations. A lower threshhold makes the agent slower, but more alert to uncommon opportunities.

[3]K allows us to balance the relative importance of need, expressed by activation, and opportunity, expressed by sensory information.

$s(n)$ is a weighted vote of precondition features for that node, and T_A is another global threshhold like T_F. The node with greatest $F(n)$ is picked out of the queue, its role bindings verified, and the first unexecuted operator in it is used to control the effectors. If the role fillers fail to verify, that node can be "suspended" by construction of a memory pool, or a different node can be taken off the queue. Only a fixed number of nodes are checked, and the queue is discarded after each cycle.

Action selection is also constant in time relative to the input, and is logarithmic in the size of the network. Cycle time is thus constant, and adjustable via the two global threshholds T_F and T_A.

When the current action node is usurped by a node with greater $F(n)$, it is suspended. A memory pool is set up for it which saves the context at time of suspension. This memory pool is treated like an action node in subsequent cycles: it receives activation from the action node's sponsor goal, it is queued and evaluated like action nodes, and when it is selected the action node it is attached to resumes execution. Memory pools have a decay term in their $F(n)$ which grows increasingly negative with time, making their resumption less and less likely. When their $F(n)$ itself becomes negative, they "evaporate" and the planner loses any trace of having been in the midst of their plans.

6 Learning

Optimization is plausible in our architecture because the flow of information is restricted to specific pathways between knowledge structures, greatly simplifying credit assignment, and because information is restricted to scalars, allowing us to construct a mathematical characterization of the network's performance.

In the network, goals are served both by feature detectors, which report goal satisfaction and action nodes, which attempt goal satisfaction. Using the feature detectors as reference signals, it is easy to collect statistics on an action node's success *vis-à-vis* its sponsoring goal. The first optimization open to us is to strengthen the weights on activation links between goals nodes and the action nodes that most reliably serve them. This allows local improvements in the ability to select plans.

A more subtle and important optimization applies to the relationship between action nodes and pressed by sensory information.

the feature nodes that detect their conditions of applicability. Here it is important to learn which features best cue an action node, and thus are most deserving of the activation that the action node can distribute. Here we use some simple tools from signal detection theory [Tanner, Swets, & Green 56, Green & Swets 66] to provide a platform from which we can do numerical optimization.

By comparing records of feature node firings with the statistics described above, we can tabulate the feature's utility (via the plan fragment) to the goal in terms of hits $p(F \cdot A)$, false alarms $p(\neg F \cdot A)$, misses $p(F \cdot \neg A)$, and correct rejections $p(\neg F \cdot \neg A)$. F refers the the presence of the feature and A refers to the decision to take an action on the basis of that feature.

From the costs and activation assigned to each node we can construct a payoff matrix. Using these and the statistics described above, we can adapt from signal detection theory the equation describing the expected value of relying upon that feature:

$$EV = W_{A \to F} p(F \cdot A) + C_A p(F \cdot \neg A) +$$
$$C_F p(\neg F \cdot A) + C_G p(\neg F \cdot \neg A) \quad (1)$$

In this notation, $W_{A \to F}$ is the weight on the activation link from the action node to the feature node, C_A is the fixed cost of evaluating the action node, C_F is the fixed cost of the feature node, and C_G is a global cost assessed for missing opportunities.

By toggling $W_{A \to F}$ between two close values and collecting statistics on the relative values of EV, we discover local information about the first derivative of the actual probability curve relating feature firing to plan appropriateness.[4] For local hillclimbing, we can simply choose to remain with the value of $W_{A \to F}$ that produces the greater EV.

More interesting is the case when we apply a global optimization technique. We are investigating the use of simulated annealing [Kirkpatrick, Gelatt & Vecchi 83] in the selection of weights. Under simulated annealing, one chooses one value of $W'_{A \to F}$ over another $W_{A \to F}$ with the probability

$$e^{-\frac{EV' - EV}{T}}$$

for some temperature T which determines the "volatility" of the decision. This is a particularly

---

[4]There is a strong assumption of Gaussian noise in the functioning of the network in order for this to work. We can rely on the obsolescence of some features for noise, but it is not clear that it will approximate a Gaussian.

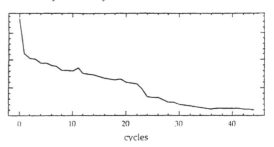

Symmetry on a 4-unit Retina

Figure 2: Error curve of a primitive variant of the optimization algorithm applied to learning symmetry in a 4-bit vector.

interesting prospect because we may be able to regulate the temperature of the annealing decisions as a function of the accuracy reported at the nodes involved.

Simulated annealing is appropriate here because it allows us to globally optimize the interactions between "opaque" functions. By "opaque" we mean that the functions in the nodes are arbitrary, and we cannot expect to have information about their first derivatives (especially if they are symbolic!) as in backpropagation, or have the time to reason about their internal structure (since we have no search).

We have been experimenting with this optimization scheme in miniature systems, as a prelude to committing to it with a full realtime multiplanner. Our first miniature merely tested the ability of the algorithm to select connections between nodes computing miscellaneous functions in order to detect symmetry in a vector of bit-values. The network was seven layers deep, and included both numeric and logical (symbolic) functions indiscriminately connected as start. The learning curve is shown in figure 2.

We are currently working on a miniature which, given the operators toggle-bit and swap-bits, will learn how to make the vector symmetrical with a minimal number of operators.

7 Determining the Content of the Nodes

AI systems that move away from "universal" methods such as search depend heavily on well-chosen and well-organized knowledge to compensate for their limited power. Especially crucial in our variety of planner are the repertoire of plans, how they are broken up into planning fragments for storage in action nodes, and features which serve these nodes. The planner designer must steer a course between plan fragments that are too general to be served by any reasonable set of features, and plan fragments that are so specific that each one requires its own special set of features. Ideally, we would like to have moderately general plan fragments that can be cued by relatively low-level features.

How to organize and mediate between behaviors is an open question in agent-based architectures. Architectures such as the Society of Mind [Minsky 86] and Subsumption Architectures [Brooks, Connell, & Peter Ning, 88] rely upon the idea of increasingly sophisticated layers of behavior, each higher layer handling circumstances that are too subtle or complicated for the layer below. We have avoided this layering approach for two reasons. First, the low-level process model of our architecture already mediates between competing behaviors. Second, layering clouds the prospects of an implicit ideal of these systems: that behaviors can be added or altered without having to modify all other behaviors already in the system.

In looking for an organizing principle for the construction of our behavior corpus, we are more concerned with the retrieval issues discussed above. An insight that we find useful in the selection of plan fragments is the following line of reasoning:

- Plan fragments can be classified by strategy, for example, *hoard, assume availability of item*, or *wait until item is more accessible*.

- Strategies in turn can be organized by resource types, for example, *perishable, permanent, core*, or *self-replicating*.

- Resource types often correlate with relatively low-level features, for example *is-food* with perishable resources, *is-moving* with time-specific resources, or *is-anchored* with location-specific resources.

Consequently, there is a useful link between relatively low-level features and highly abstract characterizations of plans. To exploit this in the design of our planner, we are collecting a set of low-level features which effectively organize a list of strategy-types we would expect a forest animal to use. These features are then used to group a corpus of plan frag-ments. Within each group we then determine which middle-level features would be necessary to distinguish between plan fragments, and which additional features are necessary to identify possible fillers for plan preconditions. Thus we are able to produce a full specification of the features an agent would need to compute, given an environment.

8 Problems and Acts of Faith

A realtime multiplanner is capable of acting in constant time because of the severe limitations we have placed on its means of computation. Many of these are inspired by the challenges of a real, volatile world. Others stem from the need to work around the lack of a "universal" computational mechanism. Although this planner may prove to be a good set of commitments in view of the environmental demands, it is not ideal. There are several useful properties of search-based projective planners which realtime multiplanning lacks.

8.1 Labelling is Hard

Naming is hard for an agent that doesn't have labels supplied to it by the environment or tutor (e.g. "the red block"). Naming not only presumes that the agent has a category for an object it encounters, but that it has some basis for distinguishing the object from other category exemplars it may encounter, even if this is the first such object it has ever seen. This means it has to know what is unique about the object with respect to other possible exemplars of the category. Without this ability to discriminate within categories, the agent is incapable of powers such as object permanence. The agent may often begin a task with one object, be interrupted, and continue the task with another object in the same role, oblivious to the change. This is disastrous if, for example, the agent is building its shelter, stops, and resumes in another place, completing the shelter of a rival.

One possible solution lies in more detailed descriptions of contexts in a memory pools. Presumably there are some features which are not important to an object's role in the plan, but distinguish it both from other objects in the same category and from the larger scene in which it was noticed. A fairly reliable example of this kind of distinguishing feature is location.

8.2 Planning without Protections

Most conspicuous of our planner's shortcomings is a lack of protections. The extreme parsimony in use of variables, the difficulty of labelling, and the sheer number of plans that may be simultaneously active all make checking for protection violations prohibitive. Every time the planner selects a plan it is making resource commitments: effectors in the short term and objects in the environment in the long term. When the planner suspends a plan it does not forfeit those commitments. But it *doesn't* check to see if any of those commitments are violated by subsequent plan inceptions. This would be too expensive, checking every resource against every plan. It is easy to imagine an agent picking up a tool and then promptly putting it down because it saw another, and then picking up the first again.

There are two reasons why a lack of protections may not be a stumbling block. The first is a variation on the Friendly World Assumption: in most environments the range of useful plans makes little use of protections, and where protection violations lead to trouble, the environment will soon change so that only one of the plans competing for the resource is still applicable.

The second we may call the Underspecification Assumption: many goals which seem to require protections need them only because they contain too little information in their specification. The classic example, stack block A on block B and block B on block C, would be beyond our agent. The stack two blocks plan fragment would put A back on B every time the agent figured to clear B to put it on C . However, a plausible real-world alternative, stack-the-blocks-in-size-order, is easily handled by repeated executions of the put-the-biggest-free-block-on-the-pile plan fragment.

9 Acknowledgements

This work was supported in part by the Defense Advanced Research Projects Agency and monitored by the Air Force Office for Scientific Research under contract number F49620-88-C-0058, and in part by a National Science Foundation Graduate Fellowship. The Institute for the Learning Sciences was established in 1989 with the support of Andersen Consulting, part of The Arthur Andersen Worldwide Organization.

References

[Agre 88] P. Agre. *The Dynamic Structure of Everyday Life.* PhD Thesis, MIT Department of Electrical Engineering and Computer Science, 1988. Available as Report AI-TR 1085.

[Agre & Chapman 87] Philip E. Agre and David Chapman. Pengi: An Implementation of a Theory of Activity. In *Proceedings of AAAI-87*, 1987.

[Birnbaum 86] L. Birnbaum *Integrated Processing in Planning and Understanding.* PhD Thesis, Yale University Computer Science Department, 1986. Available as Report RR-489.

[Brooks, Connell, & Peter Ning, 88] Rodney Brooks, Jonathon Connell, and Peter Ning, Herbert. A second generation mobile robot, AI Memo 1016, MIT Artificial Intelligence Laboratory, 1988.

[Firby 89] R. James Firby. *Adaptive Execution in Compplex Dynamic Worlds.* PhD Thesis, Yale University Computer Science Department, 1989. Available as Report RR-672.

[Green & Swets 66] David M. Green and John A. Swets. *Signal detection theory and psychophysics.* New York: J. Wiley & Sons. 1966.

[Kirkpatrick, Gelatt & Vecchi 83] Scott Kirkpatrick, C. D. Gelatt, Jr., and M. P. Vecchi. Optimization by simulated annealing. *Science* 220:671-680. 1983.

[Maes 89] Pattie Maes. The Dynamics of Action Selection. In *Proceedings, IJCAI-89.* 1989.

[Minsky 86] Marvin Minsky. *The Society of Mind,* New York: Simon and Schuster, 1986.

[Tanner, Swets, & Green 56] W. P. Tanner, Jr., J. A. Swets, and D. M. Green. Some general properties of the hearing mechanism. University of Michigan: Electronic Defense Group, 1956. Technical Report No. 30.

Recognizing Novel Uses for Familiar Plans

Beth Adelson[1]
Dept. of Computer Science
Tufts University
Medford, MA 02155
adelson@tufts.cs.edu

Abstract

Analogical design and invention is a central task in human cognition. Often during the process the designer/inventor gets stuck; backs off from the problem; and only later, after having put the problem aside, discovers that some familiar plan can be used in a novel way to solve the problem. We describe a system which uses a causal *case memory* to check the side effects, preconditions, etc. of incoming events in order to model this phenomenon.

The method used makes this work relevant to case-based reasoning as well as design. It also forms a companion issue to execution-time planning.

1   Motivation

Analogical design/invention is a task which arises continually. Sometimes the task occurs in a form so simple as to pass almost unnoticed, as when picnickers find they have forgottten their knives. Sometimes the task requires intense and extended effort, as when computer engineers find they must develop a new architecture. Difficulty notwithstanding, the scenario often runs as follows: the designer finds that the tack he has been taking is not producing the desired solution; finding he is stuck, he puts the problem aside; he then recognizes in some later situation, that a familiar device, instrument or plan can be used in a novel way to solve the problem.

Problem Statement:
This scenario of the design process implies that cognitively based design systems need a mechanism that allows the recognition of situations that can contribute to the attainment of goals which previously could not be fulfilled.

The problem we are addressing is related to the problem of *execution-time planning*, in which a planning system needs to be able to recognize conditions that unblock previously blocked goals even though the system cannot predict when those conditions will occur (Hammond, 1989; Alterman, 1988; Firby, 1987; Georgeff & Lansky, 1987; Simmons & Davis, 1987). Hammond describes such a system in his work on *opportunistic memory* (1989): His system

---

[1]This work was funded by Carnegie-Mellon's NSF funded EDRC and by a grant from NSF's Engineering Directorate.

contains a detailed taxonomy of the conditions under which goals which were blocked for various reasons might later be fulfilled. As a result, under Hammond's model when a goal is blocked it is suspended and memory is tagged for the conditions which might allow its satisfaction. When these conditions are later encountered, becuase of the tags placed in memory, they are recognized as unblocking conditions and the goal is reactivated[2] and then pursued.

Design systems face a somewhat different problem. They need to recognize conditions that will contribute to goal satisfaction even though they can predict neither when the conditions will occur, nor what the conditions will be. In this paper we describe the mechanism we have developed for addressing this recognition problem. The mechanism is one that considers the implications (side effects, etc.) of well-known plans in order to discover their relevance to blocked goals. The effect of the mechanism is that the system is able to recognize novel uses for familiar plans.

2 The Need for Recognizing Plans During Design

2.1 Previous work: Debugging analogically acquired plans

We are developing our recognition mechanism in the context of our work on analogical learning and analogical design. We began by concentrating on analogical debugging. This work then led us to our current concern with recognition.

Our initial system (Adelson, 1989a&b) was developed to acquire plans for programming operations such as **pop**, **push** and **sort**. The plans took the form of executable models. This allowed the plans to be used in either of two ways: They could be run for purposes of debugging; or they could drive a module that generated both code and box-and-arrow drawings (Adelson, 1989a&b; Burstein & Adelson, 1987; Burstein and Adelson, in press).

As described on page 3, when the plans were being used for debugging they were passed to a mechanism that, via simulation, identified functionally analogous plan entities in the more and less familiar base and target domains. This entailed addressing: 1. The role of causal reasoning; and 2. The use of target domain knowledge in analogical learning.

When the plans were being used for debugging they were passed to a mechanism that, via simulation, identified entities in the target domain that were functionally analogous to entities in the original base domain plan[3]. This entailed addressing: 1. The role of causal reasoning; and 2. The use of target domain knowledge in analogical learning.

In addition to producing programming plans, the system has modeled Edison's description of modifying the phonograph to produce the kinetoscope and Morse's account of developing

---

[2]Hammond's model has the advantage of allowing goals to be quiescent during their suspension. Additionally, because of its detail, Hammond's indexing scheme results in both a high rate for hits, and a low rate for false alarms.

[3]The base and target domains are the more and less familiar domains. The reason for identifying functionally analogous entities is that one purpose of analogical debugging is to find target domain entities that should replace base domain entities in order to produce a model appropriate to the target domain.

telegraphic relay stations (Brian, 1926; Okagaki & Koslowski, 1987)[4].

Example: Morse's telegraphic relay station

The debugging behavior we have previously focussed on and the recognition behavior we turn to here are illustrated by the following example (Okagaki & Koslowski, 1987):

> Initially, in trying to transmit telegraphic signals across significant distances Morse tried the strategy of building successively stronger generators. He found however, that the signals still degraded with distance. The solution to the problem came to him in the following way. While riding on a train, he happened to look out of the window and notice a Pony Express depot, at which horses were being fed and watered. Morse realized that the *relay station* strategy constituted a solution to the telegraph problem as well.

There are two interesting pieces of reasoning in this example, recognizing that the Pony Express offers a useful analogical model; and then modifying the Pony Express model to fit the telegraphy domain. First we describe the modification performed by our system's debugger (Adelson, 1989a & in press) and then we go on to describe our recognition mechanism.

The debugger

In modifying the Pony Express model to fit the telegraphy domain, the system determines, via simulation (Schank & Riesbeck, 1989; Falkenhainer, Forbus & Gentner, 1988; Hammond, 1989a; Simmons & Davis, 1987), the causal effects produced by the use of horses traveling between relay stations (the information in the message can successfully be sent a long distance as a result of the medium of conveyance being repeatedly refreshed at each leg of the journey). In an attempt to construct a mechanism that will reproduce this effect in the target domain, the system again uses simulation to identify already existing appropriate pieces of mechanism in the target domain; ones that could be used in a larger schema for repeatedly refreshing and sending information short distances. This results in the system producing a model in which the existing generators are arranged in series at appropriate intervals.

3 Recognizing the analogy

As mentioned above, in order to produce the model of generators arranged in series, Morse must first recognize that the relay station strategy employed by his competitors can serve as a model for the telegraph problem. We propose a mechanism that accounts for this class of recognition phenomenon, in which it is noticed that a familiar case in memory; a plan, operation or device, can serve a purpose that is radically different from those which it has previously served. In essence, the mechanism is one in which the changing environment is examined for opportunities which allow the fulfillment of blocked goals (Birnbaum & Collins, 1984; Birnbaum & Selfridge, 1981). In this scheme, a blocked goal is placed on a list with other goals that have also been suspended because they were blocked. The system then sets about to parse any incoming plan in order to determine if the plan can unblock it[5].

---

[4]Although these may not be completely accurate accounts of particular discoveries, they persist because they are accurate accounts of our *experience* of the discovery process.

[5]Along with others any others already on this list.

At a very general level, under this model Morse realizes that the relay station strategy will meet his need because as he backs off from his plan of building stronger generators he starts looking at the features of other plans and assessing their utility in unblocking his goal. That is, when he encounters the Pony Express station he notices that it has the effect of sending messages long distances and so recognizes it as a plan that meets his goal.

The next section provides a detailed description of how this phenomenon is captured in our system. We begin with an overview of the system's function.

4   The Recognition Mechanism

4.1   System Function

Our system is designed to monitor the environment for plans which will be useful in satisfying blocked goals. In doing so the system takes the following steps:

1. Detecting and saving blocked goals:
   When the system is unsuccessful in meeting a goal, the goal is placed on a BLOCKED GOAL LIST.

2. Monitoring the environment for opportunities:
   The system then begins to evaluate events in the environment[6] in terms of their relevance to the blocked goal. In order to do so the system uses an EVENT LEXICON which can be thought of as a memory for causal relations. The EVENT LEXICON stores features of previously encountered events such as intended effects, side effects, etc.

   Because the system is looking at these effects to see if they fulfill a blocked goal, and therefore should be reproduced, each effect has a pointer to a plan which if run would give rise to the effect. That is, an event may produce a side effect which matches the desired effect of the blocked goal and if it does the system can reproduce the side effect in order to meet the blocked goal.

   The monitoriing process has two parts:

   (a) Parsing incoming events:
       When an event occurs, the system retreives the representation of that event from the EVENT LEXICON, instantiates it and places the instantiated representation in the system's short term memory.

   (b) Testing potential opportunities:
       The system now matches the features of the retrieved event representation against the blocked goal in order to see if some feature of the event will help in unblocking the goal (Hammond, 1989). If a match is found, the plan indexed under the feature is retreived.

---

[6]Events are provided as input to the system.

3. Seizing the opportunities:
   At this point the goal is removed from the BLOCKED GOAL LIST. The plan satisfying the goal can now be instantiated and run. If the plan, when run, meets the goal it will be indexed under the goal in the system's PLAN MEMORY.

4.2 The Morse Example

In the Morse example this translates into the following steps:

1. Detecting and saving blocked goals:
   The system is given the goal shown just below, of sending a telegraph message over a long distance:

```
(GOAL: send
       (OBJECT:  message
(TYPE: telegraph signal))
       (DISTANCE: >1,000 mi.))
```

   The system finds that the goal cannot be satisfied by any of the existing plans in the system's PLAN MEMORY. The goal is therefore placed on the BLOCKED GOAL LIST.

2. Monitoring the environment for opportunities:
   The system is then given a set of inputs representing the objects and events Morse encounters during the train ride: The indifferent dinner in the dining car, the elaborately feathered bonnet of his compartment mate, and the Pony Express relay station which he sees as he looks out the window[7].

   (a) Parsing incoming events:
       The system retreives its representation of the events from its EVENT LEXICON. The representations are instantiated and placed in the system's short term memory.

   (b) Testing potential opportunities:
       The system then finds that SIDE EFFECT1 in the representation for the Pony Express matches the blocked goal.

       Representation for Pony Express:

```
(EVENT: Pony Express
(GOAL: deliver mail)
(PRECONDITIONS: (...)...(...))
(SIDE EFFECTS:
       (SIDE EFFECT1: send
           (OBJECT:  message
```

---

[7]Not all inputs are given equal attention. We discuss the differences in attention given to different inputs in the context of the system's attention mechanism in Section 4.3 below.

```
(TYPE: mail))
                    (DISTANCE: >1,000 mi.)
                    (CAUSED-BY-PLAN: relay stations)))

(INTENDED EFFECTS: (...)...(...)))
```

That is, looking at the sbove EVENT LEXICON representation of the Pony Express, the system determines that through the use of relay stations, the Pony Express has the effect of sending messages across long distances.

3. Seizing the opportunities:
The system retreives the RELAY STATION plan indexed under SIDE EFFECT1 and passes it to the system to be run[8]. The plan is found to satisfy the goal and so it is indexed under the goal in the system's PLAN MEMORY.

4.2.1 Range of Examples: Einstellung and Archimedes

Our system has also been used to model a result representative of the results obtained in the classic gestalt *einstellung* experiments.

The example is as follows (Meyer, 1977):

> Experimental Situation: A subject is shown into an otherwise bare laboratory, in which two cords are suspended from a ceiling and a hammer has been left on the windowsill. The subject is asked to tie the ends of the two cords together, however the distance between the cords is great enough that the ends of the cords cannot be brought together simply by grasping the first one and walking towards the second.
>
> Result: The problem can be solved by tying the hammer to the end of the first string and then using the hammer as a pendulum to swing the first string towards the second.
>
> Often subjects do not hit upon the solution themselves, In these instances the experimenter walks by one of the strings and 'accidentally' sets it in motion. This hint invariably allows the subject to solve the problem.

Our noticing mechanism, in modelling the above result, offers an account of the processes behind the insights which occur in these experiments. Under our model, at the outset of the experiment no plan for tying ropes which are more than an arm's length apart resides in memory. The subject gets stuck and the goal is placed on the BLOCKED GOAL LIST. When the rope swing occurs an underlying representation of the event is retreived. This is where the insight occurs; the representation of the rope swing contains bringing the ropes together as a side effect. Because this side effect matches the desired effect the rope swing is perceived as a solution to the problem. The retrieved representation also points to the

---

[8]Because the retreived plan is an analog to the one actually being sought it will be modified by the system's debugger before it is run.

258

'pendulum plan' which can reproduce the effect. When the plan is retreived, the hammer is seen as an appropriate weight for the pendulum.

This account includes an explanation of how in these situations problem-solvers come to see the environment differently after they have backed off from the problem-solving (Gick & Holyoak, 1980, 1983).

As a third example, and one which also illustrates the issue of attention, our system models Archimedes' realization that he could calculate the volume of the king's irregularly shaped crown by submerging it in water. Initially, because the system only has plans for calculating volumes of regularly shaped objects, the system places the goal of 'calculating the volume of the irregularly shaped crown' on the BLOCKED GOAL LIST. The system is then given 'Archimedes' bath' as an input event. None of the side effects of bathing: the cooling of the water, the increase in the volume of the tub's contents, etc., match the blocked goal of 'calculating the volume of the irregularly shaped crown'. However, the side effect of the increase in the volume of the tub's contents is treated as promising because it is relevant to the blocked goal's concern with volume. The system therefore pays more attention to it in the form of further processing: The system looks in EVENT MEMORY for the effects of increasing the volume of the tub's contents. It finds that one side effect is that the volume of the object that causes the increase can be obtained by calculating the difference between the new volume and the original. This side effect matches the blocked goal and is treated as a solution to the problem.

4.3 The attention mechanism

What attentional phenomena do we want a discovery system to capture and how should we implement the mechanisms giving rise to them? We have addressed this problem to a limited extent. At minimum we would would want to explain: Why Orville Wright but not Samuel Morse would notice a feathered bonnet; and why Morse certainly and Wright only perhaps would notice the Pony Express[9]. Although it is for a different reason, we also want to explain why Archimedes would notice the implications of the rise in water level but would not bother to trace the implications of the water cooling. In summary, we want to explain the fact that things which are either psychologically charged or conceptually relevant may receive more attention.

In order to model these effects we have implemented the system so that it does more retrieval if an event looks relevant to a blocked goal in either of these ways. That is, if an event mentions a competitor or a mentor the features not only of the event, but also, if needed, of the event's effects will be retrieved from memory and examined by the system. Additionally, as illustrated in the Archimedes example, if a feature of an event is conceptually relevant to the blocked goal the features of the feature will be retrieved and examined. As a result, we have made a first pass at attentional issues.

---

[9]At the time the Pony Express was Morse's competition.

5   Summary and Relevance to other Research

Analogical design and invention is a central task in human cognition. In our system a causal *case memory* is used to check the side effects, preconditions, etc. of incoming events, this allows the system to put familiar plans to use in novel ways. This can account for the reasoning that often is needed in analogical design and invention.

In addition to the relevance of our work to case-based reasoning, our design task is a companion task to execution time-planning. In execution-time planning, a planning system needs to be able to recognize conditions that unblock previously blocked goals even though the system cannot predict when those conditions will occur (Hammond, 1989; Hammond, Converse, & Marks, 1988; Kolodner, Simpson, & Sycara-Cyranski, 1985). Design systems need to recognize conditions that will contribute to goal satisfaction even though they can predict neither when the conditions will occur, nor what the conditions will be. It is our hope that the mutual relevance of these tasks will motivate work on the integration of design, cased-based reasoning and planning systems.

6   References

Adelson, Beth. Cognitive modeling: Uncovering how designers design. *The Journal of Engineering Design.*. Vol 1,1. 1989.

Adelson, B. The role of model-based reasoning in analogical learning. *Proceedings of the IJCAI-89 Workshop on Model-Based Reasoning.*

Adelson, B. Characterizing the nature of analogical reasoning. In Design Theory and Methodology. M. Waldron (Ed.). Springer-Verlag. NY. In press.

Alterman, R. Adaptive planning. *Cognitive Science*, Winter, 1988.

Birnbaum, L. and Selfridge, M. In *Inside Computer Understanding.* 1981. Erlbaum, Hillsdale:NJ.

Birnbaum, L. and Collins, G. Opportunistic Planning and Freudian Slips.

Brian, George. Edison: *The man and his work.* Knopf: Garden City, NY. 1926

Burstein, M. and Adelson, B. Mapping and Integrating Partial Mental Models. *Proceedings of the Tenth Annual Meeting of the Cognitive Science Society,* 1987.

Burstein, M. and Adelson, B. Analogical Reasoning for Learning. in *Applications of Artificial Intelligence to Educational Testing.* R. Freedle (Ed.) In press. Erlbaum: Hillsdale, NJ.

Firby, R.J. An investigation into reactive planning in complex domains. In: *Proceedings of the Sixth National Conference on Artificial Intelligence,* Seattle, Washington, July 1987.

Georgeff, M.P.& Lansky, A.L. Reactive reasoning and planning. In: *Proceedings of the Sixth National Conference on Artificial Intelligence,* Seattle, Washington, July 1987.

Hammond, K. Opportunistic Memory. *Proceedings of the Machine Learning Workshop,* 1989.

Hammond, K. *Case-based planning: Viewing planning as a memory task.* Academic Press, Cambridge, Massachusetts, 1989.

Hammond, K., Converse, T., & Marks, M. Learning from opportunities: Storing and reusing execution-time optimizations. In: *Proceedings of the Seventh National Conference on Artificial Intelligence,* St. Paul, Minnesota, August 1988.

Kolodner, J. In *Proceedings of the Seventh Annual Conference of the Cognitive Science Society.* Boulder, CO: Cognitive Science Society, 1985.

Kolodner, J.L., Simpson, R.L., & Sycara-Cyranski, K. A process model of case-based reasoning in problem solving. In: *Proceedings of the Ninth International Joint Conference on Artificial Intelligence,* Los Angeles, California, August 1985.

Okagaki, L. and Koslowski, B. Another look at analogies and problem-solving. *Journal of Creative Behavior,* 1987, *21*, 1.

Schank, R. and Riesbeck, C. *Inside Computer Understanding.* Erlbaum: Hillsdale, NJ. 1981.

Simmons, R., & Davis, R. Generate, test, and debug: Combining associational rules and causal models. In *Proceedings of the Tenth International Joint Conference on Artificial Intelligence,* Milan, Italy, August 1987.

Planning to Learn

Lawrence Hunter
National Library of Medicine
Bldg 38A, MS-54
Bethesda, MD 20894
HUNTER@NLM.NIH.GOV

Abstract:
The thesis of this paper is that learning is planful, goal-directed activity – that acquiring knowledge is intentional action. I present evidence that learning from one's experiences requires making decisions about what is worth learning, regardless of the specific mechanisms underlying the learning or of the degree of consciousness or automaticity or level of effort of the learning. Decisions about what is worth learning are the expressions of *desires about knowledge*. I then sketch a theory of whence desires for knowledge arise, how they are represented, and how they are used. A taxonomy of learning actions is also proposed. This theory has been partially implemented in two computer models, which are briefly described.

Introduction

The central claim of this paper is that learning is planful, goal-directed activity – that acquiring knowledge is intentional action. If true, this thesis raises the relevance of both action psychology and AI planning to theories of learning. Action psychology (e.g. Tolman (1932) or Frese & Sabini (1985)) is based on the ideas that human behavior is directed towards the accomplishment of goals, that it is directed by plans, that those plans are hierarchically arranged, and that background knowledge and the environment interact in the creation and execution of plans for the guidance of action. As Frese & Sabini observe (p. xxiii) such a view is no doubt a good model of some behaviors and a poor model of others. Here I will try to demonstrate that this view plays an important role in understanding how people and machines learn from complex experiences.

Machine learning research has been dominated by the view that learning is a kind of search (see, e.g., Langley, Gennari & Iba, 1987). I believe that *planning* forms a better foundation than search for learning. In AI, planning is a set of techniques for selecting and combining actions to achieve explicit goals; see, e.g. Sacerdoti, (1971) or Charniak & McDermott (1985). The AI work originally focused on decomposing abstract goals into "primitive" actions expected to achieve the goal given specific resource limitations (such as time and energy). It has since evolved to consider issues such as uncertain environments, managing complex action over time, revising plans during their execution, taking advantage of unexpected opportunities, avoiding unexpected dangers (Birnbaum 1986), and "situating" the planner in the environment generally (Chapman 1985). The goals and actions considered in AI planning are grounded in the physical world. Domains tackled by AI planners thus far include stacking blocks, scheduling deliveries, creating recipes, suggesting battle tactics, and many others. Applying this research to the task of learning requires mapping work on planning in physical domains onto planning in mental domains. That is, a theory of planning to learn must describe the origins and nature of goals to learn, the actions that can be taken to learn, the mental and physical resources those actions contend for, the aspects of the environment that a learner must take into account when planning, and a process for selecting among and combining actions to accomplish the goals, given limited resources and the embedding of the learner in its environment. This paper sketches such a theory.

Learning Requires Decision-making

What is the evidence that learning is goal driven? There are several converging lines of argumentation. The simplest is the widespread use of goal/plan language by people discussing the acquisition of knowledge. "Inquiring minds *want to know*," "prerequisites for courses," and "research strategies" are references to goals, action preconditions and plans (respectively) for gaining knowledge. People can easily enumerate many different kinds of plans for learning, and the situations in which they are appropriate. Some general examples of common plans to learn include: ask an expert, look it up in a book, watch for it in the newspaper, try it yourself and see, wait until it happens again, or even run a scientific experiment. People are also capable of generating a variety of very specific knowledge acquisition plans for commonly occurring knowledge acquisition goal types. For example, when asked how to find Marvin Minksy's home phone number, one person suggested seven different potential plans: try Boston directory assistance, call MIT and ask in the CS department, ask some other senior AI researcher, try the AAAI membership directory, send him email, ask the reporter who interviewed him for Science recently, or call the publisher of *Society of Mind* and ask them. He was also able to rate the likelihood of success of each of these plans, and could suggest general principles about how to get similar information in various circumstances. The widespread use of goal/plan language in describing learning, and the ability of people to easily generate plans when given statements of desired knowledge is, for now, merely anecdotal. A stronger line of argument comes from an analysis of the combinatorics of inductive learning from complex experience.

Inductive inference is limited in at least two ways. First, a recent proof by Deitterich (1989) demonstrated that learning algorithms, very broadly defined, can evaluate only a small proportion of the hypotheses compatible with the experiences they have. That is, there are far more hypotheses consistent with experience than can be distinguished among using that experience. A brief sketch of the proof is as follows: Consider inferential effort required to learn from experience, even in the drastically simplified situation assumed in the PAC-learnablity literature (Valient 1984). This simple task used for computational complexity analyses, involves a learner attempting to induce a subset h of the set of all Boolean n-tuples by processing m distinct examples, where an example is an n-tuple labelled as to its membership in h. There are $2^{(2^n-m)}$ hypotheses that are consistent with the m examples seen so far. That is, each of the 2^n-m possible n-tuples that are not examples could be in h or not. The size of that hypothesis space grows *double exponentially* in the complexity of the experiences. Information in the experiences grows only exponentially in their complexity. Learning by searching a space whose size is proportional to the space of hypotheses consistent with experience is therefore intractable.

The second problem with inductive algorithms stems from the fact that all known machine learning algorithms require time proportional to the number of features that can appear in their inputs, that is, the number of features they can "perceive." Learning systems that take time dependent on the number of perceptable features in the universe will be unable to account for human behavior, and are unlikely to be adequate for applying machine learning to desirable technological tasks (e.g. analyzing data from the human genome project). This is not to say that these algorithms may not prove to explain a *portion* of human learning, but alone they cannot form a sufficient theory.

To see how daunting the problem of learning algorithms that take time proportional to the complexity of their experiences is, consider the complexity of human experience. An order of magnitude estimate of the amount of afferent (incoming) information can be sketched easily: approximately 10^{10}–10^{12} nerve cells in the body, conservatively 1% to 10% of them sensory nerves, each capable of carrying between 100 and 1000 bits per second. Combining to find a very conservative lower bound, humans routinely handle at least $10^{10} \times 10^{-2} \times 10^2 = 10^{10}$ bits per second at their sensory surfaces over their entire (waking) lifetimes, and quite possibly as much as 10^{13} or more bits per second. There is simply more information available in human-like experience than inductive algorithms can handle.

Machine learning theories of induction are not generally proposed as cognitive models of human learning generally (although they are sometimes advanced as models of category formation or categorical perception), and this is one of the reasons. The computational complexity of searching the hypothesis space generated by experiences anywhere near as complex as human experience would take computational power far exceeding even generous estimates of the computational power of the human brain. And since people use extensive background knowledge in learning, the complexity of the search space of is further increased by the interaction between experiences and all of memory. Schank, Collins and Hunter (1986) argued that inductive category formation approaches fails on other pragmatic grounds as well.

It is important to note here that parallelism does not provide a simple solution to these problems. The number of hypotheses consistent with a set of experiences grows *double exponentially* in the complexity of the experiences. Straightforward parallelization of the search through this space would require a number of processors exponential in the complexity of inputs to make this even an exponential time task. For comparison, current artificial neural net technology (e.g. Rummelhart, McClelland & the PDP group, 1986), typically uses a number of processors proportional to the complexity of the inputs; there are typically far fewer hidden nodes than input nodes in these networks, since too many hidden nodes reduces the usefulness of the learning these networks do.

Since the hypothesis space generated by human-like experience is far too large to be searched, even sublinearly, and all induction algorithms take time dependent on the complexity of their inputs, what can people be doing when they learn from their experiences? The inescapable conclusion is that they must somehow drastically restrict the space of hypotheses that they consider during learning. How?

A key first step is the transformation of inputs to more compact representations of experience, capturing the "important" aspects and reducing the amount of "irrelevant" information. This process is hardwired perceptual processing and is likely to be automatic and fast (Fodor, 1985). However, even the transformed representational space will be quite large in systems capable of human-like behavior. It is simply the case that people are sensitive to a very large number of potentially relevant stimuli, and that this large number of "features" is overwhelming to known learning algorithms. So what can be done to restrict the size of *this* space to manageable proportions?

Existing machine learning methods have restricted the size of this space by applying *inductive biases*, e.g. Utgoff (1986), or by *a priori* limitations on the structure of the hypothesis space, through, for example, the use of decision trees or neural networks. These approaches can be considered *syntactic*, in that they constrain the *form* of the hypotheses considered, rather than their content.

I propose that the method of restricting potentially learnable hypotheses for both people and effective machine learning systems should be *content*-based. Explicit characterizations of *desirable knowledge* provide a principled method for restricting the realm of experience and background knowledge considered in learning, and thereby the size of the hypothesis space that must be considered. Having goals specifying what (kind of) knowledge is desirable provides a significant advantage for systems trying to learn from very complex experience.

Why does having explicit knowledge acquisition goals provide an advantage? The idea is to exert the broadest effective top-down constraint on the space of possible concepts to learn. Bidirectional inference, i.e. the ability to use top-down constraints (in this case, goals) as well as bottom-up information (here, processed perceptual data), is the most effective known technique for reducing the size of a space that has to be searched to find desired concepts (Birnbaum 1986).

This claim is consistent with a large body of psychological research on goal direction in selection of focus of attention, particularly from social psychology. Zukier's (1986) review concludes: "Experimental studies have clearly demonstrated that a person will structure and process information quite differently, depending on the future use he or she intends to make of it. Information integration clearly is preceded by future-oriented decision-making processes, which guide data selection and the choice of an appropriate strategy or mode from among the several that are available," (p. 495).

Hoffman, et al (1981) demonstrate that different goal orientations (e.g. "form an impression of a person in the following story" or "remember as much as you can from the following story.") may influence not only to the use of different representations, but also the selection and use of different kinds of information processing. Although the goal orientations tested in that work are quite abstract, they significantly constrain the space of hypotheses consistent with the experimental materials. Srull & Wyer's (1986) results, although divergent in important respects from those of Hoffman, et al, also provide evidence that different goal orientations have a strong effect on learning. These results bear an interesting relationship to the one of the implications that Deitterich (1989) draws from his proof about machine learning algorithms (p. 128):

> [D]ifferent classes of learning problems may call for different learning algorithms. An important problem for future research is to attempt to identify relationships between types of learning problems... and types of hypothesis spaces....

That is, the combinatorics of learning require the selection of learning methods that are appropriate to particular kinds of problems, and goal orientation clearly effects the results of learning. This convergence of evidence from both psychological studies and from computational complexity analysis in machine learning suggests a hypothesis about the control of learning: *Goals about what would be desirable to learn are central to making required decisions about what and how to learn.*

Related Previous Research
Other cognitive theories have also included reference to desires for knowledge, although there are significant differences between those prior theories and the current claims. For example, consider the D-KNOW (delta-knowledge) class of goals, which are part of the conceptual dependency representation proposed by Schank & Abelson (1977). They are goals to "change knowledge state," i.e.

to learn something. Examples of D-KNOW goals were to find out the location of food (in order to go to it and then eat it) or to find out the price of an item (in order to buy it). The generation of D-KNOW goals was always tied very specifically to a physical supergoal (e.g. satisfy hunger), and were not mentioned in the author's later theories of learning (e.g. Schank, 1982). Other theories, particularly from the animal learning psychology literature, have proposed general motivations to learn: a "will to perceive" (Thorpe), a "motivation for learning" (Thacker), and a "search by an information hungry organism" (Pribram – all reported in Livesey, 1986, p. 20-21), but these theorists did not propose any specific desires, just diffuse drives. Social psychologists have used various "goal orientations" as explanatory phenomena in theories of attention, recall and judgement, which are close in spirit to the goals to learn proposed here. However, social psychologist's goal orientations are generally specified at a very abstract level (e.g. "Form an impression," or "make predictions"), and as Zukier's (1986) review notes, "In general, however, little systematic research is available on goal orientation in inference, and no comprehensive taxonomies of 'middle-level' or concrete goals have emerged from these studies."

Also related to the current claims is the work of Horvitz, et al, (1989). They present a calculus for deciding when to do more inference (versus when to act) in medical decision making. Although based on highly idealized functions for estimating the expected value of additional inference (in their model, inference includes data gathering), it provides an attempt to model content-based decisions about *when* it is worthwhile to acquire knowledge. Although their model does not specify *what* is worth learning, it may be useful in deciding whether it is worth learning at all, potentially reducing the size of the potential hypothesis space to zero. Minton (1988) also proposes a model of judging whether it is worth learning, although his model involves computing the effect of learning on future performance *after the new concept is formed*, and is hence not useful for constraining the hypothesis space.

Both failure-driven (e.g. Schank 1982) and success-driven (e.g. DeJong & Mooney, 1986) computer models of learning posit very direct connections between experiences and (implicit) desires to learn. In these systems,. the learning always takes place at the time of the failure (or success), and anything can be learned at that time is learned. A system that plans to learn may generate learning goals as a result of a success or failure, and may (or may not) be able to achieve those goals at that time. The role of failure (or success) in planning to learn systems is to identify knowledge that is worth pursuing, not (necessarily) to signal the time when knowledge can be acquired; they are failure (or success) *motivated*, not failure (or success) *driven*.

In the remainder of this paper, I sketch a theory of the origins and uses of explicit goals about what to learn. Some aspects of this theory of knowledge acquisition goals and knowledge acquisition planning are presented in greater detail in Hunter (1989, 1990a and 1990b).

Learning Goals
In order to make learning computationally feasible, learners must have goals specifying what they wish to learn, which are used to constrain the space of possibly inducible concepts. How are these goals represented? Where do they come from? How do they influence the learning process?

Desires about knowledge can be represented in at least two distinct ways. The first representational format is based on a description of the function that the desired knowledge will fulfill. These are generally stated as "desires to know how," such as the desire to know how to distinguish between mushrooms and toadstools, or how to recognize a potential good deal in the real estate ads. The other representational format is a description of the relationship of the desired knowledge to a set of existing knowledge; for example, the desire to know the capitols of all 50 states, or the names of your boss's children.

The relation-to-other-knowledge representation of learning goals is similar to Lehnert's (1978) work on representation of questions in natural language understanding. In her computer model, questions were represented by the same knowledge structures that held memories, but with some of the unfilled slots in those structures identified as the subject of a question. It is also possible to use her representational strategy for the internal representation of knowledge acquisition goals: goals can be represented as pointers to certain unfilled slots in memory structures. Ram (1989) presented a theory where relation-to-other-knowledge representations of questions were used to drive natural language understanding. Many of Ram's results apply to the design of knowledge acquisition planners generally.

Where do unfilled slots in memory structures come from? In general terms, they come from the incomplete instantiation of knowledge schemas. In order to generate relation-to-other-knowledge goal representations, a learner must have some knowledge of the structure of its knowledge. Consider a simple example: in order to represent the goal to find the capitols of all 50 states, a learner must know that states have capitols. That knowledge implies that the representation for each state will have a "Capitol" slot, and (presumably) the values for some of those slots are unfilled. Those unfilled slots can be the subject of a desire for knowledge. That is, the relation-to-other-knowledge representation of a goal to learn is the result of the application of some knowledge about the structure of knowledge to form a characterization of a gap, which is a representation of desired knowledge. Ram (1989) presents a much more detailed mechanism for generating these kinds of goals during the process of understanding natural language.

The other form of knowledge goal representation, based on the function of the desired knowledge, arise from inferences about knowledge useful for particular tasks. The knowledge underlying these inferences provide mappings from desired performance to desired knowledge. The resulting representations specify the processes in which the knowledge will be used, and the role that it will play in those processes. Another simple example: in order to do diagnosis, one must know (a) the kinds of things that can effect the behavior of a system and (b) methods for distinguishing among alternative potential causes of the to-be diagnosed behavior. When the need to diagnose, say, computer disk-drive failures arises, that high level knowledge can be used to generate goals to find out about the ways disk drives can fail and how to distinguish among them. The general knowledge must identify where in the diagnostic process the desired information will be used and for what, so that when it is found the information can be stored in the appropriate place for later use. See Hunter (1989) for detailed examples of the generation and representation of this kind of knowledge goal in a diagnosis domain.

Planning to Learn
The generation and representation of goals to learn is only the beginning of the learning process. The theoretical justification for generating them depends on their effectiveness at constraining combinatorics of learning from complex experience. I indicated briefly that learning should involve bidirectional inference: top-down, from learning goals *and* bottom-up, from experiential data. How can this be accomplished?

The idea is to use AI planning techniques for making decisions about which learning actions should be taken in what order to achieve the knowledge goals of an actor situated in the world. Generally speaking, these decisions are based on knowledge about available resources, knowledge about actions and knowledge about the current state of the world (including the actor's current knowledge state). Planning to learn is much like other kinds of planning, so here I will just try to describe the kinds of knowledge about resources, actions and states of the world that are necessary for planning about learning, rather than describe the process itself. The source of following characterizations are the computer models IVY and INVESTIGATOR. IVY was primarily an exploration in deciding what was worth learning, and INVESTIGATOR focuses on how to learn given a set of learning goals. They are described in detail in Hunter (1989) and (1990a), respectively.

Learning Actions
The actions that people take to acquire knowledge span a tremendous range, from looking up an answer in a reference book to designing and running scientific experiments. In order for a planner to select actions appropriate to goals, the actions must be annotated with the resources that they require, preconditions to executing the actions and expected outcomes of the actions (and perhaps information about possible alternative outcomes and relative probabilities of the alternatives). Here we will consider some of those actions and their representations.

In a system capable of taking a large number of possible actions, hierarchies of action classes can improve the combinatorics of the planning process. Classes of knowledge acquisition actions are, in effect, hypotheses about the component cognitive processes involved in learning. IVY and INVESTIGATOR, two computer models of planning to learn, use very different actions and learn from very different sorts of data, but their actions can nevertheless be grouped into four clearly defined classes:

• *Finding examples of specified phenomena.* This class of actions maps abstract characterizations (phenomena) to specific instances (examples). In IVY and INVESTIGATOR, these actions fall into two subclasses: explicit data gathering and perceptual processing. INVESTIGATOR maps characterizations to instances by doing various kinds of database lookups. IVY works "perceptually," checking for inputs that match a desired characterization while doing its main task of diagnosis. Both subclasses require as preconditions representations of the desired phenomena that can be used to acquire or recognize examples. In addition, the data gathering actions require access to the sources of data. Each particular action further specifies the general preconditions; e.g. to look up bibliographic records from Medline[tm], INVESTIGATOR must form a query in the Elhill retrieval language and be able to open a network connection to the Medline[tm] server. The resources consumed by this class of actions (see below for a discussion of learning resources) are the time it takes to find the desired example, and the memory required to store the found examples. The expected time to find examples perceptually can be large (i.e. you do not know when you will find what you are looking for). The expected amount of memory required for some database searches can also be large.

• *Grouping examples.* The actions in this class create collections of related examples. Subclasses of these actions include finding similar examples (using various metrics), clustering examples into equivalence classes, and building hierarchical clusters. The precondition to this class of actions is a collection of examples. For example, given a genetic sequence (say, retrieved from a database) INVESTIGATOR can use sequence matching algorithms to find other genetic sequences it knows about that are similar to it. Very few resources are required for this action. INVESTIGATOR can also use Cheeseman's (1989) Bayesian classification program Autoclass II to divide a collection of objects into clusters. That action requires significant amounts of time and CPU cycles. Some other grouping actions (e.g. hierarchical clustering) also require an applicable distance metric as a precondition.

• *Generating Abstract Characterizations of Groups.* This diverse class of learning actions includes many of the techniques traditionally associated with machine learning: concept formation, statistical analyses of collections of examples, and forming explanations of phenomena. This class of actions maps from a collection of examples and a collection of existing abstractions to a new abstract characterization of the collection of examples. INVESTIGATOR's abstraction actions so far include an inductive category formation algorithm (which generates conjunctive definitions from groups of positive and negative examples) and ANOVA algorithms for determining the statistical features of collections of examples. These actions do not use existing characterizations: they map directly from a set of examples to an abstract characterization. Any learning method that uses domain knowledge uses both examples and existing abstractions (the domain knowledge) to form new abstractions (e.g. explanations of the examples). Although the actions in this class vary a great deal, their preconditions and expected results are similar enough so that it is possible to formulate useful planning knowledge that refers to this general class.

• *Mapping Abstract Characterizations from One Group to Another.* This class of learning actions transfers characterizations from one group to another. INVESTIGATOR currently has only one action in this class: a marker passing method for mapping a distinction in one hierarchy into another. The preconditions are two hierarchies, a distinction in one, and a mapping between the leaves of the hierarchies. This action was used to map a distinction in a taxonomy hierarchy (grouping organisms into classes) into a protein family hierarchy. The individual proteins were labelled with the organism that they came from, i.e. there was a map from the leaves of the protein hierarchy to leaves of the taxonomy hierarchy. Executing the action found protein families that were associated with specific taxa. Although not implemented in either program, this class also contains all of the learning actions involving analogy, as well as methods for mapping knowledge across dissimilar groups of examples (e.g. intersection search).

Individual learning actions are rarely able to satisfy knowledge acquisition goals; they must be assembled into sequences of actions – into plans to learn. In INVESTIGATOR, the generation of learning plans is done by top-down subgoal decomposition. Decomposition rules embody knowledge about what the various knowledge acquisition actions and classes of actions are good for. Knowledge acquisition goals are transformed into subgoals, and the subgoals are further decomposed until the process bottoms out in specific knowledge acquisition actions whose total resource consumption does not exceed preset limits, and all of whose preconditions can be satisfied. IVY did not do its own subgoal decomposition, but used programmer assembled stereotypical plans. However, INVESTIGATOR is strictly top-down, and cannot currently take advantage of unexpected opportunities, whereas IVY was able to select among potential knowledge acquisition plans based on opportunities detected during routine performance.

Work is currently underway to make INVESTIGATOR's planning more sensitive to its situation, creating a mechanism for exploring data and partial results in a more bottom-up, opportunistic fashion.

Learning Resources

With unlimited resources, planning is trivial. Unfortunately, there are always limits. Physical planners have to manage resources like energy, money and time. Planning to learn is similarly constrained, although the resources are different. In particular, learners have limitations on the amount of memory they have and on the amount of time they can spend on inference. Programs like INVESTIGATOR may also have limits on the amount of network traffic they generate. Traditional physical planning resources may also come into play, e.g. database access may cost money. Planners may have strict limits on resource consumption, or may merely try to avoid waste. INVESTIGATOR has estimates of the resources each of its actions will consume, and selects among alternative plans for accomplishing a goal by minimizing the resources consumed. It can also reject plans that exceed preset limits, e.g. would take thousands of CPU hours or gigabytes of storage.

For INVESTIGATOR, memory and CPU cycles are the constraining resources. Some of its knowledge acquisition actions are directly annotated with a formula for estimating the resources consumed. The resources consumed by others can be inferred from generalizations associated the class of which the action is a member. For example, grouping examples is assumed to take time and memory proportional to the number of examples. The Autoclass II grouping method overrides those defaults, specifying that it takes a large amount of time initially, plus time proportional to the number of examples times times the complexity of the examples times the number of expected classes). Because INVESTIGATOR tries to conserve resource consumption, Autoclass is not used unless the other grouping methods fail or unless its particular kind of output is a prerequisite for some other action.

The question of managing resources in learning raises the issue of learning over time. Existing machine learning research has focused on learning from a particular dataset. Conversely, human-like learning occurs over an entire lifetime. Learners need to decide not only whether and what to learn, but when to learn. IVY is able to keep "questions in the back of its mind," in the form of pending learning plans, which are executed as opportunities arise. A more sophisticated planner might manage a complex and interacting set of learning goals, making decisions about when to pursue a particular goal, based on its relationship to the program's other learning and performance goals and on on the current state of the world.

Conclusion: Decision-making in Learning

The space of possible lessons from experience is so large that it is combinatorically implausible to learn them all. A learner situated in a complex world must therefore make decisions about what is worth learning. The results of these decisions are explicit (although not necessarily conscious) goals about the knowledge a learner desires. Learning is not a passive process: learners act in order to learn. Their goals can be used to direct the selection of the actions taken.

Planning is decision-making based on expectations about the outcomes of actions. Effective learning decisions require knowledge about the kinds of actions that can be taken to acquire and transform knowledge, and the resources that those actions consume. Knowledge about learning actions used in planning includes information about the prerequisites for taking an action and about its expected results. Algorithms modeled on AI planners in physical domains can be used to select courses of action that can be expected to yield the desired results under resource constraints. Unlike physical planning domains, the limiting resources in learning are often inferential effort (CPU cycles for computer systems) and memory capacities.

The evidence for viewing learning as a planning process comes from both combinatoric arguments and empirical results in action psychology. This view raises a variety of issues not traditionally dealt with in the machine learning or cognitive psychology literature: How do learners come to have specific desires about knowledge? What kinds of desires to people have about knowledge? For example, can they fear specific kinds of knowledge? How do large numbers of goals to acquire knowledge interact? Can they interfere with each other the way physical goals can? How are they prioritized? The planning process raises questions of its own: How can learners recognize unexpected opportunities to learn? What are the actions that people take to learn? How are those actions organized and selected among? What do people know about the learning actions themselves, and can new actions be learned? Answers to these questions await future research.

References

Birnbaum, L. (1986). Integrated Processing in Planning and Understanding. PhD. thesis, Yale University, New Haven, CT. (Technical Report YALEU/CSD/RR#489)

Chapman, D. (1985). Planning for Conjunctive Goals. (Technical Report 802). Boston, MA: MIT AI Laboratory.

Charniak, E., & McDermott, D. (1985). Introduction to Artificial Intelligence. Reading, MA: Addision-Wesley.

Cheeseman, P., Kelly, J., Self, M., Stutz, J., Taylor, W. & Freeman, D. (1988). AutoClass: A Bayesian Classification System. in Proceedings of the Fifth International Conference on Machine Learning. University of Michigan, Ann Arbor. : Morgan Kaufman.

Deitterich, T. (1989). Limitations on Inductive Learning. in Proceedings of the Sixth International Workshop on Machine Learning. Cornell University, Ithica NY. (pp. 125-128). San Mateo, CA: Morgan Kaufman

DeJong, J., & Mooney, R. (1986). Explanation-based Learning: An Alternative View. Machine Learning, 1(2), pp. 145-176.

Fodor, J. (1985). The Modularity of Mind. Boston, MA: MIT Press.

Frese, M., & Sabini, J. (1985). Goal Directed Behavior: The Concept of Action in Psychology. Hillsdale, NJ: Lawrence Erlbaum Associates.

Hoffman, C., Mischel, W., & Mazze, K. (1981). The Role of Purpose in the Organization of Information About Behavior: Trait-based Versus Goal-based Categories in Person Cognition. Journal of Personality and Social Psychology, 39, 211-255.

Horvitz, E., Cooper, G., & Heckerman, D. (1989). Reflection and Action Under Scarce Resources: Theoretical Principles and Empirical Study. (Knowledge Systems Laboratory Working Paper No. KSL-89-1). Stanford University, Stanford, CA

Hunter, L. (1989). Knowledge Acquisition Planning: Gaining Expertise Through Experience. PhD. thesis, Yale University, New Haven, CT. (Technical Report YALEU/DCS/TR-678)

Hunter, L. (1990a). Knowledge Acquisition Planning for Inference from Large Datasets. in Proceedings of the 23rd annual Hawaii International Conference on System Sciences, Software Track. Vol. 2 Kona, Hawaii. (pp. 35-44). Washington, DC: IEEE Press.

Hunter, L. (1990b). Deciding What to Learn. Submitted to the Seventh International Conference on Machine Learning. Austin, TX.

Langley, P., Gennari, J., & Iba, W. (1987). Hill Climbing Theories of Learning. Proceedings of the Fourth International Workshop on Machine Learning. Irvine, CA. (pp. 312-323). : Morgan-Kaufman.

Lehnert, W. (1978). The Process of Question Answering. Hillsdale, NJ: Lawrence Erlbaum Associates.

Livesey, P. (1986). Learning and Emotion: A Biological Synthesis. Volume 1, Evolutionary Processes. Hillsdale, NJ: Lawrence Erlbaum Associates.

Ram, A. (1989). Question-driven Understanding: An Integrated Theory of Story Understanding, Memory and Learning. PhD. thesis, Yale University, New Haven, CT. (Tech report YALEU/CSD/RR#710)

Rumelhart, D., McClelland, J., & the PDP Group (1986). Parallel Distributed Processing: Explorations in the Microstructure of Cognition (Volumes 1, 2 & 3). Cambridge, MA: MIT Press.

Sacerdoti, E. (1971). A Structure for Plans and Behavior. New York, NY: American Elsvier.

Schank, R. (1982). Dynamic Memory: A Theory of Reminding and Learning in Computers and People. Hillsdale, NJ: Lawrence Erlbaum Associates.

Schank, R., & Abelson, R. (1977). Scripts, Plans, Goals and Understanding. Hillsdale, NJ: Lawrence Erlbaum Associates

Schank, R., Collins, G., & Hunter, L. (1986). Transcending Inductive Category Formation In Learning. Behavioral and Brain Sciences, 9(4), pp. 639-687.

Srull, T., & Wyer, R. (1986). The Role of Chronic and Temporary Goals in Social Information Processing. in R. Sorrentino, & E. Higgins (eds.), Handbook of Motivation and Cognition: Foundations of Social Behavior. (pp. 503-549). Guilford, CT: The Guilford Press.

Tolman, E. (1932). Purposive Behavior in Animals and Men. New York: Century Press.

Utgoff, P. (1986). Shift of Bias for Inductive Concept Learning. in R. Michalski, J. Carbonell, & T. Mitchell (editors.), Machine Learning 2 Los Altos, CA: Morgan Kaufmann.

Valient, L. (1984). A theory of the learnable. Communications of the ACM, 27(11), 1134-1142.

Zukier, H. (1986). The Paradigmatic and Narrative Modes in Goal-Guided Inference. in R. Sorrentino, & E. Higgins (eds.), Handbook of Motivation and Cognition: Foundations of Social Behavior. (pp. 465-502). Guilford, CT: Guilford Press.

Medline is a trademark of the National Library of Medicine.

Brainstormer: A Model of Advice-Taking*

Eric K. Jones
Institute for the Learning Sciences
Northwestern University

Abstract

Research on advice-taking in artificial intelligence is motivated by the promise of knowledge-based systems that can accept high-level, human-like instruction [11]. Examining the activity of human advice-taking is a way of determining the key computational problems that a fully-automated advice taker must solve.

In this paper, we identify three features of human advice-taking that pose computational problems, and address them in the context of BRAINSTORMER, a planning system that takes advice in the domain of terrorist crisis management.

1 The Advice-Taking Task

Advice is information communicated with the intent of helping an agent make progress on a problem. Taking advice therefore involves understanding how the advice is relevant to solving a problem and acting on this understanding. We have identified three characteristic features of the human advice-taking task, each of which imposes important computational demands on the advice taker. We believe that a fully-automated advice taker has to give an account of each of these features.

1. **Empowerment:** Taking advice empowers an agent to do something by furnishing him or her with information. Consequently, an advice taker must be capable of translating initial, high-level advice into instructions that can be carried out.

2. **Situatedness:** Advice addresses the needs of an agent situated in the context of trying to solve a particular problem. It follows that an advice taker should be able to relate advice to needs for information that have arisen in the course of problem solving.

3. **Communication:** People never communicate everything that is relevant; instead, they provide only information sufficient for a recipient to reconstruct the intended message from context. Advice is communicated information; an advice taker thus has to be able to infer information that is relevant but not explicitly provided.

In the remainder of this section, we describe the computational demands that each of these features of advice-taking place on an advice taker, and discuss the extent to which past research has addressed these demands.

1.1 Advice-taking as empowerment

Most past research on advice-taking has focused on showing how taking advice can empower an agent to do something. Research into this aspect of advice-taking falls into two categories. One category of research has investigated the problem of converting high-level, human-like advice into concrete or *operational* instructions that a machine can carry out [6, 11, 12]. This research advocates that view of an advice taker as a kind of compiler for a very high-level language. Mostow's program FOO [12], for example, translates high-level advice about playing the game of hearts, (*"avoid taking points"*), into a heuristic-search problem solver that can carry out that advice.

*This research was supported in part by the Air Force Office of Scientific Research (AFOSR). The Institute for the Learning Sciences was established in 1989 with the support of Andersen Consulting, part of The Arthur Andersen Worldwide Organization.

269

A second category of research starts with the observation that that a major difficulty in empowering knowledge-based systems is the so-called knowledge acquisition bottleneck: the problem of getting knowledge into the system sufficient for it to perform interesting tasks. This leads naturally to the view of an advice taker as mechanism for streamlining knowledge acquisition [1, 2, 3, 14]. The TEIRESIAS system [1, 2], for example, guides knowledge acquisition in a way that encourages completeness and consistency with existing knowledge, and also provides high-level tools to facilitate debugging problems that arise from faulty or missing knowledge.

1.2 Advice-taking as a situated activity

Unfortunately, more is involved in taking advice than converting it into an operational vocabulary and ensuring consistency. Once one considers advice-taking as a *situated* activity, further demands are placed on the advice taker. In particular, a situated advice taker must be able to use the advice it receives to address needs for information that arise in the context of current problem solving.

Systems such as FOO and TEIRESIAS do not treat advice-taking as a situated activity. In FOO, for example, there is no current problem solving because no problem solver exists prior to advice-taking. Instead, FOO builds a complete problem solver from scratch during advice-taking, using the input advice as a specification. TEIRESIAS is concerned with acquiring knowledge for unspecified future problem solving, not acquiring knowledge needed to progress on a current problem.

There are systems that direct advice towards current problem-solving, ([5, 10, 16] for example), but they all make assumptions that drastically simplify the interaction between advice giver and advice taker: they assume that advice is supplied immediately after a need for information arises, and that the advice comes with detailed instructions about how it is to be used. For example, the Soar system [5] can use search-control advice in current problem solving, but advice is provided as soon as an operator selection difficulty is encountered, and the system simply presumes that any advice it receives is intended to be used to resolve that particular difficulty.

In a more realistic setting, neither of these simplifying assumptions holds. First, an advice-giver cannot be expected to be on hand the instant a need for information arises. A problem solver that is engaged in a complex problem solving task can be expected to have a large set of current needs, some of which it may succeed eventually in satisfying by itself, others of which may require outside assistance. An advice giver should be able to give advice that relates to any current need, whether or not it is in the current "focus of attention" of the problem solver.

Second, in a real-world setting, an advice giver cannot be expected to give detailed instructions about how advice is to be used. An ability to give such instructions requires that the advice giver know the exact nature of the problem solver's needs, which in turn requires that it have a detailed knowledge of the arcane internal workings of the problem solver. For example, the instructible Soar system described above requires that the user know about operator selection and about the details of particular operators, both of which kinds of knowledge should be hidden from the user.

For these reasons, a fully automated advice taker must be equipped to relate advice to the problem solver's current needs for information. This implies that the advice taker know what these needs are. At the very least, the advice taker should be able to record needs for information as they arise, and store them in such a way that they can be accessed when advice is presented that addresses them.

1.3 Advice-taking as communication

Advice is not just information relevant to a specific problem, it is *communicated* information. An advice taker is guided by the expectation that the advice giver intends the advice to be helpful in current problem solving. For the advice to be helpful, it should address a current need for information. If there is an operational form of the advice that can easily be seen to satisfy a current need, then the advice taker's task is simple. But there will also arise situations where adducing the advice giver's intentions is less straightforward.

People expect discrepancies between the information that advice ostensibly provides and the information that they actually need. These discrepancies can arise in the course of human communication for reasons of communicative efficiency, or because the advice giver has an incorrect or incomplete understanding of the needs of the advice taker. In either case, the advice taker expects to have to bridge the gap between an initial, "literal" interpretation of the advice and a derived interpretation that makes clear how the advice addresses an actual need for information.

Furthermore, even if a need for information can be determined that the advice plausibly addresses, the advice may not be presented in sufficient detail for it to adequately satisfy the need. In that case, the advice taker should try to fill in the missing details; failing that, it should ask the advice giver for more information.

While some existing advice-taking systems are capable of asking the user to fill in missing details [2], few are capable of inferring these details on their own, (the MOLE system [3] is a noteworthy exception). Furthermore, existing systems cannot bridge the gap between ostensible and actual needs for information. In the remainder of this paper, we introduce the BRAINSTORMER system, and show how considering advice-taking as situated activity that involves communication has informed BRAINSTORMER's design.

2 Brainstormer: A Planner That Takes Advice

Our theory of advice-taking is implemented in BRAINSTORMER, a planning system that takes advice in the domain of terrorist crisis management. BRAINSTORMER translates abstract advice into specific directives about how to make progress on a problem it is working on. Advice is presented in the form of proverbs, represented in an abstract vocabulary of planning-relevant knowledge[7, 13, 15]. BRAINSTORMER uses the advice to come up with plans for countering terrorism.

BRAINSTORMER has two top-level modules: the **planner** and the **adapter**. The planner is BRAINSTORMER's problem solver and is similar in some ways to STRIPS [4]. It suggests plans for countering terrorism. The adapter is BRAINSTORMER's advice taker. It acts as an intelligent assistant to the planner, using advice it receives to address pre-existing needs of the planner for information. In principle, the planner could operate on its own, but in practice it relies heavily on the adapter for assistance.

BRAINSTORMER provides an account of each of the aspects of advice-taking discussed above.

1. **Advice-taking as empowerment.** Like other advice takers, BRAINSTORMER's adapter has rules for translating initial, high-level advice into the operational vocabulary of the planner. Once this advice has been transformed into an operational vocabulary, it is in a form that can directly match the planner's needs for information. If suitable needs can be found, then the advice empowers the planner to make forward progress in planning.

2. **Advice-taking as a situated activity.** BRAINSTORMER is presented with advice during ongoing problem solving. The planner is first handed a planning problem and allowed to run to quiescence. Only then is advice presented. Although the planner come up with a variety of plan suggestions on its own, it will also have discovered needs for information that it is unable to satisfy by itself, and which if satisfied would allow it to make further progress in planning. These needs arise whenever the planner tries to retrieve a knowledge structure and fails. BRAINSTORMER monitors needs for information as they arise, recording them in memory as *queries*.

   Queries are stored in terms of features of potential answers. Once advice has been converted into the operational vocabulary of the planner, features of the advice are used as cues for retrieving queries that the advice might address. Attached to each query is a procedure that specifies how the planner should use answers to it. If a query is retrieved, and if the advice used to retrieve it constitutes an adequate answer, then the query's procedure is invoked. Planning can then continue at the point in the planning process where the need for information originally arose.

3. **Advice-taking as communication.** Taking advice in BRAINSTORMER, then, is defined as turning a proverb into an adequate answer to a pre-existing query. Proverbs are a very minimalist form of communication in which all details of the specific problem that they are intended to address are omitted. BRAINSTORMER thus expects input advice to be sketchy and incomplete. After translating advice into an operational vocabulary, there may still be no query

PROBLEM SITUATION: *A terrorist crisis involving terrorists from the P.L.O., in which five American hostages were taken and one was killed.*
GOALS: *Prevent future terrorist crises similar to the problem situation, and take action against the agents responsible for the terrorist crisis.*

Figure 1: An example planning problem.

1. *Find a plan for the goal of preventing future hostage holdings similar to the one in the problem situation*
2. *Find a plan for the goal of preventing future killings similar to the one in the problem situation*
3. *Find a plan for the goal of preventing future terrorist crises similar to the one in the problem situation*
4. *Find an explanation for the hostage holding*
5. *Find an explanation for the killing*
6. *Find an explanation for the terrorist crisis*

Figure 2: Some queries posted during planning.

in memory that directly matches it, or if there is, the advice may supply insufficient information to serve as an adequate answer.

It follows that BRAINSTORMER must confront the following problems: (1) finding queries that advice addresses and (2) turning advice into adequate answers. The adapter is equipped with two sets of inference strategies for coping with these problems. These strategies add elements to the advice that were not explicitly present in the input but which the advice giver may have intended to communicate implicitly. The first set of strategies allows the adapter to hypothesize additional components of the advice sufficient to retrieve a query that the advice addresses. Once a query is found, the second set of strategies allows the adapter to fill in missing details needed for the advice to provide an adequate answer to the query. In carrying out these kind of inferences, the adapter operates on the assumption that the user intended the input advice to be helpful but omitted certain details for the usual reasons that information is often left implicit in ordinary communication.

3 An Example Planning Problem and Initial Planning

In this section, we sketch a typical planning problem in BRAINSTORMER and describe some of the queries that arise from planning for this problem, prior to the presentation of advice. Planning problems are represented using **problem situations** and **goals**. A natural-language paraphrase of a representative planning problem is shown in figure 1, above. The plans that BRAINSTORMER comes up with are plans for goals in this problem.

BRAINSTORMER's planner is first invoked on this planning problem without the help of any advice and permitted to run to quiescence. In the process of planning, numerous queries are posted, each of which signals a potential opportunity for further planning. Some of these queries are listed in figure 2, above. Queries 1, 2, and 3 were posted when the planner failed to directly retrieve a plan for a goal. Queries 4, 5, and 6 request knowledge structures that can match preconditions of an abstract counterplanning rule. Given an explanation for the occurrence of an undesirable event, this rule can transform a goal to prevent the recurrence of a similar event into a goal to prevent the recurrence of the conditions that led to it[1]. Queries 4, 5 and 6 were posted on separate occasions where the planner tried to run this rule and failed to retrieve suitable explanations.

When the planner can make no further progress on its own, a user presents BRAINSTORMER with advice in the form of a proverb. BRAINSTORMER's

[1] In the context of goals to prevent future occurrences of similar events, an event is considered similar to a second event if there is an explanation for the first, a non-vacuous generalization of which is also an explanation for the second.

Figure 3: An example that illustrates the problem of producing adequate answers

adapter then has the task of turning this proverb into an adequate answer to a query. In the previous section, we noted that in carrying out this task, the adapter must confront the problems of finding a query that the advice addresses and of fleshing out the advice into an adequate answer to it. As intimated above, these problems follow directly from the demands imposed by considering advice-taking as a situated activity involving communication. In the next two sections, we sketch BRAINSTORMER's approach to dealing with these problems.

4 Producing Adequate Answers

We start with the problem of adequate answers. Once a query has been found that advice addresses, BRAINSTORMER's adapter must fill in any details needed for the advice to constitute an adequately specific and plausible answer to the query. An apt illustration of this kind of processing arises during BRAINSTORMER's processing of the proverb "*he who has suffered more than is fitting will do more than is lawful.*" BRAINSTORMER's input-output behavior is summarized in figure 3.

BRAINSTORMER came up with this output by using the proverb to answer query 6 above, ("*find an explanation for the terrorist crisis*"). One way that the proverb cen be represented in the operational vocabulary of the planner is as an *explanation for the occurrence of an illegal action: the illegal action happened because some agent was suffering, and that explains why the agent carried out the illegal action.* This interpretation directly matches queries 4, 5, and 6 above: hostage-holdings, killings, and terrorist crises can all be viewed as illegal actions, and the proverb can therefore provide an explanation for each. BRAINSTORMER prefers queries whose answers subsume answers to other queries; in this case, an explanation for the terrorist crisis subsumes explanations for the killing and hostage holdings, because each of these actions was part of the terrorist crisis.

Consequently, BRAINSTORMER assumes that the advice is best treated as answering query 6[2].

Although the adapter possesses an operational representation of the advice and a query that it plausibly addresses, its task is not over. The advice is still missing important details which it is the adapter's responsibility to fill in. Once the adapter has committed to answering query 6, the representation of the advice can be paraphrased as follows: *the terrorists were suffering, and that explains why they carried out the terrorist crisis.* As it stands, this representation constitutes a hypothesis, that the terrorists were suffering, and that this explains why they carried out the terrorist crisis. For BRAINSTORMER to accept this hypothesis as an adequate answer to query 6, it requires that any unsupported components of the hypothesis be justified.

The adapter has a small set of strategies for justifying unsupported components of hypotheses. These include the following.

- **Memory search:** Use an unsupported component of a hypothesis as an index into memory for retrieving a knowledge structure that supports it.

- **Communicative assertion:** If only one unsupported component of a hypothesis remains, assume that the user intended the advice to assert that this component in fact holds.

- **Ask the user.**

Asking the user is hardly a novel idea: a variety of existing systems treat advice-taking as mixed-initiative knowledge acquisition, in which the system directs a user to fill in all missing details. In BRAIN-

---

[2]Our discussion here omits many important issues, including how the proverb is initially represented, how it is transformed into the operational vocabulary of the planner, and how the operational interpretation is used to retrieve relevant queries. For a discussion of these and other issues, see [7, 8, 9].

INPUT:	• The planning problem and queries described in section 2.
	• The proverb an *old poacher makes the best keeper*.
OUTPUT:	• (Plan suggestion) *Hire a former terrorist to defend against terrorism*

Figure 4: An example that illustrates the problem of finding relevant queries.

PRECONDITIONS:	plan: a *plan of defense*
	parameter: *the actor of the plan*
	situation: *the plan of defense is part of a goal conflict involving stereotyped attackers and defenders*
POSTCONDITION:	*A new plan whose actor satisfies the attacker's stereotype*

Figure 5: The proverb *"an old poacher makes the best keeper"* represented as a plan refinement operator.

STORMER however, asking the user is a strategy of last resort. Wherever possible, the adapter attempts to arrive at an adequate plausible interpretation of the advice on its own.

In the current example, there are two unsupported hypothesis components: that *the terrorists were suffering*, and that *this suffering explains why they carried out the terrorist crisis*. The adapter employs its **memory search** strategy to justify the first. Specifically, it uses the fact that the terrorists are members of the P.L.O. to retrieve a standard explanation for Palestinian suffering: poor living conditions in the refugee camps. The **communicative assertion** strategy is then sufficient to justify the second component.

Once the adapter has come up with what it judges to be an adequate answer to a query, the planner is reinvoked at the point in its processing that the query arose. Recall that this query was posted when the planner was trying to satisfy a precondition of a general counterplanning rule. The rule uses explanations of the occurrence of an undesirable event to transform a goal to prevent the recurrence of a similar event into goals to prevent the recurrence of the conditions that led to it. In the current instance, the undesirable event was the terrorist crisis. Failure to retrieve a suitable explanation from memory led the planner to post the query. The proverb provides the missing explanation: the terrorist crisis happened because of poor living conditions in the refugee camps. Now that it has this explanation, the planner can apply the counterplanning rule. This leads the planner to establish a new goal of improving living conditions in the refugee camps and eventually, to propose building public housing projects.

5 Finding Relevant Queries

In the preceding example, BRAINSTORMER encountered little difficulty trying to find a relevant query, because the operational form of the advice, (an explanation), directly matched a pre-existing query. In other cases however, this lucky state of affairs does not obtain. For example, suppose BRAINSTORMER is handed the proverb *"an old poacher makes the best keeper"*. BRAINSTORMER's input-output behavior is summarized in figure 4.

This time, the relevant operational form of the proverb is a *plan refinement operator*, which is a rule that the planner can use to elaborate plans it proposes. The representation of this operator is paraphrased in figure 5. This operator does not directly match any existing queries. If a suitable query already existed, the planner would have to have already considered a plan of defense for one of its goals, and be looking for ways to refine it. This however is not the case in the current example. Consequently, further work is necessary to find the query that the advice addresses.

The following is a highly informal sketch of the reasoning that the adapter goes through in searching for a relevant query. (For a more technical discussion, see [8]).

- The user has suggested a way of refining a plan of defense. She is giving me advice, so she is trying to help me solve my current problem, namely preventing future terrorist crisis similar to the one in the problem situation, (see figure 1). Thus, she believes that this plan refinement operator supplies information that is useful for this purpose. For this operator to be useful, a plan of defense would also have to be useful. But I haven't considered any plans of defense. Maybe I should have considered a plan of defense for one of my goals.

- One of my goals is preventing future terrorist crises similar to the one in the problem situation. Could a plan of defense be useful in planning for this goal? Yes, it could. A plan of defense can be effective at preventing future occurrences of the kinds of events it defends against, because it raises their expected cost.

- OK, I'll *hypothesize* that a plan of this sort is actually useful for this goal in the current context. After all, maybe the user intended to communicate this hypothesis. That would explain why she believes that I should find this operator useful. Now I know how to use the operator.

In carrying out the above reasoning, the adapter locates a query that the advice addresses by elaborating the representation of the advice to include a hypothesis that a plan of defense is appropriate for the goal of preventing future terrorist crises. Next, control returns to the planner, which goes on to apply the plan refinement operator to this hypothesized plan and eventually suggests *hire a former terrorist to defend against terrorism*.

There are two important morals to draw from this example. First, the inference that the defense plan might be appropriate was *licensed by* the assumption that the user was trying to be helpful in the context of the given problem. This assumption both legitimates the final interpretation of the advice and justifies the inferential effort expended in finding it. An advice-taking system that does not reflect the idea that taking advice involves making sense of *information communicated with the intention of being helpful* is unable to make these inferences; consequently, in this situation at least, such an advice-taking system would be unable to profit from the advice.

The second moral of this example is that an advice taker needs knowledge about the problem solver's problem solving *process* in order to carry out this kind of inference. The requisite knowledge is over and above information about the advice-taker's dynamic needs for information. In the above example, the adapter had to be able to reason about how the planner *uses* plan refinement operators: it uses them when it has already considered a plan of defense for one of its goals. Carrying out this reasoning requires that the adapter know that the planner's planning process takes goals as input, suggests plans for those goals, and then suggests refinements to those plans. Previous advice-taking systems lack this kind of self-knowledge, and are consequently unable to perform this kind of reasoning.

6 Conclusion

We began this paper by identifying three characteristic features of human advice taking that should inform a computational theory of advice-taking. Advice *empowers* an advice taker, advice-taking is *situated* in the context of ongoing problem solving, and advice-taking involves *communication*.

BRAINSTORMER is an advice-taking system that takes account of these features of human advice-taking. First, advice helps BRAINSTORMER's planner to come up with plans for countering terrorism. Second, the planner's needs for information are recorded during planning as they arise, allowing BRAINSTORMER to use advice to facilitate ongoing problem solving. Third, BRAINSTORMER is equipped with inference strategies that allow it to infer some of the kinds of details that are commonly left implicit in ordinary human discourse. In summary, BRAINSTORMER represents a more comprehensive model of human advice-taking than earlier advice-taking systems, and constitutes a step in the direction of problem solvers that can accept high-level, human like instruction.

Acknowledgements

Thanks to Eric Domeshek for comments on a draft of this paper, and to Andy Fano for help with the program.

275

References

[1] Randall Davis. Knowledge acquisition in rule-based systems — knowledge about representation as a basis for system construction and maintenance. In D.A. Waterman and F. Hayes-Roth, editors, *Pattern Directed Inference Systems*. Academic Press, New York, 1978.

[2] Randall Davis. TEIRESIAS: Applications of meta-level knowlege. In Randall Davis and D.B. Lenat, editors, *Knowledge-Based Systems in Artificial Intelligence*, pages 229–484. McGraw-Hill, New York, 1982.

[3] Larry Eshelman and J. McDermott. MOLE: A knowledge acquisition tool that uses its head. In *Proceedings AAAI-86 Fifth National Conference on Artificial Intelligence*, pages 950–955, Philadelphia, PA., August 1986. AAAI.

[4] Richard E. Fikes and N.J. Nilsson. STRIPS: A new approach to the application of theorem proving to problem solving. *Artificial Intelligence*, 2:189–208, 1971.

[5] Andrew Golding, P.S. Rosenbloom, and J.E. Laird. Learning general search control from outside guidance. In *Proceedings of the Tenth International Joint Conference on Artificial Intelligence*, Milan, Italy, August 1987. IJCAI.

[6] Frederick Hayes-Roth, P. Klahr, and D.J. Mostow. Advice-taking and knowledge refinement: An iterative view of skill acquisition. In John R. Anderson, editor, *Cognitive Skills and Their Acquisition*, pages 231–253. Lawrence Erlbaum Associates, Hillsdale, N.J., 1981.

[7] Eric K. Jones. Case-based analogical reasoning using proverbs. In Kristian Hammond, editor, *Proceedings: Case-Based Reasoning Workshop*, Pensacola Beach, FL., May 1989. Defense Advanced Research Projects Agency, Morgan Kaufmann Publishers, Inc.

[8] Eric K. Jones. Learning by taking advice: The need for a model of the problem-solving process. Paper submitted to the Seventh International Conference on Machine Learning, 1990.

[9] Eric K. Jones. BRAINSTORMER: A situated advice taker. Paper submitted to the Eighth National Conference on Artificial Intelligence, 1990.

[10] Richard L. Lewis, A. Newell, and T.A. Polk. Towards a SOAR theory of taking instructions for immediate reasoning tasks. In *Proceedings of the Eleventh Annual Conference of the Cognitive Science Society*, pages 514–521, Ann Arbor, Michigan, August 1989. Cognitive Science Society.

[11] John McCarthy. Programs with common sense. In Marvin Minsky, editor, *Semantic Information Processing*. MIT Press, Cambridge, MA., 1968.

[12] David J. Mostow. Machine transformation of advice into a heuristic search procedure. In Ryszard S. Michalski, J.G. Carbonell, and T.M. Mitchell, editors, *Machine Learning: An Artificial Intelligence Approach*, pages 367–404. Tioga Publishing Company, Cambridge, MA., 1983.

[13] Christopher Owens. Domain-independent prototype cases for planning. In Janet Kolodner, editor, *Proceedings of a Workshop on Case-Based Reasoning*, pages 302–311, Clearwater, FL., May 1988. Defense Advanced Research Projects Agency, Morgan Kaufmann Publishers, Inc.

[14] Michael D. Rychener. The instructible production system: A retrospective analysis. In Ryszard S. Michalski, J.G. Carbonell, and T.M. Mitchell, editors, *Machine Learning: An Artificial Intelligence Approach*, pages 429–460. Tioga Publishing Company, Cambridge, Mass, 1983.

[15] Roger C. Schank. *Explanation Patterns: Understanding Mechanically and Creatively*. Lawrence Erlbaum Associates, Hillsdale, NJ., 1986.

[16] Donald A. Waterman. Generalization learning techniques for automating the learning of heuristics. *Artificial Intelligence*, 1:121–170, 1970.

Representing abstract plan failures

Christopher Owens
The University of Chicago

An intelligent agent must be able to recover from and learn from its failures. This involves building a causal explanation of why the failure occurred and using that causal explanation as the basis of further reasoning about how to deal with the failure. This paper argues that the tasks of building the explanation and reasoning from the explanation should be tightly coupled, to avoid the problem of factually correct but pragmatically useless explanations. This integration can be accomplished by using a model of reasoning about plan failures that is based upon knowledge structures that link descriptions of stereotypical plan failures with descriptions of repair and recovery strategies appropriate to those failures.

1 Dealing with failures

An intelligent agent operating in an uncertain environment must constantly face the fact that its plans may fail. Knowledge about the world is incomplete, knowledge about the necessary preconditions for a particular course of action is likely to be underspecified, and the state of the world might change between the time a particular action is planned and the time it is executed.

While some failures are the result of circumstances that are genuinely beyond the control and predictive abilities of the agent, others result from planning errors which can be corrected if the agent understands the connection between the planning error and the failure. A widely-accepted paradigm for dealing with failed plans (see, for example, [Sussman, 75], [Hayes-Roth, 83], [Hammond, 86], [Birnbaum and Collins, 88]), is that an agent must:

- **Explain** the failure. Assign blame for the failure to some condition over which the agent could have had control. (Or, if no such condition can be found, identify the failure as an unforseeable, unavoidable one.)

- **Recover** from the failure. Plan some activity that will lead toward the original goals, taking into account the changed world resulting from the failure. Or, if achieving the original goal now looks too expensive, work on some other goal.

- **Repair** the plan that resulted in the failure. If the explanation assigns blame to some condition internal to the planner, for example failure to look for a certain contraindicating condition before commencing a particular activity, modify the plan so that future uses of the same plan will not result in the same failure.

It is clear that under this model, the steps of recovering from a failure and repairing the plan depend upon a good explanation – one that assigns blame to some state of the world or state of the planner's knowledge that is both responsible for the failure and within the power of the agent to change. It is also true, though less immediately clear, that whatever process builds the explanation of the plan failure must be informed by the system's knowledge of recovery and repair.

To understand this latter point, consider the example of a robot that, given the instruction to carry two chairs from one room to the next, picks up both chairs together and, in the process of trying to maneuver through a narrow doorway, damages the chairs. Some potential explanations of the failure are:

1. The doorway was too narrow.

2. The chairs were too large.

3. The robot is poor at judging the widths of passageways.

4. The robot did not know to re-estimate its size when carrying loads.

5. The robot knew to re-estimate its size, but is poor at it.

6. The robot did not know about the vulnerability of chairs to impact damage.

7. The robot chose the plan of carrying two chairs at once even though the plan was risky, because it considered the decrease in time worth the increased risk of damage (This might not be an error, but might in fact be a reasonable course of action if, for example, the room were on fire.)

Although each of these explanations refers to the same manifestation of a failure (i.e. dented chairs), the repairs and recoveries derived from each will be different. The first two explanations assign blame to states of the world that aren't reasonably within the robot's control. The recoveries or repairs they suggest (make the doorway larger, for example) are not feasible. The next four explanations deal with errors or omissions in the robot's knowledge about carrying objects, and the repairs they suggest involve modifying or adding to that knowledge. The final explanation deals with the mechanism the robot uses to mediate between competing goals, and it suggests modifying that mechanism.

Examining the difference between the first two explanations and the others points out that the goodness of an explanation depends not only upon the degree with which it faithfully captures some aspect of the causality leading up to the failure, but also upon the degree to which it suggests an operational repair. This dependency has implications for the role of memory in reasoning about failures.

2 Building explanations

There are basically two mechanisms whereby a system can build a useful explanation of a failed plan: "Build from scratch", which involves chaining together causal rules into an explanation that connects the unexpected failure with known conditions, and "Retrieve and apply", whereby the system maintains a library of abstract explanations that can be matched against the circumstances of a failure and instantiated with the particulars of the situation.

The "retrieve and apply" method of explanation construction is discussed in [Schank, 86] and [Kass *et al.*, 86]. The fundamental idea is that certain fairly complex patterns of causality tend to recur in the course of an agent's interaction with the world. These are not in principle different than the patterns that the system could recognize via the "build from scratch" approach, but the number of them that the system actually encounters is small relative to the total number of syntactically valid patterns that the system could build by chaining together its primitive causal rules. Caching these large and frequently-encountered causal patterns is not only useful from the point of view of efficiency, but also, as has been argued in [Kass and Owens, 88], from the point of view of likely utility in the face of incomplete knowledge.

In the context of reasoning about plan failures, there is a third advantage to the "retrieve-and-apply" approach to explanation, and this advantage pertains to the above-discussed question of how the system's notion of repair and recovery should guide its choices when it builds an explanation of a failed plan. The remainder of this paper deals with the representational form and content of a class of knowledge structure that addresses the task of understanding, recovering from and repairing failed plans.

3 What to represent

As has been argued in more detail in [Schank, 86] and [Owens, 88], there is an interesting correspondence between the type of stereotypical plan failure that an intelligent agent needs to represent, and common advice-giving proverbs and aphorisms. *The lazy man's load*, for example, refers to the failure resulting from trying to minimize the number of trips required to move some number of objects by moving all of them at one time. A more generally applicable pattern describing the same class of error might be the *too many irons in the fire* pattern, which deals with the general problem resulting from overdoing the optimization of combining tasks and executing them simultaneously.

These proverbs categorize situations in some useful way. All *too m y irons* situations share certain causal properties, for example that the failure is related to the fact that multiple tasks are being combined. It is generally easy for people to decide based on a *post facto* description, whether or not a particular situation is of the *too many irons in the fire* type. There is a common set of failure recovery strategies that should be successful in all *too many irons* situations, for example interleaving fewer tasks, putting some tasks on hold or finding someone to help. People are able to enumerate these strategies when asked about *too many irons* situations in the abstract. The goal for knowledge structures to be used as part of an intelligent planning system, is to similarly categorize experiences into meaningful abstract classes or clusters.[1]

It is the observation that proverbs seem to link abstract failure descriptions with abstract recovery strategies that addresses the question of how the tasks of explaining, recovering from and repairing failures can be better integrated. They are done so via a knowledge structure that combines an abstract description of a plan failure with recovery and repair strategies. It is called a **plan failure explanation pattern**, or PFXP, and it is an extension and specialization of the XPs described in [Schank, 86] and [Kass *et al.*, 86].[2]

3.1 Understanding the failure

The central content of a PFXP is a template that can be used to build a causal model of the class of situation represented by that knowledge structure. The template characterizes, in abstract terms, the common causality that all situations covered by this PFXP share. In the case of the *Too many irons in the fire* situation, the causal pattern that characterizes the failure, when written out in English, looks something like:

> Simultaneously executing multiple tasks can fail if several of the tasks have time-critical steps, in that the agent will be busy attending to one time-critical step at the time that another time-critical step requires the agent's attention, or if the total workload of the tasks exceeds the agent's capabilities, in that the agent will be overloaded.

By deciding that this particular causal pattern applies to the current situation, the system makes several commitments about which features of the current situation will participate in the explanation. The fact that the object being moved is a chair, for example, is not involved in matching the situation against this pattern, and is consequently ignored, while the fact that the situation involved scaling the size of a task is highlighted. When it comes time to repair the problem, the system can ignore the former and focus on the latter.

3.2 Recovering from the failure

A recovery strategy, such as the decision to restart the plan using less interleaving of tasks, could be calculated dynamically from the causal model. Since the causal model shows that the interleaving is implicated in the plan failure, reformulating the plan to use less interleaving is not a particularly complicated inference. Other recovery strategies, like deciding to look for help, are not quite so easily and cheaply inferred from the initial causal explanation of the plan failure.

---

[1]See also [Lehnert, 81], [Schank, 82], [Dyer, 82] for a more general discussion of the relationship of proverbs to abstract thematic structures in the context of story understanding.

[2]See also the planning TOPs discussed in [Hammond, 86] for another abstract characterization of planning failures

In a system based on PFXPs, though, there is very little advantage to dynamically calculating repair strategies by inferring them from the causal model. Since the causal model is a static object stored as part of the knowledge structure, a set of potential repair strategies can also be packaged with a PFXP in memory. The system's task can therefore be to choose from among several possible recovery strategies rather than to try to build one from scratch. By comparison, in a system that builds explanations from scratch by chaining primitives together there is no obvious place to put recovery strategies in memory.

While the abstract strategies stored with a PFXP are static, the instantiation must of course be handled dynamically, since the abstract knowledge structure cannot know in advance the details of the situations to which it will be applied. The variables that are instantiated in the process of matching the causal model of the PFXP to the current situation, are carried over and used to instantiate the recovery strategy into a specific course of action.

The two recovery strategies mentioned above are representative of two distinct general classes of strategies. The first, re-executing with less interleaving, is basically an application of a general strategy that could be applied to any failure:

> *If some fact* x *is causally implicated in the failure, then cause* x *not to hold and try the plan again.*

While this strategy is general and simple, it is fraught with problems. A large number of conditions are causally implicated in the failure; yet many of them cannot or should not be changed by the planner, either because they are present in service of some goal or because they are beyond the control of the planner. This recovery strategy, given some of the explanations from the beginning of this paper, could easily generate the "solution" of making the doorway larger.

The second recovery strategy, looking for help, is much more specific to the *too many irons* failure. As a design principle, PFXPs should be set up with this more specific type of recovery strategy whenever possible. There is less inferential complexity involved in instantiating the strategy in the context of the failure, and because the inference chain is shorter, we can have more confidence that the strategy will be appropriate.

3.3   Identifying the bad planning decision

The role of a PFXP in allowing a system to correct its inappropriate planning behavior is that it provides a pointer to a planning decision believed likely to be the one responsible for the failure characterized by this particular PFXP. Often the decision pointed to will be a plan transformation. In the case of the *Too many irons* PFXP, the bad decision suggested looks something like:

> *Enhance this plan by simultaneously performing similar steps*

The type of bad decision that is pointed to by a PFXP can take several forms, among them:

Spurious action Some action was taken that caused the plan to fail; had it not been taken the plan would have succeeded. This is the type of failure that the *too many irons* PFXP embodies.

Omitted action Some action could have been taken to prevent this particular failure, but was not taken. This is the type of failure implicated in, for example, the PFXP corresponding to the proverb *A stitch in time saves nine*, which typifies failures in which some low-cost preventive measure would have avoided a high-cost outcome.

Inappropriate plan choice The choice of plan to accomplish some particular goal or subgoal was inappropriate. This type of bad decision can be referred to by PFXPs such as the one corresponding to the proverb *You can catch more flies with honey than you can with vinegar.*

Inappropriate resource choice The choice of resource with which to implement some plan was inappropriate. An example of this can be found in a PFXP corresponding to some interpretations of the proverb *You can't make a silk purse out of a sow's ear* or *A handsaw is a good thing, but not to shave with* – each of which warns against applying a resource to some task for which it is manifestly unsuited.

Ignored factor Some factor was not taken into account that, if it had been taken into account, would have avoided the failure. An extremely general instance of this failure is found in the *Look before you leap* PFXP.

Spurious factor Some factor was considered that, if it had been ignored, would have avoided the failure. The system paid too much attention to an insignificant or irrelevant factor. A number of decisions related to risk-taking fall into this category, such as those implicated in the proverb *He who waits for a fair wind misses many a voyage*

Inappropriate goal prioritization Some goal was given either excess or insufficient consideration, relative to the other goals on which the system was working at the time. This corresponds to the final explanation for the damaged chairs suggested at the beginning of this paper.

Incorrect assumption From the point of view of credit and blame attribution, this type of bad decision is different from the others in that it isn't really a decision that is pointed to here – the system didn't do anything wrong that led it into the failure, but rather it relied on information that is not correct. The **bad decision** field of this type of PFXP points to the offending assumption.

Some of these descriptions are oversimplified here. For example, **spurious factor**, **ignored factor**, **spurious action** and **omitted action** need not be boolean descriptors as suggested above. In fact, this type of error is much more often a matter of degree than it is of absolutes. The description of a bad decision is less likely to be something like

You paid attention to something you should have ignored

than it is to be something like

282

You paid more attention to this factor than you should have.

The basic idea behind encoding a bad decision as part of the representation of a PFXP is analogous to the credit assignment function of the basic causal model of the PFXP. Just as the basic causal model attempts to focus credit assignment on aspects of the world that are potentially under the planner's control, the **bad decision** field provides a means to focus internal credit assignment on aspects of the system's planning behavior that are modifiable.

A problem with this kind of credit assignment is that there is no guarantee of accuracy. The particular plan transformation or other decision pointed to is neither necessary nor sufficient as an explanation of the failure. Clearly the decision to interleave tasks does not always result in a bad outcome. Generally, in fact, it is a desirable thing to do. Furthermore, and more importantly from the point of view of constructing explanations, not all instances of the *Too many irons* situation result from an explicit decision to interleave tasks. Sometimes the situation might result from, for example, failing to notice a problem developing as more and more situations requiring immediate attention arise. Or, the situation might result from the conjunction of several seemingly unrelated planning decisions. The contents of the **bad decision** field are of heuristic value rather than of provable correctness.

3.4 Modifying the bad planning decision

Just as each description of a failure in the world has associated with it a recovery strategy, likewise each description of a bad planning decision has associated with it a repair strategy. The role of a PFXP in repair is, however, less clear-cut than it is in the area of developing a causal explanation or recovering from specific failures. This is partially due to the fact that internal credit attribution is not so clear-cut as external credit assignment. In the case of the robot moving the chairs, what, exactly, is the bad decision that resulted in the damage? Was it the decision to carry two chairs at once? To move quickly through the door? Or was it the result of placing too much importance on getting the job done quickly, or not enough importance on preserving the chairs.

If, a system constantly encounters errors of the same type, say *too many irons*, it should be less willing to perform the plan transformation that says to enhance a plan by allocating multiple agents to work on it. If, on the other hand, this type of error never occurs, that is a sign that the system is probably missing opportunities to enhance plans by being too conservative – it should be less fussy about applying that particular plan transformation. Ideally, the way to make the system more fussy about a particular plan transformation is to add preconditions for that transformation, and the way to make it less fussy is to drop preconditions. A very crude approximation to this behavior that requires much less knowledge on the part of the system, is to adjust some numerical parameter corresponding to the likelihood of a particular plan transformation being applied based upon the number of errors encountered that point to that transformation. While the latter approach is easier to implement, it does not allow the kind of learning enabled by the former.

4 Conclusions

Reasoning about failed plans by using an approach based upon matching large causal structures is more than just an efficiency issue related to the compilation of rules into larger rules with more detailed applicability conditions. The approach addresses the question of how to more closely link the task of understanding a plan failure with the task of acting based upon that understanding. Because the only knowledge structures available for matching are those that are linked to operational repair and recovery strategies, the system avoids the problem of generating factually correct but pragmatically useless explanations.

References

[Birnbaum and Collins, 88] L. Birnbaum and G. Collins. The transfer of experience across planning domains through the acquisition of abstract strategies. In J. Kolodner, editor, *Proceedings of a workshop on Case-based Reasoning*, pages 61–79, Palo Alto, 1988. Defense Advanced Research Projects Agency, Morgan Kauffmann.

[Dyer, 82] M. Dyer. In-depth understanding: A computer model of integrated processing for narrative comprehension. Technical Report 219, Yale University Department of Computer Science, May 1982.

[Hammond, 86] K. Hammond. *Case-based Planning: An Integrated Theory of Planning, Learning and Memory*. PhD thesis, Yale University, 1986. Technical Report 488.

[Hayes-Roth, 83] F. Hayes-Roth. Using proofs and refutations to learn from experience. In R. Michalski, J. Carbonell, and T. Mitchell, editors, *Machine Learning: An Artificial Intelligence Approach*, pages 221–240. Tioga, Palo Alto, 1983.

[Kass and Owens, 88] A. Kass and C. Owens. Learning new explanations by incremental adaptation. In *Proceedings of the 1988 AAAI Spring Symposium on Explanation-Based Learning*. AAAI, 1988.

[Kass et al., 86] A. M. Kass, D. B. Leake, and C. C. Owens. SWALE: A program that explains. In *Explanation Patterns: Understanding Mechanically and Creatively*, pages 232–254. Lawrence Erlbaum Associates, Hillsdale, NJ, 1986.

[Lehnert, 81] W. Lehnert. Plot units and narrative summarization. *Cognitive Science*, 5:293–331, 1981.

[Owens, 88] C. Owens. Domain-independent prototype cases for planning. In J. Kolodner, editor, *Proceedings of a Workshop on Case-Based Reasoning*, pages 302–311, Palo Alto, 1988. Defense Advanced Research Projects Agency, Morgan Kaufmann, Inc.

[Schank, 82] R. Schank. *Dynamic Memory: A Theory of Learning in Computers and People*. Cambridge University Press, 1982.

[Schank, 86] R. Schank. *Explanation Patterns: Understanding Mechanically and Creatively*. Lawrence Erlbaum Associates, Hillsdale, NJ, 1986.

[Sussman, 75] G. Sussman. *A computer model of skill acquisition*, volume 1 of *Artificial Intelligence Series*. American Elsevier, New York, 1975.

Reasoning With Function Symbols In A Connectionist System

Venkat Ajjanagadde*
Department of Computer and Information Science
University of Pennsylvania

Abstract

One important problem to be addressed in realizing connectionist reasoning systems is that of dynamically creating more complex structured objects out of simpler ones during the reasoning process. In rule based reasoning, this problem typically manifests as the problem of dynamically binding objects to the arguments of a relation. In [1,7], we described a rule-based reasoning system based on the idea of using *synchronous activation* to represent bindings. As done in almost all other connectionist reasoning systems developed so far, there, we restricted our focus on the problem of binding only *static objects* to arguments. This paper describes how the synchronous activation approach can be extended to bind *dynamically created objects* to arguments, to form more complex dynamic objects. This extension allows the rule-based reasoning system to deal with function symbols. A forward reasoning system incorporating function terms is described in some detail. A backward reasoning system with similar capabilities is briefly sketched and the way of encoding long-term facts involving function terms is indicated. Several extensions to the work are briefly described, one of them being that of combining the rule based reasoner with a parallelly operating equality reasoner. The equality reasoner derives new facts by substituting equivalent terms for the terms occurring in the facts derived by the rule-based reasoner.

1 Introduction

Suppose, someone told us "At around 7PM last Thursday, as John was walking on Chestnut street,...". Virtually immediately after hearing this very small piece of explicitly stated information, we would have performed a lot of inferences, say, for example, that "John was awake", "He was moving", "His eyes were open", "His feet were touching the ground", "It was probably quite dark " and so on... . In doing this, we would have applied our general knowledge about 'walking', 'light conditions at around 7PM' etc. to make inferences about the particular case of John's walking. One of the well explored approaches of modelling this inferencing phenomenon is the following: Represent the general knowledge using rules such as[1],

$walk\text{-}on(x,y) \Rightarrow awake(x)$, $awake(x) \Rightarrow open(eye\text{-}of(x))$, $walk\text{-}on(x,y) \Rightarrow touch(feet\text{-}of(x),y)$ etc.. Now, given the fact $walk\text{-}on(john,chestnut\text{-}st)$, binding $john$ and $chestnut\text{-}st$ to appropriate variables in the rules, facts such as $awake(john)$, $touch(feet\text{-}of(john),chestnut\text{-}st)$ can be derived.

We believe that this attempt to model the human inference process as reasoning with rules and facts is *a step* in the right direction. But, at the same time, we also find compelling reasons to adopt a connectionist framework in further explorations of this approach. One primary reason is that of inferencing speed. To characterize the knowledge underlying human cognition, a very very large number of rules of the form mentioned above will be

---

*This work was partially supported by NSF grants IRI 88-05465, MCS-8219196-CER, MCS-83-05211, DARPA grants N00014-85-K-0018 and N00014-85-K-0807, and ARO grant ARO-DAA29-84-9-0027. I am indebted to Lokendra Shastri, whose ideas and suggestions have greatly contributed to this work. John Barnden provided useful comments; my thanks to him.

[1]When not mentioned otherwise, the variables occurring in a rule are assumed to be universally quantified and have scope over the whole rule.

needed. In spite of possessing that vast a knowledge base, human beings perform a broad class of inferences involved in cognition extremely fast, within a few hundred milliseconds. To be acceptable, any computational account of cognition should be able to explain this remarkable phenomenon. One necessary (but not sufficient) condition for achieving such an efficiency is massive parallelism at the knowledge level - the kind of parallelism that is characteristic of connectionist models. Another important reason that suggests the use of connectionist approach is the brittleness of logical rules. Inherent to the connectionist methodology are elegant mechanisms for avoiding this brittleness in a natural fashion.

As a preliminary step towards the realization of a connectionist soft reasoning system, we have addressed the problem of how to reason with hard logical rules in a connectionist system[2]. That meant devising a scheme for encoding rules and facts as a connectionist network and finding a way of realizing the inference process as spread of activation in the network, there being no central controller. Unfortunately, in doing this, many challenging problems surface, which need to be solved.

One of the major problems to be addressed is "How do we represent structured objects *dynamically*[3], i.e., as temporary patterns of activity generated during network's operation?". Let us look at this problem more closely with an example of reasoning.

Consider the rules $fly(x, y, z) \Rightarrow move(x, y, z)$ and $move(x, y, z) \Rightarrow reach(x, z)$. Now, starting from the fact $fly(tweety, tree1, tree2)$ (i.e., *tweety* flew from *tree1* to *tree2*), using the first rule we can infer $move(tweety, tree1, tree2)$. From this newly derived fact, using the second rule, we can, in turn, infer $reach(tweety, tree2)$. In a connectionist network performing this reasoning, activity patterns representing the facts $move(tweety, tree1, tree2)$ and $reach(tweety, tree2)$ will have to be generated during the reasoning process.

Let us look at the problem of representing the dynamic objects $move(tweety, tree1, tree2)$, and $reach(tweety, tree2)$ more closely. These are structured objects formed by binding some objects to the arguments of relations. For example, $move(tweety, tree1, tree2)$ is formed by binding the objects *tweety*, *tree1*, and *tree2* respectively to the first, second, and third arguments of the relation *move*. Thus, the problem of representing these facts boils down to the connectionist variable binding problem[3,8]: How do we represent the binding of an object to an argument of a relation?

In [1,7], we described what we refer to as the *synchronous activation approach* to represent argument bindings. Simply stated, the idea is just this: Corresponding to every argument of a predicate, have a distinct node in the network. Imagine every clock[4] cycle as divided into some number of slots, which we will refer to as *phases*. Associate distinct phases of the clock cycle with distinct objects participating in a reasoning episode[5]. Thus, in the example of reasoning given above, we would have chosen distinct phases, say, first, second, and third phases of clock cycles to correspond respectively to the objects *tweety*, *tree1*, and *tree2*. The binding of an object to an argument is represented by having the node corresponding to that argument become active in the phase associated with the object. More than one argument node can be active in a phase of a clock cycle denoting that the object associated with the phase is bound to all of those arguments.

Based on this idea of representing bindings, we developed a fairly powerful rule-based reasoning system[1,7]. This system, whose size is only linear in the size of the knowledge base, is capable of performing a large number of inferences involving rules and facts in parallel. The time taken to perform a single inference is proportional to the length of the derivation, and hence, optimal. However, as done in almost all connectionist reasoning systems developed so far, we had placed an important restriction on the kind of reasoning performed by the system. The

---

[2] Some ideas on how to render a degree of softness to the system thus arrived at, are mentioned later in the paper.

[3] Hence, the name *dynamic objects*, to objects represented that way.

[4] Actually, no global clock is necessary, as discussed in detail in [7]. However, for simplifying the discussion, here we are assuming that there is a global clock.

[5] Since the number of phases in a clock cycle is bounded, only a limited number of objects can participate in a particular reasoning episode. This restriction confirms with the psychological observation that human reasoning can focus only on a small number of objects at any time[6]. For detailed discussions of the neurological and psychological plausibilities of the synchronous activation approach to represent bindings, please refer to [7].

variable binding mechanism employed there was restricted to binding only *static objects* to arguments. For example, in the example of infering $move(tweety, tree1, tree2)$, and $reach(tweety, tree2)$ given above, the arguments of the relations are bound only to the static objects $tweety$, $tree1$, and $tree2$. An example of binding dynamic objects would be binding the dynamically created object $move(tweety, tree1, tree2)$ itself to an argument of some other other relation. The restriction that bound objects be static precluded us from having function symbols in rules and facts, since, to deal with function terms, the ability to bind dynamic objects to arguments is required. For example, consider the simple rule

$walk$-$on(x,y)$ $\Rightarrow$ $touch(feet$-$of(x),y)$

Now, suppose we have the fact *walk-on(john,street6)*. From this fact, we can infer the fact *touch(feet-of(john),street6)*. Notice that here, *feet-of(john)* is a dynamic object created during the reasoning process by binding the argument of the function symbol *feet-of* to the object *john*. In infering the fact *touch(feet-of(john),street6)*, the dynamic object *feet-of(john)* should itself be bound to the first argument of the relation '*touch*'.

In this paper, we describe how the synchronous activation approach can be extended to handle the above general kind of binding. That extension allows reasoning with function symbols and opens up interesting ways of enhancing the power of our earlier reasoning system, still retaining its nice features. Before we go into the details of these, we will digress a little to make a few comments on related research works.

To the best of our knowledge, no connectionist reasoning system has so far addressed the problem of reasoning with function symbols in any significant detail. Hence, our comments on related work is limited to the abilities of other proposed variable binding solutions to bind dynamic objects [6]. In [5], Lange and Dyer suggest the use of *signatures* to represent variable bindings. They permanently allocate a distinct signature to each static object and represent a binding by propagating the signature of the appropriate object to the argument to which it is bound. Now, to bind a dynamically created object to some argument, a signature will have to be recruited for the dynamic object on the fly during the reasoning process. Doing this appears very problematic. This is especially so, if signatures are learnt patterns, as suggested in [5]; that will mean that learning has to take place during an inference step. In [8], Smolensky addresses the variable binding problem in its abstract form and presents a tensor product based solution. He deals with the issue of nested bindings also. But, the way in which the proposed technique can be used in the context of reasoning remains to be seen. Barnden's 'Conposit'[2] is probably the only reasoning system other than the one presented in this paper, that is capable of handling nested bindings. However, the variable binding capabilities of Conposit come with a very significant sacrifice in knowledge level parallelism; in Conposit, only one rule can fire at a time. DCPS[9] is another reasoning system that is restrictive in its use of knowledge level parallelism. There does not appear to be any obvious way of extending the binding mechanism of DCPS to handle nested bindings.

2 Overview

Cognition requires both *forward reasoning* and *backward reasoning*. In forward reasoning, the system starts with a collection of facts and these facts trigger some rules leading to the inference of some other new facts. These newly derived facts in turn trigger some other rules and so on, the process leads to the derivation of a large set of facts that are deducible from the starting set of facts. A connectionist forward reasoning system dealing with function terms is discussed in some detail in section 3. That section describes the activity patterns chosen to represent function terms, the encoding of rules involving function symbols and how inferences involving function symbols is done in the network. Section 4 briefly sketches how a backward reasoning system incorporating function terms in rules and facts can be built. In that context, we indicate how long-term facts involving function terms (such as,

---

[6] Detailed comparisons of the synchronous activation approach with other proposed solutions, based on other relevant criteria, such as network size, reasoning speed, neurological plausibility etc., have been made elsewhere[7].

say, *hate(john,brother-of(tom))* are encoded in the network. Section 5 discusses some extensions to the work on reasoning with function symbols. One of the major extensions is that of combining the rule based reasoner with a parallelly operating equality reasoner.

3 A Forward Reasoning System that Deals with Function Terms

Before explaining how a reasoning system incorporating function terms is realized, let us discuss the dynamic representation of function terms.

A function term f of n arguments gets represented in the system using a relation R_f of $(n + 1)$ arguments[7]. The first n arguments of R_f correspond to the n arguments of f respectively and the $(n+1)$th argument of R_f can be thought of as corresponding to the value of the function for those arguments. A dynamic object $f(c_1, c_2, ..., c_n)$[8] gets represented as follows: Recall from the discussion of section 1 that distinct objects participating in a reasoning process are associated with distinct clock phases. Suppose that the phases associated with the objects $c_1,...,c_n$ are respectively $p_1,...,p_n$[9]. As said above, the first n arguments of R_f correspond to the arguments of f and hence are bound to $c_1, c_2,...,c_n$ respectively. Using the synchronous activation approach, these bindings get represented by having the ith argument node of R_f become active in the p_ith phase of every clock cycle ($i = 1, ..., n$). Corresponding to the dynamic object $f(c_1, ..., c_n)$,[10] a free phase (i.e., a phase that is currently not assigned to any object) is assigned. The $(n + 1)$th argument node of R_f is activated in this phase, thereby denoting that it is bound to the object $f(c_1, ..., c_n)$.

Summarizing, the following pattern of activity represents the function term $f(c_1, ..., c_n)$:

- The ith argument node of R_f becomes active in the p_ith phase of every clock cycle.

- A currently free phase (let it be p_*) is found and that phase is associated with the dynamic object $f(c_1, ..., c_n)$. The $(n + 1)$th argument node of R_f will be active during the p_* phase of clock cycles.

Now, consider the problem of binding the object $f(c_1, ..., c_n)$ to an argument of some relation, say jth argument of the relation K. All that is to be done for this, is to activate the jth argument node of K in the phase p_*.

With that introduction, let us proceed to the encoding of rules involving function symbols. Consider the rule

$$P(x, y, z) \Rightarrow Q(f(y, x), z) \tag{1}$$

Associated with the relations P and Q, there are three and two argument nodes respectively (shown as diamond shaped nodes in Fig. 1)[11]. To represent the binary function f, a ternary relation R_f is used. The correspondences between the arguments of relations are denoted by the links between the appropriate argument nodes. For example, as per the above rule, the second argument of Q gets bound to the same object that binds the third argument of P. This is denoted by a link between the argument node a3 and the argument node a5 . Ignore the hexagonal box marked B for the time being.

Using the rule (1), starting from the fact $P(a, b, c)$, we can infer $Q(f(b, a), c)$. Let us see how this gets done with the rule encoding shown in Fig.1. Suppose that the objects a, b, and c are assigned the first, second, and third phases of clock cycles. Thus, the bindings in the starting fact are denoted by having the first, second, and third argument nodes of P active in the first, second, and third phases of clock cycles. The link from the argument node

---

[7] The reader is urged to remember the notation 'R_f'. In all the examples and figures, we use this notation.

[8] It is not required that c_is be distinct. In addition, c_is can be static or dynamic objects. Hence, nested function terms such as $f(g(h(a1, a2), a3))$ are allowed.

[9] If $c_i = c_j$, then, p_i will be equal to p_j.

[10] It may help to view this object as the value of the function f for the argument objects $c_1, ..., c_n$.

[11] We won't be explaining the role of the nodes drawn as pentagons in Fig.1. Due to space limitations, we have focussed on conveying the essential ideas and have omitted some details.

a3 to the node a5 causes a5 also to become active in the third phase of clock cycles - thereby, binding a5 to the object c, as desired.

The argument nodes a6 and a7 are connected respectively to the nodes a2 and a1. This causes a6 and a7 to become active in the second and first phases of clock cycles respectively. That is, a6 and a7 get bound respectively to b and a, thereby creating a part of the representation of $f(b, a)$. As discussed at the beginning of the section, now, a free phase in the clock cycle has to be found for the object $f(b, a)$. This is done by the hexagonal box labelled B, which we will refer to as *phase requester*. This box is not a single connectionist node; instead, it is a small piece of circuitry. There exists a global record maintainer that keeps track of the currently assigned phases. Box B communicates with this record maintainer to determine a free phase. We are suppressing the details of the phase requester and the record maintainer. For further discussions, it is assumed that the output of B is a pulse in the chosen free phase. The output of B goes to the third argument node of R_f. Thus, a8 becomes active in the phase chosen for the object $f(b, a)$. The link from a8 to a4, in turn, causes a4 to become active in the chosen phase. That is, the first argument of Q gets bound to the object $f(b, a)$. Now, we have the complete representation of the inferred fact $Q(f(b, a), c)$.

Above we discussed how a single rule is encoded and inference gets performed with that rule. Fig.2 shows how a collection of rules can be encoded. With this arrangement, an inferred fact in turn can spontaneously trigger other rules leading to the derivation of further facts. It is common to have one predicate occurring in the antecedent of many rules. When a fact involving a predicate is inferred, this triggers all those rules in which this predicate is the antecedent. Thus triggered rules derive further facts in parallel.

4   A Backward Reasoning System Dealing with Function Terms

Previous section described a *forward reasoner* incorporating function terms. Cognition also requires *backward reasoning*, where the task performed is essentially that of verifying whether a given fact is derivable from the rules and facts stored in the system. Two major tasks involved in performing backward reasoning are : (i) applying rules in the backward direction , (ii) checking whether a long-term fact is stored in the system.

The first of these tasks can essentially be achieved by having links in the reverse of the directions marked in Fig. 2 (A few other small changes will also be necessary.).

To see how the second task is performed, we would like to emphasize the two kinds of representations of facts: long-term facts are represented in the network as an interconnection of nodes while short-term facts get represented by a temporary pattern of activity. To check whether a particular long-term fact is present in the system, the pattern of activity corresponding to the short-term representation of that fact is induced in the network. The interconnection encoding a long-term fact is such that the activity of a particular node in the interconnection goes high when and only when the activity corresponding to the short-term representation of that fact is present in the network[12]. Such an interconnection corresponding to the long-term encoding of the fact $P(a, f(b))$ is shown in Fig.3. In figures, we use links with dark circles at their ends to denote inhibitory connections and links with solid arrows at their ends to denote enabling connections. Nodes marked with the names of the constants a and b are referred to as *constant nodes*; they will be active in the respective clock phases assigned to these objects in a reasoning episode. Node marked N is a coincidence detector; it sends a high output if and only if all of its inputs are active and synchronous. The node marked K sends a continuous high output. Node M, drawn as a horizontal pentagon is a *temporal-AND* node, which becomes active if and only if it receives activation throughout a clock cycle. Recalling the short-term representation of function terms discussed earlier, one can easily verify that the condition for M to become active gets satisfied when and only when the pattern of activity corresponding to the short-term representation of the fact $P(a, f(b))$ is present in the network.

---

[12]Thus, the activity of this node can be used in answering the question whether a particular long-term fact exists or not.

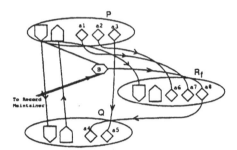

Figure 1: Encoding of the rule $P(x, y, z) \Rightarrow Q((f(y, x), z))$.

Using the above discussed technique for encoding long-term facts involving function terms, a backward reasoning system can be realized along the lines described in [1,7].

5 Extensions of the Work

5.1 Combining with an equality reasoner

In previous sections we discussed how a rule-based reasoning system incorporating function terms can be realized. Such a rule-based reasoner can be elegantly interfaced with a parallelly operating equality reasoner to obtain a more powerful reasoner. The operation of these two components is as follows: The main reasoner derives new facts and the equality reasoner substitutes equivalent terms for the terms occurring in those facts to derive some other facts. Those new facts derived by the equality reasoner can in turn trigger rules in the main reasoner. Here, we will only sketch some of the ideas involved in the realization of such a hybrid reasoner and will report the details elsewhere.

The equality reasoner operates with two kinds of equalities. Substitutions involving these two types are accomplished in different ways. The first type of equality states that an entity described using a function symbol is same as a known domain individual. An example of this kind of equality is *maternal-uncle-of(tom)=dave*. Reasoning with this kind of equality is accomplished by extending the mechanism for answering *wh-queries* reported in [7].

The second kind of equality states equalities between two entities both of them being described using function symbols. An example of this kind of equality is $\forall x$ *brother-of(mother-of(x))=maternal-uncle-of(x)*. A piece of circuitry to apply this equality to substitute *maternal-uncle-of(x)* for *brother-of(mother-of(x))* is shown in Fig. 4. This is accomplished by viewing this operation as the application of the rule *brother-of(p,q)∧mother-of(q,r)* ⇒*maternal-uncle-of(p,r)*. Network realization of this is analogous to the encoding of conjunctive antecedent rules described in [1,7] and is indicated in Fig.4. There, the rectangular shaped node marked B is a coincidence detector whose output will be high if and only if its two inputs are active and synchronous. This node ensures that the same object binds the second argument of *brother-of* and the first argument of *mother-of*, as required by the above rule.

In the derivation of a particular fact both of the above two types of equalities may be made use of. Thus, if the main reasoner derives *live-in(brother-of(mother-of(tom)),boston)*, then the network may first derive *live-in(maternal-uncle-of(tom),boston)* using the second kind of equality and then derive *live-in(dave,boston)* using the first kind of equality.

5.2 Evidential reasoning

As mentioned in section 1, our primary focus so far has been on exploring how reasoning with logical rules and facts can be efficiently realized in a connectionist network. In achieving this, we assumed all the link weights to be unity. A certain degree of softness can be rendered to this reasoning system by making the rules to be probabilistic and associating a measure of certainity with the facts. These modifications can be easily realized in the network architecture developed, by having non-uniformly weighted links.

5.3 Multiple Dynamic Facts

In the description of the system presented in this paper, we have assumed that only one dynamic fact involving a relation is present at any time. Though this is a common assumption made in connectionist reasoning systems[4,5], there are situations in which this restriction is unacceptable. In [7], we discuss some techniques of relaxing this restriction in the case of our system.

6 Conclusion

We described a connectionist rule-based reasoning system incorporating function terms. The system is extremely efficient both in network size and the time taken to perform inferences. The extended variable binding capability introduced in the system opens up many interesting avenues for realizing *broad, yet, efficient, reasoning* - the characteristic feature of human cognition. They are currently being investigated.

References

[1] Ajjanagadde, V.G., and Shastri, L., Efficient inference with multi-place predicates and variables in a connectionist system, *Proceedings of the Cognitive Science Conference*, August 89, pp. 396-403.

[2] Barnden, J., Neural-net implementation of complex symbol-processing in a mental model approach to syllogistic reasoning, *Proceedings of IJCAI-89*, pp. 568-573.

[3] Feldman, J.A., Dynamic connections in neural networks, *Bio-Cybernetics*, 46:27-39, 1982.

[4] Hinton, G., Implementing semantic networks in parallel hardware, In G.Hinton and J.Anderson (Eds.),*Parallel Models of Associative Memory*, Erlbaum, 1981.

[5] Lange, T., and Dyer, M., High-Level inferencing in a Connectionist Neural Network. Technical Report, UCLA-AI-89-12, October. Computer Science Department, UCLA, 1989.

[6] Miller, G.A., The magical number seven, plus or minus two: Some limits on our capacity for processing information, *The Psychological Review*, 63(2), March 1956, pp. 81-97.

[7] Shastri, L. and Ajjanagadde, V., From simple associations to systematic reasoning: A connectionist representation of rules, variables, and dynamic bindings, Tech. Report, Dept. of Computer Science, Univ. of Pennsylvania, January 90.

[8] Smolensky, P., On variable binding and the representation of symbolic structures in connectionist systems, Technical Report CU-CS-355-87, Department of Computer Science, University of Colorado at Boulder, 1987.

[9] Touretzky, D. and Hinton, G., A Distributed Connectionist Production System. *Cognitive Science*, 12(3), pp. 423-466.

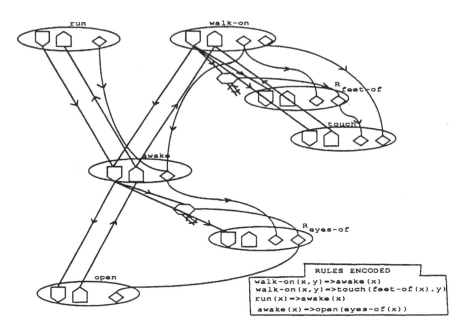

```
          RULES ENCODED
walk-on(x,y)=>awake(x)
walk-on(x,y)=>touch(feet-of(x),y)
run(x)=>awake(x)
awake(x)=>open(eyes-of(x))
```

Figure 2: An example network.

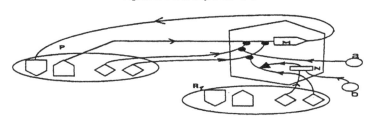

Figure 3: Encoding of the long term fact $P(a, f(b))$.

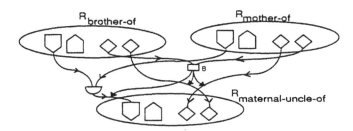

Figure 4: Interconnection for substituting $maternal\text{-}uncle\text{-}of(x)$ for $brother\text{-}of(mother\text{-}of(x))$.

292

NOT ALL POTENTIAL CHEATERS ARE EQUAL: PRAGMATIC STRATEGIES IN DEDUCTIVE REASONING

VITTORIO GIROTTO (*CNR, Rome, Italy*)
PAOLO LEGRENZI (*University of Trieste, Italy*)

ABSTRACT

This work briefly discusses one of the central problems in the current psychology of reasoning: that of explaining the effects of content. Two competing theories recently proposed to explain such effects (pragmatic reasoning schemas and social contract theories) are illustrated with reference to an experiment on reasoning in children employing a selection problem, which requires a search for the potential counterexamples of a conditional rule. On the one hand, the theory of pragmatic schemas (i.e. clusters of rules related to pragmatically relevant actions and goals) predicts that correct selection performance derives from the activation of specific contractual schemas, such as obligation and permission, the production rules of which correspond to the logic of implication. On the other hand, according to the social contract theory, people are able to detect potential counterexamples only when they correspond to the potential cheaters of rules having the form 'If benefit A is received, then cost B must be paid'. The results of the experiment show that performance on tasks of this kind is not determined simply by the possibility of representing the rule in question in cost-benefit terms; to predict performance one necessary factor is knowledge of the nature of the possible cheating behaviour that one is requested to check.

ACKNOWLEDGEMENTS. Preparation of this paper was supported by CNR grants. Correspondence should be sent either to V. Girotto, Istituto di Psicologia, CNR, Viale K. Marx 15, 00137, Roma, Italy (e.mail: vittorio@irmkant.bitnet) or to P. Legrenzi, Dipartimento di Psicologia, Via dell'Università 7, 34127, Trieste, Italy).

The ability to search for counterexamples has a central role in reasoning, since the ability to search for them can be regarded as the basis of the discovery and evaluation of hypotheses, concept attainment, and deductive inferences. However, a great deal of empirical evidence exists that adults perform poorly in reasoning problems requiring a search for potential counterexamples, for example in general statement evaluation problems. Studies that utilized the well-known Wason four-card selection task (Wason, 1966, 1968), showed that the majority of adult subjects did not search for counterexamples to a rule such as "If a card has a vowel on one side, then it has an even number on the other side". Most adults typically fail to select a card with an odd number, one of the potentially falsifying cards. In general terms, the rule used in such problems is a universal statement, typically a conditional statement, *if p then q,* and the relevant cases are *p and not-q,* in the above indicated example "a card with a vowel" and "a card with an odd number".

The long tradition of research with tasks of this type has shown that in some cases people are able to search for counterexamples, particularly when problems are phrased in "concrete" terms (Johnson-Laird, Legrenzi and Sonino-Legrenzi, 1972; for reviews see Griggs, 1983; Wason, 1983).

Among the different proposals for explaining the ensemble of findings produced with selection problems, the most convincing seems to be the pragmatic reasoning schemas interpretation (Cheng and Holyoak, 1985). Pragmatic schemas, such as permissions, obligations and causations, are clusters of rules which concern pragmatically relevant actions and goals. Under certain circumstances, some of these schemas lead to the correct solution of problems demanding a search for counterexamples. In particular, the activation of a permission or obligation schema can help people to solve a selection problem. Although their production rules go beyond those of the logic of material implication (for example, by including modal verbs such as "must" and "can"), their productions lead to card selections which *correspond* to those prescribed by a logical analyis of the task. For example, a permission rule *'If you want to do action A, then you have to satisfy precondition B ',* implies the contrapositive rule *'If you do not satisfy precondition B, then you are not allowed to do action A '.* This equivalence makes clear that the potential violators of the permission rule are people who have done action A without satisfying precondition B.

Cheng and Holyoak (1985) obtained empirical findings that corroborate the pragmatic schemas hypothesis. They have shown that adult subjects are able to search for potential violators of unfamiliar but rationalized permission rules, and that succesful performance is also elicited with an abstract description of a permission situation. Moreover, facilitation of selection performance in conditions concerning permission and obligation rules has been obtained with preadolescent children (Girotto, Light and Colbourn, 1988).

A different interpretation of the content effect in reasoning performance has been recently proposed by Cosmides (1989). According to her "social contract theory", people process information regarding social exchanges using specific, naturally evolved algorithms. In particular, social contract algorithms express an exchange in which an individual is obliged to pay a cost in order to be entitled to receive a benefit. They contain an inferential procedure ('*look for cheaters* ') that enables people to detect potential cheaters (i.e. individuals who have not paid the required cost, and individuals who have accepted the benefit). In a series of experiments, Cosmides (1989) showed that wording a selection problem in terms of a social contract (*If one accepts benefit A, then one has to pay cost B*) can produce formally correct performance when the cases indicating possible cheating ('benefit accepted' and 'cost not paid') correspond to the formally relevant cases, i.e. the potential counterexamples.

There has been a lively and still open debate between the two described positions. According to Cosmides' theory, only social contracts, which are a subset of all permission rules, produce "robust and replicable content effects" on selection tasks.

Cheng and Holyoak (1989) have criticized this position, in which only the cost/benefit representation is considered to be psychologically real. Moreover, a number of empirical studies have shown that correct reasoning performance, both for adult and child subjects, can be obtained in conditions which, following social contract theory predictions, should not activate the described 'look for cheater' procedure This has been the case, in particular, of certain prudential (Cheng and Holyoak, 1989; Girotto, Gilly, Blaye and Light, 1989; Manktelow and Over, 1990), obligation (Girotto, Blaye and Farioli, 1989) and permission (Light, Girotto and Legrenzi, in press) rules which did not directly map the cost/benefit structure of standard social contracts.

In the present paper, we will briefly present the results of a research about children's reasoning on conditional promises and permissions (reported in detail in Light *et al.*, in press). We will discuss their theoretical implications in relation to the indicated debate.

Consider a conditional contractual promise, like the following, made by a teacher to her pupils:

"If you get at least 10 points, then you can have a sweet "

And suppose that there are four pupils:

Mary (who had 10 points), Ben (4 points), Sue (who has received a sweet) and Rob (who has not received a sweet).

Clearly, in this scenario it is unlikely that the promisor (the teacher) will violate her own promise (by not giving the reward to the deserving pupils).

A more likely outcome is that some promisees will try to cheat by taking a reward which they do not deserve.

A teacher-promisor who decides to check whether her promise has been respected should thus make sure that Ben (the pupil with 4 points) and Sue (the pupil with the sweet) have not cheated, that is, that they have not respectively taken a sweet and obtained less than 10 points.

If this checking condition is considered as a version of the selection task, it is clear that the pragmatically correct choice will be that of examining the two pupils just mentioned (Ben and Sue), whose formal values are respectively *not-p* and *q* (which are different from those indicating the potential counterexamples of a conditional rule '*if p then q* ', namely the values *p* and *not-q*).

Now, if we consider a condition in which the teacher-promisor has delegated a specific pupil to administer the promise, this agent may commit two types of infraction. If the agent acts selfishly, he will tend to withhold the cake from the pupil who deserves it. For this reason, a teacher-promisor wishing to check the agent's behaviour should ensure that Mary (the pupil with 10 points) and Rob (the pupil with no sweet) have not been unfairly deprived of the reward. If instead the agent has behaved nepotistically, then the teacher-promisor will have to check not only the two pupils just indicated but also the others (Ben and Sue), who might have received the reward, although underserving, because they were friends of the agent. In the first case (selfish agent) the formal values of the cases to be checked are *p* and *not-q*; in the second case (nepotistic agent) all four values must be checked: *p*, *not-p*, *q*, *not-q*.

As can be seen, for a conditional contractual promise there can be various possible combinations of cases that indicates a violation. The formal values of these cases do not always correspond to the combination *p* and *not-q*.

Three versions of a selection task concerning these three possible situations of promise violation were presented by Light *et al.* (in press) to some English children aged 11-12 years (a fourth condition, which serves as a control, concerned a permission rule *"If you want a sweet, then you must get at least 10 points"*, which could be violated by Sue, formally *p*, and Ben, formally *not-q*).

The results of this research have shown that preadolescent children do master the complex pragmatic factors underlying the control of conditional contractual promises and permission. Their patterns of responses correspond, in most cases, to the selection of the different combinations of the potential violations above indicated: In the condition where the pupils-promisee could violate the promise by themselves ('direct promise' condition), the most frequent choice (50%) was the selection of the cards *not-p* and *q*. In the two conditions where the teacher-promisor had to check agent's behaviour, children' s selection turned out to be different. In the 'selfish agent' condition, the *p* (10 points) and *not-q* (no sweet) cards were indeed selected most regularly (90% and 83% respectively). However, only 22% of the subjects selected just these two cards. In addition, 'sweet' card (*q*) continued to be selected by many children. In the 'nepotistic agent' condition, the prevalent choices was the combination of *all cards* (39%). Finally, in the permission condition, the correct pattern *p* and *not-q* was most frequently selected (78%).

It is possible to compare, although indirectly, these data with those reported by Cosmides (1989). Some of the social rules used in her experiments are in fact conditional contractual promises. For example, in two experiments, her subjects had to check the behaviour of the promisor (an African hunter, called Bo) of the following deal *"If you give me your ostrich eggshell, then I'll give you duiker meat"*. This condition is similar to Light et al. 's *'selfish agent '* condition: In both cases, in order to detect the possible cheaters one has to check whether the deserving promisee (pupil with 10 points or man who gave Bo eggshells) had received the earned reward (sweet or meat), excluding, at the same time, that the persons who actually ran the deal (the selfish agent or the promisor himself, Bo) had illegally kept it. In other words, in both cases, the relevant cards correspond to *p* and *not-q*. Now, despite this similarity in the structure of the two problems, the elicited performance turned out to be different. While Cosmides' scenario elicited about 70% of *p* and *not-q* selections, in Light et al. 's selfish agent condition, this pattern of response was produced only by 22% of the subjects.

If we compare the ways in which the runners of the deal are presented in the two scenarios, several differences seem to appear.

In the story used by Cosmides, the subjects had to check a promisor (Bo) who was, at the same time, 1) *owner* of the goods (duiker meat) that he should have given to the others in exchange for the fulfillment of the contractual requirements; 2) *motivated to keep* for himself the maximum amount of these goods (Bo was actually presented as an "unscrupulous man...(who) had very little duiker meat and a large family to feed"); 3) personally *motivated to obtain* the fulfillment of the contract (Bo was presented as someone who was "always accidentally breaking his ostrich eggshells and would like to 'stockpile' some").

In Light et al. 's 'selfish agent' condition, the agent of the promise, 1) was *not* the *owner* of the goods (sweets) that he should allocate to the deserving pupils; 2) even if he was allowed to keep for himself the non allocated goods, it was *not specified* whether he was really *motivated* to do so (i.e. whether he was a glutton); 3) he was *not* personally *interested* in obtaining the fulfillment of the contractual requirements (i.e. the successful school performance of the classmates); 4) his *relationships* with the promisees were *not* specified (i.e. he could be a good friend or an enemy of the other pupils).

Thus, while in the Cosmides' stories it was clearly specified that the promisor was motivated to a selfish cheating behavior, in Light et al. 's condition the agent of the promise could plausibly behave both nepotistically and selfishly. This possibility to attribute different goals to the agent can explain why Light et al. 's children did not limit themselves to the selection of the 'selfish' cards *p* and *not-q*.

This comparison shows the importance of the *information about the nature of the cheating behaviour* that one is requested to check. Both children (selfish agent condition) and adults (cf. Politzer and Nguyen-Xuan, 1988) seem to have difficulties in performing consistently this check when this information is not sufficient. However, it should be noted that in conditions where sufficient information about the goals of the possible cheaters is given, children can produce consistent selection performance. This was the case of the permission and direct promise conditions in Light et al. 's study, where the nature of the potential cheating behaviour could only be 'selfish' (as the pupils acted alone). In the former case, children consistently (78%) checked the two pupils who could have violated the permission rule (the pupil with the sweet and the pupil with 4 points, i.e. *p* and *not-q*). Children (50%) still consistently selected these two cases in the latter condition, even if their logical values (i.e. *not-p* and *q*) where different from those of the cards selected in the permission condition. This specific response pattern is similar to that obtained by Cosmides (1989) in versions of the task in which a contractual promise (social contract) was modified to a sort of obligation (switched social contract). For examples, the original Bo's promise (*"If you give me your ostrich eggshell, then I'll give you duiker meat "*) was modified to *"If I give you duiker meat, then you must give me your ostrich eggshell "*. In this case, people had still to check Bo's behaviour, and they still selected the cards corresponding to 'benefit for Bo' and 'cost unpaid by Bo', which have formal values (*q* and *not-p* , respectively) different from those of the original condition (*p* and *not-q*).

In conclusion, the results presented by Light *et al* (in press) show: a) that, regardless of the similarity of rules and scenario, reasoning performance can dramatically change as a function of the *actor* who could have infringed a conditional promise (and his/her goals); b) despite the possibility of recognizing a situation as one of social exchange (*sensu* Cosmides), subjects do not consistently look for potential cheating behaviour, when complete information about it is not provided. Therefore, while previous research has demonstrated that succesful reasoning performance can be obtained even in conditions which cannot be represented in the cost/benefit terms of a social contract, Light *et al* 's study demonstrates that conditions which can be represented in these terms do not necessarily elicit the pattern of responses predicted by the social contract theory.

REFERENCES

Cheng, P.W., & Holyoak, K.J. (1985). Pragmatic reasoning schemas. *Cognitive Psychology, 17*, 391-416.

Cheng, P.W., & Holyoak, K.J. (1989). On the natural selection of reasoning theories. *Cognition, 33* , 285-313.

Cosmides, L. (1989). The logic of social exchange: has natural selection shaped how humans reason? Studies with the Wason selection task. *Cognition, 31* , 187-296.

Girotto, V., Blaye, A., & Farioli, F. (1989). A reason to reason. Pragmatic basis of children's search for counterexamples. *European Bulletin of Cognitive Psychology, 9*, 297-321.

Girotto, V., Gilly, M., Blaye, A., & Light, P.H. (1989). Children's performance in the selection task: Plausibility and experience. *British Journal of Psychology, 80* , 79-95.

Girotto, V., Light, P. H., & Colbourn, C. (1988). Pragmatic schemas and conditional reasoning in children. *Quarterly Journal of Experimental Psychology, 40A* , 469-482.

Griggs, R.A. (1983). The role of problem content in the selection task and THOG problem. In J. St B.T. Evans (Ed.) *Thinking and reasoning: Psychological approaches.* London: Routledge and Kegan Paul.

Johnson-Laird, P.N., Legrenzi, P., & Sonino-Legrenzi, M. (1972). Reasoning and a sense of reality, *British Journal of Psychology, 63*, 395-400.

Light, P.H., Girotto, V., & Legrenzi, P. (in press). Childen's reasoning on conditional promises and permissions, *Cognitive Development.*

Politzer, G. & Nguyen-Xuan, A. (1988). Pragmatic reasoning schemas: Promises and the four-card selection task. Unpublished manuscript, Centre National de la Recherche Scientifique, Paris.

Wason, P.C. (1966). Reasoning. In B. Foss (Ed.), *New horizons in psychology,* Harmondsworth: Penguin Books.

Wason, P.C. (1968). Reasoning about a rule. *Quarterly Journal of Experimental Psychology, 20*, 273-281.

Wason, P.C. (1983). Realism and rationality in the selection task. In J. St B.T. Evans (Ed.), *Thinking and reasoning: Psychological approaches.* London: Routledge and Kegan Paul.

Explanations in Cooperative Problem Solving Systems

Thomas Mastaglio and Brent Reeves

Department of Computer Science and
Institute of Cognitive Science
University of Colorado, Campus Box 430
Boulder, CO 80309
email: brentr@boulder.colorado.edu

Abstract

It is our goal to build cooperative problem solving systems, knowledge-based systems that leverage the asymmetry between the user's and the system's strengths and thus allow the dyad of user and computer system to achieve what neither alone could achieve. Our experience has shown that in these cooperative systems, the need for explanations is even more evident than in traditional expert systems. This is due to the fact that these new systems are more open-ended and flexible and therefore allow for more possibilities in which a user can reach an impasse, a point at which it is not clear how to proceed.

Observation of human-human problem solving shows that people are sensitive to the domain under discussion and the other's knowledge of that domain. People tend to construct explanations that are minimal in the number of concepts or chunks. These explanations are not comprehensive, and the communication partner is able to follow up on aspects which are still unclear.

1 Introduction and Theoretical Basis

Our research focuses on how to build cooperative knowledge-based systems that take advantage of the different strengths of users and computer systems. Computers can be a source of expert domain knowledge, knowledge they can use to make suggestions to users. The computer system's role in this dyad must include the ability to explain those suggestions. For various reasons, current explanation systems often fail to satisfy users. Too frequently they are based on an implicit assumption that explaining is a one-shot affair and that the system will be able to produce or retrieve a complete and satisfying explanation provided it is endowed with *artificial intelligence*.

Our approach takes advantage of existing information and knowledge-based systems technology already available to provide the user access to explanations at different levels of detail and complexity. Development efforts focused on the concepts requiring explanation rather than on selecting a complete prestored explanation. A conceptual model of the domain and a user model provide that set of concepts. Explanation giving requires establishing a suitable conceptual context for a dialogue between the user and the system. The system must know what concepts are required to understand an entity in the domain and furthermore which subset of those concepts are unfamiliar to a given user. Forming such an idiosyncratic explanation is a construction rather than a selection process.

We are investigating how to design systems that serve users as they are actively engaged in their own work — cooperative problem solving systems. These systems provide a task-based environment which users employ to accomplish some goal. We want them to be more than a communication medium with which to describe a problem. In the context of these task-based environments we analyzed the reasons people seek explanations. The common triggering condition is that they experience an impasse that stops or limits their work. We call these "task-oriented impasses" and have cataloged them to better understand how explanation giving can help to overcome the impasses. The four categories of task-oriented impasses are: action impasses, communication impasses, motivation impasses, and curiosity impasses.

1. *Action impasses* occur when users do not know what to do next. Some action impasse questions are: What should I do next? Is *action* the right thing to do next? How do I do *action*? What did the system just do? What are the results of doing *action*? Can I do *action* now?

2. A *communication impasse* is a failure to understand a given object in the environment. Representative questions are: What is *object*? Why is *object1* shown instead of what I expected, namely *object2*?

3. *Motivation impasses* fall into the realm of behavioral psychology; their basis is an anthropomorphic view of the computer system: Representative questions are: Why did the system do *action*? Why did the system just communicate with me? Why did the system just say X? Why should I do *action*? Why is $action_1$ better than $action_2$?

4. *Curiosity impasses* are a bit different. The other categories consist of questions that arise when users encounter a problem. Curiosity impasses are not necessarily impasses, in a strict sense, but rather a diversion from continuing with the task. They are circumstances in which users seek to gather information that is interesting or might be helpful, but *the lack of which* will not preclude them from further work. For consistency we will refer to them also as "impasses". Questions that illustrate curiosity impasses are: Is *object* a concept X? How do $object_1$ and $object_2$ differ?

To overcome these impasses, explanations in cooperative problem solving systems serve four functions; functions that are similar to findings of empirical work on explanation giving in expert systems [16]. The functions of explanations in cooperative problem solving systems are:

1. To allow users to examine the system's recommendations,

2. To relate recommendations to domain concepts — understanding "what is suggested",

3. To provide a rationale for recommendations — understanding "why this would be better",

4. To educate a user about underlying domain concepts.

These four functions are not mutually exclusive. A single explanation episode by a cooperative problem solving system will often accomplish several of these functions.

Even in cases where explanation systems have been designed with the above functions in mind, the result has typically been a system that explains too much, and therefore not enough. A familiar example to many computer system users is the *man page*, which contains everything a user might want to know, from the system's perspective, and for that very reason is often too much to be of use.

In observing problem-solving interactions between salesmen and customers in a large hardware store, we noticed that explanation never took the *man page* approach. When explanations were required, the approach was one of minimizing the explanation, then following up on unclear concepts when necessary [13]. This is interesting if you consider the fact that the particular store carries over 350,000 different items in over 33,000 square feet of retail space. If salesmen took the approach found in many computer systems, the explanations they gave would be extraordinarily long, in order to be complete, and complex, in order to take into account the relationships to other items in the store.

As an example of computer systems with extensive documentation, consider the Symbolics Lisp machine, which comes with over 4000 pages of documentation, most of which is available online in hypertext format. Issuing a query (i.e. a request for an explanation) can result in pages and pages of text and examples; frequently too much to digest and make sense of. As computer systems increase in power, they also increase in complexity. Simply having more powerful computers will not solve the problem of explanation, it will only exacerbate it.

In order to model the "minimalist explanation" approach found in human-human interactions in a knowledge-based system, we designed an extension to LISP-CRITIC, a knowledge-based source transformation system. Supporting idiosyncratic explanation giving requires a user model that contains a detailed representation of users' knowledge. The explanation approach needs something more than classifying users by level of expertise. Our framework uses a fine-grained user model and a minimalist approach [6]. More theoretical basis for the minimalist explanation approach is found in related work on discourse comprehension:

1. Short-term memory is a fundamental limiting factor in reading and understanding text [2, 1]. The best explanations are those that contain no more information than absolutely necessary, since extra words increase the chances that essential facts will be lost from memory before the entire explanation is processed.

2. It is important to relate written text to readers' existing knowledge [11, 5].

Similar guidelines are also offered as principles of rhetoric. Flesch developed formulae to evaluate the readability of text [9] that emphasize brevity. Computer explanation systems should comply with similar standards, therefore short sentences and known vocabulary as important criteria. Other support is found in Strunk and White's familiar manual; it contains similar advice. Writers of explanatory text are told "Don't explain too much" [15].

2 An Explanation Approach

Supporting explanation requires the system to have enough knowledge to describe what is going on and why. Operational knowledge is often captured in rule form (If *condition* then *action*). For users to understand a rule means that they must know the concepts underlying a rule. A conceptual domain model provides the entire set of prerequisite knowledge and a user model filters that set for an individual.

The user model helps select which subexplanations to actually present. One view of explanation is that users are engaged in an understanding process that is based on generating explanations to themselves [14]. It follows that the explanation component has to provide users with sufficient information so they can develop their own self-explanation, and yet not with so much information that it interferes with a person's ability to construct meaningful explanations.

Determining what to explain to a user requires decomposition; the system must execute a GPS-like process [3]. Prerequisite knowledge is the knowledge a user must know in order to understand a given concept. This is a recursive process, understanding those domain concepts that are prerequisites for the given concept requires, in turn, understanding their prerequisites and so on. To support such an approach a deep structure for the domain is queried to obtain the set of prerequisites. Still, a satisfactory explanation approach will do more, namely identify the concepts in that set that do not need explaining because the user already knows them. Then the system reasons about the best way to explain the remaining concepts. Based on this general schema, we developed a framework consisting of several levels of explanations.

It is also important to incorporate a fallback capability, allowing the user some recourse when the initially provided explanation fails. No computer-generated explanation system can be expected to satisfy users completely — people are not able to achieve this and we do not expect any more of computer systems. The situation where a user does not understand an initial explanation or wants more detailed information must be accommodated. One technique is the reactive approach [12]; our approach is simpler in that it makes use of existing hypertext capabilities.

3 LISP-CRITIC Explanation System

We have developed an explanation component for a LISP critiquing system in accordance with this framework. LISP-CRITIC is that system [7, 4]. It is a knowledge-based interactive system that operates in a programmer's editing environment, providing suggestions on how to improve user LISP programs. When called on to examine a piece of code, the system informs the programmer of each suggestion it has for improving the program. As each suggestion is provided, the programmer can accept the suggestion, reject it outright or ask for an explanation. Users seek explanation to help them understand the suggestion well enough to make the accept/reject decision. When a suggestion is accepted the system actually rewrites that piece of code in the user's editing buffer.

We developed an approach that provides information in four layers of increasing detail. The first two layers are not necessarily explanations in a specific sense of the word but we found that in many situations they provide enough information to satisfy system users.

1. A fundamental piece of information is the name of the rule that identifies a suggested transformation. The rule name is an abstract reference to a chunk of domain knowledge, that chunk is an instance of the domain object class LISP-CRITIC rule; it may or may not have meaning to users. Sometimes when it does have meaning, users are satisfied just knowing which rule fired and no further explanations is required. They have sufficient information on which to base an accept/reject decision.

2. The transformed code, as recommended by the system, can be compared to the user's code. The system shows the user's code and its recommended version. Often this is sufficient for users to understand the suggestion and they can make a decision on whether to accept or reject the advice.

3. The minimal explanation layer is the point where our theoretical investigations comes into play. The user is provided with a textual description of the system's advice based on the domain concepts behind that transformation.

4. The underlying computational environment already includes a hypertext-based information space, the Symbolics Document Examiner. LISP-CRITIC facilitates access to this information for users who are not satisfied with the minimalist explanation of the advice. Users navigate through the hypertext space themselves; the system first locates them in an appropriate context.

The approach used in the current implementation evolved from attempts to provide explanations for an earlier version of LISP-CRITIC [10]. The approach taken involved rule-tracing and prestoring textual descriptions for each transformation (layer 1 and 2 above). A suite of alternative canned explanations for each rule were provided; each one designed to meet the needs of a user with a particular level of expertise. To provide the correct explanation, the system classified a user as a novice, intermediate or expert programmer. This approach was of limited success. A major finding from that work was the need for a finer grained approach to modelling individual users than classification: An approach that also supports dynamic update as users' expertise changes.

The theoretical framework discussed above led us to emphasize concise and readable explanations. Metrics with which to evaluate, or guidelines to help construct such explanations do not exist. We decided that it would be best to provide terse explanations tailored individuals, while recognizing that at times users require additional information. To provide that information, we provided the hypertext "hooks" into an existing on-line documentation system.

The explanation levels shown in Figure 1 capture the necessary and sufficient conditions for an adequate explanation, each level incrementally improving on the work done at a lower level by using additional knowledge about the user and the domain. A level 0 explanation does not require knowledge about individual users. It uses the conceptual domain model to meet the necessary condition that it knows everything required to understand the entity needing to be explained. The set of prerequisite concepts required in order to understand the object the user wants explained is provided by a deep domain model. Level 1 brings the user model into the process; the prerequisite concepts are "filtered" through the user model to determine the subset of them appropriate for explaining to a given individual. What remains is often larger than what would be reasonably explained in a single dialogue episode. Therefore the explanation component uses knowledge about what makes a good explanation at level 2 to order and prioritize the concepts that are to be explained.

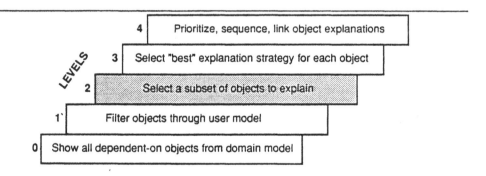

Five levels of explanation have been identified. Level 0 insures that all prerequisite knowledge for a given domain object is available to the explanation component. Level 1 builds on top of level 0 and so forth. The current implementation provides level 2 explanations. The domain and user model can also support levels 3 and 4.

Figure 1: Explanation Levels

Level 3 makes use of additional domain knowledge or perhaps other information in the user model to determine a "best" strategy for explaining each concept. For example, a system could make use of the links between objects in the domain model and the user model to determine candidate concepts or functions for use in a differential description [8]. One object can be described differentially in terms of another object that the user already knows. Level 4 performs "syntactic sugaring". Here the individual explanations from level 3 are ordered and linked in an appropriate manner. This is a nontrivial process

305

and requires the system to have knowledge of discourse as well as natural language generation capabilities that exceed the present state of the art.

4 Role of the user model in explanations

Cooperative problem solving systems must tailor explanations in order to adequately perform the four functions of explanation. The basis for this tailoring is the user model. The user model is an essential component. A simple approach is to classify users by their expertise (e.g., novice, intermediate, expert). The use of stereotyping and classification schemes can accommodate those systems that provide one-shot advise but cooperative problem solving systems need a finer grained representations of the user.

The user model contains a representation of the user's domain knowledge adequate to support any of the five "levels" of explanation shown in Figure 1. The implication is that it must be based, at least partially, on the conceptual model of the domain in order for it to serve as the filter for level 2 explanations. The model needs to capture the user's goals in order to support level 3 explanations.

Supporting level 4 explanations are more difficult. Explanations at this level are at the frontier of research on natural language generation and human-computer dialogue technology. We will not know everything required of a user model to support explanations at this level until that research matures. At this point we conjecture various user model capabilities needed to support this level, such as knowing the education and reading comprehension level of a user.

5 Summary and Conclusions

The problems with current explanation systems are widely recognized, but most efforts to improve them attempt either to emulate human-to-human communication in inappropriate ways or to provide a complete explanation in "one shot". Theoretical results in discourse comprehension and principles of rhetoric are a suitable starting point but it must be kept in mind that all human-to-human communication techniques are not appropriate for computer-based explaining.

In studying human-human problem solving, we note that one aspect that is less important than expected is the ability to produce and understand natural language. People rarely talk in grammatically correct or even complete sentences, yet they manage to communicate and solve problems. We call this 'natural communication,' rather than natural language. We have attempted to map natural communication over to human-computer systems by supporting minimalist, layered explanations with the capability for further follow-up via hypertext.

The approach we used provides several layers of explanation for advice from a knowledge-based system. The first two layers are not explanations in the strictest sense, although they can help users achieve understanding, but are detailed descriptions of what was recommended. The 3rd layer clarifies the recommendations and exposes the user to the underlying rationale for that recommendation. These are minimal explanations that query a user model to find out what is necessary for the user to understand a LISP concept, LISP function, or LISP-CRITIC rule. The highest layer of information provides users a fallback capability using a rich hypertext information space in they are free to explore details or examine concepts which they still do not understand.

References

[1]   Bruce K. Britton, John B. Black (editors).
        Understanding Expository Text.
        Lawrence Erlbaum Associates, London, 1985.

[2]   T.A. van Dijk, W. Kintsch.
        Strategies of Discourse Comprehension.
        Academic Press, New York, 1983.

[3]   G.W. Ernst, A. Newell.
        ACM Monograph Series: GPS: A Case Study in Generality and Problem Solving.
        Academic Press, London - New York, 1969.

[4]   G. Fischer.
        A Critic for LISP.
        In J. McDermott (editor), *Proceedings of the 10th International Joint Conference on Artificial Intelligence (Milan, Italy),* pages 177-184. Morgan Kaufmann Publishers, Los Altos, CA, August, 1987.

[5]   G. Fischer, S.A. Weyer, W.P. Jones, A.C. Kay, W. Kintsch, R.H. Trigg.
        A Critical Assessment of Hypertext Systems.
        In *Human Factors in Computing Systems, CHI'88 Conference Proceedings (Washington, D.C.),* pages 223-227. ACM, New York, May, 1988.

[6]   G. Fischer, A.C. Lemke, T. Mastaglio, A. Morch.
        Using Critics to Empower Users.
        In *Human Factors in Computing Systems, CHI'90 Conference Proceedings (Seattle, WA).* ACM, New York, April, 1990.

[7]   G. Fischer, T. Mastaglio.
        Computer-Based Critics.
        In *Proceedings of the 22nd Annual Hawaii Conference on System Sciences, Vol. III: Decision Support and Knowledge Based Systems Track,* pages 427-436. IEEE Computer Society, January, 1989.

[8]   G. Fischer, T. Mastaglio, B.N. Reeves, J. Rieman.
        Minimalist Explanations in Knowledge-based Systems.
        In *Proceedings of the Twenty-Third Annual Hawaii Conference on System Sciences, Vol. III: Decision Support and Knowledge Based Systems Track,* pages 309-317. IEEE Computer Society, January, 1990.

[9]   R. Flesch.
        The Art of Readable Writing.
        Harper & Brothers, New York, 1949.

[10]   J. Frank, P. Lynn T. Mastaglio.
        Using A Critic Methodology as a Computer-aided Learning Paradigm: extending the concepts.
        1987.
        Final Project Report for CS659 - Fall Term 1987.

[11]   W. Kintsch.
        The Representation of Knowledge and the Use of Knowledge in Discourse Comprehension.
        Language Processing in Social Context.
        North Holland, Amsterdam, 1989, pages 185-209.
        also published as Technical Report No. 152, Institute of Cognitive Science, University of Colorado, Boulder, CO.

[12]   J. Moore.
         A Reactive Approach to Explanation.
         Technical Report, USC/Information Sciences Institute, 1988.

[13]   B. Reeves.
         *Finding and Choosing the Right Object in a Large Hardware Store -- An Empirical Study of
             Cooperative Problem Solving among Humans.*
         Technical Report, Department of Computer Science, University of Colorado, Boulder, CO, 1990.
         forthcoming.

[14]   R.G. Schank.
         Explanation Patterns: Understanding MEchanically and Creatively.
         Lawrence Erlbaum Associates, Hillsdale, NJ, 1986.

[15]   W. Strunk, E.B. White.
         The Elements of Style.
         Harcourt-Brace?, New York, 1957.

[16]   J.W. Wallis, E.H. Shortliffe.
         Customized Explanations Using Causal Knowledge.
         *Rule-Based Expert Systems: The MYCIN Experiments of the Stanford Heuristic Programming
             Project.*
         Addison-Wesley Publishing Company, Reading, MA, 1984, pages 371-388, Chapter 20".

Improving Explanatory Competence[1]

Kenneth S. Murray
murray@cs.utexas.edu
Department of Computer Sciences
University of Texas at Austin
Austin, Texas 78712

Abstract

Explanation plays an important role in acquiring knowledge, solving problems, and establishing the credibility of conclusions. One approach to gaining explanatory competence is to acquire proofs of the domain inference rules used during problem solving. Acquiring proofs enables a system to strengthen an imperfect theory by connecting unexplained rules to the underlying principles and tacit assumptions that justify their use. This paper formalizes the task of improving explanatory competence through acquiring proofs of domain inference rules and describes KI, a knowledge acquisition tool that discovers proofs of rules as it integrates new information into a knowledge base. KI's learning method includes techniques for controlling the search for proofs and evaluating multiple explanations of a proposition to determine when they can be transformed into proofs of domain inference rules.

1. Introduction

Knowledge-based systems must be capable of explaining their conclusions. One approach to gaining explanatory competence is to acquire proofs of the domain inference rules used during problem solving. Possessing proofs of rules used during problem solving has several advantages. First, a rule's proofs identify support for the rule, that is, the domain principles that justify the rule's correctness. Second, a rule's proofs explicate the tacit assumptions being made when the rule is used. By identifying the underlying principles and assumptions, proofs of inference rules enable the system to justify and qualify its conclusions to the user [SWAR83], guide knowledge refinement [SMIT85], and, in the case of default reasoning when assumptions are not met, improve problem solving [STAL77]. This paper formalizes the task of improving explanatory competence through acquiring proofs and describes a system that discovers proofs of domain inference rules as it integrates new information into a knowledge base.

Acquiring proofs strengthens an imperfect theory when new information enables proving previously unsupported rules. Initially, a knowledge base (or person) often includes tentative, default rules such as "birds can fly" or "leaves are green." However, as the knowledge base is extended, and competence in the domain improves, these default rules may be annotated with deeper causal support when explanations of the rules are discovered. Gagne [GAGN85] illustrates this behavior in people with the following example:

> A student is told *In vitro experiments show that Vitamin C increases the formation of white blood cells.* The student has prior knowledge that white blood cells destroy viruses, and intuitively knows that Vitamin C is taken to fight colds, which are caused by viruses. The student realizes that Vitamin C is capable of fighting colds *because* it stimulates the creation of white blood cells, which subsequently kill cold-causing viruses.

The student identified a causal explanation of an existing belief that was neither stated in the new information nor previously known. Having discovered this explanation the student possesses greater insight into why Vitamin C is taken to fight colds. For example, the student could now explain why Vitamin C is not taken in response to similar symptoms having causes unrelated to viruses (e.g., allergies).

---

[1] Support for this research is provided by the Air Force Human Resources Laboratory under RICIS grant ET. 14.

This paper describes research aimed at modeling this learning behavior. In Section 2, the learning task of proof acquisition is formulated, and a terminating, although incomplete, method of performing this task is developed in Section 3. Section 4 describes KI, a knowledge acquisition tool that implements this method to discover proofs of domain inference rules as it integrates new information into a knowledge base.

2. The Learning Task

Proofs of an inference rule identify sentences in a theory that ensure its truth. However, the contents of logical proofs are not restricted to sentences having explanatory (e.g., causal) significance. For example, a proof of a rule could include an arbitrary number of trivial tautologies (e.g., $p \Rightarrow p$) not relevant to the truth of the rule. Therefore, a distinction must be made between the set of all logical proofs and proofs acceptable as explanations. Let e be a predicate on proofs such that $e(p)$ is satisfied exactly when proof p is acceptable as an explanation. For example, e might restrict proof steps to be applications of modus ponens to a particular subset of rules. Let R be a domain theory and r_i be a sentence in R. The notation p_e denotes a proof that satisfies e, and $(R - r_i) \vdash_{pe} r_i$ denotes proof p_e is a derivation of r_i from the theory $(R - r_i)$.

Each proof of a rule identifies a set of underlying principles and assumptions that justify the rule's use; different proofs may elucidate different principles and assumptions. Therefore, the goal of acquiring proofs of rules for explanation includes identifying every p_e for each rule rather than any single p_e. This learning task may be characterized as the following information processing task:

Given: a rule set R
a predicate e on proofs

Find: for each $r_i \in R$
the proof set $P_i = \{p_e \mid (R - r_i) \vdash_{pe} r_i\}$

Unfortunately, when the language used to encode rules is as expressive as first order logic (FOL) this task is not solvable. However, this task becomes decidable when the following restrictions are adopted:

Let R_e be the subset of R including only rules that may be represented as horn clauses without functions.

1) U_e, the universe of discourse for R_e, is a finite subset of U, the universe of discourse for R.

2) e admits only proofs containing non-cyclic applications of rules in R_e.

These restrictions enable the existence of a terminating method by sacrificing completeness. Intuitively, decidability is achieved by restricting the universe of discourse to a finite set. A theory equivalent to R_e can be constructed by replacing each $r_i \in R_e$ with the set of ground implications that includes every possible binding of the variables in r_i to elements of U_e. The finiteness of U_e makes such a construction possible. The result is a propositional theory and is therefore decidable.

The restricted learning task may be characterized as:

Given: a rule set R
a predicate e on proofs

Find: for each $r_i \in R$
the proof set $P_i = \{p_e \mid (R_e - r_i) \vdash_{pe} r_i\}$

While this task is guaranteed to have a terminating solution, the restrictions cannot guarantee tractability. In practice, solutions cannot be expected to discover all proofs enabled by the restricted theory. Therefore, solutions must include some mechanism to bias their search for proofs. The next section describes a method of guiding search for restricted proof acquisition.

310

3. Discovering Proofs through Hypothetical Reasoning

One approach to guiding deduction involves separating inference from the process of instantiating quantified formulae [MCAL80]. Inference is then limited to computing the entailment of a small but "representative" set of ground propositions. This sections describes a *generate and test* search procedure that manipulates a set of ground propositions and implications to guide search for proofs of rules in R. This search is summarized by the following cycle:

1) generate a hypothetical context: a set of propositions over hypothetical instances of some small subset variables referenced by rules in R

2) generate all ground explanations (i.e., sequences of deductions) enabled by repeatedly applying rules in R_e to the propositions

3) determine if any resulting explanation can be generalized into a proof of some rule in R

4) extend the context with propositions over new hypothetical instances of variables referenced by rules in R; goto step 2.

To initiate the search, select a very restricted set of rules called *Training*; the search will be biased towards discovering proofs that make use of these rules.[2] Let *Context* be some small set of propositions that satisfy every sentence in *Training*. For example, if *Training* = {[$isa(x$ $Person)$ $\&$ $location(x$ $Austin) \Rightarrow location(x$ $Texas)$]}, then the proposition set {$isa(Person_1$ $Person)$, $location(Person_1$ $Austin)$, $location(Person_1$ $Texas)$} satisfies *Training*.

Second, generate ground explanations enabled by the propositions in *Context* and the rules in R_e. This involves computing all possible deductions by repeatedly applying rules in R_e to the propositions in *Context* (i.e., by exhaustive forward-chaining). While termination is guaranteed, exhaustive forward-chaining has the potential for exponential combinatorics. However, the rules are chaining on a very restricted set of instances, so, in practice, restrictions on proof construction will typically be sufficient to prevent intractable chaining.[3]

Finally, determine if any resulting explanation can be generalized into a proof of some rule. This is accomplished using techniques developed for explanation-based learning to generalize and compile explanations (e.g., [MOON88]). To continue the search for proofs, extend *Context* with additional hypothetical instances and add some set of propositions on these new instances. Then repeat the generation and evaluation of explanations as before.

Under this strategy, the search for proofs is controlled by the extensions made to *Context*. One way to generate hypothetical instances is to instantiate Skolem functions appearing in the rule set R. For example if $isa(Fred$ $Person)$ is a proposition in *Context*, and [$isa(x$ $Person) \Rightarrow mother(x$ $fn_1(x))$] is a rule in R, $Person_1$ could be a new hypothetical instance and $mother(Fred$ $Person_1)$ a new proposition for *Context*. Now R_e can be extended with the ground implication [$isa(Fred$ $Person) \Rightarrow mother(Fred$ $Person_1)$]. This enables limited representation in R_e of rules from R that involve predicates on functions (e.g., Skolem functions). The next section describes a program that implements this method and illustrates it with an example.

---

[2] To model learning by discovery, *Training* can be any subset of R. Alternatively, when existing knowledge is being extended with new information, it is natural to prefer discovering explanations enabled by the new information. In this context, *Training* is the set of axioms being added to R.

[3] To guarantee tractability, additional restrictions can be imposed on proof construction, such as a bound on the execution time allotted to compute explanations.

Figure 1: New information and the initial context

1a) New Information Provided to KI

[∀ x isa(x Chloroplast)
⇒
∃ y isa(y Chlorophyll) & hasPart(x y)]

1b) Propositions satisfying the new information

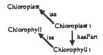

4. Acquiring Proofs During Knowledge Integration

KI is an interactive knowledge-acquisition tool being developed to help knowledge engineers integrate new information into the Botany Knowledge Base [MURR88, PORT88]. This knowledge base currently contains over four thousand frames representing plant anatomy, physiology, and development; it has been constructed in collaboration with MCC's CYC project [LENA89].

This section describes an implemented example of KI extending the Botany Knowledge Base with new information relating chloroplasts and chlorophyll. The knowledge base already contains extensive partonomic knowledge of plants and some knowledge of photosynthetic pigments, such as chlorophyll. A knowledge engineer wishes to extend the knowledge base to represent the fact that chlorophyll is a constituent part of chloroplasts (see Figure 1a). The task of KI is, in general, to identify interesting consequences of this new information and, in particular, to identify how this new information can explain existing beliefs. KI's model of knowledge integration comprises three prominent activities:

1) Recognition: identifying the knowledge relevant to new information
2) Elaboration: applying the expectations provided by relevant knowledge to determine the consequences of the new information
3) Adaptation: modifying the knowledge base to accommodate the elaborated information

4.1 Recognition

During recognition KI identifies concepts in the knowledge base that are relevant to the new information. This involves maintaining a *learning context* – a set of propositions about hypothetical instances of concepts deemed relevant to the new information. When presented with new information, KI initializes the context with propositions that satisfy the new rules (e.g., Figure 1b). To extend the learning context, KI uses *views* to determine which concepts in the knowledge base, beyond those explicitly referenced in the context, are relevant.

Views are sets of propositions that interact in some significant way and should therefore be considered together. Views are created by applying a generic *view type* to a domain concept. Each view type is a parameterized semantic net, represented as a set of paths emanating from a root node and used during knowledge integration as a reminding schema. Applying a view type to a concept involves binding the concept to the root node and instantiating each path. Figures 2a and b present an example view type and the view created by applying it to chloroplast.

To extend the learning context, KI identifies the views defined for concepts already contained in the learning context. Each candidate view is scored with a heuristic measure of relevance: the percentage of concepts contained in the view that are also contained in the learning context. KI presents the list of candidate views, ordered by their relevance score, to the knowledge engineer, who selects one for use.[4] The set of propositions contained in the selected view are added to the learning context. This results in a learning context comprising those concepts in the knowledge base considered most relevant to the new information.

---

[4] Alternatively, an autonomous version of KI selects the view having the highest relevance score.

Figure 2: An example view and view type

2a) Qua Component   **2b) Chloroplast Qua Component**

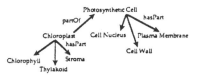

2c) [∀ s isa(s Chloroplast) ⇒ ∃ tuvwxyz isa(t Chlorophyll) & hasPart(s t) & isa(u Thylakoid) & hasPart(s u)
        & isa(v Stroma) & hasPart(s v) & isa(w Photosynthetic-cell) & partOf(s w)
        & isa(x Cell-nucleus) & hasPart(w x) & isa(y Cell-wall) & hasPart(w y)
        & isa(z Plasma-membrane) & hasPart(w z)]

View type *Qua Component* identifies two paths emanating from a concept relevant to its role as a part of a physical structure (the shaded node designates the root concept). Applying this view type to chloroplast identifies the segment of the knowledge base representing chloroplast as a part of a photosynthetic cell. The path variables may have multiple bindings (e.g., the chloroplast parts include chlorophyll, stroma, and thylakoid). 2c) expresses in FOL the inference this view supports.

In addition to adding propositions contained in the selected view to the learning context, KI adds the implications that characterize the conditions under which these propositions are assumed to be true. Whenever the preconditions of a view are satisfied, the propositions contained in the view are assumed to hold. For example, when the proposition $partOf(chloroplast_1\ photosynthetic\text{-}cell_1)$ is added, the following implications are also added:

1) $isa(chloroplast_1\ chloroplast) \Rightarrow partOf(chloroplast_1\ photosynthetic\text{-}cell_1)$

2) $isa(photosynthetic\text{-}cell_1\ photosynthetic\text{-}cell) \Rightarrow partOf(chloroplast_1\ photosynthetic\text{-}cell_1)$

The first implication follows from view *ChloroplastQuaComponent* (see Figure 2c); the second follows from *PhotosyntheticCellQuaStructure* (see Rule 6 of Figure 6). Since there is high overlap among views, many such implications are added to the learning context. This enables limited representation in R_e of rules from R that involve predicates on functions (e.g., Skolem functions). The use of these implications is often essential for completing proofs of domain inference rules.

4.2 Elaboration

During elaboration KI determines how the new information interacts with the existing knowledge within the learning context. Rules in R_e are allowed to exhaustively forward-chain, propagating the consequences of the training throughout the context. For example, one consequence of chloroplasts having chlorophyll is that their color is green. Some of the domain inference rules applicable to this example are listed in Figure 3a, and the resulting conclusions are presented in Figure 3b.

KI enters a cycle of recognition (i.e., selecting views) and elaboration (i.e., applying inference rules) that explicates the consequences of the training while searching for new proofs of rules. This cycle continues until the user intervenes or the relevance scores of all candidate views fall below a progressive threshold. Figure 4 illustrates the second round of this cycle. The recognition phase extends the context of Figure 3b with the set of propositions relevant to a photosynthetic cell in its role as a producer during cell photosynthesis. The elaboration phase propagates the consequences of the new information throughout the extended context.

4.3 Adaptation

During adaptation KI determines if elaboration has revealed any new proofs of inference rules. An interesting prerequisite of discovering proofs of rules is that multiple ground explanations for some proposition must exist. When this occurs, KI determines whether any explanation can be generalized into a proof of some inference rule.

Figure 3: Example rules and inferences

3a) Example Inference Rules

1. Rule: **@partOf-Preserves-Color**
   Color may be inferred from the color of the parts
   $[\forall\ xyz\ partOf(x\ y)\ \&\ color(x\ z) \Rightarrow color(y\ z)]$

2. Rule: **@Chlorophyll_color**
   Inheritance rule: Chlorophyll is inherently green
   $[\forall\ x\ isa(x\ Chlorophyll) \Rightarrow color(x\ Green)]$

3. Rule: **@Leaf_color**
   Inheritance rule: Leaves are assumed to be green
   $[\forall\ x\ isa(x\ Leaf) \Rightarrow color(x\ Green)]$

3b) The Elaborated Context

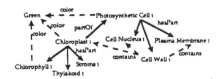

The dashed arrows indicate propositions inferred during elaboration; subscripts denote category instances (e.g., $isa(Chloroplast_1\ Chloroplast)$).

Figure 4: Recognition and elaboration during cycle 2

4a) Photosynthetic Cell Qua Producer   **4b) The Elaborated Context**

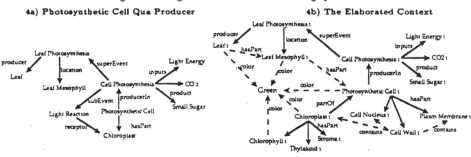

Let E be the set of explanations of some proposition, and let r_i be the last rule applied in some explanation $e_i \in E$. KI evaluates each alternative explanation in E to determine if it can be transformed into a proof of r_i. First KI uses explanation-based generalization to compute the maximal generalization of each $e_j \in E\text{-}e_i$. Let ge_j be the generalization of explanation e_j. Then KI compares the consequence of ge_j to the consequence of r_i. When the consequence of ge_j is equivalent to (or subsumes) the consequence of r_i, KI searches ge_j for sub-explanations whose weakest preconditions entail the consequence of ge_j and are equivalent to (or subsume) the preconditions of r_i; each such sub-explanation constitutes a proof of r_i.

In the example, KI's elaboration of the chloroplast training produces several explanations of the proposition $color(Leaf_1\ Green)$, two of which are presented in Figure 5. Explanation e_1 involves a single application of rule r_3 whose precondition is $isa(x\ Leaf)$. Since this is identical to the preconditions of the generalization of explanation e_2, the generalization of e_2 is a new proof of **@Leaf_color**. Note the importance of implications that explain propositions arising from views. As shown in Figure 6, the views $LeafQuaStructure$, $MesophyllQuaStructure$, $PhotosyntheticCellQuaStructure$ and $ChloroplastQuaStructure$ all chain together to demonstrate that leaves contain chlorophyll.

This example shows how KI discovers a proof for the existing rule *leaves are green* while integrating the new information *chloroplasts have chlorophyll*. This proof improves the system's explanatory competence by revealing the tacit assumptions (e.g., *mesophyll contains photosynthetic cells*) and domain principles (e.g., *an object's color is determined by the color of it's parts*) that justify the rule's use. For example, the proof provides an answer the query *why are leaves green?*

314

explanation e_1
$color(Leaf_1 \ Green)$
$\Leftarrow_{r_3} isa(Leaf_1 \ Leaf)$

explanation e_2
$color(Leaf_1 \ Green)$
$\Leftarrow_{r_1} partOf(Mesophyll_1 \ Leaf_1)$
$\quad \Leftarrow_{r_4} isa(Leaf_1 \ Leaf)$
$\quad color(Mesophyll_1 \ Green)$
$\quad \Leftarrow_{r_1} partOf(Photosynthetic\text{-}cell_1 \ Mesophyll_1)$
$\qquad \Leftarrow_{r_5} isa(Mesophyll_1 \ Mesophyll)$
$\qquad \quad \Leftarrow_{r_4} isa(Leaf_1 \ Leaf)$
$\quad color(Photosynthetic\text{-}cell_1 \ Green)$
$\quad \Leftarrow_{r_1} partOf(Chloroplast_1 \ Photosynthetic\text{-}cell_1)$
$\qquad \Leftarrow_{r_6} isa(Photosynthetic\text{-}cell_1 \ Photosynthetic\text{-}cell)$
$\qquad \quad \Leftarrow_{r_5} isa(Mesophyll_1 \ Mesophyll)$
$\qquad \qquad \Leftarrow_{r_4} isa(Leaf_1 \ Leaf)$
$\quad color(Chloroplast_1 \ Green)$
$\quad \Leftarrow_{r_1} partOf(Chlorophyll_1 \ Chloroplast_1)$
$\qquad \Leftarrow_{r_7} isa(Chloroplast_1 \ Chloroplast)$
$\qquad \quad \Leftarrow_{r_6} isa(Photosynthetic\text{-}cell_1 \ Photosynthetic\text{-}cell)$
$\qquad \qquad \Leftarrow_{r_5} isa(Mesophyll_1 \ Mesophyll)$
$\qquad \qquad \quad \Leftarrow_{r_4} isa(Leaf_1 \ Leaf)$
$\quad color(Chlorophyll_1 \ Green)$
$\quad \Leftarrow_{r_2} isa(Chlorophyll_1 \ Chlorophyll)$
$\qquad \Leftarrow_{r_7} isa(Chloroplast_1 \ Chloroplast)$
$\qquad \quad \Leftarrow_{r_6} isa(Photosynthetic\text{-}cell_1 \ Photosynthetic\text{-}cell)$
$\qquad \qquad \Leftarrow_{r_5} isa(Mesophyll_1 \ Mesophyll)$
$\qquad \qquad \quad \Leftarrow_{r_4} isa(Leaf_1 \ Leaf)$

The notation $p \Leftarrow_i q$ denotes p is infered from q by rule i (see Figures 3 and 6).

Figure 6: Inferences enabled by views and required for the proof

Rule 4) $LeafQuaStructure$
$[\forall \ w \ isa(w \ Leaf) \Rightarrow (\exists \ xyz \ isa(x \ Mesophyll) \ \& \ partOf(x \ w) \ \& \ isa(y \ Epidermis) \ \& \ partOf(y \ w)$
$\& \ isa(z \ Vascular\text{-}network) \ \& \ partOf(z \ w))]$

Rule 5) $MesophyllQuaStructure$
$[\forall \ x \ isa(x \ Mesophyll) \Rightarrow (\exists \ y \ isa(x \ Photosynthetic\text{-}cell) \ \& \ partOf(y \ x))]$

Rule 6) $PhotosyntheticCellQuaStructure$
$[\forall \ v \ isa(v \ Photosynthetic\text{-}cell) \Rightarrow (\exists \ wxyz \ isa(w \ Cell\text{-}nucleus) \ \& \ partOf(w \ v) \ \& \ isa(x \ Cell\text{-}wall) \ \& \ partOf(x \ v)$
$\& \ isa(y \ Chloroplast) \ \& \ partOf(y \ v) \ \& \ isa(z \ Plasma\text{-}membrane)$
$\& \ partOf(z \ v))]$

Rule 7) $ChloroplastQuaStructure$
$[\forall \ w \ isa(w \ Chloroplast) \Rightarrow (\exists \ xyz \ isa(x \ Chlorophyll) \ \& \ partOf(x \ w) \ \& \ isa(y \ Thylakoid) \ \& \ partOf(y \ w)$
$\& \ isa(z \ Stroma) \ \& \ partOf(z \ w))]$

(e.g., *leaves are green because they contain chlorophyll*). Alternatively, the proof guides dependency-directed backchaining to identify assumptions that explain why a particular leaf is not green (e.g., *the leaf's mesophyll has no photosynthetic cells*).

4.4 Strengths, Limitations, and Future Work

KI's approach to knowledge integration involves creating a *hypothetical model* comprising concepts relevant to the new information, and then using the model to derive the consequences of the new information for concepts represented in the model. Reasoning with a single, propositional model (e.g., a model of a hypothetical leaf), rather than reasoning about entire classes of objects (e.g., models of all possible leaves) provides greater focus and tractability. However, this prevents KI from discovering many proofs that alternative models would reveal. Furthermore, KI is currently not capable of exploring all the alternative, and often mutually-inconsistent, behaviors of a model that frequently arise during qualitative simulations [KUIP87]. This prevents KI from discovering many proofs that a single model may be capable of revealing under varying assumptions. Future work should develop methods for guiding the exploration of alternative models and the *possible worlds* for a single model.

The inferences completed with the model are not explicitly selected: rules exhaustively forward-chain. This type of reasoning corresponds to what Johnson-Laird calls *implicit inference* – the automatic, seemingly effortless inferences humans make during mundane tasks, such as discourse comprehension [JOHN83]. The complement of implicit inference is *explicit inference* – the intentional and conscious reasoning humans perform during problem solving. Currently, KI is not capable of demonstrating this kind of goal-directed elaboration. Future research must address developing methods for interleaving these two types of inference.

5. Summary

Explanation plays an important role in a system's ability to acquire knowledge, solve problems, and establish the credibility of its conclusions. One approach to gaining explanatory competence is acquiring proofs of the inference rules used during problem solving. Acquiring proofs enables a system to strengthen an imperfect theory as previously unexplained rules are connected to the underlying principles and tacit assumptions that justify their use.

KI is a knowledge acquisition tool that strengthens an existing domain theory by discovering new proofs of inference rules. When new information is provided, KI actively searches for proofs of existing beliefs that are enabled by the new information. This requires methods for restricting both the universe of discourse and the use of inference rules that include predicates on functions.

KI exploits a type of domain knowledge called *views* to precisely manage a context comprising ground propositions used during the search for proofs. Views are knowledge-base segments composed of interrelated propositions that should be considered collectively. Each view embodies the use of functions to create entities over which propositions are asserted. Separating the use of functions to create entities from the problem of proving theorems enables KI to guide its search for proofs of domain inference rules.

References

[GAGN85] Gagne, E.D. *The Cognitive Psychology of School Learning*, Boston: Little, Brown and Company, 1985.

[JOHN83] Johnson-Laird, P.N. *Mental Models*, Harvard University Press, 1983.

[KUIP87] Kuipers, B.J., and Chiu, C. Taming Intractable Branching in Qualitative Simulation. *Proceedings of the Tenth International Joint Conference on Artificial Intelligence* (1987).

[LENA89] Lenat, D.B., and Guha, R.V. *Building Large Knowledge-Based Systems: Representation and Inference in the CYC Project*, Addison-Wesley, 1989.

[MCAL80] McAllester, D.A. An Outlook on Truth Maintenance. AI Memo No. 551, Artificial Intelligence Laboratory, Massachusetts Institute of Technology, 1980.

[MOON88] Mooney, R.J. *A General Explanation-Based Learning Mechanism and Its Application to Narrative Understanding*, PhD Dissertation, Computer Science Department, University of Illinois at Urbana-Champaign, 1988.

[MURR88] Murray, K.S. KI: An Experiment in Automating Knowledge Integration. Technical Report AI-88-90, Artificial Intelligence Laboratory, Department of Computer Sciences, University of Texas at Austin, 1988.

[SMIT85] Smith, R.G., Winston, H.A., Mitchell, T.M., Buchanan, B.G. Representation and Use of Explicit Justification for Knowledge Base Refinement. *Proceedings of the Ninth International Joint Conference on Artificial Intelligence* (1985).

[STAL77] Stallman, R.M., and Sussman, G.J. Forward Reasoning and Dependency Directed Backtracking in a System for Computer-Aided Circuit Analysis. *Artificial Intelligence 9* (1977).

[SWAR83] Swartout, W.R. XPLAIN: A System for Creating and Explaining Expert Consulting Programs. *Artificial Intelligence 21* (1983).

[PORT88] Porter, B., Lester, J., Murray, K., Pittman, K., Souther, A., Acker, L., and Jones, T. AI Research in the Context of a Multifunctional Knowledge Base: The Botany Knowledge Base Project. Technical Report AI-88-88, Department of Computer Sciences, University of Texas at Austin, 1988.

Incremental Envisioning: The Flexible Use of Multiple Representations in Complex Problem Solving

Malcolm I. Bauer   Brian J. Reiser

Cognitive Science Laboratory
Princeton University

Abstract: In this paper we describe two properties of most psychological and AI models of scientific problem solving: they are one-pass, and feedforward. We then discuss the results of an experiment which suggests that experts use problem solving representations more flexibly than these models suggest. We introduce the concept of *incremental envisioning* to account for this flexible behavior. Finally, we discuss the implications of this work for psychological models of scientific problem solving and for AI programs which solve problems in scientific domains.

1 Introduction

Complex problem solving often involves the use of several representations. For example, when problem solving in scientific domains, people often use formal mathematical equations, many types of diagrams, and informal conceptual intuitions in the course of reasoning. In this paper, we consider people how coordinate the use of several representations while solving a problem in a scientific domain.

2 The Traditional View

In his book, *How to Solve It*, Polya (1945) described what he believed were the four phases of problem solving: 1) understanding the problem 2) developing a plan to solve it 3) carrying out the plan, and 4) checking over the solution. Most psychological models of mathematics and science problem solving (e.g., Larkin, McDermott, Simon, & Simon, 1980; Chi, Feltovich, & Glaser, 1981; Ri-

ley, Greeno, & Heller, 1983) and programs in AI which solve problems in science (de Kleer, 1975; Skorstad & Forbus, 1989) may be considered instantiations of this view within specific domains. For example, Larkin et al. (1980) propose that physics experts solving mechanics problems will begin by sketching a picture of the described problem and selecting a set of principles. From these they construct a representation of the problem containing relevant physical entities (i.e. understanding the problem). This conceptual representation of the problem is then re-represented as a set of physics equations (constructing a plan). Finally the equations are solved algebraically (carrying out the plan). In AI, de Kleer's (1975) Newton program solves simple kinematics problems in a similar manner. Given a description of a physical scenario and a question about that scenario (e.g. "How fast will the block be traveling at point A?"), Newton first constructs an *envisionment* or representation of what will happen in the scenario. Second, it constructs a general plan of what must be done to solve the problem. Finally it accesses the relevant mathematical knowledge and solves associated equations until the desired quantity is found.

In both models, as in most subsequent models of scientific problem solving, problem solving is accomplished by proceeding sequentially through the phases described by Polya. First some sort of general conceptual model of the problem situation is constructed (in the case of Newton, this conceptual model is called an envisionment). Second, a general plan for solving the problem is constructed, embodied either as the general principles operating or as the crucial states that must be solved for. Finally, the plan cues the relevant equations, which are then solved. Polya's fourth phase, checking over the solution, is rarely included. To summarize, these models can be characterized as comprised of some or all of the following phases.

1. Construct a conceptual understanding of what is occurring in the problem.

2. Develop a plan to solve the problem. Typically this involves deciding what principles are relevant and which equations will be used.

3. Construct and solve the relevant equations.

4. Check the solution.

The models have two key properties. First, the models are *feed-forward* because information flows from earlier phases to later phases, but never in the other direction. For example, inferences made while solving equations are never passed back to earlier phases to enhance conceptual understanding.

Second, the models are *one-pass serial*. All processing within each phase is completed before the next phase is initiated. There is a block of processing using to understand the problem conceptually followed by a planning phase, which is followed by a solving phase. This property is distinct from the first one in that it is possible to have an iterative model rather than a one-pass model which would still be feed-forward. Such a model would loop through the phases several times but only passing information "forward," for example, never using phase 3 inferences in later phase 1 processing.

For fairly simple problems, there is psychological evidence that expert problem solving fits this one-pass, feed-forward model (Larkin et al., 1980). Similarly, in AI, this model has been used to solve several types of physics problems (Skorstad & Forbus, 1989; de Kleer, 1975). However, there are several reasons to believe this model does not completely characterize how experts solve all types of problems. Similarly, there are reasons to believe that this kind of AI architecture will not be able to solve many kinds of problems.

First, for complex problems, short-term memory restrictions may require people to cycle through the phases, solving pieces of the problem each time, to put together a coherent complete solution, rather than doing all the required reasoning in each phase before initiating the next phase.

Second, memory considerations aside, for difficult problems, experts may need to use several kinds of representations simultaneously to characterize a problem conceptually. This may include particular equations, theoretical models from physics, and commonsense intuitions. Roschelle and Greeno (1987) give anecdotal evidence to support this in protocols where expert physicists use both Newtonian physics models and commonsense intuitions about a physical situation to how objects will behave.

Third, de Kleer (1975) describes a class of problems he terms *indefinite* that his program is unable to solve. He claims it can't solve these problems because the program lacks flexibility. It needs to access information from different phases of its problem solving, but cannot because it is a one-pass feed-forward model. For example, certain problems may require some calculations be performed (phase 3) in order to complete conceptual understanding (phase 1).

Finally, recent work in qualitative reasoning (Sacks, 1988) has focused on interpreting formal symbolic solutions qualitatively. In many scientific disciplines, coming up with a formal symbolic solution to a problem (the result of phase 3) is not the final goal, as it is in the models above. Instead the goal is to understand what the solution means at a conceptual level (phase 1). The work in qualitative reasoning focuses on interpreting the results of phase 3 in terms of the conceptual representations utilized in phase 1. In one-pass feed-forward models, this is impossible as passing back results from phase 3 to phase 1 does not occur.

3 An Empirical Investigation of Multiple Representations

The present research is concerned with understanding expert performance in situations that experts find more challenging. The psychological models described above were typically derived from expert performance on problems requiring little effort for the experts. For the reasons above,

318

we suggest that a one-pass feed-forward model will be inadequate to completely characterize expert performance on more complex problems. We examine expert performance on moderately difficult mechanics problems in physics. Expert performance on "easy" problems has been studied extensively in mechanics so this provides a good basis for comparison. We are interested in investigating whether one-pass feed-forward models are inadequate to explain expert behavior, and if not, what is it that experts do beyond these models in those situations.

3.1 Design and Materials

We selected four hard mechanics problems. Three of the four were taken from a review text (Wells & Slusher, 1983). The fourth was created by one of us. Simplified versions of each of the hard problems were constructed. These used the same principles necessary to solve the hard problems, but the physical scenarios in which those principles had to be used were greatly simplified. Examples are shown in Figure 1.

Subjects were graduate students drawn from the Mechanical Engineering and Physics departments at Princeton University. There were 16 subjects in total, although the analyses in this paper focus on the first 6 subjects. Each subject solved four problems, two easy and two hard. No subject was given a hard problem and its corresponding easy problem. Subjects were asked to "think out loud" while solving the problems. The sessions were videotaped. We transcribed all subjects' actions which included verbal statements, writing an equation, drawing a diagram, modifying an equation or diagram, and pointing to an equation or diagram. Because we wished to examine the transitions among the kinds of representations used, we coded protocol statements according to the kind of information used and the type of action being performed. Our analyses consider only the *information heeded* by the subject, rather than attempting to categorize the actual processes which are acting upon that information (Ericsson & Simon, 1984). Recognizing the transitions was also facilitated by the fact that, in addition to the verbal protocols, the transcripts also contained all cases where subjects modified or pointed to an equation or diagram. Protocol statements were classified into one of the eight basic categories described below:

Categorization: Subject states a category to which the problem belongs.

Rehearsal: Subject reads or re-reads problem, or restates a fact previously found.

Physical Reasoning: Subject identifies a particular physical quantity in problem, or states what occurs in the scenario, without the use of equations.

Diagram Use: Subject draws, labels, or points to a diagram.

Miscellaneous: This category includes explicit statements involving planning, and stating basic physics principles.

Mapping: Subject explicitly maps information from one representation to another.

Formal Symbolic Manipulation: Subject recalls, writes down, or performs any operation on an equation.

Qualitative Mathematical Reasoning: Subject considers an equation and reasons about it qualitatively.

Setting Goals, Hitting Impasses: Subject states a goal, or makes a statement that he or she has hit an impasse (e.g. "I'm stuck.")

Each general category was divided in several subcatgories to code the kind of action performed, if one was explicit. For example, Diagram Use had three subcategories: writing down part or all of a diagram, pointing to a diagram, and labeling part of a diagram with an equation or symbol.

3.2 Analyses

First, subjects indeed found the hard problems more difficult that the easy problems. On average it took the subjects 4.3 minutes to solve the easy problems and 18 minutes to solve the hard problems. In terms of the coding scheme, transcripts for the easy problems contained an average of 38.3 steps and for the hard problems, 122.3. All of the easy problems were solved correctly, but only 75% of the hard problems.

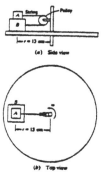

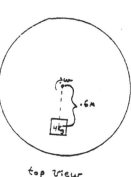

Figure 1: A hard problem (left) and its corresponding easy problem (right)

There are several analyses which can be used to evaluate the types of problem solving sequences. As a first step towards investigating these reasoning events, we divided each protocol into quarters according to the total number of codes in the protocol, and plotted the average percentage of each category of action within a quartile. The graph in Figure 2 is a quartile plot for the most prevalent codes.

The most dramatic effect is the rise in the percentage of formal symbolic manipulation, starting at 13% in the first quartile and rising fairly linearly to 60% in the fourth quartile. In addition, the physical, diagrammatic, and rehearsal codes start at around 20% in the first quartile, and slowly drop until they are all about 4% in the last quartile. This overall trend of the increase in formal manipulation and decrease in actions of with conceptual understanding is generally in keeping with the one-pass feed-forward model. However, the fact that there is even 15% formal manipulation in the first quartile and some actions of conceptual understanding in the last quartiles suggests that the one-pass feed-forward model of phases does not tell the whole story. In fact, some solving of equations

(associated with phase 3) occurred before physical reasoning (associated with phase 1) thus the strict ordering of the phases is not being followed completely (the "one-pass" property).

Another way to evaluate the model is to examine the number of transitions between the formal and conceptual representations. A one-pass model would predict very few. Transitions would occur only when creating the formal equations from the conceptual representation. For the easy problems the average number of transitions was 4, while for the hard, 14. This again is evidence which supports the claim that subjects are not strictly "one-pass." Looking at the step/transition ratio, we find that this is approximately 1 transition for every 9 steps, which seems to be many more than would be expected if problem solving occurs as a long episode of conceptual work followed by an episode of planning, followed by an episode of formal symbol manipulation. Instead, it appears that subjects shift between phase 1 and phase 3 relatively frequently.

There is also evidence that subjects were not strictly feed-forward (property 1) while solving these problems as well. In many instances subjects

320

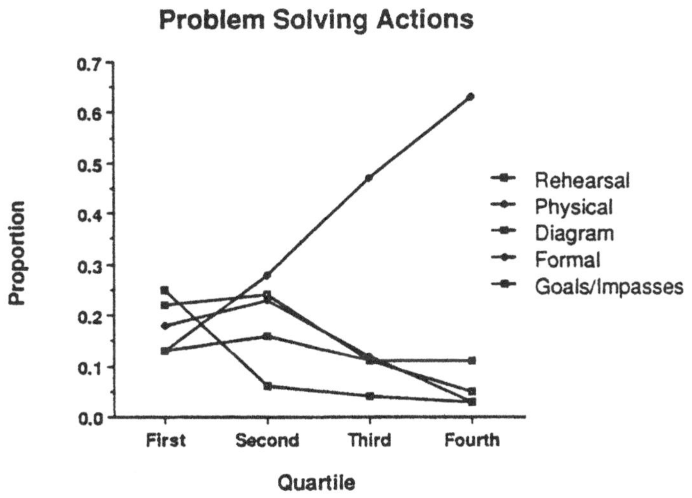

Problem Solving Actions

Figure 2: Quartile Plot of Problem Solving Actions

actually interpret derived equations to enrich their conceptual understanding in the course a problem. This *backward mapping* violates the feed-forward property described above. A typical example of this type of episode occurred when one subject was solving a problem about a falling rope:

> "Here's an old equation: $V^2 = V_0^2 + 2as$ [subject writes equation down] This is 0 [subject crosses out V_0 leaving the equation $V^2 = 2as$], so the velocity as it hits the table [points to rope in diagram] is gonna be a function of how far away from the table it was."

Here the subject has recalled an equation, applied some known quantitative information ($V_0 = 0$) and then interpreted the meaning of the expression conceptually, updating his conceptual understanding of the problem. The subject has done some work which would be classified as phase 3, but then applied it to work which would be classified as phase 1. For hard problems, this type of backward mapping occurred an average of 3.6 times per problem. This type of shift cannot occur in any model which is purely feed-forward. A more flexible model of reasoning is required.

4 Discussion

We have presented evidence that suggests that often people do not completely follow the one-pass feed-forward model. Their behavior is not strictly one-pass: they shift between understanding (phase 1) and solving (phase 3) many times in the course of reasoning about a problem. Similarly, their behavior is not strictly feed-forward: often they will use the results of solving aspects of a problem (phase 3) to enhance their conceptual understanding of the problem (phase 1) which will in turn enable them to solve other parts of the problem. Interestingly, there are different representations associated with each phase. Phase 1 is associated with building a conceptual understanding of a problem. In previous models, conceptual understanding is represented as a mental model (Roschelle & Greeno, 1987; Hegarty, Just, & Morrison, 1988), or an envisionment of what could happen (de Kleer, 1975; Roschelle & Greeno,1987). The representation used in the solution phase (phase 3) is a set of formal symbolic equations (Larkin et al, 1980). In this section, we discuss how experts coordinate these representations in problem-solving.

In most models of scientific problem solving, all of the understanding phase occurs at the beginning. Experts read the problem description, construct a representation of what's going on, and then set about to solve the problem. Instead, we propose that experts perform *incremental envisioning*: they successively refine their conceptual understanding of a problem as they work through it. There are two general ways in which subjects shift from one representation to the other. The first is a shift from envisioning to a representation associated with another phase. The second is a shift from working on the equations back to increasing the conceptual understanding of a problem.

We propose that the first kind of shift occurs largely to reduce the load of working memory. Here subjects will be thinking about what's going on in a problem and discover something relevant to one of the other phases – either an equation will be cued, an important subgoal discovered, or an important physical insight gained. The subject will then stop developing their conceptual understanding and shift to preserve that relevant piece of information, either by writing down the equation and doing some formal symbolic manipulation, by adding the physical insight to a diagram, or by stating clearly what that new goal is. In this type of shift, envisioning is momentarily halted and the important ramifications of it are propagated to other representations and preserved. Then envisioning is resumed. This is still feed-forward in that work in the other representations does not affect the envisioning, however, in contrast to the one-pass models described earlier, the process is incremental. By propagating new relevant information to other representations, the other representations are built up as the envisionment progresses. In this way, neither the entire envisionment, nor its ramifications for the other representations, have to be held in memory all at once.

To investigate this kind of incremental envisioning more precisely, we constructed the transition table containing the probability of each kind of action directly following a physical reasoning (envisioning) event (see Table 1). It is clear from the transition table that all the physical reasoning does not occur in one block, but instead shifts to other kinds of actions quite regularly. The probability of shifting to working on diagrams, shifting to working on equations, and shifting to setting goals, are all close to, if not greater than the probability of continuing with the physical reasoning.

Categorization	0.015
Rehearsal	0.073
Physical Reasoning	0.188
Diagram Use	0.272
Miscellaneous	0.019
Mapping	0.042
Formal Symbolic Manipulation	0.226
Qualitative Mathematical Reasoning	0.004
Setting Goals, Hitting Impasses	0.153

Table 1

The following examples demonstrate these feed-forward shifts:

Physical cuing Formal:

we have the man..of mass M ..on the ladder which is a force Mg..

Here the subject began to describe the scenario (man on ladder) and shifted to writing the symbolic expression for the weight of the man (force Mg).

Physical cuing Diagram:

that's the force needed to keep that thing going in the circle.. [subjects adds arrow to diagram]

In this example, the subject envisioned what a particular force is going to do, and then preserved that inference by adding an arrow (drawn in a circle) to a diagram.

physical cuing goals:

...we remain on the same circle, but I am moving on the circle and he's not..so the maximum time it's going to take is the time I need to make a complete circle, and that will be the worst case...so all I know have to know is the tangential speed...

Here the subject reasoned conceptually about what will happen, and then recognized a new goal to be acheived (phase 2).

In second kind of shift, the conceptual understanding phase is resumed because of an event that occurs in one of the other representations. Often, though not always, the subject returns to phase 1 to help resolve a difficulty arising in another phase. Envisioning might be resumed because of the realization that the problem cannot be solved from the current equations, for example the subject realizes that there are too few equations for the number of unknowns. This kind of shift also may be necessary to solve indefinite problems. Often it involves interpreting the results of symbolic manipulation (phase 3), as in the rope example given in the previous section. This may be done to check the validity of the derived equation, (if the interpreted equation makes sense conceptually it's more likely to be true). Occasionally, this kind of shift occurs simply to update the conceptual understanding of the problem, not to resolve any particular difficulty. However, this may cause the subject to gain new insight into the problem. Again, the rope protocol above is an example of this. Each of these cases is an example of iterative refinement as the understanding of the problem is updated with each return to envisioning. Some examples of this second type of shift are:

Too few equations:

that's   for   that equation so that's two equations two unknowns.. no wait a minute two equations four unknowns<laughs> but we have two more equations.. which are the uhhh... wait a minute, [points to problem diagram] why does l interfere here?.... uh mmm.. well let's see physically what happens? If we start at this point....

Here the subject was working on the equations when he realized there are too few equations for the number of unknowns. In trying to come up with the other two equations, the subject shifted back to thinking about the problem conceptually.

Shift after finding impossible results:

and we don't want a negative because we have to take a square root... and I screwed up the sign somewhere here.. A minus B... [points at minuses in equations] that's a minus, minus, minus, minus 2.... b....where did I lose my sign?.. [pointing at equations] T zero minus minus minus .. did I .. mess up...my forces while on this little thing?..... [points to diagram and checks equations against diagrams] where are my forces going here?..tension.... $muMg...muMg$ that's gotta be the opposite of that one... that one going that way...

Here the subject, in the course of solving the problem came up with the square root of a negative number. In trying to track down the error, he switched back to reasoning conceptually about what happens in the physical scenario.

To summarize, incremental envisioning occurs in two main ways. The first is done to preserve the results of envisioning and involves propagating each new result to other representations. In the second, an event in phase 3 causes envisioning to be resumed often to help resolve a difficulty arising in phase 3 processing. In this case, results from phase 3 are propagated back to phase 1.

5 Conclusions

In this paper we have described a class of scientific problem solving models called one-pass feed-forward models. We then described an experiment which suggested that expert problem solving behavior involved more than could be accounted by these models. Finally, we proposed that experts perform *incremental envisioning* as a way of describing the kinds of behaviors not characterized by one-pass feed-forward models. In this section, we briefly elaborate the implications of this work for AI and psychology.

At first glance, the first type of incremental envisioning, feed-forward shifts, may not seem useful for AI programs that solve scientific problems. We suggested this first type is used to overcome short-term memory constraints in humans. However, computers have no such limitations, so there

323

is less need to preserve the representational ramifications of envisioning in the course of performing envisioning. Instead, the entire envisionment may be saved, and used as a whole to help in planning and solving the problem. Indeed, most scientific problem solvers work this way (de Kleer, 1975; Skorstad & Forbus, 1989). However, there are many scientific problems in which a complete envisionment need not be performed. Creating one, without reference to what must be solved for in the problem, is inefficient in these cases. Also, there are many problems for which it is impossible to construct a complete envisionment from the given information, yet the problems are solvable for the particular question being asked. In these cases, creating partial envisionments and propagating the results of envisioning during the course of envisioning is essential to deriving a solution.

The importance of the second type of incremental envisioning, backward mapping, is clear. In many cases, it may be necessary to solve part of a problem in order to complete an envisionment to solve the rest of the problem. De Kleer's indefinite problems fall into this class. Similarly, in other circumstances, it may be desirable to interpret equations conceptually. Work in AI along these lines is already being done (Sacks, 1988; see Forbus, 1988 for comprehensive review).

For psychological models, this work demonstrates that experts use representations more flexibly than has been thought. Models of expert problem solving must take into account this added flexibility. We are currently developing a computational model of incremental envisioning in problem solving. Roschelle and Greeno's (1988) relational model is a step in this direction as well.

Acknowledgments: The research reported here was supported in part by contract MDA903-87-K-0652 from the Army Research Institute, by a research grant from the James S. McDonnell Foundation, and by a grant-in-aid of research from the Sigma Xi, The Scientific Research Society. The views and conclusions contained in this document are those of the authors and should not be interpreted as necessarily representing the official policies, either expressed or implied, of the U.S. Army or the McDonnell Foundation.

References

Chi, M. T. H., Feltovich, P. J., & Glaser, R. (1981) Categorization and representation of physics problems by experts and novices. *Cognitive Science*, 5,121–152.

de Kleer, J. (1975). *Qualitative and quantitative knowledge in classical mechanics.* Master's thesis, Department of Electrical Engineering, Massachusetts Institute of Technology, Cambridge, MA.

Ericsson, K. A., & Simon, H. A. (1984). *Protocol Analysis.* Cambridge, MA: MIT Press.

Forbus, K. D. (1988). Qualitative physics: Past, present, and future. In H. E. Shrobe (Ed.), *Exploring Artificial Intelligence*, San Mateo, CA: Morgan Kaufmann.

Larkin, J. H., McDermott, J., Simon, D. P., & Simon, H. A. (1980). Models of competence in solving physics problems. *Cognitive Science*, 4, 317–345.

Polya, G. (1945). *How to Solve It.* Princeton, NJ: Princeton University Press.

Riley, M. S., Greeon, J. G., & Heller, J. I. (1983). Development of children's problem solving ability in artihmetic. In H. P. Ginsberg (Ed.), *The development of mathematical thinking*, NY: Academic Press.

Roschelle, J., & Greeno, J. G. (1987). mental models in expert physic reasoning. *Report No. GK-2*, University of California, Berkeley.

Sacks, E. (1988). Qualitative analysis by piecewise linear approximation. *Artificial Intelligence in Engineering*, 3, 3.

Skorstad, G. & Forbus, K. (1989). Qualitative and Quantitative Reasoning about Thermodynamics. *Proceedings of the 11th Annual Conference of the Cognitive Science Society*, Ann Arbor, Michigan: Lawrence Erlbaum.

Wells, D. A., & Slusher, H. S. (1983) *Physics for Engineering and Science.* U.S.A: McGraw-Hill.

Task-Based Criteria for Judging Explanations[1]

David B. Leake

Center for Research on Concepts and Cognition, Indiana University

leake@cogsci.indiana.edu

Abstract

AI research on explanation has not seriously addressed the influence of explainer goals on explanation construction. Likewise, psychological research has tended to assume that people's choice between explanations can be understood without considering the explainer's task. We take the opposite view: that the influence of task is central to judging explanations. Explanations serve a wide range of tasks, each placing distinct requirements on what is needed in an explanation.

We identify eight main classes of reasons for explaining novel events, and show how each one imposes requirements on the information needed from an explanation. These requirements form the basis of dynamic, goal-based explanation evaluation implemented in the program ACCEPTER. We argue that goal-based evaluation of explanations offers three important advantages over static criteria: First, it gives a way for an explainer to know what to elaborate if an explanation is inadequate. Second, it allows cross-contextual use of explanations, by deciding when an explanation built in one context can be applied to another. Finally, it allows explainers to make a principled decision of when to accept incomplete explanations without further elaboration, allowing explainers to conserve processing resources, and also to deal with situations they can only partially explain.

Introduction

It seems obvious that people who explain usually do so for a reason— that explanation is done to serve an overarching task. Explanations allow people to understand unexpected situations, in order to deal with them more effectively. However, the effect of overarching tasks on explanation has received little attention in psychology and artificial intelligence. Attribution theory [Heider, 1958], the central current in psychological study of people's judgement of explanations, tries to account for their judgements in a context-independent way. AI work in explanation-based learning (EBL) also fails to address the influence of changing goals on explanation (see [DeJong, 1988] for an overview of EBL research).

Context-independent theories fail in two main ways. First, they simply cannot account for the choices that people make. Second, in an AI system, they limit system performance by sometimes failing to accept explanations that are useful, sometimes accepting explanations that are not. Context-independent theories often require complete explanations, showing

---

[1]This work was conducted in part at the Center for Research on Concepts and Cognition at Indiana University, supported by a grant from Indiana University, and at Yale University, supported in part by the Defense Advanced Research Projects Agency, monitored by the Office of Naval Research under contract N0014-85-K-0108 and by the Air Force Office of Scientific Research under contract F49620-88-C-0058.

necessary and sufficient conditions for occurence of the outcome being explained. However, a robbery victim who wants to keep from being robbed again does not need to form a complete picture of the robbery to benefit in the future: as long as he realizes that leaving a window open made the robber choose to rob his house, he can prevent future robberies. Nor is a complete explanation guaranteed to be useful: An account of the robber's motivation, no matter how complete, would not help the victim make his house more secure.

To develop useful criteria for evaluating explanations, we must consider how explanations are used. The following sections identify eight purposes for explanation, and illustrate how each purpose places different requirements on the information that an explanation needs to provide. These requirements in turn determine the goodness of an explanation. We illustrate the effect of purpose on explanation with output from evaluation of an explanation for two different purposes by ACCEPTER, a program that examines the information provided in explanations, according to the information requirements for a range of user-specified tasks.[2] We conclude with a discussion of how task-based evaluation allows explanation-based approaches to be applied despite the lack of a a complete explanation.

Attribution theory

Seminal work by Heider [1958] initiated psychological research into how people decide to favor certain explanations. Heider originated *attribution theory*, which investigates how people decide whether to explain an action in terms of features of its actor, or features of the environment. (Most work in attribution theory assumes that either personal or situational factors will apply, but not both.) Kelley's *covariation principle* gives a hypothesis for how people make this decision [Kelley, 1967]. It suggests that people look at covariation across different people, other entities, and time, in order to decide which type of factor applies. For example, if John dislikes a movie, but most other viewers are enthusiastic, Kelley's covariation principle suggests that John's dislike should be explained by aspects of John, rather than the movie.

The covariation principle makes no reference to how the explanation might be used. More recent work has noted one area in which attributions are influenced by overarching goals: *excuse theory* shows how people displace blame by focusing on external reasons when explaining their own bad performance (see, for example, [Mehlman and Snyder, 1983]). Excuse theory is built on Kelley's model, and shows how the desire to form excuses makes an explainer manipulate the balancing that would otherwise be determined by covariation. However, attribution theory has not addressed the role of other goals in explanation. We will show both that other goals exert strong influences, and that they require characterizing information along dimensions beyond the person–situation distinction that is central to attribution theory.

Explanation-based learning

AI research on explanation-based learning (EBL) has shown that explanations provide valuable guidance for feature selection in new situations. However, EBL research concentrates on how to learn from an explanation presented to the system, giving less attention to

---

[2] ACCEPTER is a system that detects gaps in its knowledge that require explanation, and that evaluates explanations' plausibility as well as the type of information they provide. Those phases of the system are beyond the scope of this paper, but are described further in [Leake, 1988].

explanation selection. To the extent that it has addressed intended use, it has concentrated on explaining for a single purpose: efficient object recognition (*e.g.*, [Mitchell *et al.*, 1986] and [Kedar-Cabelli, 1987]). Keller [1988] points out that studying EBL only in the context of object recognition has had a strong, and falsely limiting, effect on analysis of explanations: an explanation that permits effective object recognition may not be useful for other tasks.

Some AI systems do apply their explanations to other tasks (*e.g.*, plan repair in [Hammond, 1986]), but rely on being presented with good explanations. This cannot be assumed when using explanations from external sources, or re-using explanations built in other contexts. For example, if we want to find out why our brand X car will not start, in order to repair the problem, we might ask a friend. If he had previously urged us to buy a different brand, he might reply "because brand X is junk." A person would not be satisfied with this answer; nor should an EBL system.

Tasks that drive explanation

In order to understand human explanation, and to build systems that can explain effectively, we must first look at *why* explanation is done. Once we know the purposes for explanation, we can investigate what makes explanations good for those purposes— what information the explanations must provide.

We have identified eight primary tasks served by explanation, each of which imposes different requirements on what constitutes a good explanation. We sketch these tasks below, and describe the requirements they impose. As we describe the requirements, we build up a vocabulary of *evaluation dimensions*, which categorize the aspects of causes that are important to deciding an explanation's usefulness for a given task. We show at the end of this paper how those dimensions are used to implement task-based evaluation in the program ACCEPTER.

We consider that explanations have the form of a belief-support chain [Schank and Leake, 1989]. Belief-support chains are belief dependency networks, tracing inferences that lead from a set of premises to the outcome being explained. The inferences are plausible connections, not deductions: a belief-support chain increases the tendency to believe the outcome, but does not prove that it must occur.

The sections below sketch eight tasks that drive explanation, and examine the types of information they require from an explanation. We concentrate on tasks that arise when people explain surprising events for their own benefit, going beyond simply trying to make sense of those events.

Learning when to predict the event

When an event is surprising, it may be important to learn how *not* to be surprised by it in the future— how to predict it before it happens next time. For example, a college admissions officer might try to explain why a student who had seemed promising had dropped out, to better predict problems when next looking at applications.

Explanations useful for future predictions must have four properties. First, the links from the explanation's premises to the outcome must be strong enough to make the explainer expect the same outcome, the next time the premises recur. The degree to which an explanation licenses future predictions is its *predictive force*.

Second, the premises must be factors that the predictor is likely to know about in the future. For example, suppose a gambler explains a team's surprising loss by their lack of concentration. Since he is unlikely to know the team's concentration level in advance of future games, the explanation probably will not help him predict future losses in time to profit. However, a coach might be able to tell in advance, from observing the team in the locker room, so he might be able to use the explanation to predict before future games. How easy it is for an actor to recognize that a premise holds is its *knowability*. But the usefulness of knowable causes depends on a both knowability, and a third property, their *timeliness*: they need to happen far enough in advance for the explainer to benefit from revising his predictions. For example, it would not help the gambler to know that the team would lose after he saw the first play, if he had to bet before the game started.

Finally, the explanation can only be used predictively if it shows an unusual factor of the situation. Even if a team's lack of concentration is a contributing factor to its loss, accounting for the loss by bad concentration will not be helpful if the team never concentrates— what the explanation needs to focus on is the unusual aspect of the situation (*e.g.*, that their superstar was injured). Thus an explanation must trace a surprising event to at least one cause with *distinctiveness*.

Controlling future occurrence of the surprising event

Obviously, preventing future occurrence of an event involves finding premises with *causal force*— that cause the outcome— and that the explainer can block (*controlability*). However, this is not sufficient. For example, if someone burns a cake he is baking, he knows the basic cause of the burning— that the cake became too hot— and how to prevent it— turning down the oven. However, he still needs to know *when* to turn down the oven in the future. If he uses a lower temperature for everything, the things that used to come out perfectly will be underdone. Thus for an explanation to help in preventing an outcome, it must show when to apply the preventative steps: it must allow prediction of the bad outcome, early enough to take steps to block it.

To learn how to achieve the outcome that was surprising, an explainer needs to find a set of causes that are all either controllable, or that have *routineness*, so that they are likely to hold in the future, even without the actor taking action to achieve them himself.

Assigning responsibility and blame

If an actor could have prevented an event's occurrence, or contributed voluntarily to its causes, he bears some responsibility. Depending on the *desirability* of the outcome, the actor may be blameable. He can also be blamed, even if he could not predict or control an outcome, if he contributed to it through an undesirable act. For example, we might blame a drug dealer for an addict's death by overdose, even if overdose deaths are relatively unlikely.

Focusing repair of an undesirable current situation

In order to fix a problem, we need to find problems that both have causal force, and *repairability*. We could explain any automobile breakdown by "there's something wrong with the engine," but the only repair possible at that level of detail is to replace the entire engine, which is not within the financial constraints of most drivers. In addition, we need to find a cause with *independence* from prior causes: if a burned-out transformer in a television is caused by a short circuit, replacing only the transformer will not be an effective repair: unless the short circuit is also fixed, a new transformer would immediately burn out also.

Focusing repair is an instance of a more general category of explanation task: clarifying the current situation to choose an appropriate response. The explainer needs to find an explanation that allows selection of a feasible plan, or the choice between competing alternatives. The competing plans determine which distinctions an explanation must make. For example, an insurance company might try to determine whether a death was suicide or not, in order to determine whether to pay the claim, or refuse. If an explanation for the death shows that the victim were killed in the crash of an airliner, the company would not need further information. However, a lawyer for the family might still want to explain the crash further, to determine whether negligence was involved, and sue those who were responsible.

Sketch of additional purposes

We briefly sketch some additional purposes for explanation, that also affect the type of information a good explanation must provide:

- **Learning a new plan, or refining plan selection:** We can sometimes learn new plans by explaining surprising actions. For example, if we ride home with someone who takes an unusual route, we might explain that the route avoids rush hour traffic, and start using it ourselves. This task for explanation is investigated in [Mooney and DeJong, 1985], which argues that explanations for learning new plans must account for actions in terms of known plan schemas.

- **Changing others' view of an outcome:** An explainer might try to focus on causes that absolve an actor of blame (which is closely related to the task studied in excuse theory), or causes that associate an effect with something desirable or undesirable, to make people see the causes in a new light. For example, if someone took a wrong turn, he might try to make his passengers take a more positive view of the incident, by attributing the turn to distraction because conversation in the car was so captivating.

- **Testing or extending a special-purpose theory:** In order to test a theory, we might require that an explanation use a particular class of rules. For example, an economist might explain layoffs to substantiate his economic theory, by showing it would have predicted them.

ACCEPTER

ACCEPTER is a story understanding program that requests explanations when it encounters anomalies, and judges user-selected explanations both in terms of whether they resolve the anomaly, and in terms of whether they provide the information needed for user-selected goals (see [Leake, 1988] for an overview of the system). Thus ACCEPTER makes the judgement needed for an EBL system to assure that it starts from an explanation relevant to its goals. ACCEPTER was developed as part of SWALE (*e.g.*, [Kass *et al.*, 1986]), a system that uses ACCEPTER's judgements to determine which explanations to accept and generalize for future use.

ACCEPTER implements simple heuristics for judging explanations' premises along the dimensions identified above: predictive force, knowability, timeliness, distinctiveness/routineness, desirability, repairability, and independence. These heuristics allow it to evaluate explanations for four of the purposes above: learning to predict the outcome in the future, repairing device defects, preventing recurrence of the outcome, and assigning blame.

The example below shows ACCEPTER's evaluation of two plausible explanations for a hypothetical Audi recall:

1. The mechanical problems resulted from the car being manufactured by Acme Car Company, under contract as a supplier, due to Acme's bad quality control.

2. The defect resulted from a flaw in the transmissions, which aren't checked by Audi's quality control department.

It would be possible for both the explanations to reflect the facts of the recall. However, the following output, in which ACCEPTER evaluates their usefulness for repairing the defect, shows that they are not equally useful to a mechanic. A mechanic needs to find a state that he can repair— causes that happened in the past, and no longer affect the situation, are unimportant to him, because past events can no longer be repaired. Although the first explanation gives information on factors that led to the defect, it doesn't show a continuing cause that can be repaired in the current situation, so that explanation is useless for him:

```
Checking detail for repair.
  To aid in repair, explanation must show a cause that:
    1. Is repairable.
    2. Is predictive of the problem occurring.
    3. Will not be restored by another state if repaired.

    Checking whether some antecedent satisfies the following tests:
    CAUSAL FORCE TEST (does fact cause consequent?),
    REPAIRABILITY, PREDICTIVENESS, and INDEPENDENT CAUSE.

      Applying test for REPAIRABILITY to AUDI'S PRODUCTION-CONTRACT to ACME.

        Searching up abstraction net for pointers to standard repair plans.
        ... test failed.

      Applying test for REPAIRABILITY to ACME'S NOT M-QUALITY-CONTROL.

        Searching up abstraction net for pointers to standard repair plans.
        ... test failed.

      ... Detail is unacceptable.
```

The second explanation involves two factors that continue to contribute to the car's bad condition: the transmission's defect, and the fact that it is part of the car. ACCEPTER finds that a plan exists for correcting one of them, so that a repair can be done:

```
Applying test for REPAIRABILITY to TRANSMISSION-743'S
PART-OF-RELATIONSHIP to AUDI'S ENGINE.

  Checking repairability of features of TRANSMISSION-743'S
  PART-OF-RELATIONSHIP to AUDI'S ENGINE.
```

```
Searching up abstraction net for pointers to standard repair plans.

AUDI'S ENGINE AS CONTAINER OF TRANSMISSION-743'S
PART-OF-RELATIONSHIP to AUDI'S ENGINE is repairable, since
CONTAINERs of PART-OF-RELATIONSHIPs can usually be repaired
by the standard plan REPLACE-COMPONENT.
... test passed.

... Detail is acceptable.
```

Thus even if both explanations are accurate, an explanation-based system doing repair needs to reject one, and use the other.

Conclusion

Judging explanations according to explainer task provides a way of deciding when to accept one of the many explanations that can be constructed for an event, and finding out what information an incomplete explanation lacks. For example, after a robbery, different tasks make different information important to find out: the victim might focus on what made him a target, to prevent it next time; a policeman might focus on the lack of patrols enabling the crime, to blame his superiors; a social worker rehabilitating the robber might focus on the robber's motivations, to decide how to proceed. The range of purposes and explanations possible for a single event has been discussed in philosophical works such as [Hanson, 1961], but has not been addressed in research on EBL or attribution.[3]

In addition to helping to choose between complete explanations, task-based criteria allow an explainer to use partial explanations in a principled way. Even if the explanation does not completely account for an outcome, it can be useful. For example, if we know just one of the factors that contributed to an event, we may be able to block its occurrence: people who know that high-fat diets contribute to heart attacks can lower their risk, even if they do not know all the other factors necessary to predict heart-attacks. However, traditional approaches to EBL require that learning start from a complete explanation, giving necessary and sufficient conditions for an event, which will be impossible to generate in many situations.

Goal-based focusing is needed because of the complexity of real-world situations. No real-world explanation can include *all* the causally-relevant factors in an event, so that explanations necessarily highlight a few causes out of many. If those causes are irrelevant to the explainer's goals, the explanation will be useless. In order for explanation-based processing to be effective in complex situations, AI systems need to be able to identify which of the many causes of an event are important to their goals, and require that those causes be highlighted in the explanations they use.

---

[3][Souther *et al.*, 1989] presents an argument close in spirit to ours— that it is essential to be able to generate explanations from a given viewpoint— and identifies classes of explanations that students might seek when studying college-level botany. However, since they discuss only tutoring applications, they do not connect their classes to over-arching goals that make them important, beyond simply doing well in a course.

References

[DeJong, 1988] G. DeJong. An introduction to explanation-based learning. In H.E. Shrobe, editor, *Exploring Artificial Intelligence: Survey Talks from the National Conferences on Artificial Intelligence*. Morgan Kaufmann, Palo Alto, 1988.

[Hammond, 1986] K.J. Hammond. *Case-based Planning: An Integrated Theory of Planning, Learning and Memory*. PhD thesis, Yale University, 1986. Technical Report 488.

[Hanson, 1961] N. Hanson. *Patterns of Discovery*. Cambridge University Press, Cambridge, 1961.

[Heider, 1958] F. Heider. *The Psychology of Interpersonal Relations*, volume XV of *Current Theory and Research in Motivation*. John Wiley and Sons, New York, 1958.

[Kass et al., 1986] A. M. Kass, D. B. Leake, and C. C. Owens. Swale: A program that explains. In *Explanation Patterns: Understanding Mechanically and Creatively*, pages 232–254. Lawrence Erlbaum Associates, Hillsdale, NJ, 1986.

[Kedar-Cabelli, 1987] S.T. Kedar-Cabelli. Formulating concepts according to purpose. In *Proceedings of the Sixth Annual National Conference on Artificial Intelligence*, pages 477–481, Seattle, WA, July 1987. AAAI.

[Keller, 1988] R. Keller. Operationality and generality in explanation-based learning: Separate dimensions or opposite endpoints? In *Proceedings of the 1988 AAAI Spring Symposium on Explanation-based Learning*. AAAI, 1988.

[Kelley, 1967] H. H. Kelley. Attribution theory in social psychology. In D. Levine, editor, *Nebraska Symposium on Motivation*, pages 192–238. University of Nebraska Press, Lincoln, 1967.

[Leake, 1988] D.B. Leake. Evaluating explanations. In *Proceedings of the Seventh National Conference on Artificial Intelligence*, pages 251–255, Minneapolis, MN, August 1988. AAAI, Morgan Kaufman Publishers, Inc.

[Mehlman and Snyder, 1983] R. Mehlman and C. Snyder. Excuse theory: A test of the self-protective role of attributions. *Journal of Personality and Social Psychology*, 49(4):994–1001, 1983.

[Mitchell et al., 1986] T.M. Mitchell, R.M. Keller, and S.T. Kedar-Cabelli. Explanation–based generalization: A unifying view. *Machine Learning*, 1(1):47–80, 1986.

[Mooney and DeJong, 1985] R. Mooney and G. DeJong. Learning schemata for natural language processing. In *Proceedings of the Ninth International Joint Conference on Artificial Intelligence*, pages 681–687, Los Angeles, CA, August 1985. IJCAI.

[Schank and Leake, 1989] R.C. Schank and D.B. Leake. Creativity and learning in a case-based explainer. *Artificial Intelligence*, (40), 1989.

[Souther et al., 1989] A. Souther, L. Acker, J. Lester, and B. Porter. Using view types to generate explanations in intelligent tutoring systems. In *Proceedings of the Eleventh Annual Conference of the Cognitive Science Society*, pages 123–130, Ann Arbor, MI, August 1989. Cognitive Science Society.

Are there developmental milestones in scientific reasoning?[1]

Anne L. Fay   David Klahr   Kevin Dunbar
Carnegie Mellon   McGill
University   University

Abstract

This paper presents a conceptual framework that integrates studies on scientific reasoning that have been conducted with different age subjects and across different experimental tasks. Traditionally, different aspects of scientific reasoning have been emphasized in studies with different aged subjects, and the different literatures are somewhat unconnected. However, this separation leads to a disjointed view of the development of scientific reasoning, and it leaves unexplained certain adult behaviors in very difficult scientific reasoning contexts. In this paper we attempt to integrate these three approaches into a single framework that describes the process of scientific reasoning as a search in an hypothesis space and an experiment space. We will present the results from a variety of studies conducted with preschool, elementary school, and adult subjects, and will show how differences in performance can be viewed as differences in the knowledge and strategies used to search the two spaces. Finally, we will present evidence showing that, in sufficiently challenging situations, adults exhibit deficits of the same sort that young children exhibit, even though one might have expected that these developmental milestones were long since passed.

Experimental studies of the development of scientific reasoning skills have produced three distinct and somewhat disjoint literatures. Studies focusing on what Klayman and Ha (1987) call "positive test bias" (the tendency to seek

[1] Address correspondence to Anne L. Fay Department of Psychology, Carnegie-Mellon University, Pittsburgh, PA 15213, USA. E-mail address: fay@psy.cmu.edu. The first author was supported by a Post-doctoral Fellowship from the James S. McDonnell Foundation Program in Cognitive Studies for Educational Practice. The second author was supported in part by the Personnel and Training Research Program, Psychological Sciences Division, Office of Naval Research, Contract N00014-86K-0349, and in part by grants from NICHHD (R01-HD25211-01A1) and the A.W. Mellon Foundation. The third author was supported in part by a grant from the Natural Sciences and Engineering Research Council of Canada, grant number OGP0037356 .

instances that are expected to confirm one's current hypothesis) have concentrated on adult performance; studies on subjects' faulty strategies for the "coordination of theory and evidence" (Kuhn, 1989) have been conducted primarily with adolescents; and studies examining the understanding of necessity and possibility have been conducted with preschoolers. Rarely is one of these phenomena studied in a different age group (i.e., we know of no studies focusing on adults' understanding of the logic of indeterminacy, nor any of preschoolers' positive test bias.)

One possible justification for the different foci is that there might be a sequence of developmental milestones in the acquisition of a complete set of scientific reasoning skills. If so, then it would be prudent for investigators interested in different age levels to address the most obvious inadequacies of their subjects. However, this separation leads to a disjointed view of the development of scientific reasoning, and it leaves unexplained certain adult behaviors in very difficult scientific reasoning contexts. In this paper we attempt to integrate these three approaches into a single framework that describes the process of scientific reasoning as a search in an hypothesis space and an experiment space. We will present the results from a variety of studies conducted with preschool, elementary school, and adult subjects, and will show how differences in performance can be viewed as differences in the knowledge and strategies used to search the two spaces. Finally, we will present evidence showing that, in sufficiently challenging situations, adults exhibit deficits of the same sort that young children exhibit, even though one might have expected that these developmental milestones were long since passed.

Components of Scientific Reasoning

Klahr & Dunbar (1988) have conceptualized the process of scientific reasoning as a dual search in an experiment space and an hypothesis space. Figure 1 depicts the two spaces and the logical relations between them. The upper box is the hypothesis space, which consists of specific hypotheses related to the domain. The lower box is the experiment space. Within this space are the experiments that can be conducted in the domain. The arrows connecting the boxes in the two spaces specify how the experimental outcomes bear on the hypotheses. The heavy arrow between Hypothesis A and Experiment 1 indicates that only Hypothesis A is consistent with the outcome of Experiment 1. This reflects a

Determinate relation. The light arrows between Hypothesis A and Experiment 2 and between Hypothesis B and Experiment 2 indicate that both Hypothesis A and Hypothesis B are consistent with the outcome of Experiment 2. This reflects an *Indeterminate* relation, whereby the outcome of Experiment 2 cannot discriminate between Hypothesis A and Hypothesis B. The absence of arrows between Hypothesis B and Experiment 1, Hypothesis B and Experiment 3, and Hypothesis A and Experiment 3, indicates that these hypotheses are inconsistent with each of these outcomes, reflecting an *Impossible* relation.

The goal of scientific discovery is to generate experiments and hypotheses that will eventually result in a relation of determinacy, whereby only one hypothesis remains consistent with all the experimental outcomes.[2] Thus, the components of scientific reasoning consist of: 1) Identification and understanding of the relations between experiments and hypotheses (i.e., understanding the logic of necessity and possibility); 2) Generation of informative experiments,(i.e, generating experiments that further specify the relations between the two spaces so as to prune the search in the space of hypotheses); 3) Hypothesis generation and revision (i.e., generation of hypotheses from either analogy or via induction from experimental outcomes.)

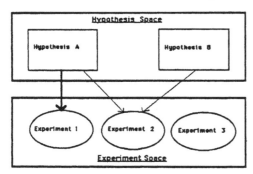

Figure 1. Schematic representation of the two spaces and the relations between them. Heavy arrow indicates a determinant relation between experimental outcome and hypothesis. Light arrows indicate an indeterminate relation and no line indicates an impossible relations.

These three general abilities are fundamental to

the process of scientific reasoning, and their deficits are characteristically associated with specific age groups. Adults recognize and understand the implications of indeterminacy, and have heuristics for designing informative experiments, but are notoriously biased toward confirmation in rule discovery tasks (Gorman & Gorman, 1984; Gorman, Stafford & Gorman, 1987; Wason, 1960, 1968).[3] Adolescents, like adults, understand the notion of indeterminacy, but in addition to their bias toward confirmation, they lack the strategies and knowledge for designing informative experiments. Preschool children demonstrate all these deficits, but also show a failure to recognize and/or understand the the implications of determinate vs indeterminate situations. Thus, acquisition of these three abilities might be viewed as *milestones* in the development of scientific reasoning skills. However, the picture is not that straightforward, as we shall argue below. First, however, we will further elaborate each of the three components enumerated above.

Identifying the relation between experiments and hypotheses

One of the basic components of scientific reasoning is the ability to recognize and understand the implications of confirming, and disconfirming evidence. Understanding the implications of these conditions is based on the distinction between determinate and indeterminate outcomes. In Indeterminate situations, the evidence is insufficient to discriminate one hypothesis from another. Until this concept is available, the process of scientific discovery will be severely flawed. Failing to recognize a situation as indeterminate will result in premature termination of the generate-experiment process because a confirming instance will be erroneously identified as sufficient to accept a theory.

Research with preschool children has shown they lack the concept of indeterminacy. In terms of Figure 1, they fail to realize the relation between Experiment 2 and the Hypothesis space. In a study extending Pieraut-Le Bonnic's (1980) investigations of childrens' understanding of possibility and necessity, Fay & Klahr (1990), presented kindergarten children with two boxes of building materials, and a series of objects, one at a time, made from materials taken entirely from one box or the other. For example, Box A might contain sticks and curves and Box B might have sticks and squares. A probe object comprised of

---

[2] In real-world situations, one never has a determinate relation, as there are an infinite number of possible hypotheses, and there is always te possibility that new evidence will disconfirm the current hypothesis. Nonetheless, the goal of science can be seen as the elimination of all *current* competing hypotheses until only one remains consistent with the existing evidence.

[3] But see Farris & Revlin (1989) for a novel reinterpretation.

only sticks would be *indeterminate* because it could have been constructed from either box. A *determinate* probe object would be one constructed from sticks and curves (only Box A could have been used to make it). The children were asked whether they could tell which box was used to make the object .

Figure 2 shows a schematic of the problem. As can be seen, the task can be mapped directly onto the components shown in Figure 1, with the boxes representing hypotheses and the probe objects representing experiments. Thus in this context the child is presented with a finite hypothesis space (e.g. box with sticks and curves vs. box with sticks and squares) and an experimental outcome (stick & curve object vs. stick-only object) but must determine the relations that exist between them (stick & curve object is determinate vs. sticks-only is indeterminate). *All* the children correctly identified the determinate situation, but only 53% consistently identified the indeterminate situation. Those who failed to recognize the indeterminate situation misidentified it as determinate, claiming that they *could* tell for sure which box had been used to construct the indeterminate probe object.

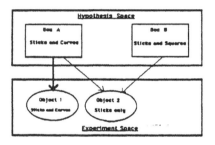

Figure 2. Experimental setup for the Possiblity-Necessity study. Heavy arrows indicate a determinate relation and lights arrows indicate an indeterminate relations.

This failure can be explained, in part, by a lack of understanding of the concept of logical necessity. Evidence for this interpretation comes from children's justifications for their responses on determinate problems, which were coded as being based on either positive or negative reasoning. Children were scored as using positive reasoning if their justification was based on the confirmatory relation between the determinate box and the object (e.g. "you used this box because it has sticks"). They were scored as using negative reasoning if their justification referred to the necessity of disconfirmation of the other response (e.g."you had to use this box

because the other box doesn't have any curves"). Negative reasoning implies an understanding of logical necessity. That is, it suggests that the child recognizes the insufficiency of confirmation alone and therefore searches the entire hypothesis space to determine the other experiment-hypothesis relationships. Table 1 shows the relation between the type of reasoning used on the determinate problems and performance on the indeterminate problems. The results suggest that the tendency to use negative reasoning is related to the recognition of indeterminate situations.

TABLE 1: Children who use negative reasoning on determinate problems are more likely to be correct on indeterminate problems.

	PERFORMANCE ON INDETERMINATE PROBLEMS (cell entries are number of responses)	
REASONING ON DETERMINATE PROBLEMS	Incorrect	Correct
Positive Reasoning	22	20
Negative Reasoning	6	19
(Chi Square=5.19, p<.025)		

Young children demonstrate a lack of understanding of logical necessity, a prerequisite of scientific reasoning. Failing to recognize an indeterminate situation, or to understand its implication, will result in a premature termination of the search based on finding a confirmatory relation between data and theory.

Generating Informative Experiments

The ability to recognize the relations between hypotheses and experiments can be seen as a prerequisite for the skill of generating informative experiments. Informative experiments are designed for the purpose of pruning the hypothesis tree, that is, eliminating impossible hypotheses, and reducing the set of consistent hypotheses. In this situation, the subject is provided with an hypothesis, or enters with a prior hypothesis, and must generate experiments which will lead to the confirmation or disconfirmation of the hypothesis. In reference to Figure 1, the subject is provided with an hypothesis (e.g. Hypothesis B), and the task is to generate experiments that will either disconfirm the hypothesis (e.g. E3), or will discriminate between existing confirming hypotheses (e.g. Experiment 1). Subjects want to avoid writing experiments that fail to discriminate between existing hypotheses (e.g. Experiment 2), or at the least, recognize them as being undiscriminating. Thus, this ability is dependent upon the ability to recognize and understand the relations between

335

experiments and hypotheses. In addition, it involves an understanding of the goal of experiment generation (reducing the hypothesis tree), and the skills for constructing experiments that will serve these goals.

In a series of experiments with children (8 to 13 years old), and adults, we examined subjects' ability to generate informative experiments (Klahr, Dunbar & Fay, 1990; Klahr, Fay & Dunbar 1990). Subjects were trained to operate a simple programmable device by entering commands (for moving forward, backward, turning right and left, and firing its cannon) and then pressing a GO key to execute the program. This would move an icon on a workstation screen according to the program the subject had entered.[*] Once trained to criterion, they were then asked to discover how an additional function, the REPEAT key, worked. They were then provided with an hypothesis (which was always incorrect), and were asked to write programs to find out if the hypothesis was correct or, if it wasn't, to find out how REPEAT worked.

The design of the study (See Table 2) crossed the plausibility of the given and actual hypotheses. Thus, subjects could be given either a highly plausible or highly implausible hypotheses for how REPEAT worked, and the device was actually programmed to interpret REPEAT in some different, but either plausible or implausible, way. Subjects were given one of the rules and the device actually worked according to a different rule. This effect of these given-actual hypotheses conditions will be expanded on in the following section.

Table 2: Design of "negative feedback" study

	Actual	
	Plausible	Implausible
Given		
Plausible	Theory refinement	Theory replacement
Implausible	Theory replacement	Theory refinement

.
Overall, children performed poorly in discovering the correct rule. Only one-third of the younger children, and half of the older children discovered the rule, compared to 83% of the adults.

---

[*]This "microworld" was a simulated version of the BigTrak, a programmable robot toy that moved around on the ground, originally used by Shrager & Klahr, 1986.

One contributing factor to this trend is the degree of informativeness of the programs that the subjects wrote. First, children appear to differ from adults in terms of their awareness of the goals of experimentation. Whereas 83% of the adults made statements referring to experimental design goals, only 20% of the younger children and 47% of the older children made such comments. The quality of these statements also differed. The adults stated experiment goals in terms of increasing the observability and informativeness. The youngest children, on the other hand, primarily made output goal statements (e.g. move it in a square) and some observability goals (e.g. use N=1 otherwise it's too confusing). The older children focused on observability goals (e.g. shorten programs, use easily traced commands).

The above data is based on verbal reports, and as such the tendency to verbalize may be different for the different age groups. A second analysis examined the types of programs that were written. The experimental space for this problem can be viewed along two dimensions, one dimension being the number of commands in the program (lambda) and the other being the magnitude of the argument for REPEAT (N). The ideal experiment is one which maximizes the informativeness of the outcome while minimizing the complexity (i.e. maximizing observability or interpretability of outcome). In the current setting, this means writing minimum length programs that can discriminate the effect of the REPEAT function. By this criterion, the "best" program has a length (lambda) of 3 and a REPEAT argument value (N) of 2. The three age groups differed in their tendency to write programs with these properties. Compared to a random model, the children were 1.5 times *less* likely to generate the ideal experiment whereas the adults were 5 times *more* likely to run such an experiment. In addition, adults were much more systematic in the way that they moved in the experiment space. Their experiments had more of the flavor of a careful experimental series than did the children's.

In summary, children appear to lack the knowledge required to generate informative experiments. Part of this deficit involves a failure to understand the goals of experimentation. Whereas adults' goals were directed toward informativeness and observability, children's goals were directed toward producing a desired effect, and, for the older children, observability. However, even though the older children recognized the importance of observability, they were not overly successful at designing interpretable experiments.

Generating and revising hypotheses

The final component of scientific reasoning is the ability to generate and revise hypotheses in response to experimental outcomes. Combined with the other abilities, this situation can be depicted in Figure 1 by having no boxes specified or present in either the experimental or hypothesis space. Thus all the components of the task must be generated by the subject. In series of studies using the physical BigTrak device, adults and third to sixth grade students were trained on all the functions of the device except the REPEAT and were then asked to write programs to figure out how REPEAT worked (Klahr & Dunbar, 1988; Dunbar & Klahr, 1988). There are two main differences in these studies as compared to the studies mentioned in the previous section: First, in these studies subjects were not given any hypothesis, and had to generate their own hypotheses from the start, and second, there was only one rule for REPEAT, it caused the device to repeat the last N instructions once, where N refers to the argument for REPEAT. There was a strong age effect: 19 of the 20 adults, but only 2 of the 22 children successfully discovered the correct rule, although over half of the children *believed* that they had correctly identified it. Part of the failure can be attributed to the non-informative programs that the children wrote. However, both the adults and the children had the same proportion of experiments from the most informative region of the experiment space, where lambda > N and N > 1. Based on the outcomes from experiments conducted in this region adults were able to induce the correct hypothesis but the children were not.

The hypotheses that were generated by the subjects in this study can be classified into two frames based on the function of N. One frame, Counter-Frame, assigned a role to N where the number indicated how many times something got repeated. The other frame, Selector-Frame, assigned a role to N where the number indicated which instructions got repeated. Children and adults demonstrated an initial preference for the Counter-Frame hypotheses, (which is incorrect in this study). But, whereas adults were able to abandon this hypothesis frame in light of disconfirming evidence and generate the Selector-Frame, the children tended to maintain Counter-

Frame hypotheses in spite of disconfirming evidence. Thus the children's search of the hypothesis space was constrained to Counter hypotheses.

Further evidence for this comes from the negative feedback studies described earlier, in which subjects were given an initial hypothesis that could be either from the same frame as the actual hypothesis or from the other frame as the actual hypothesis . Figure 3 shows the effect for Given-Actual Hypothesis conditions. The children were successful when the device worked as a (plausible) Counter, but failed to get the correct rule when it worked as a (implausible) Selector.

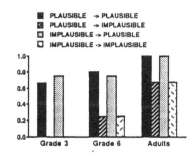

Figure 3. **Proportion of subjects discovering correct rule when given a Plausible (counter) or implausible (selector) hypothesis and actual rule was Plausible (counter) or Implausible (Selector).**

Prior to running any programs, children and adults differed in terms of there willingness to entertain a Selector hypothesis. Table 3 shows the proportion of subjects in each age group that initially accepted the Given hypothesis or one from the same frame as the Given. The children, especially the younger ones, find the Selector hypothesis very implausible. More than half of the children who rejected the Selector proposed a Counter hypothesis instead. Adults, on the other hand, demonstrated some skepticism over their Given Selector hypothesis, but rather than reject it, they proposed other hypotheses *in addition to* it, and these alternative hypotheses were most likely to be Counters.

Table 3. Proportion of subjects accepting Given Frame prior to running first experiment.

	Given Frame	
Group	Counter	Selector
3rd Grade	1.00	.12
6th Grade	.89	.63
Adults	1.00	1.00

Children's strategies and goals for searching the hypothesis space appear to be different from adults. Children's prior hypotheses constrain their search of the hypothesis space to those areas they consider plausible, in this case, counter hypotheses. Although adults also have prior hypotheses, their search of the hypothesis space is not so constrained, and they will entertain the possibility of implausible hypotheses. Thus adults will abandon a more plausible hypothesis frame given disconfirming evidence, and search the space for a new, less plausible frame, children continue to search within the plausible frame for particular hypotheses that will explain the experimental outcomes.

Milestones or fragile acquisitions?

Given the characteristic deficits associated with each age range, and given the logical necessity for each of the three skills to be in place before the next one can be reliably assessed, it is tempting to view this as a sequence of developmental milestones, in which a skill, once acquired, can be reliably invoked in a wide range of situations and can provide the basis for the subsequent acquisition. However, in other careful analysis of children's strategy acquisition (e.g, Siegler and Jenkins, 1989), it has been shown that the story is not so simple. A new strategy or skill may appear for a while, and then disappear for a protracted period. Or a strategy that seemed quite robust, may, in contexts of sufficient complexity, be abandoned, as subjects revert to simpler, and inadequate, strategies. In the domain of scientific reasoning, we have found just this situation. Dunbar (1989) found that strong prior beliefs about hypotheses can overly constrain search of the hypothesis space, and produce behavior that , at its core, reveals a severely limited ability to discriminate determinate from indeterminate outcomes.

Adult subjects were given training in a simulated molecular genetics laboratory and were shown how to go about discovering how certain genes control the enzyme production of other genes by switching them on when a nutrient is present. This mechanism was *activation*. Subjects were shown the different variables that could be manipulated (e.g. amount of nutrient present, genetic mutations), and how they could use this informatin to run experiments and induce the control mechanism. Subjects were then given a new set of genes and were asked to discover how

the enzyme producing genes were controlled. However, the mechanism in this set was *inhibition*: controller genes turn other genes off until a nutrient is present. This can be compared to the Given-Plausible, Actual-Implausible hypothesis condition in the simulated BigTrak studies, as shown in the top-right cell of Table 2. Only 25% of the subjects discovered the inhibition mechanism, similar to the success rate of 6th grade students in the BigTrak study. Subjects often conducted experiments that could have been consistent with many hypotheses, but interpreted the results as confirming their prior (plausible) hypothesis. Sixty-five percent of the subjects remained within the Activation-frame of the hypothesis space, despite experimental evidence that disconfirmed this frame. Thus, like the children in the previous study, their prior hypothesis overly constrained their search of the hypothesis space and also affected their search of the experiment space.

Conclusion

The child-as-scientist view suggests that.children go about the world gathering information and building theories (Brewer & Samarapungavan, in press; Karmiloff-Smith, 1988). Other researchers argue that although children may generate theories of their worlds, the process of theory generation and revision is different from that of adults (Kuhn, 1989). The view presented here is that children of different ages have certain characteristic conceptual deficits, which limit their ability to engage in the process of scientific reasoning. We have attempted to show how the three relatively diverse literatures on scientific reasoning can be integrated into a single framework that views discovery as a dual search in a space of hypotheses and experiments, but we have cautioned against a simple view of developmental milestones because of the tendency for people to regress to earlier deficits in sufficiently complex situations. Perhaps this tendency to regress accounts for the substantial educational and institutional supports that provide practicing scientists with the means to maximize the rationality and effectiveness of their efforts at scientific discovery.

References

Brewer, W. F. & Samarapungavan, A. (in press). Child theories versus scientific theories: Differences in reasoning or differences in knowledge? In R. R. Hoffman & D. S. Palermo (Eds.), *Cognition and the symbolic processes: Applied and ecological perspectives* (Vol. 3). Hillsdale, NJ: Erlbaum

Dunbar, K. (1989). Scientific reasoning strategies in a simulated molecular genetics environment. *Proceedings of the 11th annual meeting of the Cognitive Science society,* 426-433. Ann Arbor, MI: Lawrence Erlbaum Associates.

Dunbar, K., & Klahr, D. (1989). Developmental differences in scientific discovery strategies. In D. Klahr & K. Kotovsky (Eds.), *Complex information processing: The impact of Herbert A. Simon.* Hillsdale, NJ: Erlbaum.

Farris, H.H., & Revlin, R. (1989). Sensible reasoning in two tasks: Rule discovery and hypothesis evaluation. *Memory & Cognition,* 17, 221-232.

Fay, A. L. & Klahr, D. (1990). Cognitive precursors to scientific reasoning: the development of the concepts of possibility and necessity. Working Paper, Dept. of Psychology, Carnegie-Mellon University.

Gorman, M.E., & Gorman, M.E. (1984). A comparison of disconfirmatory, confirmatory, and control strategies on Wason's 2-4-6 task. *Quarterly Journal of Experimental Psychology,* 36a, 629-648.

Gorman, M.E., Stafford, A., & Gorman, M.E. (1987). Disconfirmation and dual hypotheses on a more difficult version of Wason's 2-4-6 task. *Quarterly Journal of Experimental Psychology,* 39a, 1-28.

Karmiloff-Smith, A. (1988) The child is a theoretician, not an inductivist. *Mind and Language,* 3, 183-195.

Klahr, D., & Dunbar, K. (1988). Dual space search during scientific reasoning. *Cognitive Science.* 12, 1-48.

Klahr, D., Dunbar, K. & Fay, A. L. (1990) Designing good experiments to test "bad" hypotheses. In J. Shrager & P. Langley (Eds.), *Computational models of discovery and theory formation.* Morgan-Kaufman.

Klahr, D., Fay, A.L., & Dunbar, K. (1990). *Developmental differences in experimental heuristics.* Working paper, Department of Psychology, Carnegie Mellon University..

Kuhn, D. (1989) Children and adults as intuitive scientists. *Psychological Review,* 96, 674-689.

Klayman, J., & Ha, Y. (1987). Confirmation, disconfirmation and information in hypothesis testing. *Psychological Review,* 94, 211-228.

Pieraut-Le Bonniec, G. (1980). *The Development of Modal Reasoning.* New York, NY: Academic Press.

Shrager, J., & Klahr, D. (1986). Instructionless learning about a complex device. *Journal of Man-Machine Studies,* 25, 153-189.

Siegler, R. S. & Jenkins, E. (*1989*) How children discover new strategies. Hillsdale, N. J.

Wason, P. C. (1960). On the failure to eliminate hypotheses in a conceptual task. *Quarterly Journal of Experimental Psychology,* 12, 129-140.

Wason, P.C. (1968). On the failure to eliminate hypotheses: A second look. In P.C. Wason & P.N. Johnson-Laird (Eds.), *Thinking and Reasoning.* Middlesex: Penguin Books.

Why Fodor and Pylyshyn Were Wrong: The Simplest Refutation

David J. Chalmers
Center for Research on Concepts and Cognition
Indiana University

Abstract

This paper offers both a theoretical and an experimental perspective on the relationship between connectionist and Classical (symbol-processing) models. Firstly, a serious flaw in Fodor and Pylyshyn's argument against connectionism is pointed out: if, in fact, a part of their argument is valid, then it establishes a conclusion quite different from that which they intend, a conclusion which is demonstrably false. The source of this flaw is traced to an underestimation of the differences between localist and distributed representation. It has been claimed that distributed representations cannot support systematic operations, or that if they can, then they will be mere implementations of traditional ideas. This paper presents experimental evidence against this conclusion: distributed representations can be used to support direct structure-sensitive operations, in a manner quite unlike the Classical approach. Finally, it is argued that even if Fodor and Pylyshyn's argument that connectionist models of compositionality must be mere implementations were correct, then this would still not be a serious argument against connectionism as a theory of mind.

Introduction

The trenchant critique by Fodor and Pylyshyn (1988) threw a scare into the field of connectionism, at least for a moment. Two distinguished figures, from the right side of the tracks, were bringing the full force of their experience with the computational approach to cognition to bear on this young, innocent field. It was enough to get anybody worried for a while. But after the initial flurry, connectionists gradually settled down to the view that while Fodor and Pylyshyn had posed a challenge for the field, it was certainly not an unanswerable one. A spate of "refutations" quickly followed. These generally took two forms: argument (e.g. Clark 1989, Smolensky 1987, van Gelder 1990), or counterexample (Elman 1990, Pollack 1990, Smolensky 1990). (One is reminded of Nietzsche's observation: "It is not the least charm of a theory that it is refutable.")

The point of this paper is to offer a few observations on the whole business. The primary purpose is to offer a particularly simple refutation of Fodor and Pylyshyn's argument that I do not believe has been presented elsewhere. Straightforward considerations about the structure of their argument will show that it cannot have succeeded in its intended purpose. Furthermore, simple as these considerations are, they lead into deeper issues about just *why* their argument was wrong, and about the vital properties of connectionist models that were not taken into account. In particular, the role of *distributed representation* will be gone into. The ability of distributed representations to support structure-sensitive operations will be demonstrated with some experimental results. Finally, this will lead into the issue of the possible *implementation* of Classical ideas by connectionist models, and expose the shortsightedness of some of Fodor and Pylyshyn's claims here.

Refutation

Recall the major thrust of Fodor and Pylyshyn's argument: that connectionist models cannot admit of a compositional semantics. Or, more accurately, not unless they are an implementation of a Classical architecture. Manifestations of compositional semantics are certainly ubiquitous in our thought, particularly in our language, through its *compositionality* (the meaning of "the girl loves John" is a function of the meaning of its constituent parts, "the girl", "loves", and "John"),

340

and its *systematicity* (the ability to think "John loves the girl" is tied to the ability to think "the girl loves John"). So if connectionism cannot handle compositional semantics, then that's a problem for connectionism.

The refutation of F&P's argument can be stated in one sentence, then explained. *If F&P's argument is correct as it is presented, then it implies that no connectionist network can support a compositional semantics; not even a connectionist implementation of a Turing Machine, or of a Language of Thought.* But this is a problem for F&P, as it is well-known that connectionist networks can be used to implement Turing Machines (or at least Turing Machines with arbitrarily large but finite tape), and it is well-known that Turing Machines can be used to support a compositional semantics. Furthermore, the *human brain* is like a connectionist network in many ways, and the human brain certainly supports a compositional semantics. So if F&P's argument really establishes that *no* connectionist network can support a compositional semantics, then it establishes a false conclusion. So, applying the contrapositive of the italicized sentence above, F&P's argument is not correct as it stands.

Of course, Fodor and Pylyshyn do not *want* to imply such a conclusion. Indeed, they take great care to point out that the best future for connectionism will lie in using it as an *implementation* strategy. Connectionist implementations of Classical systems will certainly support a compositional semantics, if not in a particularly interesting way. Well and good; of course they must say such a thing: it may be slightly embarrassing that the brain is made of neurons and not directly out of symbolic structures, but it is a *fact*, and as a fact it must be dealt with. But what they *say* is one thing. Their actual *argument* is a different matter.

The substantive argument in F&P's paper, that connectionist models cannot support a compositional semantics, takes up only a few pages (pp. 15-28). This starts with a simple localist connectionist network (that is, a network with one node representing one concept). F&P show that this network cannot possibly possess a compositional semantics, and argue that this applies equally to networks with distributed semantics (that is, a network with one concept being represented over many nodes). Therefore, the argument concludes, it is impossible for the semantics of a connectionist network to be compositional, whether these semantics are localist or distributed.

There is something very strange about this conclusion. It is plainly false; it is universally recognized that *some* connectionist networks have compositional semantics: namely, connectionist implementations of Classical architectures. So why are these not excluded from the argument? Going through the argument, the reader expects that at any point soon, there will be an *escape clause* — a clause showing why the argument as it stands does not apply to connectionist implementations of Classical architectures. But this clause never appears; nothing close to it, in fact. F&P are left in the improbable position of having "proved" that even connectionist implementations of Classical models have no compositional semantics. Faced with such a situation, we can only conclude that the argument is defective. Supporters of F&P might argue that the flaw simply lies in the lack of an escape clause, which can easily be supplied; but no such escape clause is in evidence, and the onus lies with these people to provide it. In the meantime, we can conclude that the defect lies elsewhere: very likely, in the generalization from localist to distributed semantics. More on this in a moment, after an analogy.

Say a mad scientist comes up to us with a "proof" that the Earth is the only inhabited planet in the universe. She runs through an impressive *a priori* argument, showing why it is impossible that the right kinds of biochemicals could be assembled in the right way, that the requisite organizational complexity could not arise, and so on. She concludes: life could not have arisen on any planet in this universe. But then, of course, it is an obvious fact that life arose on Earth. "That's OK," she answers, "that suits me fine. We knew that already. So what I've established is that life cannot have arisen anywhere but Earth." Now this will strike us as ad hoc, and as extremely poor logic. Their main argument never mentioned Earth; there was no *escape clause* showing just why the argument doesn't apply to Earth. To modify the conclusions of one's argument by considerations *external* to the argument is to admit that the argument is faulty. ("Mars is inhabited? OK, our argument demonstrates that life cannot have arisen anywhere but Earth or Mars.") If the argument can be fixed so that Earth is excluded from its force, very likely other planets will be excluded also. Analogously: if F&P's argument can possibly be fixed up so that it excludes Classical implementations from the scope of its conclusion, then the same fixes will probably exclude many other connectionist models too.

Refuting Fodor and Pylyshyn in Four Easy Steps

All this has been a long-winded way of making the following simple argument:

(1) In F&P's argument that no connectionist models can have compositional semantics, there is no escape clause excluding certain models (such as Classical implementations) from the force of the conclusion. (By observation.)

(2) If F&P's argument is correct as it stands, then it establishes that *no* connectionist model can have compositional semantics. (From (1).)

(3) But some connectionist models obviously *do* have compositional semantics; namely, connectionist implementations of classical models. (By observation, accepted by all.)

(4) Therefore, F&P's argument is not correct as it stands. (From (2), (3).)

Summing things up: Let C denote the class of all possible connectionist models, together with all possible associated semantics. Let FP denote the subset of C of models whose semantics are not compositional. Let L denote the subset of C consisting of models with localist semantics. Let IMP denote the subset of C consisting of connectionist implementations of Classical models. The conclusion that F&P *want* to establish is that FP = C − IMP.

In their argument, F&P first establish that L ≤ FP. (Here "≤" denotes set inclusion.) Let us grant them this, though some might argue. They then argue that it makes no difference whether the semantics are localist or distributed. Now, clearly the two possibilities of localist and distributed semantics exhaust the set C, so this argument, if correct, establishes that FP = C. But this is plainly false, as IMP < C but it is not the case that IMP < FP.

We may conclude that *all* F&P have established is that L ≤ FP ≤ C − IMP. The step in the argument that generalizes to *all* distributed semantics is plainly defective. Although F&P would like to hold that it generalizes to all distributed semantics *except* those used to implement Classical models, the burden rests with them to show that this is the case. The conclusion established is a much weaker statement than FP = C − IMP. As things stand, it is just as likely that FP = L as that FP = C − IMP, though no doubt the truth lies somewhere in the middle.

Localist and Distributed Representation

So far, we have given a simple logical demonstration that F&P's argument must be flawed. It remains to precisely locate the weak spot in the argument. Fortunately, this is not hard to do. To find this, we must think about just *why* certain models, implementations and possibly others, slip through the argument's net. By now, no doubt, supporters of F&P are lining up in droves, waiting to say: "But of *course* the argument doesn't apply to implementations of Classical models. Implementations are *different* — the representations of Classical symbols in such a network will not exist at the level of the *node*, but at a much higher level. These symbols will be able to combine compositionally and autonomously." To such a person we might reply "Congratulations! You have just discovered the power of distributed representation."

Many connectionists have noted that the small localist network that F&P used as their chief example was most unrepresentative of the connectionist endeavour of a whole. When one asks what is the deepest philosophical commitment of the connectionist movement, the answer is surely this: the rejection of the atomic symbol as the bearer of meaning. Connectionists feel that atomic tokens simply do not carry enough information with them to be useful in modeling human cognition. Rather, distributed, subdivisible, malleable representations are the cornerstone of the connectionist endeavour. For this reason, localist networks are regarded by many connectionists as not really connectionist at all. These networks employ precisely the traditional notion of atomic symbols, with a new twist added by connecting all of these by associative links. (We might thus call localist connectionism "symbolic AI with soft constraints.")

The use of a localist network by F&P, then, betrays a lack of understanding of the connectionist endeavor. They believe that nothing depends on the localist/distributed distinction; the connectionist, on the other hand, believes that everything depends on it. To F&P, a connectionist distributed representation is just a spread-out version of a single node (this comes out clearly in the footnote to p. 15). To the connectionist, a group of nodes functioning separately has functional properties far beyond those of an isolated unit. Small differences in the activity of a subset of nodes can make subtle or unsubtle differences to later processing, in a way that no single node can manage. A group of nodes carries far more *information* than a single node, and as such to the connectionist is a far more likely candidate for for semantic interpretation. And most importantly, a distributed representation has a great deal of internal structure. (The point that Fodor and Pylyshyn underestimate the power of distribution is by no means original. It was first made by Smolensky (1987).)

Before moving on, we should briefly examine F&P's demonstration of why their argument applies equally to localist and distributed networks. This will be brief, as the relevant material is brief. On the bottom of p. 15, we find

> To simplify the argument, we assume a more 'localist' approach, in which each semantically interpreted node corresponds to a single Connectionist unit; but nothing relevant to this discussion is changed if these nodes actually consist of patterns over a cluster of units.

No argument to be found there. And later (p. 19)

> To claim that a node is neurally distributed is presumably to claim that its states of activation correspond to changes in neural activity — to aggregates of neural 'units' — rather than to activations of single neurons. The important point is that nodes that are distributed in this sense can perfectly well be syntactically and semantically atomic: Complex spatially-distributed implementation in no way implies constituent structure.

No-one will begrudge F&P this passage. As it stands, it is perfectly true. But it would only be interesting as argument if the last two sentences changed so that the "can" became a "must" and the "in no way implies" became "forbids". But it is precisely this that F&P cannot establish. We can conclude that their argument against distributed representation (and this is the extent of it) is weak. F&P go on to argue against connectionist models whose semantics are "distributed over microfeatures". But, as elsewhere, the kinds of semantics they consider bear little resemblance to those found anywhere in connectionism. This is the fundamental flaw in F&P's argument: lack of imagination in considering the possible ways in which distributed representations can carry semantics. It is a different variety of distributed semantics that would be carried by a connectionist implementation of a Turing Machine (and this, then, accounts for the logical flaw detailed above.) And it is a different variety again of distributed semantics that can yield connectionist models of compositionality in important new ways.

It is no accident that three of the most prominent *counterexamples* to F&P's argument — the models of Elman, Pollack, and Smolensky — all use distributed representation in an essential way. Smolensky's tensor-product architecture simply could not work in a localist framework. Its multidimensional tensor representations are by their nature spread over many nodes. Elman's implicit structure which develops in a recurrent network could also not succeed in a localist framework — the many subtle adjustments needed for various syntactic distinctions to develop could not be made. And Pollack's Recursive Auto-Associative Memory has a deep commitment to distribution — if it were one-concept-to-one-node, then its recursive encoding scheme could never get off the ground.

Structure-Sensitive Operations on Distributed Representations

The Classicist might now reply: "All this talk of distributed representations is all very well. Maybe you can *encode* compositional information into such a representation. But can you *use* it?" This point is initially plausible. If the structural information is present but cannot be processed, then it is useless. The Classicist might hold that connectionist compositional structure might be buried too deeply, too implicitly, to be accessed in a useful way. Indeed, in a recent paper, Fodor and McLaughlin (forthcoming) argue that to support structure-sensitive processing, a compositional representation must be a concatenation of explicit tokens of the original constituent parts. If this argument is correct, then connectionist representations that represent structure only in a distributed, implicit way will not have the causal power to support structure-sensitivity.

One obvious reply that the connectionist might make is that clearly *some* structure-sensitive operations can be supported by such representations: namely, the operation of extraction of the original constituents. Both Smolensky's and Pollack's models, for instance, include decodal processes that go from a compositional representation back to its parts. This reply, while valid, is not very interesting. If structure-sensitive processing must always proceed through an initial stage of decomposition into constituents, then what we are dealing with is essentially a connectionist implementation of a Classical symbol processing. In such processing, distributed representation is used as a mere implementational technique.

Fortunately, this is not always the case. In fact, distributed representations of compositional structure *can* be operated on directly, without proceeding through an extraction stage. This offers the promise of a connectionist approach to compositionality that is in no sense an implementation of the Classical notion. (It should be noted that Pollack and Smolensky have addressed this issue briefly in their models, but in a more limited way than outlined below.)

I have performed a series of experiments demonstrating the possibility of effective structure-sensitive operations on distributed representations. I can only outline them very briefly here; they are presented in more detail in (Chalmers, forthcoming). The experiments used a Recursive Auto-Associative Memory (RAAM; see Pollack 1988, 1990) to encode syntactically structured

Figure 1. Examples of sentences to be represented.

344

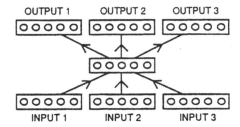

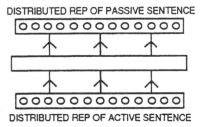

Figure 2. The basis of the RAAM network.　　**Figure 3.** The Transformation network.

representations of sentences in distributed form. Following this, a back-propagation network learned to perform syntactic transformations directly from one encoded representation to another.

The sentences represented were all of similar syntactic form to "John loves Michael" (active) or "Michael is loved by John" (passive). Five different names/verbs were used as fillers for each slot of subject, verb or object, giving 125 possible sentences of each type altogether. These sentences were assigned syntactic structure as shown in Figure 1. A RAAM network was trained to encode 125 sentences of each kind into a distributed form. (Pollack 1990 gives details of the RAAM architecture.) This is done by assigning each word a primitive localist representation (over 13 units), and then training a 39-13-39 backpropagation network (Figure 2) to auto-associate on the three leaves descending from every internal "node" (in the trees in Figure 1).

This gives us a 13-node distributed representation of the three leaves. Where necessary, this 13-node distributed representation is repropagated as part of the input to the 39-13-39 network, leading to higher-order structures being encoded. Eventually, we have a distributed representation of the entire tree. This process can be used, in principle, to encode any tree of valence 3 recursively.

The RAAM network learned to represent all 250 sentences satisfactorily, so that the distributed encodings of each sentence could be decoded back to the original sentence. These distributed representations were then used in modeling the process of syntactic transformation. In particular, the transformation of *passivization* was modeled: that is, the passing from sentences like "John loves Michael" to sentences like "Michael is loved by John". (No commitment to any particular linguistic paradigm is being made here; syntactic transformations are simply being used as a clear example of the kind of structure-sensitive operations with which connectionist models are supposed to have difficulty.)

150 of the encoded distributed representations (75 active and and the corresponding 75 passive sentences) were randomly selected for the training of the Transformation Network. This was a simple 13-13-13 backpropagation network (Figure 4), which took a representation of an active ("John loves Michael") sentence as input, and was trained to produce a representation of the corresponding passivized sentence ("Michael is loved by John") as output.

Training proceeded satisfactorily. The interesting part was the test of generalization, to see if the network was truly sensitive to the syntactic structure encoded in the distributed forms. The Transformation network was tested on the 100 remaining sentences from the original corpus. The 50 active sentences were encoded by the RAAM and fed to the Transformation network, yielding a 13-node output pattern. This was fed to the RAAM network for decoding. In all 50 cases, the output pattern decoded to the correct passivized sentence. Thus, not only was the Transformation network able to be trained to optimal performance, but the generalization rate on new sentences of the same form was 100%. The reverse transformation was also modeled (from passive to active). Performance was equally good, with a generalization rate of 100%.

These results establish without doubt that it is possible for connectionist networks to model structure-sensitive operations directly upon distributed representations. This bears on the arguments at hand in two ways.

(1) It demonstrates that not only can compositional structure be *encoded* in distributed form, but that the structure implicitly present within the distributed form can be *used* directly for further processing. This provides a direct counterexample to the Fodor and McLaughlin argument. Despite the lack of explicit concatenative structure in the RAAM representations, they support structure-sensitive processing anyway.

(2) It demonstrates the possibility of structure-sensitive operations in connectionist models which are in no sense implementations of Classical algorithms. To see this, note that when a structure-sensitive operations is being performed upon a Classical compositional representation, all processing *must* first proceed through a step of explicit decomposition, with particular tokens being explicitly extracted. In the connectionist model above, the transformation operation takes place without ever having to extract those constituent parts. Instead, the operation is direct and holistic.

The Relationship Between the Approaches

A argument made frequently by Fodor and Pylyshyn is that connectionists have two choices: either (1) ignore the facts of compositionality and systematicity, and thus have a defective theory of mind, or (2) accept compositionality and systematicity, in which case connectionism merely becomes a strategy for implementing Classical models. The following passage is typical:

> ...if you need structure in mental representations anyway to account for the productivity and systematicity of minds, why not postulate mental processes that are structure sensitive to account for the coherence of mental processes? Why not be a Classicist, in short? [p. 67]

This argument is rather curious. It is not only that it contradicts the evidence, demonstrated above, that connectionism might model structure-sensitive processes in a non-Classical way. There is also a deeply-embedded false assumption here: the assumption that *compositionality is all there is*.

To see the role that this assumption plays, shift the temporal position of the debate back a few decades. Let us imagine two traditional behaviorists, Fido and Pavlovian, who are rather distressed at the current turn of events. The revolutionary "cognitivists" have recently appeared on the screen, and are doing their best to undermine the basic assumptions of decades of solid research in psychology. Our behaviorists have difficulty grasping the idea of this movement. They express their bewilderment as follows: "Surely you all recognize that Classical Conditioning is a fact of human nature. The empirical evidence is overwhelming. But your cognitivist ideas do not take it sufficiently into account. There is no guarantee of stimulus-response association in your models as they stand. It seems to us that you have two choices: either (1) ignore the facts of Classical Conditioning, and therefore have a defective theory of mind, or (2) accept Conditioning and stimulus-response association, in which case cognitivism merely becomes a strategy for implementing the Behaviorist agenda."

Presumably a cognitivist (such as Fodor or Pylyshyn) would quickly see the flaw in this argument. To be sure, Conditioning is an empirical fact, and any complete theory must account for it. But it's certainly not the *only* fact, or even the most important fact, about the human mind. The cognitivists may pursue their own research agenda, making progress in many areas, and paying as much or as little attention to Conditioning as they like. Eventually they will have to come up with some explanation of the phenomenon, and who knows, it may well end up looking much like the Behaviorist story, *as far as conditioning is concerned*. But this doesn't mean that the cognitivist theory of *mind* looks much like the behaviorist theory overall, for the simple reason that *conditioning is only one part of the story*.

Similarly, compositionality is only one part of the story. Connectionists are free to pursue their own agenda, explaining various aspects of the mind as they see fit. Sooner or later, they will have to explain how compositionality fits into the picture. The story that connectionism tells about compositionality may prove quite similar to the Classical picture, or it may prove different. But even if it proves similar, this diminishes the status of connectionism not at all. The fact that connectionism might implement Classical theories of *compositionality* does not imply that connectionism would be implementing Classical theories of *mind*. Compositionality is just one aspect of the mind, after all. (Aspects of cognition for which compositionality seems relatively unimportant include: perception, categorization, motor control, memory, similarity judgments, association, attention, and much more. Even within language processing, compositionality is only part of the story, albeit an important part.)

Behaviorism was very good at explaining conditioning, but it had a problem: it was *only* good at explaining conditioning. Fodor and Pylyshyn's Classicism is good at explaining compositionality and compositional semantics, but it's not necessarily good at explaining much else. Both conditioning and compositionality are only small aspects of the mind; it seems to be an illusion of perspective that led to behaviorists and Classicists putting so much respective emphasis on them.

Fodor and Pylyshyn's arguments establish that compositionality *exists*, but for their arguments above to succeed, they would need to establish a rather stronger claim: that compositionality is *everything*. Such a claim is obviously false, so connectionism can go on happily trying to explain those areas of the mind that it chooses to. If the connectionist story about compositionality ends up looking a little like the Classical story, then well and good — it implies that the Classicists haven't been wasting their time completely all these years, and there may be room for a healthy amount of ecumenicism. In the meantime, preemptive relegation of either approach to a subsidiary role is probably a bad idea.

Acknowledgements: Thanks to Indiana University for support, and to Bob French, Liane Gabora and Doug Hofstadter for comments.

References

Chalmers, D. J. (forthcoming). Syntactic transformations on distributed representations. *Connection Science*.

Clark, A. (1989). *Microcognition*. Cambridge, MA: MIT Press.

Elman, J. L. (1990). Structured representations and connectionist models. In Gerald Altmann (ed.), *Computational and Psycholinguistic Approaches to Speech Processing*. New York: Academic Press.

Fodor, J. A.,& Pylyshyn, Z. (1988). Connectionism and cognitive architecture: A critical analysis. *Cognition*, 28: 3-71.

Fodor, J.A., & McLaughlin, B. (forthcoming). What is wrong with tensor product connectionism? In T. Horgan and J. Tienson (eds.), *Connectionism and the Philosophy of Mind*. Cambridge, MA: MIT Press.

Pollack, J. B. (1988). Recursive auto-associative memory: Devising compositional distributed representations. In *Proceedings of the Tenth Annual Conference of the Cognitive Science Society*. Montreal, Canada, pp. 33-39.

Pollack, J. B. (1990). Recursive distributed representations. *Artificial Intelligence*, forthcoming.

Smolensky, P. (1987). The constituent structure of connectionist mental states: A reply to Fodor and Pylyshyn. *Southern Journal of Philosophy*, 26: 137-163.

Smolensky, P. (1990). Tensor product variable binding and the representation of symbolic structures in connectionist systems. *Artificial Intelligence*, forthcoming.

Van Gelder, T. (1990). Compositionality: A connectionist variation on a Classical theme. *Cognitive Science*, 4.

Phonological Rule Induction: An Architectural Solution

David S. Touretzky[1], Gillette Elvgren III[1], and Deirdre W. Wheeler[2]

[1]School of Computer Science
Carnegie Mellon University
Pittsburgh, PA 15213

[2]Department of Linguistics
University of Pittsburgh
Pittsburgh, PA 15260

Abstract: Acquiring phonological rules is hard, especially when they do not describe generalizations that hold for all surface forms. We believe it can be made easier by adopting a more cognitively natural architecture for phonological processing. We briefly review the structure of M^3P, our connectionist Many Maps Model of Phonology, in which extrinsic rule ordering is virtually eliminated, and "iterative" processes are handled by a parallel clustering mechanism. We then describe a program for inducing phonological rules from examples. Our examples, drawn from Yawelmani, involve several complex rule interactions. The parallel nature of M^3P rule application greatly simplifies the description of these phenomena, and makes a computational model of rule acquisition feasible.

1. Introduction

In previous publications [10-14] we described our work on a connectionist approach to phonology inspired initially by the ideas of John Goldsmith [2] and George Lakoff [6,7]. Our "Many Maps Model of Phonology," M^3P, is an attempt to provide a computational account for both the regularities and peculiarities of human phonological behavior. The parallel rule formalism we developed is constrained by properties of an underlying connectionist sequence manipulation architecture. We suggested that rule acquisition should be easier in this parallel formalism than in the classical generative formalism, because rule ordering constraints are virtually eliminated, and iterative rule application, such as required for vowel harmony, is replaced by a single application of a clustering rule.

In this paper we present some experimental evidence to support our claim that rule acquisition is more tractable in the M^3P formalism. We describe a rule-learning program that examines a set of underlying and surface forms and induces rules to account for the differences. Our program is language-independent, but for reasons of space we will confine our discussion to examples from a single language. We choose the Yawelmani dialect of Yokuts (an American Indian language from California) because it combines several interesting processes in a small number of examples: epenthesis, lowering, shortening, and vowel harmony. Our Yawelmani data come from Kenstowicz & Kisseberth [4], who draw on data from Newman [9] and the analysis of Kuroda [5]. Lakoff offers an alternative to the Kenstowicz & Kisseberth analysis in [7].

Of course, humans are not supplied with underlying forms when they learn their language, so in this respect at least, our program is not a realistic model of human language acquisition. However, we view it as an important first step toward more ambitious, human-like models. We are aware of no other phonological rule learning program, connectionist or otherwise, that can deal with complex rule interactions of the sort found in Yawelmani and many other languages. Phonological rule acquisition is simply a hard problem. Our purpose here is to show that it can be made less hard by adopting a more cognitively natural architecture. We include a detailed discussion of Yawelmani phonology below to underscore the complexity of the task. Non-linguists can safely skim the following section.

2. The Facts of Yawelmani

In the following discussion we will focus on four rules from Yawelmani, all involving vowels. The (underlying) phonemic and (surface) phonetic vowel systems for Yawelmani are given below. Colons denote long vowels. Note that there are no long high vowels (/i:/ or /u:/) at the surface, and that /e/ and /e:/ do not exist phonemically.

	Phonemic (underlying)	Phonetic (surface)	
i/i:	u/u:	i	u
	o/o:	e/e:	o/o:
	a/a:		a/a:

For typographical convenience, following Kenstowicz & Kisseberth, the short and long mid vowels are represented here as 'e' and 'o', although phonetically they are actually [ɛ] and [ɔ]. Given this phonemic inventory, we have evidence for the following distinctive feature analysis of the vowels of Yawelmani:

	i	u	o	a	i:	u:	o:	a:
high	+	+	–	–	+	+	–	–
round	–	+	+	–	–	+	+	–
long	–	–	–	–	+	+	+	+

Suffixes in Yawelmani exhibit alternations between non-round and round vowels. The basic pattern is that a vowel is pronounced round (and back) if immediately preceded by a round vowel of the same height, that is, u-i becomes u-u, and o-a becomes o-o. Note the alternation of -hin/-hun and -al/-ol below:

xat-hin	'eats'	xat-al	'might eat'
bok'-hin	'finds'	bok'-ol	'might find'
xil-hin	'tangles'	xil-al	'might tangle'
dub-hun	'leads by the hand'	dub-al	'might lead by the hand'

Rounding applies iteratively, throughout an entire word, as illustrated in the following examples:

Underlying	Surface	Gloss
/dub-wis-mi/	[dub-wus-mu]	'having led each other by the hand'
/t'ul-sit-hin/	[t'ul-sut-hun]	'burns for'

Returning now to the vowel inventories of Yawelmani, it is worth noting again that there are no underlying segments /e/ and /e:/. The surface segments [e] and [e:] are derived from /i:/ through the application of two rules: Lowering and Shortening. All long vowels lower, and vowels in closed syllables shorten. These rules are shown below; the $ denotes a syllable boundary.

Yawelmani Lowering

$$\begin{matrix} V \\ [+\text{long}] \end{matrix} \rightarrow [-\text{high}]$$

Yawelmani Shortening

$$V \rightarrow [-\text{long}] / \_ C \$$$

Evidence for shortening comes from paradigms like the following, which show an alternation in vowel length (such as o:/o or a:/a) in the root. Notice that the short variants are followed by *two* consonants; their syllable structure is CVC$CV(C), with the first vowel satisfying the environment for shortening.

Nonfuture	Imperative	Dubitative	Future	
dos-hin	dos-k'o	do:s-ol	do:s-en	'report'
lan-hin	lan-k'a	la:n-al	la:n-en	'hear'

We now argue, in agreement with previous researchers, that not only does [e] derive from a high underlying vowel, but some occurrences of [o] do as well. In particular, the underlying form of the root [c'om-] "destroy" should be /c'u:m-/. One source of evidence for this is harmony. If the underlying form were /c'o:m-/, the non-future form would be *[c'om-hin], but it is actually [c'om-hun]. Lowering and shortening apply only after harmony has had its effect. This also explains why we get [c'om-al] (no rounding of the suffix vowel), not *[c'om-ol]. Compare this with the root meaning 'report,' which is underlyingly /do:s-/, and triggers harmony as expected, giving [do:s-ol], not *[do:s-al].

c'o:m-al	'might destroy'	do:s-ol	'might report'
c'om-hun	'destroys'	dos-hin	'reports'

The interaction of harmony, lowering, and shortening is illustrated below:

	/c'u:m-al/	/c'u:m-hin/
harmony	—	u
lowering	o:	o:
shortening	—	o
	[c'o:mal]	[c'om h u n]

There is another set of apparent counterexamples to harmony, in that a sequence of vowels that agree in height at the surface do not agree in rounding (o-e), and vowels that disagree in height do agree in rounding (u-o):

bok'-en	'will find'	xat-en	'will eat'
dub-on	'will lead by the hand'	giy'-en	'will touch'

Notice that in [dub-on] the surface *non*-high vowel of the suffix appears rounded after a *high* vowel in the root. Here again, the regularity in the system reemerges if we assume that the future suffix is underlyingly long and high, i.e., /-i:n/. It surfaces as [-en] through the combined effects of lowering and shortening, or as [-on] if harmony has applied first.

There is one additional rule involving vowels that interacts with vowel harmony, namely epenthesis. There is a class of roots of the form CVCC- which have alternants of the form CVCiC- or CVCuC- depending on the preceding vowel and the effects of harmony.

?ugn-al	'might drink'	?ugun-hun	'drinks'
logw-ol	'might pulverize'	logiw-hin	'pulverizes'

Clearly, epenthesis precedes vowel harmony. This is further supported by examples like [logiw-xa] 'let's pulverize', derived from /logw-xa/, in which the appearance of the epenthetic vowel blocks rounding from applying to the final vowel.

To summarize, the phonological system of Yawelmani offers an example of a very complex set of interactions between independently-motivated rules. The classical generative analysis of this data depends heavily on ordered application [4,5], but learning these rules would be easier in an architecture where they could apply simultaneously. Another factor complicating learning is that the environment of vowel harmony is only regular at the abstract underlying level; the alternations attributable to harmony are not completely systematic based solely on surface forms.

3. The "Many Maps" Architecture

As an alternative to standard generative analyses involving long lists of ordered rules, Lakoff [6,7] develops a theory of phonology which is essentially non-derivational in character. "Rules" are replaced by "constructions," which state well-formedness constraints within levels and correlations between levels. He recognizes three levels: a morphophonemic level (M), a phonemic level (P), and a phonetic level (F). Our attempts to actually implement Lakoff's work in a connectionist framework led to several revisions in the analysis of Yawelmani [11,14]. In this section we will describe our analysis, then turn to the question of learning this complex set of phonological rules in the next section.

In a generative analysis, shortening comes *after* lowering because only long vowels can lower. In our model, both these processes are P-F constructions that apply simultaneously. Both have their environments satisfied at P-level and their changes realized at F-level. The rules are presented below using Lakoff's parallel mapping notation:

Lowering: P: [+syll,+long]   Shortening: P: [+syll,+long]   C $
                 | |
           F: [−high]   F: [−long]

Vowel harmony is traditionally extrinsically ordered before both lowering and shortening, because of the restriction that vowels undergoing harmony must agree in height. If harmony followed lowering, there would be no rounding in the final vowel of examples like [c'omhun] 'destroys' (underlying form /c'uːm-hin/). But in our model, vowel harmony is another P-F construction. It applies simultaneously with the other two P-F rules; all three rules therefore have their environment at P. Ignoring iteration for the moment, the vowel harmony rule might be stated as:

Vowel Harmony: P: [+syll,+round, αhigh] C_0 [+syll, αhigh]
                                                                    |
                F: [+round]

An example of the interaction of these three constructions is given below.

    P: c'uːm-hin
            | | lowering and shortening of 1st vowel, harmony on 2nd
    F: c'o m-hun

The above formulation of harmony does not allow for iterative application in words like [t'ul-sut-hun] (from /t'ul-sit-hin/). In our model, harmony is actually stated as a P-F "cluster rule." Cluster rules use special circuitry described in [11,14] to process groups of segments undergoing the same change. The cluster rule for harmony first identifies the cluster "trigger" (a round vowel), and then marks as cluster "elements" all subsequent vowels in sequence that agree with it in height. The change sanctioned by the rule is applied to all these elements simultaneously. Our cluster rules are stated in a tabular format:

    P-F Cluster Rule for Vowel Harmony:
          Cluster type: [+syllabic]
          Trigger: [+round, αhigh]
          Element: [αhigh]
          Change: [+round]

Our model also includes a syllabifier component that is part of the mapping from M-level to P-level [13]. Epenthesis and deletion processes in most languages are necessitated by the requirement that strings be fully syllabified. In Yawelmani, epenthesis serves to break up consonant clusters which would otherwise be unsyllabifiable, because its syllable types are restricted to CV and CVC [5]. Since epenthesis is an M-P rule and harmony processes are always P-F, we correctly predict that the epenthetic vowel [i] will be visible at P-level, and thus undergo or block harmony, depending on the height of the preceding vowel.

The following examples illustrate the interactions of the four rules in our parallel formalism:

```
M:    du:ll-al                       M:    du:l l-hin
                                            |              epenthesis
P:    du:ll-al                       P:    du:lil-hin
       |        shortening                  | | |        lowering, harmony
F:    doll-al   'might climb'        F:    do:lul-hun   'climbs'
```

With all three mutation rules, lowering, shortening, and harmony, stated as P-F rules, the problem of rule induction is considerably simplified, since there is no need to stipulate constraints on rule application. These are determined by the architecture of the model. We're now in a position to consider the problem of rule induction.

4. The Rule Learning Program

Our rule learning program takes as input a set of of M-level forms and their corresponding F-level realizations. Its output is a set of rules that collectively account for the differences between the two levels. We will discuss the process of learning the shortening rule to illustrate how mutation rules in general are acquired. Each rule accounts for a single change to a single segment. Rule environments are induced using Mitchell's version space technique [8]. Rules have two environments, a most specific environment (SPEC) and a most general (GEN). The SPEC is the intersection of all environments in which the rule has been seen to apply. Initially the SPEC is the string consisting of the changed segment of the first example seen, and up to three segments of context on either side. The GEN states the minimal conditions required for the rule to apply. Initially it contains just the major class features of the first input, i.e., sequences of [+cons] and [+syll], represented below as Cs and Vs. When the SPEC and GEN match, the rule has been refined completely.

Assume the first pair of inputs the learner examines is /do:shin/ and [doshin]. A comparison of the two strings reveals a difference in length of the initial vowel, so a prototype shortening rule is created. The shortening rule's initial SPEC is <d>o<s$hi>, where segments in angle brackets denote context, and the $ indicates a syllable boundary that was detected by the syllabifier. The /o:/ is not marked [+long] by convention in the SPEC, because this feature is the one changed by the rule. The rule's initial GEN is <C>V<CCV>. When shortening is seen to operate in other environments, the GEN will contract to the minimal common substring that characterizes all examples, namely <C>V<C>.

Suppose the second input happens to be /c'u:mhin/ and [c'omhun]. There are three differences in this string: the initial vowel lowers and shortens, and the final vowel rounds. The learner will hypothesize a separate rule for each change. Rules are indexed by the changes they cause, so the previously-formulated rule for shortening will be expected to account for this case as well. Further examples of shortening help to relax the SPEC by eliminating overly-restrictive features. After incorporating the /c'u:mhin/ example, the proto-rule's SPEC is <C>[V,+round]<C$hi>. And after processing the next pair, /bok'i:n/ and [bok'en], the SPEC becomes <C>V<C$>, and the GEN contracts to <C>V<C>.

352

Examples where shortening doesn't apply are also important, because they force the learner to make the GEN more specific. The underlying form /do:sal/ satisfies the GEN for shortening of the first vowel, but the surface form [do:sol] shows that shortening did not in fact happen. This causes the learner to look for some feature of the SPEC that is absent from the GEN and uniquely accounts for the rule's failure to apply. In this case, the only such feature is the coda marking of the final consonant. The GEN is updated to <C>V<C$>, which matches the SPEC, and the rule is now complete. The lowering rule is learned in a similar fashion.

When a sequence of vowels is observed to undergo the same change, a cluster rule is postulated. On the basis of examples such as /t'ul-sit-hin/, [t'ul-sut-hun], where the second and third high vowels undergo rounding, the learner creates a cluster rule for rounding. It generates single-segment GENs and SPECs for the trigger and element portions of the rule, and refines them as it processes additional examples, such as /do:s-al/, [do:s-ol]. The trigger GEN eventually settles on [+syll,+round], and the element GEN remains [+syll]. Unfortunately, these specifications do not explain certain cases where vowel harmony fails to apply, such as /do:s-hin/, which does not become *[dos-hun], but rather surfaces as [dos-hin].

The learner collects correlation statistics on trigger and element features in order to detect agreement relationships that would be expressed with α variables in conventional rules. The correlation matrix indicates that in all cases where harmony applies, triggers and elements agree in height, and in cases where harmony fails to apply, they disagree. Therefore the learner abandons the original harmony rule and generates a pair of rules. In one, the trigger and element specifications are both [+high], while in the other they are [−high]. We find this solution preferable to introducing variable binding for a feature [αhigh] into the clustering machinery. That would increase the complexity of the connectionist architecture that must implement these rules.

Although we are covering epenthesis last in this section, the learner is actually designed to detect and account for epenthesis and deletion phenomena first. They can generally be explained by syllabification, an M-P process. At this stage in the development of the model, the syllabifier relies on language-specific parameters which we supply for Yawelmani; it does not yet acquire these parameter values on its own. Learning the M-P epenthesis process in cases such as /?ugn-hin/, [?ugunhun] is simple and straightforward given the phonotactic constraints of Yawelmani. The syllabifier predicts an epenthetic vowel will appear in this example; all the rule learner needs to do is specify the quality of the vowel. The interaction of epenthesis with other rules follows from the architecture of the model. Notice that this automatically predicts that epenthesis (M-P) will feed harmony (P-F), as it does in the [?ugunhun] example.

After epenthesis applies to the M-level form /?ugn-hin/, its P-level representation is /?ugIn-hin/. The /I/ is a [+high,−long] segment left unspecified for roundness, because the epenthetic vowel surfaces as either [i] or [u] depending on context. The P-level sequence then forms part of the data for learning the harmony rule. Thus we see that when learning P-F rules, the actual input strings must be obtained by applying previously-acquired M-P processes to the M-level strings, rather than looking at the M-level strings themselves. This also lets the model naturally account for the failure to round the final vowel in /logw-xa/. If the harmony rule looked at the underlying representation we would expect it to apply, but the epenthetic high vowel /I/ appearing at P-level in /logIw-xa/ blocks it, since it does not agree in height. This correctly predicts the surface form [logiw-xa], not *[logiw-xo].

As this section has shown, our rule learner has several components. One component learns SPECs and GENs for ordinary rules. Another learns the components of cluster rules: the cluster type, SPECs and GENs for the trigger and element, and the desired change. A third component recognizes insertion and deletion phenomena that can be accounted for by epenthesis, and so do not need separate rules. Each component corresponds to a different piece of the connectionist architecture that implements these rules.

5. Discussion

Our treatment of vowel harmony is notably different from the proposals of Gasser & Lee [1] and Hare [3], both of which are based on properties of sequential recurrent networks. Their models are trained directly on surface sequences, and do not derive underlying representations to express regularities, although they do develop internal "hidden" representations. They focus on just harmony, and do not consider possible interactions of this process with other phonological rules. Hare's model suggests that a vowel will undergo harmony to become more like the trigger only if it is already sufficiently similar to the trigger. In Yawelmani the crucial similarity governing harmony is height, but the [αhigh] constraint applies only at the abstract underlying level. It is violated on the surface, because long high vowels serving as triggers or elements subsequently undergo lowering.

Insertions and deletions are always handled at M-P in our model (usually by the syllabifier), and mutations at P-F. This works fine for the examples we've tried from Yawelmani and other languages, and is suggestive of a more general pattern across languages. However, it remains an open question whether all languages fall into this pattern. If necessary, we can introduce additional mechanisms to allow rules to migrate between M-P and P-F to establish the correct feeding and blocking relations. We suspect such mechanisms will ultimately be needed.

Our model would be more impressive if it developed its own underlying representations from exposure to annotated surface forms alone. We see no reason why this cannot be done in principle, once a lexical component is added to provide the necessary information (syntactic or semantic) for recognizing allomorphs. We are exploring various possibilities.

The main result of our work to date is that rule learning can be made tractable by adopting a more cognitively natural (less sequential) formalism. Our M^3P architecture has another advantage: it is compatible with a connectionist implementation, and therefore does not violate any fundamental computational constraints associated with neural processing.

Acknowledgements

This research was supported by a contract from Hughes Research Laboratories, by the Office of Naval Research under contract number N00014-86-K-0678, and by National Science Foundation grant EET-8716324. We thank David Evans for helpful comments on an earlier draft of this paper.

References

[1] Gasser, M., and Lee, C.-D. (1989) Networks that learn phonology. Indiana University Computer Science Technical Report #300.

[2] Goldsmith, J. (to appear) Phonology as an intelligent system. To appear in a festschrift for Leila Gleitman, edited by D. Napoli and J. Kegl.

[3] Hare, M. (1989) The role of similarity in Hungarian vowel harmony: a connectionist account. Technical report, University of California at San Diego.

[4] Kenstowicz, M., and Kisseberth, C. (1979) *Generative Phonology: Description and Theory.* San Diego, CA: Academic Press.

[5] Kuroda, S.-Y. (1967) Yawelmani Phonology. Cambridge, MA: The MIT Press.

[6] Lakoff, G. (1988) A suggestion for a linguistics with connectionist foundations. In D. S. Touretzky, G. E. Hinton, and T. J. Sejnowski (eds.), Proceedings of the 1988 Connectionist Models Summer School, pp. 301-314. San Mateo, California: Morgan Kaufmann.

[7] Lakoff, G. (1989) Cognitive phonology. Draft of paper presented at the UC-Berkeley Workshop on Constraints vs. Rules, May 1989.

[8] Mitchell, T. M. (1978) Version Spaces. Doctoral dissertation, Stanford University. Available as technical report STAN-CS-78-711.

[9] Newman, S. (1944) Yokuts Language of California. New York: Viking Fund Publications in Anthropology.

[10] Touretzky, D. S. (1989) Toward a connectionist phonology: the "many maps" approach to sequence manipulation. Proceedings of the Eleventh Annual Conference of the Cognitive Science Society, pp. 188-195. Hillsdale, NJ: Erlbaum.

[11] Touretzky, D. S., and Wheeler, D. W. (1990) A computational basis for phonology. In D. S. Touretzky (ed.), Advances in Neural Information Processing Systems 2. San Mateo, California: Morgan Kaufmann.

[12] Touretzky, D. S., and Wheeler, D. W. (1990) Rationale for a "many maps" phonology machine. Proceedings of EMCSR-90: the Tenth European Meeting on Cybernetics and Systems Research. Vienna, Austria, April 1990.

[13] Touretzky, D. S., and Wheeler, D. W. (unpublished) Two derivations suffice: the role of syllabification in cognitive phonology. Manuscript draft.

[14] Wheeler, D. W., and Touretzky, D. S. (1989) A connectionist implementation of cognitive phonology. Technical Report CMU-CS-89-144, Carnegie Mellon University School of Computer Science. To appear in J. Goldsmith (ed.), Proceedings of the UC-Berkeley Workshop on Constraints vs, Rules in Phonology, University of Chicago Press.

Discovering Faithful 'Wickelfeature' Representations in a Connectionist Network

Michael C. Mozer

Department of Computer Science and
Institute of Cognitive Science
University of Colorado
Boulder, CO 80309-0430
e-mail: mozer@boulder.colorado.edu

Abstract. A challenging problem for connectionist models is the representation of varying-length sequences, e.g., the sequence of phonemes that compose a word. One representation that has been proposed involves encoding each sequence element with respect to its local context; this is known as a *Wickelfeature* representation. Handcrafted Wickelfeature representations suffer from a number of limitations, as pointed out by Pinker and Prince (1988). However, these limitations can be avoided if the representation is constructed with a priori knowledge of the set of possible sequences. This paper proposes a specialized connectionist network architecture and learning algorithm for the discovery of *faithful* Wickelfeature representations — ones that do not lose critical information about the sequence to be encoded. The architecture is applied to a simplified version of Rumelhart and McClelland's (1986) verb past-tense model.

A challenging problem for connectionist models is the manipulation and representation of varying-length sequences. Consider the problem of representing a sequence of symbols, say letters. Using symbolic, LISP-like structures, this is straighforward: A short string like ARM can be represented as (A R M), and a longer string like FIREARM can be represented by concatenating extra symbols onto the list — (F I R E A R M). However, using connectionist activity patterns to represent these strings is a more complex matter. The activity pattern must indicate not only what the symbols are, but their positions in the string. This suggests the straightforward idea of reserving a processing unit for for every possible symbol in every position, but this scheme requires knowing the maximum length of the sequence in advance. It also suffers from the serious difficulty that two sequences containing common subsequences may appear quite different. For example, using the notation x/n to refer to a unit that is activated by the symbol x in position n, activity patterns corresponding to { A/1, R/2, M/3 } and { F/1, I/2, R/3, E/4, A/5, R/6, M/7 } have no overlap. The common subsequence ARM is not represented by an overlap in the activity patterns because ARM appears in a different position in each string. Overlap between similar activity patterns is critical in connectionist representations because it determines how a connectionist network will generalize to novel instances: if a network responds a certain way to ARM, one might like it to respond similarly to FIREARM, yet the position-specific letter encoding will not facilitate this.

Any representation of sequences should satisfy four criteria.

- The representation must be *faithful* (Smolensky, 1987), meaning that a one-to-one mapping exists between sequences and activity patterns. This requirement may be relaxed somewhat in the context of a particular task: The representation need only be sufficient to perform the desired input-output mapping. If two sequences have exactly the same consequences in all situations, there is no need to encode them distinctly. Task-irrelevant features do not have to be captured in the representation.

- The representation must be capable of encoding sequences of varying lengths with a fixed number of units.

- The representation must be capable of encoding relationships between elements of a sequence.

- The representation should provide a natural basis for generalization. It is on this ground that the position-specific encoding fails.

Wickelgren (1969) has suggested a representational scheme that seems to satisfy these criteria and has been applied successfully in several connectionist models (Mozer, 1990; Rumelhart & McClelland, 1986; Seidenberg, 1990). The basic idea is to encode each element of a sequence with respect to its local context. For example, consider the phonetic encoding of a word. Wickelgren proposed context-sensitive phoneme units, each responding to a particular phoneme in the context of a particular predecessor and successor. I will call these units *Wickelphones*, after the terminology of Rumelhart and McClelland. If the word *explain* had the phonetic spelling /eksplʌn/, it would be composed of the Wickelphones $\_e_k$, $_ee_s$, $_ks_p$, $_sp_l$, $_pl_A$, $_lA_n$, and $_An\_$. (where the dash indicates a word boundary). Assuming one Wickelphone unit for every such triple, activation of a word would correspond to a distributed pattern of activity over the Wickelphone units. With a fixed number of Wickelphone units, it is possible to represent arbitrary strings of varying length. Generally, this representation is faithful. In such cases, the unordered set of Wickelphones is sufficient to allow for the unambiguous reconstruction of the ordered string.

Rumelhart and McClelland devised a more compact and distributed encoding of phoneme sequences that depended on *features* of the phonemes rather than the phonemes themselves. Units in this *Wickelfeature* representation encode triples of phonemic features (such a "voiced" or "dental"). Smolensky (1987) provides a formalism that allows the Wickelphone and Wickelfeature encodings to be viewed in a uniform representational framework, as tensor products of feature vectors. In the remainder of this paper, I use the term "Wickelfeature" to denote a context-sensitive encoding of features of sequence elements or of the elements themselves, thereby subsuming the term "Wickelphone" and allowing the representation to be applied to arbitrary sequences.

Pinker and Prince (1988; Prince & Pinker, 1988) point to several serious limitations of handcrafted Wickelfeature representations, in particular the representation used by Rumelhart and McClelland in their model of learning past tenses of English verbs. One critical limitation is that if the class of sequences to be represented contain repeated subsequences of length two or more, the resulting representation is ambiguous. For example, the set of Wickelfeatures { $_AB$, $_AB_A$, $_BA_B$, $_AB\_$ } could correspond to the sequence ABAB or to ABABAB or an infinite number of other such strings. Similarly, the set { $_AB$, $_AB_X$, $_BX_A$, $_XA_B$, $_AB_Y$, $_BY_A$, $_YA_B$, $_AB\_$ } could correspond either to sequence ABXABYAB or ABYABXAB. Thus, the Wickelfeature representation can lose order information.

There are potential ways around these problems. One quick solution is to represent more contextual information in the Wickelfeatures. If a Wickelfeature consists of v sequence elements rather than just three, confusions arise only if the strings contain repeated subsequences of length $v-1$ or greater. As v grows, however, the representation becomes more and more localist and loses the advantages that we set out to attain. Another solution is to have the Wickelfeature units be activated in a graded fashion, not all-or-nothing. This would allow a unit to signal the number of instances of that Wickelfeature in a sequence, which handles the ABAB problem. Alternatively, the amount of activity could correspond to the position in a sequence; in the ABXABYAB example, the $_AB_X$ unit could be less active than the $_AB_Y$ unit, indicating its primacy in the sequence.

Hand coding Wickelfeature representations of this sort gets quite tricky. In this paper, I report on an alternative approach using connectionist learning algorithms to discover Wickelfeature-like representations. The advantage of leaving the job to learning is that whatever representations the system develops, they are assured of being sufficient for the domain at hand, i.e., they will satisfy the faithfulness criterion mentioned above. A further advantage of using learning is that by discovering only domain-relevant Wickelfeatures, the overall representation can be more compact. For instance, a system whose task is to encode English letter strings as Wickelfeatures will not develop a $_pK_T$ unit.

A network architecture to learn Wickelfeatures

The approach I have taken involves training a network to map input sequences to target output patterns through a layer of units that learn to respond as Wickelfeatures. It does not much matter what the output patterns are; they could be localist representations of the sequences, responses to the sequence, or perhaps sequences themselves. Figure 1 shows a schematic drawing of an architecture that performs this mapping. The input layer represents a small window on the sequence. At any time, the input layer views several consecutive elements of the sequence — three elements in the Figure. Presenting a complete sequence to the network involves sliding the sequence through the window. More concretely, time is quantized into discrete *steps*, and at each time step, the sequence is advanced by one position in the input window. Once the entire sequence has been presented, the output units should respond appropriately. The output layer is activated by the context layer, the purpose of which is to remember those elements of the input sequence that are critical for performing the input-output mapping. At each time step, units in the context layer integrate their current values with the new input to form a new context representation.

357

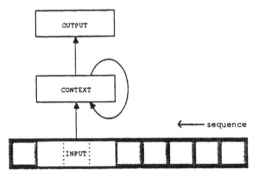

Figure 1. A three-layered recurrent network consisting of input, context, and output units. Each labeled box indicates a set of processing units. The arrows indicate complete connectivity from one layer to another.

The context layer thus forms a *static* internal representation of the dynamic input sequence. The goal of learning, of course, is for this to become a Wickelfeature representation. The use of a sliding input window does part of the job: At each time, the context units can only see a local "chunk" of the sequence. This allows the context units to detect local conjunctions of sequence elements, or conjunctions of features of sequence elements. Once activated by a pattern in the input, the context units should remain on. Thus, it seems sensible to have self-connected context units, but not to connect each context unit to each other, using an activation function like:

$$c_i(t+1) = d_i c_i(t) + s[net_i(t)] ,$$

where $c_i(t)$ is the activity level of context unit i at time t, d_i is a decay weight associated with the unit, s is a sigmoid squashing function, and $net_i(t)$ is the net input to the unit:

$$net_i(t) = \sum_j w_{ji} x_j(t) ,$$

$x_j(t)$ being the activity of input unit j at time t, w_{ji} the connection strength from input unit j to context unit i. Thus, a context unit adds its current activity, weighted by the decay factor, to the new input at each time. The decay factor allows old information to fade over time if d_i is less than one.

To summarize, the Wickelfeature-learning architecture differs from a generic recurrent architecture for temporal sequence recognition in three respects: (1) the input layer consists of a small temporal window holding several elements of the input sequence; (2) connectivity in the context layer is restricted to one-to-one recurrent connections; and (3) integration over time in the context layer is linear.

A training algorithm for the Wickelfeature architecture

The standard procedure for training a recurrent network with temporally-varying inputs using the back-propagation algorithm is to "unfold" the network in time (Rumelhart, Hinton, & Williams, 1986), transforming the recurrent network into a feedforward network. The unfolding procedure requires that each unit remember a temporal history of its activation values and is computation intensive. For the Wickelfeature architecture, however, the unfolding procedure can be avoided, as described by Mozer (1989). To summarize the result, consider a sequence with s elements and an architecture with a v-element window. The number of time steps, t, required to slide the sequence through the window is simply $s-v+1$. Consequently, at time t the network receives a target vector over the output units and an error E can be computed. Using the ordinary back propagation procedure, the error derivative with respect to each context unit i,

$$\delta_i(t) = \frac{\partial E}{\partial c_i(t)}$$

can be computed. The weight update rule for the recurrent connections, d_i, is then:

$$\Delta d_i = -\varepsilon \delta_i(t) \alpha_i(t) \, ,$$

where $\alpha_i(t)$ is defined by the recurrence relation

$$\alpha_i(\tau) = c_i(\tau-1) + d_i \alpha_i(\tau-1)$$

with boundary value $\alpha_i(0) = 0$. Similarly, the weight update rule for the input-context connections, w_{ji}, is:

$$\Delta w_{ji} = -\varepsilon \delta_i(t) \beta_{ji}(t) \, ,$$

where $\beta_{ji}(0) = 0$ and

$$\beta_{ji}(\tau) = s'[net_i(\tau)] x_j(\tau) + d_i \beta_{ji}(\tau-1) \, .$$

Thus, explicit back propagation in time is not necessary. Bachrach (1988), Gori, Bengio, and De Mori (1989), and Williams and Zipser (1989) have independently discovered the idea of computing an activity trace during the forward pass as an alternative to back propagation in time. However, this is the first use of the architecture for the purpose of learning Wickelfeature-like representations.

Simulation results

Implementation details

In the simulations to be reported, an additional parameter z_i — called the *zero point*, was added to the context-unit activation function, for reasons described by Mozer (1989). The complete activation function is:

$$c_i(t+1) = d_i c_i(t) + s[net_i(t)] + z_i \, ,$$

where the value of z_i is determined by gradient descent as for the other parameters.

The initial input-context and context-output connection strengths were randomly picked from a zero-mean gaussian distribution and normalized such that the L1 norm of the fan-in (incoming) weight vector was 2.0. The z_i were initially set to -0.5, and the d_i picked from a uniform distribution over the interval .99-1.01. The weights were updated only after a complete presentation of the training set (an *epoch*). Momentum was not used. Learning rates were adjusted dynamically for each set of connections according to a heuristic described by Mozer (1989).

Learning Wickelfeatures

Starting with a simple example, the network was trained to identify four sequences: _DEAR_, _DEAN_, _BEAR_, and _BEAN_. Each symbol corresponds to a single sequence element and was represented by a random binary activity pattern over three units. The input layer was a two-element buffer through which the sequence was passed. For _DEAR_, the input on successive time steps consisted of _D, DE, EA, AR, R_. The input layer had six units, the context layer two, and the output layer four. The network's task was to associate each sequence with a corresponding output unit. To perform this task, the network must learn to discriminate D from B in the first letter position and N from R in the fourth letter position. This can be achieved if the context units learn to behave as Wickelfeature detectors. For example, a context unit that responds to the Wickelfeatures _D or DE serves as a B-D discriminator; a unit that responds to R_ or AR serves as an N-R discriminator. Thus, a solution can be obtained with two context units.

Fifty replications of the simulation were run with different initial weights. The task was learned in a median of 488 training epochs, the criterion for a correct response being that the output unit with the largest value was the appropriate one. Figure 2 shows the result of one run. The weights are grouped by connection type, with the input-context connections in the upper-left array, followed by the decay connections (d_i), zero points (z_i), and context-output connections. Each connection is depicted as a square whose *area* indicates the relative weight magnitude, and shading the weight sign — black is positive, white is negative. The sizes of the squares are normalized within each array such that the largest square has sides whose length is equal to that of the vertical bars on the right edge of the array. The absolute magnitude of the largest weight is indicated by the number in the upper-right corner. Because normalization is performed within each array, weight magnitudes of different connection types must be

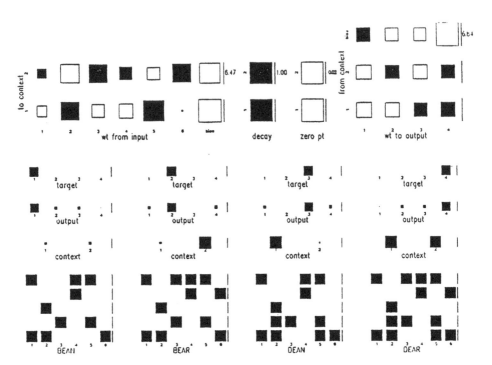

Figure 2. The **DEAR/DEAN/BEAR/BEAN** problem. The upper half of the figure shows learned weights in the network, the lower half activity levels in response to each of the four input sequences.

compared with reference to the normalization factors. The units within each layer are numbered. The weights feeding into and out of context unit 1 have been arranged along a single row, and the weights of context unit 2 in the row above. Bias terms (i.e., weight lines with a fixed input of 1.0) are also shown for the context and output units.

For the activity levels in the lower half of the figure, there are four columns of values, one for each sequence. The input pattern itself is shown in the lowest array. Time is represented along the vertical dimension, with the first time step at the bottom and each succeeding one above the previous. The input at each time reflects the buffer contents. Because the buffer holds two sequence elements, note that the second element in the buffer at one time step (the activity pattern in input units 4-6) is the same as the first element of the buffer at the next (input units 1-3). Above the input pattern are, respectively, the context unit activity levels after presentation of the final sequence element, the output unit activity levels at this time, and the target output values. The activity level of a unit is proportional to the area of its corresponding square. If a unit has an activity level of 0, its square has no area — an empty space. The squares are normalized such that a "unit square" — a square whose edge is the length of one of the vertical bars — corresponds to an activity level of 1. While the input, output, and target activity levels range from 0 to 1, the context activity levels can lie outside these bounds, and are, in fact, occasionally greater than 1.

With these preliminaries out of the way, consider what the network has learned. At the completion of each sequence, the context unit activity pattern is essentially binary. Context unit 1 is off for _BEAN_ and _BEAR_, and on for _DEAN_ and _DEAR_; thus, it discriminates B and D. Context unit 2 is off for _BEAN_ and _DEAN_, and on for _BEAR_ and _DEAR_; thus it discriminates N and R. However, the context units do not behave in a straightforward way as Wickelfeatures. If context unit 1 were sharply tuned to, say, _D, the input-context weights should serve as a matched filter to the input pattern _D. This is not the case: the weights have signs -+--+- but the _D input pattern is 110011. Nor is context unit 1 tuned to the DE, whose input pattern is 011010. Instead, the unit appears to be tuned equally to both patterns. By examining the activity of the unit over time, it can be determined that the unit

360

is activated partly by _D and partly by DE but by no other input pattern. This makes sense: _D and DE are equally valid cues to the sequence identity, and as such, evidence from each should contribute to the response. To get a feel for why the detector responds as it does, note that _D (110011) is distinguished from _B (110001) by activity in unit 5; DE (011010) from BE (001010) by activity in unit 2. The weights from inputs 2 and 5 to context unit 1 are positive, allowing the unit to detect D in either context. The other weights are set so as to prevent the unit from responding to other possible inputs. Thus, the unit selects out key features of the Wickelfeatures _D and DE that are not found in other Wickelfeatures. As such, it behaves as a _DE Wickelfeature detector, and context unit 2 similarly as a AR_ detector.

Generalization testing supports the notion that the context units have become sensitive to these Wickelfeatures. If the input elements are permuted to produce sequences like AR_BE, which preserves the Wickelfeatures AR_ and _BE, context unit responses are similar to those of the original sequences. However, with permutations like _RB_, _DAER_, and DEAR (without the end delimiters), which destroy the Wickelfeatures AR_ and _BE, context unit responses are not contingent upon the D, B, N, and R. Thus, the context units are responding to these key letters, but in a context-dependent manner.

Learning the regularities of verb past tense

In English, the past tense of many verbs is formed according to a simple rule. Regular verbs can be divided into three classes, depending on whether the past tense is formed by adding /^d/ (an "ud" sound), /t/, or /d/. Examples of the classes are /dEpend/ (*depend*), /fAs/ (*face*), and /dEscrIb/ (*describe*), respectively. Each string denotes the phonetic encoding of the verb in italics, and each symbol a single phoneme. The phoneme notation and the examples have been borrowed from Rumelhart and McClelland (1986). The rule for determining the class of a regular verb is as follows.

> If the final phoneme is dental (/d/ or /t/), add /^d/;
> else if the final phoneme is an unvoiced consonant, add /t/;
> else (the final phoneme is voiced), add /d/.

A network was trained to classify the twenty examples of each class. Each phoneme was encoded by a set of four trinary acoustic features (see Rumelhart & McClelland, 1986, Table 5). The input layer of the network was a two-element buffer, so a verb like /kamp/ appeared in the buffer over time as _k, ka, am, mp, p_. The underscore is a delimiter symbol placed at the beginning and end of each string. The network had eight input units (two time slices each consisting of four features), two context units, and three output units — one for each verb class.

In fifteen replications of the simulation, the network performed at 90% within 100 epochs, learned the training set perfectly in under 1000 epochs. A verb was considered to have been categorized correctly if the most active output unit specified the verb's class. The network has learned the underlying rule, as evidenced by perfect generalization to novel verbs. Typical weights learned by the network are presented in Figure 3, along with the output levels of the two context units in response to twenty verbs. These verbs, though not part of the training set, were all classified correctly.

The response of the context units is straightforward. Context unit 1 has a positive activity level if the final phoneme is a dental (/d/ or /t/), negative otherwise. Context unit 2 has positive activity if the final phoneme is unvoiced, near zero otherwise. These are precisely the features required to discriminate among the three regular verb classes. In fact, the classification rule for regular verbs can be observed in the context-output weights (the rightmost weight matrix in Figure 3). Connections are such that output unit 1, which represents the "add /^d/" class, is activated by a final dental phoneme; output unit 2, which represents the "add /t/" class, is activated by a final non-dental unvoiced phoneme; and output unit 3, which represents "add /d/" class, is activated by a final non-dental voiced phoneme.

Note that the decay weights in this simulation are small in magnitude; the largest is .02. Consequently, context units retain no history of past events, which is quite sensible because only the final phoneme determines the verb class. This fact makes verb classification a simple task: it is not necessary for the context units to hold on to information over time. Simulations were also conducted giving the network the same verb classification task, but reversing the order of the phonemes; instead of /dEpend/, /dnepEd/ was presented. In this problem, the relevant

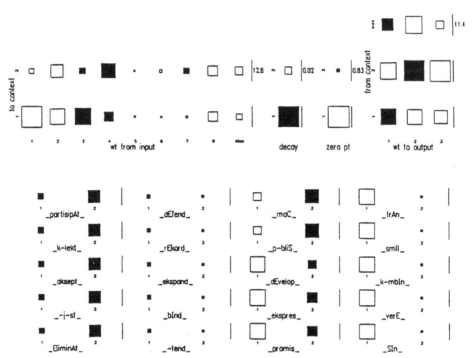

Figure 3. The regular verb problem. The upper half shows learned weights in the network, the lower half shows the final activity levels of the context units in response to a variety of verbs. Verbs in the first column all end with /t/, in the second column with /d/, in the third column with an unvoiced consonant, and the fourth column with a voiced consonant or vowel.

information comes at the *start* of the sequence and must be retained until the sequence is completed. Nonetheless, the network is able to learn the task. Interestingly, a more standard network architecture was unsuccessful at learning the task.

Large verb simulation

To study a more difficult task, the regular-verb categorization problem was extended to a larger corpus of verbs. As before, the task was to classify each verb according to the manner in which its past tense is formed. The complexity of the task was increased by including both regular and irregular verbs, 136 training instances altogether, and a total of thirteen response categories — three for regular forms and ten for irregular (see Mozer, 1989, for examples of these categories). The categories are based loosely on a set suggested by Bybee and Slobin (1982).

The corpus of verbs was borrowed from the Rumelhart and McClelland (1986) model. The model, designed to account for children's acquisition of verb past tenses, produces the past tense of a verb given its infinitive form as input. The representation used at both input and output ends is a handcrafted Wickelfeature encoding of the verb, built into the model. The purpose of this simulation is to demonstrate that a network, given a sequence of phonemes, can *learn* a representation like that presupposed by Rumelhart and McClelland's model.

The task is difficult. The verb classes contain some internal regularities, but these regularities are too weak to be used to uniquely classify a verb. For instance, all verbs in category 3 end in a /d/ or /t/, but so do verbs in categories 4, 5, and 11. Whether a verb ending in /d/ or /t/ belongs in category 3 or one of the other categories depends on whether it is regular, but there are no simple features signaling this fact. Further, fine discriminations are necessary because two outwardly similar verbs can be classified into different categories. *Swim* and *sing* belong to category 10, but *swing* to category 12; *ring* belongs to category 10, but *bring* to category 8; *set* belongs to

362

category 4, but *get* to category 11. Because the category to which a verb belongs is somewhat arbitrary, the network must memorize a large number of special cases.

The network architecture was similar to that used in the regular verb example. The input layer was a two-phoneme buffer, and the encoding of phonemes was the same as before. The output layer consisted of thirteen units, one for each verb class, and the context layer contained 25 units.

In ten replications of the simulation, the network learned to select the correct category in about 500 epochs. At intermediate stages of learning, verbs are sometimes "overregularized", as when the past tense of *eat* was considered to be *eated*. Overgeneralization occurs in other respects, as when *sit* was misclassified in the category of verbs whose past tense is the same as the root — presumably by analogy to *hit* and *fit* and *set*. Interpretation of the behavior of individual context units is difficult, but by examining similar input sequences that are classified differently, e.g., /riN/ and /briN/, one can pinpoint context units responsible for certain behaviors.

These simulations demonstrate the feasibility of constructing faithful Wickelfeature-like representations using connectionist learning procedures, instead of having to craft the representations by hand. Further, the simulations show that intrinsically temporal or sequential input can be dealt with as such, instead of as static patterns. This is a necessary first step in the modeling of language and speech processes.

Acknowledgements

Thanks to Jeff Elman and Yoshiro Miyata for their insightful comments and assistance. The graphical displays of network states are due to Miyata's SunNet simulator. Dave Rumelhart and Jay McClelland were kind enough to provide me with the phonological encoding and classification of verbs from their simulation work. This research was supported by Contracts N00014-85-K-0450 NR 667-548 and N00014-85-K-0076 with the Office of Naval Research, a grant from the System Development Foundation, and a Junior Faculty Development Award from the University of Colorado.

References

Bachrach, J. (1988). *Learning to represent state.* Unpublished master's thesis, University of Massachusetts, Amherst.

Bybee, J. L., & Slobin, D. I. (1982). Rules and schemas in the development and use of the English past tense. *Language, 58*, 265-289.

Gori, M., Bengio, Y., & Mori, R. de (1989). BPS: A learning algorithm for capturing the dynamic nature of speech. In *Proceedings of the First International Joint Conference on Neural Networks, Volume 2* (pp. 417-423).

Mozer, M. C. (1989). A focused back-propagation algorithm for temporal pattern recognition. *Complex Systems, 3.*

Mozer, M. C. (1990). In *The perception of multiple objects: A connectionist approach.* Cambridge, MA: MIT Press/Bradford Books.

Pinker, S., & Prince, A. (1988). On language and connectionism. *Cognition, 28,* 73-193.

Prince, A., & Pinker, S. (1988). Wickelphone ambiguity. *Cognition, 30,* 189-190.

Rumelhart, D. E., Hinton, G. E., & Williams, R. J. (1986). Learning internal representations by error propagation. In D. E. Rumelhart & J. L. McClelland (Eds.), *Parallel distributed processing: Explorations in the microstructure of cognition. Volume I: Foundations* (pp. 318-362). Cambridge, MA: MIT Press/Bradford Books.

Rumelhart, D. E., & McClelland, J. L. (1986). On learning the past tenses of English verbs. In J. L. McClelland & D. E. Rumelhart (Eds.), *Parallel distributed processing: Explorations in the microstructure of cognition. Volume II: Psychological and biological models* (pp. 216-271). Cambridge, MA: MIT Press/Bradford Books.

Seidenberg, M. S. (1990). Word recognition and naming: A computational model and its implications. In W. D. Marslen-Wilson (Ed.), *Lexical representation and process.* Cambridge, MA: MIT Press.

Wickelgren, W. (1969). Context-sensitive coding, associative memory, and serial order in (speech) behavior. *Psychological Review, 76,* 1-15.

Williams, R. J., & Zipser, D. (1989). Experimental analysis of the real-time recurrent learning algorithm. *Connection Science, 1,* 87-111.

Constraints on Assimilation in Vowel Harmony Languages

Mary Hare
UC San Diego

Abstract

Over the last 10 years, the assimilation process referred to as vowel harmony has served as a test case for a number of proposals in phonological theory. Current autosegmental approaches successfully capture the intuition that vowel harmony is a dynamic process involving the interaction of a sequence of vowels; still, no theoretical analysis has offered a non-stipulative account of the inconsistent behavior of the so-called "transparent", or disharmonic, segments.

The current paper proposes a connectionist processing account of the vowel harmony phenomenon, using data from Hungarian. The strength of this account is that it demonstrates that the same general principle of assimilation which underlies the behavior of the "harmonic" forms accounts as well for the apparently exceptional "transparent" cases, without stipulation.

I. Introduction [1]

The current paper proposes a connectionist processing account of certain aspects of vowel harmony in Hungarian. The paper has two interrelated goals. First, it offers an explanatory account of the behavior of the so-called *transparent* vowels in that language. Second, this account relies crucially on a connectionist theory of sequential processes: thus to the extent it succeeds it demonstrates the utility of connectionist models as an explanatory tool in the study of linguistic phenomena.

The paper is organized in the following manner: I first review some facts about the vowel harmony process in Hungarian which present difficulties to analysis. Second, I introduce the model of sequential processes developed by Jordan (1986). The core of the paper then involves a series of parametric studies, whose aim is to determine the conditions on assimilation in a network of this type. Having established what factors constrain assimilation in the sequential network, I return to the Hungarian data, and show that the interaction of these same factors predicts the correct pattern of behavior for both harmonic and transparent vowels in that language.

II. The data

The Hungarian vowel system is as shown below. This is a seven vowel system, and each vowel has a long counterpart which is phonemic. Notice that there is a round - nonround distinction among the non-low vowels, and that while /e:/ is a mid vowel, /e/ is analyzed as being low.

	front:		back:
	unrounded:	rounded:	
	i i:	ü ü:	u u:
	e:	ő ő:	o o:
	e		a

Hungarian exhibits front-back harmony: in general roots contain only front or only back vowels, and suffix vowels alternate to agree in backness with those of the root. The following data exemplify the harmony phenomenon. These are examples of consistent front- and back-vowel roots, followed by the dative suffix. Note that after a front root, the suffix takes the form *nek* while after a back root the same suffix is realized as *nak* (data from Vago 1979).

(1) Front roots:

iker 'twin'	iker-nek	'twin-DAT'
tükör 'mirror'	tükör-nek	'mirror-DAT'

(2) Back roots:

        varos 'city'   varos-nak   'city-DAT'
        kapu 'gate'   kapu-nak   'gate-DAT'

There are a number of exceptions to the pattern of consistent harmony within roots. The most important exception involves the class of non-low front unrounded vowels (/i/, /iː/, /eː/, and on some accounts /e/). As the following examples demonstrate, these can also appear in the same root as a back vowel. In these cases the back vowel of the root, regardless of its position, determines the backness quality of the suffix vowel.

(3)

        bika 'bull'   bika-nak 'bull-DAT'
        izom 'tendon'   izom-nak 'tendon-DAT'

(4)

        kosci 'carriage'   kosci-nak 'carriage-DAT'
        taxi   taxi-nak 'taxi-DAT'

Note, however, that in certain environments the front vowels *do* determine the backness value of the suffix. This is the case if the root contains only front vowels, as in (1), or if the root ends in a sequence of such vowels, as in the (borrowed) forms shown below (data from Kontra and Ringen 1987).

(5)

        aspirin   aspirin-nek
                * aspirin-nak
                bronkitis
                * bronkitis-nak

The problem, then, is that an identical vowel may behave harmonically in one environment, while violating harmony in another. This complication has often been dealt with in the literature by positing a number of different sources for the segment in question, and allowing the harmonic-nonharmonic distinction to follow from this (Clements 1986, van der Hulst 1985, Ringen 1989, among others). One drawback to such an approach is that there is no reason to establish these differences in derivational source except to distinguish between harmonic and nonharmonic behavior: there is no other behavior in the phonology of the language that motivates it. A preferable account would be one in which these differences in behavior follow from general conditions on the model. In what follows I will use a connectionist model of assimilation to suggest one such account.

III. Sequential processing in the connectionist framework

The account that is being developed here relies on the theory of sequential processes developed by Michael Jordan. Jordan (1986) describes an interesting series of models of coarticulation effects, using a recurrent connectionist network which learns to produce an ordered sequence of output patterns in response to a given input. The network is illustrated in Diagram I.

(6) Diagram I

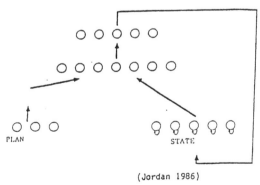

(Jordan 1986)

365

These models involve at least three layers of processing units: input, internal (or *hidden*), and output. Activation passes from the input to the output along weighted connections. Input to the model consists of two parts. The first, labeled the *plan*, is an arbitrary vector that triggers the production of a given sequence. In addition, the *state* of the system (that is, the current output) is fed back over fixed connections and constitutes part of the input at the next cycle. This serves as a temporal context and aids the system in learning what part of the sequence is the next to be produced. Learning is accomplished through the back propagation of error algorithm. After each input is presented, the output that results is compared to the desired output, and the discrepancy between the two is computed. This discrepancy is the *error* on that pattern. The weights on the connections are modified slightly to minimize this error. This process is repeated until some criterion of acceptability is reached.

In the simulations to be discussed here, as in Jordan's coarticulation model, output at any given time consists of a single phoneme represented by a vector corresponding to a distinctive feature description. A word or other longer sequence is represented over time as a string of phonemes on successive output cycles. One interesting property of this network is that particular features of a phoneme can be left unspecified for any value. This is accomplished by having no error signal propagated back from that unit. Instead of learning to match a particular teacher, the unit picks up its specification from some other pattern in the sequence.

In what follows I will use the term *assimilation* to refer to the tendency of an unspecified output unit (hereafter a *don't care* unit) to take on a value influenced by one of its neighbors in time. Jordan shows that outputs tend to follow as smooth a trajectory as possible: thus a don't care unit might be expected to assimilate most strongly to its immediate temporal predecessor. In certain cases, however, the don't care unit ignores its immediate predecessor, and takes on a value close to that of an earlier pattern in the sequence. The question, then, is to determine what factors influence the choice of assimilatory trigger. Note that this exactly the problem in the Hungarian data, as well.

IV. Conditions on assimilation in the sequential network[2]

The following set of simulations were designed to test the hypothesis that the similarity between vowels (in a sense which will be made precise below) is a crucial factor in determining the choice of assimilatory trigger. Stimuli were output sequences as in the example below.

(7)

1	0 1 0 0 0 1 0
2	1 0 1 1 1 0 1
3	* 1 0 0 0 1 0

Each output was a seven-bit distributed pattern, and for each plan the network learned to produce a three-pattern sequence whose members will be referred to as 1, 2, and 3. In each sequence the first two patterns (1 and 2) are specified for all seven units, while the third (3) has one don't care unit, in initial position in the string. (The don't care unit is indicated by the asterisk.) 1 and 2 have opposing values on this first unit.

Sets of patterns were devised in which the final two lines (2 & 3) were held constant with certain number of units in common. This measure of 'units in common' is referred to as the 'hamming distance' between 2 and 3, and is a measure of vector similarity. The first line in the sequence (line 1) was varied in similarity to the other two by manipulating the hamming distance between them This was done in the following way. The pattern given in (7) was the first 3-line sequence in one such set. Here 2 & 3 have opposing values on the last six bits, while 1 and 3 are identical. In the second sequence of this set (example 8) 2 and 3 remain unchanged while 1 is varied to differ from 3 on one unit. In the third sequence, (given in 9) 1 and 3 differ on two units.

(8)

1	0 0 0 0 0 1 0
2	1 0 1 1 1 0 1
3	* 1 0 0 0 1 0

(9)
```
1    0010010
2    1011101
3    *100010
```

This process was repeated, steadily decreasing the similarity between 1 and 3 until the set consisted of seven 3-line sequences. Note that by *similarity* I am speaking of hamming distance, a measure of overall vector similarity, and not simply the presence of similar values on any single unit.

a. Training

These sequences served as teaching output to the network described above. This network was trained on each sequence for 2000 iterations, where an iteration is one presentation of one pattern. In learning to produce the sequences, the network also assigns a value to the don't care unit. This unit is expected to simply maintain the value of the previous pattern; the goal of these simulations is to determine under what conditions the *don't care* unit reverts to the value of the first pattern instead. After 2000 iterations, the training was stopped and the actual output was examined to determine the value taht the don't care unit had taken on.

b. Results

Results from the first set of simulations show that the don't care unit in 3 consistently assimilates to the corresponding unit in 1 when these two patterns are most similar. Thus although the default case in the Jordan network is for a don't care unit to maintain the value of the immediately previous output, this unit does not exclusively influence the result. If the pattern two time steps back is strongly similar to the target, the don't care unit will take a value nearer the corresponding unit in that pattern instead.

These results are given in Graph I, which should be read as follows. Distance along the x-axis measure the similarity between patterns 1 and 3 - that is, between the first and third line of each sequence. The y-axis gives the activation level taken on by the don't care unit after 2000 iterations of learning. The boldface bar gives the average activation over a number of trials, while the line through each bar marks the limits of the variability. As the graph shows, as patterns 1 and 3 become more alike, there is a corresponding increase in the influence of 1 as assimilatory trigger.

These results are typical of a pattern which emerged over a number of pattern sets. The second graph gives the results from a second set of sequences, in which the second pattern was held constant at a hamming distance of 5 units from the target, while the first pattern was varied as before. The only difference between the simulations reported above and this set is that 2, the second pattern in the sequence, is here slightly more similar to 3, the target. In this set, the same pattern of results emerges.

Notice also that the second graph begins with an additional column, where all values are clustered near 0, indicating low assimilation to 1 and high assimilation to 2. This is the output from what will be referred to at the identity condition, where 1 and 2 are not only equal in hamming distance from 3, but are identical. This result shows that when the two potential trigger patterns are identical or nearly so, the target pattern assimilates to the second of the two in all cases. This in not surprising, given the model. A basic property of these networks is that, similar inputs produce similar outputs. Since here temporal context is treated as part of the input, patterns learned in very similar temporal contexts are expected to exhibit very similar behavior.

These simulations were repeated under a number of conditions, with the hamming distance between 2 and 3 progressively decreased. The same pattern of results continued to appear, although in an increasingly attenuated form. Consistently, the influence of the first pattern of the sequence is strongest when it is most similar to the target.

V. Analysis of Hungarian vowel harmony

This pattern of results shows that in a processor of this sort the similarity structure of output strings across time influences assimilatory behavior. Returning to the Hungarian data, let us consider how the facts of the transparent vowels of that language agree with the behavior of the sequential network.

367

Here I modeled the behavior of a series of Hungarian words in the same assimilation task. In this case the output sequences were not arbitrary bit strings chosen only for their similarity structure, but vectors corresponding to distinctive feature representations of phonemes. The features used to represent the vowels were *back*, *high*, *low*, and *round*.

(10) Vowel Code:

i	0 1 0 0	õ	0 0 0 1
e:	0 0 0 0	u	1 1 0 1
e	0 0 1 0	o	1 0 0 1
ü	0 1 0 1	a	1 0 1 0

Words being modeled were represented only by their vowels. Each sequence consisted of vectors representing two or more root vowels specified for all features, and a third which represented the vowel of the dative suffix. This was given as a low unrounded vowel unspecified for [back]. As before, lack of specification equated to a don't care condition on the relevant unit.

(11) iker - nek

i	0 1 0 0
e	0 0 1 0
e	* 0 1 0

Each pattern was learned separately, as before, for 2000 iterations. At this point the underspecified vowel had taken on a value for [back] influenced either by its immediate predecessor, or by an earlier member of the sequence.

To summarize the results of the earlier simulations, a don't care unit will generally maintain the value on the corresponding unit in the previous output. However, if the immediate predecessor is very dissimilar to the target, it is less likely to trigger assimilation. If the antepenultimate member of the sequence shows a strong similarity to the target it instead will be chosen as the trigger, and the penultimate member will be ignored. Furthermore, the similarity between the two potential triggers plays a role. If these two are identical, or markedly similar, the target will assimilate to the second of the two in all cases. The current simulations look at how these results explain the real language data.

In the data presented below, the expected (or *teacher*) output is given first, followed by the actual output of the network after 2000 iterations of training. The unspecified unit in the teacher is represented with an asterisk (*), and the corresponding output is given in boldface.

For the harmonic roots, both potential triggers have the same value for [back]. This value is straightforwardly maintained onto the don't care unit as a result of the smoothness constraint.

(12) iker - nek

i	0 1 0 0	0.053	0.824	0.173	0.059
e	0 0 1 0	0.036	0.149	0.853	0.032
e	* 0 1 0	0.030	0.093	0.910	0.023

(13) kapu - nak

a	1 0 1 0	0.951	0.099	0.911	0.086
u	1 1 0 1	0.962	0.817	0.171	0.833
a	* 0 1 0	0.947	0.120	0.886	0.111

In the mixed roots, the examples all contain a high front vowel in one syllable and a back vowel elsewhere. In these examples, the vectors representing both the suffix vowel and the back root vowel differ significantly from the root vowel *i*. Thus it is expected that even when *i* immediately precedes the underspecified vowel, it will exert little assimilatory influence. In addition, the first pattern in the string is strong similar to the target, and so is expected to have a strong influence. This is in fact the case, both in the simulation and in the real language data.

(14) taxi - nak

a	1 0 1 0	0.811	0.106	0.878	0.032
i	0 1 0 0	0.231	0.781	0.240	0.035
a	* 0 1 0	0.700	0.200	0.785	0.029

(15) bika - nak

i	0 1 0 0	0.134	0.877	0.130	0.050
a	1 0 1 0	0.845	0.110	0.883	0.025
a	* 0 1 0	0.870	0.071	0.930	0.029

However, the situation changes when the root contains a sequence of non-low front vowels. In these examples the target is preceded by a sequence of identical vectors. Here the identity of temporal context is the strongest factor, and the don't care unit is expected to assume the value of its immediate predecessor. Again, this behavior parallels the Hungarian facts.

(16) aspirin - nek

a	1 0 1 0	0.758	0.252	0.750	0.060
i	0 1 0 0	0.138	0.794	0.198	0.014
i	0 1 0 0	0.175	0.671	0.330	0.026
e	* 0 1 0	0.174	0.633	0.372	0.032

VI. Conclusion

To summarize, although the expected pattern in Hungarian is that all vowels of a word will agree in backness, certain front vowels in some environments respect this pattern, and in other environments do not. This more complex behavior is a function of both segmental identity and temporal context. Here I have suggested a processing treatment of the Hungarian facts which predicts harmonic behavior for these vowels on the basis of the overall similarity relationships among the vowels of the word.

A number of factors argue in favor of such an analysis. First, if offers a simpler and more explanatory account of Hungarian data. The vowels which exhibit transparent behavior, and the environments in which this behavior will change, must be stipulated arbitrarily under traditional accounts, while both follow automatically from the account proposed here. Second, this account makes strong claims about the existence of possible harmony patterns. As was demonstrated above, it is a general property of the sequential network that the assimilation process is sensitive to similarity in the temporal context. This predicts substantive constraints on what patterns of harmony may or may not exist. Whether these predictions can be maintained as a general principle requires further research, but available data suggest them to be correct.

Finally, although this accounts suggests that modifications of the autosegmental treatment of harmony are necessary, it is heavily influenced by the autosegmental notion of assimilation as the spread of a value for a particular phonetic feature. As the simulations demonstrate, a properly constrained treatment of temporal spread correctly predicts those harmonic patterns which exist in Hungarian, while failing to produce non-attested patterns. This result argues strongly in favor of the use of processing models as sources of constraint and explanation which can potentially enrich linguistic theory.

Notes

[1] I am grateful to Jeff Elman, Rob Kluender, Steve Poteet, Robert Port, George Lakoff, Sanford Schane, Gary Cottrell, Ann Thyme, Errapel Mejias-Bikandi and Kathleen Carey for useful comments and discussion.

[2] Results reported here are from a recurrent network with two input (plan) units, seven output and consequently seven state units, and six hidden units. The learning rate in simulations was 0.1; *mu* (the multiplier on the recurrent connections from each state unit to itself) was 0.6, and momentum was set to 0.

Bibliography

Archangeli, Diane. 1984. Underspecification in Yawelmani Phonology and Morphology. MIT PhD dissertation.

Archangeli, Diane and Douglas Pullyblank. 1986. The Content and Structure of Phonological Representations. ms.

Clements, George N. 1976. Vowel harmony in non-linear generative phonology. IULC.

Goldsmith, John. 1976. Autosegmental Phonology. PhD dissertation, MIT. Published 1979, New York: Garland Press.

Goldsmith, John. 1985. Vowel harmony in Khalkha Mongolian, Yaka, Finnish, and Hungarian. Phonology Yearbook 2. 251-275.

Goldsmith, John. 1989. Autosegmental and Metrical Phonology. Basil Blackwell.

Hulst, H. van der. 1985. Vowel harmony in Hungarian: A comparison of segmental and autosegmental analyses. In van der Hulst and Smith 1985.

Hulst, H. van der and Norval Smith (eds) 1985. Advances in nonlinear phonology. Dordrecht: Foris.

Jensen, J.T. 1978. A reply to "Theoretical implications of Hungarian vowel harmony". Linguistic Inquiry 9, 89-97.

Jordan, Michael. 1986. Serial Order: a Parallel Distributed Processing Approach. Institute for Cognitive Science Report #8604. UC San Diego.

Kontra, M. and Catherine Ringen. 1987. Stress and harmony in Hungarian loanwords. in Redei 1987.

McClelland, James L., Daved E. Rumelhart, and the PDP Research Group. 1986. Parallel Distributed Processing: Explorations in the Microstructure of Cognition. Volume 2: Psychological and Biological Models. Cambridge, Mass.: MIT Press/Bradford Books.

Pullyblank, Douglas. 1988. Underspecification, the feature hierarchy, and Tiv vowels. Phonology S.2.

Redei, K. (ed) 1987. Studien sur Phonologie und Morphonologie der uralischen Sprachen. Studia Uralica, Wein: Verbund der wissenschaftlichen Gesellschaften Osterreichs. 81-96.

Ringen, Catherine. 1988. Transparency in Hungarian Vowel Harmony. Phonology Yearbook 5.2.

Rumelhart, David E., James L. McClelland, and the PDP Research Group. 1986. Parallel Distributed Processing: Explorations in the Microstructure of Cognition. Volume 1: Foundations. Cambridge, Mass.: MIT Press/Bradford Books.

Vago, Robert M. 1976. Theoretical implications of Hungarian vowel harmony. Linguistic Inquiry 7, 243-263.

Graph I

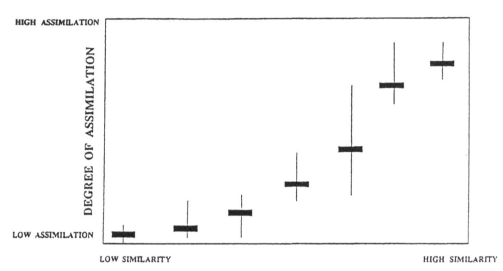

Graph II

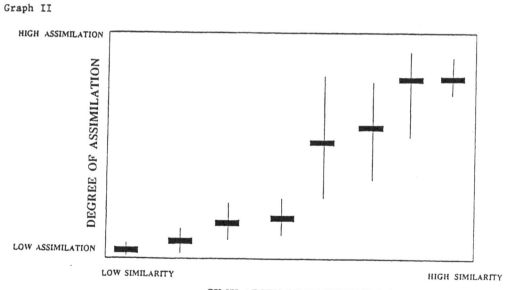

Recency Preference and Garden-Path Effects

Edward Gibson
Department of Philosophy, Carnegie Mellon University
Pittsburgh, PA 15213-3890, USA
electronic mail: gibson@cs.cmu.edu

Abstract

Following Fodor (1983), it is assumed that the language processor is an automatic device that maintains only the best of the set of all compatible representations for an input string. One way to make this idea explicit is to assume the serial hypothesis: at most one representation for an input string is permitted at any time (*e.g.*, Frazier & Fodor (1978), Frazier (1979), and Pritchett (1988)). This paper assumes an alternative formulation of local memory restrictions within a parallel framework. First of all, it is assumed that there exists a number of structural properties, each of which is associated with a processing load. One structure is preferred over another if the processing load associated with the first structure is markedly lower than the processing load associated with the second. Thus a garden-path effect results if the unpreferred structure is necessary for a grammatical sentence.

This paper presents three structural properties within this framework: the first two– the Properties of Thematic Assignment and Reception– derivable from the θ-Criterion of Government and Binding Theory (Chomsky (1981)); and the third– the Property of Recency Preference– that prefers local attachments over more distant attachments. This paper shows how these properties interact to give appropriate predictions– garden-path effects or not– for a large array of local ambiguities.

1 Introduction

Perhaps the best-known theory of garden-path effects is that developed by Frazier and her colleagues (Frazier & Fodor (1978), Frazier (1979), Frazier & Rayner (1982)). This theory assumes the serial hypothesis: that at most one representation can be maintained for the input string at each parse state. In order to decide which structure to choose at a given parse state, the principles of Minimal Attachment and Late Closure are invoked. These principles are given in (1) and (2) respectively (from Frazier & Rayner (1982)):

(1) Minimal Attachment: Attach incoming material into the phrase-marker being constructed using the fewest nodes consistent with the well-formedness rules of the language.

(2) Late Closure: When possible, attach incoming lexical items into the clause or phrase currently being processed (*i.e.*, the lowest possible nonterminal node dominating the last item analyzed).

The principles of Minimal Attachment and Late Closure inside a serial processing model correctly predict a large array of garden-path effects and preferred readings of ambiguous input. Consider the following well-known examples:[1]

(3) # The horse raced past the barn fell.

(4) a. # Since she jogs a mile seems light work.

  b. Bill thought John died yesterday.

Minimal attachment predicts the garden-path effect in (3). At the point of parsing the word *raced*, fewer nodes need to be constructed for the matrix verb reading than for the reduced relative clause reading, so the matrix verb reading is preferred. Since it is the reduced relative clause reading that is necessary for (3), a garden-path effect results.

Late Closure predicts the garden-path effect in (4a) and preferred reading in (4a). In (4a), there is a syntactic ambiguity at the point of parsing the noun phrase *a mile*: this NP may attach as either direct object of the verb *jogs* or as subject of the matrix clause to follow. Since the direct object attachment is within the same clause as the preceding words, this attachment is preferred by the principle of Late Closure. However, the matrix subject attachment is the attachment that is necessary for a successful parse of (4a). Thus a garden-path effect is correctly predicted.

Similarly, the nominal adverb *yesterday* can attach to either the embedded clause or to the matrix clause in (4b). Since the embedded clause occurs more recently in the input string, this attachment is preferred. Thus there is a preferred reading of (4b): that which associates *yesterday* with the embedded clause.

Although the principles of Minimal Attachment and Late Closure correctly account for numerous other garden-path effects, they also make a number of incorrect predictions, as noted in Pritchett (1988). For example, it is predicted that (5) should induce a garden-path effect:

(5) John knew Bill liked Sue.

---

[1] I will prefix sentences that are difficult to process with the symbol "#".

The NP *Bill* may attach in one of two locations: as direct object of the verb *knew* or as subject of the complement clause of the verb *knew*. Since the direct object attachment requires fewer nodes, it is preferred because of the principle of Minimal Attachment. Thus when the verb *liked* is processed, reanalysis must take place and a garden-path effect results. Since people have little difficulty parsing sentences like (5), Frazier's principles are in error in this case.

As a result, Pritchett proposes an alternative processing theory which collapses the Principles of Minimal Attachment and Late Closure into a single parsing principle:

(6) Σ-Attachment: Every principle of the Syntax attempts to be satisfied at every point during processing.

The syntactic principles that Pritchett assumes are those from Government and Binding Theory (Chomsky (1981), Chomsky (1986a)). In particular he appeals to the θ-Criterion:

(7) The θ-Criterion: Each argument bears one and only one θ-role (thematic role) and each θ-role is assigned to one and only one argument (Chomsky (1981) p. 36).

The garden-path effect in (3) is derived in Pritchett's theory as follows. When the word *raced* is input it can attach either as matrix verb or as a reduced relative clause modifier of *the horse*. In the matrix verb attachment, the NP *the horse* receives a thematic role from the verb *raced*. No such thematic role is assigned to *the horse* in the modifier attachment. Thus the matrix verb attachment is locally preferred since it better satisfies the θ-Criterion than does the modifier attachment. When the word *fell* is processed, no attachments are possible and reanalysis is necessary to obtain a parse for the sentence. Thus the garden-path status of (3) is predicted.

In order to account for the non-garden-path status of (5), Pritchett hypothesizes the existence of the Theta Reanalysis Constraint:

(8) Theta Reanalysis Constraint: Syntactic reanalysis which interprets a θ-marked constituent as outside its current θ-Domain is costly.

(9) θ-Domain: α is in the γ θ-Domain of β iff α receives the γ θ-role from β or α is dominated by a constituent that receives the γ θ-role from β.

Consider (5) with respect to the Theta Reanalysis Constraint. At the point of parsing the word *liked*, reanalysis is necessary. The NP *Bill* initially receives its θ-role from the verb *knew*; after reanalysis this NP receives its θ-role from the verb *liked*. Pritchett hypothesizes that this reanalysis is not costly because of the Theta Reanalysis Constraint: after reanalysis the θ-marked constituent *Bill* is still within its original θ-Domain since the θ-role initially assigned to *Bill* is now assigned to a constituent dominating *Bill*, the complementizer phrase *Bill liked*.[2,3]

Note that the definition of the Theta Reanalysis Constraint still predicts a garden-path effect in (3). At the parse state just before the word *fell* is input, the NP *the horse* receives the θ-role from the verb *raced*. When the word *fell* is input, the NP *the horse* must be reanalyzed as THEME of *fell* rather than as AGENT of *raced*. Since this reanalysis interprets the NP *the horse* as outside its original θ-Domain, this reanalysis is expensive and a garden-path effect results.

In addition, Pritchett's theory predicts a garden-path effect in (4a), thus partially collapsing Frazier's principles of Minimal Attachment and Late Closure. However, Pritchett's theory does not predict the preferred reading in (4b): no principle of the syntax is better satisfied by attaching the adverb *yesterday* to the embedded rather than to the matrix clause. Thus the preferred reading of (4b) is unexplained in Pritchett's theory: his theory will be forced to include a principle like Late Closure in order to account for examples like (4b).

Furthermore, both the theories of Pritchett and Frazier make incorrect predictions with respect to the data in (10):

(10) a. I gave her earrings on her birthday.

b. I gave her earrings to Sally.

Although the input string *I gave her earrings* is ambiguous between two possible readings, neither is difficult to process, as is demonstrated by the lack of garden-path effects in either of the sentences in (10). Since both Frazier's and Pritchett's models are serial models, there can be at most one representation for the input string *I gave her earrings*.

---

[2] The category complementizer phrase (CP) is the equivalent of the traditional S' node (Chomsky (1986b). Furthermore, tense and agreement information are assumed to reside in the category *Infl*. The category IP (Infl phrase) is the modern equivalent of the traditional S node.

[3] It turns out that there are difficulties with Pritchett's analysis when Case Theory is considered. If the Theta Reanalysis Constraint is not to be stipulative, then it should follow from (6). Since Pritchett appeals to Case Theory in many of his garden-path derivations, there should be a corresponding Case Reanalysis Constraint. However there cannot be such a constraint because of examples like (5). If the Case Filter is to be locally satisfied, then the preferred attachment of the NP *Bill* is as direct object of the verb *knew* so that it receives accusative Case. Case reanalysis is necessary when the verb *liked* is encountered: the noun *Bill* now receives nominative Case. Since this sentence is not difficult to process, this reanalysis should not be costly. Thus either (5) violates the Case Reanalysis Constraint or there is no Case Reanalysis Constraint and hence the Theta Reanalysis Constraint is stipulative.

Frazier's model therefore predicts a garden-path effect for one of the two sentences. Since Pritchett's model allows reanalysis as long as the Theta Reanalysis Constraint is not violated, it is necessary to check whether or not this constraint is violated by the parse of one of the sentences in (10). Consider the state of the parse after the input *I gave her earrings* has been processed. Since the verb *give* assigns two thematic roles, the representation that would best satisfy the θ-Criterion has both of these roles assigned. Thus Pritchett's theory predicts that the preferred reading at this parse state represents *her* and *earrings* as separate noun phrases, each receiving thematic roles from *gave*. Hence reanalysis is necessary in order to parse (10b). Furthermore, this reanalysis violates the Theta Reanalysis Constraint, since the NP *earrings* must be reanalyzed as within a new θ-Domain. Thus it is incorrectly predicted that (10b) should induce a garden-path effect.

I propose here that the difficulties encountered by these models can be overcome by the use of similar principles inside a constrained parallel model (*cf.* Gibson & Clark (1987), Clark & Gibson (1988)). By including a principle like Late Closure within a constrained parallel model, two structures can be maintained in parallel for the sentences in (10). Thus neither of these sentences will cause a garden-path effect.

2 A Parallel Model of Sentence Processing

Following Fodor (1983), it is assumed that the language processor is an automatic device that maintains only the best of the set of all compatible representations for an input string. One way to make this idea explicit is to assume the serial hypothesis: at most one representation for an input string is permitted at any time (*e.g.*, Frazier & Fodor (1978), Frazier (1979), and Pritchett (1988)). This paper assumes an alternative formulation of local memory restrictions within a parallel framework.[4] First of all, it is assumed that there exists a number of structural properties, each of which is associated with a processing load, in Processing Load Units or PLUs.[5] One structure is preferred over another if the processing load associated with the first structure is markedly lower than the processing load associated with the second.[6] That is, I assume there exists some preference quantity P corresponding to a processing load, such that if the processing loads associated with two representations for the same string differ by load P, then only the representation associated with the smaller of the two loads is pursued. Given the existence of a preference factor P, it is easy to account for garden-path effects and preferred readings of ambiguous sentences. Both effects occur because of a local ambiguity which is resolved in favor of one reading. In the case of a garden-path effect, the favored reading is not compatible with the whole sentence. Given two representations for the same input string that differ in processing load by at least the factor P, only the less computationally expensive structure will be pursued. If that structure is not compatible with the rest of the sentence and the discarded structure is part of a successful parse of the sentence, a garden-path effect results. If the parse is successful, but the discarded structure is compatible with another reading for the sentence, then only a preferred reading for the sentence has been calculated. Thus if we know where one reading of a (temporarily) ambiguous sentence becomes the strongly preferred reading, we can write an inequality associated with this preference:

(12)
$$\sum_{i=1}^{n} A_i x_i - \sum_{i=1}^{n} B_i x_i > P$$

where:

P is the preference factor in PLUs,

x_i is the number of PLUs associated with property i,

A_i is the number of times property i appears in the unpreferred structure,

B_i is the number of times property i appears in the preferred structure.

Three structural properties will be presented within this framework: the first two– the Properties of Thematic Assignment and Reception (Gibson (1990))– derivable from the θ-Criterion of Government and Binding Theory (Chomsky (1981)); and the third– the Property of Recency Preference– that prefers local attachments over more

---

[4]See Kurtzman (1985), Gorrell (1986) and Carlson & Tanenhaus (1989) for psycholinguistic evidence in favor of parallel processing.

[5]I also assume the existence of semantic and pragmatic properties that require processing load, but I will only consider structural properties here. The existence of further properties may help to explain the data presented in Crain & Steedman (1985) and Ni & Crain (1989).

[6]See Gibson (1990) for a description of how these same properties can be used to predict processing overload in sentences like (11):

(11) # The man that the woman that the dog bit likes eats fish.

distant attachments (*cf.* Frazier & Fodor (1978), Frazier (1979), Frazier & Rayner (1982)).

3 The Properties of Thematic Assignment and Reception

Recall the θ-Criterion:

(7) The θ-Criterion: Each argument bears one and only one θ-role (thematic role) and each θ-role is assigned to one and only one argument.

Note that the θ-Criterion can be violated in one of two ways: an argument can be missing a thematic role or a thematic role can be left unassigned. Thus I propose that the θ-Criterion has two corresponding parsing properties, each of which requires processing load:

(13) The Property of Thematic Reception (PTR):

Associate a load of x_{TR} PLUs of short term memory to each thematic element that is in a position that can receive a thematic role in some co-existing structure, but lacks a thematic role in the structure in question.

(14) The Property of Thematic Assignment (PTA):

Associate a load of x_{TA} PLUs of short term memory to each thematic role that is not assigned to a node containing a thematic element.

Note that the Properties of Thematic Assignment and Reception are stated in terms of *thematic* elements.[7] Thus the Property of Thematic Reception doesn't apply to functional categories, whether or not they are in positions that receive thematic roles. Similarly, if a thematic role is assigned to a functional category, the Property of Thematic Assignment does not notice until there is a thematic element inside this constituent.

Since the Properties of Thematic Assignment and Reception are both derived from the θ-Criterion, it is reasonable to assume as a default that the loads associated with these two properties is the same:

(15) $x_{TR} = x_{TA} = x_{\theta}$

Consider (5) with respect to the Properties of Thematic Assignment and Reception:

(5) John knew Bill liked Sue.

As pointed out earlier, the verb *knew* is ambiguous: either taking an NP complement or a CP complement. Thus the NP *Bill* may attach as either the direct object of the verb *knew* or as subject of the CP to come.[8]:

(16) a. $[_{IP} [_{NP} \text{John}] [_{VP} \text{knew} [_{NP} \text{Bill}]]]$

  b. $[_{IP} [_{NP} \text{John}] [_{VP} \text{knew} [_{CP} [_{IP} [_{NP} \text{Bill}] e]]]]$

In (16a) the NP *Bill* is attached as the NP complement of *knew*. In this representation there is no load associated with either of the Properties of Thematic Assignment or Reception since no thematic elements need thematic roles and no thematic roles are left unassigned. In (16b) the NP *Bill* is the specifier of a hypothesized IP node which is attached as the complement of the other reading of *knew*. This representation is associated with at least x_{θ} PLUs since the NP *Mary* is in a position that can be associated with a thematic role (the subject position), but does not yet receive one in this structure. No load is associated with the Property of Thematic Assignment, however, since both thematic roles of the verb *knew* are assigned to nodes that contain thematic elements.

Since there is no difficulty in processing sentence (5), the load difference between the structures in (16) cannot be greater than P PLUs, the preference factor assumed in inequality (12). Thus the inequality in (17) is obtained:

(17) $x_{\theta} \leq P$

Since the load difference between the two structures is not sufficient to cause a strong preference, both structures are maintained. Note that this is a crucial difference between the theory presented here and the theory presented in Frazier & Fodor (1978), Frazier (1979) and Pritchett (1988). In each of these theories, only one representation can be maintained, so that either (16a) or (16b) would be preferred at this point. As noted earlier, Pritchett's theory accounts for the lack of difficulty experienced in parsing (5) by appeal to the Theta Reanalysis Constraint, (8). However, no such stipulation is required in the theory presented here: all reanalysis is assumed to be expensive.

---

[7] Following early work in linguistic theory, two kinds of categories are distinguished: *functional* categories and *thematic* or *content* categories (see, for example, Fukui & Speas (1986) and Abney (1987) and the references cited in each). Thematic categories include nouns, verbs, adjectives and some prepositions; functional categories include determiners, complementizers, and inflection markers. There are a number of properties that distinguish functional elements from thematic elements, the most crucial being that functional elements mark grammatical or relational features while thematic elements pick out a class of objects or events.

[8] I assume some form of hypothesis-driven node projection so that noun phrases are projected to the categories that they specify (Gibson (1989)).

Now consider once again (3):

(3) # The horse raced past the barn fell.

The structure for the input *the horse raced* is ambiguous between at least the two structures in (18):

(18) a. $[_{IP} [_{NP}$ the horse $] [_{VP}$ raced $]]$

    b. $[_{IP} [_{NP}$ the $[_{N'} [_{N'}$ horse$_i$ $] [_{CP} O_i$ raced $]]] [_{I'}]]$

Structure (18a) has no load associated with it due to either the PTA or the PTR. Crucially note that the verb *raced* has an intransitive reading so that no load is required via the Property of Thematic Assignment. On the other hand, structure (18b) requires a load of $2 * x_\theta$ PLUs since 1) the noun phrase *the horse* is in a position that can receive a thematic role, but currently does not and 2) the operator O_i is in a position that may be associated with a thematic role, but is not yet associated with one.[9] Thus the difference between the processing loads of structures (18a) and (18b) is $2 * x_\theta$ PLUs. Since this sentence is a strong garden-path sentence, it is hypothesized that a load difference of $2 * x_\theta$ PLUs is greater than the allowable limit, P PLUs:

(19) $2 * x_\theta > P$

Consider now (20), a sentence whose structure and local ambiguities are very similar to those in (3):

(20) The bird found in the room was dead.

Although the structures and local ambiguities in (20) and (3) are similar, (3) causes a garden-path effect while, surprisingly, (20) does not. To determine why (20) is not a garden-path sentence we need to examine the local ambiguity when the word *found* is read:

(21) a. $[_{IP} [_{NP}$ the bird $] [_{VP} [_{V'} [_V$ found $]]]]$

    b. $[_{IP} [_{NP}$ the $[_{N'} [_{N'}$ bird$_i$ $] [_{CP} O_i$ found $]]] [_{I'}]]$

The crucial difference between the verb *found* and the verb *raced* is that *found* is obligatorily transitive, while *raced* is optionally intransitive. Since the θ-grid of the verb *found* is not filled in structure (21a), this representation is associated with x_θ PLUs of memory load. Like structure (18b), structure (21b) requires $2 * x_\theta$ PLUs. Thus the difference between the processing loads of structures (21a) and (21b) is $2 * x_\theta - x_\theta$ PLUs = x_θ PLUs. Since this difference is less than the preference factor P, both structures are maintained and a garden-path effect is avoided as desired.[10]

The Properties of Thematic Assignment and Reception make many further garden-path predictions, among them:

(23) a. # I put the candy on the table in my mouth.

    b. # The Russian women loved died.

    c. # John told the man that Mary kissed that Bill saw Phil.

See Gibson (1990) for derivations of the garden-path status of these sentences within the framework described here.

4 The Property of Recency Preference

Although the Properties of Thematic Assignment and Reception account for numerous garden-path effects and preferred readings of ambiguous input, they do not account for the Late Closure effects presented in (4):

(4a) # Since she jogs a mile seems light work.

---

[9]In fact, this operator will be associated with a thematic role as soon as a gap-positing algorithm links it with the object of the passive participle *raced*. However, when the attachment is initially made, no such link yet exists: the operator will initially be unassociated with a thematic role.

[10]Note that the principle of Minimal Attachment makes the wrong prediction in (20): this example is wrongly predicted to be identical to (3) and thus a garden-path.

Pritchett attempts to account for the lack of garden-path effect in (20) by altering the Theta Reanalysis Constraint in such a way that (20) does not violate the new constraint while garden-path sentences like (3) still do. Crucial to his argument is his claim that there is a strong preference for the matrix clause reading of the word *found* when it is initially input. However, Kurtzman (1985) found that both matrix clause and reduced relative clause readings of verbs like *found* were equally easy to process as soon as they were read, contrary to Pritchett's claim. For example, consider the sentences in (22):

(22) a. The monkeys chased his...

    b. The monkeys chased were...

Kurtzman found that partial sentences like those in (22) did not vary significantly in parsing difficulty. Thus Pritchett's claim that words like *found* or *chased* are initially analyzed as matrix verbs appears to be incorrect. Furthermore, note that a parallel model of processing makes exactly the right predictions here.

(4b) Bill thought John died yesterday.

First consider (4a). There are two possible attachments of the NP *a mile*: 1) as direct object of the verb *jogs*; and 2) as subject of the matrix clause to follow. Consider these two structures:

(24) a. $[_{IP} [_{CP}$ since $[_{IP} [_{NP}$ she $] [_{VP} [_{V'} [_{V}$ jogs $] [_{NP}$ a mile $]]]]] [_{IP}]]$

    b. $[_{IP} [_{CP}$ since $[_{IP} [_{NP}$ she $] [_{VP}$ jogs $]]] [_{IP} [_{NP}$ a mile $] [_{I'}]]]$

There is no load associated with structure (24a) by the Properties of Thematic Assignment and Reception since all arguments receive thematic roles and all thematic roles are assigned. Structure (24b), on the other hand is associated with x_θ PLUs since the NP *a mile* currently lacks a thematic role in this structure. However this is the only load associated with (24b). Thus the load difference between the two structures is only x_θ PLUs by the Properties of Thematic Assignment and Reception, not enough to cause a garden-path effect.

It turns out that this problem is solved by incorporating a structural property derived from a principle similar to Late Closure into the framework described thus far. The intuition behind the Principle of Late Closure and its predecessors (Kimball (1973)) is that new structures prefer to be attached to structures associated with more recent words in the input string. For example, in (4b), the preferred attachment for the adverb *yesterday* is as modifier of the more recently occurring clause: the most deeply embedded one. The property that I present here, the Property of Recency Preference (PRP), makes this intuition explicit.

(25) The Property of Recency Preference (PRP):
The load associated with the structure resulting from an attachment of structure X = (number of more recent words that would also allow an attachment of structure X) $*x_{RP}$ PLUs.

Hence given two possible attachment sites, the structure resulting from attachment to the more recent word will be associated with no load via the Property of Recency Preference, while the structure resulting from attachment to the less recent word will be associated with x_{RP} PLUs.

Consider the PRP with respect to sentence (4b). At the point of parsing the word *yesterday*, there are two possible attachments: either as a modifier of the embedded clause headed by *died* or as modifier of the matrix clause headed by *thought*. The structure that results from attaching this adverb as modifier of the embedded clause is associated with no load via the Property of Recency Preference, since the word *died* is the most recently occurring attachment site in the input string. However, the structure that results from attaching this adverb to the matrix clause is associated with x_{RP} PLUs, since there is a more recent word in the input string, the word *died*, to which this adverb could attach. Since the interpretation which links the adverb *yesterday* with the embedded clause is the strongly preferred reading in (4b), I hypothesize that the load difference between the structures resulting from the two possible attachment sites is significant:

(26) $x_{RP} > P$

The existence of a garden-path effect in (4a) can now be explained. Structure (24a) is associated with no load via the Property of Recency Preference since the NP *a mile* is attached to a structure headed by the most recent word in the input string, *jogs*. Structure (24b), on the other hand, represents attachment to the CP headed by *since*. Thus this structure is associated with x_{RP} PLUs by the PRP. Since this structure also contains a thematic role-less NP, the total load associated with this structure is $x_{RP} + x_\theta$ PLUs. Structure (24a) is associated with no load whatsoever. Thus the load difference between the two structures is $x_{RP} + x_\theta$ PLUs, enough to cause a strong local preference and hence a garden-path.

Although the Property of Recency Preference is very similar to Frazier's principle of Late Closure, there is an important difference. Unlike the principle of Late Closure, the PRP is not stipulated to act on its own: it can interact with other properties. Thus we expect to find situations where the PRP interacts with the Properties of Thematic Assignment and Reception in the prediction of behavior in ambiguous situations. In fact, many such cases occur. First consider (27), a sentence whose garden-path effect is unexplained without the PRP:

(27) # I convinced her children are noisy.

(27) is locally ambiguous over the span of the words *her children*. Two parses for the input string *I convinced her children* are given in (28):

(28) a. $[_{IP} [_{NP}$ I $] [_{VP} [_{V'} [_{V}$ convinced $] [_{NP}$ her children $]]]]$

    b. $[_{IP} [_{NP}$ I $] [_{VP} [_{V'} [_{V}$ convinced $] [_{NP}$ her $] [_{CP} [_{IP} [_{NP}$ children $]]]]]]$

In structure (28a) the words *her children* correspond to the noun phrase object of *convinced*. In (28b), the word *her* is the noun phrase object of *convinced* and the word *children* is the subject of the complement clause of *convinced*. Structure (28a) is strongly preferred over (28b) and a garden-path effect results for (27).

In order to see how this garden-path effect can be predicted in this framework, consider the loads associated with each of the structures in (28). First, let us consider the Property of Recency Preference. The attachment of the NP representation of the word *children* to form (28a) requires no PRP load since the attachment involves the most recent word in the input string, *her*. On the other hand, the attachment of *children* as the subject of the CP complement to *convinced* involves making an attachment to the verb *convinced*, a less recent word in the input string. Thus there is a load of x_{RP} PLUs associated with (28b).

Consider now the Properties of Thematic Assignment and Reception. Structure (28a) has a load of x_θ PLUs since the verb *convinced* has a yet unassigned thematic role. Structure (28b) is associated with a load of x_θ PLUs since the noun phrase *children* requires a thematic role and does not yet receive one. Thus the total load difference between the two structures is $x_\theta + x_{RP} - x_\theta$ PLUs $= x_{RP}$ PLUs. Thus (27) induces a garden-path effect, as desired.

Furthermore, the combination of the properties also explains the lack of difficulty in the sentences in (10):

(10a) I gave her earrings on her birthday.
(10b) I gave her earrings to Sally.

In order to formulate an inequality representing the state of affairs in (10), consider the parse state after the word *earrings* is read:

(29) a. $[_{IP} [_{NP} \text{I}] [_{VP} [_{V'} [_V \text{gave}] [_{NP} \text{her earrings}]]]]$

    b. $[_{IP} [_{NP} \text{I}] [_{VP} [_{V'} [_V \text{gave}] [_{NP} \text{her}] [_{NP} \text{earrings}]]]]$

The verb *gave* subcategorizes for either two noun phrases or for a noun phrase and a prepositional phrase (*cf.* Kayne (1984), Larson (1988)). First consider the load associated with the structures in (29) with respect to the Property of Recency Preference. The derivation of this load is similar to that for the structures in (28). Structure (29a) is associated with no load by the PRP since *earrings* attaches to *her*, the most recent word. However, structure (29b) is associated with a load of x_{RP} PLUs since the attachment necessary to form this structure involves a less recent word, *gave*. Now consider the loads associated with the structures in (29) with respect to the Properties of Thematic Assignment and Reception. Structure (29a) is associated with a load of x_θ PLUs since a thematic role is yet unassigned by the verb *gave* in this structure. On the other hand, structure (29b) is associated with no load due either the PTA or the PTR since all thematic roles are assigned and all thematic elements receive thematic roles. Note that this is the crucial difference between (10) and (27). Thus the load difference between structures (29a) and (29b) is $x_{RP} - x_\theta$ PLUs. Since neither (10a) nor (10b) is a garden-path sentence, I hypothesize that this load difference is not significant:

(30) $x_{RP} - x_\theta \leq P$

Thus we have the following inequalities:

(31) a. $x_\theta \leq P$

    b. $2 * x_\theta > P$

    c. $x_{RP} > P$

    d. $x_{RP} - x_\theta \leq P$

This set of inequalities is consistent. It identifies the solution space depicted in Figure 1.

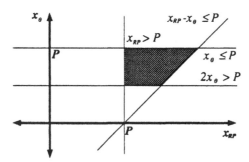

Figure 1: The Solution Space for the Inequalities in (31)

378

5 Conclusions

This paper has presented a parallel model of human sentence processing in which it is assumed that the ease or difficulty in parsing a given sentence is due to multiple coexisting properties of the sentence. Three independent properties were presented: two that follow from the θ-Criterion, and the third, a property that prefers attachments involving more recent words. These three properties were shown to interact to correctly predict previously unexplained results with respect to a number of local ambiguities. Furthermore, no stipulations regarding reanalysis are necessary: all reanalysis is assumed to be expensive. Thus the framework presented here makes better predictions with respect to the data considered here than the currently accepted serial models of language processing.

6 References

Abney (1987) *The English Noun Phrase in its Sentential Aspect*, MIT Ph.D. dissertation, Cambridge, MA.

Carlson, G.N., & Tanenhaus, M.K. (1989) "Thematic Roles and Language Comprehension", in Wilkins, W. (ed.), *Syntax and Semantics Volume 21: Thematic Relations*, Academic Press, San Diego, CA.

Chomsky, N. (1981) *Lectures on Government and Binding*, Foris, Dordrecht, The Netherlands.

Chomsky, N. (1986a) *Knowledge of Language: Its Nature, Origin and Use*, Praeger Publishers, New York, NY.

Chomsky, N. (1986b) *Barriers*, Linguistic Inquiry Monograph 13, MIT Press, Cambridge, MA.

Clark, R. & Gibson, E. (1988) "A Parallel Model for Adult Sentence Processing", *Proceedings of the Tenth Cognitive Science Conference*, McGill University, Montreal, Quebec.

Crain, S., & Steedman, M. (1985) "On Not Being Led Up the Garden Path: the Use of Context by the Psychological Parser", in D. Dowty, L. Karttunen, & A. Zwicky (eds.), *Natural Language Processing: Psychological, Computational and Theoretical Perspectives*, Cambridge University Press, Cambridge, U.K.

Fodor, J.A. (1983) *Modularity of Mind*, MIT Press, Cambridge, MA.

Frazier, L. (1979) *On Comprehending Sentences: Syntactic Parsing Strategies*, University of Massachusetts Ph.D. dissertation.

Frazier, L., & Fodor, J.D. (1978) "The Sausage Machine: A New Two-stage Parsing Model", *Cognition* 6, pp. 291-325.

Frazier, L. & Rayner, K. (1982) "Making and Correcting Errors During Sentence Comprehension: Eye Movements in the Analysis of Structurally Ambiguous Sentences", *Cognitive Psychology* 14, pp. 178-210.

Fukui, N., & Speas, M. (1986) "Specifiers and Projections", *MIT Working Papers in Linguistics* 8, Cambridge, MA.

Gibson, E., & Clark, R. (1987) "Positing Gaps in a Parallel Parser," *Proceedings of the Eighteenth North East Linguistic Society Conference*, University of Toronto, Toronto, Ontario.

Gibson, E. (1989) "Parsing with Principles: Predicting a Phrasal Node Before Its Head Appears", *Proceedings of the First International Workshop on Parsing Technologies*, Carnegie Mellon University, 1989.

Gibson, E. (1990) "Memory Capacity and Sentence Processing", *Proceedings of the 28th Annual Meeting of the Association for Computational Linguistics*, Pittsburgh, PA.

Gorrell, P.G. (1987) *Studies of Human Syntactic Processing: Ranked-Parallel versus Serial Models*, University of Connecticut Ph.D. dissertation.

Kayne, R. S. (1984) *Connectedness and Binary Branching*, Foris, Dordrecht, The Netherlands.

Kimball, J. (1973) "Seven Principles of Surface Structure Parsing in Natural Language," *Cognition* 2, pp. 15-47.

Kurtzman, H. (1985) *Studies in Syntactic Ambiguity Resolution*, MIT Ph.D. dissertation.

Larson, R.K. (1988) "On the Double Object Construction," *Linguistic Inquiry*, 19, pp. 335-391.

Ni, W. and Crain, C. (1989) "How to Resolve Structural Ambiguities," *Proceedings of the Twentieth North East Linguistic Society Conference*, Pittsburgh, PA.

Pritchett, B. (1988) "Garden Path Phenomena and the Grammatical Basis of Language Processing", *Language* 64 pp. 539-576.

A Connectionist Treatment of Grammar for Generation

Nigel Ward

Computer Science Division
University of California at Berkeley

Abstract

Connectionist language generation promises better interaction between syntactic and lexical considerations and thus improved output quality. To realize this requires a connectionist treatment of grammar. This paper explains one way to do so. The basic idea is that constructions and their constituents are nodes in the same network that encodes world knowledge and lexical knowledge. The principal novelty is reliance on emergent properties. This makes it unnecessary to maké explicit syntactic choice or to build up representations of sentence structure. The scheme includes novel ways of handling constituency, word order and optional constituents; and a simple way to avoid the problems of instantiation and binding. Despite the novel approach, the syntactic knowledge used is expressed in a form similar to that often used in linguistics; this representation straightforwardly defines parts of the knowlege network. These ideas have been implemented in FIG, a 'flexible incremental generator.'

1 Introduction

A generator is faced with a great number of interdependent options: lexical, syntactic, and conceptual. To produce a good utterance a generator must arrive at a consistent set of choices. The best way to do this seems to be with explicit parallel consideration of all possible options and parallel computation of their interdependencies [Ward 89c]. This ensures that the relevant information is all available, something which is difficult for generators which make choices in sequence [Ward 89b].

For syntax, this implies considering many possible constructions at once. This technique appears to be used by human speakers – analysis of speech errors suggests that even normal speech is the result of competing 'plans' [Baars 80]. [Stemberger 85] realized that, in particular, human speakers can be modeled as having many 'phrase structure units' being 'partially activated' simultaneously, and stressed the importance of emergents.

I have written an intrinsically parallel generator, 'FIG,' motivated by considerations of cognitive modeling [Ward 89c]. FIG is a structured (aka localist) connectionist system. Structured connectionism allows parallelism while making it relatively easy to build, explain, and debug the system. (A distributed connectionist system would have other advantages but would be harder to develop.)

This paper presents a new approach to grammar for language generation. The key innovation is reliance on emergent properties, instead of making explicit choices and doing explicit structure-building. Despite the novel approach to processing, there is a declarative representation for linguistic knowledge.

To see that this approach works for syntactically non-trivial examples, consider that FIG's outputs include: "once upon a time there lived an old man and an old woman," "one day the old man went into the hills to gather wood," "a big peach bobbed down towards an old woman from upstream," "an old woman gave a peach to an old man," and "Mary was killed;" and corresponding Japanese sentences: "mukashi mukashi aru tokoro ni ojiisan to obaasan ga sunde imashita," "aru hi ojiisan wa yama e shibakari ni ikimashita," "kawakami kara ookii momo ga donburiko donburako to obaasan e nagarete kimashita," "ojiisan wa meeri ni momo o agemashita," and "meeri o koroshimashita."

Section 2 overviews contrasting and related treatments of syntax in generation, Section 3 summarizes the FIG approach to generation, Section 4 presents a representation for grammatical knowledge, Section 5 describes how this knowledge is used, Section 6 discusses the implementation, and Section 7 suggests fu-

---

[0]Thanks to Daniel Jurafsky, Robert Wilensky, and Dekai Wu. This research was sponsored by the Defense Advanced Research Projects Agency (DoD), monitored by the Space and Naval Warfare Systems Command under N00039-88-C-0292, and the Office of Naval Research under contract N00014-89-J-3205.

ture research directions.

2 Previous Research

Problems of grammar for generation have received a fair amount of attention in AI. Of the work which is concerned with the details of language, almost all is based on syntactic mechanisms adopted from linguistic theories. Most linguistic grammars come complete with mechanisms: transformations, parse-tree traversals, unification, and so on. Yet these mechanisms are not intended to be computational models. They are typically inspired by the goal of explaining sentence structure, a goal probably originally due to linguistics' focus on grammaticality.

Independent of linguistic theories, the most common metaphor for generation is as a sequence of choices among alternatives. For example, a generator may chose among words for a concept, among ways to syntactically realize a constituent, and among concepts to bind to a slot. These decisions are generally made in a fairly fixed (and generally top-down) order, thus most generators are not easily parallelizable.

In FIG grammar is important but grammaticality is not. Grammar is a tool used in the process of expressing meaning, not a goal in itself. Structure building, structure mapping, and explicit syntactic choice are dispensed with. In FIG the structure of the output is emergent, and choices are also largely emergent. One advantage of relying on emergents is that there is no need to order choices [Ward 89b], and thus the process is naturally parallelizable.

Previous connectionist research has in general not strayed far from traditional approaches to grammar. [Stolcke 89] directly implemented unification grammar. [Kalita and Shastri 87] implemented a standard symbolic generator [McDonald 1983]. Perhaps the most original connectionist generator is Gasser's CHIE [Gasser 88]. Yet even in CHIE there are choices (represented by neuron firings) and these happen sequentially, in order. The exact timing of firings seems crucial. CHIE freely uses winner-take-all subnetworks, which also cuts down on the amount of effective parallelism.

3 The FIG Approach to Generation

The task is generation of natural language from thoughts. (Most generators, presume that the input has been pre-processed by a 'what-to-say' component, and thus only need to take the 'message' and do some language-specific processing. I think this division of the task is unnecessary and unwise [Ward 88b].) Reduced to bare essentials, a generator's task is to get

from concepts (what the speaker wants to express) to words (what he can say). From this point of view, the key problem in generation is computing the relevance (pertinence) of a particular word, given the concepts to express. Syntactic and other knowledge mediates this computation of relevance. Therefore FIG is based on word choice – every other consideration is analyzed in terms of how it affects word choice.

Processing in FIG is done with spreading activation in a network. The basic FIG algorithm is:

1. each node of the input conceptualization is a source of activation
2. activation flows through the network
3. when the network settles, the most highly activated word is selected and emitted
4. activation levels are updated to represent the new current state
5. steps 2 through 4 repeat until all of the input has been conveyed

An utterance is simply the result of successive word choices, thus FIG is incremental in a strong sense.

Activation represents relevance; flow of activation represents implications of relevance; and updating the activation of a node represents computing its relevance. The general direction of activation flow is from concepts to words, but nodes representing syntax 're-distribute' activation also, and feedback is pervasive.

The network must be designed so that, when it settles, the node which is most highly activated corresponds to the best next word. This paper discusses the design of the network structures which encode syntactic knowledge.

4 Knowledge of Syntax

FIG's treatment of syntax is based on Construction Grammar [Fillmore et al 89]. This approach describes the grammar of a language 'directly, in terms of a collection of grammatical constructions' [Fillmore 88]. The key characteristics here are that Construction Grammar is declarative and that the units of syntactic knowledge, namely constructions, are densely related to words, meaning, and each other.

The encodings of syntactic knowledge shown below are taken directly from FIG. These are for illustrative purposes only. I do not claim that these represent the facts of English, nor the best way to describe them in a grammar. The examples are intended simply to illustrate the representational tools and computational mechanisms available in FIG.

Figure 1 shows FIG's definition of **noun-phr,** representing a simplification of the English noun-phrase construction. This construction has three constituents:

```
(defp noun-phr
  (constituents (np-1  obl  article    ((article .8) (a-w .2) ))
                (np-2  opt  adjective((adjective .6)))
                (np-3  obl  noun       ((noun .9))) ))
```
Figure 1: The English Noun-Phrase Construction

```
(defp go-p
  (constituents (gp-1  obl  go-w    ((go-w .1)))
                (gp-2  opt  epart   ((vparticle .6) (directionr .2)))
                (gp-3  opt  noun    ((prep-phr .6) (destr .2)))
                (gp-4  opt  verb    ((purpose-clause .6) (purposer .2))) ))
```
Figure 2: Representation of the Valence of "Go"

```
(defp ex-there
  (inhibit subj-pred passive)
  (constituents (et-1  obl  therew ((therew .9)))
                (et-2  obl  verb    ((verb .9)))
                (et-3  obl  noun    ((noun .5))) ))
```
Figure 3: Representation of the Existential "There" Construction

```
(defw peachw    (cat noun)   (expresses momoc) (grapheme "peach")
      (nebors (initial-phoner consnt-initial .5)) )

(defs noun    (maximals (noun-phr .4)))

(defw go-w   (cat verb) (expresses ikuc) (valence (go-p .2))
      (grapheme (inf "go") (past "went") (pastp "gone") (presp "going")) )

(defc introductoryc   (english (ex-there .1) (a-w .1)) )

(defr purposer (english (to2w .4) (purpose-clause .1))
      (japanese (ni-w .6)))
```
Figure 4: Some Knowledge Related to Constructions

np-1, np-2, and np-3. np-1 and np-3 are obligatory, np-2 is optional. Glossing over the details for the moment, the list at the end of the definitions specifies how to realize the constituent. For example, np-1 should be realized as an article, with the default being a-w (representing the word "a"), and so on.

Figure 2 shows the construction for the case frame of the word "go." First comes go-w, for the word "go," which is obligatory. Next come (optionally): a verb-particle representing direction (as in "go *away*" or "go *back* home" or "go *down* to the lake"), a prepositional phrase to express the destination, and a purpose clause.

Figure 3 shows the representation of the existential "there" construction, as in "there was a poor cobbler." The 'inhibit' field indicates that this construction is incompatible with the passive construction and also with subj-pred, the construction responsible for the basic SVO ordering of English.

Figure 4 shows knowledge about when and where constructions are relevant. Constructions are associated with words. For example noun-phr is the 'maximal' of noun (actually, of all nouns), and go-p is the 'valence' (case frame) of go-w. These links encode knowledge about constructions and their heads; other relations between words and constructions are discussed in Section 5.5. Constructions are also associated with the meanings they can express. For example, ex-there is listed under the concept introductory, representing that this construction is appropriate for introducing some character into the story, and purpose-clause is listed as a way to express the purposer relation. Constructions are also associated with other constructions. For example, the fourth constituent of go-p subcategorizes for purpose-clause (Figure 2); and there are associations among incompatible constructions, for example the 'inhibit' link between ex-there and subj-pred (Figure 3).

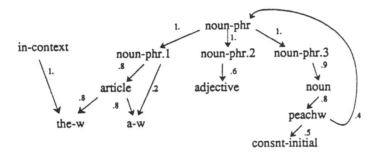

Figure 5: A Fragment of the Network

5 Using This Knowledge

While the above representations resemble those used by several modern linguistic theories, FIG uses them in a novel way.

5.1 Constructions in the Network

In FIG constructions and constituents are nodes in the knowledge network. Their activation levels represent their current relevance. Constructions receive activation from nodes linked to them, and transmit activation to other nodes. Figure 5 shows a fragment of FIG's network, where the numbers on the links are their weights. This is partially specified by the knowledge shown in the previous figures [1]. It is generally possible to give procedural interpretations to links. For example, the link from peachw to noun-phr 'advises' that: if you want to say a noun, you should 'consult' the knowledge in noun-phr.

Activation flow among the various nodes in the network provides, among other things, pervasive interaction among lexical choices and syntactic considerations. The rest of this section explains how this handles some basic functions of syntax.

5.2 Constituency

The links defined above suffice to handle constituency. Consider for example the fact that nouns need to be preceded by articles in this particular kind of noun phrase. Suppose that peachw is activated, perhaps because a peachc concept is in the input. Activation flows from peachw to noun-phr, from noun-phr to article, and from there to a-w and the-w. a-w also

receives activation via a direct link from noun-phr.

In this way the relevance of a noun increases the relevance rating of articles. Provided that other activation levels are appropriate, this will cause some article to become the most highly activated word, and thus be selected and emitted. Note that FIG does not first choose to say a noun, then an article; both 'decisions' are considered and made together, as activation levels settle.

If there are additional sources of activation (such as in-context) then the-w will receive more activation, and thus "the" will be output. Also, if the node vowel-initial is more highly activated than the node consnt-initial, "an" instead of "a" will be output, thanks to the inflection mechanism (not described further).

There is also the question of specifying where a given concept should appear and what syntactic form it should take. This problem, subcategorization, is handled in FIG by simultaneously activating a concept and the syntactic form it should take. For example, the third constituent of go-p specifies that 'the direction of the going' be expressed as a 'verbal particle.' Activation will thus flow to an appropriate word node, such as downw, both via the concept filling the directionr slot and via the syntactic category vparticle. Thanks to this sort of activation flow, FIG tends to select and emit an appropriate word in an appropriate form [Ward 88a].

Syntactic considerations manifest themselves only through their effects on the activation levels of words. Syntax is never 'in control' of word choice [2]; the syntactic structure of the result is emergent.

---

[1] The mapping from s-expressions to network structures is not always trivial. For example, the link from noun to peachw comes from the statement that peachw had 'cat' noun; and the link from peachw to noun-phr is inherited by peachw from the 'maximals' information on noun.

[2] Post hoc examination of FIG output might make one think, for example, 'this exhibits the choice of the existential-there construction.' In FIG there is indeed an inhibit link between the nodes ex-there and subj-pred, and so when generating the network tends to reach a state where only one of these nodes is highly activated. The most highly activated construction can have a strong effect on word choices, which is why the appearance of syntactic choice arises.

5.3 Word Order

FIG is an incremental generator, that is, it selects and emits words one by one in order. At each time the activation level of a word must represent its *current* relevance. To this end, one job of constructions is to activate things which are currently syntactically appropriate. In FIG the current syntactic state is represented in the state of each construction node, namely, their activation levels and 'cursors.' The cursor of a construction points to the currently appropriate constituent and ensures that it is relatively highly activated. To be specific, the cursor gives the location of a 'mask' specifying the weights of the links from the construction to constituents. The mask specifies a weight of 1.0 for the constituent under the cursor, and for subsequent constituents a weight proportional to their closeness to the cursor [3]. This is parallelism among constituents.

For example, if the cursor of **noun-phr** points to **np-1**, then articles will receive a large proportion of the activation of **noun-phr**. Thus, an article is likely to be the most highly activated word and therefore selected and emitted. After an article is emitted the cursor is advanced to **np-2**, and so on. Advancing cursors is described in Section 5.5.

In this way constructions 'shunt' activation to words which should appear early in the input. FIG has no central process which plans or manipulates word order. Each construction simply activates nodes which it 'thinks' currently are relevant. In this sense word order is emergent.

5.4 Optional Constituents

When building a noun-phrase a generator should emit an adjective if semantically appropriate, otherwise it should ignore that option and emit a noun next. FIG does this without additional mechanism.

To see this, suppose "the" has been emitted and the cursor of **noun-phr** is on its second constituent, **np-2**. As a result adjectives get activation, via **np-2**, and so to a lesser extent do nouns via **np-3**. There are two cases: If the input includes a concept linked (indirectly perhaps) to some adjective, that adjective will receive activation from it. In this case the adjective will receive more syntactic activation than any noun does, and hence have more total activation, so it will be selected next. If the input does not include any concept linked to an adjective, then a noun will have more activation than any adjective (since only the noun receives semantic activation also), and so a noun will be se-

lected next.

Most generators use some syntax-driven procedure to inspect semantics and decide explicitly whether or not to realize an optional constituent. In FIG, the decision to include or to omit an optional constituent (or adjunct) is emergent — if an adjective becomes highly activated it will be chosen, in the usual fashion, otherwise some other word, most likely a noun, will be.

5.5 Updating Constructions

Recall that FIG, after selecting and emitting a word, updates activation levels to represent the new state. In particular, it must advance the cursors of constructions as their constituents are completed [4]. Why is a separate update mechanism necessary? Most generators simply choose a construction and then 'execute' it straightforwardly. However, in FIG no construction is ever 'in control.' For example, one construction may be strongly activating a verb, but activation from other constructions may 'interfere,' causing an adverbial, for example, to be emitted instead. Therefore, in FIG constructions need feedback on what words have been output.

The difference between obl and opt constituents is whether or not the update mechanism can skip over them. (Since, for example, if there are no adjectives, the cursor of **noun-phr** should not remain stuck forever at the second constituent.) More than one construction may get updated after a word is output. For example, emitting a noun may cause updates to both the **prep-phr** construction and the **noun-phr** construction. Constructions which are 'guiding' the output should be scored as more relevant, so the update process adds activation to those constructions whose cursors have changed. It also sets a floor under their activation levels. After the last constituent of a construction has been completed, the cursor is reset and the floor is removed.

This type of bottom-up influence on constructions models an important factor affecting the syntactic form of utterances. [Bock and Warren 85] has shown that people can realize, after emitting some words, that in order to continue they must use a certain construction, for example, a passive. Similarly, FIG may output some words without any syntactic plan, then, based on the words output, the update mechanism will activate appropriate constructions, and those constructions will henceforth help guide production.

---

[3] For unordered construction the weight on all construction-constituent links is uniform and unchanging.

[4] Determining when a constituent is complete is not trivial. The current implementation uses a simple matching process, using the 'triggers' or each constituent (the third atoms in their descriptions).

5.6 No Instantiation or Binding

Most generators employ special mechanisms for instantiation and binding. One thing these are used for is handling multiple copies, for example, several noun phrases, or several instances of "a" in a single sentence. A connectionist system must also address this issue. An example of a problem that might occur otherwise is: in the case where several words of a category are highly activated, a node linked to all of them would receive more activation than when only one such word were active. For example **noun-phr** might receive activation from many words of category **noun**.

For this reason FIG uses a special rule for activation received across inherited links: the maximum (not the sum) of these amounts is used. For example, this rule applies to the 'maximal' links from nouns to **noun-phr**, which means that **noun-phr** effectively 'ignores' all but the most highly activated noun.

An earlier version of FIG handled this differently: by making copies of words and constructions. For example, it would make a copy of **noun-phrase** for each noun-expressible concept, and bind each copy to the appropriate concept, and to copies of **a-w** and **the-w**. Once I had started using instances and binding, it seemed natural to use those mechanisms for other problems (notably slots and cases). This approach worked, but it meshed so poorly with the basic activation-flow mechanism that I went back to a more pure spreading activation model. I conjecture that everything which seems to require 'instantiation' or 'binding' can be handled better by an appropriate refinement to the spreading activation mechanism.

5.7 Extended Example

This section describes how FIG produces "the old woman went to a stream to wash clothes." For this example the input is the set of nodes **ikuc1**, **old-womanc1**, **sentakuc1**, **kawac1**, and **pastc**. These nodes are linked to each other as follows: **ikuc1**'s **agentr** is **old-womanc1**, its **purposer** is **sentakuc1**, and its **destr** is **kawac1**; and **old-womanc1**'s **pragroler** is **topicc**. The concepts here have Japanese names because the input is the result of parsing the Japanese sentence "obaasan wa kawa e sentaku ni ikimashita," (old-woman TOPIC stream DEST washclothes PURPOSE go-POLITE-PAST).

Initially, each node of the input has 12 units of activation. Figure 6 shows the activation levels of selected nodes after activation flows, before any word is output. At this point the most highly activated word node is **the-w**, thus it will be selected and emitted first. The major source of activation for **the-w** is the first constituent of **noun-phr**, **np-1** (shown in capitals to indicate that it is the constituent currently under the cursor.) **np-1** receives energy from **noun-phr**, **noun-phr** receives most of its activation from **old-womanw**, which receives activation from **old-womanc1** and from **noun**. **noun** is activated, among other reasons, by the first constituent of **subj-pred**.

One construction not mentioned previously is **back-forep**, the construction responsible for putting adverbials of time and place at the beginning of a sentence. This construction has no effect on this sentence, since there are no concepts present expressible in this way.

After "the" is emitted **noun-phr** becomes even more highly activated and its cursor is moved to **np-2**. The most highly activated word becomes **old-womanw**, largely due to activation from **np-3**.

After "old woman" is emitted **noun-phr** is reset – that is, the cursor is set back to **np-1** and it thereby becomes ready to guide production of another noun phrase. Also, now the cursor on **subj-pred** advances to **sp-2**. As a result verbs, in particular **go-w**, become highly activated.

go-w is selected. Because **pastc** has more activation than **presentc** etc., **go-w** is inflected and emitted as "went." After this **subj-pred**'s cursor advances to its third constituent. At the same time, **go-p**'s cursor advances to its second constituent, thus it activates directional particles, although it happens that there is no semantic input to any such word. The most highly activated words are prepositions, due to activation from the first constituent of **prep-phr**, which in turn receives its energy from **sp-3** and to a lesser extent from **gp-3**. Of the various prepositions, **to1w** receives the most activation from **directionr**, which also receives its activation from the third constituent of **go-p**.

After "to" is emitted, the cursor of **prep-phr** is advanced. The key path of activation flow is now from the second constituent of **prep-phr** to **noun** to **streamw** to **noun-phr** to **article** to **a-w**. Thus "a" is emitted.

Then the cursor of **noun-phr** advances and "stream" is emitted. It is "stream" rather than some other noun because **streamw** is linked to **kawac**, **kawac** fills a **destinationr** relation, and **destinationr** is listed in **gp-3**.

At this point the cursor of **go-p** is on **gp-4**. From this constituent activation flows to **purpose-clause**, and in due course "to" and "wash clothes" are emitted.

In this way FIG has produced: "the old woman went to a stream to wash clothes." All the nodes of the input having been expressed, FIG ends.

6 Implementation

```
---PATTERNS---              ----WORDS-----          ---CONCEPTS---
   16.0  BACK-FOREP            21.3  THE-W            23.6  IKUC1
         BF-1 bf-2 bf-3        21.0  A-W              19.7  OLD-WOMANC1
    4.9  NOUN-PHR              12.6  OLD-WOMANW       16.7  KAWAC1
         NP-1 np-2 np-3        10.7  STREAMW          15.5  SENTAKUC1
    3.1  SUBJ-PRED             10.6  GO-W             12.0  PASTC
         SP-1 sp-2 sp-3         8.6  RIVERW            9.5  CONSNT-INITIAL
    2.1  GO-P                   5.5  WASH-CLOTHESW     6.1  VOWEL-INITIAL
         GP-1 gp-2 gp-3 gp-4    3.4  TO2W              5.9  TOPICC
    1.8  PURPOSE-CLAUSE         ---                   ----OTHER-----
         PC-1 pc-2 pc-3         ---                   16.0  TIMES
    0.3  PREP-PHR               ---                    3.8  ARTICLE
         PP-1 pp-2              ---                    2.6  NOUN
         ---                    ---                    1.8  AGENTR
```

Figure 6: Activation Levels of Selected Nodes After Activation Flow

FIG currently has six types of nodes: concepts, relations, words, constructions, constituents, and instances of concepts. They are distinguished for clarity and efficiency but not for activation flow. The cursor update process and semantic update process (not described further) do, however, examine node types; and of course only words are selected and emitted.

Although links have been differentiated above in terms of their intended meaning, activation flows across all links in the same way, except: 1. there are **english** and **japanese** links; no activation flows across the ones for the language not in use, 2. the weights of links from constructions to constituents are modified by the mask according to the cursor, and 3. inhibit links transmit negative activation.

In accordance with the intuition that a word is not truly appropriate unless it is both syntactically and semantically appropriate, the activation level for words is given by the product (not the sum) of incoming syntactic and semantic activation. 'Syntactic activation' is activation received from constituents and syntactic categories.

Currently FIG has 284 nodes and about 600 links. Before each word choice, activation flows until the network settles down, with cutoff after 8 cycles. This takes about .15 seconds on average (simulating parallel activation flow on a Symbolics 3670), thus FIG outputs words faster than a human speaker.

The correct operation of FIG depends on having correct link weights. This is not a major problem. Many of the link weights are uniform. For example, all links from syntactic categories to their members have weight .8, all 'inhibit' links have weight .7, and so on. Many of the others have a rationale: for example, the link from **np-1** to articles has relatively high weight because articles get very little activation from other sources. No single weight is meaningful; the way it

functions in context is. For example, the exact weight of the link from the first constituent of **subj-pred** to **noun** is not crucial, as long as the product of it and the weight on the **agentr** relation is appropriate.

Also crucial in generation is the flow of activation through the network structures encoding world-knowledge. World knowledge is also used when monitoring the output and updating activation levels. For details see [Ward 88a].

FIG is, of course, extensible. Adding new concepts, words or constructions is generally straightforward; they can be encoded by analogy to similar nodes, and usually the same link weights suffice. Occasionally new nodes and links interact in unforeseen ways with other knowledge in the system, causing other nodes to get too much or too little activation. In these cases it is necessary to debug the network. Sometimes trial-and-error experiments are required, but often the acceptable range of weights can be determined by examination. This is a kind of back-propagation by hand; it could doubtless be automated.

Besides just increasing the amount of knowledge in FIG's network, I would like to make it model human speech errors and to use its grammatical knowledge structures for parsing also.

7 Summary

FIG's treatment of syntax is connectionist and novel. It relies heavily on parallelism and emergents. It does not build up any syntactic structures, nor even make explicit syntactic choices. The only explicit choices needed are the successive choices of words. It is also novel in that the network representations of linguistic knowledge affect word choice and order directly, rather than just affecting a parse tree. Thus the implementation corresponds clearly and directly to the knowledge-level theory.

This treatment of syntax works well with the rest of FIG — all types of knowledge are well integrated and interact freely at run time. I have explained elsewhere how this is important for: accurate and flexible word choice [Ward 88a], producing natural-sounding output for machine translation [Ward 89a], and modeling the key aspects of the human language production process [Ward 89c].

This work is not traditional linguistics, artificial intelligence, or connectionism, but uses techniques from all three fields. I have presented a syntactic mechanism which is compatible with intuitions about syntactic knowledge and also with connectionist processing. I hope this will stimulate further work in empirical computational linguistics, modeling human language production, and building and useful parallel generation systems.

References

[Baars 80] Baars, Bernard K,. The Competing Plans Hypothesis: an heuristic viewpoint on the causes of errors in speech, in *Temporal Variables in Speech*, Hans W. Dechert and Manfred Raupach (eds.), Mouton, 1980.

[Bock and Warren 85] Bock, J. K., and Richard Warren, Conceptual Accessibility and Syntactic Structure in Sentence Formulation, *Cognition* 21, 1985.

[Dell 86] Dell, Gary S., A Spreading Activation Theory of Retrieval in Sentence Production, *Psychological Review* 93, 3, 1986.

[Fillmore 88] Fillmore, Charles, *On Grammatical Constructions*, course notes, UC Berkeley Linguistics Department, 1988.

[Fillmore et al 89] Fillmore, Charles, Paul Kay, and M. C. O'Connor, Regularity and Idiomaticity in Grammatical Constructions: The Case of Let Alone, *Language* 64, 3, pp 501-538, 1988.

[Gasser 88] Gasser, Michael, A Connectionist Model of Sentence Generation in a First and Second Language, PhD Thesis, also Technical Report UCLA-AI-88-13, Los Angeles, 1988.

[Kalita and Shastri 87] Kalita, Jugal, and Lokendra Shastri, Generation of Simple Sentences in English Using the Connectionist Model of Computation, *9th Cognitive Science Conference*, Erlbaum, 1987

[McDonald 1983] McDonald, David, Description Directed Control: Its Implications for Natural Language Generation, *Computers and Mathematics with Applications*, 9, 1 1983.

[Stemberger 85] Stemberger, J. P., An Interactive Activation Model of Language Production, in *Progress in the Psychology of Language, Volume 1*, Andrew W. Ellis, ed., Erlbaum, 1985.

[Stolcke 89] Stolcke, Andreas, Processing Unification-based Grammars in a Connectionist Framework, *11th Cognitive Science Conference*, Erlbaum, 1989.

[Ward 88a] Ward, Nigel, Issues in Word Choice, *COLING-88*, Budapest, August 1988.

[Ward 88b] Ward, Nigel, An Open Design for Generation, *Proceedings of the AAAI Workshop on Text Planning and Realization*, St. Paul, MN, August 1988.

[Ward 89a] Ward, Nigel, Towards Natural Machine Translation, Proceedings of the EIC Workshop on Artificial Intelligence, Published as Technical Research Report AI89-29 ̄ 37, Institute of Electronics, Information, and Communication Engineers, Tokyo, June 1989.

[Ward 89b] Ward, Nigel, On the Ordering of Decisions in Machine Translation, *Proceedings of the National Conference of the Japanese Society for Artificial Intelligence*, Tokyo, July 1989.

[Ward 89c] Ward, Nigel, Capturing Intuitions about Human Language Production, *Proceedings, Cognitive Science Conference*, Ann Arbor, August 1989.

Harmonic Grammar - A formal multi-level connectionist theory of linguistic well-formedness: Theoretical foundations

Géraldine Legendre[1,2], Yoshiro Miyata[1,3,4], Paul Smolensky[1,3,4]

[1]*Institute of Cognitive Science,* [2]*Department of Linguistics,* [3]*Department of Computer Science,*
& [4]*Optoelectronic Computing Systems Center, University of Colorado at Boulder*

Abstract

In this paper, we derive the formalism of *harmonic grammar,* a connectionist-based theory of linguistic well-formedness. Harmonic grammar is a two-level theory, involving a low level connectionist network using a particular kind of distributed representation, and a second, higher level network that uses local representations and which approximately and incompletely describes the aggregate computational behavior of the lower level network. The central hypothesis is that the connectionist well-formedness measure *harmony*[1] can be used to model linguistic well-formedness; what is crucial about the relation between the lower and higher level networks is that there is a harmony-preserving mapping between them: they are *isoharmonic* (at least approximately). In a companion paper (Legendre, Miyata, & Smolensky, 1990; henceforth, "LMS[1]"), we apply harmonic grammar to a syntactic problem, unaccusativity, and show that the resulting network is capable of a degree of coverage of difficult data that is unparalleled by symbolic approaches of which we are aware: of the 760 sentence types represented in our data, the network correctly predicts the acceptability in all but two cases. In the present paper, we describe the theoretical basis for the two level approach, illustrating the general theory through the derivation from first principles of the unaccusativity network of LMS[1].

Introduction

Our starting point is the approach to connectionist cognitive modeling called the *subsymbolic paradigm* (Smolensky, 1988):

(1)   **Hypotheses of the subsymbolic approach to cognitive modeling**

a.   There are two important levels for cognitive modeling.

b.   At the lower level, the natural description of the cognitive architecture is as a massively interconnected network of simple parallel processing units: call this LNet (Lower level Network).

c.   In LNet, elements of the problem domain (e.g., in syntax, words and phrases) are represented not by individual units, but as distributed patterns of activity; a given unit in LNet has no semantic interpretation by itself: it plays a small part in the representation of many different elements.

d.   When the representations and computational processing of LNet are described at the higher level of the semantically meaningful activity patterns, we get descriptions of the cognitive architecture at the higher level. Such descriptions will often be approximate, idealized, or incomplete.

e.   Unlike the lower level, descriptions of the higher level are not computationally uniform. Some of these descriptions involve symbolic computation with hard rules. Others involve local connectionist networks, in which individual units have semantic interpretations corresponding to those of the patterns of LNet. Such networks will be called HNets (Higher level Networks).

f.   The symbols and rules of symbolic accounts correspond in LNet to patterns of activity and to the aggregate effects of groups of connections on these patterns of activity.

g.   An important goal of connectionist modeling is to develop LNets supporting higher level descriptions that are simultaneously (i) sufficiently close to symbolic cognitive theory to explain the successes of symbolic accounts, yet (ii) sufficiently different to improve upon these successes.

The central idea of harmonic grammar is to start by partially specifying a LNet for a domain of linguistic interest, and then, rather than fully specifying and simulating it, as is conventionally done in connectionist modeling, to embody the most important aspects of LNet in a higher-level net HNet. This model, or rather a notational variant of it, HNet', is what gets simulated. HNet' (or, equivalently, HNet) is interpreted as grammar fragment expressing linguistic regularities via *soft rules.* Whereas symbolic rules of well-formedness have the form (2a), the soft rules of harmonic grammar have the form (2b).

(2)   a.   Condition X must never be violated in well-formed structures.

b.   If Condition X is violated, then the well-formedness (harmony) of the structure is diminished by C_X.

The status of the two networks LNet and HNet are rather different. The level of LNet is presumably closer to the neural level, and therefore provides a more appropriate model for questions related to neurolinguistics (although the problematic relationship between connectionist and neural models, emphasized in Smolensky, 1988, suggests caution here). For language acquisition and real-time language processing models, as well, LNet would presumably be the more appropriate network. But for grammar, it is HNet that is the focus of attention.

This paper procedes as follows. We begin with a number of technical preliminaries which, after brief introduction of the linguistic problem of unaccusativity, motivate LNet, a partially specified lower level model for the unaccusativity data. We then derive a corresponding higher level model, HNet, and then its notational variant, HNet', which is the model discussed in LMS_1. HNet' allows standard connectionist learning to automatically extract from the data the constants C_X in the soft rules (b) of harmonic grammar. We close by summarizing the methodology and identifying some of its novel features.

Technical preliminaries

The subsymbolic approach outlined in (1) and its application to the domain of language presents the following research challenges, among others.[2]

(3) A. Representation:

      1. Develop a formalism for higher level description of distributed representations: a calculus of patterns of activity (it is these patterns that correspond to symbols; (1f))

      2. Apply this calculus to the representation of constituent structure

  B. Processing:

      1. Develop a formalism for higher level description of connectionist processing: a calculus of the aggregate effects of groups of connections on patterns of activity (it is these effects that correspond to rules; (1f))

      2. Apply this calculus to the processing of constituent structure

The next four subsections successively address these four problems: A.1, A.2, B.1, and B.2.

A calculus of patterns of activity

A natural "calculus of patterns of activity" is straightforward: vector calculus, where the vectors are the lists of activation values for the units. The central idea of distributed representation (1c) can be stated very simply: it is activity vectors (not, e.g., individual units) that have semantic interpretations, i.e., interpretations as elements of the problem domain (the kind of information that is represented by symbols in the symbolic paradigm).

If different symbols are represented by different patterns of activity over the same set of units, as hypothesized in (1c), how is it possible to represent several such symbols at once? Vector calculus suggests a simple answer: by *superimposing*, i.e, adding together, the vectors representing the individual symbols. In the symbolic paradigm, structures are formed by some kind of (e.g., string or tree) concatenation of their constituents; in the subsymbolic approach, patterns combine by superposition rather than concatenation. This principle is discussed at some length in Smolensky (1986b), where an important consequence is derived: to a given network using distributed superpositional representations, there corresponds another network using local representations which provides a higher level description of the distributed network. The formal relation between the lower and higher level models can be thought of as a "rotation of the coordinates" in the activation space, so that the new coordinate axes lie along the directions of the distributed patterns with semantic interpretation; alternatively, we can think of this relation as changing variables from the lower level variables — units' activation values — to higher level variables — the strength of semantically interpretable patterns.[3]

Vectorial representation of constituent structure

How can simple vector addition replace concatenation? One basic problem that immediately suggests itself is that the former is a commutative operation, while the latter is not; e.g., $\mathtt{concat(a,b)} = \mathtt{ab} \neq \mathtt{ba} = \mathtt{concat(b,a)}$, while $\mathtt{sum(a,b)} = \mathtt{a+b} = \mathtt{b+a} = \mathtt{sum(b,a)}$. A solution to this and related problems, called tensor product representations, is formalized and analyzed in Smolensky (in press 1). The first step is to recognize that vector superposition really represents *conjunction* rather than *concatenation*, and that concatenation, and other structure-building operations, can be achieved through conjunction together with *filler/role decompositions*. In such decompositions, a structure, e.g. abc, is described as the conjunction of an unordered set of propositions of the form, *structural role r is filled by f*, which are denoted by the *filler/role bindings f/r*; thus, e.g., abc is identified with the conjunction of the filler-role bindings $\{a/r_1, c/r_3, b/r_2\}$. The vector representing abc, under this filler/role decomposition, is abc $= a/r_1 + c/r_3 + b/r_2$ The vectors representing filler/role bindings, e.g. b/r_2, are constructed from vectors representing the unbound fillers and vectors representing unbound roles, e.g., b and r_2, by an operation from vector calculus called *the tensor product*: $b/r_2 = b \otimes r_2$. The tensor product is similar to the outer product of matrix algebra, e.g. $(x, y, z) \otimes (\alpha, \beta) = (x\alpha, x\beta, y\alpha, y\beta, z\alpha, z\beta)$ except that the result is interpreted not as a matrix but as another vector; the resulting vector can in turn be used recursively in further products, allowing recursive representations employing higher-order tensors. Smolensky (in press 1) analyzes these ideas — decompositions of structures into conjunctions of filler/role bindings, the superpositional representation of conjunction, and representation of filler/role variable bindings via the tensor product — and shows that together they formalize and generalize a number of previous connectionist approaches to representing structure, and that they represent structured data in a way that naturally permits the usual features of connectionist processing, e.g., massively parallel (and structure-sensitive) associative processing, graceful degradation, and statistical learning.[4]

389

Thus, for the purposes of this paper, we assume:

(4) **Tensor product representation of structure**

At the lower level, in LNet, a structure s is represented by the activation vector $s = \sum_\alpha c_\alpha$, where each c_α represents a constituent of s, which is a filler/role binding f_α/r_α with respect to some filler/role decomposition of s; the constituent vectors are $c_\alpha = f_\alpha \otimes r_\alpha$, where f_α and r_α are activity vectors respectively representing f_α and r_α (possibly recursively defined as tensor product representations themselves).

A calculus for connectionist processing

Viewed at the lowest level, connectionist processing is the spread of numerical activation by some set of numerical equations in which the connection strengths enter as parameters. A calculus of the aggregate effects of connection strengths on patterns of activity relies on the idea that these activation equations are trying to achieve some characterizable end product: a pattern of activity that encodes a set of inferences which is justifiable from some notion of statistical inference. Smolensky (1983, 1986a) developed such a higher level description, deriving from a well-defined statistical inference problem a measure called the *harmony function H* whose global maximum constitutes the solution to the inference problem. In a large variety of connectionist models, the activation functions turn out to be implementing local maximization of this function, which can be written very simply:

(5) $\qquad H(\mathbf{a}) = \sum_{i,j} a_i w_{ij} a_j = \mathbf{a}^T \mathbf{W} \mathbf{a}$

where $\mathbf{a} = (a_1, a_2, \ldots)$ is the total activity vector of the network, and $\mathbf{W} = \{w_{ij}\}$ is the matrix of connection weights. (The negative of H is often referred to as "energy"; Hopfield, 1982; Hinton & Sejnowski, 1983, 1986.)[5] In a variety of networks, including both feed-back and feed-forward architectures, each update of the units' activations will increase H (Cohen & Grossberg, 1983, Golden, 1986, 1988, Hopfield 1982, 1984, 1987, Smolensky, 1983, 1986a, Hinton & Sejnowski, 1983, 1986.) Thus for a major subset of connectionist models, it is appropriate to regard the goal of the spread of processing to be the creation of an activation vector that maximizes H. For the purposes of formulating approximate higher level accounts of connectionist processing, we will thus assume that such harmony maximization is what processing in LNet achieves, even though a more detailed lower level account might well need to consider conditions under which the network fails to actually find the global maximum of H. Thus for our purposes we assume that under suitable approximation or idealization, the following holds:

(6) **Principle of harmony maximization**

Given an input vector i and connection weights $\mathbf{W}$, processing in LNet establishes activity vectors h and o over the hidden and output units, respectively, that maximize $H(\mathbf{a})$, where $\mathbf{a} = (\mathbf{i}, \mathbf{h}, \mathbf{o})$ and the harmony function H is defined in (5).

Given the connection between H and statistical inference, this principle can be interpreted as follows: the network draws a set of inferences that provides a best fit to the input data and the statistical constraints embodied in W (e.g., the "Best Fit Principle" of Smolensky, 1988; Golden 1988). The value of H that is achieved in this maximization process is a quantitative measure of the degree to which it is possible to meet the statistical constraints in W by appropriately processing the given input data. This motivates the following central assumption of harmonic grammar:

(7) The H value achieved in processing an input is a quantitative measure of that input's well-formedness. An informant's judgements of acceptability of sentences can be modeled as a monotonic function f of the harmony values achieved in processing those sentences (the higher the harmony, the more acceptable).

In this paper, we take f to be the particular monotonically increasing function $f(x) = (1 + e^{-x})^{-1}$: a logistic; the same methodology could be carried out for any other choice of (differentiable) f.

Connectionist processing of constituent structure

Now we bring together (4) and (5), assuming that the activity vector a in (5) is the structure representation s in (4). Then (6) states that processing in LNet maximizes:

(8) $\qquad H(s) = s^T \mathbf{W} s = \sum_\alpha c_\alpha^T \mathbf{W} \sum_\beta c_\beta = \sum_\alpha H_\alpha + \sum_{\alpha,\beta} H_{\alpha,\beta}$

Here, the sum $\sum_{\alpha,\beta}$ is understood to include *one* term for each pair of distinct constituents $c_\alpha \neq c_\beta$ in s, and the first- and second-order harmony terms are defined by:

(9) a. $H_\alpha = c_\alpha^T \mathbf{W} c_\alpha = \sum_{i,j} (c_\alpha)_i w_{ij} (c_\alpha)_j$

b. $H_{\alpha,\beta} = c_\alpha^T \mathbf{W} c_\beta + c_\beta^T \mathbf{W} c_\alpha = c_\alpha^T [\mathbf{W} + \mathbf{W}^T] c_\beta = \sum_{i,j} (c_\alpha)_i [w_{ij} + w_{ji}] (c_\alpha)_j$

For example, if s = abc is decomposed as $\{a/r_1, c/r_3, b/r_2\}$, then $H(\text{abc}) = H_{a/r_1} + H_{b/r_2} + H_{c/r_3} + H_{a/r_1, b/r_2} + H_{a/r_1, c/r_3} + H_{b/r_2, c/r_3}$. H_α is the internal harmony associated with constituent c_α, and $H_{\alpha,\beta}$ is the pairwise harmony arising from combining the constituents c_α and c_β in the same structure. Note that terms depending on more than two constituents cannot arise because H is quadratic.

Now if our specification of LNet were sufficiently complete that we knew the weight matrix W and the activity patterns representing the constituents c_α, we could compute each of the terms in (8) through the equations (9). This would amount to computing at the lower level. Alternatively, *we can operate with the harmony terms in (8) directly*, treating each H_α and $H_{\alpha\beta}$ as an independent variable; this is computing at the higher level. Exploitation of this alternative is a central innovation of harmonic grammar.

The distinction between computing at the lower and higher levels can be viewed as follows. Equation (5) expresses the harmony as a function of the *lower level variables*: activities of individual units and strengths of individual weights. Equation (8), on the other hand, expresses the harmony as a function of the *higher level variables*: the constituents in the structure. The derivation of (8) from (5) [and (4)] amounts to a *change of variables* from the lower level variables associated with units and connections to the higher level variables associated with constituents. These higher level variables will shortly be used to define HNet.

We conclude these preliminaries with a few remarks.

(10) a. In a given problem, some of the constituents c_α will be "inputs," others will be "outputs," and still others will be "hidden" constituents. E.g., a sentence interpretation model might take as input constituents a string of words, might produce as output constituents the elements of some meaning representation, and might fill in as hidden constitents, say, non-terminal nodes in a parse tree. The "inferred" constituents — the hidden and output constituents — are determined through the principle of harmony maximization (6): they are the choice of c_αs that maximize H in (8).

  b. The higher level harmony values H_α and $H_{\alpha\beta}$ will later be interpreted as the constants in the soft rules of (b). They will be computed by a numerical fit to data. When is this parameter fitting exercise appropriately constrained? Note that, since H in (8) is quadratic in the constituents, the number of different terms that may appear on the right-hand-side of (8) scales as $(\#fillers)^2$, while the number of possible structures on the left-hand-side of (8) scales roughly as $(\#fillers)^{\#roles}$. Thus, as the number of roles in the structure increases, the formalism rapidly becomes more and more constrained, and the significance of good parameter fit becomes increasingly more meaningful.

  c. Is it correct to treat the higher level harmony variables H_α and $H_{\alpha\beta}$ as independent? This clearly depends on the structure assumed in LNet. Crudely speaking, if there are many more lower level variables than higher level variables, it is likely that any set of values for the higher level variables H_α and $H_{\alpha\beta}$ can be achieved by some choice of the lower level variables, the representations c_α and weights W. On the other hand, if it is possible to identify some strong constraints on the lower level variables — e.g., if a large number of different constituents were constrained to be represented as different activity patterns over a much smaller number of units — then, effectively, there might be fewer lower level variables than higher level ones, so that the space of possible values for the higher level variables might be genuinely constrained by the fact that they are derived from the lower level.

A sample application: Unaccusativity in French

Unaccusativity

Since the problem of unaccusativity is discussed in some detail in LMS$_1$, we are extremely brief here. In many languages, in particular French, intransitive verbs divide into two classes: *unergatives* and *unaccusatives*, which yield different acceptability judgements in certain syntactic environments called *diagnostic contexts* (here, simply "contexts"). Consider, for example, the sentence *La glace est facile à faire fondre* "Ice is easy to make melt." Here, the diagnostic context is Object Raising or "OR," which is a sentence frame _____ *est facile à faire* _____ having two slots; the first, "argument," slot is filled by the NP *La glace*, and the second, "predicate," slot is filled by the intransitive verb *fondre*. The data of LMS$_1$ are 760 such French sentences, generated from four different diagnostic contexts, 143 different intransitive verbs, and arguments with varying semantic features. The pattern of acceptability judgements for these 760 sentences is quite complex. The acceptability patterns across different contexts of roughly half the verbs can be explained by a standard symbolic syntactic account which postulates that all the diagnostic contexts have well-formedness conditions requiring the argument to be a deep Direct Object of the predicate, and that each intransitive verb is marked in the lexicon as requiring its argument to be either a deep Subject (unergative verbs) or a deep Direct Object (unaccusative verbs). The other half of the data can only be explained by assuming that the acceptability reflects not only these "structural features" (deep Subject, Direct Object), but also semantic features of the argument and predicate. At the same time, these semantic features alone do not seem to be sufficient either; structural and semantic features are both required to explain these data.

LNet

Applying (1g) and (4) to the case at hand, we assume:

(11) a. Symbolic structural descriptions of sentences are approximate higher level descriptions of the patterns of activity in a lower level model LNet representing those sentences. In particular, the argument of an intransitive verb fills, among other roles, either the structural role of deep Subject or that of deep Direct

Object.

b. In particular, these patterns of activity can be approximated as tensor product representations based on a role filler/role decomposition exemplified as follows for the vector representing the Object Raising (OR) sentence *La glace est facile à faire fondre*:

La_glace_est_facile_à_faire_fondre =

La_glace/ARG + OR/CONTEXT + fondre/PRED + DIRECT_OBJECT/STRUCTURE =

A + C + P + S

That is, the vector representing a sentence can be approximated as the sum of four vectors, each of which represents a kind of constituent that is specially designed for the particular data under study: an argument A, a context C, a predicate P, and a "structure" (deep grammatical function) S (either Subject or Direct Object).

We will not further specify this partial description of LNet; in particular, we will not specify vectors representing the individual fillers and roles. In the most general case, these vectors may be presumed to be fully distributed, giving rise to a representation of sentences in which every unit is part of the representation of each constituent; it will not matter to our analysis whether this fully distributed case or a more localized special case obtains, e.g., one in which the four roles of (11b) are localized to disjoint regions of the network.

There is no particular point in drawing a picture of LNet; we need only imagine a large network holding a representation of the sentence as a pattern of activity which is the sum of four constituent patterns (each of which may well involve activation over the entire network), according to (11b). Three constituents of this vector — the argument, context, and predicate — are specified in the input: the surface word string of a given sentence. The fourth constituent — the structure feature — is not given in the input; it is "hidden" (10a), and must be inferred by the network through activation spread to maximize harmony. Following (7), the degree of acceptability of the sentence to the network is taken to be $f(H)$, where H is the harmony of this activation pattern, and f is the logistic function. In LNet, acceptability is a distributed property; there is no "output unit" giving the network's acceptability judgement.

Why do we assume the filler/role decomposition of (11b)? Because it is the simplest imaginable one with which to start. The remarkable success of the consequent model provides some evidence in favor of this very simple assumption. It should be made clear, however, that the methodology permits assuming a different filler/role decomposition of the sentences, and following it through to a corresponding higher level model HNet operating in terms of the different constituent filler/role pairs, just as we now do for the filler/role decomposition assumed in (11).

HNet

Combining (6), (7), (8), and (11b), we have:

(12) The acceptability of a sentence s consisting of the argument A, the context C, and the predicate P is:

acceptability$(s) = f[\max_S H(A+C+P+S)]$

where S ranges over the two possible structures, Subject and Direct Object, and

$H(A+C+P+S) = H_A + H_C + H_P + H_S + H_{AC} + H_{AP} + H_{AS} + H_{CP} + H_{CS} + H_{PS}$

This equation for H involves a prohibitively large number of higher-level parameters H_α and $H_{\alpha\beta}$. We eliminate a great many of these parameters by appealing to a number of linguistically motivated constraints:

(13) a. H_A: assume all arguments in the sentences used are equally well-formed internally

b. H_P: assume all predicates in the sentences used are equally well-formed internally

c. H_S: assume the grammar has no intrinsic preference between deep Subjects and deep Direct Objects

d. H_{AC}: assume the grammatical restrictions on the diagnostic context can refer only to general semantic features of the argument (not, e.g., to specific NPs); we take these features to be VO (volitionality) and AN (animacy)

e. H_{AP}: assume the lexical entry for the predicate can only express preference for general semantic features of the argument (again, VO and AN)

f. H_{AS}: assume the grammatical preferences for semantic/structural correspondences of the argument can only depend on its general semantic features (VO, AN)

g. H_{CP}: assume the grammatical restrictions on the diagnostic context can refer only to general semantic features of the predicate (not, e.g., to specific verbs); we take these features to be TE (telicity) and PR (progressivity)[5]

h. H_{CS}: assume the grammatical restrictions on the diagnostic context can refer to the structure (Subject vs. Direct Object) of the argument

i. H_{PS}: assume the lexical entry for a predicate can include a structural preference, but not an absolute bias on grammaticality

Assuming these constraints to hold, and dropping H_A, H_P and H_S because they do not vary across sentences (13a-c), we can rewrite the harmony function:

(14) $H(A+C+P+S) = H_C + H_{VO, C} + H_{AN, C} + H_{VO, P} + H_{AN, P} + H_{VO, S} + H_{AN, S} + H_{C, TE} + H_{C, PR} + H_{C, S} + H_{P, S}$

Now we recognize this as the harmony function of another network, HNet, illustrated in Figure 1. HNet uses a local representation, with a single unit for each each context, argument feature, predicate feature, structural feature, and individual predicate. The units in HNet correspond to patterns in LNet; HNet is a higher level network that is *isoharmonic* to LNet: the harmony of corresponding states in the two models are the same.

This network can be used to compute acceptability as follows. A given sentence is represented over the input units. We activate which ever of the hidden units gives the greatest harmony; this can be achieved by having the two units compete so that the unit with the greater net input wins: the net input to each hidden unit is precisely the contribution to the total harmony that that hidden unit would make if it were to have activity value 1. The hidden units thus are a little "winner-take-all" group in which the winning unit gets activity value 1, and the other, 0. Now we compute the harmony H of the network as a whole using (5) (with the variables H_α and $H_{\alpha\beta}$ now playing the roles in (5) of the weights W). Putting this value H into f, we get the acceptability $f(H)$, following (7).

The weights in this network are the harmony values H_α and $H_{\alpha\beta}$ of (10); from the point of view of the original lower level model, each of these weights represents the aggregate harmony of a set of weights and activity vectors, as indicated in (9). We'd like to work backwards from the data to infer what these aggregate values must be in order to produce the observed well-formedness pattern, but training the harmony values that are distributed throughout this network is not straightforward. A few simple modifications in the network, though, will fix this.

HNet´

In order to perform standard supervised learning from the data, we now create a network HNet´ that is precisely equivalent to HNet, but which possesses a single output O unit which explicitly computes acceptability. The main trick, illustrated in Figure 2, is simple: replace the connection between input units α and β of HNet, carrying weight $H_{\alpha\beta}$, by a conjunction unit $c_{\alpha\beta}$ whose activity is the product $a_\alpha a_\beta$, and connect $c_{\alpha\beta}$ to O with a connection of strength $H_{\alpha\beta}$. Then the contribution to O's net input coming from $c_{\alpha\beta}$ is $a_\alpha a_\beta H_{\alpha\beta}$, which is just the amount of harmony in HNet contributed by the original connection between α and β. Thus the total net input to O is the total harmony H. If O uses f to transform its net input to its activation value, then its value is exactly the acceptability judgement of Figure 1.

The only remaining step concerns the hidden units. In defining HNet´, the trick of replacing HNet connections with conjunction units should not be applied to the connections to the hidden units; these connections just stay as in HNet. As noted above, the net input to each hidden unit is precisely the contribution to the total harmony that that hidden unit would make if it were to win the competition. Suppose we define the activation functions of HNet´'s hidden units so that their activity values prior to competition are just equal to their net inputs; this is also their contribution to H. To maximize H, we let these two units compete so that the one with the higher activity value retains its value, while the other has its value set to zero. Now, the hidden units send their activation values to O (along connections with strength 1); the hidden unit capable of contributing the greatest harmony sends that harmony value up O, whose net input now includes the correct contribution from the hidden units, namely, the harmony arising from picking the structural feature that maximizes harmony.

The network HNet´ we have just defined, shown in Figure 3, is precisely the network used in LMS$_1$; and we have completed its derivation from basic principles. This network can now be trained using the appropriate form of standard back propagation (Rumelhart, Hinton, & Williams, 1986), as described in LMS$_1$. Note that the assumption of independence of the higher level variables, discussed in (10c), is relevant here, if the training procedure incorporates no constraints between weights. Note also that the "learning" in HNet´ is not a plausible model of language acquisition (for one thing, positive and negative data are crucial); "learning" in HNet´ is purely a computational procedure for parameter fitting, a formal trick for automating (a particularly nasty) part of the job of the harmonic grammarian: determining the numerical constants C_X in the soft rules (b). Presumably, a plausible model of real language acquisition would operate at the lower level, in LNet, rather than in HNet´.

Summary of the methodology

The methodoloy of harmonic grammar exemplified above can be summarized as the following series of steps.

(15) a. Choose a filler/role decomposition for the structures whose well-formedness is to be accounted for.

   b. Postulate a lower level model LNet using a tensor product representation with this filler/role decomposition.

   c. Take the formula (5) for the harmony of LNet in terms of its weights and activities, and change variables ...

   d. ... to get a formula (8) for the harmony as function of the constituents of the structure being represented; this function involves aggregated harmony values indexed by pairs of constituents; treat these values as independent high level variables.

   e. Prune the number of these variables by appealing to linguistic constraints (at least) until the number of variables is considerably fewer than the number of data points to be accounted for.

   f. Embody the resulting harmony function as a local connectionist network HNet whose connection strengths are the high level harmony variables.

   g. Create HNet´ by adding to HNet an output unit that explicitly computes the harmony and corresponding acceptability value by means of additional conjunctive units and winner-take-all linear hidden units.

   h. Train HNet´ using more-or-less standard connectionist supervised learning.

393

    i.   Interpret HNet' as embodying soft grammatical and lexical rules.

    j.   Analyze these rules for new linguistic insight into the original linguistic problem.

Step (15j) is the subject of current research.

The method exhibits the following novel features:

(16) a. It is founded on a distributed lower level connectionist model that is only partially specified.

      b. It operates primarily through a higher level formalism that approximately describes certain aspects of the aggregate behavior of the lower level network in terms of another, local, connectionist network.

      c. The grammatical and lexical rules of the formalism are soft, and represent a set of quantified tendencies; but the model is fully formal, in that it makes precise predictions (even graded ones) of acceptability or well-formedness.

      d. The strength of the soft rules is determined automatically from the data.

      e. Existing linguistic knowledge plays the important role of constraining the form of the grammar.

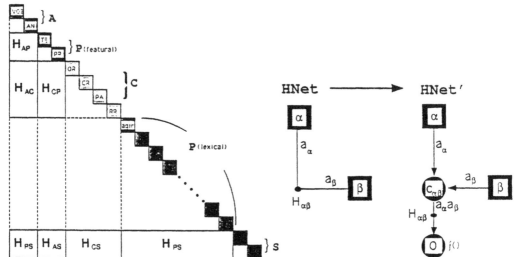

Figure 1.

Figure 2.

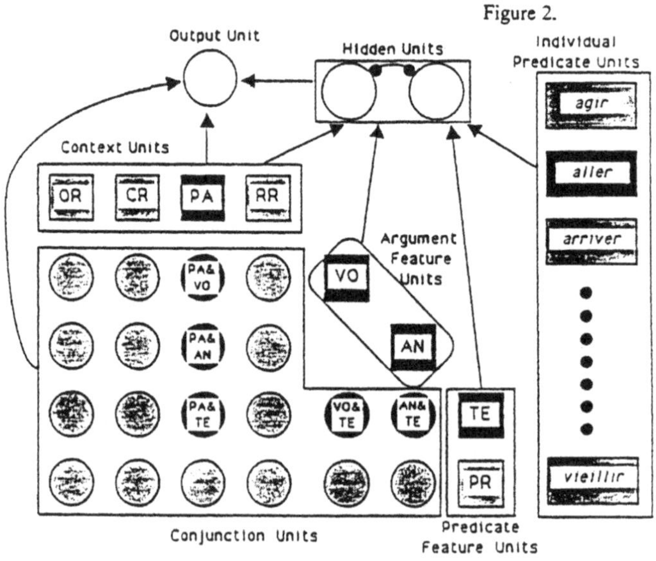

Figure 3.

394

Acknowledgements

Warm thanks to Alan Prince, for very helpful discussions, and especially, a great pot of chicken soup and the term "isoharmonic." This work owes its existence to Mike Mozer, who failed to convince us not to do it. Thanks also to Jim Martin for his valuable comments on an earlier version. This work has been supported by NSF grants IRI-8609599 and ECE-8617947 to PS, by a grant to PS from the Sloan Foundation's computational neuroscience program. PS (in part) and YM have also been supported by the Optical Connectionist Machine Program of the Center for Optoelectronic Computing Systems, which is sponsored in part by NSF/ERC grant CDR-8622236 and by the Colorado Advanced Technology Institute, an agency of the State of Colorado. GL has been supported in part by a Junior Faculty Development Award from the Council on Research and Creative Work, University of Colorado, Boulder. The authors are listed in alphabetical order.

Footnotes

1. Other connectionist approaches to linguistics appealing to the notion of harmony include John Goldsmith's "harmonic phonology" (Goldsmith, to appear) and George Lakoff's "cognitive phonology" (Lakoff, 1988).

2. In addition, there are corresponding problems related to learning, but these are not yet relevant to this research.

3. In Smolensky (1986b), the dynamical question is also considered: do the lower and higher level models evolve isomorphically in time? In this paper, we do an end run around the dynamics, working directly with the optimal equilibrium states the (incompletely specified) dynamics is trying to find.

4. Smolensky (in press 2) uses this technique as the technical basis for a reply to the putative dilemma of Fodor & Pylyshyn (1988): connectionism must choose between associationist and structure-sensitive processing.

5. This simple form for H arises from treating biases as weights to an extra unit with constant value 1, and treating input lines as though they originated in units interior to the network. In this form, H in the text is maximized when each unit achieves its maximum or minimum activation values. Networks whose units are not driven to their limits — e.g., quasi-linear units with sigmoid non-linearities, discussed in Smolensky (1986b) and very popular since Rumelhart, Hinton, & Williams (1986) in "back-propagation networks" — can be analyzed by adding to H a term $-\sum_i h(a_i)$ which does not introduce further interactions among the units, but is designed to penalize units with extreme values. E.g., for the popular logistic non-linearity $a_i = (1+e^{-input_i})^{-1}$, we set $h(a) = a \ln a + (1-a) \ln (1-a)$. This function h, like the other terms in H, has an interpretation in terms of statistical inference and information theory.

6. This constraint is particularly important since without it, every pair of context and individual predicate would have its own free parameter, giving rise to 572 parameters of this type alone — with only 760 data points to fix the parameters.

References

Cohen, M. A. & Grossberg, S. (1983). *Absolute stability of global pattern formation and parallel memory storage by competitive neural networks.* IEEE Trans SMC-13, 815–825.

Fodor, J. A. & Pylyshyn, Z. W. (1988). Connectionism and cognitive architecture: A critical analysis. *Cognition*, 28, 3–71.

Golden, R. M. (1986) The "Brain-State-in-a-Box" Neural Model Is a Gradient Descent Algorithm. *Mathematical Psychology*, 30-1, 73–80.

Golden, R. M. (1988) A Unified Framework for Connectionist Systems. *Biological Cybernetics*, 59, 109–120.

Goldsmith, J. (to appear). Harmonic phonology. To appear in J. Goldsmith (ed.) *Proceedings of the Berkeley Workshop on Nonderivational Phonology.* Univ. of Chicago Press.

Hinton, G.E. & Sejnowski, T.J. (1983). Analyzing cooperative computation. *Proceedings of the Fifth Annual Conference of the Cognitive Science Society.* Rochester, NY.

Hinton, G.E. & Sejnowski, T.J. (1986). Learning and Relearning in Boltzmann Machines. In D. E. Rumelhart, J. L. McClelland, & the PDP Research Group, *Parallel distributed processing: Explorations in the microstructure of cognition. Volume 1: Foundations.* Cambridge, MA: MIT Press/Bradford Books.

Hopfield, J.J. (1982). Neural networks and physical systems with emergent collective computational abilities. *Proceedings of the National Academy of Sciences, USA* 79, 2554–2558.

Hopfield, J.J. (1984). Neurons with graded response have collective computational properties like those of two-state neurons. *Proceedings of the National Academy of Sciences, USA* 81, 3088–3092.

Hopfield, J.J. (1987). Learning algorithms and probability distributions in feed-forward and feed-back networks. *Proceedings of the National Academy of Sciences, USA* 84, 8429–8433.

Lakoff, G. (1988). A suggestion for a linguistics with connectionist foundations. In D. Touretzky, G. Hinton, & T. Sejnowski (eds.), *Proceedings of the 1988 Connectionist Models Summer School.* Morgan Kaufmann Publishers.

Legendre, G., Miyata, Y. & Smolensky, P. (1990) *Harmonic Grammar - A formal multi-level connectionist theory of linguistic well-formedness: An application.* Technical report #90-4, Institute of Cognitive Science, University of Colorado at Boulder.

Rumelhart, D.E., Hinton, G.E., & Williams, R.J. (1986). Learning internal representations by error propagation. In D. E. Rumelhart, J. L. McClelland, & the PDP Research Group, *Parallel distributed processing: Explorations in the microstructure of cognition. Volume 1: Foundations.* Cambridge, MA: MIT Press/Bradford Books.

Smolensky, P. (1983). Schema selection and stochastic inference in modular environments. *Proceedings of the National Conference on Artificial Intelligence.* Washington, DC.

Smolensky, P. (1986a). Information processing in dynamical systems: Foundations of harmony theory. In D. E. Rumelhart, J. L. McClelland, & the PDP Research Group, *Parallel distributed processing: Explorations in the microstructure of cognition. Volume 1: Foundations.* Cambridge, MA: MIT Press/Bradford Books.

Smolensky, P. (1986b). Neural and conceptual interpretations of parallel distributed processing models. In J. L. McClelland, D. E. Rumelhart, & the PDP Research Group, *Parallel distributed processing: Explorations in the microstructure of cognition. Volume 2: Psychological and biological models.* Cambridge, MA: MIT Press/Bradford Books.

Smolensky, P. (1988). On the proper treatment of connectionism. *The Behavioral and Brain Sciences.* 11, 1–23.

Smolensky, P. (in press 1). Tensor product variable binding and the representation of symbolic structures in connectionist networks. *Artificial Intelligence.*

Smolensky, P. (in press 2). Connectionism, constituency, and the language of thought. In B. Loewer & G. Rey (Eds.), *Fodor and his critics.* Blackwell's.

A Parallel Constraint Satisfaction and Spreading Activation Model for Resolving Syntactic Ambiguity

Suzanne Stevenson
Department of Computer Science
University of Maryland, College Park

Abstract

This paper describes a computational architecture whose emergent properties yield an explanatory theory of human structural disambiguation in syntactic processing. Linguistic and computational factors conspire to dictate a particular integration of symbolic and connectionist approaches, producing a principled cognitive model of the processing of structural ambiguities. The model is a hybrid massively parallel architecture, using symbolic features and constraints to encode structural alternatives, and numeric spreading activation to capture structural preferences. The model provides a unifying explanation of a range of serial and parallel behaviors observed in the processing of structural alternatives. Furthermore, the inherent properties of active symbolic and numeric information correspond to general cognitive mechanisms which subsume a number of proposed structural preference strategies.

1 Introduction

It has been repeatedly demonstrated that people have little trouble in processing structurally ambiguous sentences; moreover, they yield consistent structural preferences in the face of ambiguity. Yet theories of human structural preferences have progressed little beyond the stage of unrelated descriptions of each piece of the psychological data. The research described here aims to shed light on the cognitive principles used in structural disambiguation by exploring the computational mechanisms which underlie them. The goal is not to create a parser in which human structural preferences are built in, but to design a parsing architecture whose basic properties *predict* those preferences.

A predictive theory of structural disambiguation emerges from the active, distributed nature of the computational model described here. The model is a hybrid massively parallel architecture, combining symbolic constraint satisfaction and numeric spreading activation. Symbolic features and constraints based on Chomsky's (1981, 1986) Government-Binding theory

(GB) capture multiple structural alternatives in parallel in a linguistically motivated way. Numeric spreading activation guides the choice between these structural alternatives by encoding and integrating the degree of featural compatibility, the recency of activation, and the strength of lexical preference for each possible attachment. The preference for a particular structural attachment is thus uniformly determined by an inherent mechanism of the architecture.

The remainder of this paper discusses the model and its consequences in more detail. Section 2 describes the key psycholinguistic issues which must be addressed by an explanatory theory of structural disambiguation. Section 3 presents the details of the hybrid architecture and describes the properties from which its structural disambiguation behavior emerges. In Section 4, the explanatory power of the mechanism is demonstrated. Section 5 discusses some related work on structural disambiguation, and Section 6 concludes the paper with a summary of the contributions of this research.

2 The Psycholinguistic Data

A structural ambiguity gives rise to multiple attachment possibilities for a syntactic phrase. Any model of structural disambiguation must address the two issues of how to process the valid structural alternatives for the phrase, and how to capture the structural preference factors which choose between them. This section describes some of the psycholinguistic observations related to these issues.

Serialism versus parallelism

One of the first issues that must be addressed in building a predictive model of structural preferences is the degree to which structural alternatives are processed in parallel. This is, in fact, a major open question in psycholinguistic research. Clear evidence for a serial mechanism comes from experiments which demonstrate consistent strong preferences for one resolution over another of a temporary ambiguity (Frazier, 1978). For example, in the sentence beginning:

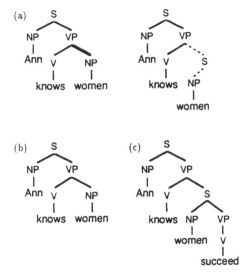

(a) ——— preferred ······ non-preferred

(b) preferred resolution of the ambiguity.

(c) non-preferred resolution of the ambiguity.

Figure 1: Attachment possibilities for *women*.

Ann knows [NP women] ...,

the attachment of the NP is temporarily ambiguous, as shown in Figure 1. The sentence may end after *photo* or continue "...succeed," each case resolving the ambiguity in a different way. The consistent preference for the first of these resolutions of the NP attachment indicates that the parser chooses one of the possible structural alternatives and pursues it serially.

However, equally convincing evidence for a parallel architecture emerges from experiments which reveal the availability of multiple structures in on-line processing of these temporary ambiguities (Gorrell, 1987). That is, experiments indicate that in the above example, both the NP-to-VP and the NP-to-S attachment possibilities are maintained in parallel. A major contribution of the model proposed here is that it naturally accounts for these apparently contradictory results, while other models have failed to do so. Exploiting the interesting interaction of serial and parallel qualities in fact leads to the model's ability to provide an architectural explanation for the range of serial and parallel behaviors attested in a number of psycholinguistic experiments. Section 3 describes the hybrid model which turns this tension between serial and parallel processing to its advantage.

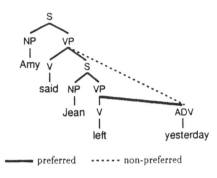

——— preferred ····· non-preferred

Figure 2: Attachment possibilities for *yesterday*.

Structural preference accounts

Numerous principles have been proposed to account for the consistent structural preferences displayed by the human parser in the face of syntactic ambiguity. For example, Minimal Attachment asserts that when the parser has a choice between two or more ways of attaching the current phrase into the parse tree, it will pick the one which requires the creation of the fewest number of new nodes (Frazier, 1978). The preference in Figure 1 for the NP to attach as the object of the verb is a clear case of Minimal Attachment: the parser prefers to attach the NP directly to the VP, rather than creating the S node to serve as its attachment site.

Another principle, Late Closure, states that the parser will prefer to keep a constituent open (that is, available to attach into) as long as possible, entailing that people will prefer to attach a phrase into the most recent open constituent (Frazier & Rayner, 1982). Late Closure accounts for the preferences indicated in Figures 2 and 3. In each case, the non-preferred attachment would require first closing off the open subordinate verb phrase.

Theories of lexical preferences claim that verbs have varying strengths of expectation for their possible arguments. For example, in these sentences taken from Ford, Bresnan, & Kaplan (1982):

Joe included [NPthe package [PPfor Susan]].
Joe carried [NPthe package] [PPfor Susan].

the PP attachment preferences indicated by the given bracketings result from a difference in how strongly the verbs *include* and *carry* expect a PP argument.

These are just a few of the many such accounts of the factors involved in structural disambiguation (for example, Kimball, 1973; Frazier & Fodor, 1978; Nicol, 1988; McRoy & Hirst, 1989). Although valuable as concise descriptions of a wealth of psycholinguistic phenomena, these accounts do not explain *why* the parser

(a)

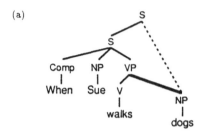

(b)

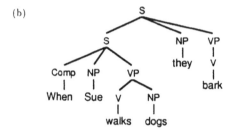

(c)

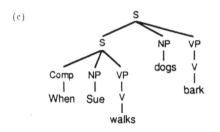

(a) —— preferred   ····· non-preferred

(b) preferred resolution of the ambiguity.

(c) non-preferred resolution of the ambiguity.

Figure 3: Attachment possibilities for *dogs*.

follows these particular patterns of structural preferences and not others. On closer examination, many of these psycholinguistic principles can be shown to be specific statements of the results of more general cognitive processes: the impetus to immediately structure incoming material, the decrease in salience of a structure over time, and the increase in salience given higher frequency or priming. In the model described here, these processes are precisely mirrored in its inherent qualities of active distributed computation, decay of activation, frequency-encoding weights, and activation of expectations. The properties of its active distributed computation are in turn strongly influenced by the model's integration of serial and parallel processing. Section 4 presents in detail how these emergent properties of the architecture predict the observed pattern of preferences.

3 The Hybrid Architecture

The rise over the past decade of the connectionist approach to cognitive modeling has generated much debate over the relative merits of serial symbolic processing models and massively parallel architectures restricted to numeric spreading activation. The debate has sparked an interest in so-called "hybrid" models which attempt to exploit the desired properties of each approach, while avoiding their respective pitfalls. A precise formulation of the components of the structural disambiguation process has motivated the design of a hybrid model in the research presented here.

Structural disambiguation involves two distinct parsing processes: identifying the allowable attachments for a phrase, and choosing between them. The first process involves the linguistic *competence* of the parser; it uses grammatical knowledge to select the valid structural alternatives. The second process is a matter of linguistic *performance*; extragrammatical factors are taken into account in determining the structural preferences. The motivation for a hybrid approach to a computational explanation of structural disambiguation arises from the necessity of capturing within a single model the properties relevant to both of these processes. Traditional serial symbolic processing models have been good at encoding discrete competence knowledge, while connectionist models are quite successful at integrating the multitude of factors affecting performance.

The question, of course, is how to combine these divergent approaches in a principled way. This can be achieved more naturally than might be expected. Properties of competence and performance themselves each converge on some type of massively parallel architecture. On the competence side, a recent trend in linguistic theory has been away from unwieldy, construction-specific rule-based systems toward a so-called "principles and parameters" approach. Government-Binding theory (GB), founded on this approach, is a constraint-based theory in which the validity of syntactic structures is determined by local licensing relations among constituent phrases. An active, distributed architecture lends itself well to the formulation of grammatical knowledge as a set of simultaneous declarative constraints which must be satisfied locally.

On the performance side of the issue, processing structural attachments requires some interesting interaction of serialism and parallelism, as noted in Section 2. Spreading activation through a parallel network inherently combines aspects of serial and parallel processing. Although highly parallel in its simultaneous communication to all neighboring nodes, activation is intrinsically serial in its spread through the space of the network. Furthermore, the massive parallelism of activation must be harnessed through some kind of focusing mechanism, or its sole effect will be network saturation.

Thus the problem domain itself strongly supports a massively parallel architecture combining symbolic constraint satisfaction and numeric spreading activation.

The design of a hybrid architecture must address the issue of how to integrate the seemingly incompatible properties of the symbolic and connectionist processing paradigms. As shown in Table 1, traditional symbolic models typically manipulate symbols serially, building new structure to solve a problem. Connectionist models, on the other hand, compute numeric activation functions in parallel, solving problems by activating the appropriate built-in structures. In the model described here, linguistic and computational principles have converged on a profitable synthesis of these approaches along each of the three relevant dimensions.

First consider the units of information. In the model, symbolic constraint satisfaction naturally encodes GB, while numeric spreading activation acts as a uniform mechanism to capture diverse sources of structural preference information. Many possibilities have previously been explored for effectively integrating symbolic and numeric computation in a cognitive model: Symbolic and numeric computation may operate at different levels of abstraction (Hendler, 1987); they may operate at the same level of abstraction, but independently (Waltz & Pollack, 1985); and activation may constrain the passing of symbolic information (Hendler, 1986). The model here incorporates a new approach, in which symbolic features constrain the spreading of activation. Symbolic constraint satisfaction directly affects the numeric activation of a node, and determines the paths along which activation can spread beyond the node. This is accomplished by using an activation function which depends in part on the *state* of a node, which is a numeric estimation of its degree of constraint satisfaction.

Both linguistic and computational reasons motivate this technique. Symbolic features, which represent linguistic competence, control what is affected by numeric activation, which guides performance. The primacy of symbolic information has a positive computational effect, since it restrains the unwanted spreading of activation. For example, many nodes represent potential syntactic attachments which will be determined to not satisfy the necessary grammatical constraints. If activation could spread across these bad attachments, lending

Symbolic Processing	Connectionism
symbols	numeric activation
serialism	parallelism
dynamic structure (creation)	fixed structure (recognition)

Table 1: Properties of Symbolic Processing and Connectionist Models.

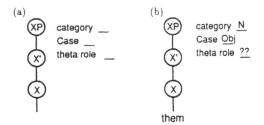

(a) $\overline{X}$ template and sample features.

(b) template instantiated and initialized by *them*.

Figure 4: The parser's generic syntactic phrases.

other nodes false support, it would make the determination of structural preferences based on activation much more difficult. Instead, a negative *state*, indicating invalid feature values, forces a node's activation to zero even when it is receiving external stimuli.

Second, the issue of dynamic versus fixed structure must be resolved. Most massively parallel parsers are based on a fixed network of nodes (Cottrell, 1985; Selman & Hirst, 1985); only the model of Waltz & Pollack (1985) has made use of dynamic structure creation. However, their model uses a traditional serial structure-building parser to construct a network corresponding to the parse(s) of the input. The model here strikes a compromise between a totally fixed network structure and the ability to create an arbitrary network structure on the fly. The parser is limited to a single fixed phrase structure template, but it may instantiate this template at will and connect the instances to the input. This "generic" syntactic phrase is then passed initializing features by the associated input. Figure 4 shows the template and a sample instantiation. All logical possibilities of inter-phrase attachments are represented by dynamically allocated attachment nodes; constraint satisfaction rules out those attachments that are invalid.

Once more, this approach is motivated by both linguistic and computational factors. The generic phrasal template is inspired by the lack of general phrase structure rules in GB. $\overline{X}$ theory, a subsystem of GB, conceives of all phrases as having the same fixed structural shape, with differences in grammatical behavior entailed by features projected from the input. From a computational perspective, this vastly simplifies the structure-building component by restricting it to uniform instantiation of fixed templates. The approach also incorporates a lexically-driven aspect which allows the model to respond to conditions in the input in a straightforward way. For example, a verb can easily determine the weights on its connections to attachment nodes, dynamically taking into account the frequency

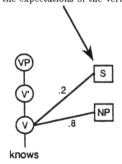

Attachment nodes corresponding to
the expectations of the verb.

knows

The verb sets the weights on the connections to nodes
which represent potential attachments.

Figure 5: Weights capture lexical frequencies.

of its various arguments, as shown in Figure 5.

Finally, the model incorporates elements of both serial and parallel computation. In other massively parallel parsers, the serial aspect of spreading activation is
the only constraint on the parallelism of the computation. Here the parallelism is further restricted, by pro-
hibiting top-down precomputation of phrase structure.
An $\overline{X}$ node may trigger multiple attachment alternatives, but it cannot cause instantiation of phrase structure based solely on an expectation. For example, in
Figure 5 the verb may establish attachment nodes corresponding to its NP and S expectations, but it cannot
license the building of an $\overline{X}$ phrase for either of these alternatives. Although quite restricted, the model is still
highly parallel in that alternative attachments based
on expectations and on phrases built by bottom-up evidence exist in parallel and compete for activation.

Again, both linguistic and computational concerns
support this approach. According to GB, phrase struc-
ture is projected from a lexical item; no $\overline{X}$ phrase can exist without being licensed in this way. Interpreting this
principle computationally as a constraint on structure
building, rather than one which checks already computed structure, increases the efficiency of the approach.
Disallowing precomputation in the model not only limits the number of nodes that are created, but also simplifies the structure building, constraint satisfaction, and
spreading activation algorithms significantly.

Not only do each of these decisions receive independent linguistic and computational support, these issues
are in fact a set of interrelated choices. The motivation for integrating symbolic and numeric computation
was presented above. By granting symbolic information a primary role in the processing of the network,

the opportunity for building structure arises. Dynamically creating structure in turn discourages top-down
precomputation. The fact that these are mutually constraining decisions yields a hybrid architecture with a
coherent cluster of properties. The following section
demonstrates that the combined result of these interdependent choices is a principled architecture from which
the desired structural disambiguation behavior emerges.

4 Predictions of the Model

Section 2 presented the two types of psycholinguistic
observation which a theory of structural disambiguation
should explain: the conflicting evidence concerning the
degree to which structural alternatives are maintained
in parallel, and the pattern of structural preferences
which people exhibit. This section describes the behavior of the model relevant to these two issues. First,
the critical properties which underlie the model's behavior will be presented. Next, the model's restricted
parallelism will be seen to resolve the seemingly contradictory evidence for serial and parallel processing of
structural alternatives. Finally, the preference behavior of the model on some illustrative cases of structural
ambiguity will be discussed.

The property of the model which yields a unified
theory of structural disambiguation is the process of
active communication of symbolic and numeric information within the parsing network. When a phrase
is created, the parser establishes nodes for the potential attachments of the phrase into the parse tree. The
phrase must then actively communicate features to its
neighbors in order to determine which attachments are
valid. These attachment nodes are the structural alternatives for the phrase; their activation level encodes
their relative preference. They receive numeric activation from their neighbors across weighted connections; these weights encode the frequency with which
one phrase expects to attach to another. Activation
decays over time if it is not reinforced. A competitive
activation method (Reggia, Marsland, & Berndt, 1988)
provides a focusing mechanism to sharpen the preference for an alternative.

Integrating serial and parallel behavior

Parallelism is restricted in the model by disallowing top-down precomputation. Thus a phrase which
is actively seeking an attachment can only communicate with other structures which have received evidence
from the input. In addition, a competitive mechanism
required to control spreading activation attempts to focus activation on a single alternative. These two properties lead to observed serial behavior in the parser, accounting for the results of psycholinguistic experiments
which support a serial mechanism. For example, the

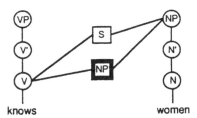

The NP may attach as the S object of *know* or as the NP object of *know*. Since the features of the first attachment expectation are incompatible with the NP, only the second attachment node remains active.

Figure 6: Initial attachment possibilities for *women*.

consistent preference for the NP-to-VP attachment in Figure 1 is simply due to the fact that it is the *only* attachment initially available for the NP. The parser has not encountered any overt evidence of a sentential object, so the NP can only make the attachment directly to the VP, as shown in Figure 6. In cases where multiple attachments are available, as was the case in Figure 2, the competitive activation mechanism will focus on one of them, also leading to seemingly serial behavior.[1] In either case, evidence that the initially preferred attachment is incorrect leads to a delay in processing, since the new structural alternative must compete for activation with the established attachment. This serial behavior mimics that of the human parser demonstrated in the analysis of eye-movements recorded while people read these types of temporarily ambiguous sentences (Frazier & Rayner, 1982).

This behavior is not inconsistent with a fundamentally parallel architecture, however. The model maintains multiple structural alternatives for which evidence exists, and projects active expectations. These expectations are particularly relevant in accounting for data showing that multiple alternatives are in some form available to the parser even when evidence from the input has not been encountered. Gorrell (1987), using a lexical decision task immediately following the NP, showed that the non-preferred structural alternative in Figure 1 (that is, the NP-to-S attachment) could prime a verb. Gorrell took this as clear evidence of precomputation of all possible structural alternatives. However, the active expectations of the model here can easily account for the observed behavior. Figure 7 shows that since the verb *know* actively expects either an NP or S argument, the S expectation primes the subsequent occurrence of a verb in the input.[2]

[1] The factors involved in focusing preferences will be discussed below.
[2] The verb in English carries tense features which trigger the building of an S node. More precisely, it is the attachment of this

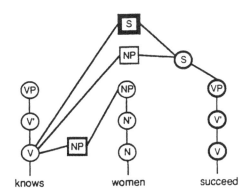

The verb's active attachment nodes encode the expectation of an NP or S object. The S expectation primes the S projected from the tense features of the verb.

Figure 7: Priming of a subsequent S.

Thus, even with the restriction of only maintaining the knowledge of alternative possibilities, rather than precomputing their structure, the model predicts the results of experiments supporting parallelism in situations of structural ambiguity. On the other hand, the restrictedness of the parallelism accounts for the serial effects displayed in experiments testing structural preferences. This explanation of the range of behaviors in processing structural ambiguities is the result of the inherent integration of aspects of serialism and parallelism in the model.

Unifying structural preferences

Fundamental properties of the model directly relate to the cognitive principles responsible for human structural preferences that were noted in Section 2. The need for a phrase to actively determine its valid attachments predicts that people will show a preference for attachments which allow immediate structuring of input. The decay of activation explains recency effects in structural preference, which correspond to a decrease in salience of older attachment sites. Weights increase salience by strengthening activation of more frequent alternatives. And finally, activation of expectations primes certain alternatives. These structural preference mechanisms interact in the resolution of each instance of structural ambiguity. A predictive model of structural disambiguation thus arises from these natural properties.

For example, the active attachment behavior of the model, in conjunction with the restricted parallelism discussed above, provides a simple account of many of the Minimal Attachment and Late Closure cases. Fig-

S node to the VP which is primed by the S expectation.

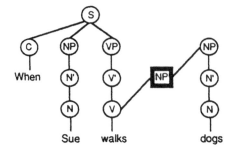

Only one attachment is initially available for the NP: as the NP object of *read*. (No main clause S node has been projected.)

Figure 8: Initial attachment possibilities for *dogs*.

ures 6 and 8 demonstrate that the alternative attachments are just not available at the time the NP is processed. Thus Minimal Attachment, represented in Figure 6, results not from an explicit comparison of the complexity of various choices as in previous models (for example, Frazier, 1987; Gorrell, 1987; Clark, 1988), but from the active nature of the model's syntactic phrases. Furthermore, cases of Late Closure as in Figures 8 are accounted for by the same properties of the model. That is, when the NP begins to actively seek an attachment, the parser has not yet projected a main clause S node, so the embedded VP is the only possible attachment site. This gives a uniform explanation of a range of structural preferences for which two attachment strategies were previously thought to be required.

The other standard cases of Late Closure, which were exemplified in Figure 2, are predicted by the recency effects which result from the decay of activation. Although both attachments are available, the higher attachment has less activation because that verb is more distant in the input and its activation has decayed. As the two verbs actively compete for the adverbial attachment, the more recent verb has the advantage of more activation and will "win" the competition. A similar effect arises from lexical frequencies, which are encoded by the weights on connections to possible arguments of a verb, and provide more or less advantage to potential attachments. (See Figure 5.) Priming in the form of an expectation also leads to the active advantage of an attachment, as discussed above and demonstrated in Figure 7.

Thus we have a model which accounts for a wide range of structural preferences with the single principled mechanism of active symbolic and numeric information. Not only does the model predict the various preferences, but it does so with a spreading activation mechanism which naturally integrates their interaction

as well.

5   Related Approaches

Recent work of McRoy & Hirst (1989) similarly attempts to unify a broad range of syntactic influences on structural preferences. However, the timing effects they seek are not a natural result of their parsing architecture; in fact, they must explicitly build in the interaction of preferences and timing. Furthermore, their serial, race-based parser is unable to account for the parallel aspects of the processing of ambiguities, as is the similar model of Frazier & Rayner (1982). Cottrell's (1985) connectionist parser results in Minimal Attachment behavior due to the nature of spreading activation, but falls short of accounting for the related principle of Late Closure with the same mechanism. In the parallel models of Gorrell (1987) and Clark (1988), the ranking mechanisms proposed for determining structural preferences are not a fundamental aspect of the parsing architecture, and each fails to capture recency and lexical preference effects.

6   Conclusions

This paper has presented a hybrid massively parallel parsing architecture which integrates symbolic and numeric processing in a linguistically and computationally motivated way. Behavior mimicking human processing of structural ambiguities emerges from the inherent properties of this architecture. The serial aspects of spreading activation and the restriction on top-down precomputation provide a natural explanation for the seemingly irreconcilable range of serial and parallel behaviors in processing structural alternatives. The property of active symbolic and numeric information leads to a principled account of structural preferences, unifying with a single mechanism the effects of various previously proposed preference strategies, such as Minimal Attachment and Late Closure.

Acknowledgments

This work has been supported by University of Maryland Graduate School Fellowships, NSF Grant IST-8451430, and the University of Maryland Institute for Advanced Computing Studies (UMIACS).

Thanks to Amy Weinberg, James Reggia, and Sven Dickinson for helpful comments on earlier drafts of this paper.

References

Chomsky, N. (1981). *Lectures on Government and Binding: The Pisa Lectures*. Dordrecht: Foris Publications.

Chomsky, N. (1986). *Barriers*. Cambridge: MIT Press.

Clark, R. (1988). "Parallel Processing and Local Optimization." Talk given at the University of Maryland Processing Workshop, December 9, 1988.

Cottrell, G. W. (1985). "Connectionist Parsing." *Proceedings of the Seventh Annual Conference of the Cognitive Science Society*, 201–211.

Ford, M., J. Bresnan, and R. Kaplan (1982). "A competence-based theory of syntactic closure." In J. Bresnan (Ed.), *The Mental Representation of Grammatical Relations*. Cambridge: MIT Press.

Frazier, L. (1978). *On Comprehending Sentences: Syntactic Parsing Strategies*. Unpublished doctoral dissertation, University of Connecticut. Distributed by Indiana University Linguistics Club.

Frazier, L. (1987). "Sentence processing." In M. Coltheart (Ed.), *Attention and Performance XII*. Hillsdale, NJ: LEA.

Frazier, L., and J. D. Fodor (1978). "The Sausage Machine: A new two-stage parsing model." *Cognition* 6, 291–325.

Frazier, L., and K. Rayner (1982). "Making and correcting errors during sentence comprehension: Eye movements in the analysis of structurally ambiguous sentences." *Cognitive Psychology* 14, 178–210.

Gorrell, P. (1987). "Structural ambiguity and syntactic priming: Toward a theory of ranked-parallel parsing." Manuscript, University of Maryland.

Hendler, J. (1986). Integrating Marker-Passing and Problem Solving: A Spreading Activation Approach to Improved Choice in Planning." Technical Report 1624, Computer Science Department, University of Maryland, College Park, Maryland.

Hendler, J. (1987). "Marker-passing and Microfeatures." *Proceedings of the Tenth International Joint Conferences on Artificial Intelligence*, 151–154.

Kimball, J. (1973). "Seven principles of surface structure parsing in natural language." *Cognition* 2:1, 15–47.

McRoy, S. and G. Hirst (1989). "Race-Based Parsing and Syntactic Disambiguation." Manuscript, University of Toronto. Submitted for publication.

Nicol, J. (1988). "Coreference Processing During Sentence Comprehension: A Review of On-Line Research." Manuscript, University of Arizona.

Reggia, J., P. Marsland, and R. Berndt (1988). "Competitive Dynamics in a Dual-Route Connectionist Model of Print-to-Sound Transformation." *Complex Systems*.

Selman, G., and G. Hirst (1985). "A Rule-Based Connectionist Parsing Scheme." *Proceedings of the Seventh Annual Conference of the Cognitive Science Society*, 212–219.

Waltz, D., and J. Pollack (1985). "Massively parallel parsing: A strongly interactive model of natural language interpretation." *Cognitive Science* 9, 51–74.

FUNCTIONAL CONSTRAINTS ON
BACKWARDS PRONOMINAL REFERENCE

Catherine L. Harris
Elizabeth A. Bates

Department of Cognitive Science
University of California, San Diego

ABSTRACT

How does the syntax of a sentence constrain speakers' selection of pronominal referents? Drawing on work by functionalist grammarians, we describe the communicative effect of using a pronoun vs. a definite noun phrase, a matrix vs. a subordinate clause, and the simple past tense vs. anterior/imperfective aspect. Our analysis allowed us to predict differences in coreference judgements for the following three sentence types:

> He worked on a top-secret project when John was ordered to quit.
> He was working on a top-secret project when John was ordered to quit.
> When he worked on a top-secret project, John was ordered to quit.

Coreference judgements from 70 speakers supported our predictions and our research program: An adequate characterization of how syntax constrains sentence comprehension requires reference to the communicative functions performed by syntactic forms.

INTRODUCTION

Pronouns are typically used to refer to persons or objects previously identified by name in a sentence or discourse, as illustrated by (1). In some sentences, pronouns can precede their referents, as in (2), while in others, such as (3), native speaker intuitions are that coreference between an initial pronoun and a subsequent lexicalized noun is blocked.

(1)   Harry met Sally when he moved to New York.
(2)   When he moved to New York, Harry met Sally.
(3)   He moved to New York when Harry met Sally.

Because the only change in form across these examples is syntactic, syntax must be responsible for differences in perceived meaning and differences in coreference judgements. How should these changes in syntactic form be characterized, and how do these forms aid listeners in determining the referent intended by speakers?

Linguists have long noted that the relationship between nodes in a phrase-structure tree appears to constrain coreference assignment. Reinhart (1983) has argued that coreference is blocked (prohibited) when an anaphoric element **c-commands** a lexical noun. If the anaphoric element does not c-command the candidate referent, then coreference is free to vary with semantic and pragmatic factors.

A relatively accessible definition of c-command is provided by Radford (1988): A node c-commands its sisters (those nodes on the same level) and their descendants. In the tree at the right, node D c-commands E, F, G, but not A, B, or C. In example (3), *he* is the sentence subject, and thus c-commands *Harry* as well as all other sentence elements. In (2), however, *Harry* c-commands *he*.

404

Numerous linguistic analyses have questioned whether c-command makes the right predictions in all cases where it is applicable (Bolinger, 1979; Bosch, 1984; Kuno, 1987). For example, because *he* is the sentence subject in (4) and (5), it c-commands *John*. The prediction is thus that coreference should be blocked in both of these sentences. Linguistic intuition is, however, that an interpretation of coreference is odd in (4) but reasonably felicitous in (5). (Examples are from Carden, 1980, cited in Kuno, 1987.)

(4)   Near John, he found a snake.
(5)   Near the girl John was talking with, he found a snake.

From a functionalist perspective, even if c-command (or some other statement of a surface relation between sentence elements) did perfectly divide all utterances into categories such as blocked and free, the job of understanding how syntactic form constrains meaning would be incomplete. What would remain to be developed is an explanation of why this syntactic device (eg., level and direction of embedding) predicts speaker coreference judgements. If the surface devices that comprise c-command prove to be only partially predictive of coreference judgements, we would still want to determine the communicative reasons why this partial correlation between form and meaning is a useful one for selecting pronominal referents.

GENERALIZATIONS ABOUT SOME FORM-FUNCTION MAPPINGS

The sentences in (6)-(9) differ in the grammatical devices they use, but they contain almost identical lexical items and describe roughly the same events. Next to each sentence we have noted our intuitions about whether coreference between the proper name and pronoun is possible.

(6)   **likely:** Bill stayed with some underground writers when he was ordered to leave the country.

(7)   **optional:** When he stayed with some underground writers, Bill was ordered to leave the country.

(8)   **optional:** He was staying with some underground writers when Bill was ordered to leave the country.

(9)   **blocked:** He stayed with some underground writers when Bill was ordered to leave the country.

The obvious changes in form between these sentences are the differences between lexicalized noun (*Bill*) and pronoun, the difference between subordinate and matrix clause, and the difference between imperfective aspect (*was staying*) and the completive aspect which is typically indicated in English with the simple past tense (*stayed*).

In the following sections, we sketch a functionalist explanation of how these differences in syntactic forms lead to differences in coreference judgements. We will then investigate the extent to which speaker judgements of coreference support our hypotheses about form-function mappings.

PRONOUNS AND DEFINITE NOUN PHRASES

What factors influence whether a speaker will use a pronoun or a full nominal to indicate reference to a person or object? Givon (1984) and Prince (1981) have described how pronouns are typically used when the intended referent is the discourse topic, or is otherwise recoverable from context. Use of a pronoun thus tends to be a signal to the listener that the current topic is unchanged: "I'm still talking about the same thing." In contrast, a speaker uses a full lexical noun to indicate a change in topic or when the identity of the pronoun can not be recovered from context. Even if a listener could, with some effort, infer the identity of a referent from the context, a lexical noun may still be used if substantial time has passed since last mention of the entity, or if other discourse characters have been discussed in the interim since last mention of the intended referent.

In the likely assignment example in (6), coding *Bill* as the sentence subject establishes him as the discourse topic. It is thus most natural to interpret the following *he* as referring to *Bill*. In the blocked case (9), a pronoun (*he*) is the sentence subject and thus established as the current discourse topic.[1] The lexicalization of *Bill* in the following clause signals that *Bill* is new information, and that either a shift in topic has occurred or that the speaker wishes to refer to a discourse entity other than the current topic. The resulting inference is that *he* has an extrasentential reference, and that Bill and *he* refer to different people.

This helps explain the difference in referent selection between the **blocked** and **likely** assignment cases, but does not shed light on why backwards pronominalization is allowed when the pronoun appears in a subordinate clause. The next section addresses this point.

MATRIX AND SUBORDINATE CLAUSES

Clauses conjoined with conjunctives/adverbials such as *when, because, before, after, while* are typically viewed by syntacticians to be matrix-subordinate pairs: the clause introduced by the adverbial is the subordinate clause, and the clause beginning with a head noun is the matrix clause. For the purposes of the current paper we will accept this definition of matrix and subordinate.

What is the communicative function of conjoining two events in a matrix-subordinate pair? Matthiessen and Thompson (1988) note that crosslinguistically, matrix-subordinate clause combining involves some type of circumstantial relation: the subordinate clause signals a condition, reason, purpose, cause, setting, manner, or means. The matrix clause is understood to be the main or focal assertion. The subordinate clause thus functions as the *context* in which to interpret or evaluate the speaker's main assertion.

A similar conception of the role of subordinate clauses has been advanced by Chafe (1988), who views matrix-subordinate clause combining as a grammaticization of what he calls *event linking*. He notes that when the subordinate clause is placed before the matrix, the clause linkage is anticipatory: the first clause must be followed by a second clause (barring a change of mind on the part of the speaker). When the matrix clause appears first, however, the listener may not know until the second clause is actually encountered that the utterance is an instance of event linking.

Why might **listeners** be willing to let a pronoun in a sentence-initial *subordinate* clause -- but not a pronoun in a sentence-initial *matrix* clause -- be coreferential with a lexical noun in a subsequent clause? Because sentence-initial subordinate clauses require a following clause, listeners know that material relevant to the current clause is immediately forthcoming. Because subordinate clauses function as a context in which to evaluate or interpret a main point, listeners will attempt, where possible, to integrate material across the clauses, or to seek reasons why material in the first is relevant to the second.

Why would **speakers** place a pronoun before a referent, violating the convention that a pronoun signals continued reference to an established topic? We doubt that the speaker's *goal* is to violate this convention. Instead, violation should be viewed as a side-effect of other communicative goals. One tendency in English and other languages is that important information, such as establishing the identity of a central discourse participant, is coded with syntactic forms which draw attention to it, such as the sentence subject (Bates and MacWhinney, 1989). How does this tendency to signal importance with sentence-subject coding interact with the subordinate-matrix asymmetry? Speakers place the context or supporting material (the subordinate clause) before the main assertion to produce an effect: it is placed first so that when the information in the main clause is encountered, it is evaluated appropriately. What happens if the supporting material needs to refer to *Bill*? This will be the case if the point of the supporting material is to situate *Bill* in space or time, or to describe some circumstantial or otherwise relevant event. If the topic is identified with a full lexical noun in the supporting material, then the situating force of this material is lessened. Instead of scene setting, the initial clause will be construed as having the

---

[1]Discourse topic is not to be equated with sentence subject. In naturally occurring text, the discourse topic is often so obvious and available that it is either not explicitly mentioned, or it is pronominalized (Givon, 1984). In interpreting sentences which do not have a prior context (such as the first sentence in a text such as a newspaper article) speakers must use what surface cues are available to determine the topic. Sentence subject is the surface device most commonly used to rapidly establish or re-establish a topic.

function of introducing a new discourse character. Example (10), as well as other sentences from Carden's (1982) corpus, illustrate this point.

(10) While *he* hadn't read the Gifford article, *Associate Dean of Yale College Martin Griffin* said that the 'best administrators are scholars', and that... (*Yale Daily News*, 31, Jan. 78).

Our hypothesis that a subordinate clause licenses backwards pronominalization by virtue of a backgrounding or scene-setting function is complemented by Bolinger's (1979) discussion of loose and tight connectives. He notes that connectives such as *and, although, before,* and *when* are "loose" connectives: they allow a change in agent or topic, and, when such adverbials are sentence-initial, they are typically accompanied by an intonation break. It is most natural for a speaker to reidentify the referent of a pronoun after a break of some kind.

Thus far, the system of explanation we have developed makes the same blocked vs. free predictions as Reinhart's c-command description: backwards reference is blocked if the pronoun is the sentence subject, but free if it is in an initial subordinate clause. In the next section, we turn to a case where c-command incorrectly predicts blocked coreference. We argue that backwards pronominalization is possible in sentences such as (8) because the imperfective or anterior aspect serves to background the initial clause with respect to a clause encoded with the simple past tense.

THE SIMPLE PAST VERSUS IMPERFECTIVE ASPECT

In this section, we investigate a case of backwards pronominal reference which has not received explicit linguistic analysis (although see Bolinger, 1979; Bosch, 1983). Although the pronoun is the sentence subject in examples (11)-(13), either an intrasentential or an extrasentential reference appears to be possible.

(11) He had been staring at the control panel for over an hour when Jack received a message from his commander.

(12) She had just reached the door to her apartment when Lois heard a shriek from the street.

(13) He was busy looking over the stolen exam when Michael heard someone opening the door.

In English, the simple past tense is typically used to denote discrete, punctate, completed events, as in (14). Events which are encoded with the simple past tense are typically construed as a narrative sequence in which the order of mention reflects the real world order of occurrence. An imperfect marker such as the progressive tense *ing* can be used to indicate that one event overlaps another, as in (15). The past perfect marker *had* signals that an event was completed prior to some reference point, as in (16). We will refer to these types of verbal aspect as **marked** to distinguish them from clauses containing the simple past tense.

(14) He walked to the store, decided what he wanted, and returned home.

(15) Walking to the store, he decided what he wanted. Upon returning home...

(16) He had walked to the store before, but this time...

When narrating a story, speakers need to convey to their listeners which events are part of the story line, and which events are to be interpreted as *comments* or *amplifications* of the story line. Drawing on an analysis of speakers of 20 different languages describing a 6 minute silent film, Hopper (1979) argues that the language of the story line (what he calls the **foreground**) differs from the language of the supporting material (the **background**). One important device for signaling the narrative foreground is the use of the completive aspect (the simple past tense in English). In contrast, when one event is simultaneous with another, or when an event is static or descriptive, the event can be construed as narrative background.

The sentences in (11)-(13) were problematic for c-command because the subject of the sentence is a pronoun, and thus c-commands all other nodes in the tree. But from the perspective of Hopper's analysis of verb aspect in discourse, the initial clause of each of these sentences is a backgrounded event. We thus hypothesize that coreference is possible in these sentences for the same reasons that coreference is possible with sentence-initial subordinate clauses: because the initial clause functions as the setting or context for evaluating the material in the following clause.

SPEAKER JUDGEMENTS

In the previous section we demonstrated that the canonical communicative functions of clause type (matrix vs. subordinate), NP type (pronoun vs. full noun), and verbal aspect (simple past versus marked aspect) could be related to our linguistic intuitions about coreference assignment. Cases of marked aspect are unusual: backgrounding is achieved in a matrix clause by describing an action with imperfective or anterior aspect. Would a survey of speakers, questioned on a substantial number of such sentences, support our intuitions that verbal aspect functions to background the event, thus allowing backwards pronominalization? Is manipulating aspect as valid or strong a cue to backgrounding as syntactic subordination?

EXPERIMENTAL MATERIALS

In the exploration of constraints on intrasentential coreference, linguists typically make judgements of blocked versus free coreference for single, isolated sentences. As mentioned previously, the most common function of pronouns is to refer back to already established discourse entities (Givon, 1984). A very stringent test of speakers' willingness to allow a pronoun to precede its antecedent would thus be to give speakers a choice between discourse characters occurring before as well as after the pronoun.

We composed 61 three-sentence passages in which the first sentence introduced two characters and the second sentence topicalized one of them. These two sentences functioned as the discourse context for the third sentence, called the **target**. For each of the 61 passages, there were three versions of the target sentence, designed to corresponded to the sentence types in (7)-(9). In the **matrix** sentences, the initial clause was not introduced by an adverbial, and occurred in the simple past tense. In the **subordinate** cases, the initial clause was prefaced with an adverbial and contained simple past tense. In the **aspect**, the initial clause was the matrix clause of the sentence, and contained anterior or imperfective aspect.

CONTEXT	THREE VERSIONS OF TARGET SENTENCE
Kenneth and Andrew helped prepare each other for the big sumo wrestling match. Andrew weighed in at 193 kilos.	He put on the wrestler's outfit just as... (**matrix**) As he put on the wrestler's outfit... (**subordinate**) He had just put on the wrestler's outfit when... (**aspect**)

... Kenneth/Andrew learned the match was canceled.

In each target sentence, either of the two discourse characters could be named. In the **relexicalization condition** the character who had been established as the discourse topic in the second sentence was renamed in the target sentence. In the **new name** condition, the non-topic was lexicalized in the target sentence.

Thirty-four raters were asked to read the 61 passages (along with filler passages) while sitting at a computer display. Each subject saw only one version of a passage. A question about the target sentence and a list of response options appeared simultaneously with each passage. For the passage above, the question and response options were as follows:

Question: Who got into wrestling gear?

Options:	Kenneth Best	Kenneth Better	Either	Andrew Better	Andrew Best	Someone Else	Ungrammatical

An additional 36 raters were asked to make reference judgements to just the target sentence from the 61 passages (the **no context** condition). Instead of being seated at a computer display, raters were given a paper-and-pencil questionnaire. Because only the target sentences were to be rated, the response options included only one proper name. Response options for the target sentence described above were as follows:

Options: Kenneth   Kenneth   Either   Someone   Ungrammatical
          Best   Better   Else

Our two factors were thus sentence type (three levels: **matrix, aspect, subordinate**) and discourse condition (three levels: **relexicalization, new name, no context.**)

HYPOTHESES

The **aspect** sentence type resembles the **matrix** in syntactic form, but resembles the **subordinate** in terms of its foreground-background structure. Will coreference judgements to the **aspect** targets be more similar to the pattern for the **subordinate** case or the **matrix** case? Our hypothesis is that the **aspect** sentences will be midway between the two. The reason for this is that these sentence types contain conflicting cues: the sentence-initial pronoun is a cue to extrasentential reference, while the verbal aspect, as a cue to backgrounding, signals the listener to delay pronominal selectional until its relevance of the following clause is assessed.

We predict that the **no-context** condition will elicit a higher frequency of intrasentential referents than the **relexicalization** and **new name** conditions. This prediction comes from our characterization of the discourse function of pronouns: pronouns are used to refer to established or known discourse entities. In the absence of syntactic or semantic cues that the pronoun refers to a following NP, raters will try to find an extrasentential referent for the pronouns in our sentences. But without a previous context, raters will have to construct a context and populate it with a candidate referent. The "principle of least effort" suggests that raters will want to *minimize* the number of hypothesized discourse entities (Prince, 1981). Without a context, speakers will, if at all possible, attempt to find a reading of the sentence in which the intrasentential discourse character is the referent for the pronoun.

If this prediction is supported, it implies that judgements of blocked vs. free reference for sentences in isolation provide an inflated estimate of the conditions under which backwards pronominal reference is possible. Including a **no context** condition in the current study allows us to compare judgements of intrasentential reference for our three sentence types under two different discourse environments: an environment which encourages extrasentential reference (the **new name** condition), and an environment which encourages intrasentential reference (the **no context** condition).

RESULTS

For each passage, we calculated the percent of judgements in which raters decided that something *other* than the intrasentential proper name was the referent for the pronoun. Selection of the non-intrasentential proper name, or the "someone else" response, or the "ungrammatical" response was coded as a judgement that coreference between the pronoun and intrasentential NP was blocked (or non-preferred). ("Ungrammatical" responses were rare: only four passages received more than six such judgements.)

Figure 1 shows the percent of passages in which raters judged intrasentential reference to be blocked or non-preferred. An item-analysis anova revealed highly reliable main effects for sentence type, $F(2,120) = 72$, $p < .001$, and discourse condition $F(2,120) = 201$, $p < .001$, as well as a sentence type X discourse condition interaction, $F(4,420) = 5.2$, $p < .001$.

It is not surprising that syntactic differences in sentence type and discourse condition result in significantly different reference judgements. Of greater interest is quantifying how the *interaction* of cues affects reference selection. Within the **no context** condition, **matrix** sentence types received more blocked coreference judgements than the **aspect** sentences, $F(1,60) = 18$, $p < .001$, and **aspect** sentences

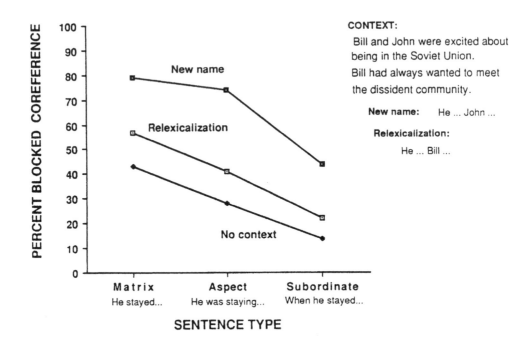

FIGURE 1: Percent of target sentences in which raters judged intrasentential reference to be blocked or non-preferred.

received more blocked judgements than **subordinate** sentences, $F(1,60) = 22$, $p < .001$. Comparable F values were obtained for the **relexicalization** condition. In the **new name** condition, however, the **aspect** sentences did not differ significantly from the **matrix** sentences, $F(1,60) = 2.1$, $p = .15$, although the **aspect** sentences did differ significantly from the **subordinate** sentences, $F(1,60) = 51$, $p < .001$.

DISCUSSION

In the first part of this paper we drew on work by functionalist grammarians to describe the communicative function of pronouns compared to lexical nouns, of subordinate clauses compared to matrix clauses, and of completive aspect compared to imperfective and anterior aspect. In the absence of other compelling syntactic or semantic information, listeners will look to the previous discourse context for a antecedent to a pronoun (Givon, 1984; Prince, 1981). What types of information would compel listeners to suspend this default strategy? We hypothesized that both syntactic subordination and durative/anterior aspect cause information to be perceived as background, context or supporting material. Because the listener knows that relevant information immediately follows a backgrounded clause, the default strategy of looking for an antecedent in the previous discourse may be relaxed.

Our survey of raters' judgements strongly supported our hypotheses. When provided with a backgrounding cue (either an aspect cue or syntactic subordination) subjects were more likely to allow a pronoun to precede its antecedent than when no backgrounding cue was present. As we predicted, however, aspect was not as strong a cue as syntactic subordination: in all discourse conditions, more intrasentential judgements were obtained for the **subordinate** sentences than for the **aspect** sentences.

What is the significance of the sentence type by discourse condition interaction? Recall that we analyzed the **aspect** sentences as containing two conflicting cues: the backgrounding cue signals that an antecedent may be coming up, but coding the pronoun as the sentence subject signals that it refers to established material. In the **no context** and **relexicalization** condition, both cues appear to be contributing to reference judgements, since the percent of blocked/non-preferred intrasentential judgements for the **aspect** case is intermediary between the two other sentence types. Why, in the **new name** condition, was the **aspect** case indistinguishable from the **matrix** case? It appears that when raters are given a legitimate choice between an intrasentential and extrasentential referent, the aspect cue is not strong or salient enough to overwhelm the pronoun-in-subject position cue. However, in a conflict situation -- such as when speakers must decide whether relexicalization of a referent following pronominalization is possible, or must choose a referent in the absence of context -- then the aspect cue does succeed in allowing backwards pronominalization.

Functional approaches to understanding constraints on anaphoric reference have sometimes been represented as attempts to "indicate that coreference is not dependent at all on properties of the syntactic tree" (Reinhart, 1983, p. 94). Our own view -- supported by the data from speakers' judgements presented here -- is that the surface form of a sentence has a strong effect on referent selection. A more accurate characterization of the functionalist position is that speakers have communicative reasons for selecting a particular syntactic encoding (Givon, 1984; Kuno, 1987). An adequate characterization of the constraints on anaphoric reference will thus need to make reference to the communicative functions performed by syntactic forms. Furthermore, the interaction we found between discourse condition and sentence type suggests that syntactic cues do not operate in isolation from each other or from the discourse environment.

In the current paper, we showed that characterizing syntactic forms in terms of their communicative functions allowed us to predict a range of coreference judgements. Future work will be required to better understand the principles constraining the interaction of several syntactic cues and discourse contexts.

REFERENCES

Bates, E.A. & MacWhinney, B. (1989). Functionalism and the competition model. In B. MacWhinney and E. A. Bates (Eds.), *The crosslinguistic study of sentence processing*. New York: Cambridge University Press.

Bolinger, D. (1979) Pronouns in discourse. In T. Givon (Ed.), *Discourse and Syntax: Syntax and Semantics* **12**. New York: Academic Press.

Bosch, P. (1983). *Agreement and anaphora: A study of the role of pronouns in syntax*. New York: Academic Press.

Carden, G. (1980). Blocked forward anaphora: C-command the surface-interpretation hypothesis. Presented at the Fifty-fifth Annual Meeting of the Linguistic Society, of America, San Antonio.

Carden, G. (1982). Backwards anaphora in discourse context. *Journal of Linguistics*, **18**, 361-387.

Chafe, W. (1984). How people use adverbial clauses. *Berkeley Linguistic Society*, **10**, 437-449.

Chafe, W. (1988). Linking intonation rules. In J. Haiman and S. Thompson, (Eds.), *Clause combining in grammar and discourse*. Philadelphia: J. Benjamins.

Givon, T. (1984). *Syntax: A functional-typological introduction, Vol. 1*. Philadelphia: J. Benjamins.

Hopper, P.J. (1979). Aspect and foregrounding in discourse. In T. Givon, (Ed.), *Discourse and Syntax, Syntax and Semantics* **12**. New York: Academic Press.

Kuno, S. (1987). *Functional syntax: Anaphora, discourse and empathy*. Chicago: Chicago University Press.

Matthiessen, C., & Thompson, S. (1988). The structure of discourse and 'subordination.' In J. Haiman and S. Thompson, (Eds.), *Clause combining in grammar and discourse*. Philadelphia: J. Benjamins.

Prince, E. (1981). Toward a taxonomy of given-new information. In P. Cole, (Ed.), *Radical pragmatics*. New York: Academic Press.

Radford, A. (1988). *Transformational grammar*. Cambridge: Cambridge University Press.

Reinhart, T. (1983). *Anaphora and semantic interpretation*. London: Croom Helm.

A semantic analysis of action verbs based on physical primitives

Jugal K. Kalita and Norman I. Badler
Department of Computer & Information Science
University of Pennsylvania
Philadelphia, PA 19104-6389

Abstract

We develop a representation scheme for action verbs and their modifiers based on decompositional analysis emphasizing the implementability of the underlying semantic primitives. Our primitives pertain to mechanical characteristics of the tasks denoted by the verbs; they refer to geometric constraints, kinematic and dynamic characteristics, and certain aspectual characteristics such as repetitiveness of one or more sub-actions, and definedness of termination points.

1 Introduction

Suppose a human agent is asked to perform the following commands in a suitable environment:

- *Put the block on the table.*
- *Turn the switch to position 6.*
- *Roll the ball across the table.*
- *Open the door.*

Each of these sentences specifies an underlying task requested of an agent. In order to perform the task, the performing agent has to "understand" the command. Understanding the imperatives requires understanding the meanings of the action verbs such as *put, turn, open* and *roll*, and the meanings of prepositional words such as *on, in* and *across*. One has to integrate the meanings of the constituents and produce a meaning of the sentence as a whole taking pragmatic factors into consideration, wherever appropriate. Having done so, one has to construct a plan for execution of the task in the environment. Only then the agent may perform the action. All the above steps need to be followed even if the agent is not human, but program-controlled such as an animated agent in a computer graphics environment or a robotic agent.

Among the myriad issues involved in the comprehension of imperatives in a physical domain and the execution of the underlying tasks, this paper primarily deals with developing a representation for the meanings of verbs and prepositions in order to characterize underlying actions. Following Badler [Badler 1989b], we develop a representation in which movements denoted by action verbs can be decomposed into "primitives" with implementable semantics.

2 Identifying the nature of components

Case frames [Fillmore 1980], or its variations have been used extensively for representing the semantic roles between noun phrases and the verb in a clause. Comprehensive analysis of case frames have indicated limitations of their representational capabilities [Palmer 1985, Levin 1979, Jackendoff 1972]. These include the existence of a large number of exceptions, lack of consensus in establishing a universal set of cases, invalidity of multiple case assignments to a noun phrase, unsubstantiated semantic overloading of the names of cases, lack of explicit characterization of inter-relationships among cases, and inadequacy of cases for representing the full complexity of concepts denoted by verbs. Considering the fact that a decompositional analysis obviates most of the above drawbacks [Palmer 1985], we opt for such an approach.

Palmer's research [Palmer 1985] in the domain of word problems in physics is similar to ours in objective and approach. However, our approach is "active", laying emphasis on implementability of the primitives, which is not the case in her study. Although her study considers some simple motion verbs, she treats them in a "static" fashion. Miller's analysis [Miller 1972] provided English paraphrases of some complex motion verbs in terms of "simpler" ones; Okada's analysis [Okada 1980] lacks in coherence and proper justifications. Schank's representation of verbs [Schank 1972], though impressive, suffers from the lack of uniformity in the levels of decomposition and explicit semantic anchoring of the primitives in terms of executability at a non-linguistic level.

Componential analysis performed here involves working from bottom up rather than from the language end. Our goal is to obtain representations as close to the physical world as possible. We obtain the components of the verbs from an analysis of the "real" actions they represent taking into consideration physical attributes only. Thus, we use the linguistic technique of componential analysis for the representation of verbal meanings, but confine ourselves to consideration of mechanistic components only. This view of verbal semantics, albeit incomplete, is not short-sighted; such a study has not been carried out in an elaborate fashion to date and is vitally essential for understanding the physical nature of actions.

The attributes we identify for the characterization of the nature of tasks denoted by action verbs deal with the following criteria: kinematic/dynamic distinctions; the type and operational nature of relevant geometric constraints, aspectual considerations such as repetitiveness, whether termination condition(s) for the verb's underlying task are naturally well-defined, or need to be inferred contextually, etc. In prevalent characterizations of actions, kinematic and dynamic characteristics of verbs have not been considered in detail. Badler mentions these attributes, but does not elaborate [Badler 1989b].

2.1 Geometric constraints

Geometric constraints can be used to clearly describe certain movements and configurations of physical objects. They provide information regarding how one or more objects or sub-parts of objects relate to one another in terms of physical contact, absolute or relative location, inter-object distance, absolute and relative orientation, or path of motion. Nelson [Nelson 1985], Rossignac [Rossignac 1986] and Barzel [Barzel and Barr 1988] use geometric constraints to describe the motion of "simple" objects. Badler discusses specification of motions through constraints for succinct expression of activities of articulated human figures composed of hierarchic sub-parts performing natural actions or tasks [Badler 1989b, Badler 1989a].

2.1.1 Constraint types

Some verbs' underlying actions can be primarily described by positional or orientational constraints.

1. *Positional constraints*: This refers to situations in which a 0-, 1-, 2- or 3-dimensional object is constrained to a 0-, 1-, 2- or 3-dimensional region of space. For example, in order to execute the command *Put the ball on the table*, an arbitrary point on the surface of the ball has to be brought in contact with (or constrained to) an arbitrary point on the surface of the table. Another example is seen in the action underlying the imperative *Put the block in the box* where one needs to constrain the block (or the volume occupied by the block) to the interior volume of the box.

2. *Orientational constraints*: Consider the meaning of the preposition *across* in the sentence *Place the ruler across the table*. The interpretation of the preposition involves several components, one of which requires that the longitudinal axis of the ruler and the longitudinal axis of the table top be perpendicular to each other. This requirement can be expressed in terms of an orientational constraint.

2.1.2 Constraint operation

Verbs dealing with constraints can be classified considering whether they denote establishment, removal, maintenance or modification of (existing) geometric constraints.

1. Verbs whose central action requires that constraints established continue to hold: attach, hold, engage, fix, grab, grasp, hook.

2. Verbs whose central action requires that already existing constraints *cease* to hold. Examples include: detach, disconnect, disengage, release.

3. Verbs which refer to modification of an already existing constraint: loosen, tighten. We do not discuss such verbs in this paper.

2.2 Aspectual components

Aspect is an inherent semantic content of a lexical item pertaining to the temporal structure of the situation denoted by the lexical item, independent of context [Passonneau 1988]. Nakhimovsky's notion of aspectual class refers to internal temporal structuring of generic situations [Nakhimovsky 1988]. Moens's use of the term aspectual category is different in that it takes speaker's perspectives into consideration [Moens and Steedman 1988]. Below, we consider two aspectual characteristics: repetitiveness and telicity.

413

2.2.1 Repetitiveness or frequentation

1. Verbs whose underlying tasks definitely need repetitions of one or more sub-actions: roll, calibrate, screw, scrub, shake, rock.

2. Verbs for which repetitions may or may not be performed (i.e., whether repetitions are performed depends on the object(s) involved, information gathered from linguistic input, etc). Some example verbs are: cut, fill, lace, load, tamp.

2.2.2 Terminal conditions

We can divide the tasks identified by verbs into two categories based on this criterion. Nakhimovsky [Nakhimovsky 1988] also discusses the telicity property of actions denoted by verbs and verbal phrases.

1. Atelic verbs: The tasks denoted by such verbs do not have properly defined end conditions. The termination point may be determined by accompanying linguistic expressions or by context-dependent, task-dependent criteria such as default resulting states of affected object(s), or obtained through reasoning from commonsense knowledge, or knowledge of the goal to achieve, or defined by explicit feedback from simulation. For example, *cut* is atelic because an object can be cut and recut repeatedly, unless the linguistic imperative specifies that the object be cut once, or twice, etc., or specifies the size of the resultant pieces. Other examples of such verbs are: fold, hold, press, scrub, shake.

2. Telic verbs: These are verbs whose underlying tasks have properly defined built-in terminal points that are reached in the normal course of events and beyond which the processes cannot continue. Some examples are: align, assemble, attach, close, detach, drop, engage, fix, fill, place, release.

2.3 Kinematic—dynamic characterization of actions

Badler [Badler 1989b] states that an approach to movement (action) representation should be able to characterize (qualitative) specifications of kinematic and dynamic information, whenever appropriate. Dynamics describes the force or effort influencing motion. Kinematics deals with direct path or goals, and motion specification. Often movements along the same spatial path and toward the same spatial goal may be represented by different verbs such as *touch*, *press* and *punch*. These distinctions can be formulated in terms of dynamic specification.

1. *Kinematic:* These are verbs whose underlying actions can be expressed as a movement along an arbitrary path or at an arbitrary velocity. Some examples are turn, roll, rotate.

2. *Dynamic:* For a verb in this category, its underlying action can be characterized by describing the force which causes it. Examples include: push, shove, pull, drag, wring, hit, strike, punch, press.

3. Both kinematic and dynamic: These are verbs which have strong path as well as force components: swing, grip/grasp (vs. touch), twist.

3 Obtaining a representation for the verbs: primitives

The primitives we use are anchored outside the linguistic domain. Currently, we work in the domain of graphical animation and hence, our primitives are executable directly in a graphics environment called JACK [Phillips 1988]. The expression of linguistic semantics in terms of tested primitives vindicates the usefulness and "completeness" of our approach. Implementation of the dynamic primitives used can be found in [Otani 1989]. They pertain to forces, torques, mass and balance. We do not discuss dynamic primitives here since they are not directly relevant to the examples in this paper. Implementation of the primitives concerned with geometric relations are discussed in [Zhao and Badler 1989].

3.1 Geometric relations and geometric constraints

We specify geometric relations in terms of the following frame structure.

Geometric-relation: spatial-type:
                      source-constraint-space:
                      destination-constraint-space:
                      selectional-restrictions:

Spatial-type refers to the type of the geometric relation specified. It may have one of two values: *positional* and *orientational*. The two slots called *source-constraint-space* and *destination-constraint-space* refer to one or more objects, or parts or features thereof which need to be related. For example, in order to execute the command *Put the cup on the table*, one brings the bottom surface of the cup into contact with the top surface of the table. The command *Put the ball on the table* requires bringing an arbitrary point on the surface of the ball in contact with the surface of the table top. Since, the items being related may be arbitrary geometric entities (i.e., points, surfaces, volumes, etc.), we call them *spaces*; the first space is called the source space and the second the destination space. The slot *selectional-restrictions* refers to conditions (static, dynamic, global or object-specific) that need to be satisfied before the constraint can be executed.

Geometric constraints are geometric goals; they are specified as follows:

Geometric-constraint: execution-type:
                      geometric-relation:

Geometric constraints are of four types. They are distinguished by the *execution-type* component. The execution class or type of a constraint may be *achieve, break, maintain* or *modify*.

3.2 Kinematics

The frame used for specifying the kinematic aspect of motion is the following:

Kinematics: motion-type:
          source:
          destination:
          path-geometry:
          velocity:
          axis:

Motions are mainly of two types: *translational* and *rotational*. In order to describe a translational motion, we need to specify the source of the motion, its destination, the trajectory of the path, and the velocity of the motion. In the case of rotational motion, the path-geometry is always circular. The velocity, if specified is angular. An axis of rotation should be specified; otherwise, it is inferred by consulting geometric knowledge about the object concerned.

3.3 Kernel actions

The central part of an action consists of one or more components: *dynamics, kinematics* and *geometric-constraints*— along with control structures stating aspectual or other complexities involved in the execution of an action. The constructs we use in the paper are: *repeat-arbitrary-times* and *concurrent*. The keyword *concurrent* is specified when two or more components, be they kinematic, dynamic or geometric constraints, need to be satisfied or achieved at the same time. The keyword *repeat-arbitrary-times* provides a means for specifying the frequentation propery of certain verbs. The verbs' semantic representation need not specify how many times the action or sub-action may need to be repeated. However, since every action is presumed to end, the number of repetitions of an action will have to be computed from simulation (based on tests for some suitable termination conditions), or by inference unless specified linguistically as in *Shake the block about fifty times*.

3.4 Representation of verbal and sentential meaning

Since our meaning representation is verb-based, the template for the representation of the meaning of a verb is also the frame for representation of meanings of sentences. The representation for a sentence has the following slots.

Verbal-representation: agent:
                   object:
                   kernel-actions:
                   selectional-restrictions:

Selectional restrictions may refer to dynamic or static properties of objects or the environment.

4 Some example verbs

4.1 A verb of establishment of positional constraint: *put*

Webster's dictionary [Woolfe 1981] defines one sense of the meaning of the verb *put* as *to place in a specified position or relationship*. We consider only the positional aspect of the meaning to obtain a lexical definition. The nature of the positional constraint is dependent upon the nature of the object, and the location specified by a locative expression. The lexical entry is

```
put (l-agent, l-object, l-locative) ⟵ agent: l-agent
                                      object: l-object
                                      kernel-action:
                                             geometric-constraint:
                                                    execution-type:achieve
                                                    spatial-type:   positional
                                                    geometric-relation: l-locative
```

This representation tells us that *put* requires us to *achieve* a *positional* constraint between two objects, parts or features thereof. It does not indicate the type of positional relation to be achieved. The details of the geometric relation to be achieved have to be provided by the locative expression used which may be in terms of prepositions such as *in, on* or *across*.

4.2 A kinematic verb: *roll*

The verb *roll* refers to two motions occurring concurrently: a rotational motion about the longitudinal axis of the object and a translational motion of the object along an arbitrary path. The rotational motion is repeated an arbitrary number of times. The representation for the verb *roll* we use is as follows:

```
roll (l-agent, l-object, path-relation)⟵
      agent: l-agent
      object:l-object
      kernel-action:
          concurrent { { kinematic:
                                motion-type:  rotational
                                axis:         longitudinal-axis-of (l-object)
                          } repeat-arbitrary-times }
                          { kinematic:
                                motion-type:  translational
                          .   path:          path-relation } }
      Selectional Restrictions:   has-circular-contour (l-object, longitudinal-axis-of (l-object))
```

4.3 A verb that removes constraints: *open*

We consider just one sense of *open*—the sense defined by Webster's Dictionary [Woolfe 1981] as *to move (as a door) from closed position*. The meaning is defined with respect to a specific position of the object under consideration. The closed position of the object can be viewed as a *constraint* on the position or orientation of the object. Thus, *open* can be considered as a verb whose underlying task undoes an existing *constraint*. The object under consideration is required to have at least two parts: a solid 2-dimensional part called the *cover* and an unfilled 2-dimensional part defined by some kind of frame: the *hole*. The meaning must capture that the agent performs an action whose result is to remove the constraint that object's cover and its hole are in one coincident plane. Additionally, the object's cover must occupy the total space available in object's hole in the constrained position. This is fulfilled by requiring that the two (sub-)objects (the hole and the cover) are of the same shape and size.

The definition for *open* is:

```
open (Ag, Obj) ⟵ agent: Ag
                 object: Obj
                 kernel-action:
                       geometric-constraint:
                             execution-type:break
```

416

```
             spatial-type:    positional
             geometric-relation: source-constraint-space: Obj • hole
                                 destination-constraint-space: Obj • cover
Selectional Restrictions:  contains-part (Obj, hole)
                           contains-part (Obj, cover)
                           area-of (Obj.cover)  = area-of (Obj • hole)
                           shape-of (Obj.cover) = shape-of (Obj • hole)
```

5 Representing meanings of prepositions

In order to provide precise, implementable meanings of prepositions, we have been influenced by Badler [Badler 1975] and Gangel [Gangel 1984]. The semantics of the linguistic locative expression has also been discussed by Herskovits [Herskovits 1986]. Talmy's work [Talmy 1983] on the relation between language and space also discusses semantic representation of prepositions. We obtain lexical entries for a selection of prepositions in [Kalita 1990]. We include one such example below. Our definitions are limited in that they work with simple, solid, non-deformable geometric objects.

5.1 A representation for *on*

Among the senses of *on* defined by Herskovits [Herskovits 1986], the one we are interested in is: *spatial entity supported by physical object*. Examples of its use are seen in sentences such as *Put the block on the table* and *Put the block on the box*. The support can come in various forms as discussed by Herskovits. One situation which is commonplace or prototypical, is the one in which the located object rests on a free, horizontal, upward facing surface of the reference object; this need not be a top surface of the reference object, though it almost always is an *outer* surface (otherwise *in* is preferred). Webster's dictionary [Woolfe 1981] defines this meaning as *a function word to indicate a position over and in contact with*. We describe this meaning of *on* as

```
on (X,Y) ←─ geometric-relation:
             spatial-type:            positional
             source-constraint-space:      any-of (self-supporting-spaces-of (X))
             destination-constraint-space: any-of (supporter-surfaces-of (Y)))
         selectional-restrictions:
             horizontal (destination-constraint-space)
             equal ((direction-of (normal-to destination-constraint-space) "global-up")
             area-of (source-constraint-space) ≤ area-of (destination-constraint-space)
             free-p (destination-constraint-space)
```

Given a geometric object, the geometrical function *self-supporting-spaces-of* obtains a list containing surfaces, lines or points on the object on which it can support itself. For example, a cube can support itself on any of its six faces, and a sphere on any point on its surface. The function *supporting-surfaces-of* finds out the surfaces on an object on which other objects can be supported. The functions *direction-of, normal-to, horizontal-p* and *area-of* are self-evident. The two directional constants *global-up* and *global-down* are defined with respect to a global reference frame.

6 Processing the sentence *Put the block on the table*

The sentence consists of the action verb *put*. The object is specified as the subject of the sentence and the location as a prepositional phrase. The meaning of the whole sentence, obtained by composing the meanings of its constituent parts [Kalita 1990] as specified by the definitions for *put* and *on*, is

```
agent: "you"
object: block-1
kernel-action: geometric-constraint:
                 execution-type:      achieve
                 spatial-type:        positional
                 geometric-relation:
                     spatial-type:            positional
                     source-constraint-space:      any-of (self-supporting-spaces-of (block-1))
```

        destination-constraint-space: any-of (supporter-spaces-of (table-1)))
    selectional-restrictions:
        horizontal-p (destination-constraint-space)
        equal (direction-of (normal-to destination-constraint-space) "global-up")
        area-of (source-constraint-space) $\leq$ area-of (destination-constraint-space)
        free-p (destination-constraint-space)

In order to execute the action dictated by this sentence, the program [Kalita 1990] looks at the knowledge stored about the block to find a part or feature of the block on which it can support itself. It can be supported on any one of its faces and no face is more salient than any other for supporting purposes. A cube (the shape of the block) has six faces and one is chosen randomly as the support area. The program searches the knowledge stored about the table for a part or feature which can be used to support other objects. It gathers that the table's function is to support "small" objects on its top which is also horizontal as required by a selectional restriction. Finally, the system concludes that one of the sides of the cube has to be brought in contact with the top of the table. Herskovits [Herskovits 1986] gives a very general discussion on the properties or attributes of objects reqired for such inferences. A planning module is needed to make the interface between the semantic representation level and the animation level complete. Details of object knowledge representation and planning can be found in [Kalita 1990]. Finally, the simulation program YAPS [Esakov and Badler 1990] performs appropriate computations and inferences where necessary, taking into consideration many aspects such as detailed geometric knowledge, default states, and knowledge of strengths and dimensions of the various parts of the body of the agent, and perform a graphical animation of the task's execution.

7   Conclusions

We have demonstrated that operational meanings of action verbs and their modifiers can be represented in terms of components pertaining to aspectuals, constraints, and kinematic/dynamic characterization. For additional examples of decomposition, the reader is referred to [Kalita 1990].

We have implemented a system incorporating the semantic processing discussed in this paper in Common Lisp on a HP workstation. The semantic output is further processed in consultation with the detailed knowledge stored about the objects under consideration. Finally, this interpreted output is used by YAPS [Esakov et al 1989, Esakov and Badler 1990] to drive a graphical animation. The successful animation of tasks starting from natural language input provides a sound anchoring for our semantic representation.

In this paper, we have not discussed the classification of lingusitic arguments of a verb as obligatory or optional, and the treatment of different classes of arguments. This issue is discussed in [Kalita 1990]. We have not also considered significant aspects of language usage such as intention, non-geometric goals and beliefs of agents. The reason is that ours is an in-depth study of the purely physical aspects of actions; thus, direct physical realizability is of primary importance. Our study has to be complemented by augmenting it with such intensional considerations for a fuller understanding.

Acknowledgements

This research is partially supported by Lockheed Engineering and Management Services (NASA Johnson Space Center), NASA Ames Grant NAG-2-426, FMC Corporation, Martin-Marietta Denver Aerospace, NSF CER Grant MCS-82-19196, and ARO Grant DAAL03-89-C-0031 including participation by the U.S. Army Human Engineering Laboratory.

References

[Badler 1975]   Badler, Norman I., 1975. *Temporal Scene Analysis: Conceptual Description of Object Movements.* Technical Report TR-80, University of Toronto, Toronto, Ontario. (University of Pennsylvania, Department of Computer and Information Science, Technical Report 76-4).

[Badler 1989a]   Badler, N.I., 1989. Artificial Intelligence, Natural Language and Simulation for Human Animation. In Magnenat-Thalmann, M. and Thalmann, D. (editors), *State-of-the-Art in Computer Animation.* Springer Verlag, New York.

[Badler 1989b]   Badler, N.I., 1989. A Representation for Natural Human Movement. In Gray, J.A. (editor), *Dance Technology: Current Applications and Future Trends.* AAHPERD Publications, Reston, VA.

[Barzel and Barr 1988]   Barzel, R. and Barr, A.H., 1988. A Modeling System Based on Dynamic Constraints. *Computer Graphics* 22(4):179–188.

[Esakov and Badler 1990]   Esakov, Jeffrey and Badler, Norman I., 1990. An Architecture for High-Level Human Task Animation Control. In Fishwick, P.A. and Modjeski, R.S. (editors), *Knowledge-Based Simulation: Methodology and Aplications.* Springer Verlag, New York.

[Esakov et al 1989]   Esakov, J.; Jung, M.; and Badler, N. I., 1989. An investigation of language input and performance timing for task animation. In *Proceedings of Graphics Interface 89*, pages 86–93. Morgan-Kaufmann, Palo Alto, Ca.

[Fillmore 1980]   Fillmore, C., 1980. The Case for Case. In Bach and Harms (editors), *Universals in Linguistic Theory*, pages 1–88. Holt, Reinhart and Winston, New York.

[Gangel 1984]   Gangel, Jeffrey, 1984. A Motion Verb Interface to a Task Animation System. Master's thesis, Department of Computer and Information Science, University of Pennsylvania.

[Herskovits 1986]   Herskovits, Annette, 1986. *Language and Spatial Cognition. Studies in Natural Language Processing.* Cambridge University Press, Cambridge, England.

[Jackendoff 1972]   Jackendoff, R.S., 1972. *Semantic Interpretation in Generative Grammar.* MIT Press, Cambridge, Massachussetts.

[Kalita 1990]   Kalita, J.K., 1990. Analysis of Some Actions Verbs and Synthesis of Underlying Tasks in an Animation Environment. Forthcoming Ph.D. Thesis, Department of Computer and Information Science, University of Pennsylvania.

[Levin 1979]   Levin, B., 1979. Predicate-Argument Structures in English. Master's thesis, MIT.

[Miller 1972]   Miller, G.A., 1972. English Verbs of Motion: A Case Study in Semantics and Lexical Memory. In Melton, A. W. and Martin, E. (editors), *Coding Processes in Human Memory*, pages 335–372. V.H. Winston and Sons.

[Moens and Steedman 1988]   Moens, Marc and Steedman, Mark, June 1988. Temporal Ontology and Temporal Reference. *Computational Linguistics* 14(2):15–28.

[Nakhimovsky 1988]   Nakhimovsky, A., June 1988. Aspect, Aspectual Class and the Temporal Structure of Narrative. *Computational Linguistics* 14(2):29–43.

[Nelson 1985]   Nelson, G., 1985. Juno, a Constraint-based Graphics System. *Computer Graphics* 19(3):235–243.

[Okada 1980]   Okada, N., 1980. A Conceptual Taxonomy of Japanese Verbs for Understanding Natural Language and Picture Patterns. In *Proceedings of ICCL*, pages 127–135.

[Otani 1989]   Otani, Ernest, 1989. Software Tools for Dynamic and Kinematic Modeling of Human Motion. Master's thesis, Department of Mechanical Engineering, University of Pennsylvania, Technical Report, MS-CIS-89-43, Philadephia, PA.

[Palmer 1985]   Palmer, Martha, 1985. *Driving Semantics in a Limited Domain.* PhD thesis, University of Edinburgh, Scotland.

[Passonneau 1988]   Passonneau, R.J., June 1988. A Computational Model of the Semantics of Tense and Aspect. *Computational Linguistics* 14(2):44–60.

[Phillips 1988]   Phillips, C.B., 1988. *JACK User's Guide.* Computer Graphics Research Laboratory, Department of Computer and Information Science, University of Pennsylvania, Philadelphia, PA.

[Rossignac 1986]   Rossignac, J.R., 1986. Constraints in Constructive Solid Geometry. In *Proceedings of Workshop on Interactive 3-D Graphics*, pages 93–110. ACM.

[Schank 1972]   Schank, Roger, 1972. Conceptual Dependency: A Theory of Natural Language Understanding. *Cognitive Psychology* 3(4).

[Talmy 1983]   Talmy, Leonard, 1983. How Language Structures Space. In Pick, H. and Acredols, L. (editors), *Spatial Orientation: Theory, Research and Application*, pages 225–282. Plenum Press, New York.

[Woolfe 1981]   Woolfe, Henry (editor), 1981. *Webster's New Collegiate Dictionary.* G. & C. Merriam Company, Springfield, MA.

[Zhao and Badler 1989]   Zhao, J. and Badler, N.I., 1989. *Ral Time Inverse Kinematics with Joint Limits and Spatial Constraints.* Technical Report MS-CIS-89-09, Department of Computer and Information Science, University of Pennsylvania.

Some Principles of the Organization of Verbs in the Mental Lexicon

Christiane Fellbaum
Cognitive Science Laboratory
Princeton University

Roger Chaffin
Trenton State College

We tested the organization of verbs in semantic memory in terms of five semantic relations. These relations are modeled on, but different from, those commonly assumed to organize the noun lexicon. In a restricted association task, subjects were given 30 seconds to generate verb-only responses to a verb stimulus, and the responses were classified in terms of the five relations. 28 different verb stimuli were selected from pairs that had been identified as examples of the relations under study. When idiosyncratic responses were discounted, the five relations accounted for 94% of all responses. The dominant relation, accounting for about 25% of the answers, turned out to be troponymy, the hyponymic *manner-of* relation, which links verbs like *munch, eat,* and *consume.* The second most frequent responses (14.4%) were examples of entailment, as between *dream* and *sleep*, followed by synonymy (*shout-holler-yell*) with 13.5% of the answers, and opposition relations (such as *enter-exit*) with 8%. The least frequently generated responses (4.1% of the total) represented the presupposition relation (exemplified by *cure-treat.*) For verbs that have a "tree" structure with three or more lexicalized taxonomic levels, associations seem to be strongest between the superordinate and what might be a "basic" level, while higher-level verbs are rarely generated. The semantically more elaborate troponyms also enter into opposition relations with each other, unlike the verbs on the superordinate level. Some verbs have a relatively "flat" structure, and are linked only to antonyms and synonyms; the organization of these verbs, which tend to cluster in the *change* verb lexicon, resembles that found for adjectives. The results lend support to a model of the structure of the verb lexicon based on these relations.

1. Conceptual Relations Among Verbs as the Organizing Principle of the Mental Lexicon

The typical high school graduate knows upwards of 40,000 words (Miller, 1988.) The organization of such a large number of words in the mental lexicon is commonly assumed to be in terms of semantic relations connecting the words to each other (see Evens, 1988, for a summary.) Miller (1969) noted that much of the available association data (Kent and Rosanoff, 1910; Russell and Jenkins, 1954; and Woodrow and Lowell,

The authors gratefully acknowledge the assistance of the members of the Experimental Methods Class at Trenton State College, Spring, 1989.

1916) could be interpreted in the light of two semantic relations, hyponymy and meronymy. Hyponymy, a relation based on category membership, links words such as *robin*
and *bird*, where the former can be said to be *a kind of* the latter. Words related by hyponymy are believed to be stored together (Collins and Quillian, 1969, Neisser, 1988, and
others), making this relation a major organizer of the mental lexicon. Evidence also
exists for an organization in terms of meronymic (or part-whole) relation, which relates
words like *wheel-car* and *tree-forest* (Chaffin, Herrmann, and Winston, 1988; Winston,
Chaffin, and Herrmann, 1987). Hyponymy and meronymy are relations that appear to be
best fitted to nouns and noun concepts (Beckwith, Fellbaum, Gross, and Miller, to
appear.) Less attention has been focused on the relations among other parts of speech.
Gross, Fischer, and Miller (1989) showed that adjectives are organized in terms of antonymy and similarity relations, and that these relations hold between individual lexical
items, rather than between entire concepts that can be expressed by more than one word.

The purpose of the present inquiry is to identify the major semantic relations
between verbs by means of an association task.

Few attempts have been made to study the organization of verbs (but see Rifkin,
1985, and Rips and Conrad, 1989.) Fellbaum and Miller (to appear) suggest, contrary to
Rips and Conrad (1989), that the organization of verbs differs substantially from that of
nouns. Instead of hyponymy, they posit a manner, or "troponymy", relation (from Greek
tropos, fashion or manner). Thus, *nibble*, *munch*, and *gorge* are troponyms of *eat*, in that
they refer to manners of eating ("manner" here denotes a variety of semantic elements,
such as speed, direction, location, time, intent, quantity, etc.)

The relation of troponymy has been extensively employed in the construction of
WordNet, an on-line lexical database constructed on the basis of theories of human lexical organization (Miller et al., 1988; Beckwith et al., to appear; Fellbaum, ms.) Postulating this relation made it possible to cast the English verb lexicon into a tight network, but
its usefulness in constructing such a network did not in itself constitute any evidence for
the existence of troponymy as an organizer of the mental lexicon. The present study was
intended to provide just such evidence.

The relation of synonymy has also been assumed to be a strong organizer of both
the noun and the verb lexicon. Furthermore, we test the status of antonymous relations as
organizers of the verb lexicon. Such pairs as *rise-fall*, *shout-whisper*, and *enter-exit*
represent different kinds of opposition (Cruse, 1986; Lyons, 1977.) The verbs in each
pair are always co-troponyms, i.e., daughters of the same superordinate, but they elaborate the concept expressed by that superordinate in contrasting ways. In such opposite
pairs as *tie-untie*, one member refers to the undoing or reversing of the action denoted by
the other member. Opposite pairs like *give-take* and *question-answer* are converse and
symmetric, in that the action denoted by one member results in the action referred to by
the other member, but performed by a different participant.

Three additional relations have been postulated as organizers of the verb lexicon.
They are variations of a relation termed "entailment" by Fellbaum and Miller (to appear).
It was argued there that this relation is the analog of the part-whole relation among
nouns. In most cases, verbs denoting activities cannot be broken down into other verbs
referring to sequentially ordered subactivities. The closest approximation to meronymy

among verbs can be found in such verb phrases as *write a paper*, denoting events or "script"-like activities (Schank and Abelson, 1977) that can be broken down into sub-activities like *submit, proofread*, etc. Note that these component activities tend not to be lexicalized, but are referred to by entire verb phrases. To derive "parts" of most English verbs, one could undertake a semantic decomposition. However, this approach would, in most cases, not yield verbs but, rather, such components as causation (cf. the celebrated example of *kill*,) negation, and aspect. While these meaning components often have a morphological surface realization (such as affixes of various kinds,) they can usually not be expressed as independently lexicalized verbs. The "entailment" relation that Fellbaum and Miller postulate instead is based on the notion of entailment, or strict implication, in logic, where a proposition P is said to entail a proposition Q iff there is no conceivable state of affairs that could make P true and Q false. Entailment here denotes the relation between two verbs V_1 and V_2 that holds when the statement *Somebody V_1-s* entails the statement *Somebody V_2-s*. For example, entailment relates such verbs as *snore* or *dream* and *sleep*, and also *drive* and *ride*, where the former activity always entails, and overlaps temporally with, the latter (i.e., you cannot snore or dream without sleeping at the same time.)

Another, similar, relation is a kind of backward presupposition; this relation is illustrated by such pairs as *succeed-try* and *digest-ingest*. Unlike the verbs in the entailment relation, the verbs in this relation are not linked by temporal inclusion: you must have performed the presupposed action prior to the presupposing one.[1]

The purpose of the present study was to see whether the semantic relations described above (synonymy, troponymy, antonymy, entailment, and presupposition) really do serve to organize people's verb lexicon. Subjects' generation of verbs associated with a stimulus verb shows whether the relations of the stimulus and the subject-generated verbs are of the kind we have postulated here. Another study, which we will report on separately, tests subjects' ability to recognize our hypothesized relation by distinguishing one verb pair from a set of pairs as being an instance of that relation and as differing from other relations. This has been shown to be the case for hyponymy and meronymy among nouns. People recognize that *robin:bird* and *oak:tree* are examples of the same relation, and that these pairs differ from those like *neck:giraffe* and *petal:flower* (Chaffin and Herrmann, 1988a.) In the present study, we tested subjects' ability to produce verbs related in the five ways outlined above.

2.0 The Restricted Association Task

Our specific aim was to test the reality of the semantic relations between verbs that underlie the structure of WordNet. In the association task that we report here subjects were asked to restrict the associations they produced to verbs. This restriction is

---

[1] Verbs linked by troponymy, such as the pair *traipse-walk*, are always linked by a (temporally including) entailment relation: a verb referring to the elaboration of another verb always entails the unelaborated verb. Similarly, entailment always accompanies certain kinds of opposition or antonymy (e.g., both members of the pair *enter* and *exit* entail *walk*.) And some verb pairs are linked by both an opposition and a presupposition relation: *tie-untie*. These secondary relations are not the subject of our study here.

somewhat artificial in that people clearly do not form mental associations between words and concepts represented by one type of syntactic category only. We also performed an unrestricted association task experiment, where subjects' responses to verb stimuli were not restricted to verbs; the results of this study, which will be reported on elsewhere, should reflect the structure of the mental lexicon more accurately.

2.1 Method

Eleven subjects were each given 28 verbs as stimuli. The 28 verbs were chosen from pairs representing typical examples of the five different relations used to code verbs in WordNet (synonymy, antonymy, troponymy, entailment, and presupposition.) From each such pair, only one verb was chosen. All of the stimuli are words occurring relatively frequently in the language (X=32.4, Francis and Kucera, 1982.) Thus, *rise* was chosen from the pair *rise-fall*, coded in WordNet as opposites, and *waltz* was selected from the pair *waltz-dance*, illustrating the relation of hyponymy (troponymy). Besides its one prominent relation to another verb, each verb is usually connected further to other verbs, and we expected the different responses to show these diverse relations.

Eleven students in an Experimental Methods Class at Trenton State College were each given a note pad on which they were instructed to write down all the verbs that came to their minds after the stimulus verb had been read aloud. They were told to use a different page to record their responses to each stimulus. For each stimulus, they were given 30 seconds to respond.

2.3 Results

The two authors independently rated the responses in terms of the five semantic relation holding between the stimulus and the response. For each relation, we had formulated an illustrative sentence with one slot each for the stimulus and the response verb. When appropriate, we differentiated between the cases where the response occurred either in the first or in the second slot in the sentence. For example, the sample sentence for the troponymy relation was *To____is to ___in some manner*. If the troponym constituted the response (in the first slot), the answer was rated as *T1*. If the superordinate term (in the second slot) was generated, the response was classified as *T2*. This directional distinction was also relevant in the cases of entailment and presupposition, but not for the "symmetric" relations of synonymy and antonymy. The overall agreement rate was 83.5%. Disagreements, which were resolved by discussion, were generally due to a coder's failing to recognize a low frequency sense of the response.

The average number of responses by the eleven subjects to each of the 28 stimuli was 36.85. Of these responses, an average of 23.96 per stimulus fell into one of the categories we had identified. Table 1 lists the frequencies with which the eleven subjects responded to each stimulus word. The frequencies are means taken across the 28 different stimulus words. Frequencies are given separately for each of the five relations under study, totalled across the five relations, and for responses that could not be classified in terms of the five relations. The relations under study accounted for 65% of all responses. The first row of the table gives the frequencies for all responses. When idiosyncratic responses were eliminated by looking only at words generated by more than

423

two subjects, the proportion of responses accounted for by the relations under study rose to 94%. Frequencies for words given by more than two subjects are listed in the second row of the table.

Inspection of the top row of Table 1 shows that the relation that appeared most frequently in the subjects' responses was troponymy (25.1%), with entailment (14.4%), synonymy (13.5%), and antonymy or opposition (8%) appearing with intermediate frequencies, and presupposition (4.1%) having the lowest frequency. These differences were significant, $F(4,108)=6.43$, $p<.001$. The ordering of frequencies was the same for words given by more than two subjects, shown in the second row of Table 1, $F(4,108)=4.86$, $p<.001$. The ordering of relations was also largely the same when only the first response to each stimulus was counted. The frequencies for first responses are shown in the third row of Table 1. Again, troponymy accounted for the most frequent (27.0%), and presupposition for the least frequent (3.2%) responses. The ordering of the relations with intermediate frequencies differed from that for all responses. Synonymy appeared almost as frequently as troponymy (22.1%), with antonymy (15.9%) and entailment (13.3%) appearing somewhat less frequently. The difference in the frequency of the five relations for the first responses was reliable, $F(4.108)=3.38$, $p<.001$.

3.0 Discussion

The results of this experiment lends support to our hypothesis about the mental organization of the verb lexicon, in that 65% of the responses could be classified in terms of the semantic relations postulated; this figure rises to 94% when idiosyncratic answers given by less than two subjects are eliminated. These answers often denote verbs that are in a co-ordination relation with the stimulus (such as *read-write*), or co-troponyms of the stimulus (such as the responses *rumba, cha-cha,* and *mambo* given to the stimulus *waltz.*) The results permit a more fine-grained analyis of the structure of the verb lexicon and the distribution of some of the semantic relations within the verb lexicon.

3.1 Troponymy

Troponyms elaborate the concepts expressed by their superordinate by adding some fairly specific manner component, which, in a semantic decomposition, could be expressed by means of an adverb or an adverbial phrase. Lexicalization is richest on the subordinate level of the troponyms, because a number of manner elaborations are usually possible for a given superordinate. Opposition relations among verbs tend to be found only among the troponyms, where the oppositions derive from the manner elaboration (e.g., *gobble* and *nibble* constitute a pair of opposing co-troponyms of *eat.*) The same kind of manner relation does not exist between the superordinates (such as *eat, drink,* and *write*) and their respective superordinates (*consume* and *communicate,* respectively), which seem somewhat more "remote." The same turned out to be true for contact verbs, such as *hit* and *break,* which are rich in troponyms but tend not to have antonyms on the superordinate level. Fellbaum (ms.) notes the general infelicitousness of transivity statements involving verbs, which can be attributed to subtle differences in the relations between verbs that are separated by more than one level. On the analogy of Rosch's et al. (1976) important work on noun concepts, one might argue that the troponyms constitute "basic-level" verbs. The manner elaborations that are part of the troponyms' elaborate semantics and whose differentiating function shows up in the opposition relations between the troponyms correspond to the large number of attributes characteristic of the basic level noun concepts studied by Rosch et al. Our results indicate that associations are strongest between the level of the troponyms and their superordinate (e.g., *munch* and *eat*,) rather than between the superordinate and its higher term (such as *eat* and *consume*.)

Subjects generated troponyms and superordinates with about equal frequency (12.6% and 12.3%, respectively.) The number of troponymic and superordinate responses to a particular stimulus depended on the level of the stimulus in its particular hierarchy. Some verbs do not have lexicalized superordinates, such as the verb *hit*, which elicited mostly troponyms like *bang, knock, punch,* and *slap*. Others do not have troponyms, such as *waltz*, which elicited its superordinate, *dance*, 11 times. In the cases of verbs that have three or more lexicalized taxonomic tiers, responses were generally limited to verbs on what might be termed the "basic" and "superordinate" levels, and subjects did not generate words from further "up" or "down" in the hierarchy. "Basic-level" verbs elicited most frequently their superordinates (for example, *sip* elicited *drink* 10 times,) while a superordinate, such as *eat*, elicited its respective superordinate "genus" term, *consume*, only once, and generated more troponyms, such as *gobble, gorge, dine, crunch, devour, binge,* and *stuff*.

3.2 Synonymy and Antonymy

While some verbs have the "vertical" structure with at least three taxonomic levels that we saw in the cases of *eat* and *drink*, there are other verbs whose structure seems to be flat, or "horizontal." These verbs are related to synonyms and verbs expressing an opposition, but they have no superordinate and few troponyms. The stimulus *shout*, for example, produced mostly synonyms, such as *bellow, yell, holler*, and only a few superordinates, such as *tell, voice, talk, interject* and *speak* (24 and 5 responses, respectively.) Another example is *close*, which generated both its antonym *open* and its synonym *shut* with equal frequency (10 responses each,) but only 5 hyponyms. Similarly, *respond* elicited most frequently a synonym *answer* (10 times) and an opposite term *question* (5 times); the superordinate term *talk* was given only twice. *Exhale* elicited its lexical and semantic opposite *inhale* (7 times,) and its entailed verb *breathe* (10 times.) *Enter* elicited its "clang" opposite, *exit*, most often, but also two other opposites, *leave* and *go*. *Enter* and *respond* exhibit a structure resembling the one found for adjectives (Gross et al., 1989), where two adjectives form a strong opposition, and where each of these "direct antonyms" in turn is related to its synonyms, which constitute "indirect antonyms." In WordNet, verbs with such a relatively "flat" structure tend to cluster in the *change* verb group, where opposition is heavily represented as a major relation in this part of the lexicon.

3.3 Entailment and Presupposition

The entailment relation with temporal overlap between the activities denoted by the two verbs was represented in a number of responses, such as *snore* and *dream* to the stimulus *sleep*. Here, the stimulus constitutes the entailed verb, and the responses the entailing activity. By contrast, *steer* elicited the entailed verbs *drive* (four times); and *chase* most frequently generated its entailed activities *run* (7 times) and *follow* (6 times). In terms of a taxonomic structure, the subjects generally moved "up", rather than "down."

Finally, we also found evidence that the presupposition relation functions as an associative link. Subjects responded to the stimulus *marry* with the presupposed verbs *love* (4 responses) and *engage* (2 responses). *Win* elicited *try, compete*, and *gamble*. Other clear examples were the frequent responses *treat* and *medicate* for the stimulus *cure*. As in the examples of entailment, subjects generally moved "up" in the hierarchy, from presupposing to presupposed verb.

4.0 Conclusion

The results of our study give evidence for the mental organization of the verb lexicon in terms of semantic relations between verbs. The five relations that were specifically tested all appear to serve as links between verbs, with some relations playing a more prominent role within the verb lexicon than others. The responses elicited by our stimuli indicate that the *manner-of* relation, or troponymy, is the most important organizer of the verb lexicon, followed by entailment, synonymy, opposition relations, and presupposition.

References

Beckwith, R. C. Fellbaum, D. Gross, & G. A. Miller (to appear). WordNet: A Lexical Database Organized on Psycholinguistic Principles. To appear in: *Proceedings of the First International Workshop on Lexical Acquisition*, ed. U. Zernik. Hillsdale, NJ: Erlbaum.

Chaffin, R. and D. J. Herrmann (1988a). The nature of semantic relations: A comparison of two approaches. In M. Evens (1988), 289-334.

Chaffin, R. and D. J. Herrmann (1988b). Effects of relation similarity on part-whole decisions. *Journal of General Psychology*, **115**, 131-139.

Chaffin, R., D. J. Herrmann, and M. Winston (1988). An empirical taxonomy of part-whole relations: Effects of part-whole relation type on relation identification. *Language and Cognitive Processes*, **3**, 17-48.

Collins, A. M., & M. R. Quillian (1969). Retrieval time from semantic memory. *Journal of Verbal Learning and Verbal Behavior*, **8**, 240-247.

Cruse, D.A. (1986). *Lexical Semantics*. New York: Cambridge University Press.

Evens, M. W. (ed.)(1988). *Relational Models of the Lexicon*. Cambridge: Cambridge Unversity Press.

Fellbaum, C. (ms). The English verb lexicon as a semantic net. Princeton University, Cognitive Science Laboratory.

Francis, W. N., and H. Kucera (1982). *Frequency Analysis of English Usage: Lexicon and Grammar*. Boston, MA: Houghton Mifflin.

Gross, D., U. Fischer, & G. A. Miller (1989). The organization of adjectival meanings. *Journal of Language and Memory*, **28**, 92-106.

Kent, G. H., and A. J. Rosanoff (1910). A study of association in insanity. *American Journal of Insanity*, **67**, 317-390.

Lyons, J. (1977). *Semantics.* 2 vols. New York: Cambridge University Press.

Miller, G. A. (1969). The organization of lexical memory: Are word associations sufficient? In: G. A. Talland and N. C. Waugh (eds.), *The Pathology of Memory.* New York: Academic Press.

Miller, G. A., C. Fellbaum, J.Kegl, & K. Miller. (1988). WordNet: An electronic lexical reference system based on theories of lexical memory. *Revue quebecoise de linguistique,* **17,** 181-213.

Miller, G. A. (1988). The challenge of universal literacy. *Science,* **24,** 1293-1299.

Neisser, U. (ed.) (1988). *Concepts and conceptual development: Ecological and intellectual factors in categorization..* Cambridge: Cambridge University press.

Rifkin, A. (1985). Evidence for a basic level in event taxonomies. *Memory and Cognition,* **13,** 538-556.

Rips, L. J., & F. G. Conrad (1989). Folk psychology of mental activities. *Psychological Review,* **96,** 187-207.

Rosch, E., C. B. Mervis, W. Gray, & P. Boyes-Braem (1976). Basic objects in natural categories. *Cognitive Psychology,* **8,** 382-439.

Russell,W. A., and J. J. Jenkins (1954). *The complete Minnesota Norms for Responses to 100 Words From the Kent-Rosanoff Word Association Tests.* Mimeograph, Department of Psychology, Minneapolis: University of Minnesota.

Schank, R. C. & R. P. Abelson (1977). *Scripts, Plans, Goals, and Understanding.* Hillsdale, NJ: Erlbaum.

Winston, M. Chaffin. R., & D. J. Hermann (1987). A taxonomy of part-whole relations. *Cognitive Science,* **11,** 417-444.

Woodrow, H., and F. Lowell (1916). Children's association frequency tables. *Psychological Monographs,* **22,** No. 97.

Appendix

Table 1
Mean Response Frequencies Across Stimulus Words (N=28),
Classified by Relation, for Eleven Subjects

Relation of Response to Stimulus

	Synonym	Antonym	Troponym	Entailment	Presupp.	Total for all Relations	Other Responses
All Responses	4.93	2.93	9.18	5.46	1.50	23.96	12.89
Responses given by more than two subjects	3.61	2.39	5.89	3.86	.86	16.60	1.29
First Response	2.43	1.75	2.93	1.46	.36	8.93	2.07

Semantic Classification of Verbs from their Syntactic Contexts: Automated Lexicography with Implications for Child Language Acquisition

Michael R. Brent
MIT AI Lab
545 Technology Square
Cambridge, Massachussets 02139
michael@ai.mit.edu

Abstract

Young children and natural language processing programs share an insufficient knowledge of word meanings. Children catch up by learning, using innate predisposition and observation of language use. However, no one has demonstrated artificial devices that robustly learn lexical semantic classifications from example sentences. This paper describes the ongoing development of such a device. An early version discovers verbs with a non-stative sense by searching in unrestricted text for verbs in syntactic constructions forbidden to statives. Our program parses unrestricted text to the extent necessary for classification. Once the parsing is done recognizing the telltale constructions is so easy even a two-year-old child could do it. In fact, Landau and Gleitman (1985) and especially Gleitman (1989) argue that children must, can, and do use the syntactic constructions in which verbs appear to support meaning acquisition. In this paper we use our program to examine the difficulty of exploiting two particular syntactic constructions to discover the availability of non-stative senses, concluding that only very little sophistication is needed. This conclusion bolsters the general position of Gleitman (1989) that children can exploit syntactic context to aid in semantic classification of verbs.

1 Introduction

Young children and natural language processing programs face a common problem: everyone else knows a lot more about words. Children indisputably catch up by learning, using innate predisposition and observation of language use. However, no one has succeeded in creating artificial devices that robustly learn lexical classifications from example sentences. This paper describes the ongoing development of such a device. An early version discovers verbs with a non-stative sense by searching in edited text[1] for verbs in syntactic constructions forbidden to statives. To do this, it must partially parse the sentence, which in turn requires knowing the major syntactic categories of most of the words. Once the partial parsing is done, recognizing the telltale constructions is so easy even a two-year-old child could do it. In fact, Landau and Gleitman (1985) and especially Gleitman (1989) argue that children must, can, and do use the syntactic constructions in which verbs appear as an aid to meaning acquisition.[2] In the first part of this paper we use our program to examine the difficulty of using two particular syntactic constructions to discover the availability of non-stative senses. We conclude that only very modest syntactic and lexical capability are needed to exploit observation of these syntactic constructions for lexical semantic classification of verbs. This conclusion bolsters the general position of Gleitman (1989) that children can exploit the syntactic structure to aid in semantic classification of verbs.[3]

The second part of this paper describes current work on expanding the scope of the acquisition program both in terms of the lexical classifications it can learn and the quantity and type of text it can learn from. One of several benefits of this extension will be the ability to apply our learning program to corpora of maternal speech, thereby bringing it closer the child acquisition questions.

We have argued for the pursuit of automatic lexical classification based on syntactic context as it relates to questions about children's lexical acquisition, but we would also like to motivate it as technology.

There is wide agreement that language users, whether natural or artificial, need detailed semantic and syntactic classifications of words. However, most current approaches to satisfying that need for artificial devices do not involve learning from examples. Interpreting the information published in machine-readable dictionaries (e.g. Boguraev and Briscoe, 1987), entering it manually in conjunction with knowledge-base construction (Knight, 1989), and studying word collocations statistically (Church and Hanks, 1990) are alternative pro-

---

[1] The text source we've used so far is the Lancaster/Oslo/Bergen (LOB) Corpus, a balanced corpus of one million words of British English. All but a small percentage is edited prose.

[2] See Pinker (1984) and Pinker (1989) for a different perspective how child learners use constraints between lexical syntax and lexical semantics.

[3] We do not intend to claim that child learners exploit our particular syntactic constructions, which merely represent our earliest attempts; instead, we mean to model the general process of meaning classification based on the syntactic environments in which verbs appear.

posals. When learning from examples is proposed, it is usually tutored learning in a controlled environment (Zernik and Dyer, 1987). Ultimately, however, any language user must be able to add new words to its lexicon, if only to accommodate the many neologisms it will encounter. Moreover, researchers rarely agree on the necessary lexical classifications, and our lexicographic needs grow with our understanding of language. Any method that requires explicit human intervention — be it that of lexicographers, knowledge engineers, or "tutors" — will lag behind both the growth of vocabulary and the growth of linguistics, as well as being subject to the uncertainties of introspection. Further, the cost of maintaining dictionaries manually in the face of this growth will remain high. By contrast, dictionaries constructed by automated learners from real sentences will not lag behind vocabulary growth; examples of current language use are free and nearly infinite. And the ability of such dictionaries to keep pace with theoretical developments is limited only by the difficulty of coming up with syntactic tests and programming the system to detect revealing sentences. Judging by our experience so far, the former task will be the more challenging one.

2 Detecting Verbs with Non-Stative Senses

In this section we discuss our study of two syntactic constructions that reveal the availability of non-stative senses for verbs. This work focuses on three questions to determine the difficulty of discovering the availability of non-stative senses:

1. Is it possible to robustly detect sentences of the type illustrated in (1) and (2) using only a simple syntactic parse tree? How simple can the parse tree be?

2. Do the progressive and rate adverb tests actually behave as advertised in text, which is subject to performance limitations? Specifically, are the syntax-semantics constraints regular enough to support semantic classification under a broad range of psychologically plausible learning strategies?

3. Can a parse tree sufficient for Item 1 be reliably, automatically recovered using only a simple parser, a relatively compact grammar description, and knowledge of the major syntactic categories of the words involved?

Section 2.1 describes the two syntactic constructions we have studied and demonstrates their relation to the semantic category in question. Sections 2.2, 2.3, and 2.4, respectively, answer the three questions in the affirmative. Section 2.5 briefly describes the mechanism and resources used by the parser behind our lexical semantic learning program.

2.1 Revealing Constructions

The distinction between stative and non-stative verbs has been a subject of interest in linguistics at least since Lakoff (1965). Giving a precise semantic characterization of statives is rather involved (see Dowty, 1979); but, roughly speaking, they are verbs that, when asserted at some time, are assumed by default to hold at all later times. Classic examples of stative verbs are *know*, *believe*, *desire*, and *love*. A number of syntactic tests have been proposed to distinguish between statives and non-statives (again see Dowty, 1979). For example, stative verbs cannot normally appear in the progressive, (1). In

(1)   a.   OK   Jon is fixing his car
         b.   *   Jon is knowing calculus

addition, statives cannot be modified by rate adverbs such as *quickly* and *slowly*, (2). We have chosen the stative/non-stative distinction, and in particular the

(2)   a.   OK   Jon fixes his car quickly
         b.   *   Jon knows calculus quickly

two tests shown (1) and (2), as test cases for our approach to learning lexical semantic classifications from the syntax of example sentences.

2.2 Required Precision of Parse Trees

Consider first how much syntactic structure is needed to detect the progressive and rate adverb constructions. To begin with, let us assume that the availability of a non-stative sense is an intrinsic property of a verb independent of factors such as the subcategorization frame in which it appears.[4] To detect progressives one need only parse the auxiliary system. Rate adverbs, by contrast, require determining what the adverb modifies. For example, adverbs may appear after the direct object, (3a), and this must not be confused with the case where they appear after the subject of an embedded clause, (3b).

(3)   a.   Jon fixed the robot quickly
         b.   Jon knew his hostess rapidly lost interest in such things

Thus it is necessary to determine the boundaries of NPs and Ss. However, it is not necessary to know much about the internal structure of these phrases.

---

[4]This is a reasonable approximation for the stative/non-stative distinction. (The obvious exceptions are verbs like *think* that are stative with a propositional argument.) Subcategorization frames are essential for determining many other lexical semantic categorizations. See Section 3.

For example, it is not necessary to know the structure of noun-noun predications, or (except in contrived cases) the attachment of PPs. Finally, there are some truly ambiguous cases that cannot be resolved by any syntactic parser not already possessed of the distinctions we are attempting to learn, (4). When

(4) a. Jon fixed the robot that had spoken slowly
     b. Jon believed the robot that had spoken slowly

encountering such sentences the strictly monotonic learner must recognize the ambiguity and decline to draw any conclusion. In summary, to the question: "Is it possible to detect sentences containing constructions (1) and (2) using only a simple syntactic parse?" we answer cautiously, "Yes, in principle."

2.3   Behavior of Test Constructions in the LOB

We now proceed to the question of whether the syntactic tests behave as advertised in real text, which is subject to the hazards of our linguistic performance as well as the rigors our competence. This question is addressed in two stages: first, we estimate the reliability of the progressive and rate-adverb constructions as indicators of non-stativity; next, we evaluate the implications of the reliability estimates for a broad range of psychologically plausible learning strategies. To investigate the reliability of our two constructions as indicators of non-stativity we processed the Lancaster/Oslo/Bergen (LOB) corpus of one million words of edited British English text. After partially parsing each sentence, our program automatically examined the parse trees and the words to see whether or not each clause in fact contained a progressive verb or a verb modified by a rate adverb. When the clause was determined to contain such a construction our program noted that in its dictionary entry for the appropriate verb. It also stored the example sentence for analysis by the researchers.[5]

Before considering the reliability estimates, note that we are exploring syntactic constructions that imply the availability of a **non-stative** sense for a verb, but not constructions that imply the availability of a **stative** sense. Accordingly, in conjecturing that a verb has a non-stative sense, we are quite concerned with false positives. Since we are not currently attempting to conjecture that verbs lack a non-stative sense there is no false negative case.[6]

If the progressive and rate-adverb tests behave ideally then every verb that shows up in one of these constructions ought to have a non-stative sense. To estimate how closely the test constructions approach that ideal, we examined by hand the observations our program recorded for the 100 verbs that occur

---

[5] Storing sentences is not, of course, required for the learning models under consideration here.

[6] After a thorough statistical analysis of our data we hope to explore the possibility of making negative conjectures stochastically. While such stochastic learning may prove valuable technologically, it is less relevant to the current focus.

most frequently in the LOB corpus. These 100 verbs occur about 50,000 times in the corpus, accounting for 50% of all verb occurrences. Of these 100 verbs, 89 occurred in either progressive or rate-adverb constructions at least once, according to our parser. Of the 89 appearing in the test constructions, only one verb, *mean*, lacks a non-stative sense. Of the 100 verbs, a total of six lack non-stative senses: *know, seem, mean, like, believe,* and *understand.* The lone false positive, *mean*, appears in a non-stative construction only once, in the anomalous sentence "It's a stroke, that was what he was meaning." The six verbs lacking non-stative senses appeared 3,835 times in the corpus with only this single occurrence in the progressive and no occurrences modified by rate adverbs.

Now we must translate the estimates of the reliability of the syntactic tests into conclusions about the reliability of various learning strategies that might employ them. The most obvious learning strategy, and the only one we have implemented so far, is to conclude that a verb has a non-stative sense immediately and irrevocably as soon as one of the telltale constructions is seen, independent of what has been seen in the past. This strategy requires no resources on the part of the learner. In particular, it requires no storage or counting of examples and no inference of any kind. Using this strategy, a learner exposed to our one-million word corpus would have mis-classified one in 89 of our verbs as non-stative, given six opportunities. However, it is obviously unrealistic to apply such a learning strategy over an unbounded body of examples — eventually any verb will show up in an anomalous context. Indeed, it is well-known that children retract overgeneralizations at many points in their language development (Brown, 1973). Nonetheless, the reliability of the syntax/semantics correlation in our sample was so strong that even the null strategy provided nearly one-hundred percent accuracy. Given only modest, psychologically plausible strategies and resources a learner could be expected to achieve one-hundred percent accuracy on the sample data. Although a more articulated and realistic learning strategy is beyond the scope of this paper, we hope to develop one shortly.

2.4   The Sufficiency of the Parser

In Section 2.2 we discussed how much structure must be imposed on sentences if the progressive and rate-adverb constructions are to be detected. In Section 2.3 we determined that the progressive and rate-adverb constructions are indeed reliable indicators of the availability of a non-stative sense. In this section we discuss the accuracy with which we can recover the parses deemed necessary in Section 2.2.

The question at hand is whether a sufficient parse tree can be reliably, automatically recovered using only a simple parser, a relatively compact grammar description, and knowledge of the major syntactic categories of the words involved. As mentioned above, we automatically parsed the LOB corpus. More precisely, we parsed each sentence to the extent necessary to determine whether or not each clause in fact contained a progressive verb or a rate adverb. Let us consider the accuracy of our parser/analyzer in terms of the all-important measure of false positives. In other words, let us consider how many verbs that were judged to be either progressive or modified by a rate adverb in fact were not. It is not practical to check manually every verb occurrence that our program judged to be progressive. Instead, we checked 300 such sentences selected at random from among the most commonly occurring verbs. This check revealed only one sentence that was not truly progressive. That sentence is shown in (5a). Recognizing pseudo-cleft constructions like (5a) would require some

(5) a. *go*: What that means in this case **is going** back to the war years...

  b. *see*: The task was solely **to see how speedily** it could be met...

  c. *compare*: ...the purchasing power of the underdeveloped countries in the commonwealth **will rise slowly compared** with that of Europe.

thought and might entail additions to our grammar description or tree-analyzer that go beyond the merely cosmetic.[7] By contrast with the progressives, rate adverbs are infrequent enough that we were able to verify manually all 281 cases our program found. In four of those cases the rate adverb actually modified a verb other than the one that our program chose. Three of these four cases had the structure of (5b), where a wh- relative is not recognized as signaling the beginning of a new clause. This reflects an oversight in our grammar description that can be corrected trivially. The one remaining case of a mis-attributed rate adverb, (5c), would again require some attention to correct. The rate of false positives in sentence detection, then can be estimated at about one serious hazard in 300 for both tests. However, none of these wrongly identified sentences occurred with verbs lacking a non-stative sense, so none resulted in false positives in word classification.

2.5   Mechanism of the Parser

Having discussed the sufficiency of our parser for the task at hand, it is worth mentioning briefly the nature of the parser. It is a local, heuristic parser developed by DeMarcken (1990). De Marcken's parser is local in that its decisions about the boundaries of phrases are independent of its decisions about their attachment. For example, a grammar writer might choose to build PPs but not attach them. Whether or not they are attached does not affect the legitimacy of phrases or their boundaries. De Marcken's parser is heuristic in that the descriptions of legal structures and the decisions about where to look for those structures are decoupled. In other words, if the only NPs that are

---

[7] A gross but effective solution would be merely to ignore all sentences beginning with wh-words. This approach would simplify the subcategorization problem as well.

relevant are those that follow verbs and prepositions then the grammar writer can describe the structure of NPs in general, but attempt to build that structure only after a verb or preposition. The fact that the subject NP would then remain unparsed poses no problem for the parsing algorithm.

Beyond the parsing engine, the major resources are the parser rules and the lexical sources. The approximately one-hundred[8] parser rules we used are a subset of a fairly large grammar written by DeMarcken (1990). The subset was selected with the aim of meeting the requirements for structure described in Section 2.2. There is no reason not to use a more complete grammar other than the goal of demonstrating how little syntactic knowledge is needed to use the progressive and rate-adverb tests. The lexical syntactic categories used by the parser are a subset of those defined by the tagged LOB corpus. These include about ten open categories, roughly the ones found in any collegiate dictionary.[9] Even the most basic subcategorization information, such as whether a verb is transitive or intransitive, is unavailable.

In addition to the parsing engine, parsing rules, and dictionary, we used a variation on the DeRose (1988) statistical disambiguator (described in De-Marcken, 1990) to deal with lexical ambiguity. Fortunately, the LOB corpus is also available in a tagged form, where each word has been manually disam-biguated. In order to check the effects of errors in statistical disambiguation on our conclusions we compared our results using the disambiguator to the results we got using the hand-tagged corpus. Specifically, we compared the number of progressive and rate-adverb constructions found for each of the verbs in the corpus. To our great surprise, the results were absolutely identical whether we used the disambiguator or the hand-tagged corpus. Although our disambiguator is fairly accurate, this identical performance on 100,000 verb occurrences dra-matically demonstrates how insensitive the identification of these constructions is to lexical syntactic error. This one observation is perhaps the most impressive of all our results so far in demonstrating the ease of using these tests under the adverse circumstances with which children are faced.

3   Scaling Up

In order to realize the promise of the approach we have taken to semantic classification we must scale it up beyond the demonstration described above. Indeed, we are currently scaling it up both in terms of the quantity and type of text it can learn from and in terms of the lexical semantic classes it can learn. The ability to deal with text from diverse sources and in diverse formats

---

[8]It is impossible to convey precisely the power of the rules. They are more compact than context-free rules, but they seem not to be greatly so.

[9]Nominally, the LOB uses 132 categories, but most of these are either closed categories (such as all inflections of *do*, *be*, etc.) or inflections of open categories. We ignore the inflec-tions, using our own morphological recognizer instead.

will have both psychological and technological benefits. On the psychological side, we hope to process corpora of transcribed maternal speech as well as the written text we have used so far. That will allow us to model much more accurately the challenges and opportunities that children would face in doing semantic classification from syntactic context. On the technological side, the log-normal frequency distribution of words in text[10] requires us to process very large quantities of text in order to compile a substantial lexicon. The sources of text that are available to us on the hundred-million words scale are completely raw, so a great deal of work is needed merely to divide the text into sentences. In addition we need sources for the major categories of the words, and these will be unavailable for many words, especially proper names. Indeed, even identifying the boundaries of proper names requires work. Despite the technological hurdles, we hope to be learning from newspaper text sometime this year.

The other way in which we must scale up is in terms of the number and diversity of semantic categories in which we can classify verbs. We are currently working on telicity, the distinction between processes and accomplishments/achievements (Brent, 1989). Work is also underway on the distinction between stage-level and object-level stative predicates (Dowty, 1979). Many of the semantic categorizations that we hope to learn, including telicity, are properties of the subcategorization frame in which a verb appears as well as of the verb itself. This means that our parser needs to be able to determine subcategorization frames. Although it currently goes a long way toward doing so, several hurdles remain. Nonetheless, as our ability to determine subcategorization improves we hope to be able to classify verbs of locomotion by their strong tendency to occur with directional prepositions and no direct object. Indeed, there are many classifications that can be learned using this type of subcategorization information. By expanding in this direction, we hope to make contact with the data on child language acquisition collected by Gleitman (1989), Pinker (1989), and others.

4   Conclusions

The data presented in this paper suggest that, with very modest syntactic and lexical capabilities and no semantic knowledge, it is possible to exploit the progressive and rate-adverb constructions to readily determine the availability of non-stative senses for many verbs. This conclusion is significant both for the study of child language acquisition and for the technology of automated, scientific lexicography. We do not claim that child learners exploit these particular constructions to do semantic classification. Rather, the psychological significance of this work lies in its demonstration that the syntactic contexts of verbs provide reliable information about their semantics which can be recovered with

---

[10]Zipf (1949)

minimal sophistication. The significance of our conclusion for scientific lexicography is its promise of permitting the automatic construction of large-scale lexica from primary sources. The automatic construction of such lexica is, in turn, one of the most promising paths in natural language processing technology.

References

[Boguraev and Briscoe, 1987] B. Boguraev and T. Briscoe. Large Lexicons for Natural Language Processing: Utilising the Grammar Coding System of LDOCE. *Comp. Ling.*, 13(3), 1987.

[Brent, 1989] M. Brent. Earning dividends on lexical knowledge: How the rich can get richer. In *Proceedings of the First Annual Workshop on Lexical Acquisition*. IJCAI, 1989.

[Brown, 1973] R. Brown. *A First Language: The Early Stages*. Harvard University Press, Cambridge, MA, 1973.

[Church and Hanks, 1990] K. Church and P. Hanks. Word association norms, mutual information, and lexicography. *Computational Linguistics*, 16, 1990.

[DeMarcken, 1990] C. DeMarcken. Parsing the LOB Corpus. In *Proceedings of the Association for Computational Linguistics*. Assocation for Computational Linguistics, 1990.

[DeRose, 1988] S. DeRose. Grammatical category disambiguation by statistical optimization. *Comp. Ling.*, 14(1), 1988.

[Dowty, 1979] D. Dowty. *Word Meaning and Montague Grammar*. Synthese Language Library. D. Reidel, Boston, 1979.

[Gleitman, 1989] L. Gleitman. The structural sources of verb meanings. Keynote address at Child Language Conference, 1989.

[Knight, 1989] K. Knight. Integrating language acquisition and knowledge acquisition. In *Proceedings of the First Annual Workshop on Lexical Acquisition*. IJCAI, 1989.

[Lakoff, 1965] G. Lakoff. *On the Nature of Syntactic Irregularity*. PhD thesis, Indiana University, 1965. Published by Holt, Rinhard, and Winston as *Irregularity in Syntax*, 1970.

[Landau and Gleitman, 1985] B. Landau and L. Gleitman. *Language and Experience*. Harvard University Press, Cambridge, MA, 1985.

[Pinker, 1984] S. Pinker. *Language Learnability and Language Development*. Harvard University Press, Cambridge, MA, 1984.

[Pinker, 1989] S. Pinker. *Learnability and Cognition: The Acquisition of Argument Structure*. MIT Press, Cambridge, MA, 1989.

[Zernik and Dyer, 1987] U. Zernik and M. Dyer. The self-extending phrasal lexicon. *Comp. Ling.*, 13(3), 1987.

[Zipf, 1949] G. Zipf. *Human Behavior and the Principle of Least Effort*. Addison-Wesley, New York, NY, 1949.

Sense Generation

or

How to Make the Mental Lexicon Flexible

Bradley Franks   Nick Braisby

Centre for Cognitive Science
University of Edinburgh
2 Buccleuch Place
Edinburgh EH8 9LW
UK

Abstract

In this paper we address some key issues in the psychology of word meaning, and thereby motivate a *Sense Generation* approach to the diversity of senses that a word may have. We note that an adequate account must allow for the flexibility and specificity of senses, and must also make appropriate distinctions between default and non-default senses of a word, and between different senses for vague and ambiguous words. We then discuss two central components of a theory of sense. Firstly, *lexons*, the stable representations, in a "mental lexicon", of word meanings; secondly, *senses*, the mentally represented descriptions associated with particular *uses* of words. We argue that the crucial issues in accounting for the diversity of sense, are: the number of lexons we need to postulate, and the relationship between the contents of those lexons and their associated senses. *Sense Selection* accounts, of which we distinguish Strong and Weak versions, both of which find considerable support in the cognitive science literature, fail to account for the flexibility and specificity of senses in a way that is consonant with linguistic evidence regarding the ambiguity of words, and psychological evidence regarding the coherence which underlies their use. We will show how the *Sense Generation* approach, by positing a nonmonotonic relationship between lexons and their senses, respects these considerations. We sketch this approach, and finally note some of its promising implications for other aspects of word meaning.

1 Introduction

In this paper, our aim is to consider some possibilities for certain aspects of a theory of word meaning, and thereby to motivate what we call *Sense Generation*. We briefly outline the crucial phenomena of flexibility and specificity of senses in Section 2. In Section 3 we sketch some of the sorts of object which might be required in a theory of sense, and, most importantly, the relations between them. This provides the apparatus for a discussion of some possible theories of senses, in Section 4. In Section 5, we turn to a more detailed exposition of Sense Generation, indicating how it may account for flexibility and specificity. Finally, we sketch some implications of this view and touch on some wider concerns for theories of word meaning.

2 Preliminaries

The phenomena of flexibility and specificity are best illustr~,'ed by example.

> Mary is giving a dinner party at her home in the country. Unfortunately, her cupboards are bare. The appetites of her voracious guests are, however, whetted by the sight of Mary's pet mouse, Midge, tucking into some mouse food, and by the sight of Mary's pet canary eating some bird food. Aware of all this food-eating, one of Mary's less subtle guests asks "Do you have any food, Mary?". Mary replies that there is none but proceeds to feed her dog, Mungo.

How are we to resolve the semantical nature of the guests' problems? They are led to believe that Mary has no food and yet they can clearly see that she has: that she has pet food, but no food fit for human consumption. We require that any theory of word meaning respect the intuition that there are different but related senses attached to the word *food*, senses, for example, which apply to different types of food: human food, dog food, bird food, etc. We employ "sense" in a similar manner to Clark (1983): as the mentally represented aspects of the semantic content of a word on a particular occasion of use; we will be more precise about this in 3. The fact that the same word can seemingly have many different senses, illustrates what we call *diversity*. One aspect of the diversity of senses is illustrated by the fact that *food* seems to have senses corresponding to both types and subtypes of food. In this case, it has senses ordinarily associated with *pet food*, and its subtypes, for example *mouse food*. This aspect of diversity is what we call *specificity*: some senses of a word appear to be more specific than others. The fact that *food* may have senses for different types, for example, senses for "mouse food", "dog food", "mouse food", etc., illustrates another aspect of diversity, *flexibility*.

Our discussion of theories of sense will concentrate on several factors: we will be concerned to respect the arguments of, among others, Clark (1983) and Murphy & Medin (1985), which we will outline in more detail later. We also require that any plausible account of reflect two important distinctions between types of senses: between senses that express default information and those that express non-default information, and between senses of vague and ambiguous words. Throughout, our overriding concern is to provide an evaluation which not only respects basic linguistic intuitions, but does so in a way that is consonant with a broad range of psychological considerations.

3 Some Components of a Theory of Sense

In this section, we will set out some aspects of a theory of sense. Two categories of object play a central role in our discussion. The first, *Senses*, are descriptions that we take to mediate relations between uses of words and their referents. These descriptions are both publicly specifiable and mentally representable. The notion of sense as employed here, although derived from that of Frege, does not carry a commitment to Frege's abstract semantical "third realm", distinct from the realms of mental and physical objects. The most important aspect of senses for our purposes is the way in which they guide linguistic behaviour. The application of a word to an entity (objects, events, substances - any individuum) is mediated by the sense of that word: in particular, the description that constitutes the sense subsumes the description of the object. So the uses of a word must be explicable in terms of the sense or senses which that word possesses. In this way, senses may be taken to classify the linguistic behaviour of agents.

The description of the phenomena of flexibility and specificity relied upon the various senses noted for *food* being different. This assumption was motivated by the application of what Evans (1976) labels the "intuitive criterion of identity" for senses. This determines that if a rational agent can both assent to and remain agnostic about the application of a referring expression to an entity when used in utterances of the same sentence, then that referring expression must have two different senses. As an illustration, reconsider Mary's dinner guests. Here, *food* is being used in different ways: sometimes it is being used to refer to all food, and at other times to types of food. So it is possible that one of Mary's guests could both assent to, and dissent from the statement, "Mary has food in her house". So it is quite felicitous for Mary to say, of the same entity (i.e., some mouse food, say), both that it is food, and that it is not. The intuitive criterion of identity for senses then requires that we treat *food* as having such different senses. Different senses express the fact that an entity may have different "modes of presentation" with respect to an agent: different ways the agent may refer to that entity. They also correspond to different ways of cognizing that entity: they are indicative of different perspectives that an agent may adopt.

The second type of object that we require is *lexons*. Most accounts of the psychology of language presuppose the existence of a "mental lexicon", in which words have "entries", that contain orthographic, phonological, morphological, syntactic and semantic information. The semantic component has been variously referred to as a "concept" or "lexical concept"; in order to avoid correlative unwarranted assumptions, we will refer to it as the lexon. A lexon, then, is a description that defines the stable mental representation in this mental lexicon; it also forms the semantic contribution of a word to the meaning of the expressions of which it forms a part. We also assume that senses are derivative in some way on lexons. That is, language users arrive at a sense for a word through first accessing its lexon. Given the multiplicity of senses which a word may have it is clear that a major problem for theories of is the relation between senses and lexons. Our discussion of such theories rests primarily on the way this issue is addressed.

Pre-theoretically, we are led to believe that senses usually outnumber the words with which they are associated: that is, the senses of a given word always number one or more. Considering the relations between words and their senses in terms of lexons then gives rise to two crucial questions. One concerns the *number* of lexons we postulate in order to effect these relations; and the other concerns the relations between the *contents* of senses and lexons.

In order to facilitate our discussion we will describe the contents of lexons and senses in terms of feature-structures like the following, which may describe the lexon for *chair*:

$$
\begin{bmatrix}
\text{legs:} & \begin{bmatrix} \text{number:} & 4 \end{bmatrix} \\
\text{seat:} & \begin{bmatrix} \text{number:} & 1 \end{bmatrix} \\
\text{made-of:} & \text{wood}
\end{bmatrix}
\tag{1}
$$

This feature-structure is not intended to be an exhaustive specification of the content of the lexon for *chair*; it is presented for illustrative purposes only. If any lexon or sense has the same feature-structure as this one, we may conclude that they are in fact identical lexons/senses. There may be cases where one feature-structure subsumes another, by having the same content or some addition of features. Another possible case is where two feature-structures cannot be ordered by this relation. The former is indicated by the relationship between the structures for *chair* and *arm-chair*, and the latter by that between *chair* and *rocking chair*:

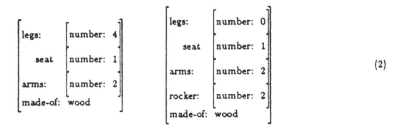

$$
\begin{bmatrix}
\text{legs:} & \begin{bmatrix} \text{number:} & 4 \end{bmatrix} \\
\text{seat} & \begin{bmatrix} \text{number:} & 1 \end{bmatrix} \\
\text{arms:} & \begin{bmatrix} \text{number:} & 2 \end{bmatrix} \\
\text{made-of:} & \text{wood}
\end{bmatrix}
\qquad
\begin{bmatrix}
\text{legs:} & \begin{bmatrix} \text{number:} & 0 \end{bmatrix} \\
\text{seat} & \begin{bmatrix} \text{number:} & 1 \end{bmatrix} \\
\text{arms:} & \begin{bmatrix} \text{number:} & 2 \end{bmatrix} \\
\text{rocker:} & \begin{bmatrix} \text{number:} & 2 \end{bmatrix} \\
\text{made-of:} & \text{wood}
\end{bmatrix}
\tag{2}
$$

The subsumption relation amounts to the kind of relation that holds between a type and one of its tokens; typically, we might assume that that defining features of a type are possessed by a token that can be categorised as a member of that type.

On just these two dimensions, the number and contents of lexons and senses, we distinguish three classes of theory. The first, Strong Sense Selection (S), is that which Clark demonstrated to be unsound; we will note some additional problems. S may appear to be a straw man; a more plausible alternative is the second class, Weak Sense Selection (W). W has two variants, both of which appear to be flawed. The third class, Sense Generation, avoids these difficulties, and is the one we would like to endorse.

4 Problematic Theories of Sense

4.1 Strong Sense Selection

Two assumptions identify S. Firstly, the number of lexons: there is a lexon for each and every sense of a given word. Secondly, the contents of the lexons and senses: S assumes that the contents of each lexon and its corresponding sense are identical. S accords well with standard model-theoretic analyses of word meaning. For example, the approach taken in Montague-style semantics requires that different interpretations for the same syntactically unambiguous linguistic string result from the same word having different basic expressions. In the case of *bank*, for example, there would be two distinct basic expressions, $bank'_1$ and $bank'_2$, in the lexicon. S then offers the possibility of being able to treat the diversity of senses which might be associated with *food* in the same way, and thus to provide a precise semantics. All of the idiosyncratic information which demarcates senses is thus represented in lexons.

The diversity of senses that might be attached to *mother* provides another illustration of S. Such senses include "adoptive mother", "biological mother", "surrogate mother", "foster mother" and "step-mother". According to S each of these senses is assigned a distinct lexon whose content expresses that of the sense.

Despite its prevalence in formal approaches to word meaning, S has some irremediable deficits. Some of these, relating to flexibility, coherence and ambiguity, are also problems of W and we will turn to these in 4.3.

However, there are also problems unique to S. One concerns the number of lexons we are led to hypothesise in order to capture diversity. This is essentially the same point that Clark made in respect of "nonce" senses; however, as we have seen, even for common nouns such as *food* and *mother* the number of senses greatly exceeds the number of words. Accordingly, in S, so does the number of lexons. This is problematic since the multiplication of lexons must make psychological sense. It is unclear that this is so in the case of S since such a multiplication places an intolerable burden on memory and presumably would result in a highly complex search procedure. These problems are difficult enough in the case of the interpretation of single words: in the case of combinations, such as simple noun phrases, there would be an explosion of combinatorial possibilities, in which the appropriate sense would have to be selected from a list comprising each and every permutation of all of the lexons associated with each constituent.

Regarding flexibility, S appears to proffer a solution that treats vagueness and context-sensitivity in the same way as ambiguity: by postulating independent lexons for each sense of a vague word. We will return to this in 4.3. It is also clear that specificity raises difficulties for S. The issue is whether we can have a limitless number of ever more specific senses for a given word. We remain agnostic about this possibility though it is clear that very many senses may be associated with the same word. However, S rules out the possible unboundedness of specificity by *fiat*. That is, the only way that S can possibly capture specificity is via the multiplication of lexons, and, given the uncontroversial assumption of a finite lexicon, the possible unboundedness of specificity could not be captured by S.

S also appears unable to distinguish between senses which express default information and those which express non-default information. For instance, the default sense for *mother* is, presumably, "biological mother" yet this sense is accorded the same status as the other senses of *mother*. That is, they are each assigned a separate lexon. Of course, S theorists may have in mind some other bit of theoretical apparatus which to capture this distinction. The fact is, though, that as it stands, S does not respect this very important distinction. An alternative to this rather straw-mannish way of trying to capture the phenomena is offered by Weak Sense Selection.

4.2   Weak Sense Selection

W is characterised by three assumptions: firstly, there may be more than one lexon for a given word; secondly, there may be more than one sense for a particular lexon. Thirdly, it is assumed that the contents of senses and the contents of corresponding lexons lie in the relation of subsumption: that is, the only possible difference between a sense and the lexon from which it comes, is that the sense may have had features added. W is more appealing than S in the following ways. Firstly, senses seem to be intrinsically context sensitive: in conventional circumstances *mother* has the sense of "biological mother", but in a social work inquiry, for example, *mother* may have the sense of "biological mother who is also a carer". A way in which this context-sensitive specificity can be captured is through some process by which features are added to the contents of lexons in a manner appropriate to context. Though W does not specify such a process it is clearly implicit in its definition. This aspect of W is in the spirit of the findings of Barsalou (1982): different senses may be different "context-dependent" elaborations of a single "context-independent" lexon.

Another appeal of W is the fact that it allows lexons to express generalisations with respect to the category to which a word applies. That is, W allows that *lion* may have various senses but that the lexon for *lion* may be a description that applies to all (and only) lions. This is again quite appealing given standard assumptions about word meaning. The arguments of Kripke (1972) and Putnam (1975) for example, assume that senses apply to all and only those individuals to which the word applies. Further, the fact that W distinguishes between the different senses deriving from a lexon, that is, between those whose content is the same as the lexon and those whose content is an elaboration of the lexon's, *may* allow for the expression of default information. That is, default information might be expressed as part of the content of lexons.

There are two extreme versions of the W thesis: one is that the number of senses and lexons are equal, which forces equivalence with S; another is what we might term the "Generality" option. This results from the assumption that a word has only one lexon, whose content may be added to and made more specific. W allows that the number of lexons may be intermediate between the number of words and the number of senses: what we will term an "Intermediate" option. Our previous discussion of S allows us to consider just the Generality and the Intermediate options of W. The Generality option would operate in the following way. *Mother*, for example, would be assigned a single lexon whose content would subsume all the senses that *mother* can have. So all of its senses result from the addition of features to this lexon's content. Given the diversity of senses for *mother* such a lexon must needs be maximally unspecific. In contrast, the Intermediate option allows *mother* to have more than one lexon underlying its senses. For example, we might have lexons for "biological mother" and "surrogate mother", say. The latter might be further specified to yield senses for "adoptive mother", "step-mother" and so on.

There are a number of problems with W some of which we will deal with in 4.3. However, we will outline some problems unique to W here. A critical problem of the Generality option is that it appears to be unable to express default information. Reconsider the example of *mother*. The appropriate lexon cannot express a relation of genetic inheritance because although some mothers are related this way to their children and some are not (e.g., foster mothers). To specify such a feature in the lexon would be to exclude mothers such as these from the domain of application of the lexon and all its associated senses, since features can only be added to the lexon and not taken away. For similar reasons, the lexon cannot express any relation of caring between mothers and children. And so on for any other feature-specification which we might ascribe to the lexon for *mother*. Arguments such as these indicate that in many cases the Generality option leaves us with a maximally unspecific lexon. This, however, flies in the face of the strong intuition that words *do* have default senses. The fact that this option renders the expression of such defaults as difficult to obtain as the expression of exceptions is a major deficit.

The Intermediate option postulates a *certain* multiplicity of lexons: there might be more than one lexon for *mother* (in contrast to the Generality option), but less than would be postulated by S. The critical problem here is exactly how the number of lexons might be determined. Whereas for S and the Generality option, there is an overt constraint on the number of lexons postulated, it is not clear what principle there could be for deciding on the number of lexons in Intermediate option. For example, what lexons might we postulate for *chair* so that it may have a sense corresponding to "rocking-chair"? Since feature-adding is the only way in which senses may be derived from lexons, the sense for "rocking-chair" shown in (2) can only be derived from a lexon which either does not specify the number of legs or specifies no legs. Under this Intermediate option we are allowed to postulate several lexons for *chair*: one corresponding to (1), say, and one corresponding to that for "rocking-chair" in (2). A problem may arise, however, in the case of a special type of rocking-chair having no legs and no rockers. Assuming that *chair* can have this sense, the question arises as to how it is derived from the lexons we have postulated. If we only have feature-adding at our disposal, such a sense simply cannot be derived from either of the lexons for chair we have postulated. Our only option is to suppose that there is another lexon for chair. The problem is that, in principle, there seems to be no bound to the number of exceptional chairs we can imagine and for each type, we would be led to posit an additional lexon. The issue then would be, what degree of exception do we rule out as invoking a new lexon? One way of constraining the number of lexons might be to determine a threshold for permitted specificity of lexons: if a particular sense is more specific than the threshold level, it must be represented as a sense deriving from a particular lexon (and not as a lexon in itself). Three problems render such a criterion untenable.

Firstly, it is not clear just how we could go about comparing the relative specificity of senses that have non-overlapping contents; for example, is "biological mother" less specific than "adoptive mother"? The operation of this criterion is perspicuous within groups of senses that *can* be ordered according to specificity (i.e., where the only difference between senses is in the degree of specification of the same set of features), but not in groups that cannot be so ordered. The general application of such a criterion would require a complete theory of content for lexons and senses, and some precise and motivated means for comparison. Neither are at present available. Secondly, to stipulate that lexons must be relatively non-specific may mean that they cannot express default information, since this is typically quite detailed and specific in nature. A third problem concerns the plausibility of postulating independent lexons to account for senses that are discriminable though related. This will be picked up in the next section.

4.3   Difficulties with Sense Selection

There are three principal flaws common to Sense Selection accounts. The first concerns the multiplication of lexons. The second concerns the ability of Sense Selection to account for the full range of flexibility. And the third concerns the underlying commitment to monotonicity, which gives rise to the first two problems.

The difficulty with assuming multiple lexons is that it is not clear to what extent they plausibly reflect mental representations. Arguments from linguistics and psychology caution against unprincipled multiplication. The linguistic considerations concern the difference between ambiguity and vagueness. Accounting for the diversity of senses by postulating distinct underlying lexons assumes that they are, synchronically, wholly independent. That is, supposing different lexons for a given word assumes they are as different as different lexemes with a single orthographic/phonological form. Postulating two lexons for *food* ("animal food" and "human food") treats *food* as an ambiguous item like *bank*. This amounts to making no distinction between different senses of a vague term, and different senses of an ambiguous term. However, if we consider any of the standard linguistic tests for ambiguity (Cruse, 1986), then we find that the independence of content assumed by postulating different lexons does not hold for examples such as *food*. For example, consider zeugmatic contexts (those which give rise to two different senses of a word at one time): "He sat on the bank whilst fishing and put his cheque in it". The strong contrast or opposition between the two senses of *bank* requires the postulation of independent lexons to account for them. In contrast, the various senses for *food* or *mother*, noted earlier, do not produce an opposition of sufficiently marked character. The examples are, rather, characterised by the relatedness of the various senses: they are distinct but clearly *not* independent.

Multiplication of lexons is also countered by psychological considerations raised by Murphy & Medin (1985). Murphy & Medin's discussion bears on the issue of the mental representations underlying the application of words to referents. In the current framework, these are lexons. The question for both W and S is whether the postulation of multiple lexons accords with psychological evidence. Murphy & Medin's arguments convince us that such multiplication is unwarranted. Consider whether the postulation of independent lexons for "animal food", and "human food", say, is justified on psychological grounds. The thrust of Murphy & Medin's arguments is to suggest that categories such as food are highly structured, and that the application of *food* to individuals thereof is highly dependent upon this structure. That is, the application of a word to entities in a category reveals what Murphy & Medin call "coherence". And the crucial point regarding coherence is that the application of a word to such an entity is dependent upon our theories concerning that entity. It is the fact that entities can be related by theories that allows their grouping together to be psychologically plausible. If lexons are to be psychologically plausible, then entities that form a coherent category (e.g., all different types of mother) should all fall under the extension of the same lexon.

However, even if we were to allow some multiplication of lexons - that is, even if the above considerations have no purchase - there are still cases in which the postulation of independent lexons to underly senses for a particular word would be implausible. These include the "contextual expressions", discussed by Clark (1983), and many examples noted by Nunberg (1977). Nunberg notes several different possible referents (and therefore, senses) for *newspaper*: a particular token of the newspaper (as in, "here's your newspaper, sir!"), the newspaper company as a whole (as in, "the newspaper's profits are less than expected!"), and a particular journalist (as in the case of a dubious piece of governmental behaviour: "don't say a word, the newspaper is here!"). It is clear that we would not want to claim that *newspaper*, for example, has a pre-stored lexon that expresses the sense of the third use ("journalist"). Yet this is precisely what Sense Selection accounts would have to hypothesise, since this sense of *newspaper* could not be said to be a simple specification of a lexon for *newspaper* (as W might aver). Clark argues that the parsing of contextual expressions (including certain denominal verbs, such as *to teapot*) stems from the *creation* of interpretations associated with those phrases. It is clear that the same kinds of considerations apply equally to Nunberg's examples. Since the only possibility of a creative process for Sense Selection is provided by the specification mechanism of W, the only contextual expressions that W could accommodate would be those that are mere specifications of pre-stored lexons. And this cannot capture the flexibility evidenced in, for example, denominal verbs. It is clear that, even though Clark's discussion of S might appear to have attacked a straw man, his arguments have a broader significance, and have played a central role in undermining the more plausible W.

The preceding discussion leads to the conclusion that none of the versions of Sense Selection are adequate to the task of accounting for the phenomena in a way that does justice to basic psychological and linguistic intuitions and requirements. The major problems stem from Sense Selection's adherence to monotonicity. That is, to the assumption that any alteration in the content of a lexon in the formation of a sense must be feature-addition. The Sense Generation approach (section 5) circumvents these problems by denying precisely this assumption and then tracing the ramifications.

444

5 Sense Generation

In opposition to the above types of theory, Sense Generation regards the variation we observe in senses to be due not to variation in lexons nor the generality of lexons but to some generative process which generates various senses from a (lexon) base.

5.1 Aspects of Sense Generation

Sense Generation is characterised by the following assumptions. Firstly, the number of lexons is identical to the number of non-ambiguous words. A single linguistic string is assigned more than one lexon if and only if it has genuinely unrelated senses, as indicated by tests for ambiguity. Secondly, the content of a lexon comprises the default sense of the word. Thirdly, the different senses of a word are generated from the lexon for that word. Fourthly, generation may result in a sense that is non-monotonically related to the lexon; that is, generation may result in a sense that does not simply add features to those of the lexon: features may be retracted or negated in the generation process.

Such a view can readily account for the kinds of example that are so problematic for Sense Selection. Recall the different senses for *newspaper*. In Sense Generation the lexon corresponds to the default sense of *newspaper*, perhaps as in "the newspaper hit the mat". The two other senses we have identified would then be non-monotonically derived from this lexon. The sense, for example, in "the newspaper's profits halved" would have to involve a retraction of those features expressing the facts that newspapers are material objects, made of paper, containing ink, etc. It would also need to include features expressing facts about businesses, finance, employment, etc. What Sense Generation claims is that this latter sense can indeed be generated from the lexon for *newspaper*. That is, there is some process by which features are negotiated. The precise nature of such processes is, clearly, a matter for further empirical enquiry but we suggest two possibilities. One is that argued for in Franks (1989) which involves the emergence of the features of a sense being constrained by some implicitly attached noun derived from an instantiation. For example, the sense of *fake gun* may be partly derived from the lexon for *replica* (thus adding features such as the degree of resemblance to a gun, and the way the object might be constructed), which is accessed as a result of the lexon for *fake* defeating certain features of that of *gun* (like firing bullets). Another is that suggested in Braisby (1989) where a related process of combining lexons results in the defeating of features. For example, the sense of *lion* which applies to stone lions, can be seen to result from the combination of a relational lexon such as "statue" and the lexon "lion". Similarly, for other non-default senses: they are derived from the combination of default and other lexons.

5.2 Implications of Sense Generation

The link between Sense Generation and Clark's *sense creation* should be noted. Clark's argument is that there is a restricted and well-defined group of contextual expressions, for which a sense creation process is necessary. Clark suggests that, for other kinds of expressions, a selection mechanism may be adequate. Since Clark's focus of attention is not conventional senses, the impression may be gained that these are not similarly contextual in nature. Where Sense Generation differs from sense creation is in its firm committment to the view that conventional uses are higly contextual and therefore require some generative process to explain the diversity of their senses. It follows that there is no clear dichotomy between contextual expressions and those used conventionally, rather there is a gradation.

Sense Generation is, in general, agnostic about the precise time-course of the role of *context* in determining senses. Indeed, it is meant as a formal, abstract characterisation of a class of theory. Consequently, it is compatible with more detailed accounts which suppose context to play a pre-access as opposed to a post-access role. That is, although context may choose from a number of possibilities for generation, it may also rule out certain possibilities prior to any generative process. Ultimately, this entails that exceptional senses need not require a longer time-course than default ones. Clearly, the exact time-course underlying the generation of senses is a matter for empirical enquiry: it suffices to note that Sense Generation is compatible with either outcome.

One implication of Sense Generation is that there are meanings of which senses are descriptions. Two questions arise: is there a meaning relation which the default sense of, say, *mother* describes? And, since there are many senses of *mother*, are there also many meanings to *mother*? Whereas the traditional theory of meaning may answer these questions in the negative, support for affirmative answers comes from *Situation Theory*. Indeed the notion of meaning relations as conditional constraints allows us to claim that default senses are descriptions of meanings. The assumption that there are many meaning relations underlying the uses of a word is also perfectly compatible with the framework of Situation Theory.

A further range of issues concerns the connection between Sense Generation and various hypothesised structures and contents for lexons. The Sense Generation approach allows us to endorse certain aspects of both *classical* and *prototype* representations, whilst rejecting problematic implications of both views. In terms of the epistemological rationale of the classical approach, Sense Generation rejects the search for common features or necessary conditions underlying the sense of a word (as a result of nonmonotonicity), whilst it allows us to retain the economical representations that would result were the search for necessary conditions successful. In contrast, the relations between the various generated senses for a word mirror the intuitive and epistemological underpinnings of family resemblance (as a result of nonmonotonicity and the emergence of new features), which is acheived without postulating prototype representations, with their attendant difficulties. That is, the various senses generated for a word in different contexts will be related by a family resemblance, in line with Wittgenstein's (1953) original formulation.

Senses are descriptions that mediate a word's reference. There may appear to be a tension between this fact and the unlimited scope for nonmonotonicity in Sense Generation: if generation defeats all of the default features of a word's lexon, then we may refer to an entity through a description having nothing in common with the usual properties of the type of referent. This point is countered by considering the *perspectival-relativity of categorisation*. A situated agent, in referring to an entity through a particular sense, can be seen to be adopting a perspective on that entity. Even though Sense Generation allows of the logical possibility that words may refer to any manner of entity, an important constraint is deemed to operate. Namely, the agent in making such a reference must be adopting a particular perspective. While a theory of perspectives is something we lack, we note that for such a reference to be posited there must be independent evidence concerning the perspective adopted. Further, we suppose that the nature of the perspectives that people may adopt is such as to determine the content of senses which they relate to referents. This may of itself limit the degree of permissible difference between the content of a word's lexon and its senses, since one of the purposes of perspectives is to allow mutual reference. That is, one constraint is that several agents must be able to share a single perspective.

6   Conclusion

In this paper, we have sketched some of the assumptions that underly prevalent views of the senses of words (Sense Selection views). We have also considered some of the problems that arise when such views attempt to account for some basic phenomena of word meaning in a way that is consonant with linguistic and psychological desiderata. This then motivated an alternative view that circumvents these difficulties (Sense Generation). Finally, we noted some of the other advantageous implications of Sense Generation.

References

Braisby N. R. (1989). Situating Word Meaning. Paper presented at the Conference on Situation Theory and its Applications, Asilomar, California. March, 1989.

Clark, H. H. (1983). Making Sense of Nonce Sense. In d'Arcais, G. B. F. and Jarvella, R. J. (eds.). *The Process of Language Understanding*. Chichester: John Wiley and Sons. 297-331.

Evans G. (1976). *The Varieties of Reference*. Oxford: Basil Blackwell.

Franks B. W. (1989) Criteria and Concepts: an Anti-Realist approach to Word Meaning. PhD. Thesis. Centre for Cognitive Science, University of Edinburgh.

Murphy G. L. & Medin D. L. (1985). The Role of Theories in Conceptual Coherence. *Psych. Rev., 92*, 289-316.

A DISTRIBUTED FEATURE MAP MODEL OF THE LEXICON *

Risto Miikkulainen
Artificial Intelligence Laboratory
Computer Science Department
University of California, Los Angeles, CA 90024
risto@cs.ucla.edu

Abstract

DISLEX models the human lexical system at the level of physical structures, i.e. maps and pathways. It consists of a semantic memory and a number of modality-specific symbol memories, implemented as feature maps. Distributed representations for the word symbols and their meanings are stored on the maps, and linked with associative connections. The memory organization and the associations are formed in an unsupervised process, based on co-occurrence of the physical symbol and its meaning. DISLEX models processing of ambiguous words, i.e. homonyms and synonyms, and dyslexic errors in input and in production. Lesioning the system produces lexical deficits similar to human aphasia. DISLEX-1 is an AI implementation of the model, which can be used as the lexicon module in distributed natural language processing systems.

1 Introduction

The lexicon in symbolic NLP systems is a list of word symbols and phrasal patterns, with pointers to conceptual memory. The memory contains syntactic and semantic knowledge about the lexicon entry in the form of declarations, or procedures which specify how the word should be interpreted in different environments [29; 1; 6]. This knowledge has been explicitly programmed into the system with specific examples in mind. The symbolic lexicons are intended to model the *processes* of lexical access, not the physical structures that implement the processes. Consequently, these models lack the capacity to account for lexical errors in human performance, as well as lexical deficits in acquired aphasia.

A number of connectionist models of lexical disambiguation have been proposed [5; 25; 7; 12; 8]. These models aim at explaining lexical processing with low-level mechanisms, and can better account for the timing of the process, as well as for certain types of performance errors and deficits. However, they are still primarily process models, detached from the physical structures. They are designed as controlled demonstrations, not as building blocks in larger NLP systems.

*This research was supported in part by an ITA Foundation grant and by fellowships from the Academy of Finland, the Emil Aaltonen Foundation, the Foundation for the Advancement of Technology and the Alfred Kordelin Foundation (Finland).

The main goal of the DISLEX project (DIStributed feature map LEXicon) is to develop a computational model of the human lexical system, which is plausible at the level of *physical structures* such as maps and pathways. The model is based on current cognitive neuroscience theories and accounts for several documented lexical deficits in acquired aphasia and dyslexia. A secondary goal is to build a practical implementation of the model for a distributed story understanding system [19].

In terms of the symbolic lexicon models, DISLEX contains both the symbol memory and the conceptual memory, and implements a mapping between them. However, DISLEX is based on distributed representations of the word symbols and the word semantics. The lexical system is seen more like a filter, which transforms an input word symbol into its semantic representation, and vice versa. The memory organization and the mapping are formed in an unsupervised self-organizing process, based on examples of co-occurrence of the word and its meaning. As a model of the lexical system, DISLEX is in good agreement with Caramazza's theory [3]. The architecture offers a simple explanation to several types of lexical errors and deficits.

2 Overview of DISLEX

DISLEX has separate symbol memories for each input and output modality (figure 1). These memories store distributed representations for the physical word symbols, which are used in communication with the external world. For example, an orthographic word representation for DOG consists of the visual form of the letters D, O, G, while the phonological representation stands for the string of phonemes do:g. The separation of modality-specific channels is intuitively compelling, since the modalities give rise to different representations, and are processed through different structures [3]. The symbol spaces are not identical across modalities, there are homophones and homographs. Considerable experimental evidence also supports dissociation of the lexical components [3] (section 8).

The semantic memory of DISLEX consists of distributed representations of meanings, called semantic words. The semantic word dog (or e.g. dog32) refers to a specific animal and contains information such as domestic, mammal, brown color etc. There is a pathway from the semantic memory to the higher level language processing systems, which use semantic representations. The semantic memory

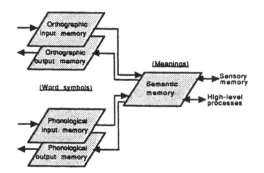

Figure 1: **The DISLEX architecture.** The physical symbol memories are modality and direction specific. The arrows indicate pathways of distributed representations.

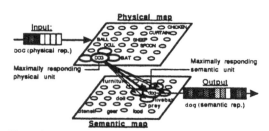

Figure 2: **Physical and semantic feature maps.** The physical input word DOG is transformed into the semantic representation of dog. The representations are vectors of real values between 0 and 1, shown by gray-scale coding. The size of the unit indicates the strength of its response. Only a few strongest associative connections are shown.

is also connected to the sensory memory, which contains visual images of objects and other sensory information. This pathway allows nonlinguistic access to the semantic memory, and provides the means for symbol grounding. The semantic word representation contains sensory information about the word referent, and the abstract word meaning originating from the high-level processes (ID and content, see [22]).

The physical and semantic memories are implemented as feature maps (figure 2). There is one map for each input and output modality and one for the semantic memory. The maps lay out each high-dimensional representation space on a 2-D area so that the similarities between words become visible. Physical words with similar form, e.g. BALL, DOLL are represented by nearby units in a physical map. In the semantic map, semantic words with similar content, e.g. livebat, prey are mapped near each other.

The physical maps are densely connected to the semantic map with associative connections. A localized activity pattern representing a symbol in the physical input map will cause a localized activity pattern to form in the semantic map, representing the meaning of the symbol (figure 2). Similarly, an active meaning activates a symbol in the physical output map. The lexicon thus transforms a physical input representation into a semantic output representation, and vice versa, and serves as an input/output filter for language processing. The physical and semantic maps are organized and the associative connections between them are formed simultaneously in an unsupervised learning process.

3 The DISLEX-1 simulation

DISLEX-1 is an AI implementation of DISLEX, designed as the lexicon module for a distributed neural network story understanding system [19]. DISLEX-1 contains a single physical modality, and the same representation space is used for both input and output. Figure 2 displays the basic architecture of DISLEX-1. Associative connections

exist in both directions (the connections from semantic to physical map are omitted from the figure), and the transformation depicted in the figure can be reversed. This is a practical design for an AI module, and illustrates the basic principles and properties of the model.

DISLEX-1 was trained with data from a sentence processing experiment [17; 21] (figure 3). In the remainder of the paper, the mechanisms and properties of DISLEX are discussed, using the DISLEX-1 simulation as an example.

4 Representations

4.1 Physical representations

A central assumption in DISLEX is that the representations in each physical modality reflect the similarities within that modality. For example, the orthographic representations for DOG and DOC are very similar, but less so in the phonological domain.

The DISLEX-1 architecture concentrates on the orthographic modality. A simple encoding scheme was used to build the distributed representations for the written words. Each character was given a value between 0 and 1 according to its darkness, i.e. how many pixels are black in its bitmap representation. The darkness values of the word's characters were then concatenated into one representation vector (figure 3). This simple representation adequately reflects the visual similarities of the orthographic word symbols.

4.2 Semantic representations

The semantic representation is a distributed representation of the meaning of the word. Semantic representations are used internally for processing in cognitive models, and they should facilitate inferencing, expectations, generalizations etc. [15; 22]. A possible solution is to compose the representation from an ID part, representing the sensory referent of the word, and a content part, which encodes the processing properties of the word in relation to other words [22]

448

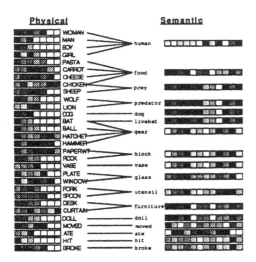

Physical

WOMAN
MAN
BOY
GIRL — human
PASTA
CARROT
CHEESE — food
CHICKEN
SHEEP — prey
WOLF
LION — predator
DOG — dog
BAT — livebat
BALL
HATCHET — gear
HAMMER
PAPERWT — block
ROCK
VASE — vase
PLATE — glass
WINDOW
FORK
SPOON — utensil
DESK
CURTAIN — furniture
DOLL — doll
MOVED — moved
ATE — ate
HIT — hit
BROKE — broke

Semantic

Figure 3: **The training data for DISLEX-1.** The physical representations code the orthographic word symbols, while the semantic representations stand for distinct meanings. Gray-scale boxes indicate component values within 0 and 1. The connections depict the mapping between the symbols and their meanings.

Category	Semantic words
animal	prey predator livebat dog
fragileobj	glass vase
breaker	gear block
hitter	gear block vase
possession	gear vase doll dog
object	gear block vase glass food furniture doll utensil
thing	human animal object
verb	hit ate broke moved

Table 1: **Semantic categories.** Each slot in the sentence templates specifies a category, and can be filled with any semantic word in that category. In other words, the categorization determines how the words are used in the sentences.

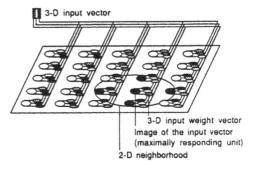

3-D input vector

3-D input weight vector
Image of the input vector
(maximally responding unit)

2-D neighborhood

Figure 4: **A self-organizing feature map network.** A mapping is formed from a 3-dimensional input space onto a 2-dimensional network. The values of the input components, weights and the unit output are shown by gray-scale coding.

With the FGREP-mechanism [21] it is possible to extract the processing content of the word from examples of its use, and code it into a distributed representation. An FGREP-module is a three-layer backpropagation network which automatically developes distributed representations for its input items as it is learning a processing task.

For simplicity, and without restricting the generality of the model, the sensory part was omitted from the training data for DISLEX-1. The semantic representations for DISLEX-1 were formed with FGREP in the sentence case-role assignment task. The input to the FGREP network consisted of the syntactic constituents of the sentence and the network was trained to assign the correct semantic case roles to them. The sentences were generated from templates, by filling each slot in the template with a word from a specified category (table 1). The actual sentences and the specifics of the task are not important for this discussion (see [21]). However, the meanings embedded in the semantic representations originate from the categorization in table 1.

The representations that result from the FGREP process reflect the use of the semantic words (figure 3). Words belonging to the same category have a number of uses in common, and their representations become similar. The total usage is different for each word, and consequently, they stand for unique meanings.

5 Word maps

5.1 Topological feature maps

A 2-D topological feature map [13] implements a topology-preserving mapping from a high-dimensional input space onto a 2-D output space. The map consists of an array of processing units, each with N weight parameters (figure 4). The map takes an N-dimensional vector as its input, and produces a localized pattern of activity as its output. In other words, an input vector is mapped onto a location on the map.

Each processing unit receives the same input vector, and produces one output value. The response is proportional to the similarity of the input vector and the unit's weight vector. The unit with the largest output value constitutes the image of the input vector on the map. The weight vectors are ordered in such a way that the output activity smoothly decreases with the distance from the image unit, forming a localized response.

The ordering of the weight vectors retains the topology of the input space. This means roughly that nearby vectors in the input space are mapped onto nearby units in the map. This is a very useful property, since the complex similarity relationships of the high-dimensional input space become visible on the map.

449

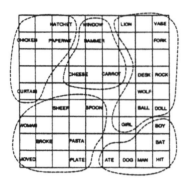

Figure 5: **The physical map.** Each unit in the 9×9 network is represented by a box in the figure. The labels indicate the image unit for each physical word representation. The map is divided into major subareas according to word length.

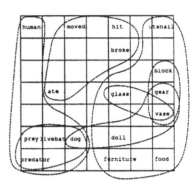

Figure 6: **The semantic map.** The labels on this 7×7 map indicate the maximally responding unit for each semantic word representation. The map is organized according to the semantic categories (table 1).

5.2 Self-organization

The organization of the map, i.e. the assignment of the weight vectors, is formed in an unsupervised learning process [13]. Input items are randomly drawn from the input distribution and presented to the network one at a time (figure 4). The weight vector of the image unit and each unit in its neighborhood are changed towards the input vector, so that these units will produce an even stronger response to the same input in the future. The parallelism of neighboring vectors is increased at each presentation, a process which results in a global order.

The process starts with very large neighborhoods, i.e. weight vectors are changed in large areas. This results in a gross ordering of the map. The size of the neighborhood decreases with time, allowing the map to make finer and finer distinctions between items.

There are several alternatives for implementing the similarity metric, neighborhood selection, and weight change. A biologically plausible process would be based on scalar products of the weight and input vectors, lateral inhibition and redistribution of synaptic resources [14; 20]. These mechanisms can be abstracted and replaced with computationally more efficient ones without obscuring the process itself. The similarity in DISLEX-1 is measured by Euclidian distance, the neighborhood consists of the area around the maximally responding unit, and the weight changes are proportional to the Euclidian difference. More specifically, the output η_{ij} of unit (i, j) is

$$\eta_{ij} = \begin{cases} 1.0 - \frac{\|x - \mu_{ij}\|}{\|x - \mu_{max}\|} & \text{if } (i, j) \in N_c(t) \\ 0.0 & \text{otherwise} \end{cases} \quad (1)$$

where μ_{ij} is the unit's weight vector, x is the input vector, $N_c(t)$ is the neighborhood around the maximally responding unit (shrinking with time), and μ_{max} is the weight vector least similar to x in the neighborhood. This forms a nice concentrated activity pattern around the maximally responding unit. With $\alpha(t)$ as the gain, the weight components are changed according to the input vector – weight

vector difference:

$$\Delta\mu_{ij,k} = \begin{cases} \alpha(t)[x_k - \mu_{ij,k}] & \text{if } (i, j) \in N_c(t) \\ 0.0 & \text{otherwise} \end{cases} \quad (2)$$

5.3 Physical and semantic maps

The physical and semantic maps are organized independently, albeit simultaneously, so that associative connections between them can be developed at the same time (see next section). The ordered maps in DISLEX-1 (figures 5 and 6) were obtained in 150 epochs, i.e. by presenting each physical/semantic representation pair (figure 3) to the appropriate map 150 times in random order.

In the self-organizing process, the physical and semantic representations become stored in the weights of the units. For each e.g. physical word, there is an image unit in the physical map, and this unit's weight vector equals the physical representation of that word. The weight vectors of the intermediate units represent combinations of representations. For example, an unlabeled semantic unit between **dog** and **predator** would have features of both domestic and carnivorous animals.

Both maps exhibit hierarchical knowledge organization. Large areas are allocated to different categories of words, and each area is divided into subareas with finer distinctions. The physical map is mainly organized according to the word length. There are separate, adjacent areas for words with 3, 4, 5, 6 and 7 characters. Within these areas, similar words are mapped near each other. For example, **BAT** is mapped between **BOY** and **HIT**, **DOLL** is mapped next to **BALL** etc.

The semantic map has three main areas: verbs, animate objects and inanimate objects. Finer distinctions reveal the semantic categories of table 1. For example, there are subareas for hitters, possessions and fragile-objects, with **vase**, which belongs to all these categories, in the center. Note that the categorization was not directly accessible to the system at any point. It was only manifest in the sentences that were input to the FGREP-mechanism. The

450

categories were extracted by FGREP, coded into the representations, and finally made visible in the semantic feature map. The final map reflects both the syntactic and semantic properties of the words.

In the self-organizing process, the distribution of the weight vectors becomes an approximation of the input vector distribution [13]. This means that the most frequent areas of the input space are represented to greater detail, i.e. more units are allocated to represent these inputs. For example, the representations for the different animals are very similar (figure 3), yet they accommodate a large area in the map.

The two dimensions of the map do not necessarily stand for any recognizable features of the input space. The dimensions develop automatically to facilitate the best discrimination between the input items. As a result, the ordered areas on the map are likely to have complicated and intertwined, rather than linear shapes.

Feature maps have several useful properties for representing lexical information. (1) The classification performed by a feature map is based on a large number of parameters (the weight components), making it very robust. Incomplete or somewhat erroneous word representations can be correctly recognized. (2) The map is continuous, and can represent items between established categories. In other words, words can have soft boundaries. (3) The differences of the most frequent input items are magnified in the mapping, i.e. the variations of the most common word meanings or surface forms are more finely discriminated. Finally, (4) the self-organizing process requires no supervision and makes no assumptions on the form or content of the words. The properties of the representations which provide the best discrimination are determined automatically.

6 Word associations

6.1 The physical ⇌ semantic mappings

The physical words do not correspond one-to-one to semantic words. Some words have multiple meanings (homonyms), and sometimes the same meaning can be expressed with several different symbols (synonyms). The mapping between the physical and semantic representations is many-to-many.

The training data for DISLEX-1 contained several such ambiguities (figure 3). The physical word CHICKEN could mean a living chicken or food. Similarly, BAT could be a baseball bat or a living bat. There were also several groups of synonymous words in the data. MAN, WOMAN, BOY, GIRL all have the same meaning human, predator could be WOLF or LION etc. In the DISLEX model, the many-to-many mapping between the physical words and their meanings is implemented with associative connections between the physical and semantic maps.

6.2 Associative connections

The physical word maps are fully connected to the semantic map with one-directional associative connections (figure 2). There is a connection from each unit in the physical input map to each unit in the semantic map, and from each unit in the semantic map to each unit in the physical output map. The connection weight indicates the strength of the association. The weights are stored as associative output weight vectors per each unit.

The physical and semantic feature maps and the associative connections between them are organized at the same time. The physical pattern for the word is presented to the physical map, and ordinary feature map adaptation takes place. At the same time, the semantic pattern for the same word is input to the semantic map, and the feature map weight vectors in this map are adapted. At this point, both maps display concentrated patterns of activity. DISLEX learns to associate the physical word with its meaning through Hebbian learning. The weights between active units are increased proportional to their activity:

$$\Delta a_{ij,kl} = \alpha(t)\eta_{ij}\eta_{kl} \qquad (3)$$

where $a_{ij,kl}$ is the weight between the physical unit (i,j) and the semantic unit (k,l), and η_{ij} and η_{kl} indicate the activities of these units. The associative weight vectors are then normalized, which in effect decreases the weights on all nonactive output connections of the same unit. This corresponds to redistribution of synaptic resources, where the synaptic efficacy is proportional to the square root of the resource [20]. Initially the activity patterns are large, and associative weights are changed in large areas. As the two maps become ordered, the associations become more focused.

For example, DISLEX-1 was trained by simultaneously presenting pairs of physical words and their semantic counterparts from figure 3. The final associative connections form a continuous many-to-many mapping between the two maps. Unambiguous words have focused connections (figures 7a and 8b). If a physical word has several meanings, or one meaning can be expressed with several synonyms, there are several groups of strong connections (figures 7b and 8a). Units located between image units tend to combine the connectivity patterns of nearby words (figure 8a).

7 DISLEX in action

7.1 Transforming representations

A physical word is transformed to its semantic counterpart (and vice versa) through the associative connections. For example in figure 2, the physical representation of DOG is input to the physical map, which forms a concentrated activity pattern around the unit labeled DOG. The activity propagates through the associative connections (figure 7a) to the semantic map, where a localized activity pattern forms around the unit labeled dog. The semantic representation for dog is now output through the weight vector of this unit. In a similar fashion, a semantic representa-

451

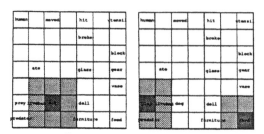
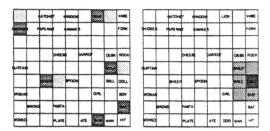

Figure 7: **Sample physical → semantic associative connections.** The darkness of the box indicates the strength of the connection from the physical unit DOG (a) or CHICKEN (b) to the semantic unit. The strongest connections concentrate around the semantic image units. CHICKEN has two possible interpretations, **food** and **prey**.

Figure 8: **Sample semantic → physical associative connections.** In (a), the connections from the intermediate unit between dog, livebat, predator and prey are shown. Possible output symbols include all animal names CHICKEN, SHEEP, WOLF, LION, BAT and DOG. In (b), weak connections from doll to nearby units might cause BALL to be output instead of DOLL in noisy conditions.

tion can be transformed to its physical counterpart. The associative connections are different in the two directions, but the same feature map weight vectors are used for both input and output.

The behaviour of the system is very robust. Even if the input pattern is noisy or incomplete, it is usually mapped on the correct unit. Even if this does not happen, the associative connections of the intermediate units provide a mapping that is close enough, so that the correct meaning or symbol can be retrieved with top-down priming.

7.2 Priming

When an ambiguous physical or semantic representation is input to the lexicon, all possible meanings (or symbols) are activated at the same time (figures 7b and 8a). A top-down priming mechanism is employed to select the correct representation. In addition to the associative activity, the map receives priming activation through its input connections. The activities add up, selecting one of the possible interpretations. If the priming arrives after a short delay, all alternatives are briefly active before one of them is selected. This complies with experimental results [24], which indicate that all meanings of ambiguous words are activated upon reading the word.

The expectations generated by the FGREP mechanism provide a possible source for semantic priming. After reading The wolf ate the, the FGREP network generates a strong expectation for prey [22]. When the physical symbol CHICKEN is read in, both the food and prey units are initially equally active in the semantic map (figure 7b). The expectation pattern, which is close to the representation for prey, is input to the semantic map and summed up with the activity propagated through the associative connections. As a result, the prey unit receives the strongest activity and becomes selected.

The weights on the associative connections represent statistical likelihoods of the associations. A very frequently active connection is much stronger than a rare connection. For example, if most of the occurrences of CHICKEN in train-

ing DISLEX-1 would have been paired up with prey, the CHICKEN unit would tend to activate the prey unit much more than the food unit. By default, the prey meaning would be selected, and stronger priming for food would be required to override it.

DISLEX-1 simply selects and outputs the representation stored at the maximally responding unit. The selection could also be implemented with lateral inhibition, where the map settles into a localized response around the maximally responding unit [20]. The settling times would most likely correspond to the reaction times observed in humans [23]. High-frequency words would have shorter reaction times, and these times could be changed with priming. With several equally likely interpretations, settling would take longer.

7.3 Errors

The DISLEX architecture is well suited into modeling dyslexic performance errors. If the system performance is degraded e.g. by adding noise to the connections, two types of input errors and two types of production errors are observed.

In the input, a physical representation may be mapped incorrectly on a nearby unit in the physical map. This corresponds to reading or hearing the word incorrectly. For example, DOLL may be input as BALL (figure 5). The activity in the physical map may also propagate incorrectly to a nearby unit in the semantic map, in which case e.g. CHICKEN would be understood semantically as livebat (figure 7b).

Analogously in production, a semantic input representation can be classified incorrectly, and a word with a similar but incorrect meaning is produced. For example, if the semantic pattern for block is accidentally mapped on vase (figure 6), the output reads VASE instead of, say, PAPERWT. Or, the activity in the semantic map may be propagated incorrectly to the physical map, and a word with a similar surface form but different meaning is output. This means generating BALL instead of DOLL (figure 8b).

452

Errors of this kind occur in noisy, stressful or overload situations in normal human performance. They are also documented in patients with deep dyslexia [4; 3]. The observed visual and semantic paralexic errors can be explained by above mechanisms, giving strong support to the physical/semantic feature map architecture.

If priming is used in the model, there is also a possibility for another type of error, the Freudian slip. This occurs when very strong semantic priming interferes with the output function. For example, if doll is input to the semantic map, together with simultaneous priming for gear, the activity is propagated through the associative connections of both. As a result, the physical BALL might receive the strongest activation, and would be output instead of DOLL. The output symbols are similar, but the meaning of BALL reveals the semantic priming.

8 Modeling aphasia

The DISLEX architecture is in good agreement with the current theories of the human lexical system [3; 27; 26]. Many observed lexical deficits in acquired aphasia have straightforward explanations in the model.

A common feature of the aphasic deficits is category specificity. The patient may have difficulties only with words belonging to a specific syntactic or semantic category. In certain patients the lexical access to e.g. function words is selectively impaired, in other cases the patient has trouble with verbs [3; 4]. More specific impairments seem to occur in semantic hierarchies. Some patients have trouble with e.g. concrete words, or inanimate objects [28], or even as specific classes as names of fruits and vegetables [10].

Deficits of this kind can be explained by the topological organization of the semantic memory. The semantic map in DISLEX is hierarchically organized, and reflects both the syntactic and semantic properties of the words. Localized lesions to the map produce selective impairments, like the above.

In some cases the impairments cover all modalities, sometimes they are limited only to verbal input or output, or even only to orthographic or phonological domain. This suggests that the semantic memory, visual input, and verbal input/output modalities are represented in separate structures, strongly supporting the distributed DISLEX architecture.

For example, some patients were unable to access the specific meanings from verbally as well as visually (with pictures) presented cues [26; 28]. This implies that the semantic memory itself, i.e. the map, had been damaged. Another patient could not give definitions for aurally presented names of living things such as "dolphin", although he was able to describe other objects. But when shown a picture of a dolphin, he could name it and give an accurate verbal description of it [16]. This suggests that the visual pathway to the semantic memory, the semantic memory itself, and the verbal output were preserved, but the verbal access to the semantic memory had been damaged. In an-

other case, the patient was unable to name fruits and vegetables, although he was able to match their names with pictures, and classify them correctly when their names were presented aurally [10]. In other words, his semantic memory and verbal input were preserved, and the verbal output function was selectively impaired.

The impairment of semantic categories which is restricted to a single input or output modality can be explained in DISLEX by severed pathways between physical and semantic maps. The pathways are not single axons, but consist of interneurons, which also exhibit map-like organization. Close to the semantic map, the organization is semantic, close to the physical map it parallels the physical map. If the pathway is severed close to the semantic map, semantic impairment within this modality results.

The dissociation of the orthographic and phonological modalities is also well-documented. Some patients have deficits only in one of the input or output channels, or different deficits in different channels [2]. For example, a patient may have spelling difficulties exclusively in the orthographic output domain [9; 18]. The types of errors in visual and phonological dyslexia (section 7.3) further indicate that the channels are organized according to the physical forms of the words. The DISLEX model predicts that it would be possible to lose access to specific types of physical symbols, as a result of localized damage to a physical map.

In the aphasic impairments, the high-frequency words are often better preserved than rare words. This is also predicted by the feature map organization. The most often occurring words occupy larger areas in the map, making them more robust against damage.

9 Discussion

The DISLEX model can be locally lesioned, and it displays deficits similar to human patients. This suggests that the model successfully represents some of the physical structure underlying the lexical system in the brain. The architecture is based on word maps, where different units are selectively sensitive to different words in the data. Several low-level sensory maps are known to exist in the central nervous system, e.g. retinotopic maps, tonotopic maps, and also tactile and motor maps. Recently it was found that neurons in the hippocampus respond selectively to visually presented words [11]. These response characteristic could be explained by a map-like structure.

DISLEX still finesses much of the fine neural structure, and the mapping to the neuron level is nontrivial. The units and connections in the model do not necessarily correspond one-to-one to neurons and synapses, but rather, to connected groups of neurons. For example, the weight vectors in the maps are used both for input and output, which is not a plausible model of the synaptic efficacies. However, these two-way connections could be implemented with tightly interconnected (or phase-locking) groups of neurons in the brain.

The associative connections between two feature maps

learn a many-to-many mapping from one distributed representation space to another, which is hard to do with other neural network mechanisms such as backpropagation. In the maps, several representations can be active at the same time, whereas e.g. in an assembly-based representation all the different alternatives would be combined into a single average representation pattern [22].

DISLEX is primarily a model of single word processing. It does not have special mechanisms for representing and processing phrasal structures and morphology. There are two possible ways of doing this, and it seems that both of them are involved. Common morphological forms and phrases, such as nationalism or The Big Apple could be represented like words, as single entries in the physical and semantic maps. More complex phrases and unusual, constructive forms, e.g. kick the bucket or non-preemptive could be represented in the lexicon by their constituents, and parsed/generated by a higher-level language processing module.

10 Conclusion

The DISLEX architecture models the human lexical system at the level of physical structures. The architecture accounts for many observed dyslexic performance errors and lexical deficits in acquired aphasia. DISLEX-1, the AI implementation of the model, can be used as an input/output filter for a natural language processing system, which communicates with the external world with physical symbol representations, but internally processes semantic representations.

References

[1] Yigal Arens. CLUSTER: An Approach to Contextual Language Understanding. PhD thesis, Computer Science Division, University of California, Berkeley, 1986.

[2] A. Basso, A. Taborelli, and L. A. Vignolo. Dissociated disorders of speaking and writing in aphasia. Journal of Neurology, Neurosurgery and Psychiatry, 41:526–556, 1978.

[3] Alfonso Caramazza. Some aspects of language processing revealed through the analysis of acquired aphasia: The lexical system. Annual Reviews in Neuroscience, 11:395–421, 1988.

[4] Max Coltheart, Karalyn Patterson, and John C. Marshall, editors. Deep Dyslexia. International Library of Psychology, Routledge and Kegan Paul, 1980.

[5] Garrison W. Cottrell and Steven L. Small. A connectionist scheme for modelling word sense disambiguation. Cognition and Brain Theory, 6(1):89–120, 1983.

[6] Michael G. Dyer. In-Depth Understanding: A Computer Model of Integrated Processing for Narrative Comprehension. MIT Press, Cambridge, MA, 1983.

[7] Michael Gasser. A Connectionist Model of Sentence Generation in a First and Second Language. PhD thesis, Computer Science Department, UCLA, 1988.

[8] Helen Gigley. Process synchronization, lexical ambiguity resolution and aphasia. In Steven L. Small, Garrison W. Cottrell, and Michael K. Tanenhaus, editors, Lexical Ambiguity Resolution, Morgan Kaufmann Publishers, Los Altos, CA, 1988.

[9] R. A. Goodman and Alfonso Caramazza. Aspects of the spelling process: Evidence from a case of acquired dysgraphia. Language and Cognitive Processes, 1(4):263–296, 1986.

[10] John Hart, Rita Sloan Berndt, and Alfonso Caramazza. Category-specific naming deficit following cerebral infarction. Nature, 316(1):439–440, August 1985.

[11] Gary Heit, Michael E. Smith, and Eric Halgren. Neural encoding of individual words and faces by the human hippocampus and amygdala. Nature, (333):773–775, 1989.

[12] Alan H. Kawamoto. Distributed representations of ambiguous words and their resolution in a connectionist network. In Steven L. Small, Garrison W. Cottrell, and Michael K. Tanenhaus, editors, Lexical Ambiguity Resolution, Morgan Kaufmann Publishers, 1988.

[13] Teuvo Kohonen. Self-Organization and Associative Memory, chapter 5. Springer-Verlag, Berlin; New York, 1984.

[14] Teuvo Kohonen. Self-organized formation of topologically correct feature maps. Biological Cybernetics, (43):59–69, 1982.

[15] Geunbae Lee, Margot Flowers, and Michael G. Dyer. Learning distributed representations of conceptual knowledge and their application to script-based story processing. Connection Science, 1990. (In press).

[16] Rosaleen A. McCarthy and Elizabeth K. Warrington. Evidence for modality-specific meaning systems in the brain. Nature, 334(4):428–430, August 1988.

[17] James L. McClelland and Alan H. Kawamoto. Mechanisms of sentence processing: Assigning roles to constituents. In James L. McClelland and David E. Rumelhart, editors, Parallel Distributed Processing: Explorations in the Microstructure of Cognition. Volume II: Psychological and Biological Models, MIT Press, 1986.

[18] G. Miceli, M. C. Silveri, and Alfonso Caramazza. Cognitive analysis of a case of pure dysgraphia. Brain and Language, 25:187–212, 1985.

[19] Risto Miikkulainen. A Neural Network Model of Script Processing and Memory. Technical Report UCLA-AI-90-03, Artificial Intelligence Laboratory, Computer Science Department, University of California, Los Angeles, 1990.

[20] Risto Miikkulainen. Self-Organizing Process Based on Lateral Inhibition and Weight Redistribution. Technical Report UCLA-AI-87-16, Artificial Intelligence Laboratory, Computer Science Department, UCLA, 1987.

[21] Risto Miikkulainen and Michael G. Dyer. Encoding input/output representations in connectionist cognitive systems. In David S. Touretzky, Geoffrey E. Hinton, and Terrence J. Sejnowski, editors, Proceedings of the 1988 Connectionist Models Summer School, Morgan Kaufmann Publishers, 1989.

[22] Risto Miikkulainen and Michael G. Dyer. Natural language processing with modular neural networks and distributed lexicon. 1989. Submitted to Cognitive Science.

[23] Greg B. Simpson and Curt Burgess. Activation and selection processes in the recognition of ambiguous words. Journal of Experimental Psychology: Human Perception and Performance, 11(1):28–39, 1985.

[24] D. A. Swinney. Lexical access during sentence comprehension: (Re)consideration of context effects. Journal of Verbal Learning and Verbal Behavior, 18:645–659, 1979.

[25] David L. Waltz and Jordan B. Pollack. Massively parallel parsing: A strongly interactive model of natural language interpretation. Cognitive Science, (9):51–74, 1985.

[26] Elizabeth K. Warrington. The selective impairment of semantic memory. Quarterly Journal of Experimental Psychology, 27:635–657, 1975.

[27] Elizabeth K. Warrington and Rosaleen A. McCarthy. Categories of knowledge: Further fractionations and an attempted integration. Brain, 110:1273–1296, 1987.

[28] Elizabeth K. Warrington and T. Shallice. Category specific semantic impairments. Brain, 107:829–854, 1984.

[29] Uri Zernik. Strategies of Language Acquisition: Learning Phrases from Examples in Context. PhD thesis, Computer Science Department, University of California, Los Angeles, 1987. Technical Report UCLA-AI-87-1.

Efficient Learning of Language Categories:
The Closed-Category Relevance Property
and Auxiliary Verbs

Sheldon Nicholl and David C. Wilkins

nicholl@cs.uiuc.edu
wilkins@cs.uiuc.edu
Department of Computer Science
University of Illinois
405 North Mathews Avenue
Urbana, IL 61801

Abstract

This paper describes the mechanism used by the ALACK language acquisition program for identification of auxiliary verbs. Pinker's approach to this problem (Pinker, 1984) is a general learning algorithm that can learn any Boolean function but takes time exponential in the number of feature dimensions. In this paper, we describe an approach that improves upon Pinker's method by introducing the Closed-Category Relevance Property, and showing how it provides the basis of an algorithm that learns the class of Boolean functions that is believed sufficient for natural language, and does not require more than linear time as feature dimensions are added.

1 Introduction

Within the study of language acquisition, the problem of category identification is still a challenge to formal theories of language acquisition. Even the identification of the members of a closed category such as the Auxiliary Verbs (hereinafter referred to as AUX) stands unresolved. The principal approaches to this problem include (Anderson, 1983), (Berwick, 1985), and (Pinker, 1984); Our approach is closest to that of Pinker. We share with Pinker the following five assumptions: (1) Language is learned not from a string of words alone but from the corresponding meaning (and possibly other attributes) as well. (2) Some components of the meaning can be represented with features. (3) The features are drawn from sets we will call *feature dimensions*. Examples of several feature dimensions are shown below in Table 1. (4) Candidate AUXes are not annotated with syntactic features in the input, e.g. (Berwick, 1985), nor is the input prechunked into phrase-like groupings, e.g., (Anderson, 1983). (5) Steele's cross-linguistic generalization (Steele et al., 1981), holds for AUXes: AUXes encode tense or modality or both.

Pinker's approach is based on a general learning algorithm that (i) can learn any Boolean function but (ii) takes time exponential in the number of feature dimensions. In contrast, our approach, which depends on the Closed-Category Relevance Property, defined Section 2, (i) cannot learn an arbitrary Boolean function but is conjectured to be sufficient for natural language, and (ii) does not require more than linear time as feature dimensions are added.

455

2 The Closed-Category Relevance Property

In this section, we introduce the Closed-Category Relevance Property that will be used to identify the category AUX; this is the basis of our algorithm for AUX identification. Our goal is identification only, not full control. So to recognize that **are**, for example, is an auxiliary is sufficient; to learn the rules that control when to choose **are** instead of **is** or **were**, for example, is beyond the scope of this paper.

The Closed-Category Relevance Property can be viewed abstractly as a two-place predicate R which takes a word as its first argument and a feature dimension as its second argument: $R(word, dimension)$. Its purpose is to relate words to features that control their usage. It is meant to capture the idea that *animacy*, for example, has no bearing on the word **are**, i.e., $\neg R(are, animacy)$, but that *tense*, for instance, does: $R(are, tense)$.

The Closed-Category Relevance Property is defined as follows: $R(word, dimension)$ is true iff *word* can encode some but not all of the values in *dimension*. $R(are, tense)$ is true because **are** can encode present and future time but not past time. The definition is satisfied because **are** can encode some but not all of the values on the tense dimension. $R(are, animacy)$ is false bacause **are** can be used in both animate ("The dogs are running") and inanimate ("The computers are running") contexts, so it trivially encodes both the values on the animacy dimension.

3 The AUX Learning Algorithm

The Closed-Category Relevance Property has been embodied in a computer model of language acquisition called ALACK, which runs in Common Lisp on a Sun 4.

3.1 The Input to the Algorithm

The input to ALACK relevant to this discussion consists of: (1) a segmented string of words, each of which is segmented into grammatical morphemes, (2) a list of semantic categories corresponding to each word, drawn from the set {thing,event,state,null} where thing marks a perceptually salient physical object, event marks a perceptually salient event, action, or process, state marks some ongoing state, and null is the default which applies to all other words, and (3) a list of sets of feature values, which are empty sets for words marked null, nonempty otherwise.

3.2 The Algorithm and an Example

In this section, we describe the steps of our Closed-Category Relevance algorithm, and show how each step processes the following input that is based on actual input to ALACK:

person	*1st-person, 2nd-person, 3rd-person*
number	*singular, plural*
tense	*past, present, future*
animacy	*animate, inanimate*
modality	*modal, nonmodal*
aspect	*perfective, imperfective, progressive*

Table 1: Features used as examples throughout the text. They, and the actual values within them, are used as illustration in the text, and of course do not constitute a claim as to what is indeed linguistically complete and correct.

456

```
(((the) (men) (are) (walk ing))
 (null thing null event)
 (() (3rd-person plural animate) () (present progressive)))
```

The feature values are drawn from the same sets of *feature dimensions* described in the introduction. ALACK embodies the Closed-Category Relevance Property in a manner logically equivalent to the following.

- Step 1. All words marked null are collected into a set E. In this case, $E = \{$are, the$\}$. It is this set that is tested for closed-category relevance; the treatment of the other words is beyond the scope of this paper.

- Step 2. All the feature values are collected into a set F. In this case, $F = \{$*3rd-person, plural, animate, present, progressive*$\}$. ALACK filters the input to make sure that F contains only one value from each feature dimension. Inputs violating this constraint are ignored.

- Step 3. Unless they have been built already, ALACK constructs all the triples $E \times G \times H$ where

$$G = \{z \mid z \subseteq F \wedge |z| = 1\}$$

$$H = \{dim(f) \mid f \in F\}$$

$$dim(f) = y \quad \text{if } f \in y$$

  For example, $dim(singular) = number$, since $number = \{singular, plural\}$. Three examples of $E \times G \times H$ are $(are, \{present\}, tense)$, $(are, \{animate\}, animacy)$, and $(the, \{plural\}, number)$.

- Step 4. If a triple (e, S, d) where $e \in E$ and $d \in dim(F)$ has already been constructed, set S is updated to include the new feature value $f \in F$: $S_{new} = S_{old} \cup \{f\}$. So for example, if ALACK gets the following input

```
(((the) (ball) (is) (fall ing))
 (null thing null event)
 (() (3rd-person singular inanimate) () (present progressive)))
```

  then the example triple $(are, \{animate\}, animacy)$ is updated to

$$(are, \{animate, inanimate\}, animacy)$$

- Step 5. All the updated triples are tested against the following rule:

$$(z, y, y) \Rightarrow \neg R(z, y)$$

Since $animacy = \{animate, inanimate\}$, the example triple matches the left-hand side, which forces the conclusion $\neg R(are, animacy)$; i.e., **are** is not closed-category relevant for animacy, as discussed above. But **are** is still relevant for *tense*: the triple $(are, \{present\}, tense)$ has not been changed. Pinker's model and ours agree that all dimensions not explicitly found to be irrelevant are relevant by default.

ALACK organizes some feature dimensions into a set, or *domain*, which we will call the *verbal domain*. In the current implementation of ALACK, this domain is as follows:

$$verbal = \{tense,\ aspect\}$$

Formally, category inference is done as follows. Given morpheme x and dimension y,

$$R(x, y) \wedge (y \in verbal) \Rightarrow x \in AUX$$

The rule is justified by the previous discussion on Steele's generalization (Steele et al., 1981). ALACK's implementation does not yet include modality; aspect has been included since it works well for English. For example, since $R(are, tense)$ and $tense \in verbal$, the rule allows $are \in AUX$ to be concluded.

4   Analysis of AUX Learning Algorithm

Correctness. Clearly the closed-category relevance property leads to an algorithm that is not correct for all Boolean functions. For example, suppose that English had an auxiliary **hawn** whose paradigm, or grammar chart, looked like this:

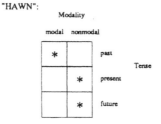

where the stars mean to use the auxiliary, and the blanks mean ϕ (the null morpheme), for instance. The auxiliary **hawn** is irrelevant along both the *tense* and *modality* dimensions, even though both dimensions are (1) important to auxiliary identification, as discussed below, and (2) important to the proper usage of **hawn**. Though Closed-Category Relevance is not correct from the standpoint of full logical generality, it is only a small stipulation beyond the generalization of (Steele 1981); English has nothing like **hawn**. This leads to the **Closed-Category Relevance Conjecture**: All the auxiliaries in all the world's languages that have auxiliaries are relevant for tense or modality or both. This Conjecture goes beyond Steele's generalization in that the Conjecture would not allow something like **hawn**, while Steele's generalization would. Steele's generalization is satisfied by any encoding of tense or modality; the Conjecture demands that the encoding satisfy the Relevance Property as well.

Complexity Analysis. We wish to examine the time complexity of determining $\neg R(w, d)$ for a given w, d as the total number of dimensions T in *features* is increased. For the sake of this argument, we can stipulate that in the implementation, the triples (e, S, d) are accessed by their dimension via a function h, where $h(d) = \{(e, S, d') \mid d' = d\}$. If h is chosen to be implemented in an array A, one may simply search A linearly for the desired dimension d, i.e., the search time is $O(T)$. If A is sorted, the time drops to $O(\log(T))$. If h is a hash function, that time can be lowered significantly.

5   Cross-Linguistic Analysis of Relevance

The idea of Closed-Category Relevance has interesting implications when applied to Bickerton's work (Bickerton, 1984). Suppose we are given the problem of identifying the auxiliaries in some

of the creole languages that Bickerton has studied. For instance, in Hawaiian Creole, three auxiliaries to try are **bin**, **go**, and **stei**. For Lesser Antilles Creole, the auxiliaries are **ka**, **ke**, and
te. Two of the auxiliaries in Saramaccan are **ta**, and **bi-o-ta**. It is possible to translate his
notation for tense, modality, and aspect (see Table 1, p. 183) into this system in the following
way. Let $features = verbal = \{tense, modality, aspect\}$ where $tense = \{anterior, nonanterior\}$,
$modality = \{realis, irrealis\}$, and $aspect = \{punctual, nonpunctual\}$. Then for Hawaiian creole, $R(stei, aspect)$, $R(go, modality)$, $R(bin, tense)$, and for Lesser Antilles Creole, $R(ka, aspect)$,
$R(ke, modality)$, and $R(te, tense)$. Now in a case like Saramaccan where auxiliaries are built up
morphologically, closed-category relevance can be applied successfully to each morpheme individually or to a whole word, e.g. $R(bi-o-ta, tense)$ or $R(ta, aspect)$. Closed-Category Relevance is
confirmed for auxiliaries in these languages. Although the above demonstration hardly constitutes
a full confirmation of Closed-Category Relevance, it does show that further tests of Relevance in
other languages are worthwhile. It also lends credence to the idea of Closed-Category Relevance as
an acquisition principle.

6 Comparison to Pinker's Learning Method

This section will do three things: show that Pinker's Method is logically correct, analyze its computational complexity, and compare it to Closed-Category Relevance.

6.1 Correctness

The set of features described in Table 1 can be viewed as an instance of the following format, where
the given set of features is simply a set of dimensions, and each dimension is simply a set of values.
To make the statement of Pinker's method more precise, we introduce here a set of *feature-names*,
with the obvious bijection between *features* and *feature-names*: $features = \{dim_1, dim_2, \ldots, dim_n\}$,
$dim_i = \{val_1, val_2, \ldots, val_{f(i)}\}$, and $feature\text{-}names = \{d_1, d_2, \ldots, d_n\}$. The input to Pinker's procedure is first a sequence of *attribute-lists*, which we will index with $q \in \{1, 2, 3, \ldots\}$. Each attribute-list
is a set of pairs, with a feature name in the first slot of the pair and a value from the corresponding
feature dimension in the second:

$$attribute\text{-}list_q = \{(d_{q_1}, val_{q_1}), (d_{q_2}, val_{q_2}), \ldots, (d_{q_n}, val_{q_n})\}$$

The procedure is also provided with a morpheme m_i on each trial, where

$$m_{i_q} \in M = \{m_1, m_2, \ldots, m_i, \ldots, m_{g(q)}\}$$

The goal is to discover (learn) the Boolean expression B_j for each m_i, where B_j is a possibly complex
Boolean expression built up from the pairs in the *attribute-lists*, using conjunction and disjunction
only, without negation, and $m_i \Leftrightarrow B_j$.

Pinker's solution to this learning problem is to build a big multi-dimensional array, a *Paradigm*,
and to fill single array locations by (1) reading each input q as a set of coordinates and (2) placing
m_{i_q} at the location specified by these coordinates. The array is built up one dimension at a time;
the dimensions to add are selected at random from the image of $\{x \mid (x, y) \in attribute\text{-}list_q\}$, for
some q. That is, the array can be built up only from dimensions that occur somewhere in the input.
Pinker does not say what to do with the morpheme entries when a new dimension is added; one
possibility would be simply to forget them all and start over with a bigger matrix. We will neglect
this problem and assume that we begin with a big enough matrix.

459

Given a sufficiently large matrix, Pinker's method is correct, since it is simply storing the examples into the matrix as they come in. Although this result is new (Pinker didn't give correctness proofs), it is very minor, and serves only to provide a background for the next result, which is the complexity result.

6.2 Complexity

Since Pinker's learning procedure P chooses feature dimensions dim_i at random, it is quite possible that P will choose an irrelevant dimension, say dim_5, even though B only requires the use of some other dimensions, say dim_1, dim_2, and dim_3. It is important to dispose of irrelevant dimensions, since, among other things, Pinker's method for finding auxiliaries does not tolerate irrelevant dimensions. We will first give Pinker's statement of his method for disposing of irrelevant dimensions, show its correctness, and then give its time complexity.

Here is Pinker's (Pinker, 1984) method for eliminating irrelevant dimensions, which he calls Procedure I3. His use of "cells" corresponds to "array locations" in this paper; similarly, "paradigm" means "array", and "affix" means "morpheme":

> If the same affix appears in all the cells defining a dimension across a given combination of values of the other dimensions, and this is true for every possible combination of values of the other dimensions, eliminate that entire dimension from the paradigm. (Pinker, 1984) p. 186.

For example, suppose that $features = \{X, Y, Z\}$, $X = \{a, b, c\}$, $Y = \{d, e, f\}$, $Z = \{j, k, l\}$, and $feature\text{-}names = \{\mathbf{X}, \mathbf{Y}, \mathbf{Z}\}$, and suppose further that the input consists of the following three input attribute-lists for morpheme m:

$$attribute\text{-}list_1 = \{(\mathbf{X}, c), (\mathbf{Y}, f), (\mathbf{Z}, j)\}$$

$$attribute\text{-}list_2 = \{(\mathbf{X}, c), (\mathbf{Y}, f), (\mathbf{Z}, k)\}$$

$$attribute\text{-}list_3 = \{(\mathbf{X}, c), (\mathbf{Y}, f), (\mathbf{Z}, l)\}$$

The (complete) array resulting from these inputs is:

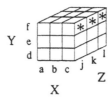

where the asterisks correspond to the three inputs. Pinker's elimination method says that the Z dimension can be eliminated from the array, leaving just dimensions X and Y. We now show that this is logically correct.

Note that the possible attribute-lists for m as shown in the array can be represented as follows:

$$cfj \vee cfk \vee cfl = cf(j \vee k \vee l) = cf(true) = cf$$

460

since $j \vee k \vee l \Rightarrow true$. Now since the resulting expression, cf, contains no reference to the Z dimension, that dimension can be eliminated. It should now be clear that this argument can be carried out in general for any number of dimensions, values, and inputs.

Procedure I3 can now be stated formally. Let $S = \{f_1, f_2, \ldots, f_k\}$ be a set of feature dimensions. Let $B(S)$ be a Boolean expression based on the members of S. Given m iff $B(S)$, dimension $f_i \in S$ can be eliminated from S only if $[B(S)$ iff $B(S - \{f_i\})]$. In our example, $S = \{X, Y, Z\}$ and $f_i = Z$. So

$$B(S) = B(\{X, Y, Z\}) = cfj \vee cfk \vee cfl = cf = B(\{X, Y\}) = B(S - \{f_i\})$$

This is just a formal way of saying that dimension Z can be eliminated from consideration, just as it was in the array realization above.

Result: Procedure I3 is NP-complete. Proof: The elimination of f_i from S requires that the expression $B(S) \Longleftrightarrow B(S - \{f_i\})$ be shown to be a tautology. The tautology problem is NP-complete.

This result will be used shortly. First, a predicate similar in spirit to our Closed-Category Relevance predicate can be defined: $R'(word, dimension)$ iff $(word \Leftrightarrow B(S)) \wedge (dimension \in S)$. Pinker's AUX identification method can now be approximated by the following expression. Pinker left several terms mathematically undefined.

$$Prob(R'(word, tense) \vee R'(word, modality), Phon(word), Syn(word)) \Rightarrow word \in AUX$$

That is, a word is an auxiliary if it satisfies an undefined predicate ($Prob$) based on a probabilistic combination of its arguments: the ability of the word to encode tense or modality (R'), an undefined predicate ($Phon$) based on certain phonological properties of the word, and an undefined predicate (Syn) based on certain other syntactic properties of the word. Now if $Prob$ is strict in its first argument, $Prob$ must be at least NP-complete. Hence Pinker's auxiliary identification procedure is at least NP-complete under the assumption that $Prob$ needs the output of R'.

6.3 Comparison to Closed-Category Relevance

Figure 1 showed that there exist logical, if not linguistic, counterexamples to Closed-Category Relevance. By contrast, section 6.1 showed that under assumptions (1) – (5) in section 1, Pinker's procedure could handle any logically possible AUX rule, including Figure 1. Section 4 showed, however, that Closed-Category Relevance leads to an algorithm that is fast, while section 6.2 showed that Pinker's procedure is NP-complete.

7 Conclusion

The Closed-Category Relevance Property has been defined and has been shown to lead to an efficient algorithm for the identification of Auxiliary Verbs. Relevance was shown to hold in several languages other than English, demonstrating that the same algorithm could be applied to Auxiliary Verb identification in those languages. Finally, Pinker's method was subjected to an analysis which, under certain reasonable assumptions, proved it logically correct but NP-complete.

Acknowledgements

The authors would like to thank Cindy Fisher, Peter Haddawy, and Steve Pinker for their very helpful comments.

References

Anderson, J. R. (1983). *The Architecture of Cognition.* Cambridge, MA: Harvard.

Berwick, R. C. (1985). *The Acquisition of Syntactic Knowledge.* Cambridge, MA: MIT Press.

Bickerton, D. (1984). The language bioprogram hypothesis. *The Behavioral and Brain Sciences,* 7:173–221.

Pinker, S. (1984). *Language Learnability and Language Development.* Cambridge, MA: Harvard.

Steele, S., Akmajian, A., Demers, R., Jelinek, E., Kitagawa, C., Oehrle, R., and Wasow, T. (1981). *An Encyclopedia of AUX: a study of cross-linguistic equivalence.* Cambridge, MA: MIT Press.

The Representation of Word Meaning

Renison J. Gonsalves, Brooklyn College

Abstract: This article shows that a substantial portion of the empirical evidence regarding the representation of word meaning can be explained by the definitional semantic theory of Jerrold J. Katz (henceforth ST). First, we look at the relative complexities of four types of negatives which, according to Fodor, Fodor, and Garrett (1975; henceforth FFG), show that definitions are not psychologically real. The ST definitional structures explain the FFG results in terms of the number of disjuncts generated by the negative elements in their ST representations. Next we look at the arguments of Gentner for componential structure from evidence from a recall experiment that considers connectedness relationships between the noun phrases of sentences with three types of verbs. Gentner's results can be explained in terms of the number of argument places in the ST representations, and the same explanation can be used with respect to evidence from studies by Fodor, Garrett, Walker, and Parkes (1980; henceforth FGWP) and Gergely and Bever (1986).

John Locke devotes a great deal of <u>An Essay Concerning Human Understanding</u> (1689) to his account of the mental representation of word meaning, and this account is essentially definitional or decompositional in character:

> The Mind being, as I have declared, furnished with a great number of simple *Ideas*, conveyed by the *Senses*, as they are found in exterior things, or by *Reflection* on its own Operations, takes notice also, that a certain number of these simple *Ideas* go constantly together; which being·presumed to belong to one thing, and Words being suited to common apprehensions, and made by use for quick dispatch, are called so united by one subject, by one name; . . . (II, xxiii, 1)

Contemporary versions of this definitional approach came into such substantial criticism (Fodor et al, 1975 and 1980) that for most of the 1980s many investigators in this area worked under the erroneous assumption that it had been completely discredited. However, three hundred years after the first publication of Locke's <u>Essay</u>, in a thorough critical review of all of the evidence and arguments, McNamara and Miller (1989) came to a pro-decompositional view, concluding that "there's little evidence against conceptual structure and there's some evidence for it." In this paper I will show that a substantial portion of the empirical evidence can be perspicuously explained by the definitional semantic theory of Katz (1972, 1976, 1989; henceforth ST).

Part 1: Fodor, Fodor, and Garrett and the Complexity of Negatives

One of the major components of the FFG argument against the psychological reality of definitional structures was the results of a psycholinguistic study involving four types of negatives: explicit negatives, e.g. "not married"; implicit negatives, e.g. "doubt," deny," fail"; morphological negatives, e.g. "unmarried"; and pure definitional negatives (PDNs) e.g. "bachelor." Subjects were presented with the sentence "If practically all of the men in the room are _____, then few of the men in the room have wives," with either "not married," "unmarried," or "bachelor" in the blank. The subjects were then asked to judge the correctness of the inference and response times were measured. FFG found that explicit negatives were the most difficult; morphological and implicit negatives were both less difficult; and PDNs were the least difficult. Based on this evidence FFG argued that "PDNs do not act as though they contain a negative element," and that "PDNs are not semantically analyzed," contrary to the definitional view.

However, in ST we might have the following representations:

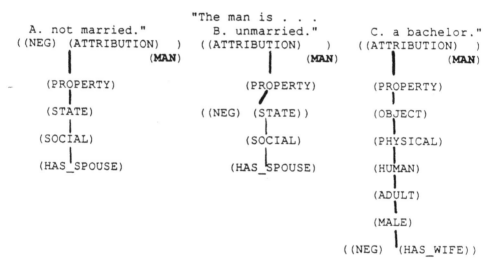

"The man is . . .

| A. not married." | B. unmarried." | C. a bachelor." |

Our reading for sentence A says that the attribution to the man of the property of being in a social state of having a spouse is negated, while our reading for B says that there is an attribution to the man of the property of not being in the social state of having a spouse, and finally our reading for C says that there is an attribution to the man of the property of being a physical, object, that is human, adult, male, and that does not have a wife.

The scopes of the negative elements in these structures explain the FFG results. In a hierarchical structure as in a semantic reading, a negation of a node in the structure results in a disjunction made by attaching the negative element to alternate nodes below the initial negative element. The following schema illustrates this format:

```
NOT(AAAAA)        (AAAAA)            (AAAAA)            (AAAAA)       NOT(AAAAA)
    |                |                  |                  |              |
 (BBBBB)   =      (AAAAA)  OR        (BBBBB)  OR  NOT(BBBBB)   OR     (BBBBB)
    |                |                  |                  |              |
 (CCCCC)          (CCCCC)         NOT(CCCCC)            (CCCCC)        (CCCCC)
    |                |                  |                  |              |
 (DDDDD)       NOT(DDDDD)           (DDDDD)             (DDDDD)        (DDDDD)
```

The taller the structure and the higher up in it the
negative element occurs, the more disjuncts or the more ORs you
get. By simple calculation we see that the complexity
relationships between explicit, morphological and definitional
negatives that FFG found are exactly mirrored by considering the
ST representations for sentences A, B, and C, taking into account
the number of disjuncts generated by the negative elements in
these structures. So a sentence like C, with the PDN "bachelor"
gets no disjunction since the negative element is at the bottom
of the semantic reading. Sentence B, with the morphological
negative "unmarried" gets three disjuncts; and sentence A, with
the explicit negative "not married" gets five disjuncts.
Sentences with an explicit negative plus a morphological negative
get fifteen disjuncts, and an explicit and a PDN get eight.

The following markers show that the relative complexities of
the explicit, morphological, and implicit negatives also
correspond to the FFG results.

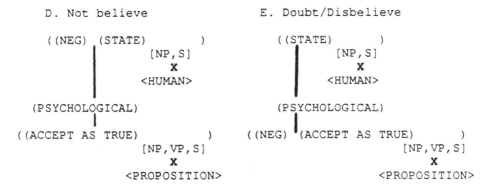

```
    D. Not believe                    E. Doubt/Disbelieve

    ((NEG) (STATE)       )            ((STATE)         )
           |       [NP,S]                    |    [NP,S]
           |         X                       |      X
           |      <HUMAN>                    |   <HUMAN>
           |                                 |
   (PSYCHOLOGICAL)                   (PSYCHOLOGICAL)
           |                                 |
    ((ACCEPT AS TRUE)      )          ((NEG) (ACCEPT AS TRUE)      )
                  [NP,VP,S]                          [NP,VP,S]
                     X                                  X
              <PROPOSITION>                       <PROPOSITION>
```

Part 2: Three Connectedness/Relatedness Studies

Unlike the FFG experiment on negatives which dealt with the
relative semantic complexity of sentence meanings, Gentner's
recall experiments dealt with the relative connectedness of noun
phrases in SVO sentences. Specifically, Gentner's experiment
compared connectedness relations in such sentences for three
different types of verbs: general verbs like "gave," connecting-
specific verbs like "sold," and non-connecting specific verbs

like "sent." When we compare the meanings of such verbs we see that a connecting specific verb like "sold," because it involves an exchange of merchandize and money between buyer and seller, provides for a greater degree of connectedness between noun phrases in its simple sentences than either the general or non-connecting specific verbs. While both "gave" and "sent" suggest a one-way transaction, "sent" is more specific or complex since it suggests a causative relation in the transaction, perhaps something like "cause to be given." One of Gentner's experiments involved reading simple sentences with these verbs to subjects and then asking them to recall the direct object, "woman" in the examples below, given the subject as a cue.

Basically, Gentner's approach was to distinguish between two hypotheses, both intended to test the definitional view. The first, the complexity hypothesis, is the one on which FFG had based their rejection of the psychological reality of definitions. The second Gentner called the connectivity hypothesis. Now, with respect to sentences like F, G, and H below the connectivity and complexity hypotheses make different predictions. The complexity hypothesis would predict that recall would be best for sentences with verbs like "gave" since the meanings of these verbs are the least complex and so leave more memory space available for recall. On the other hand, the connectivity hypothesis would predict that sentences with verbs like "sold" would bring about better recall since there is stronger connectedness between the referents of the noun phrases in such sentences.

In fact, it is the connectivity hypothesis that wins out in the Gentner results, with sentences with verbs like "sold" providing for much better recall of the object noun phrases than either sentences with verbs like "gave" or sentences with verbs like "sent." The definitional structures of ST do in fact provide a fairly straightforward explanation of these results in terms of the number of argument places in the ST representation of the verbs' meanings. Very simply, the more argument places there are in a structure the more connected the referents of the noun phrases that fill these argument places. As the following structures for sentences with the three verbs show, with arguments appearing in boldface, the sentence for "sold" has more work for the projection routine than either the sentence with "sent" or the one with "gave," which are equal in this respect. If we consider just the number of insertions of the subject noun phrase into its argument places we see that "sold" requires three, while "gave" and "sent" each require just two. If we consider the total number of argument insertions required for the subject, used as the cue in the Gentner experiment, and the direct object, which had to be recalled, then we see that while there are five argument insertions for "sold," there are three each for "gave" and "sent." This corresponds to the Gentner results.

F. The man sold the woman a book.

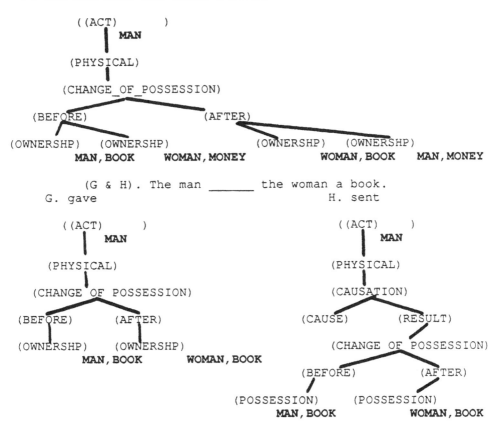

(G & H). The man _____ the woman a book.
G. gave   H. sent

Turning now to the FGWP evidence, we find that it concerns the relative degree of relatedness between noun phrases in simple sentences. Basically, FGWP claim that while on the basis of a supposedly definitional representation of causative verbs we would expect their subject and object NPs to be less related than the subject and object NPs of non-causative transitive verbs, in fact the experimental evidence shows that this is not the case. Now while FGWP choose to use the term "related" and Gentner, perhaps leaning towards the connectionist or parallel distributed processing approach, chooses to use the term "connected," and while FGWP employ a different methodology, direcly asking subjects to make relatedness ratings, the conclusions about greater or lesser relatedness or greater or lesser connectedness seem to be about the same thing. Very briefly, then, I would like

467

to show how the previous explanation of the Gentner evidence can also be applied to some of the FGWP results. Consider the following two sentences:

    I. The woman expected the man to leave.
    J. The woman persuaded the man to leave.

Gergely and Bever (1987) and FGWP both found that "the woman" and "the man" in (J) are judged to be more closely related than the same NPs in (I). FGWP offer a syntactic explanation for this which Gergely and Bever have shown not to work for other cases. In fact, Gergely and Bever suggest a semantic explanation: namely, that verbs like "persuade" whose meanings include a change in intention by the referent of the object NP brought about by the referent of the subject NP cause stronger relatedness judgements for these NPs than do other verbs which do not have this semantic structure. The Gergely and Bever study is very persuasive on this score. Nevertheless, consider the following representations of the meanings of these two sentences:

    I. The woman expected the man to leave.

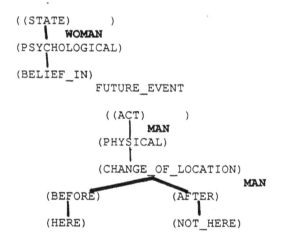

J. The woman persuaded the man to leave.

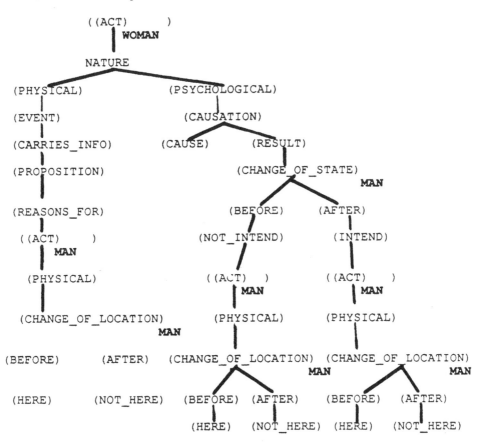

It is clear that the structure for "persuade" involves many
more argument insertions than does the structure for "expect":
eight for the former and only three for the latter. This, in my
view, is what accounts for the difference in relatedness in the
NPs in these sentences.

Moreover, this explanation would work for all verbs that
involved a change of intention on the part of the referent of the
object NP since all such verbs must have a branch in their
semantic representations similar to the CHANGE-OF-STATE branch in
the above reading for the "persuade" sentence, and this is the
branch that has in it the proliferation of argument insertions
below the highest BEFORE and AFTER nodes.

Conclusion: The explanations presented here for both the negative sentences and the NP relatedness experiments are quite natural. But what seems compelling to me is that both of these explanations depend crucially on the definitional character of the representations. Moreover, the psychological data that these explanations handle so well arise both from opponents and exponents of the definitional approach. For all these reasons psycholinguists and specialists in cognitive science interested in the mental representation of word meaning should give more credence to the definitional view.

REFERENCES

Fodor, J. A., Garrett, M., Walker, E., & Parkes, C. (1980). Against Definitions. Cognition, 8, 263-367.

Fodor, J. D., Fodor, J. A., & Garrett, M. (1975). The psychological unreality of semantic representations. Linguistic Inquiry, 6, 515-531.

Fodor, J. A. (1981). Representations: Philosophical Essays on the foundations of cognitive science. Cambridge, MA: MIT Press.

Gentner, D. (1981). Verb semantic structures in memory for sentences: evidence for componential representation. Cognitive Psychology, 13, 56-83.

Gergely, G., & Bever, T. (1986). Relatedness intuitions and the mental representation of causative verbs in adults and children. Cognition, 23, 211-277.

Katz, J. (1972). Semantic Theory. New York: Harper and Row.

Katz, J. (1977). Propositional structure and illocutionary force. New York: Thomas Y. Crowell Co.

Katz, J. (1989). Cogitations: A Study of the Cogito in relation to the philosophy of Logic and Language and a Study of them in relation to the Cogito. New York: Oxford University Press.

Locke, J. (1975). An Essay Concerning Human Understanding. Ed. P. H. Nidditch. Oxford: Oxford University Press.

McNamara, T. P. and Miller, D. L. (1989). Attributes of theories of meaning. Psychological Bulletin, 106, no. 3, 355-376.

Lexical Cooccurrence Relations in Text Generation[1]

Leo Wanner

Projekt KOMET
GMD-IPSI
Dolivostr. 15
D-6100 Darmstadt
West Germany
(*email:* wanner@ipsi.darmstadt.gmd.dbp.de)

John A. Bateman

USC/Information Sciences Institute
4676 Admiralty Way
Marina del Rey
California 90292
U.S.A.
(*email:* bateman@isi.edu)

Abstract

In this paper we address the organization and use of the lexicon giving special consideration to how the salience of certain aspects of abstract semantic structure may be expressed. We propose an organization of the lexicon and its interaction with grammar and knowledge that makes extensive use of *lexical functions* from the Meaning-Text-Theory of Mel'čuk. We integrate this approach with the architecture of the PENMAN text generation system, showing some areas where that architecture is insufficient, and illustrating how the lexicon can provide functionally oriented guidance for the generation process.

1 Introduction

In this paper we address the organization of lexis[2] giving special consideration to the expression of the salience of certain aspects of abstract semantic structure — a set of phenomena which we call **perspectives** of that structure. These have been addressed rarely in approaches in generation so far: for example, [Jacobs 85] discusses the verbs "give" and "take" as two different expressions of the same event; and Iordanskaja *et al.* [Iordanskaja, Kittredge, and Polguère 88] propose an approach to linguistic paraphrasing by adapting the Meaning-Text-Theory (MTT) [Mel'čuk and Žholkovsky 70] and its paraphrasing rules. Here, we make more extensive use of the MTT in order to provide a richer organization of lexis and its interaction with grammar and knowledge than has been proposed previously. Moreover, we develop this approach in the context of a concrete generation environment, the PENMAN system [Mann and Matthiessen, 85], showing some areas where the existing architecture is insufficient and how the richer organization of lexis we propose can help.

The following set of examples gives an impression of the variety of linguistic phenomena that we include under the term perspective.[3] All the sentences can be interpreted as verbalizations of a single abstract semantic structure with differing aspects of that structure being given expression in each case. For example, in (3), the reader is made salient as a participant of the proposition; and in (5), a particular temporal aspect of the process, namely the beginning, is put into focus. While the variation that can be seen between (1) and (2) can already be treated in, for example, the current PENMAN system by exercising meaning options available in the grammar (i.e., (2) exhibits passivization), the variation shown in the remaining examples cannot be functionally motivated as possible realizations of the base form.

1. *"We use the adjective "electronic" to indicate that the dictionaries are deeply dedicated to computers."*

2. *"The adjective "electronic" is used to indicate that the dictionaries are deeply dedicated to computers."*

3. *"The reader gets an indication that the dictionaries are deeply dedicated to computers by the adjective "electronic"".*

4. *"By the use of the adjective "electronic" we illustrate the deep dedication of dictionaries to computers."*

---

[1]We would like to thank Elisabeth Maier, Hans Müller, Erich Steiner, and Elke Teich for fruitful discussions. John Bateman acknowledges the additional financial support of IPSI during the development of the ideas reported here.

[2]We use the term 'lexis' rather than 'lexicon' to cover both the static organization of lexical information and the dynamic aspect of the *use* of that information and its *interaction* with other components of the linguistic system. Lexis, in this sense, is a term we borrow from Systemic linguistics, cf. [Matthiessen 89].

[3]The basic sentence given under (1) is chosen from the introductory note of a text concerning the development of electronic dictionaries in Japan [EDR 88].

5. *"We create an indication that the dictionaries are deeply dedicated to computers by the adjective "electronic".*

Some of the phenomena running through these examples have been treated as lexical cooccurrence [Apresjan, Žholkovsky, and Mel'čuk 69] or **collocation** [Firth 51; Halliday 66; Hausmann 85]). Most extensively they are handled by I. Mel'čuk *et al.* in the scope of the Meaning-Text-Theory by means of **lexical functions** (LFs). Our approach to adding the ability to generate this range of variation under functional control by means of perspectives takes its starting point, therefore, from the notion of lexical cooccurrence defined by Mel'čuk. There is a large body of descriptive work based on the notion of LFs which has been carried out for different languages [Mel'čuk and Žholkovsky 84; Mel'čuk *et al.* 88; Žholkovsky 70; Reuther 78; Janus 71] and we will suggest how this body of knowledge can now provide significant input to work on text generation.

2   The Nature and Organization of Lexical Functions

Lexical cooccurrence in the scope of MTT is provided in terms of lexical functions which Mel'čuk defines as follows [Mel'čuk and Polguère 87]:

> *A lexical function f is a dependency that associates with a lexeme L, called the argument of f, another lexeme (or a set of (quasi-)synonymous lexemes) L' which expresses, with respect to L, a very abstract meaning (...) and plays a specific syntactic role. For instance, for a noun N denoting an action, the LF $Oper_1$ specifies a verb (...) which takes as its grammatical subject the name of the agent of the said action and as its direct object, the lexeme N itself.*

The values for any particular application of a LF to a lexeme are provided by an **Explanatory Combinatorial Dictionary** (ECD); extensive dictionaries of this type for a number of languages have already been compiled by MTT researchers. Thus, for example, the ECD for English provides for the following applications of the LF $Oper_1$: $Oper_1$ ("influence") = "exert", $Oper_1$ ("punishment") = "administer". These give lexical verbs appropriate for use when the argument is to appear as a direct object to form a combination where an agent (optionally) acts upon some patient; e.g.: *He exerted influence on P..., He administered a punishment...,* but not, *he exerted a punishment..., he administered an influence....*

Cooccurrence relations of this kind are pervasive in natural language and need to be captured in the representation of a language's lexical resources. Such co-occurrence relations can be rather arbitrary and so are unlikely to be supportable by, for example, distinctions maintained in the knowledge base. Their *meaning* is not, however, arbitrary. An important claim of MTT is that each LF represents a particular abstract meaning which remains invariant across its various applications. Thus, for example, further LFs include: $Func_0$ with the meaning 'something takes place' ($Func_0$ ("accident") = {"occur", "happen"}, as in the sentence: *"The accident occured two hours ago."*); **Result** standing for a state following the process addressed (Result ("subject") = "master", as in the sentence: *"John mastered his subject."*); and **Liqu** expressing an active process termination. This latter LF is often used in so called *composed* LFs where a number of LFs are combined in a predefined order ($LiquFunc_0$ ("Fire") = {"extinguish", "put out"}, as in the sentence: *"The fire brigade could put out the fire quickly."*).

LFs typically correspond to knowledge at varying levels of abstraction in addition to lexical information, these classes are still very heterogenous. Previous approaches that have made use of LFs in generation (e.g., [Kittredge and Mel'čuk 83; Iordanskaja, Kittredge, and Polguère 88; Bourbeau *et al.* 89]) have been hindered by this. Work in progress at IPSI suggests that the large number of heterogeneous LFs used within MTT can be organized coherently in terms of the functions and semantic distinctions that they represent. Based on this, we have defined part of a general model of lexis with a taxonomic organization underlying it, within which the most general structures provide the representations of lexical semantics and the most delicate ones lexicalization. For the purposes of this paper, we will restrict attention to the organization of LFs that are particularly relevant for modeling situation perspectives as illustrated in our examples above. In Figure 1 we set out in network form the more general distinctions in meaning that the LFs we discuss

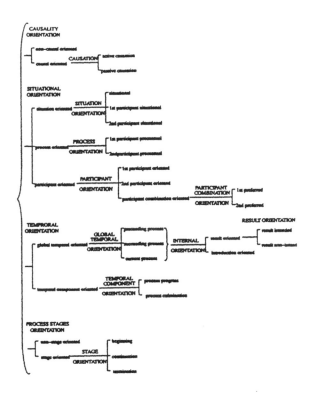

Figure 1: The hierarchical organization of lexical functions in network form

here cover.[4] The network explicates LFs by classifying each of them according to a particular set of semantic features. The general function of the network is thus to relate particular LFs to the functional conditions for their application. This defines the meaning that any LF expresses and so provides a functionally organized key into the LF-oriented dictionaries being developed within MTT. The network also shows the hierarchial arrangement lying behind the meaning of LFs and so reflects the relation of perspectives to one another.

We will now briefly describe in semantic terms a representative set of the LFs covered by the network, showing how the network relates perspectival presentation decisions to choices of LFs.[5] Then, with the organizational network of perspectives in place and motivated, we show how it can

---

[4]The notation of Figure 1 follows that used within the NIGEL grammar of the PENMAN system for the specification of grammar possibilities. Names in capitals represent the names of choice points, and names in lower case features which may be selected: one from each choice point; also square brackets represent disjunction of features and braces conjunction. Such networks can be readily expressed in a number of distinct formalisms, e.g., FUG (cf. [Kasper 88]), LOOM (cf. [Kasper, 89]).

[5]In the full version of this network, the consequences of each possible selection of features for LF selection is specified; space precludes a detailed discussion at this point, although examples are given below.

be used to guide the generation process to produce the kinds of variation illustrated in (1)-(5).

§2.1 Situation introduction

When a situation is introduced, this may be done respecting a number of varying types of salience — e.g., the salience of particular participants of a situation or the situation itself. Mel'čuk characterizes abstract situations by **key terms** which on the syntactic level are realized as nominals (or, more specifically, in most cases, as nominalized verbs) and their participants; the key term is designated by the LF S_0, the participants as S_i (i-th participant of the situation). Thus, looking at the situation of "teaching", the ECD for English offers us: S_0 ("teaching") ="teaching", S_1 ("teaching") = "teacher", S_2 ("teaching") = "pupil".

The selection of particular combinations of process and participants according to differing attributions of salience is then provided in the scope of the ECD by LFs of the groups **Func**, which stands for the salience of the lexeme labeling the situation, **Oper**, which stands for the salience of one of the participants, and **Labor** which stands for the salience of a combination of the participants. The selection of these broad groups is made in the network by the choices available under SITUATIONAL ORIENTATION, by the features 'situation oriented' (Func) and 'participant oriented' (Oper, Labor).

These are further differentiated according to which participants are affected; e.g.: $Oper_1$ makes the 'first' participant of the situation salient (i.e., the participant for which the LF S_1 provides a lexeme) and $Oper_2$ the 'second' (i.e., the participant for which the LF S_2 provides a lexeme): $Oper_2$ ("influence") = "be under". Similarly, $Func_0$ makes the key term of the situation itself salient, while $Func_1$ introduces the situation with particular respect to the first participant: $Func_0$ ("problem") = "exist", $Func_1$ ("problem") = "come [from]". $Labor_{12}$ makes the first and the second participant salient, the first more then the second, $Labor_{21}$, on the contrary, makes the second participant more salient, e.g.: $Labor_{12}$ ("authority") = "vest [with]", $Labor_{21}$ ("authority") = "owe [to]". These options are controlled by the further selections of participants to be accorded salience in the choice points SITUATION ORIENTATION and PARTICIPANT ORIENTATION.

Finally, the third option in the SITUATIONAL ORIENTATION system, 'process orientation' is responsible for the neutral LF V_0, which provides the most direct lexical verb for realizing the key term of a situation; e.g., V_0 ("influence") = "[to] influence".

§2.2 Temporal dependency

LFs also address the global arrangement of a process on the temporal axes by the definition of its preceding and succeeding processes. These considerations are reached in the network by a feature selection of {global temporal oriented, ..., } from the alternatives of the TEMPORAL ORIENTATION choice point. These alternatives call for the application of the LFs **Prox** and **Result**; examples of which from the ECD for English are: $ProxFunc_0$ ("storm") = "brew", $ResultFunc_0$ ("storm") = "subside". In addition, the internal temporal aspects of a process, represented by its stages, are reflected by the corresponding triple of "phasal" LFs: **Incep** for the beginning, **Cont** for continuing, and **Fin** for the termination stage. These meanings are reached via the features under the 'stage oriented' option in the choice point PROCESS STAGES ORIENTATION in the network.

§2.3 Results and consequences

Situations can also be expressed so as to give salience to their *results*. The treatment of this requires a consideration of the *intended* result of the situation — the actual LF chosen depends on whether that result was achieved or not. These options are found under the choice point INTERNAL ORIENTATION and RESULT ORIENTATION. If the result of the process was the intended result (i.e., the 'purpose' of the carrying out the process), then the **Real**$_i$, **Labreal**$_{ij}$, and **Fact**$_i$ groups of LFs are applicable; in the opposite case, the **AntiReal**$_i$, **AntiLabreal**$_{ij}$, and **AntiFact**$_i$ groups apply. Each of these groups provide further the salience either of the key term of the situation itself or of the various participants of the situation as determined by the simultaneous selections of features made under (in this sense $Real_i$ and $AntiReal_i$ correspond to $Oper_i$, $Labreal_{ij}$ and $AntiLabreal_{ij}$ to $Labor_{ij}$, and $Fact_i$ and $AntiFact_i$ to $Func_i$). For example: $Real_2$ ("order") = "obey", $AntiReal_2$ ("order") = "refuse".

§2.4 Causality

Situations can also be expressed so as to make the *causality* relationships that the situation enters into explicit or not; these options are considered by the choice point CAUSALITY ORIENTATION, which is responsible for application of either the LF **Caus** or **Perm**.

- The Caus function provides the active causer of the situation, as in the case of "problem"; e.g., $CausFunc_0$ ("problem") = "pose".

- Perm presupposes a 'permission', or allowance or acceptance, of the occurrence from the agent; e.g., $PermFunc_0$ (problem) = "tolerate".

3 Guiding the Generation Process by Lexis

The concrete generation system in which we are realizing the ideas proposed in this paper is the PENMAN system [Mann and Matthiessen 85]. The linguistic core of PENMAN is a large systemic-functional grammar of English, the NIGEL grammar [Matthiessen 83]. The semantic interface of NIGEL is defined by a set of *inquiries* mediating the flow of information between the grammar and external sources of information. PENMAN provides structure for some of these external sources of information, including a conceptual hierarchy of relations and entities, called the *Upper Model* (UM) [Bateman, Kasper, Moore and Whitney 89]; the UM is used as an interface between the organizational structures of the Domain Knowledge (DK) and the grammar's inquiries. PENMAN accepts demands for text to be generated in the notation of the PENMAN *Sentence Plan Language* (SPL) [Kasper 89]. SPL expressions are lists of terms describing the types of entities and the particular features of those entities that are to be expressed in English. The features of SPL terms are either semantic relations to be expressed, which are drawn from the upper model or from domain concepts subordinated to the upper model, or direct specifications of responses to NIGEL's inquiries.[6]

To generate any of the sentences (1)-(5) above using PENMAN, therefore, we must define appropriate SPL input. However, as mentioned in Section 1, these input specifications do not, at present, capture the generalization that these sentences share significant aspects of their meaning. To capture this, while still maintaining complete functional control of the generator, we introduce a more abstract input specification, from which particular SPL specifications are constructed depending on additional salience-oriented semantic distinctions. These semantic distinctions are specified in terms of the hierarchical organization of the meanings of LFs shown in the network of Figure 1. This organization provides a decision network representing the perspectives available and the functional motivations for choosing one perspective over another. Each of the decision points in this network may place constraints on the mapping between the abstract input level and SPL. These decisions themselves need to be made by a text planning component — the network represents the *capability* of generating variation under control rather than the control process itself. In this sense, lexis as the stratum containing perspective information provides a controlling mechanism for the generation process entirely analogously to the grammatical network defined by NIGEL.

4 Example of perspective-guided generation

We now illustrate the realization of some chosen perspectives in detail. Consider the clauses (1), (3), (4), and (5) given in Section 1. The SPL input specifications necessary to generate each of these clauses are set out in Figure 2.[7] As we can see, there is no connection between these since the generalization that they refer to the same situation is captured neither within the grammar, nor the upper model. Our new level of abstract input to the generation process, which corresponds more with Mel'čuk's conception of 'abstract situation' introduced in Section 2, provides this connection as follows. Abstract situations are represented in terms of a general type and a set of participants drawn from the lexemes defined with respect to the Domain Knowledge; for example, the abstract input for the situation underlying sentences (1), (3), (4), and (5) may be set out thus:[8]

---

[6] For full details of the PENMAN system and its components, see the PENMAN documentation [The PENMAN Project 89].

[7] Note that in this figure, in order to save space, we share the varables ve, N1, A1, AS1 across the distinct SPL specifications; this would not normally be done.

[8] The notation ↑ S_i is used to indicate that the value given is *not* the value of the LF S_i itself, it is rather the value of the role that the LF delivers; i.e., S_1 ("use") is "user".

```
(C1 / use
    :actor (we / person)
    :actee (N1 / adjective
               :name electronic)
    :purpose (A1 /indicate
               :actor we
               :subject-matter
                   (AS1 / dedicate
                        :domain (dictionaries / thing)
                        :range (computers / thing)
                        :manner (deep / sense-and-measure-quality))))

           SPL specification for sentence (1)

(C2 / get :actor (r / reader) :means N1 :actee A1)

           SPL specification for sentence (3)

(C3 / illustrate :actor we :actee AS1 :means N1)

           SPL specification for sentence (4)

(C4 / create :actor we :actee A1 :means N1)

           SPL specification for sentence (5)
```

Figure 2: SPL specifications for differing perspectives on a situation

$$
\begin{bmatrix}
S_0 & use \\
\uparrow S_1 & we \\
\uparrow S_2 & adjective\ 'electronic' \\
\uparrow S_3 &
\begin{bmatrix}
S_0 & indication \\
\uparrow S_2 & reader \\
\uparrow S_3 &
\begin{bmatrix}
S_0 & (deep)\ dedication \\
\uparrow S_1 & dictionaries \\
\uparrow S_2 & computers
\end{bmatrix}
\end{bmatrix}
\end{bmatrix}
$$

In order to generate sentences from this specification, we need to construct appropriate SPL expressions. This we achieve by following the semantic alternatives made in the LF network of Figure 1, applying the constraints that it specifies to compose a mapping between the abstract input and SPL.

Thus, for example, consider the context of use where a text planner has determined, in addition to expressing the situation shown in the abstract input, that that situation is to be presented textually as one in which the process is introduced neutrally, without respect for what preceded or succeeded, and with the process and the first participant (we: S_1) made relatively more salient. This corresponds to the set of LF network features {non-causal oriented, non-stage oriented, global temporal oriented, current process, introduction oriented, process-oriented, 1st participant processual}. This set of features governs the selection of the LF V_0, which is applied to the key-term of the situation, i.e., to S_0 of the input form: the lexeme associated with the DK concept *use*. The ECD for the language then supplies a candidate lexical item — in this case, the process "use".

We integrate the information from the ECD by requiring lexical items to be linked to concepts which are subordinated to the PENMAN upper model. It is then possible to determine, by inheritance, the particular set of upper model/semantic role relations that are appropriate for a process of any type. The concept for "use" is classified as a *nondirected-action* in the upper model and so the role-set :actor, :actee is inherited. The fillers of these roles are then selected from the ordered set of participants specified in the abstract input under S_1, S_2. The process then recurses for the complex filler of S_3 — filling, in this case, :purpose upper model relation — and the SPL given in Figure 2 for sentence (1) is constructed.[9]

---

[9]The association of the abstract situational roles S_i and the roles drawn from the upper model in fact offers

If the text planning component had determined that a different set of presentational LF features were necessary, then a different LF would be selected for application to the key-term of the abstract input. Thus, with the selection of the features {non-causal oriented, non-stage oriented, global temporal oriented, succeeding process, introduction oriented, participant oriented, 1st participant oriented}, which expresses the effect of the process *use* with salience on its first participant, the LF ResultOper$_1$ is selected and, here, the ECD gives the process *illustrate*. This term is then, again, selected as the main term in the corresponding SPL specification and, as before, since it is also linked into the upper model, we know that the relevant role set is :actor, :actee, :means. The further mapping of situational roles S_i to available UM-roles then provides the necessary fillers for the slots in the SPL. This gives the SPL for sentence (4).

In sentences (3) and (5), the interaction between the lexical network and the situation subordinated under S_3 in the abstract input is shown.[10] For the situation of 'indication', then, when the LF features: {non-causal oriented, non-stage oriented, global temporal oriented, current process, introduction oriented, participant oriented, 2nd participant oriented} are required, expressing that the situation is introduced with emphasis on its internal composition and participants and that the second of those participants is the more salient, then the LF Oper$_2$ is selected for application to the filler of $\uparrow S_3$ (i.e., "indication"). The ECD in this case supplies "get". Note that here, the LF Oper$_2$ also has consequences for the latter mapping between situational roles and upper model roles; the key-term itself, S_0, is now associated with the role :actee. This provides the SPL specification for sentence (3).

Finally, with the selection of LF features {non-causal oriented, stage oriented, beginning, participant oriented, 1st participant oriented, global temporal oriented, current process, introduction oriented}, the LF IncepOper$_1$ is selected. When this is applied to "indication", the ECD gives the process "create" and the SPL for sentence (5) is set up accordingly.

5 Conclusion

We have shown how lexical cooccurrence relations can be used to express the salience of particular aspects of abstract semantic structures and how they can be organized to influence the generation process. A specification of perspectival presentatation features as defined in the network of Figure 1 makes it possible to generate rather varied surface realizational forms. We can view this network as a candidate for the *textual organization* of lexis — which complements the more traditional 'propositional' organization found in lexical discrimination nets (e.g., Goldman, 1975) and thesauri. The functional meanings of LFs we propose, although arguably inherent in the MTM, have not formerly been extracted as an explicit principle of organization. We suggest that this kind of organization may substantially enhance the information collected by MTM researchers. Finally, although we have restricted ourselves in this paper to details that are particularly relevant for modeling situation perspectives, we are working at a general model of lexis including, e.g., a semantically motivated classification of verbs, relations, etc. For this we also use a set of further LFs represented on various levels of abstraction.

References

[Apresjan, Žholkovsky, and Mel'čuk 69] Yu.D. Apresjan, A.K. Žholkovsky, I.A. Mel'čuk. 'On a Possible Method of Describing Restricted Lexical Cooccurrence', In *Russkij Jazyk v Nacionalnoj Shcole*, 6, 61-72.

[Bateman and Paris 89] J.A. Bateman, C.L. Paris "Phrasing a text in terms the user can understand", In *Proceedings of IJCAI 89*.

[Bateman, Kasper, Moore, and Whitney 89] J.A. Bateman, R.T. Kasper, J.D. Moore, R. Whitney. "The PENMAN Upper Model — 1989", ISI Research Report, USC/Information Sciences Institute, Marina del Rey, CA

---

another significant source of presentation variability which may also be addressed in terms of LFs. We do not discuss this further within the confines of the present paper however.

[10]Work elsewhere (e.g., [Bateman and Paris 89]) has shown that *propositionally* embedded components of an input specification can be linguistically realized under certain textual conditions as unembedded, or as dominating, constituents. This is the case here, although space precludes a more thorough discussion.

[Bourbeau *et al.* 89] L. Bourbeau, D. Carcagno, K. Kittredge, and A. Polguère "Text Synthesis for Marine Weather Forecast", Final Report, Odyssey Research Associates Inc., Montréal

[EDR 88] "Electronic Dictionary Project", Technical Report, Japan Electronic Dictionary Research Institute, Ltd.

[Firth 51]J.R. Firth "Modes of Meaning", In *Papers in Linguistics 1934-51*, London: Longman, pp190-215.

[Goldman 75] N. Goldman. "Conceptual Generation". In R.C. Schank (ed.) *Conceptual Information Processing*, North-Holland Pub.Co., Amsterdam.

[Halliday 66] M.A.K. Halliday "Lexis as a linguistic level", in C.E. Bazell *et al.* (eds.) *In Memory of J.R. Firth*, London: Longman, pp148-162.

[Hausmann 85] F.J. Hausmann. "Kollokationen im deutschen Wörterbuch. Ein Beitrag zur Theorie des lexikographischen Beispiels", in H. Bergenholtz, J. Mugdan (eds.) *Lexikographie und Grammatik, Akten des Essener Kolloquiums zur Grammatik im Wörterbuch*, pp118-129.

[Iordanskaja, Kittredge, and Polguère 88] L. Iordanskaja, R. Kittredge, A. Polguère "Lexical Selection and Paraphrase in a Meaning-Text Model", Paper presented at the 4th International Workshop on Natural Language Generation, St. Catalina, CA. To appear in: *Natural Language Generation in Artificial Intelligence and Computational Linguistics*, Cecile L. Paris, William R. Swartout and William C. Mann (eds.), Kluwer Academic Publishers.

[Jacobs 85] P.S. Jacobs. "A Knowledge-Based Approach to Language Production", Report No. UCB/CSD 86/254, Univ. of California at Berkeley

[Janus 71] E. Janus. "Five Polish Dictionary Entries...", In *Naučno-techničeskaja informacia*, 2.11, 21-24.

[Kasper 88] R.T. Kasper "An Experimental Parser for Systemic Grammars", in *Proceedings COLING '88*

[Kasper 89] R.T. Kasper. "A Flexible Interface for Linking Applications to PENMAN's Sentence Generator", in *Proceedings of the DARPA Speech and Natural Language Workshop*, Philadelphia, 1989.

[Kittredge and Mel'čuk 83] R. Kittredge, I.A. Mel'čuk "Towards a computable model of meaning-text relations within a natural sublanguage", in *Proceedings of the IJCAI 1983*.

[Mann 85] W.C. Mann. "An Introduction to the NIGEL text generation grammar", in J. Benson, W. Greaves (eds.) *Systemic Perspectives on Discourse, Vol. I, Selected Theoretical Papers from the 9th International Systemic Workshop 1983*, NJ, Ablex, 1985

[Mann and Matthiessen 85] W.C. Mann, C.M.I.M Matthiessen. "A demonstration of the NIGEL text generation computer program", in J.D. Benson, W.S. Greaves (eds.) *Systemic Perspectives on Discourse, Vol. I, Selected Theoretical Papers from the 9th International Systemic Workshop 1983*, NJ, Ablex, pp. 50-83, 1985

[Matthiessen 83] C.M.I.M Matthiessen. "Systemic grammar in computation: the NIGEL case", in *Proceedings of the First Conference of teh European Chapter of the Association for Computational Linguistics*, Pisa, Italy, 1-2 September, 1983.

[Matthiessen 89] C.M.I.M Matthiessen. "Lexico(grammatical) Choice in Text Generation", revised version of the Paper presented at the 4th International Workshop on Natural Language Generation, St. Catalina, CA, 1988. To appear in: *Natural Language Generation in Artificial Intelligence and Computational Linguistics*, Cecile L. Paris, William R. Swartout and William C. Mann (eds.), Kluwer Academic Publishers.

[Mel'čuk and Polguère 87] I.A. Mel'čuk, A. Polguère. "A Formal Lexicon in the Meaning-Text Theory (or How to Do Lexica with Words)", *Computational Linguistics*, 13.3-4, 276-289.

[Mel'čuk and Žholkovsky 70] I.A. Mel'čuk, A.K. Žholkovsky. "Towards a Functioning Meaning-Text Model of Language", *Linguistics*, 57, pp. 10-47

[Mel'čuk and Žholkovsky 84] I.A. Mel'čuk, A.K. Žholkovsky. *Explanatory Combinatorial Dictionary of Modern Russian*, Wiener Slawistischer Almanach, Vienna 1984.

[Mel'čuk *et al.* 88]Mel'čuk, N. Arbatchewsky-Jumarie, L. Elnitsky, A. Lessard. *Dictionnaire explicatif et combinatoire du francais contemporain*, Presses de l'Université de Montréal, Montréal.

[Reuther 78] T. Reuther "Plädoyer für das Wörterbuch",, *Linguistische Berichte*, 57, 25-48.

[The PENMAN Project 89] "The PENMAN Documentation: Primer, User Guide, Reference Manual, and NIGEL Manual", USC/Information Sciences Institute, Marina del Rey, California.

[Žholkovsky 70] Žholkovsky. "Materials for a Russian-Somali Dictionary", *Mashinnij perevod i prikladnaja lingvistika*, 13, 35-63.

478

Learning Lexical Knowledge in Context:
Experiments with Recurrent Feed Forward Networks

Steven L. Small

Department of Neurology
University of Pittsburgh

Abstract

Recent work on representation in simple recursive feed forward connectionist networks suggests that a computational device can learn linguistic behaviors without any explicit representation of linguistic knowledge in the form of rules, facts, or procedures. This paper presents an extension of these methods to the study of lexical ambiguity resolution and semantic parsing. Five specific hypotheses are discussed regarding network architectures for lexical ambiguity resolution and the nature of their performance: (1) A simple recurrent feed forward network using back propagation can learn to predict correctly the object of ambiguous verb "take out" in specific contexts; (2) Such a network can likewise predict a pronoun of the correct gender in the appropriate contexts; (3) The effect of specific contextual features increases with their proximity to the ambiguous word or words; (4) The training of hidden recurrent networks for lexical ambiguity resolution improves significantly when the input consists of two words rather than a single word; and (5) The principal components of the hidden units in the trained networks reflect an internal representation of linguistic knowledge. Experimental results supporting these hypotheses are presented, including analysis of network performance and acquired representations. The paper concludes with a discussion of the work in terms of computational neuropsychology, with potential impact on clinical and basic neuroscience.

1. Introduction

Connectionist approaches to the study of language, vision, and memory have led to altered perspectives on the nature of cognition [Churchland and Sejnowski, 1987]. In particular, this work has meant the rethinking of the computer metaphor for the mind, such that human memory does not necessarily have to be a "place" to "store" information and human knowledge can be more than "facts" and "inference rules". These computational concepts can be rejected (or at least questioned) without giving up the metaphor of human mental computation [Feldman, 1989].

Parsing has always played a prominent role in the computational study of human language. One reason for this, of course, was the engineering importance of parsing to early researchers in artificial intelligence; their goal was to access newly devised information resources using "natural" language. Cognitive scientists have also focused on parsing issues, with connectionist approaches contributing increasingly to this attention [Cottrell and Small, 1983; Waltz and Pollack, 1985].

Recent work on linguistic representation in connectionist models [Elman, 1989] has profound significance for the psycholinguistic and computational study of human language. In this work, Elman constructs a feed forward connectionist network [Rumelhart, et al., 1985] with only one (easily implemented) recurrent structure [Cottrell and Fu-Sheng, 1989], and trains it to analyze sentences. For each word presented in a particular sequence, the network must predict the next word expected. When the training has been completed, the network has acquired the ability to perform the desired task. Furthermore, in analyzing (statistically) the nature of the acquired "knowledge", Elman found that similar words, both semantically and syntactically, clustered together. He subsequently used his technique to build a network to learn to predict subject/verb agreements in sentences with relative clauses (differing in number).

This work succeeds for the first time at accomplishing a task that has been attempted a number of times in the recent history of cognitive science [Small and Rieger, 1982] without as much success. This work demonstrates (to a limited, but not insignificant

Full Address: Department of Neurology, University of Pittsburgh, 325 Scaife Hall, Pittsburgh, PA 15261. Phone: (412) 648-9200. Network: small@cadre.dsl.pitt.edu.

479

degree) that a computational device can learn linguistic behaviors without any explicit representation of linguistic knowledge in the form of rules, facts, procedures, or other symbolic schemes. Furthermore, it does so using a simulation technique that has much closer analogies to the human neurobiological substrate (i.e., neurons and their connections) than do any symbol processing approaches. Of course, there are great differences between connectionist networks (of all kinds) and biological neural "networks", and there are important contributions to cognitive scientific knowledge available from the study of logical representations. However, the ability of a simple network of impoverished computational units to acquire linguistic knowledge is important.

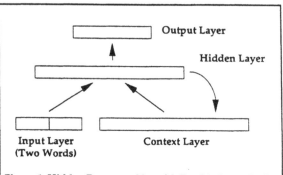

Figure 1: Hidden Recurrent Net with Double Input Buffer

2. Lexical Ambiguity Resolution

Representation of semantic and pragmatic context for lexical disambiguation has been a difficult problem, especially in contexts involving more than one sentence. In the work described here, a simple recurrent feed foward network (as in Figure 1) was trained to predict the next word in a sequence of lexical inputs. The correct desired output word depends on the semantic context of the previous sentence. A set of two sentence "stories" constituted the basic input to the system. Sentence 1a is an example "story" of this type.

(1a) "A man fights. He takes out the assailant."

As part of the experimental method, two simplifying assumptions were made initially, one of which was subsequently lifted. Throughout all of the experiments, the sentences have been simplified by removal of the articles. Sentence 1b shows the example story in the form actually used.

(1b) "Man fights. He takes out assailant."

A further simplification of the experimental method is the merging of "take" and "out" into a single word "take-out". Note that this was done in some but not all of the experiments, and constitutes an interesting part of the experimental design. Sentence 1c shows this input form of the example story.

(1c) "Man fights. He takes-out assailant."

This change simplifies the problem by (a) decreasing the number of total input words and thus the width of the input vector; and (b) decreasing the distance between the contextually important antecedent word and the ultimate ambiguity resolution task word (i.e., predicting the next word after "take out").

The input to the system on any experimental trial included sequences of three or four stories. On each trial, some textual feature or computational parameter was investigated. The two experimental endpoints consisted of the ability of the network to learn the task (i.e., convergence) and the number of trials needed to learn the task. Text comprehension features investigated included the following:

(a) Pronominal gender agreement;
(b) Equivalent contexts for different objects;
(c) Different contexts for the same objects;
(d) Distance between contextual prime and ambiguous word; and
(e) Size of the input buffer.

Computational manipulations were also studied, and aspects that could affect convergence included:

(a) Network learning parameters;
(b) Training instance presentation; and
(c) Network architecture.

The ability of the networks to find solutions to the problems presented suggest a number of things about human linguistic representations, as noted by Elman [1989]. In addition, the ways in which these networks are manipulated to effectuate or improve learning may have implications for language teaching, especially in second language learning or in language learning following damage to the nervous system.

3. Hypotheses and Experiments

All experiments were conducted with feed forward networks and learning by back propagation of error [Rumelhart, et al., 1985].

Five hypotheses motivated the work:

(1) A simple recurrent feed forward network using back propagation can learn to predict correctly the object of ambiguous verb "take out" in specific contexts;

(2) Such a network can likewise predict a pronoun of the correct gender in the appropriate contexts;

(3) The effect of specific contextual features increases with their proximity to the ambiguous word or words;

(4) The training of hidden recurrent networks for lexical ambiguity resolution improves significantly when the input consists of two words rather than a single word; and

(5) The principal components of the hidden units in the trained networks reflect an internal representation of linguistic knowledge.

The experiments were done with networks of three layers, using simple recurrence of hidden units, as shown in Figure 1. The distinct input words were each encoded as if they were orthogonal vectors in an n-dimensional space, where n is the total number of words in the trial (i.e., with six distinct input words, the first one would be encoded as 000001, the second as 000010, and so forth). When the input consists of more than one word (e.g., two words), each word is encoded as before, but with multiple buffer positions, each one consisting of the vector for one word (e.g., the input vector width for inputs of two words becomes 2n). Outputs are encoded separately, with one bit position for each possible output item (i.e., words, concept representations, or case frame data).

The use of one hidden layer (rather than two or three) and the ideal number of hidden units (generally 3 to 4 times the number of coded input units) were empirically determined through many experimental trials. The learning rate (nu or epsilon) was generally kept at 0.6 and the momentum (alpha) at 1.0. Changes in these values had little effect on convergence of the experimental network configurations. No attempt was made to minimize convergence time, and convergence was defined as achieving the correct binary output values for all inputs, with a value < 0.4 defined as zero, a value > 0.6 defined as one, and anything in between undefined, as per the suggestions of Fahlman [1988].

Experiments were conducted with three or four sentence pairs (which we call "stories"), along the lines of those shown above. The training sets presented the input data one word at a time (input buffer size = 1) or two words at a time (input buffer size = 2). Examples of both training instance types for Sentence 1b are shown in Figure 2. Example stories to study both ambiguity resolution and pronoun gender agreement are shown below. These sentences (2a-d) were presented in several different ways during the experiments. The presentations involved either (a) the first three stories or all four stories; (b) a single "take-out" word or two separate words; and (c) either one input word at a time or two input words at a time (as seen in the example training set of Figure 2).

(2a) "Man fights. He takes out assailant."
(2b) "Woman cleans. She takes out garbage."
(2c) "Man loves. He takes out licence."
(2d) "Woman eats. She takes out supper."

INPUT	OUTPUT
man	fights
fights	*
*	he
he	takes
takes	out
out	assailant
assailant	*

Single Word Input Training Set

INPUT BUFFER #1	#2	OUTPUT WORD
man	fights	*
fights	*	he
*	he	takes
he	takes	out
takes	out	assailant
out	assailant	*

Two Word Input Training Set

Figure 2: Example Training Sets with One or Two Input Words

481

Note that capital letters are not represented, but end of sentence periods are included (as the asterisk in the example training set of Figure 2).

4. Experimental Results

Approximately one hundred experiments were conducted, and some general conclusions are possible on the basis of what was learned empirically from those studies. Fourteen experiments, restricted to three and four story sequences, are summarized in Table 1, and labelled Experiments 1-14. Several parameters that were not varied in these fourteen experiments are not listed in the table, including the number of hidden layers (1), the learning rate (0.6), and the momentum (1.0).

The information included in the table consists of the following: The input buffer width is the number of vectors, each representing a single word, that were input to the network; the networks were presented with either one or two word inputs. The words "take out" were represented in some experiments as a single word "take-out" and in others as two separate words. The input of a "clear signal" (a vector of all zeros) after each epoch aided convergence, as per the empirical observations of Blumenfeld [1989]. The hidden layer fraction is the ratio of hidden layer width to input layer width (before recurrence). A network was considered to converge if it produced the correct results for the training set. This was always true when the mean squared error of the net-

work was less than 0.1. A network was considered to be monotonic when its mean squared error never increased during training. The number of trials shown consists of epochs (complete presentations of the training set).

The hypotheses enumerated above proved to be mostly correct. It was possible to construct feed forward hidden recursive networks to predict the object of the verb "take out" in context (Hypothesis 1). Experiments using the same number of contexts (e.g., "fights") as ambiguous verbs (e.g., "takes out" meaning "knock out with a punch") converged the most readily (these experiments are shown in Table 1). Experiments with more contexts than ambiguous verbs also converged, but not as readily. Experiments with a greater number of ambiguous verbs than distinct contexts did not converge. Experiments including both male and female agents converged more readily than did experiments in which all the stories contained male agents only. The networks were not only able to predict the correct pronoun in context (Hypothesis 2), but actually improved their performance by having this additional nonredundant element of context to use in forming their internal (hidden unit vector) encodings.

By using "take out" as two words in some experiments but as a single word in others, the distance between the contextually relevant antecedent word and the ambiguous word was varied. Better convergence was obtained when it was encoded as one

EXPERIMENT #	1	2	3	4	5	6	7	8	9	10	11	12	13	14
PARAMETERS														
# of stories	3	3	3	3	4	4	4	4	4	4	4	4	4	4
# of "take out" words	1	1	2	2	1	1	1	2	2	2	2	2	2	2
Input buffer width	1	1	1	1	1	1	1	1	1	2	2	2	2	2
Genders represented	M	M	M	M	M	M	M/F	M	M/F	M/F	M/F	M	M	M
# of priming verbs	3	3	3	3	4	4	4	4	4	4	4	4	4	4
# of direct objects	3	3	3	3	4	4	4	4	4	4	4	4	4	4
Clear each epoch?	N	Y	N	Y	N	Y	Y	Y	Y	N	Y	Y	Y	Y
Input width	10	10	11	11	12	12	14	13	15	30	30	26	26	26
Hidden width	40	40	44	44	48	48	56	52	60	45	45	39	65	78
Output width	10	10	11	11	12	12	14	13	15	14	14	12	12	12
Hidden fraction	4	4	4	4	4	4	4	4	4	1.5	1.5	1.5	2.5	3
RESULTS														
Convergence?	Y	Y	N	Y	N	Y	Y	N	Y	Y	Y	N	N	Y
Monotonic?	N	N	N	N	N	Y	Y	N	N	N	N	N	N	N
# of trials (epochs)	887	1294	1160	896	4232	1047	495	3874	611	855	659	2207	2078	1662

Table 1: Summary of Fourteen Prototypical Experiments

word than as two words (Hypothesis 3), though most networks were able to perform adequately when each word was represented separately. The input buffer width had a significant effect on network performance (Hypothesis 4), with two word input experiments converging more consistently and faster than one word input experiments. Hypothesis 5 concerns the nature of the hidden unit vectors following training, and whether or not they constitute a "representation" of linguistic knowledge. This will be addressed in the next section.

5. Network Analyses

Principal components analysis and contribution analysis, a variation suggested by Sanger [1989] specifically for evaluating feed forward networks, were used to analyze the hidden unit vectors. The goal of this analysis was to determine if the hidden unit layer acquired a "representation" of the linguistic knowledge as it learned enough about the structure of the presented stories to predict their outcomes (i.e., the direct object of the context-dependent verbs).

Principal components analysis (PCA) consists of several steps, explained briefly in Fukunaga [1972], aimed at determining a coordinate system for a collection of vectors that maximally separates them, i.e., that organizes them into "components". In a feed forward network with hidden units, these components can be viewed as an encoding of the distributed information acquired by the network in training and used by the network to produce desired outputs for particular inputs. The steps of PCA are as follows:

(1) Compute the hidden unit vector corresponding to each input vector;

(2) Compute the covariance matrix of this array of hidden unit vectors;

(3) Determine the eigenvectors of the covariance matrix; these vectors constitute the new coordinate system;

(4) Sort the eigenvectors by their corresponding eigenvalues;

(5) Translate each hidden unit vector into the new coordinate system.

Contribution analysis simply requires that the hidden unit activations computed in step (1) be adjusted by selected weights between the hidden layer and the output layer of the network. The numerical analysis text by Press et al [1989] includes several of the algorithms required to perform eigenvector computation.

Analyses were performed on the hidden unit layer from Experiment 9 (see Table 1): This experiment involved the collection of the four stories shown in Sentences 2a-d, in which the verb "take out" takes four direct objects, which are primed by the semantic context in a previous sentence, and in which the main actor is either male or female. Traditional principal components analysis was performed, as was a contribution analysis focussing on the distributed hidden unit responsibilities toward particular output words.

Three of the most interesting components discovered in this analysis derive from the hidden unit contributions to the output word "garbage", which is one of the primed objects of "take out" that the network learns to predict based on context. These are the components illustrated in the figures. Note that a constant has been added to the raw values to improve the graphic presentation.

Figure 3 consists of a bar

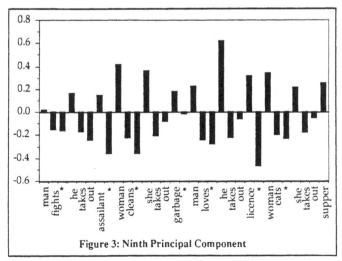

Figure 3: Ninth Principal Component

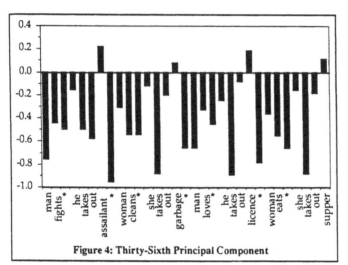

Figure 4: Thirty-Sixth Principal Component

the disambiguation task, and can be seen in a number of the principal components, which themselves appear to encode different information. Figure 5 illustrates this point in a principal component that superficially appears to represent the word "out", a word with no semantic role in the experimental stories used here. Significantly, the value of the principal component is maximal when the word "out" occurs in a sentence with a female subject. The network predicts the next word of the input stream by accumulating contextual information; in this case, a readily predictable word that precedes a highly unpredictable one (context excluded) becomes a carrier of contextual information.

graph illustrating the contribution of the ninth principal component to the decision task of the network. This component discriminates between nouns and other words (i.e., verbs and the periods at the end of sentences). Many of the principal component vectors discriminate among words and word types, and suggest learned linguistic representations (appropriate to the simple linguistic task performed). Other principal components appear not to represent typical linguistic concepts, representing instead heuristically useful information for performing the requested task. In the analyses performed for Experiment 9, for example, one principal component vector seemed to represent a category of pronouns and objects, another represented the words "woman" and all occurrences of the word "take" except the first one, and another the last word of each sentence.

Figure 4 shows that one of the principal components encodes the direct objects of the ambiguous verb "take out". Note that the gender of the sentence subject is subtly represented in these data in the magnitude of the component. The representation of gender contributes to the network's ability to perform

As expected, the knowledge gained by these networks, when presented with particular linguistic samples, pertains directly to those samples. The network thus has an inherently heuristic nature; the generalizations (are they representations?) acquired are useful and/or necessary for performing one particular task. Naturally, results based on experiments involving such small corpora of textual samples cannot necessarily be extrapolated to the entirety of human linguistic knowledge and processing.

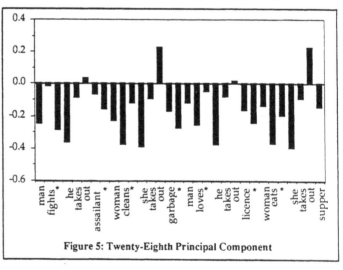

Figure 5: Twenty-Eighth Principal Component

484

6. Discussion

Much attention has been devoted to the effects of context on human comprehension of sentences and collections of sentences. The relevant context has included local syntactic and semantic features as well as broader elements of textual information. The subject of lexical ambiguity resolution [Small, et al., 1988] has been a productive domain for studies of this type, since understanding the syntactic role and semantics of a word requires knowledge of context at many different levels [Small, 1980].

Linguists have attended to the structural features of sentences and texts that bear on the unambiguous interpretation of subsequent linguistic fragments. Psychologists have employed lexical decision tasks [Tanenhaus, et al., 1979] and auditory evoked potentials [van Petten and Kutas, 1988] to gain information about the temporal sequence of steps performed by the brain to perform word or sentence understanding. While much of this work has been conducted in (presumably) normal users of language, some work has also been done in subjects with language dysfunction, such as Broca's aphasia [Bates and Wulfeck, 1989; Friederici and Kilborn, 1989] or Alzheimer's Disease [Nebes, et al., 1986].

In the current work, a simple recurrent feed forward connectionist network learned to interpret correctly the intended meaning of the words "take out" in context. As noted by Elman [1989], the distributed connectionist approach leads to linguistic performance without explicit rules. Furthermore, the syntactic and semantic structures of language (albeit the very simple examples studied so far) are represented in a distributed non-symbolic form. While in all likelihood, the brain does not employ back propagation learning, it does appear that human learning takes place by weight changes in response to input stimuli (if chemical changes at synapses are viewed as weight changes), and that repetition of stimuli potentiates learning [Lynch, 1986].

7. Conclusions and Future Work

Computational network architectures can learn to perform certain linguistic tasks without any explicitly coded pre-existing linguistic knowledge. In these experiments, simple networks were shown to gain internal linguistic representations sufficient to interpret ambiguous words in context. Furthermore, they were shown to improve performance with (a) shorter distance between contextually important antecedent word and ambiguous word; and (b) increased input buffer size from one word at a time to two words at a time. Both of these processing characteristics have a direct bearing on understanding human performance.

The linear algebraic technique of principal components analysis was used to demonstrate that the network gained a distributed internal representation of various heuristically useful concepts. These concepts include the linguistic notions of "noun" and "direct object", the interesting and useful notion of "the word 'out' in the context of a female agent", and other potentially useful heuristic concepts such as "last word in a sentence" and "period at the end of a contextually important sentence" (i.e., a two word antecedent sentence in one of the simple stories).

Finally, such networks have significant neurological importance. People are subject to a variety of neurological adversities, and the pathophysiology of many are unknown. Computer models of language that can be disrupted to produce deficits analogous to those present in human disease, such as acquired dyslexia [Hinton and Shallice, 1989; Mozer and Behrmann, 1989], may lead to better understanding of these disease processes. In addition to illness, such as stroke and dementia, which produce numerous speaking and understanding (and reading and writing) problems, normal aging also involves changes in linguistic processing. Perhaps a "computational neuropsychology" can shed some light on questions that have been unanswered since Broca [1861].

Acknowledgements

Thanks to the members of the neuroscience community at the University of Pittsburgh who provided helpful comments, advice, and support for the work described here: Audrey Holland, Mark Fitzsimmons, Mac Reinmuth, Gloria Hoffman, and Brad Tanner. Thanks also to Gary Cottrell of UCSD for his help with principal components analysis.

References

Bates, E. and B. Wulfeck, Crosslinguistic Studies of Aphasia, in *The Crosslinguistic Study of Sentence Processing*, MacWhinney and Bates (ed.), Cambridge University Press, Cambridge, 1989.

Blumenfeld, B., A Connectionist Approach to the Recognition of Trends in Time Ordered Medical Parameters, *Symposium on Computer Applications in Medical Care*, Washington, D.C., 1989.

Broca, P. P., Nouvelle Observation d'Aphémie produite par une Lesion de la Partie Postérieure des Deuxième et Troisième Circonvolutions Frontales, *Bullétin de la Societé Anatomique* , 1861, 6: 398-407.

Churchland, P. S. and T. J. Sejnowski, Neural Representation and Neural Computation, Cognitive Neuropsychology Laboratory, The Johns Hopkins University, Technical Report #34, 1987.

Cottrell, G. W. and T. Fu-Sheng, Learning Simple Arithmetic Procedures, *Eleventh Annual Conference of the Cognitive Science Society*, Ann Arbor, 1989.

Cottrell, G. W. and S. L. Small, A Connectionist Scheme for Modelling Word Sense Disambiguation, *Cognition and Brain Theory*, 1983, 6: 89-120.

Elman, J. L., Representation and Structure in Connectionist Models, Center for Research in Language, University of California, San Diego, Technical Report CRL-TR-8903, 1989.

Fahlman, S. E., An Empirical Study of Learning Speed in Back-Propagation Networks, Computer Science Department, Carnegie Mellon University, Technical Report CMU-CS-88-162, 1988.

Feldman, J. A., Neural Representation and Neural Computation, in *Neural Connections, Mental Computation*, Nadel, Cooper, Culicover, and Harnish (ed.), The MIT Press, Cambridge, 1989.

Friederici, A. D. and K. Kilborn, Temporal Constraints on Language Processing: Syntactic Priming in Broca's Aphasia, *Journal of Cognitive Neuroscience*, 1989, 1: 262-272.

Fukunaga, K., *Introduction to Statistical Pattern Recognition*, Academic Press, New York, 1972.

Hinton, G. E. and T. Shallice, Lesioning a Connectionist Network: Investigations of Acquired Dyslexia, Department of Computer Science, University of Toronto, Technical Report CRG-TR-89-3, 1989.

Lynch, G., *Synapses, Circuits, and the Beginnings of Memory*, The MIT Press, Cambridge, 1986.

Mozer, M. C. and M. Behrmann, On the Interaction of Selective Attention and Lexical Knowledge: A Connectionist Account of Neglect Dyslexia, Department of Computer Science, University of Colorado at Boulder, Technical Report CU-CS-441-89, 1989.

Nebes, R. D., F. Boller and A. Holland, Use of Semantic Context by Patients with Alzheimer's Disease, *Psychology and Aging*, 1986, 1: 261-269.

Press, W. H., B. P. Flannery, S. A. Teukolsky and W. T. Vetterling, *Numerical Recipes in Pascal: The Art of Scientific Computing*, Cambridge University Press, Cambridge, 1989.

Rumelhart, D. E., G. E. Hinton and R. J. Williams, Learning Internal Representations by Error Propagation, Institute for Cognitive Science, University of California, San Diego, Technical Report ICS-8506, 1985.

Sanger, D., Contribution Analysis: A Technique for Assigning Responsibilities to Hidden Units in Connectionist Networks, Department of Computer Science, University of Colorado at Boulder, Technical Report CU-CS-435-89, 1989.

Small, S. L., Word Expert Parsing: A Theory of Distributed Word-Based Natural Language Understanding, Ph.D. Thesis, Department of Computer Science, University of Maryland, 1980.

Small, S. L., G. W. Cottrell and M. K. Tanenhaus (ed.), *Lexical Ambiguity Resolution: Perspectives from Psycholinguistics, Neuropsychology, and Artificial Intelligence*, Morgan Kaufmann Publishers, Inc., San Mateo, California, 1988.

Small, S. L. and C. J. Rieger III, *Parsing and Comprehending with Word Experts: A Theory and Its Realization, in Strategies for Natural Language Processing*, Lenhert and Ringle (ed.), Lawrence Erlbaum Associates, Hillsdale, N.J., 1982.

Tanenhaus, M. K., J. M. Leiman and M. S. Seidenberg, Evidence for Multiple Stages in the Processing of Ambiguous Words in Syntactic Contexts, *Journal of Verbal Learning and Verbal Behavior*, 1979, 18: 427-440.

van Petten, C. and M. Kutas, Tracking the Time Course of Meaning Activation, in *Lexical Ambiguity Resolution: Perspectives from Psycholinguistics, Neuropsychology, and Artificial Intelligence*, Small, Cottrell, and Tanenhaus (ed.), Morgan Kaufmann Publishers, Inc., San Mateo, 1988.

Waltz, D. L. and J. B. Pollack, Massively Parallel Parsing: A Strongly Interactive Model of Language Interpretation, *Cognitive Science*, 1985, 9: 51-74.

How to Describe What?
Towards a Theory of Modality Utilization

Yigal Arens and Eduard Hovy*
USC/ISI
ARENS@ISI.EDU, HOVY@ISI.EDU

In this paper we outline the first steps of an investigation of the nature of representations of information, an investigation that uses as a starting point the various ways in which people tend to communicate different kinds of information. Our hope is that by identifying the regularities of presentation, in particular by finding out when people decide to switch presentation modalities and what they then tend to do, we will be able to shed light on the nature of the underlying representations and processes of communication between people.

1 Introduction: The Use of Multiple Modalities

In extended discussions of a technical nature, there invariably comes a point when someone reaches for a pen and draws a diagram or figure. Why? When and why does language, which is after all the most powerful means of communication available to humankind, fall short in expressive power? What additional features do other modalities of communication have? How do our cognitive abilities manage all the disparate kinds of information, splitting them apart during communication and allocating them to various modalities, and then integrating them again? Why is translating to another "visualization" not a simple process — for example, why do some problems seem unsolvable when presented in one way (say, in language) and straightforward when presented in another (say, diagrammatically)? What does it mean for some people to be more "visual" than others?

Questions such as these are interesting to the cognitive scientist because they may shed light both on our internal representations and on our manipulations of them, as reflected by the natures of the modalities we have developed to communicate ideas. This is a deep issue: humans *need* multiple media when they communicate. You cannot speak normally if restricted in hand gesture and facial expression. It is a rare nonfiction book that does not contain photographs, illustrations, or charts. Speakers in most workshops would consider themselves severely handicapped if denied use of overhead or slide projectors. And so forth.

The problem of display design has not yet been given a thorough computational analysis elsewhere. There does exist a general theory of graphical presentation, aimed at the human practitioner ([Bretin 83]), as well as computational treatments of certain subclasses of presentations ([Mackinlay 86, Feiner 88]).

While we do not pretend to have a theory to explain the phenomena, we believe that a careful study of the types of modalities people use, and the types of information they typically utilize them for, will single out characteristics of the underlying cognitive representations and shed light on people's communicative processes. With these issues in mind, initiating a study of the characteristics of representation as expressed through communication, we decided to examine first two aspects:

---

*This author was supported in part by the Rome Air Development Center under RADC contract FQ7619-89-03326-0001.

- communication-related characteristics of information
- modes of human-human and human-computer communication

We decided to take into account modes that are used in interactions with computers as well, in order eventually to test the rules we develop and implement on a computer against the display decisions made by people.

When identifying characteristics salient to the display of information, the vocabulary should:

- describe all features of the information that are salient for presentation purposes,
- describe all features of presentation modalities that can be utilized to convey information,
- be general enough to allow comparisons and specific enough to differentiate between different modalities and information.

We first define some useful terms, and then provide characterizations of media and information. The paper ends with an example.

2 Characterization of Modalities

2.1 Definition of Terms

The following terms are used to describe presentation-related concepts. We take the point of view of the communicator (indicating where the consumer's subjective experience may differ).

1. **Consumer:** A person interpreting a communication.

2. **Modality:** A single mechanism by which to express information. Examples: spoken and written natural language, diagrams, sketches, graphs, tables, pictures.

3. **Exhibit:** A complex exhibit is a collection, or composition, of several simple exhibits. A simple exhibit is what is produced by one invocation of one modality. Examples of simple exhibits are a paragraph of text, a diagram, a computer beep. Simple exhibits involve the placement of one or more **Information Carriers** on a background **Substrate**.

4. **Carried Item:** That piece of information represented by the carrier; the 'denotation' of the carrier.

For purposes of rigor, it is important to note that a substrate is simply one or more information carrier(s) superimposed. This is because the substrate carries information as well[1]. In addition, in many cases the substrate provides an internal system of semantics which may be utilized by the carrier to convey information. Thus, despite its name, not all information is transmitted by the carrier itself alone; its positioning (temporal or spatial) in relation to the substrate may encode information as well. This is discussed further below.

5. **Channel:** An independent dimension of variation of a particular information carrier in a particular substrate. The total number of channels gives the total number of independent pieces of information the carrier can convey. For example, a single mark or icon can convey information by its shape, color, and position and orientation in relation to a background map. The number and nature of the channels depend on the type of the carrier and on the exhibit's substrate.

2.2 Internal Semantic Systems

Some information carriers exhibit an internal structure that can be assigned a 'real-world' denotation, enabling them subsequently to be used as substrates against which other carriers can acquire

---

[1]Note that from the information consumer's point of view, Carrier and Substrate are subjective terms; two people looking at the same exhibit can interpret its components as carrier and substrate in different ways, depending on what they already know.

information by virtue of being interpreted within the substrate. For example, a map used to describe a region of the world possesses an internal structure — points on it correspond to points in the region it charts. When used as a background for a ship icon, one may indicate the location of the ship in the world by placing its icon in the corresponding location on the map substrate. Examples of such carriers and their internal semantic systems are:

Carrier	Internal Semantic System
Picture	'real-world' spatial location based on picture denotation
NL sentence	'real-world' sentence denotation
Table	categorization according to row and column
Graph	coordinate values on graph axes
Map	'real-world' spatial location based on map denotation
Ordered list	ordinal sequentiality

Other information carriers exhibit no internal structure. Examples: icon, computer beep, and unordered list.

An internal semantic system of the type described is always intrinsic to the item carried.

2.3 Characteristics of Modalities

In addition to the internal semantics listed above, modalities differ in a number of other ways which can be exploited by a presenter to communicate effectively and efficiently. The values of these characteristics for various modalities are shown in Table 1.

Carrier Dimension: Values: *0D, 1D, 2D*. A measure of the number of dimensions usually required to exhibit the information presented by the modality.

Internal Semantic Dimension: Values: *0D, 1D, 2D, >2D, 3D, #D, ∞D*. The number of dimensions present in the internal semantic system of the carrier or substrate.

Temporal Endurance: Values: *permanent, transient*. An indication whether the created exhibit varies during the lifetime of the presentation.

Granularity: Values: *continuous, discrete*. An indication of whether arbitrarily small variations along any dimension of presentation have meaning in the denotation or not.

Medium Type: Values: *aural, visual*. What type of medium is necessary for presenting the created exhibit.

Default Detectability: Values: *low, medlow, medhigh, high*. A default measure of how intrusive to the consumer the exhibit created by the modality will be.

Baggage: Values: *low, high*. A gross measure of the amount of extra information a consumer must process in order to become familiar enough with the substrate to correctly interpret a carrier on it.

2.4 How Carriers Convey Information

As part of an exhibit, a carrier can convey information along one or more **channels**. For example, with an icon carrier, one may convey information by the icon's shape, color, and possibly through its position in relation to a background map. The number and nature of the channels depends on the type of carrier and the substrate.

The semantics of a channel may be *derived* from the carrier's spatial or temporal relation to a substrate which possesses an internal semantic structure; e.g., placement on a map of a carrier representing an object which exists in the charted area. Otherwise we say the channels is *free*.

Generic Modality	Carrier Dimension	Int. Semantic Dim.	Temporal Endurance	Granularity	Medium Type	Default Detectability	Baggage
Beep	0D		transient	N/A	aural	high	
Icon	0D		permanent	N/A	visual	low	
Map	2D	2D	permanent	continuous	visual	low	high
Picture	2D	3D	permanent	continuous	visual	low	high
Table	2D	2D	permanent	discrete	visual	low	high
Form	2D	>2D	permanent	discrete	visual	low	high
Graph	2D	2D	permanent	continuous	visual	low	high
Ordered list	1D	#D	permanent	discrete	visual	low	low
Unordered list	0D	#D	permanent	N/A	visual	low	low
Written sentence	1D	∞D	permanent	discrete	visual	low	low
Spoken sentence	1D	∞D	transient	discrete	aural	medhigh	low
Animated material	2D	3D	transient	continuous	visual	high	high
Music	1D	?	transient	continuous	aural	med	low

Table 1: Modality characteristics.

Among *free* channels we distinguish between those whose interpretation is *independent* of the carried item (e.g., color, if the carrier does not represent an object for which color is relevant); and those whose interpretation is *dependent* on the carried item (e.g., shape, if the carrier represents an object which has some shape).

Most of the carrier channels can be made to vary their presented value in time. Time variation can be seen as an additional channel which provides yet another degree of freedom of presentation to most of the other channels. The most basic variation is the alternation between two states, in other words, a flip-flop, because this guarantees the continued (though intermittent) presentation of the original basic channel value.

3 Characterization of Information and Its Presentation

In this section we develop a vocabulary of presentation-related characteristics of information.

Broadly speaking, as shown in Table 2, three subcases must be considered when choosing a presentation for an item of information: intrinsic properties of the specific item; properties associated with the class to which the item belongs; and properties of the collection of items that will eventually be presented, and of which the current item is a member. These characteristics are explained in the remainder of this section.

Dimensionality: Some single items of information, such as a data base record, can be decomposed as a vector of simple components; others, such as a photograph, have a complex internal structure which is not decomposable. We define the *dimensionality* of the latter as *complex*, and of the former as the dimension of the vector.

Type	Characteristic	Values
Intrinsic Property	Dimensionality	0D, 1D, 2D, >2D, ∞D
	Transience	live, dead
	Urgency	urgent, routine
Class Property	Order	ordered, nominal
	Density	dense, discrete, N/A
Set Property	Volume	singular, little, much

Table 2: Information characteristics by type.

Since all the information must be represented in some fashion, the following must hold (where *simple* dimensionality has a value of 0, *single* the value 1, and so on, and *complex* the value ∞):

The Basic Dimensionality Rule of Presentations

☐ *Rule:* Dim(Info) ≤ Dim(Carrier) + Free Channels(Carrier) + Internal Semantic Dim(Substrate)

In addition, we have found that different rules apply to information of differing dimensions. With respect to dimensionality, we divide information into four classes as follows:

- *Simple:* Simple atomic items of information, such as an indication of the presence or absence of email.

  ☐ *Rule:* As carrier, use a modality with a dimension value of 0D.
  ☐ *Rule:* No special restrictions on substrate.

- *Single:* The value of some meter such as the amount of gasoline left. Associated rule is:

  ☐ *Rule:* No special restrictions on substrate.

- *Double:* Pairs of information components, such as coordinates (graphs, map locations), or domain-range pairs in relations (automobile × satisfaction rating, etc.).

  ☐ *Rule:* As substrate, use modalities with internal semantic dimension of 2D.
  ☐ *Rule:* As substrate, use modalities with discrete granularity (e.g., forms and tables) if information-class of both components is discrete.
  ☐ *Rule:* As substrate, use modalities with continuous granularity (e.g., graphs and maps) if information-class of either component is dense.
  ☐ *Rule:* As carrier, use a modality with a dimension value of 0D.

- *Multiple:* More complex information structures of higher dimension, such as home addresses. It is assumed that information of this type requires more time to consume (hence the last rule in this group).

  ☐ *Rule:* As substrate, use modalities with discrete granularity if information-class of all components is discrete.
  ☐ *Rule:* As substrate, use modalities with continuous granularity if the information-class of some component is dense.
  ☐ *Rule:* As carrier, use a modality with a dimension value of at least 1D.
  ☐ *Rule:* As substrate and carrier, do not use modalities with the temporal endurance value transient.

491

- *Complex:* Information with internal structure that is not decomposable, such as photographs.
  - ☐ *Rule:* Check for the existence of specialized modalities for this class of information.

Transience: Transience refers to whether the information to be presented expresses some current (and presumably changing) state or not. Presentations differ according to:

- *Live:* The information presented consists of a single conceptual item of information (that is, one carried item) that varies with time (or in general, along some linear, ordered, dimension), and for which the history of values is not important. Examples are the amount of money owed while pumping gasoline or the load average on a computer. Most appropriate for *live* information is a single exhibit.
  - ☐ *Rule:* As carrier, use a modality with the temporal endurance characteristic transient if the update rate is comparable to the lifetime of the carrier signal.
  - ☐ *Rule:* As carrier, use a modality with the temporal endurance characteristic permanent if update rate is much longer.
  - ☐ *Rule:* As substrate, unless the information is already part of an existing exhibit, use the neutral substrate.
- *Dead:* The other case, in which information does not reflect some current state, or in which it does but the history of values is important. An example is the history of some stock on the stock market; though only the current price may be important to a trader, the history of the stock is of import to the buyer.
  - ☐ *Rule:* As carrier, use ones that are marked with the value permanent temporal endurance.

Urgency: Some information may be designated *urgent*, requiring presentation in such a way that the consumer's attention is drawn. This characteristic takes the values *urgent* and *routine*:

- *Urgent:* This situation is exemplified in emergencies, whether they be imminent meltdowns or a warning to a person crossing the road in front of a car. Rules of modality allocation are:
  - ☐ *Rule:* If the information is not yet part of a presentation instance, use a modality whose default detectability has the value high (such as an aural modality) either for the substrate or the carrier.
  - ☐ *Rule:* If the information is already displayed as part of a presentation instance, use the present modality but switch one or more of its channels from fixed to the corresponding temporally varying state (such as flashing, pulsating, or hopping).
- *Routine:* The normal case.
  - ☐ *Rule:* Choose a modality with low default detectability and a channel with no temporal variance.

Density: The difference between information that is presented equally well on a graph and a histogram and information that is not well presented on a histogram is a matter of the density of the class to which the information belongs. The former case is *discrete* information; an example is the various types of car made in Japan. The latter is *dense* information; an example is the prices of cars made in Japan.

- *Dense:* A class in which arbitrary small variations along a dimension of interest carry meaning. Information in such a class is best presented by a modality that supports continuous change:
  - ☐ *Rule:* As substrate, use a modality with granularity characteristic continuous (e.g., graphs, maps, animations).
- *Discrete:* A class in which there exists a lower limit to variations on the dimension of interest. Appropriate modalities are as follows:
  - ☐ *Rule:* As substrate, use a modality with granularity characteristic discrete (e.g., tables, histograms, lists).

Volume: A batch of information may contain various amounts of information to be presented. If it is a single fact, we call it *singular*; if more than one fact but still little relative to some some task- and user-specific threshold, we call it *little*; and if not, we call it *much*. This distinction is useful because not all modalities are suited to present *much* information.

- *Much:* The relatively permanent modalities such as written text or graphics leave a trace to which the consumer can refer if he or she gets lost doing the task or forgets, while transient modalities such as spoken sentences and beeps do not. Thus the former should be preferred in this case.
  - ☐ *Rule:* As carrier, do not use a modality the temporal endurance value transient.
  - ☐ *Rule:* As substrate, do not use a modality the temporal endurance value transient.
- *Little:* There is no need to avoid the more transient modalities when the amount of information to present is *little*.
- *Singular:* A single atomic item of information. A transient modality can be used. However, one should not overwhelm the consumer with irrelevant information. For example, to display information about a single ship, one need not draw a map.
  - ☐ *Rule:* As substrate, if possible use a modality whose internal semantic system has *low* baggage.

4 An Example

We present three simple tasks in parallel.

Given: the task of presenting Paris (as the destination of a flight, say).

Available information (three separate examples): the coordinates of the city, the name *Paris*, and a photograph of the Eiffel Tower.

Available modalities: maps, spoken and written language, pictures, tables, graphs, ordered lists.

The modality characteristics are listed among those in Table 1. The information characteristics are listed in Table 3.

The allocation algorithm classifies information characteristics with respect to characteristics of modalities, according to the rules outlined in Section 3. The modality with the most desired characteristics is then chosen to form the exhibit.

Handling the coordinates: As given by the rules mentioned in Section3, information with a *dimensionality* value of *double* is best presented in a substrate with a *dimension* value of *2D*. This means that candidate substrates for the exhibit are maps, pictures, tables, and graphs. Since the *volume* is *little*, *transient* modalities are not ruled out. The value *dense* for the characteristic

	Coordinates	Name	Photograph
Information	48N 2E	Paris	Eiffel Tower
Dimensionality	*double*	*single*	*single*
Volume	*little*	*singular*	*singular*
Density	*dense*	*discrete*	*discrete*
Transience	*dead*	*dead*	*dead*
Urgency	*routine*	*routine*	*routine*

Table 3: Example information characteristics.

density rules out tables. The values for *transience* and *urgency* have no further effect. This leaves tables, maps, and graphs as possible modalities. Next, taking into account the rules dealing with the internal semantics of modalities, immediately everything but maps are ruled out (maps' internal semantics denote spatial locations, which matches up with the denotation of the coordinates). If no other information is present, a map modality is selected to display the location of Paris.

Handling the name: The name Paris, being an atomic entity, has the value *single* for the *dimensionality* characteristic. By the appropriate rule (see Section 3), the substrate should be the neutral substrate or natural language and the carrier one with *dimension* of *0D*. Since the *volume* is *singular*, a *transient* modality is not ruled out. None of the other characteristics have any effect, leaving the possibility of communicating the single word Paris or of speaking or writing a sentence such as *"The destination is Paris"*.

Handling the photograph: The photograph has a *dimensionality* value *complex*, for which appropriate rules specify modalities with *internal semantic dimension* of *3D*, and with *density* of *dense* (see Section 3) — animation or pictures. Since no other characteristic plays a role, the photograph can simply be presented.

5 Conclusion

We realize full well that this paper does not present an actual cognitive theory of how people represent and communicate information to highlight various characteristics. However, based on the pervasiveness and regularities in the use of multiple modalities in communication, we believe that any adequate cognitive theory will have to include the types of considerations and characteristics we discuss. That is to say, we believe that notions such as *dimensionality, urgency,* and *granularity* have an irrefutable cognitive reality, thanks to their essential role in the cognitive process of interhuman communication. Future refinements of these terms and identifications of others will help to uncover some of the ways in which people represent and manipulate various types of information.

References

[Bretin 83] Bretin, J. *Semiology of Graphics*, trans. by J. Berg. University of Wisconsin Press, 1983.

[Feiner 88] Feiner, S. An Architecture for Knowledge-Based Graphical Interfaces. ACM/SIGCHI workshop on *Architectures for Intelligent Interfaces: Elements and Prototypes*, Monterey, CA, 1988.

[Hovy & Arens 90] Hovy, E. & Y. Arens. When is a Picture Worth a Thousand Words?—Allocation of Modalities in Multimedia Communication. *AAAI Symp. on Human-Computer Interaction*, Stanford U., 1990.

[Mackinlay 86] Mackinlay, J. *Automatic Design of Graphical Presentations*. Ph.D. dissertation, Department of Computer Science, Stanford University, 1986.

Towards a Failure-driven Mechanism for Discourse Planning: a Characterization of Learning Impairments

Ingrid Zukerman
Department of Computer Science
Monash University
Clayton, VICTORIA 3168, AUSTRALIA
ingrid@bruce.cs.monash.oz.au

ABSTRACT

In the process of generating discourse, speakers generate utterances which directly achieve the communicative goal of conveying an information item to a hearer, and they also generate utterances which prevent the disruption of correct beliefs maintained by a hearer or the inception of incorrect beliefs. In this paper, we propose a representation scheme which supports a discourse planning mechanism that exhibits both behaviors. Our representation is based on a characterization of commonly occurring impairments to the knowledge acquisition process in terms of a model of a hearer's beliefs. As a testbed of these ideas, a discourse planner called WISHFUL is being implemented in the domain of high-school algebra.

INTRODUCTION

In the process of generating discourse, speakers generate utterances which directly achieve the communicative goal of conveying an information item to a hearer[†], and they also generate utterances which prevent the disruption of correct beliefs or the inception of incorrect beliefs due to inferences performed by a hearer.

Goal-based discourse planning systems constitute a significan. trend in the discourse planning effort. In these systems, a communicative goal, such as $KNOW(item)$, is posted, and then a plan which includes speech acts as actions is formulated to attain this goal. If, according to a model of a hearer's beliefs, a precondition to an action is not satisfied, then it is posted as a subgoal (Appelt 1982, Hovy 1988, Moore and Swartout 1989). In particular, in systems developed by Hovy and by Moore and Swartout, generated discourse plans include rhetorical relations, such as Elaboration and Evidence, from Rhetorical Structure Theory (Mann and Thompson 1987). Goal-based discourse planners model successfully the first aspect of human discourse generation. However, they fail to account for rhetorical devices such as Revisions of previous material [*"In chapter 7, we saw how to factorize expressions ... "*] and Contradictions to erroneous beliefs or inferences ["Koalas are marsupials, *not bears*"], which address beliefs that are indirectly affected by the discourse. These rhetorical devices are accounted for by discourse generation systems which apply forward reasoning (Zukerman 1990a). Thus, in order to model both types of human discourse generation strategies and to generate a range of rhetorical devices which supports competent discourse, we need to apply both forward and backward reasoning.

In this paper, we propose a uniform representation formalism which supports discourse planning by means of both types of reasoning processes, and we motivate our representation by means of a simple discourse planner which applies both reasoning processes in sequence. Our formalism relies on a characterization of impairments to the knowledge acquisition process, such as Confusion, Lack of Understanding and Loss of Interest, which is based on a model of a hearer's beliefs.

[†] The terms speaker/writer and hearer/listener/reader are used interchangeably in this paper.

In the following section, we briefly discuss a model of a listener's beliefs capable of representing uncertain beliefs and predicting inferences commonly drawn in a knowledge acquisition setting. Next, we describe a simple discourse planner which applies both forward and backward reasoning. We then present our characterization of impairments, and demonstrate its application in discourse planning.

NETWORK MODEL OF A LISTENER'S BELIEFS

In order to address beliefs presumably entertained by a particular listener, we maintain an epistemological model which represents a listener's beliefs as a result of direct and indirect inferences drawn from presented material (Zukerman and Cheong 1988, Zukerman 1990a).

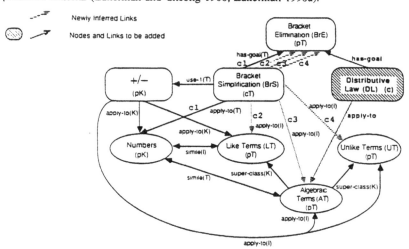

Fig. 1: Network Model of a Listener's Beliefs in High-School Algebra[†]

We represent a listener's beliefs by means of a network whose nodes contain individual information items and whose links contain the relationships between the nodes (see Figure 1). The links in the network are labeled according to the manner in which they were acquired, i.e., they can either be Inferred, Told or previously Known, where Inferred links are generated by means of generally applicable *Common-sense Inference Rules*. In addition, each link is accompanied by a *Measure of Belief (MB)* between -1 and 1, akin to Certainty Factors (Buchanan and Shortliffe 1985), which represents a user's level of expertise. The information in the network is represented at a level of detail which is consistent with the level of expertise required to learn the subject at hand, i.e., a simple and well-known concept is represented by a **p-node** (primitive), whereas a relatively new or complex concept is represented by a **c-node** (complex) which has other nodes as constituents. Like links, nodes may be Inferred, Told or previously Known, and each node has a *Degree of Expertise (DE)* between 0 and 1. The DE of a c-node is a function of the DEs and MBs of its constituent nodes and links, respectively. In this paper, we focus on technical domains, where the transmitted information typically pertains to *procedures, objects* and *goals*. Since one procedure will often achieve different goals when applied to different objects, we define a *context* as a triple composed of a procedure, an object to which it is applied, and the goal accomplished by this procedure when applied to this object (labeled c1-c4 in Figure 1).

[†] In the actual network each link may have a counterpart representing the inverse relationship. However, for clarity of presentation, only links which are relevant to our discussion are shown here.

Our inference mechanism generates plausible inferences from links in the network by means of generally applicable Common-sense Inference Rules which portray reasoning activities such as generalization, specialization and similarity-based inference (see Figure 2). These rules are inspired by rule adaptations commonly performed by students which were studied by Matz (1982), Brown and Van Lehn (1980), Van Lehn (1983) and Sleeman (1984). In order to account for the deductive abilities of a particular type of listener, we annotate each rule with a measure of uncertainty, denoted ρ, which represents a listener's belief in the validity of a conclusion given that the evidence is certain. This measure resembles the rule strength used in ACT* (Anderson 1983).

R1
; *If procedure $PROC_a$ initially uses a given set of procedures and these procedures apply to*
; *disjoint parts of a given object OBJ_m then, with likelihood ρ_1, $PROC_a$ is applicable to OBJ_m*
IF [for $i=1, \cdots, n$ $\exists$ a use-1 link between $PROC_a$ and $PROC_i$ with MB k_{ai}
    AND for $i=1, \cdots, n$ $\exists$ an apply-to link between $PROC_i$ and OBJ_m with MB k_{im}]
    THEN (with certainty ρ_1)

    Add an apply-to link of type I between $PROC_a$ and OBJ_m with MB $k_{am} = \dfrac{\rho_1}{n} \sum_{i=1}^{n} k_{ai} k_{im}$

Fig. 2: Sample Inference Rule

THE BASIC MECHANISM

As stated above, in a knowledge acquisition setting, a speaker's communicative goal not only pertains to the acquisition of a particular item of knowledge, but also to inferences a hearer is likely to draw and to other beliefs held by the hearer. Thus, given an *Intended Message (IM)* to be conveyed to a hearer, the following tasks must be performed:

1.   Generate *Peripheral RDs*, such as Contradictions and Revisions, which are related to the IM but are not directly instrumental to its acquisition.

2.   Generate *Supportive RDs*, such as Causal Explanations, Examples and Descriptions, which are directly instrumental to the attainment of the goal $KNOW(m)$, $\forall m \in \{IM, Peripheral\ RDs\}$.

3.   Sort the IM and the proposed RDs according to rhetorical considerations.

In general, these tasks should not be performed in strict sequence, but should be interleaved, since they affect each other's results. However, there are conditions under which the sequential execution of these tasks leads to coherent text (Zukerman 1990b). Hence, a two-stage discourse planner which generates Peripheral and Supportive RDs sequentially will suffice in order to illustrate the application of our characterization of learning impairments.

In the first stage, we apply forward reasoning to evaluate the impact of an IM on a listener's beliefs, and generate Peripheral RDs to counteract learning impairments which are likely to take place. To this effect, we temporarily assume that the goal $KNOW(m)$ for $m \in \{IM, Peripheral\ RDs\}$ can be attained by merely stating the message in question (this assumption is eliminated in the second step). This stage is executed as follows: initially, a network representing the IM is added to the network representing a listener's beliefs (see Figure 1). Next, a *Recognition* mechanism uses a characterization of learning impairments to anticipate whether the IM is likely to cause an impairment. If this is the case, a *Selection* procedure suggests a preventive Peripheral RD based on this impairment. A *Propagation* mechanism then performs forward reasoning by activating Common-sense Inference Rules to draw inferences from the proposed RD and the IM. The Recognition-Selection-Propagation cycle is repeated with respect to the newly drawn inferences until no impairments remain, i.e., no Peripheral RDs are proposed. This mechanism accounts for the presence of the Contradiction (in italics) in the sentence

"Pandas are bears, *but red pandas are not*," which prevents Mislearning due to an erroneous inference from the first part of the text. (A detailed description of this procedure appears in [Zukerman 1990a].)

In the second stage, backward reasoning is applied to generate Supportive RDs which fulfill the preconditions for the acquisition of each of the messages proposed in the first stage. Since the fulfillment of the preconditions to discourse actions (i.e., speech acts) is equivalent to the avoidance of learning impairments, a characterization of learning impairments may be used to determine Supportive RDs. This procedure accounts for the generation of a Causal Explanation such as "*they are raccoons*" to support the Contradiction in the above example. In the remainder of this paper we focus on our characterization of learning impairments based on our model of a hearer's beliefs, and demonstrate its use in discourse planning.

CHARACTERIZING KNOWLEDGE ACQUISITION IMPAIRMENTS

We distinguish between three main types of impairments which are responsible for a listener's failure to acquire the beliefs intended by the speaker from the presented information. Our distinction is based on the role of these impairments in the knowledge acquisition process, namely: *Comprehension-related*, *Affect-related*[†] and *Inference-related*. Comprehension-related impairments directly inhibit the acquisition of a message, while Affect- and Inference-related impairments inhibit the acquisition of a message through their effect on related beliefs held by a listener. Thus, the recognition and invalidation of possible Comprehension-related impairments is performed in the second stage of the above discourse planning procedure, yielding Supportive RDs; while the recognition and invalidation of the other learning impairments is performed in the first stage, generating Peripheral RDs.

Affect-related Impairments

Affect-related impairments occur when a hearer experiences adverse affective responses due to a conflict between the presented information and his/her existing beliefs. These conflicts inhibit the hearer's acquisition of this information even though s/he may understand it. In a knowledge acquisition setting, two common Affect-related impairments are *Confusion* and *Loss of Interest*.

Confusion occurs when an inference decreases significantly a listener's confidence in a previous belief, i.e., the absolute value of the MB of a link in a network representing a hearer's beliefs is significantly lowered due to the effect of an inference. For instance, upon reading the statement "One cannot always add Algebraic Terms," which yields a negative value for the MB of the link [+/− apply-to AT] in the network in Figure 1, a listener may erroneously infer that one cannot always add Like Algebraic Terms, in direct contradiction with his/her previous belief. The invalidation of Confusion caused by the effect of an incorrect inference on a correct link is performed by a Revision of this link, e.g., "but Like Terms can always be added"; while the invalidation of Confusion due to the effect of a correct inference on an incorrect link is performed by a Contradiction of this link.

Loss of Interest occurs when a listener who is initially motivated to acquire knowledge is presented with an IM s/he considers redundant. In terms of our model, this takes place if there exists a node B which *subsumes* a new node A, i.e., new distinguishing links incident upon A are connected to the same nodes and have MBs of compatible magnitude and sign as the corresponding links incident upon B. This situation is illustrated in Figure 1, where we try to add the node 0DL, representing distributive law, and the links [DL apply-to AT] and [DL has-goal BrE] to the network representing a listener's beliefs. However, the existence of the erroneous link [BrS apply-to AT] makes the node BrS equivalent to DL, thereby rendering the new procedure redundant and causing Loss of Interest. If Loss of Interest is caused by an incorrect link, it is invalidated by a Contradiction of this link, e.g., "One can not always simplify bracketed algebraic expressions"; whereas if all the links participating in this

---

† The term *affect* is used in this paper in the sense of *emotions*.

impairment are correct, the generation of a Motivation which adds new links to the message to be transferred is called for. Clearly, Loss of Interest may also be caused by boredom or by lack of understanding. However, in this case, Loss of Interest is a secondary learning impairment which results from other impairments.

Inference-related Impairments

Inference-related impairments take place when a hearer has failed to realize the implications intended by a speaker. That is, inferences which pertain to beliefs that the speaker intends the hearer to hold upon completion of the discourse produce either correct but weak beliefs or incorrect beliefs. These inferences may either affect previously existing beliefs or may be responsible for the inception of new beliefs. Inference-related impairments which are common in a knowledge acquisition setting are *Mislearning, Insufficient Learning* and *Insignificant Change* in a listener's knowledge status. A characterization of these impairments must take into consideration the difference between a listener's level of expertise with respect to a link and a level of expertise considered satisfactory.

Mislearning takes place when an erroneous belief with a relatively high degree of confidence is produced by an incorrect inference drawn by a listener, i.e., the link in question acquires a high MB with a wrong sign. This impairment is invalidated by a Contradiction of the inference.

Insufficient Learning occurs when a correct inference yields a correct belief with a relatively high MB, but which still falls short of a desired MB representative of proficiency. This impairment is invalidated by a Revision of the inference.

Finally, an *Insignificant Change* in a listener's knowledge status occurs when an inference produces a rather inconsequential change in a link with an MB representative of insufficient proficiency. The invalidation of this impairment in a link with a relatively high MB is performed by a Revision of the link, if it is correct, and a Contradiction, otherwise. In a link with a low MB, this impairment is considered equivalent to ignorance, and is invalidated accordingly.

The immediate invalidation of Affect-related impairments is essential for the smooth continuation of the knowledge acquisition process, since their persistence diverts a listener's mental resources from the task of acquiring further knowledge. On the other hand, the invalidation of Inference-related impairments with respect to links which are removed from the main focus of the discourse may be postponed if didactic or stylistic constraints prohibit the invalidation of all the recognized impairments.

Comprehension-related Impairments

Different Supportive RDs may accomplish the same function with respect to the comprehension process, e.g., a concept may be created in memory by means of a Description or an Analogy. Further, one Supportive RDs may perform a number of functions, e.g., a Description may be used to create a new concept or to identify a known concept. Therefore, we distinguish between three types of Supportive RDs according to their function rather than their structure, namely *Creative, Indicative* and *Explanatory*. Creative RDs are generated to build or reinforce a mental representation of a concept, Indicative RDs are generated to identify an existing concept in memory, and Explanatory RDs are produced to foster belief in a proposition. The Comprehension-related impairments characterized below determine the type of a Supportive RD to be generated.

In order to characterize Comprehension-related impairments, we have found it convenient to separate the comprehension process into three phases: (1) *Access* of the concepts in memory intended by the speaker, (2) *Construction* of a representation in memory of the presented information, and (3) *Acceptance* of the correctness of the presented information. We postulate that in a knowledge acquisition setting, if all these phases are successfully completed, then a message will be understood. In other types of settings, such as a task oriented setting, the third phase is desirable but not essential.

In order to complete the Access phase, the following subgoals must be satisfied: (1) Connection — the hearer must reconcile a referring expression used by a speaker with a node in memory which is intended by the speaker, and (2) Content — the goal *KNOW* must be fulfilled with respect to the intended node. A Content-related impairment may occur in conjunction with a Connection-related impairment, thereby requiring the generation of Supportive RDs which satisfy both subgoals. *Lack of Connection* and *Misunderstanding* are Connection-related impairments, and *Lack of Understanding* and *Insufficient Understanding* are Content-related impairments. These impairments define the preconditions to the attainment of the subgoals of the Access phase, and are characterized in terms of our network model as follows[†].

Lack of Connection occurs when one of the following conditions is satisfied: (1) a lexical item used by a speaker to refer to an intended node does not exist in the network which represents a listener's beliefs, i.e., the listener is unfamiliar with the terminology used by the speaker, (2) the lexical item exists in the network, but it is not connected to a concept, (3) it is weakly connected to the intended node (and no other node), or (4) it is connected to the intended node (and no other node), but this node is not primed in the network, i.e., it is outside the listener's *attentional state*[‡]. The last condition may occur when the discourse diverges both in time and place from the intended node, inhibiting a listener's ability to access it, even if its name has been mentioned. The invalidation of this impairment is performed by means of an Indicative RD, such as the Instantiation in the text "Like Algebraic Terms, e.g., $2x+3x$."

Misunderstanding occurs when a lexical item mentioned by a speaker is connected to a node which is not the intended node. This may be due to a true mis-connection or due to the fact that there is more than one concept with the same name, and the 'wrong' one is primed. A common example of the latter case is a scenario where two people are talking about another person, let's call her Mary, but each participant in the dialogue has a different Mary in mind. Like Lack of Understanding, this impairment is invalidated by means of an Indicative RD, such as "Mary Smith, not Jones."

Lack of Understanding takes place when there does not exist in the network representing a hearer's beliefs a node which corresponds to an intended concept. It entails a connection-related impairment, since a lexical item cannot point to an absent node. This impairment is invalidated by a Creative RD.

Finally, *Insufficient Understanding* takes place when there exists a node which corresponds to an intended concept, but the Degree of Expertise associated with this node indicates lack of proficiency. This impairment may occur in conjunction with a connection-related impairment or by itself. It is also invalidated by a Creative RD, but emphasis is placed on addressing missing or erroneous constituents of the node in question, rather than the entire concept. For example, "In completion to square, *you add and subtract* $(b/2a)^2$."

If a lexical item is used by a speaker to refer to a concept, the recognition of an impairment calls for the generation of an *Identification* which associates a proposed Supportive RD with this name, e.g., "A *crook* is a shepherd's staff." This may result in other impairments, such as Confusion or Mislearning, if the intended node is connected (either correctly or incorrectly) to another lexical item, i.e., it is identified with another name, or if the lexical item is connected (either correctly or incorrectly) to another node, i.e., there is more than one node with the same name. Both cases call for the generation of a Revision of the link in question, if it is correct, and a Contradiction, otherwise. In the above example, an impairment may take place if the hearer associates the lexical item *crook* with the concept *criminal*. If a speaker did not use a lexical item, Lack of Connection takes place, calling for the generation of an Indicative RD to enable a listener to access the node in question. In addition, a Creative RD may be required if the listener's expertise with respect to this concept is insufficient.

[†] We assume that the meaning of links, e.g., apply-to and subclass, is understood by a listener, and concentrate on nodes as possible sources of impairments.

[‡] The term *attentional state* is due to Grosz and Sidner (1986).

At present, we recognize two preconditions for a *Construction-related Impairment* with respect to a given message: (1) the recognition of a Content-related impairment in the Access phase of the comprehension of this message, or (2) a low MB in the links between the nodes in this message or between the constituents of these nodes. The first condition indicates that the hearer is unfamiliar with the concepts themselves, and, hence, is likely to be unfamiliar with the way they relate to each other. It may be invalidated by forcing Instantiations in Creative RDs proposed during the Access phase. The second condition indicates that although the listener may be familiar with the concepts in isolation, s/he is not proficient with respect to the way they relate to each other. This condition may be invalidated by means of Creative RDs with Instantiations with respect to the context at hand.

Finally, we recognize two preconditions whose satisfaction anticipates an *Acceptance-related Impairment* with respect to a given message: (1) the application of Common-sense Inference Rules to links in the network which are close to the link representing this message yields an MB for this link which indicates insufficient proficiency, or (2) there exists at least one link which has an MB indicative of an erroneous belief and is related by means of a Common-sense Inference Rule to the link representing the message in question. The first condition stipulates that the combination of the beliefs held by a listener which are related to the belief to be acquired fails to adequately explain the correctness of this belief, whereas the second condition stipulates that it is sufficient to have one belief which undermines the belief to be acquired, in order to anticipate an acceptance failure. Impairments in the Acceptance phase may be invalidated by generating Explanatory RDs, where the links targeted by these RDs are the ones with the lowest MBs. For instance, in the sample network in Figure 1, the Contradiction "Bracket simplification does not always apply to Algebraic Terms" requires a Causal Explanation such as "because you cannot always add Algebraic Terms," if the erroneous link [+/– apply-to AT] has a positive MB. The application of rule R1 in Figure 2 on this link and the link [BrS use-1 +/–] results in the link [BrS apply-to AT], thereby undermining a hearer's belief in the Contradiction.

A WORKED EXAMPLE

In this section, we briefly describe a possible behavior of our discourse planning procedure when teaching a student the distributive law. This situation is represented by the incorporation of the message [DL apply-to AT has-goal BrE], depicted by the shaded node and links in Figure 1, to the rest of the network in Figure 1. The result of this process is summarized in Table 1.

Table 1: RDs Proposed for the Intended Message [DL apply-to AT has-goal BrE]		
RD Type	*RD Contents*	*Possible Text*
Revision *Identification* *Instantiation*	**[BrS apply-to LT has-goal BrE]** (BrS, 'bracket simplification') (BrS apply-to LT)	We can always eliminate brackets in like terms by applying bracket simplification. E.g., $2(5x+3x) = 2 \times 8x = 16x$.
Contradiction *Causality*	**[BrS ¬apply-to AT]** (+/– ¬apply-to AT)	However, we cannot do this for all algebraic terms, because we cannot always add algebraic terms.
Intended Message *Identification* *Description* *Instantiation*	**[DL apply-to AT has-goal BrE]** (DL, 'distributive law') (DL) (DL apply-to AT)	In algebra, we can eliminate brackets by applying distributive law: We multiply each term inside the brackets by the term outside the brackets. For example, $2(x+y) = 2x + 2y$.

As stated above, in the forward reasoning stage, Loss of Interest is recognized due to the incorrect link [BrS apply-to AT], prompting the generation of a Contradiction of this link. The propagation of inferences from this RD cause Confusion in the correct link [BrS apply-to LT], calling for the generation of a Revision of this link. Since no further impairments are recognized in this stage, we proceed to the backward reasoning stage. During the Access phase, we recognize Lack of Understanding with respect

501

to the new concept *distributive law*, and Lack of Connection with respect to the concepts *bracket simplification* and *Like Terms*. The first of these impairments is invalidated by means of a Creative RD, such as a Description, and the rest by means of an Indicative RD, say, an Instantiation. Next, during the Construction phase, an impairment may be detected with respect to the application of distributive law to Algebraic Terms, requiring an Instantiation to complement the Description. Finally, in the Acceptance phase, an impairment may be recognized with respect to the Contradiction, calling for a Causal Explanation, as explained above.

CONCLUSION

This paper offers a discourse planning paradigm based on a characterization of impairments to the knowledge acquisition process in terms of a model of a hearer's beliefs. Our characterization provides a parsimonious representation of the preconditions for the fulfillment of a communicative goal, and it supports both backward and forward reasoning in discourse planning. This characterization requires a model of a hearer's beliefs which represents uncertain beliefs and supports the generation of inferences. At present, the forward reasoning process has been implemented with respect to the network in Figure 1, producing Peripheral RDs which are consistent with those appearing in naturally occurring texts.

REFERENCES

Anderson, J.R. (1983), *The Architecture of Cognition*, Harvard University Press, Cambridge, Massachusetts.

Appelt, D.E. (1982), *Planning Natural Language Utterances to Satisfy Multiple Goals*, Technical Note 259, SRI International, March 1982.

Brown, J.S., and Van Lehn, K. (1980), Repair Theory: A Generative Theory of Bugs in Procedural Skills. In *Cognitive Science* 4, pp. 379-426.

Buchanan, B.G. and Shortliffe, E.H. (1985), *Rule-Based Expert Systems — The MYCIN Experiments of the Stanford Heuristic Programming Project*, Addison-Wesley Publishing Company.

Grosz, B.J. and Sidner, C.L. (1986), Attention, Intentions, and the Structure of Discourse. In *Computational Linguistics*, Volume 12, Number 3, July-September 1986, pp. 175-204.

Hovy, E.H. (1988), Planning Coherent Multisentential Text. In *Proceedings of the Twenty-Sixth Annual Meeting of the Association for Computational Linguistics*, State University of New York, Buffalo, New York.

Mann, W.C. and Thompson, S.A. (1987), Rhetorical Structure Theory: A Theory of Text Organization. Technical Report No. ISI/RS-87-190, Information Sciences Institute, Los Angeles, June 1987.

Matz, M. (1982), Towards a Process Model for High School Algebra Errors. In D. Sleeman and J.S. Brown (Eds.), *Intelligent Tutoring Systems*, London: Academic Press, pp. 25-50.

Moore, J.D. and Swartout, W.R. (1989), A Reactive Approach to Explanation. In *IJCAI-11 Proceedings, International Joint Conference on Artificial Intelligence*, pp. 1504-1510.

Sleeman, D. (1984), Mis-Generalization: An Explanation of Observed Mal-rules. In *Proceedings of the Sixth Annual Conference of the Cognitive Science Society*, pp. 51-56.

Van Lehn, K. (1983), Human Procedural Skill Acquisition: Theory, Model and Psychological Validation. In *AAAI-83 Proceedings, American Association for Artificial Intelligence*, pp. 420-423.

Zukerman, I. and Cheong, Y.H. (1988), Impairment Invalidation: A Computational Model for the Generation of Rhetorical Devices. In *Proceedings of the International Computer Science Conference '88: Artificial Intelligence, Theory and Applications*, pp. 294-300.

Zukerman, I. (1990a), A Predictive Approach for the Generation of Rhetorical Devices. To appear in *Computational Intelligence — an International Journal*, Vol. 6, issue 1 or 2.

Zukerman, I. (1990b), Anticipating a Listener's Response in Text Planning. To appear in Golumbic, M.C. (Ed.), *Advances in Artificial Intelligence, Natural Language and Knowledge-based Systems*, Springer-Verlag.

Coherence Relation Reasoning in Persuasive Discourse

Horng Jyh P. Wu and Steven L. Lytinen
Artificial Intelligence Laboratory
The University of Michigan

Abstract

One major element of discourse understanding is to perceive coherence relations between portions of the discourse. Previous computational approaches to coherence relations reasoning have focused only on expository discourse, such as task-oriented dialog or database querying. For these approaches, the main processing concern is the *clarity* of the information that is to be conveyed. However, in a persuasive discourse, such as debates or advertising, the emphasis is on the *adequacy* of presenting the information, not just on clarity. This paper proposes a formalism and a system in which coherence relations corresponding to speech actions such as *clarify, make adequate* and *remind* are represented. Furthermore, in relating to human reasoning in general where studies have revealed that implicational and associative reasoning schema are prevalent across various domains, this formalism demonstrates that coherence relation reasoning is similar to this human reasoning, in the sense that coherence relations can be defined by domain independent implicational and associative schema. A prototype system based on this formalism is also demonstrated in this paper in which real world advertisements are processed.

1 Introduction

Some texts hang together better than others. To explain this fact, coherence relations have been proposed, which specify the possible ways in which sentences or other portions of discourse can connect to each other. Using coherence relations, a text's clarity can be evaluated. If an acceptable coherence relation structure can be built, then the text is clear; if not, it is not.

Most of the work in coherence relations has been done on task-oriented dialogues, or on stories. In this sort of discourse, clarity is an essential, and relatively straightforward, feature of the text. For example, in describing a task, the text is coherent if the steps of the task are specified in a well-connected manner. However, coherence is not as simple in persuasive texts, such as debates or advertisements. In these types of discourse, the author's speech actions are constantly affected by precautions such as to be objective or to be polite, etc. Hence, for understanding persuasive discourse, a formalism is needed which can represent those portions of discourse conforming not just to the clarity of the information, but also to the *adequacy* of presenting the information.

An example will illustrate the difference between clarity and persuasive coherence (adopted from Halliday's [HH76], p. 241):

> (1.a) Mary is leaving. She was never really happy here.
> (1.b) Is Mary leaving? She will be better off somewhere else.

In (1.a), after the second sentence is mentioned, the reason why Mary is leaving becomes clear to the hearer/reader. By being given this reason, the reader shall clarify his picture about the event and understand it better. However, in (1.b), the second sentence is used as a "justification" for the adequacy of the question. It explains why the speaker ask the question. That is, given that Mary shall be happier somewhere else, it is reasonable to ask the question. Similarly, by being given this justification, the hearer may be more willing to cooperate and answer the question as best he can.

In fact, in real life, many discourses can be seen in which an author/speaker will tend to draw support for his requests and beliefs, or try to concede an opinion by acknowledging other facts in order to invite the hearer's cooperation. Such discourses may include debates in an election, arguments in the court, advertisements in magazines or even everyday conversations. Consider, for example, the following two passages:

(2.a) Your oldest son can't help you take care of the other kids. But he can run errands for you.

(2.b) Your invitation is very nice. But I am not available that night.

Although these two utterances would be used in very different situations (one between two mothers, the other between a guest and a host), it is not hard to see the commonality between the two passages. Particularly, they both exhibit a counter-expectation deduced by the following implication-like schema,

The situation is A but it is not so A.

For example, A may stand for BAD in (2.a), since it is "bad" that the oldest kid cannot help take care of the other kids, however it is not so BAD because he can do something else. Similarly, A may stand for GOOD in (2.b), since being invited to a party is "good," but not able to make it is not so "good." To summarize, from a discourse point of view, the first sentence in both (2.a) and (2.b) serves as a concession to hearer's point of view so that they can cooperate and accept the second statement.

In this paper, a formalism is proposed in which coherence relations are treated as individual speech actions connecting portions of discourses. The types of speech actions categorized in this formalisms are *clarify*, *make adequate*, and *remind*. A set of 20 coherence relations originally identified by Mann & Thompson [MT88] are then categorized into the above three classes. For example, for *clarify*, there are coherence relations such as volitional-result and unvolitional-result to indicate the result of events; for *remind*, there are restatement and summary; for *make adequate*, there are evidence, justification, motivation, etc.

A set of implicational semantic relations are summarized from previous psychological studies in our formalism [TvdBS89], [CH85]. The relations included are Goal-oriented (GO), psychological-causation (PSI), physical-causation (PHI), enablement (ENB), obligation (OB), permission (PE), and material-implication (MI). For example, for (1.a) as well as (1.b), the underlying semantic connection between the two sentences is:

If A is unhappy about B then A avoids B.

This is one of the psychological causations between a state and a reaction categorized in Trabasso's [TvdBS89].

Besides implicational semantic relations, there are other underlying relations, which are called associative in our formalism. Following Chaffin and Herman's [CH84] categorization, there are: opposite (OPP), part-whole (PW) and class-inclusion (CI). These semantic relations are believed to underlie coherence relations such as contrast, elaboration and antithesis, which in turn, serve to clarify information. For example, for antithesis,

America rescued Panama. We did not invade it.

There is an opposite (OPP) semantic relation between rescuing and invading, which underlies the relation between the two sentences. The reasons for these categorizations are twofold: first, to capture subcategorizations of coherence relations due to subcategorization in semantic relations; and secondly, as a consequence of the first point, to reveal the hierarchy of coherence relations. The details will be shown in section 3.

2   Defining Coherence Relations (CR's)

In this section, a formalism is introduced which modifies and extends Hovy's system briefly sketched in his paper [Hov88]. The two major "players" in the system are denoted as S-for speaker/author, H-for hearer/reader. Each entity in this formalism has a type and can have associated attributes. Basically, the formalism assumes the representational scheme in a rule-based system such as Soar or Ops5. [1].

The major entities in the formalism are defined in the following.

---

[1] In the following, the actual representations are abbreviated for clarity of presentation

1. State of affairs, abbreviated as P. State of affairs is the direct semantic representation corresponding to a clause or entities that can be recursively defined as below. For example, "Peter is hungry" is represented as (Hungry Peter).

2. Implication relations, denoted as (IMP P Q), where P and Q are states of affairs. An implication can any one of the 7 types mentioned in section 1. For example, the relation "If A is a policeman then A can investigate people" is represented as (IMP P Q :type Permission), where P and Q denote (Is-a A Policeman) and (Investigate A people), respectively.

3. Associate relations, denoted as (ASSOC P Q), where P and Q are states of affairs. For example, If P is (Rescue America Panama) and Q is (Invade America Panama), then the associated relation between them is Opposite, that is (ASSOC P Q :type opposite).

4. Belief, abbreviated as (BEL X P). A belief has a holder and a content. For examples, the fact that a speaker uses present tense in the sentence "Peter is hungry" indicates his belief that Peter is hungry, denoted as (BEL S (Hungry Peter)).

5. Goal, abbreviated as (GOAL X P). A goal has a holder (X) and the desired state of affairs (P). Goals related to a speaker S are reflected by their speech acts. There are 3 types of major speech acts in this formalism, denoted as SACT (a) Demand actions, denoted as ACT; (b) Inform reference of a entity, denoted as INFORMREF; (c) Inform factual status of an affair, denoted as INFORMYN[2]. For example, a question, "Would you tell me where John is?", is represented as (GOAL S (INFORMREF H S P'), where P' is the proposition (Be-at John ?loc), where ?loc means the location is unknown to the speaker.[3]

6. Mutual belief, denoted as (MB X Y P), where X is the holder of the mutual belief, Y are the other partners who share mutual belief with X, and P, the content of the mutual belief.

7. Mention, denoted as (MEN S P), represents the speech action performed by an author/speaker where S it the speaker and P is the statement being mentioned. Two things should be noted for mentioning. First, the difference between (MEN S P) and (BEL S P) can be demonstrated by the following the sentence,

   > Peter might be a student.

   it is translatable as (MEN S P') where P' is (Is-a Peter student) but not as (BEL S P'). Secondly, Mention can takes English words and hence, its implied word order as its arguments). So if speaker says "P because Q" then it can be represented as (MEN S (P because Q)). If the word order is not crucial then a dot is put between the two statements, so (MEN S (P . Q)) means P and Q can be mentioned in any order.

8. Acknowledgment, denoted as (ACK X P), describes an attitude toward a belief or command. In our domain, X is usually the hearer and P is belief or command the speaker wants to implant into the hearer's mind.

9. Coherence relations to make a passage adequate, denoted as (CR S P Q), where CR corresponds to the speech actions Justify, Evidence, motivate, enablement, and concession, were S is the speaker, P and Q are the relevant state of affairs.

Given the above represented entities, coherence relations related to the three major speech actions can be defined as follows[4]

Coherence relations of *make adequate* There are 5 coherence relations included in this category: Evidence, Justification, Motivation, Enablement, and Concession. Let's take Evidence and Justification as examples.

---

[2] For the latter two types, Cf. Allen's [All83]

[3] Later on, a primed proposition P' of P indicates P' is the declarative counterpart of a question or command expressed by P, or a modal-less propositions of the one with modal

[4] We take the initial coherence relations as those listed in Mann & Thompson's Rhetorical Structure Theory.

```
(Evidence P Q)                          (Justification P Q)
If                                      If
  (MEN S P) and                           (BEL S P) and
  (BEL S Q) and                           [(MEN S Q) or
  (MB (IMP P Q :type all types)) and       (GOAL S (SACT H S Q'))]
  [(MEN S (P . Q)) or                      (MB (IMP P Q :type all except MI and ENB)) and
   (MEN S (P because Q))]                  [(MEN S (P . Q)) or
Then                                        (MEN S (Q because P)) or
  (Evidence S Q P) and                      (MEN S (P so Q))]
  (ACK H (BEL H P'))                      Then
                                           (Justify S P Q) and
                                           [(ACK H (BEL H P') or
                                            (ACK H (SACT H S Q'))]
```

The definition for evidence states that if a speaker mentions P, and he also believes in Q (i.e., Q is a declarative sentence), and there is a implicational relation from P to Q, and the speaker mentions "P because Q" or just "P Q,", then the speaker uses Q to evidence P so the hearer shall come closer to the belief of P'. An example of the Evidence CR is as follows:

Peter is hungry. (Because) he looks faint.

Since if A is hungry then A will look faint, using the second sentence the reader becomes more convinced of the claim that Peter is hungry. Note that, the above definition will all apply for all seven types of implicational relations. However, in the case of material-implication type, the direction of the implication becomes irrelevant. Hence, the condition (IMP P Q) can also be (IMP Q P :type material-implication). This can be demonstrated by the following examples,

(3.a) Peter might be able to write a poem, because he can write a letter.
(3.b) Peter can write a letter, because he can write a poem.

The second clauses both serve as evidence for the first clauses in (3.a) and (3.b), although the same material-implication is used: If A can write a poem, then A can write a letter.

The definition for justification states that, rephrasing the definition backward, if a speaker wants to justify a question, or a command, or a belief described in Q and it is mutually believed that P implies Q, then he can mention P to achieve the justification. An example of a justification coherence relation is as follows:

I am a policeman. Please show me your id.

The speaker justifies his command by indicating he is a policeman, since if A is a policeman, then A is permitted to arrest people (a PE relation). To show the definition works for other implicational relations, for example,

I want to go the London. Can you buy me a ticket by tomorrow?

In this case, the goal-oriented (GO) relation-If A wants to fly to London, then A will buy a ticket to London, together with the mentioning of the motivation, justify the request for the hearer to buy the ticket for the speaker. The other coherence relations together with Evidence and Justification are summarized in the following Taxonomy.

```
Make adequate: (MEN S (P Y Q)) where Y is optional
             --------------/\-----------------
           /              |                  \
Assume (IMP Q P)   Assume (IMP P Q))   Assume (IMP -P Q)
  & Y = because      & Y = because       & Y = BUT
     |                ----/\-----            |
  Evidence          |          |        Concession
             Justification  Enablement
                     |
                 Motivation
```

506

The taxonomy is self-explanatory. The reason why Motivation is under Justification is because Motivation is to Justify a command by resorting to the pleasure or benefit (a PSI type of implicational relation) of the hearer.

Coherence relations of _clarify_. There are ten coherence relations included in this category: Volitional-cause/result, Non-volitional-result/cause, solution, purpose, condition, otherwise, evaluation, interpretation, elaboration, antithesis, and contrast. The definitions for Contrast CR and Antithesis CR are given below:

```
(Contrast P Q)                      (Antithesis P Q)
If                                  If
  (MEN S P) and                       (BEL S -P) and
  (MEN S Q) and                       (BEL S Q)  and
  (MEN S (P Q)) and                   (MEN S (P Q))
  (MB S (ASSOC P Q :type OPP))        (MB S (ASSOC P Q :type OPP))
Then                                Then
  (MEN S (Contrast P Q))              (MEN S (Antithesis P Q)) and
                                      (ACK H (BEL S Q))
```

The definitions indicate that the difference between Antithesis and Concession in of their underlying semantic relations. Antithesis assumes a associative type relation. On the other hand, Concession assumes a implicational type relation. These relations can be summarized in the following taxonomy:

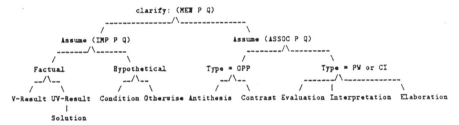

The reason why solution is a especial case of UV-result is because it requires the precedent to be a problem. Evaluation and Interpretation both assume that the situation where the state of affairs is assessed is a part of the entire belief space. The part could be the speaker's individual belief as for Evaluation or another state of affairs as for Interpretation. It is obvious that an Elaboration CR assumes class-inclusion semantical relations.

Coherence relations of _remind_ There are two such relations, they are Summary and Restatement. Restatement is a repetition of the exact terms that are mentioned in the previous context, whereas summary is a repetition of some derived terms from the previous context. Their definitions are straightforward. However, it will be shown in the next section that these CR's have an effect on the discourse stack that is not seen in the former two types of CR's.

3   Processing advertisements

The above formalism is currently under development in a system called BUYER (Cf. [LW89]). It takes propositions extracted from real-world advertisements as its input. The final output is the set of coherence relations that are derived from the entire discourse. Following are the control flow of the system and two examples:

The processing control flow.

(0) If end of passage then done, otherwise go to (1), if it is just a sentence or to (2), if it is preceded by a connective.

(1) Processing a sentence:
(1.a) Decide its referential continuity.
    (1.a.1) If not continuous then create a new segment and push the old context.
(1.b) Store potential referents in the current segment.
(1.c) Decide the speech acts of the sentences (e.g., it may a BEL, MEN, or GOAL).
(1.d) Abstraction to semantic frames, e.g., to a commodity as follows:
    Commodity Kraft-singles:
    Brand: Kraft.
    Category: Food.
    Ingredient: Milk.
    Flavor: Tasty.
(1.e) Decide implicational or semantical relations and coherence relations.
(1.f) Go to (0).

(2) Processing a connective between P and Q:
(2.a) Hypothesize the corresponding CR's.
(2.a.1) Start with the most general one if there is no clues for specific ones. For example, Connective So:
    General: Conclusion or Cause.
    Specific: Summary or Restatement.
          or Justification, etc.
(2.b) Decide the continuity of the discourse.
(2.c) Processing the latter one, Q.
(2.d) Go to (0)

The examples.

The washer ad
S1. It all comes out in the wash.
S2. You can crank-up a GE washer
S3. and get electro-mechanical effect.
S4. Or you can tap-touch a Speed-Queen Marathon
S5. and enjoy fully-programmable laundry.
S6. Match temperature to fabrics.
S7. Recall favorite cycles.
S8. GE or Speed Queen.
S9. The answer is at your figure tips.

The Kraft ad
S1. The older sister said milk is better than oil.
S2. We would never argue with such an authority.
S3. Imitation slices are made from oil and water.
S4. But Kraft singles is made from milk.
S5. Some people already know why Kraft is better than slices.
S6. They are the big brothers and sisters.

We will now describe the processing on the two examples presented above.

The washer ad. After S1 is processed, the referent of "it" is expected to be resolved. The referent is specified as of type PROBLEM, since the undergoer-slot of "comes out" is of PROBLEM type. When S2 is processed, due to referential discontinuity, a new segment is created and the old one pushed. The Coherence relation between S2 and S3 is determined to be volitional-result, since it is one of the CR's that correspond to the connective "and" and there is an underlying implicational relation: If A operates a machine then A gets the effect of the machine. Similar processing happened between S4 and S5, so the Volitional-result CR is decided. At the same time, while processing the connective "or," the relation between S2 and S4 are determined to be the Contrast CR because of the propositional structure corresponding to them is "symmetrical." Furthermore, since the expectation of PROBLEM is stacked, the Contrast CR is interpreted as an exclusive-or (adversative) instead of an inclusive-or (alternative). Thus, the referent of "it" is also resolved. S6 and S7 are evidences to S5 since "If A is a Match-temperature-to-fabric or a Recall-cycles then A is a Programmable-laundry." Meanwhile due to the referential discontinuity, the segment S2-S5 is pushed. Then, S8 is decided as a restatement of the Contrast CR, also the segment S2-S5 is popped because the restatement refers to the terms in the previous segment. R9 is an Evaluation CR, since the judgment references the reader's knowledge. The output can be summarized as:

Elaboration(S1,Contrast(S2,S4))
Volitional-Result(S2,S3)
Contrast(S2,S4)
Volitional-Result(S4,S5)

Evidence(S6,S5)
Evidence(S7,S5)
Restatement(S8,Contrast(S2,S4))
Evaluation(S9,S8)

The Kraft ad. After S1 and S2 are processed, a Justification CR between them is determined, since a implicational relation "If A is an authority then what he says is true" is recognized. S3 and S4 form a new segment because of the referential discontinuity, a Contrast CR between them is also determined, since the propositions corresponding to S3 and S4 have the same predicates but different subjects and objects. Then, the system recognizes when the claim (viz., milk is better than oil) is justified and the contrast related to the claim is given (viz., Kraft singles v.s. imitation slices), the speaker is indicating a exclusive-choice between the contrasted pairs. This causes the system to derive that Kraft singles is better than imitation slices, since milk is better than oil. S5 serves as summary of the above derived facts. S6 is an evaluation of S5, since it references the speaker belief. The output can be summarized as:

Justify(S2,S1)   Summary(S5,S1-S4)
Contrast(S3,S4)   Evaluation(S6,S5)

Top level CR sequence. One interesting observation in advertisement domains is that the top level CR's sequence tends to follow a few fixed patterns. For example, in the above two examples, they both have an assertion (either stated or justified) followed by a contrast, then followed by a Summary and Evaluation. This first part of the sequence resembles a common story plot: background, suspense and resolution. The difference is that in a persuasive discourse, the reader is reminded to reinforce the point. To study these common patterns of persuasion, called debate-plan, is just underway in our investigation.

4   Related work

Being a descriptive theory, Mann&Thompson's [MT88] Rhetorical Structure Theory proposes the initial categorization of coherence relations into presentation and subject-matter, two classes which roughly correspond to our *make adequate* and *clarify* speech actions. However, the definitions given for their Rhetorical relations tend to be too informal for a computational model. Particularly, the theory fails to capitalizes on the fact that the constraints of a Rhetorical relation actually can be conceptualized as implicational and associative semantic relations. Also, the notion of "positive-regard", which was vague in their theory, is represented explicitly in our formalism as the belief and acknowledgment of the reader. Furthermore, their multiple-nuclei Sequence Rhetorical relations, occurring in the top level of the discourse, do not tell us much about the semantic content of the passage. However, as demonstrated in processing advertisements, our system recognizes the sequence to be debate-plans that are commonly seen in persuasive discourse.

Hobbs' theory [Hob], on the other hand, captures of the general semantic relations underlying part of the CR's (those to clarify). However, little emphasis is put on the analysis of the CR's *make adequate* and *remind*.

Hovy's and Mckewon's [Hov88] [McK85] approaches work in the domain of generating answers to data-base queries. The CR's formulated are mostly concerned with clarifying a piece of information. Since their system is for text-generation, it applies knowledge in a back-chaining way. On the other hand, our system applies knowledge in forward-chaining way, and a back-chaining mechanism for understanding a discourse is being investigated for our system.

Allen and Litman's approaches [All83] [Lit86] [Lit87] share the common weakness of previous approaches in missing the CR's *make adequate* and *remind*. Furthermore, for the CR *clarify*, they did not capture the underlying implicational and associative semantical relations, which makes their approaches more domain dependent, especially in their earlier systems.

Cohen's [Coh87] is another computational approach which defines the CR of *make adequate*. However, only the Evidence CR is formulated. The argumentation structure derived from evidence coherence relations thus can not fully cover the debate-plan structure on which most advertisements are based.

5 Future Work

Three types of coherence relations are formulated in this paper: those of *make adequate*, of *clarify* and of *remind*. A prototype system based on this formalism together with other discourse processing mechanisms is shown to process advertisements. However, the formulation, as well as the system, is still rudimentary. Further enhancement can be pursued both in the formalism and the system.

In formalizing discourse reasoning, two goals are set: (1) To refine the formalism's vocabulary, so it make more use of the information deducible from grammatical morphemes for recognizing the implicational semantic relations. (2) To link up the sentence level processing with Unification Grammar based systems and investigate the possibility of even extending the unification mechanism up to the discourse level.

In enhancing the system performance, there are also two goals: (1) To refine the mechanism for deciding referential continuity. Currently the mechanism is simple-minded and works on the advertisements seen so far. A more complicated mechanism may be needed. However, if it turns out there is no need for such mechanism in advertisements, then it may contribute to our understanding of how referential continuity works in debate discourse. (2) To incorporate back-chaining inferencing in implicational relation recognition. According to our observation, advertisements make use of more "immediate" causal relations in consecutive sentences, unlike stories in which causal connections tend to involve several steps. However, there might be cases where hidden connections should exist. In those cases, assumptions should be made and a back-chaining mechanism should be incorporated.

References

[All83]   J. Allen. Recognizing intentions from natural language utterances. In M. Brady, editor, *Computational Model of Discourse*, pages 107–166. The MIT Press, 1983.

[CH84]   R. Chaffin and D. Herrmann. The similarity and diversity of semantic relations. *Memory and Cognition*, 12:134–141, 1984.

[CH85]   P. Cheng and K. Holyoak. Pragmatic reasoning schemas. *Cognitive Psychology*, 17:391–416, 1985.

[Coh87]   R. Cohen. Analyzing the structure of argumentative discourse. *Computational Liguistics*, 13:11–23, 1987.

[HH76]   M. Halliday and R. Hasan. *Cohesion in English*. Longman, 1976.

[Hob]   J. Hobbs. On the coherence and structure of discourse. In Livia Polanyi, editor, *The Structure of Discourse*. Ablex (forth coming).

[Hov88]   E. Hovy. Planning coherent multisentential text. In *26th Annual Meeting of the ACL*, pages 163–169, 1988.

[Lit86]   D. Litman. Linguistic coherence: A plan-based alternative. In *Proceedings of the 24th Annual Conference of Assoc. for Computational Linguistics*, pages 215–223, June 1986.

[Lit87]   D. Litman. A plan recognition model for subdialogues in conversation. *Cognitive Science*, 11:163–200, 1987.

[LW89]   S. Lytinen and H. J. Wu. Recognition of coherence relations. In *2nd AAAI Workshop on Plan Recognition*, 1989.

[McK85]   K. McKeown. Discourse strategies for generating natural-language text. *Artificial Intelligence*, 27:1–41, 1985.

[MT88]   W. Mann and S. Thompson. Rhetorical structure theory: Toward a functional theory of text organization. *Text*, 8:243–281, 1988.

[TvdBS89] T. Trabasso, P. van den Broek, and S. Y. Suh. Logical necessity and transitivity of causal relations in stories. *Discourse Processes*, 12:1–25, 1989.

Analyzing research papers using citation sentences

Wendy Lehnert, Claire Cardie, and Ellen Riloff
Department of Computer and Information Science
University of Massachusetts
Amherst, MA 01003
E-mail: lehnert@cs.umass.edu

Abstract

By focusing only on the citation sentences in a research document, one can get a good feel for how the paper relates to other research and its overall contribution to the field. The main purpose of a citation is to explicitly link one research paper to another. We present a taxonomy of citation types based upon empirical data and claim that we can recognize these citation types using domain-independent predictive parsing techniques. Finally, an experiment based on a corpus of research papers in the field of machine learning demonstrates that this is a promising new approach for processing expository text.

1 Introduction

One can get a reasonably good understanding of a research paper by merely skimming the sentences that reference other papers. By looking at how the author relates his work to other work in the field, a casual reader can get a good idea of what the paper is all about. As an example, consider the following opening sentence taken from a paper by (Braverman 88):

> The methods of explanation-based learning (EBL) [DeJong & Mooney, 1986] and explanation-based generalization (EBG) [Mitchell, Keller, & Kedar-Cabelli, 1986] involve two conceptual phases: explanation and generalization.

There are two important inferences that can be drawn from the sentence: (1) The paper is pigeonholing itself in the explanation-based learning (EBL) and explanation-based generalization (EBG) paradigms and (2) The distinction between the two conceptual phases is likely to be relevant to the paper. These inferences require general knowledge about research and research papers but no domain-dependent knowledge about EBL or EBG per se. Based on this observation, we contend that research documents can be understood at two distinct levels:

1. **The Semantic Level:** the domain-dependent details of the paper

2. **The Paradigmatic Level:** how the paper relates to other papers in the field

Previous work in understanding expository text has concentrated on summarization at the semantic level. Traditional approaches required extensive domain-dependent knowledge as well as an analysis of the surface structure of the text (see [Britton and Black 85] and [Voss and Bisanz 85] for discussions of these approaches). By focusing on the paradigmatic level of research documents, however, we can ignore the domain-dependent details of a paper and thereby make the task of "understanding" the text a tractable problem. Two main claims follow from this approach:

- Research documents can be understood at the paradigmatic level using a set of *conceptual references*.

- *Conceptual references* can be extracted from research documents using domain-independent predictive parsing techniques.

2 Conceptual References

A *conceptual reference* is a relation between a referencing paper and the referenced paper. Conceptual references represent the reasons behind a citation and tell us why an author references another paper. We have identified two distinct levels of conceptual references: conceptual reference categories and conceptual reference structures. In the following sections, we describe these two levels of conceptual references.

2.1 Conceptual Reference Categories

Conceptual reference categories identify the abstract object that the author is pointing to in the referenced paper. For example, the author may reference another paper to refer to a method, example, or result presented in that paper. Based on the observation that the majority of citation sentences rely on a small set of conceptual reference types, we have created a taxonomy of 18 conceptual reference categories:

1. **System:** a system is described in the referenced paper; e.g. in (Silver 88),
   "Other approaches were considered, including the use of ID3 [Quinlan]..."

2. **Method:** a method is described in the referenced paper; e.g. in (Shavlik 88),
   "Mooney [Mooney 88a] presents an algorithm for generalizing..."

3. **Concept:** a concept is described in the referenced paper; e.g. in (Keller 88),
   "Mostow's original definition of operationality [Mostow 81]..."

4. **Result:** a result is claimed in the referenced paper; e.g. in (Cohen 88),
   "In [Cohen 87] it is shown that PAs are Turing-equivalent..."

5. **Fact:** a fact is stated in the referenced paper; e.g. in (Ellman 88),
   "Standard explanation-based learning (EBL) methods apply only to domains for which a tractable domain theory is available [Mitchell 86]"

6. **Criticism:** a criticism is made in the referenced paper; e.g. in (Hunter 88),
   "A detailed criticism of such purely empirical systems can be found in [Schank 86]"

7. **Example:** an example is used in the referenced paper; e.g. in (Shavlik 88),
   "An example in [Shavlik 88a] shows that ..."

8. **More details:** the referenced paper has more details; e.g. in (Swaminathan 88),
   "For details, the reader is referred to [Swaminathan 88a]"

9. **Attribution:** an item is attributed to the referenced paper; e.g. in (Bylander 88),
   "In [Chandrasekaran 87], three types of explanation are ..."

10. **View:** a view is expressed in the referenced paper; e.g. in (Hirsh 88),
    "Generalization can be viewed as a search problem ([Mitchell 82] [Simon 74])..."

11. **Model:** a model is presented in the referenced paper; e.g. in (Mahadevan 88),
    "While there exist formal models for concept learning [Natarajan 87a] ..."

12. **Research:** research is presented in the referenced paper; e.g. in (Clancey 88),
    "Apprenticeship learning research has considered ... [Mitchell 85] [Smith 85]"

13. **Extends:** the referenced paper extends previous work; e.g. in (Cohen 88),
    "[Cohen 88a] has extended the system described in this paper ..."

14. **Application:** the referenced paper presents an application; e.g. in (Bennett 88),
    "For example, Segre has applied EBL to learning robotics tasks in a simplified blocks world [Segre 87b]"

15. **Merge:** the referenced paper merges two techniques; e.g. in (Prieditis 88),
    "[this work] is based on combining partial evaluation with other techniques (see Seki and Furukawa [37])"

16. **Proposal:** the referenced paper proposes an idea; e.g. in (Swaminathan 88),
    "[Tadepalli 85] has proposed replacing the original theory with ..."

17. **Problems:** the referenced paper identifies a problem; e.g. in (Dietterich 88),
    "[An important problem] ... is the imperfect theory problem [Mitchell 86]"

18. **Argument:** the referenced paper argues a position; e.g. in (Ginsberg 88),
    "... Kleer gives a similar argument for the ATMS [DeKleer 86]"

We created this taxonomy of conceptual reference categories based upon an exploratory empirical study of citation sentences. Our corpus contained 372 citation sentences from 40 papers in the Proceedings of the AAAI Spring Symposium Series on Explanation-Based Learning, March 1988.[1] To establish a good set of categories, we set a priori criteria for an acceptable taxonomy: (1) every category must be present in at least 2 sentences from at least 2 different papers (to limit idiosyncracies due to a particular author) and (2) the final set of categories must cover at least 90% of the citation sentences.

First, we arbitrarily selected 208 sentences (the odd-numbered sentences) from our corpus and labelled them by hand with the object being referenced by the citation – its candidate conceptual reference type.[2] Second, we compiled a list of these candidate conceptual reference types and retained only those that occurred in at least 2 sentences from 2 different papers (satisfying the first criterion). Finally, we measured the coverage of this final set and found that it covered 93.7% of the test set. Since this exceeded our 90% threshold (satisfying the second criterion), this set became our 18 conceptual reference categories.

2.2 Conceptual Reference Structures

The conceptual reference categories describe objects being pointed to in the referenced paper. Conceptual reference structures fit on top of these categories to describe the relationship between the referenced object and the current paper. The structures combine conceptual reference categories to explain exactly how a referenced object is being used by the referencing paper. For example, the author might reference a method in another paper to show how his own method *is similar to* the referenced method. There are currently three types of conceptual reference structures: similarity, difference, and flagship references:

- **SIMILARITY:** an object in the current paper is similar to an object in the referenced paper; e.g. in (Ellman 88): *"The general approach ... is similar to methods described in [Keller 87] and [Mostow and Fawcett 87]"*

- **DIFFERENCE:** an object in the current paper differs from an object in the referenced paper; e.g. in (Minton 88): *"Using a different approach, DeJong and Mooney's GENESIS system [DeJong 86b] ..."*

- **FLAGSHIP:** the current paper is pigeonholed via a group of citations of the same type; e.g. in (Prieditis 88): *"See [9,28,29,27,18,35,21] for examples of EBL systems."*

Since these conceptual reference structures fit on top of many conceptual reference categories (e.g. systems, methods, or models can be similar), we can visualize conceptual reference structures as being on a higher plane than conceptual reference categories. A citation sentence may therefore be represented as a conceptual reference category alone (e.g. if a related system is referenced) or as several conceptual reference categories that are embedded in a conceptual reference structure (e.g. if a method is compared to a related method). It is also possible for a sentence to be mapped into

---

[1] All examples used in the paper are taken from this corpus.
[2] There were actually 223 references because some of the sentences had multiple citations.

more than one conceptual reference if the author references a paper for several reasons. The next section describes how we recognize conceptual reference categories and build structures on top of them.

3 Parsing into Conceptual References

As stated earlier, we claim that understanding the relationships among research papers hinges on the ability to extract conceptual references from a document. Our second claim extends to the parsing mechanisms needed to understand these conceptual references:

1. *The parser relies strictly on predictive parsing techniques.* Predictive parsers are knowledge-based sentence analyzers that create conceptual representations for sentences. They have been used extensively in understanding narrative texts (e.g. [Lehnert 89], [Riesbeck and Schank 76], [Birnbaum and Selfridge 81], [Dyer 83]).

2. *The memory model underlying the parser contains only domain-independent knowledge.* Because we draw our examples from research literature in the field of machine learning, we distinguish between knowledge about research in general (domain-independent knowledge) and knowledge about machine learning (domain-dependent knowledge). In mapping sentences into conceptual references, the parser applies only general research knowledge.

Relationships among research papers are usually made explicit when one research paper references another. For this reason, we can recognize conceptual references without parsing the entire research document and restrict our attention to only those sentences that cite other papers. Citation analysis has been recognized as an important subfield of information retrieval since the early 1960's (e.g., [Garfield 55], [Garfield 64], [Garfield 79]). For the most part, however, researchers in information retrieval have concentrated on statistical analyses of citations to assess the value of an individual paper or the influence of a particular author (see [Salton and McGill 83], [O'Connor 83], and [Hurt 87]). They examine citations only to find the *existence* of explicit links between papers and make no attempt to attach any semantics to the links.

Because our work requires a deeper understanding of the relationships implied when one paper references another, we analyze citations within the context of the sentences in which they occur. These sentences are easily identifiable by a preprocessor that recognizes the peculiar format of citations. Occasionally, there are sentences that contain conceptual references without explicitly citing other papers. There is nothing about our parsing approach that prohibits mapping these sentences into the appropriate conceptual reference types. Identifying these sentences, however, would entail a scan of every sentence in the document. By limiting our attention to explicit citation sentences, we lose little information and only need to parse a small, easily identifiable portion of the text.

The goal of the parser is to represent a citation sentence as an instantiated form of one or more conceptual reference types. Sometimes it is adequate to map a sentence into a simple conceptual reference category. Often, however, a sentence contains more than one conceptual reference or contains one of the more complicated conceptual reference structures. In these cases, the parser returns multiple or embedded representations of the input.

Thus far, we have concentrated on recognizing 10 of the most common reference types described in section 2 — System, Method, Concept, Result, Criticism, Example, More Details, Attribution, Similarity, and Difference references. In the next section, we discuss our approach for parsing citation sentences into one or more of these types. Section 4 walks through a more detailed parse of a sentence from the machine learning corpus.

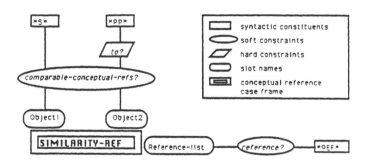

Figure 1: Case Frame Definition for a Similarity Reference

3.1 The CIRCUS Parser

We currently use the semantically-oriented CIRCUS parser [Lehnert 89] for understanding citation sentences. As a conceptual sentence analyzer, CIRCUS represents the meaning of sentences in terms of semantic case frames. Within CIRCUS, a conceptual reference is therefore represented as a case frame structure. Before sentence analysis begins, however, case frame definitions for each conceptual reference type must be hand-coded for the predictive semantics module that performs the slot-filling task. A Similarity reference, for example, has a case frame definition illustrated by Figure 1. Similarity references have three slots: Object1 and Object2 hold the two objects being compared; the Reference-list slot contains a list of citations. In addition, the case frame definition specifies that Object1 will be located in the subject of the sentence, Object2 will be in a prepositional phrase, and the special *REF* syntactic constituent[3] will contain the Reference-list.

Before filling a case frame slot, a syntactic constituent must satisfy the slot's semantic constraints.[4] For a Similarity reference, the prepositional phrase filling Object2 should begin with the preposition "to"[5], the head nouns in the subject and prepositional phrase constituents should be conceptual references that address research at the same level of generality, and the contents of *REF* should be a list of citations.[6] Below we present an example to illustrate how CIRCUS maps a sentence into a Similarity reference using the case frame definition described above.

4 An Example

Consider the following citation sentence:

---

[3] The sole purpose of the "REF" syntactic buffer is to hold citations.

[4] CIRCUS allows both *hard* and *soft* constraints. A hard slot constraint is a predicate that *must* be satisfied. In contrast, a soft constraint defines a preference for a slot filler rather than a predicate that blocks slot-filling when it is not satisfied.

[5] The Similarity reference case frame in Figure 1 recognizes citation sentences of the form "... {object1}...{ "to be" verb}...{any synonym for "similar"}...to {object2}...".

[6] Because we employ only domain-independent knowledge in mapping citation sentences into conceptual references, the semantic constraints access knowledge about research in general, but do not use any knowledge about the machine learning domain.

515

```
Similarity-ref

Object1 : Method-ref
Object2 : Method-ref
Reference-list : ([Keller 87][Mostow and Fawcett 87])
```

Figure 2: Desired Case Frame

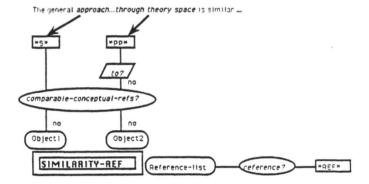

Figure 3: Case Frame Status After the Word "similar"

"The general approach of using examples to guide search through an approximate theory space is similar to methods described in [Keller 87] and [Mostow and Fawcett 87]" (Ellman 88).

CIRCUS should parse this sentence into the instantiated Similarity reference case frame shown in Figure 2. The parser scans a sentence from left to right, using its stack-oriented control to assign words/phrases to syntactic constituents until it notices a trigger for one of the predefined case frames.[7] Once a case frame is active, CIRCUS' predictive semantics module uses a marker passing algorithm to fill slots in the frame.

In our example, the presence of a "to be" verb followed by the adjective "similar" activates the Similarity reference case frame. In addition, the words "approach" and "methods" are a subset of the phrases that trigger Method references. Figure 3 illustrates the Similarity reference case frame just after CIRCUS has scanned the word "similar". The subject contains a Method reference for "approach" and the most recent prepositional phrase is "through theory space". Although CIRCUS places these constituents in the Object slots (as specified by the case frame definition), the Reference-list slot remains empty. In addition, the semantic constraints associated with Object1 and Object2 have not yet been satisfied. The prepositional phrase filling Object2 should begin with "to" and *both* Object slots should point to conceptual references.

---

[7] Some Similarity reference triggers are: "Similarly, ...","In the same way, ...", "X-like" where X can be any noun, "...is the same as...", "...is similar...".

CIRCUS continues scanning the sentence until all slots of the active frame(s) are filled without any semantic failures or until it reaches the end of the sentence. After picking up the references, the parser successfully returns the instantiated Similarity reference case frame of Figure 2 because each slot is filled with an object that satisfies the slot's semantic constraints: *REF* contains legitimate references, the preposition in the prepositional phrase constituent is "to", and Object1 and Object2 point to conceptual references that address research at the same level of generality (i.e., both are methods).

5 Evaluation

Our system currently recognizes 10 conceptual reference types — 8 conceptual reference categories (System, Method, Concept, Result, Criticism, Example, More Details, Attribution) and 2 of the higher level conceptual reference structures (Similarity and Difference). It correctly parses 69 sentences from papers in our machine learning corpus and contains over 450 lexicon entries.

To evaluate our progress, we ran an informal experiment. The goal of the experiment was to test the generality of our current set of conceptual reference case frame definitions. We selected two papers from the field of machine learning that were not part of the original corpus[8] and parsed the 28 citation sentences from those papers. We allowed the addition of lexicon entries for any new words occurring in the citation sentences, but did not define any new conceptual reference case frames or case frame triggers.

The system correctly parsed 75% of all citation sentences in the two papers. However, two of the sentences (7%) contained conceptual references whose case frames had not been predefined for CIRCUS. (They were not one of the 10 reference types listed above.) Modifying existing conceptual reference frame definitions and adding new triggers allowed 3 more of the remaining sentences to be parsed. With minor modifications to our parser definitions, we could therefore cover 86% of the test sentences. Discounting the 7% covered by undefined case frames, our success rate was then 93%.

6 Conclusion

This paper introduces an original strategy for parsing research documents using conceptual references. The work began in conjunction with the RA document summarization project which aims to summarize scientific research papers in terms of underlying research trends [Swaminathan 90]. RA models domain-independent structural relations in a research field in terms of research schemas and conceptual references. The RA system can use the conceptual references produced by our system to construct a summary of a corpus of research papers.

In closing, we emphasize that our approach to processing expository text is unique in two distinct ways. First, we model domain-independent structural relations between research papers in terms of conceptual references. This is a fundamental departure from other knowledge-based systems that emphasize the semantic content of their domains. Second, we demonstrate that expository text can be processed at the paradigmatic level using strongly predictive techniques. Our results have demonstrated that these two aspects of our system make it a promising new approach for processing expository texts.

---

[8] In order to remove any bias in the selection of papers, someone outside the parsing development group chose the papers for the experiment, [Keller 87] and [Kedar-Cabelli 87].

7 Acknowledgements

The authors would like to thank Kishore Swaminathan for commenting on earlier drafts of this paper and Stefan Wermter for his work on the project. This research was supported by the Advanced Research Projects Agency of the Department of Defense, monitored by the Office of Naval Research under contract #N00014-87-K-0238, the Office of Naval Research, under a University Research Initiative Grant, Contract #N00014-86-K-0764 and NSF Presidential Young Investigators Award NSFIST-8351863.

References

[Birnbaum and Selfridge 81] Lawrence Birnbaum and Mallory Selfridge, 1981. Conceptual Analysis of Natural Language. In R. Schank and C. Riesbeck, (Eds.), *Inside Computer Understanding*, pp. 318-353. Hillsdale, NJ; Lawrence Erlbaum Associates.

[Britton and Black 85] Bruce Britton and John Black, 1985. Understanding Expository Text: From Structure to Process and World Knowledge. In B. Britton and J. Black. (Eds.), *Understanding Expository Text*, pp. 1-9. Hillsdale, NJ; Lawrence Erlbaum Associates.

[Dyer 83] Michael Dyer, 1983. *In-Depth Understanding: A Computer Model of Integrated Processing for Narrative Comprehension*. Cambridge, MA; MIT Press.

[Garfield 55] E. Garfield, 1955. Citation Indexes for Science. *Science*. 122, pp. 108-111.

[Garfield 64] E. Garfield, 1964. Can Citation Indexing be Automated? In *Proc. of Symposium on Statistical Association Methods for Mechanized Documentation*, Washington, D.C.

[Garfield 79] E. Garfield, 1979. *Citation Indexing — Its Theory and Applications in Science, Technology and Humanities*. New York; John Wiley.

[Hurt 87] C.D. Hurt, 1987. Conceptual Citation Differences in Science, Technology, and Social Sciences Literature. *Information Processing & Management*, Vol. 23. No. 1, pp. 1-6.

[Kedar-Cabelli 87] S. Kedar-Cabelli, 1987. "Formulating Concepts According to Purpose". *Proc. of AAAI*, Seattle, WA.

[Keller 87] R. Keller, 1987. "Defining Operationality for Explanation-Based Learning". *Proc. of AAAI*. Seattle, WA.

[Lehnert 89] Wendy Lehnert, 1989. Symbolic/Subsymbolic Sentence Analysis: Exploiting the Best of Two Worlds. In: Barnden, J. and Pollack, J. (Eds.): *Advances in Connectionist and Neural Computation Theory*, Vol. 1, Ablex Publishers. in press. (Also available as COINS Technical Report 88-99, Department of Computer and Information Science, University of Massachusetts, Amherst, MA.)

[O'Connor 83] John O'Connor, 1983. Biomedical Citing Statements: Computer Recognition and Use to Aid Full-text Retrieval. *Information Processing & Management*, Vol. 19, No. 6, pp. 361-368.

[Riesbeck and Schank 76] Chris Riesbeck and Roger Schank, 1976. Expectation-Based Analysis of Sentences in Context. Research Report No. 78. New Haven, CT; Department of Computer Science, Yale University.

[Salton and McGill 83] Gerard Salton and Michael J. McGill, 1983. *Introduction to Modern Information Retrieval*. New York, NY; McGraw-Hill Book Company.

[Swaminathan 90] Kishore Swaminathan, 1990. "Knowledge Evolution and Memory Organization for Scientific Domains" — a PhD dissertation in preparation. Department of Computer & Information Science. University of Massachusetts, Amherst, MA.

[Voss and Bisanz 85] James Voss and Gay Bisanz, 1985. Knowledge and the Processing of Narrative and Expository Texts. In B. Britton and J. Black, (Eds.), *Understanding Expository Text*, pp. 173-198. Hillsdale, NJ; Lawrence Erlbaum Associates.

Printed and bound by CPI Group (UK) Ltd, Croydon, CR0 4YY

17/10/2024

01775697-0013